Spatial Econometrics

Spatial Econometrics

Harry Kelejian
Emeritus Professor at the University of Maryland, College Park, USA
Gianfranco Piras
Associate Professor, The Busch School of Business and Economics,
The Catholic University of America, Washington, D.C., USA

Academic Press is an imprint of Elsevier
125 London Wall, London EC2Y 5AS, United Kingdom
525 B Street, Suite 1800, San Diego, CA 92101-4495, United States
50 Hampshire Street, 5th Floor, Cambridge, MA 02139, United States
The Boulevard, Langford Lane, Kidlington, Oxford OX5 1GB, United Kingdom

Library of Congress Cataloging-in-Publication Data
A catalog record for this book is available from the Library of Congress

British Library Cataloguing-in-Publication Data
A catalogue record for this book is available from the British Library

ISBN: 978-0-12-813387-3

For information on all Academic Press publications
visit our website at https://www.elsevier.com/books-and-journals

Publisher: Candice Janco
Acquisition Editor: Graham Nisbet
Editorial Project Manager: Jaclyn A. Truesdell
Production Project Manager: Poulouse Joseph
Designer: Greg Harris

Typeset by VTeX

Contents

List of Empirical Illustrations

List of Figures

List of Tables

Preface

In recent years interest in spatial analysis has blossomed. The areas of application, the scope and complexity of the models, and corresponding results have moved far beyond their original borders. As expected, formal results relating to such models have also become more complex.

The purpose of this book is to provide graduate students, as well as spatial researchers, with a solid foundation in the formation, specification, and applications of spatial models. Fundamental principles are presented with a reasonable amount of rigor. In addition, great care has been taken to describe these fundamental principles in an intuitive fashion. Consistent with this, empirical illustrations relating to many of the discussed procedures are given. We also provide an appendix which describes how to empirically implement many of the procedures which are presented in the text. It is hoped that the extent of rigor and the descriptions of many of the empirical models will enable spatial researchers to have a more complete understanding of the results and issues relating to spatial models. Complete rigor of all the models and results described in this book would require a book of far greater length than this one. Such a book would be a contribution, but may not "appeal" to many spatial researchers, and may be obtuse to many others. Hopefully, this book will "strike a happy balance."

Chapters 1 and 2 are basic in the sense that basic issues, procedures, and models are discussed. In somewhat more detail, Chapter 1 describes various forms of spatial interactions, and therefore the need for spatial models. The concept of a weighting matrix is introduced, and numerous illustrations of it are given. Chapter 2 specifies basic spatial regression models, various estimation procedures, and complications associated with them. There are various issues or complications that arise in a spatial framework that do not arise in a time series setting. One of these is the triangular array. This is defined and examples are given. Implications relating to model specifications and to large sample theory, upon which inference is often based, are clearly discussed. For example, in time series, samples are assumed to "increase" in a certain and clear way, e.g., year after year, etc. In spatial models, because of triangular arrays, the growth of samples is not so straightforward.

Chapters 3 and 4 relate to direct applications of spatial models. For example, given the specifications of typical spatial models, Chapter 3 describes the calculation of resulting spillover effects. These relate to those that emanate from one unit to neighboring units, as well as those that impact a given unit which emanate from units neighboring it. Another application of spatial models relates to predictions based on them. Chapter 4 describes various predictors and their properties, and gives numerical evaluations of their efficiency.

The remaining chapters are concerned with model estimation under various complications relating to model specifications, data problems, tests of hypotheses, systems of equations, and panel data extensions. There is also a chapter on pretest procedures which are rampant in spatial analysis. That chapter contains an illustration which clearly reveals the seriousness of the issue. Finally, there is also a chapter on Bayesian analysis, which is essentially a beautiful theory of learning. Suggested applications of the Bayesian method are described. A set of problems is suggested at the end of each chapter. A solution manual is given at the end of the book.

The reader is assumed to have the equivalent of a first year graduate course in econometrics. Many of the results in this book require only a mild background in large sample theory. An appendix is provided for readers who want to review or extend their background in this area. This appendix is more than enough to understand the material in this book. Another appendix relates to the R programming language. It does not assume a background in R, and clearly describes how a researcher can implement many of the statistical procedures described in this book.

A Point to Note About This Book

It will be noticed that although the maximum likelihood procedure is well described in this book and examples are given, less space is given to it than to the instrumental variable procedure. There are two reasons for this. First, the endogenous variables spatial researchers consider are typically jointly determined in a system which involves more than one equation. This implies that the explanation in a spatial model of one endogenous variable should be in terms of other endogenous variables, as well as exogenous variables. In the literature these "other" endogenous variables are often called "additional" endogenous variables. It will typically be the case that the researcher does not know all of the equations determining the "additional" endogenous variables in his model. This rules out the maximum likelihood procedure, as well as Bayesian methods, but not the instrumental variable method. Of course, one can assume – and researchers sometimes do – that the "additional" endogenous variables are exogenous and so implement maximum likelihood. However, this leads to major statistical problems. It is reasonable to assume that over time, spatial researchers will become more inclined to recognize the endogeneity of some of their regressors. The suggestion is that the instrumental variable procedure will become even more important over time.

The second reason for this book's greater focus on the instrumental variable procedure is that the maximum likelihood procedure is typically considered in a framework which involves structurally specified error terms, e.g., the i.i.d. specification, the spatial autoregressive specification, etc. We argue at various points in this book that error terms are the unknown parts of a model and so should be nonparametrically specified in a way that allows for **unknown** patterns of heteroskedasticity, as well as spatial and time correlation. If they are so specified, the maximum likelihood procedure cannot be implemented as it typically is. On the other hand, the instrumental variable procedure, along with an HAC procedure, can be easily implemented in such a framework. HAC procedures are described in Chapter 9 and relate to the estimation of variance–covariance matrices. It should be noted that researchers stopped structurally specifying heteroskedastic errors in time series models when Halbert White (1980) explained that such *ad hoc* specifications may introduce biases, and are unnecessary for the consistent estimation of the asymptotic variance covariance matrix of the estimators. Spatial researchers should take a lesson from that time series literature.

Finally, as spatial researchers we observe correlations and infer causations. "Sometimes" errors are made. This is well illustrated by an anecdote given in Fisher (1966, pp. 2–3) for a related issue. Fisher thanks Evsey D. D__ for the "tale."

> *There was once a cholera epidemic in Russia. The government, in an effort to stem the disease, sent doctors to the worse-effected areas. The peasants of the province of S__ discussed the situation and observed a very high correlation between the number of doctors in a given area and the incidence of cholera in that area. Relying on this hard fact, they rose and murdered their doctors.*

Acknowledgements

Writing a book is certainly time consuming and, at times, frustrating. Harry Kelejian would like to thank his fiancee' Sandra Morewitz. In all sincerity, without her support and encouragement, this book would not have been written. He would also like to acknowledge the memory of his parents, Sally and Jack (Shavarsh) Kelejian. His debt to them can never be repaid! Finally, he would like to thank Henk Folmer for advice and suggestions given at an early stage in the development of this book.

Gianfranco Piras would like to thank Giuseppe Arbia, who first introduced him to the study of this topic back in college and has always been an example of dedication and passion. He also wants to thank his father and mother for being a magnificent example of a mutually caring and loving couple. Last but not least, this book is dedicated to Nancy "*ché dentro a li occhi suoi ardeva un riso tal, ch' io pensai co' miei toccar lo fondo de la mia gloria e del mio paradiso*" (Dante, Divina Commedia, Paradiso, Canto XV).

Both authors would also like to thank some referees who gave advice and suggestions at an earlier stage of the development of this book.

Harry Kelejian
Department of Economics, University of Maryland, College Park, MD

Gianfranco Piras
School of Business and Economics, The Catholic University of America, Washington DC

March, 2017

Chapter 1

Spatial Models: Basic Issues*

In this chapter we provide the reader with several basic notions that relate to the use of spatial econometric models. In Section 1.1 we give a definition of the first law of Geography, which is a basic principle behind spatial models. In many applications, space often relates to geographical distance. However, other representations of spaces can be considered. Some illustrative examples are given below. Section 1.2 introduces the concept of a neighbor and presents one of the most important tools in spatial econometrics, namely the spatial weighting matrix. Formal definitions of some typology of a weighting matrix are given in Section 1.3. Finally, the last section relates to spatial weighting matrices that are usually employed in computer studies. Nevertheless, some of the criteria used in Monte Carlo studies are also valid, *mutatis mutandis*, for real world applications.

1.1 ILLUSTRATIONS INVOLVING SPATIAL INTERACTIONS

Spatial models account for the role that space plays in determining many of the variables that economists and other social scientists (such as geographers, planners, and regional scientists, etc.) deal with. On an intuitive level, the typology of a model is based on a simple principle, namely the further apart in space are the observational units, the weaker the connections between them. In many applications space is related to geographic distances, but it can also relate to differences in products, markets, political systems, city size, and a host of other "spaces." The following examples should clarify this[1]:

1. Many empirical models try to explain the level of police expenditures per capita in given areas (e.g., counties or states).[2] Good candidates to explain such

* Basic texts in spatial analysis and econometrics are Cliff and Ord (1973, 1981), Anselin (1988), and Cressie (1993). More recent texts and compilations are Anselin and Florax (1995b), Anselin et al. (2004), Anselin and Rey (2014), LeSage and Pace (2004, 2009), Elhorst (2014), and Arbia (2006, 2014). See also a nice overview of spatial models, and the development of spatial econometrics by Anselin (2002, 2009) and Anselin and Bera (1998).

1. The interesting paper by Brueckner (2003) contains additional motivations for spatial models.

2. See, for example, Ajilore and Smith (2011); Di Tella and Schargrodsky (2004); Levitt (1997); Kovandzic and Sloan (2002), and Marvell and Moody (1996) among others.

Spatial Econometrics. http://dx.doi.org/10.1016/B978-0-12-813387-3.00001-9

a variable would be, among others, crime and unemployment rates, average levels of education and income, and the proportion of housing units that are rented in each of the considered areas. However, with respect to each given area, it might also be of interest to consider the levels of police expenditures per capita in areas surrounding that given area. That is, one might expect that the higher the expenditures in these surrounding areas, the higher the level of police expenditures in the given area. The reason for this is that, *ceteris paribus*, if neighboring areas have high levels of police protection, and a given area does not, that given area might be a magnet for criminals and so be more at risk for crime. Clearly, the further away an area is from the one considered, the less important its characteristics might be to the given area.[3] In this example distance might simply relate to geographical proximity.[4]

2. Similar spillover issues would arise if one were to consider the education budget per capita in a given city as they relate to those of other cities. In this case one would think of competitive issues between cities as they try to attract firms as well as higher income people for tax purposes. In this case the distance between cities might relate to the size of their population rather than their geographic distance. For example, New York might seek to compete with Los Angeles, rather than with College Park, Maryland even though College Park, Maryland is a lot closer to New York than is Los Angeles.[5]

3. As a third set of examples, consider the problem of explaining foreign exchange rates between countries. Clearly, the exchange rate between countries A and B will influence the rate between countries A and C. These relationships may be especially strong during times of crisis. For example, if there is a run on the currency of country A due to its "poor" macro conditions, then speculators may decide to flee from the currency of countries which are geographically close but, perhaps more importantly, have similar macro conditions. This type of spillover between countries in times of crisis is often referred to as contagion. In such cases the connectedness, or "closeness", between countries which may induce contagion may involve more than one characteristic, e.g., geographic proximity, similar credit conditions, the extent of public debt, trade shares, etc.[6]

3. This statement is, generally, referred to as the Tobler's first law of geography.
4. An example of a crime model along the lines described here was given by Kelejian and Robinson (1993). Many other studies involve geographical distance. Shroder (1995) analyzes whether or not states tend to "export" their welfare recipients by setting the level of welfare payments lower than their surrounding areas. Other studies involving geographical distance relate to housing prices, Case (1991), Fingleton (2008b), regional growth rates, LeSage and Fischer (2008), Piras et al. (2012), Dall'Erba et al. (2008), Arbia et al. (2008), Abreu et al. (2005); total factor productivity, Angeriz et al. (2009), labor productivity, Fischer et al. (2009).
5. A study along these lines was given by Vigil (1998).
6. A study involving contagion in foreign markets is Hondroyiannis et al. (2009).

Clearly, there are many other cases involving spatial "spillovers" between various types of "units" and their characteristics. Some evident examples relate to air and water pollution issues, local tax rates and migration, GDP fluctuations between countries, and the extent of foreign trade between countries. A somewhat less evident case relates to various characteristics associated with government quality, such as freedom of speech, of the press, etc. For example, citizens in a given country may be influenced in their demands on their government by political conditions observed in nearby countries!

1.2 CONCEPT OF A NEIGHBOR AND THE WEIGHTING MATRIX

In spatial models the spatial interactions described above are typically accounted for by what has been termed the "weighting (or weights) matrix", which is a concept that was introduced by Moran (1948). The (i, j)th element of this matrix, say w_{ij}, describes the "closeness" between unit i and unit j in terms of a distance measure. If $w_{ij} \neq 0$, unit j is said to be a neighbor of unit i; on the other hand, if $w_{ij} = 0$, unit j is not a neighbor of unit i. Units that are viewed as neighbors to a given unit interact with that given unit in a meaningful way. This interaction could relate to spillovers, externalities, copy-cat policies, geographic proximity issues, industrial structure, similarity of markets, sharing of infrastructure, welfare benefits, banking regulations, tax and reelection issues, just to mention a few.

The description above indicates that the weighting matrix is a matrix that selects neighbors for each unit and indicates the "importance" of each neighbor. For example, suppose we have N observations on a dependent variable, say $y' = (y_1, ..., y_N)$, where y_i is the value on the dependent variable corresponding to the ith unit, e.g., y_i might be the crime rate relating to the ith unit, which might be a region. Suppose the neighbors of unit i are units 1, 2, and 3. Then the ith row of the $N \times N$ weighting matrix, W, will only have the nonzero elements: w_{i1}, w_{i2}, and w_{i3}. If $\sum_{j=1}^{N} w_{ij} = 1$ for all i, the weighting matrix is said to be row normalized. Because a unit is not viewed as its own neighbor $w_{ii} = 0$, $i = 1, ..., N$.

As an example of use, let $W_{i.}$ be the ith row of W and let x_i be a scalar variable in unit i which is used to explain y_i. Then a model such as

$$y_i = b_0 + b_1 x_i + b_2 W_{i.} X + \varepsilon_i, \tag{1.2.1}$$
$$X' = (x_1, ..., x_N),$$

where ε_i is the corresponding error term, suggests that y_i depends upon x_i (a within unit effect), as well as $\sum_{j=1}^{N} w_{ij} x_j$, which is a weighted sum of the regressor in neighboring units. If W is specified to be row normalized then y_i depends on x_i and a weighted average of this regressor corresponding to neighboring units. Clearly, the simplest weighted average is the uniform, e.g., if y_i has 5 neighbors, then the nonzero weights in the ith row of W are all 1/5. Other weighting schemes will be considered below.

1.3 SOME DIFFERENT WAYS TO SPECIFY SPATIAL WEIGHTING MATRICES

Rewriting the above relation in scalar terms, i.e.,

$$y_i = b_0 + b_1 x_i + b_2 \Sigma_{j=1}^{N} w_{ij} x_j + \varepsilon_i, \tag{1.3.1}$$

one can clearly see that w_{ij} is part of the effect that x_j has on y_i, namely $b_2 w_{ij}$. If unit j is not a neighbor to unit i (i.e., $w_{ij} = 0$), y_i would not be effected by x_j. If unit j is a neighbor of unit i, the effect of x_j on y_i would, in part, depend upon w_{ij} which, in turn, depends upon the distance measure, or some measure of connectedness, between unit i and unit j.

There are various ways researchers have specified w_{ij}. An incomplete list of possible specifications is given below:

(A) Let N_i be the number of neighbors that unit i has. Then, if j is a neighbor to i, researchers often take $w_{ij} = 1/N_i$. In this case W would be a row normalized weighting matrix. Suppose that W is a 10×10 matrix, and that the first unit has three neighbors corresponding to units 2, 5, and 8. Then, the first row of the spatial weighting matrix will be

$$W_{1.} = [0, 1/3, 0, 0, 1/3, 0, 0, 1/3, 0, 0].$$

(B) Let j be a neighbor to i, and let d_{ij} be a distance measure between i and j. Then, one typically wants $w_{ij} \geq 0$, and also wants w_{ij} to be negatively related to d_{ij}, that is, the more distant j and i are, the smaller w_{ij} should be, see, e.g., Fig. 1.3.1 below. Some researchers take $w_{ij} = 1/d_{ij}$. In many cases d_{ij} is taken to be the geographical distance between i and j. Also, in many cases a row normalized version is specified as

$$w_{ij} = \frac{1/d_{ij}}{\Sigma_{r=1}^{N}(1/d_{ir})}, \quad i = 1, ..., N. \tag{1.3.2}$$

(C) A specification need not relate to geographical distance. As an example, let us define INC_r as the income per capita in cross-sectional unit $r = 1, ..., N$; then one specification of w_{ij} would be

$$w_{ij} = |INC_i - INC_j|^{-1}. \tag{1.3.3}$$

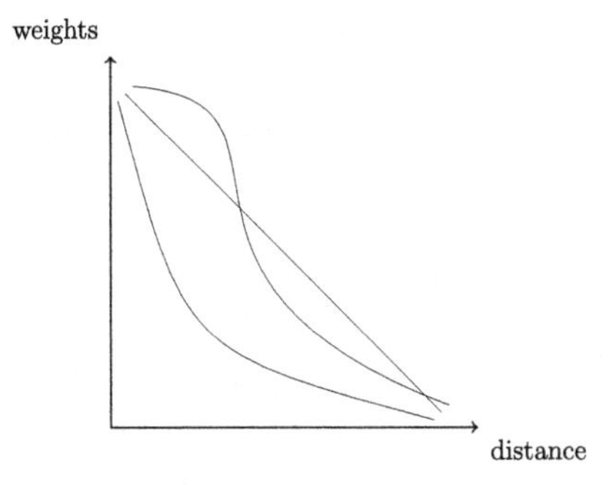

FIGURE 1.3.1 Possible patterns of weights and distance

Although this particular specification is interesting, it also presents a disadvantage. In particular, w_{ij} is not necessarily *bounded* because INC_i and INC_j could be arbitrarily close. As we will see in the next chapter, this is a serious shortcoming because many formal results in spatial econometrics assume that the elements of a weighting matrix are bounded.

Given that income is nonnegative, one possible improvement over (1.3.3) is

$$w_{ij} = 1 - \frac{|INC_i - INC_j|}{INC_i + INC_j}. \tag{1.3.4}$$

The reason for the denominator in (1.3.4) is that elements of a weighting matrix are always taken to be $w_{ij} \geq 0$, and in the absence of the denominator, w_{ij} in (1.3.4) could be negative. At first sight, one might think that w_{ij} in (1.3.4) has an evident shortcoming in that its value is bounded by 1 which occurs when $INC_i = INC_j$. However, this is not a real issue since the maximum value of w_{ij} can be viewed simply as a scaling issue which is accounted for by the coefficient of the term multiplying the spatial weights. For example, one could define a variant of w_{ij} in (1.3.4) as

$$w_{ij} = \alpha \left[1 - \frac{|INC_i - INC_j|}{INC_i + INC_j} \right] \tag{1.3.4A}$$

where α is a preselected positive constant whose value can be very large (or small). If large, the upper limit of w_{ij} would be α. However, in practice one need not be concerned with preselecting the value of a constant such as α. For example, in a model such (1.3.1) if w_{ij} is taken to be as in (1.3.4A), but with α not specified, then that model could be rewritten as

$$\begin{aligned} y_i &= b_0 + b_1 x_i + b_3 \Sigma_{j=1}^{N} \bar{w}_{ij} x_j + \varepsilon_i, \\ b_3 &= b_2 \alpha, \end{aligned}$$

where

$$\bar{w}_{ij} = \left[1 - \frac{|INC_i - INC_j|}{INC_i + INC_j}\right].$$

In this case, the weighting matrix would be defined in terms of $\bar{w}_{ij}$ and the researcher would estimate b_0, b_1, and b_3. The constant term α is not identified, and so cannot be estimated. Although there is no benefit in doing so, if a value were assigned to α, the estimated value of b_2 would be $\hat{b}_2$, where $\hat{b}_2 = \hat{b}_3/\alpha$. Generalizing, the coefficient of the term multiplying the weights, such as α, can always be viewed as accounting for the scale factor of the weights. An exception is the case in which the weighting matrix is row normalized.[7]

Another possible variant of (1.3.3) is

$$w_{ij} = F[-|INC_i - INC_j|] \tag{1.3.5}$$

where $F \geq 0$ is a cumulative distribution function – as one example, the CDF of the normal. In this case $0 < w_{ij} < 1$.

Other economic variables whose differences could signify distance between neighboring units i and j are:

(a) the average level of education
(b) the proportion of housing units that are rental units
(c) ethnic group composition differences
(d) trade shares
(e) the proportion of people in a given area that are registered in a particular political party, e.g., as democrats, republicans, etc.

Finally, in studies involving states, countries, or other geographical areas, researchers often define $w_{ij} = 1$ if area i borders area j at some point, and $w_{ij} = 0$, otherwise. Row normalized versions of such a weighting matrix are typically considered. In the examples above, each unit typically would not be specified to have **all** other units as neighboring units.

In all of the examples we gave, w_{ij} is specified in terms of a single distance measure. In some cases units may differ in important ways by more than one measure. As an example, suppose one were studying the determinants of the volatilities of the GDPs of countries. In a spatial framework, one might want the elements of the weighting matrix to involve more than one comparison of variables between countries. For example, one might want w_{ij} to involve comparisons of unemployment rates, GDP growth rates, inflation rates, etc. Then one might specify w_{ij} in terms of the Euclidean distance between the important

7. In this case we leave it to the reader to demonstrate that a scale factor such as α would cancel if the weighting matrix were row normalized.

variables of the countries such as

$$w_{ij} = 1/(d_{ij}), \qquad (1.3.6)$$
$$d_{ij} = [(z_{i1} - z_{j1})^2 + ... + (z_{ir} - z_{jr})^2]^{1/2}$$

where z_{iq} is the q-th "relevant" variable for country i, $q = 1, ..., r$.

As is, the measure in (1.3.6) has three potential problems. The first relates to the units of measurement for the variables involved. The second relates to the relative importance of each variable in the distance measure. The third relates to the possibility that w_{ij} is unbounded.

For instance, suppose there are only two variables in the comparison and they are the unemployment rate and income per capita. Unless care is taken with units of measurement, in this case d_{ij} in (1.3.6) could be completely determined by income comparisons because the unemployment rates are bounded by zero and one, and the measure of income per capita (say in dollars) could lead to much large numbers. The evident solution is that the researcher should use units of measurement such that all the variables determining the distance measure are within bounds of each other, e.g., as one example, they are all within, say, [0, 10].

Consider now the issue of relative importance. It is unlikely that the variables determining d_{ij} in (1.3.6) are all equally important, and so one might want to weight these variables. As an example, instead of (1.3.6), one might **think** of specifying d_{ij} as

$$d_{ij} = [a_1(z_{i1} - z_{j1})^2 + ... + a_r(z_{ir} - z_{jr})^2]^{1/2} \qquad (1.3.7)$$

and estimate the parameters $a_1, ..., a_r$ along with the other model parameters. As our discussion in a later chapter will indicate, the specification in (1.3.7) will lead to serious estimation problems. Therefore, in such cases we suggest that instead of defining a single distance measure with numerous weights, such as that in (1.3.7), the researcher should define r distance measures each of which relates to a single variable, such as

$$d_{ij}^q = (z_{iq} - z_{jq})^2, \quad q = 1, ..., r, \qquad (1.3.8)$$

and correspondingly, r weighting matrices whose elements are

$$w_{ij}^q = 1/d_{ij}^q, \quad q = 1, ..., r. \qquad (1.3.9)$$

Using evident notation, in this case the extended form of the basic model in (1.3.1) would be

$$y_i = b_0 + b_1 X_i + a_1 W_i^1 X + a_2 W_i^2 X + ... + a_r W_i^r X + \varepsilon_i. \qquad (1.3.10)$$

$$\begin{bmatrix} NN & NN & NN & NN & NN \\ NN & N & R & N & NN \\ NN & R & i & R & NN \\ NN & N & R & N & NN \\ NN & NN & NN & NN & NN \end{bmatrix}$$

FIGURE 1.4.1 Some neighbor types in computer studies

Finally if, for the chosen variables, the resulting elements of the weighting matrix w_{ij}^q, are not bounded, solutions such as those described in (1.3.4) or (1.3.5) should be considered.

1.4 TYPICAL WEIGHTING MATRICES IN COMPUTER STUDIES

Economists often consider computer studies relating to the properties of spatial models. These studies are typically based on data that are generated using Monte Carlo methods.

Unlike in standard econometric applications, the sample size is often taken as the square of an integer and the "geometry" underlying the sample is often taken in terms of a regular grid (i.e., checkerboard of squares). In many of these studies the elements of the weighting matrices are often determined in such a way that they relate to the game of chess. For instance, in a sample of size 25 one might have a scenario as described in Fig. 1.4.1.

There are 25 squares in Fig. 1.4.1 and each square corresponds to a unit in the computer study. Reading across the first row, the units would be 1, ..., 5; the second row starts with unit 6, etc. For the ith unit, the squares labeled N and R denote "close" neighbors; the units NN are neighbors that are further away, etc. For unit i, the close neighbors would be units 7, 8, 9, 12, 14, 17, 18, and 19. The pattern of neighbors of unit i described by R is called a rook; this corresponds to some of the movements a rook can make in the game of chess. The pattern described by N and R combined is called a queen for similar reasons. The pattern described by NN is called a double queen.

Another configuration for computer studies is the one based on the Euclidean distance between the units in a checker board of squares based on the "(x, y)" coordinates of the units as described in Fig. 1.4.2 below. For example, in the figure the origin is taken with coordinates $(0, 0)$. Again, the number of the units in the top most row are units, 1, 2, ..., 5; row 2 begins with unit 6, etc.

In this framework, the distance between unit 12, whose coordinates are $(1, 2)$, and unit 9, whose coordinates are $(3, 3)$ is

$$\begin{aligned} d_{12,9} &= [(1-3)^2 + (2-3)^2]^{1/2} \\ &= 2.236. \end{aligned} \tag{1.4.1}$$

$$\begin{bmatrix} 0,4 & 1,4 & 2,4 & 3,4 & 4,4 \\ 0,3 & 1,3 & 2,3 & 3,3 & 4,3 \\ 0,2 & 1,2 & 2,2 & 3,2 & 4,2 \\ 0,1 & 1,1 & 2,1 & 3,1 & 4,1 \\ 0,0 & 1,0 & 2,0 & 3,0 & 4,0 \end{bmatrix}$$

FIGURE 1.4.2 Neighbors types based on Euclidean distance

In some cases, a configuration such as that in Fig. 1.4.2 is used to compute a spatial weighting matrix which is based on the k-nearest neighbors criteria. That is, corresponding to each unit, the Euclidean distance from all the other units is calculated and sorted in an increasing order. The neighbors for each unit are then taken to be the nearest k of those units.

Still another method used in computer studies is the "k-ahead and k-behind" criterion in a circular world introduced by Kelejian and Prucha (1999). In this framework, each unit is assumed to have k neighbors which are ahead of it in the order of the sample, and k units which are behind it. The number k is typically chosen to be small relative to the sample size. In this scenario, each unit has $2k$ neighbors. Weighting matrices which are built on this framework are typically row normalized, and all of the nonzero elements in the matrix are $1/(2k)$. The meaning of "circular world" is best explained in terms of an illustration.

Suppose the sample size is 9, and a value of k is taken to be 3. In this case each unit would have $2 \times 3 = 6$ neighbors and the weighting matrix would be 9×9. Since the diagonal elements of a weighting matrix are always taken to be zero, the first row of that matrix, which relates to the first unit, would be

$$W_{1.} = [0, \frac{1}{6}, \frac{1}{6}, \frac{1}{6}, 0, 0, \frac{1}{6}, \frac{1}{6}, \frac{1}{6}]. \tag{1.4.2}$$

The three neighbors that are ahead of the first unit are units 2, 3, and 4. Because of the circular world condition, the three neighbors that are behind the first unit are units 9, 8, and 7. In a similar light, the second row of the weighting matrix would be

$$W_{2.} = [\frac{1}{6}, 0, \frac{1}{6}, \frac{1}{6}, \frac{1}{6}, 0, 0, \frac{1}{6}, \frac{1}{6}]. \tag{1.4.3}$$

In (1.4.3), the three units that are behind the second unit are units $1, 9$, and 8.

Many of the available software packages that deal with spatial econometric models (such as R, Stata, GeoDa/GeoDaSpace/PySAL, and Matlab) have the capability of generating weighting matrices according to the previous criteria. However, the examples presented in the book will be based on R statistical software (see Appendix B).

SUGGESTED PROBLEMS

1. Demonstrate that if w_{ij} were defined as in (1.3.4A), the scale factor α would cancel if the weighting matrix is row normalized.
2. In (1.3.5) suppose F is the CDF of the normal $(0, \sigma^2)$ distribution. If σ^2 is not known, would the model fit into the framework of (1.2.1)?
3. Suppose data are available on the annual percentage changes in the GDPs of N countries. Suggest a model which might explain these percentage changes.
4. For a general sample size, say N, which corresponds to a checkerboard of squares, what is the minimum number of neighbors a unit can have if the weighting matrix is based on a queen pattern?
5. In the k-ahead and k-behind circular world model, suppose $N = 10$ and $k = 2$. Specify the third row of the 10×10 weighting matrix.

Chapter 2

Specification and Estimation

An important class of spatial models can be traced back to the work of Cliff and Ord (1973, 1981). The models they considered have since been generalized and extended in a variety of directions.[1] In Section 2.1 we present and discuss a general linear form of a model that is specified in terms of a spatial lag of the dependent variable, spatially lagged exogenous regressors, and a spatially autocorrelated error term. Section 2.1.1 introduces the important concept of triangular arrays which is a distinctive characteristic of spatial models compared to time series analysis. More details will be given below but, essentially, the idea is that the sequence of observations on the dependent variable, as well as the other model variables, must be indexed not only by the order of the observations, but also by the sample size. Triangular arrays rarely occur in time series models. Sections 2.1.2 and 2.1.3 discuss the definition of the parameter space and various forms of normalization of the model, whereas Section 2.1.4 introduces an important condition which is assumed in the derivation of many properties of spatial estimators. Sections 2.2, 2.3, and 2.4 are the core of this chapter since they deal with the estimation of cross-sectional spatial models. Section 2.2 deals with estimation issues in various special cases of the general model. A discussion of the model assumptions and the development of a generalized moments (GM) estimator of a parameter in the disturbance process are also provided in this section. Section 2.3 presents an instrumental variable estimator of the regression parameters of the general model. Finally, in Section 2.4 the maximum likelihood approach is reviewed. Sections 2.5 and 2.6 conclude the chapter. In Section 2.5 we show that when the spatial weighting matrices are the same in the general model and there are **no** regressors, there is an identification problem concerning the spatial parameters. We also show that if there are regressors in the models, there is no such problem. In Section 2.6 we make known that certain time series procedures should not be used in a spatial framework.

---

1. Among others, see Kelejian and Prucha (2004, 2007a,b, 2010a), Lee (2003, 2004, 2007), Lee and Liu (2010), Lee et al. (2010), Baltagi and Li (2004), Baltagi et al. (2014a), Fingleton and Le Gallo (2008), Fingleton (2008a,b), Mutl and Pfaffermayr (2011), Piras (2013), Elhorst (2005), and references cited therein.

Spatial Econometrics. http://dx.doi.org/10.1016/B978-0-12-813387-3.00002-0

2.1 THE GENERAL MODEL

Let $y' = [y_1, ..., y_N]$, where y_i, $i = 1, ..., N$ is the dependent variable corresponding to the ith unit and consider the following model:

$$y_i = a + X_{i.}B_1 + \rho_1 (W_{i.}y) + (W_{i.}X) B_2 + u_i, \tag{2.1.1}$$
$$u_i = \rho_2(W_{i.}u) + \varepsilon_i, \quad |\rho_1| < 1, \ |\rho_2| < 1$$

where $X_{i.}$ is a $1 \times k$ row vector of observations on exogenous explanatory variables whose values vary over the units, $W_{i.}$ is a $1 \times N$ row vector of observations on the ith row of an observable and exogenous $N \times N$ weighting matrix defined below,[2] u_i is a disturbance term, ε_i is a random term which is i.i.d. $(0, \sigma_\varepsilon^2)$, B_1 and B_2 are $k \times 1$ parameter vectors, and a, ρ_1, and ρ_2 are scalar parameters. The term ε_i is typically refereed to as an innovation in the error process.

The model in (2.1.1) contains a fair amount of spatial spillovers. For example, the value of the dependent variable corresponding to the ith unit (which is typically a cross-sectional unit) depends upon the within unit effect of the regressor vector, $X_{i.}$, as well as the values of the dependent variable and the exogenous regressors in neighboring units. Similarly, the model also allows for spillovers in the disturbance terms by the second line of (2.1.1).

Denote the $N \times N$ weighting matrix as

$$W = \begin{bmatrix} W_{1.} \\ \vdots \\ W_{N.} \end{bmatrix}$$

so that the model in (2.1.1) can be written in stacked form as

$$y = ae_N + XB_1 + \rho_1 (Wy) + (WX) B_2 + u, \tag{2.1.2}$$
$$u = \rho_2 (Wu) + \varepsilon$$

where e_N is an $N \times 1$ vector of unit elements, and

$$X = [X'_{1.}, ..., X'_{N.}]',$$
$$u = [u_1, ..., u_N]',$$
$$\varepsilon = [\varepsilon_1, ..., \varepsilon_N]'.$$

For future reference, we note that the model in (2.1.2) is sometimes referred to as the spatial Durbin model; if $B_2 = 0$ and $\rho_2 = 0$, the model is sometimes

2. In Chapter 13 we will consider the case in which the weighting matrix is endogenous.

called a spatial lag model; if $\rho_1 = 0$ and $B_2 = 0$, the model is sometimes called a spatial error model.

Denote the ith column of X, which is the $N \times 1$ vector of observations on the ith exogenous variable, as $X_{.i}, i = 1, ..., k$. By matrix multiplication, the term WX in (2.1.2) can be expressed as

$$\begin{aligned} WX &= W[X_{.1}, ..., X_{.k}] \\ &= [WX_{.1}, WX_{.2}, ..., WX_{.k}]. \end{aligned} \tag{2.1.3}$$

In a time series setting, the time lag of a variable, say z_t, is the value of that same variable at an earlier point in time, e.g., z_{t-j}, $j > 0$. Now note that the rth element of the $N \times 1$ vector $WX_{.1}$ in (2.1.3), namely $(WX_{.1})_r$, is

$$(WX_{.1})_r = \sum_{j=1}^{N} w_{r,j} x_{j1} \tag{2.1.4}$$

where x_{j1} is the jth element of $X_{.1}$. Note that $(WX_{.1})_r$ is a weighted sum of the values of that **same** first exogenous variable over neighboring units. Also recall that the diagonal elements of weighting matrices are zero. For these reasons, the vector $WX_{.1}$ is often referred to as the spatial lag of the first exogenous variable, $X_{.1}$; generalizing, $WX_{.j}$ is the spatial lag of the jth exogenous regressor.

The model (2.1.2) contains the spatial lags of all of the exogenous variables. Typically researchers consider the spatial lags of only a subset of the exogenous variables, e.g., perhaps only $WX_{.2}$ and $WX_{.5}$.

As an example, consider a model in which the dependent variable is the price of all the transactions involving single family houses in the Washington, DC area in a specific year. To explain the price of a single family house, the structural characteristics of the house (such as number of bedrooms, number of bathrooms, square footage of the living area, age, presence of a garage, whether the house has a fireplace, the construction material, etc.) along with the neighborhood characteristics (median income, percentage of population over 65, etc.) and amenities (distance from central business district, presence of parks, lakes, or rivers, accessibility, views, etc.) are generally considered good predictors. The model postulated above could include such additional variables: the spatial lag of the dependent variable as well as the spatial lag of some, or all, of the exogenous variables. A possible explanation for including the spatial lag of the price should be evident. In determining the market price of a house, economic agents look at the price of comparable houses in the same neighborhood. The rational to include the spatial lag of one (or more) of the explanatory variables is also quite intuitive. As an example consider the age variable. A new construction surrounded by older houses is likely to be, *ceteris paribus*, less expensive than

$$\begin{bmatrix} y_{11}, & y_{12}, & y_{13}, & y_{14}, & \text{etc.} \\ & y_{22}, & y_{23}, & y_{24}, & \\ & & y_{33}, & y_{34}, & \\ & & & y_{44}, & \end{bmatrix}$$

FIGURE 2.1.1 Appearance of a triangular array

a new construction surrounded by newer houses. The spatial lag of the age variable could account for this.[3] The spatial lag of the disturbance term is supposed to capture remaining exogenous spatially correlated effects that are omitted from the model either because data on certain variables are not available, or simply they may not even be known.

2.1.1 Triangular Arrays

More formal assumptions of the model in (2.1.1) are presented later. In this section we review an important issue related to spatial models. We start by assuming that the model can be solved for y in that $(I_N - aW)$ is nonsingular for all $|a| < 1$. More on this is said below. Given this nonsingularity, the reduced form of the model can be written as follows:

$$\begin{aligned} y &= (I_N - \rho_1 W)^{-1}[ae_N + XB_1 + WXB_2 + u] \qquad (2.1.1.1) \\ &= (I_N - \rho_1 W)^{-1}[ae_N + XB_1 + WXB_2] + \\ &(I_N - \rho_1 W)^{-1}(I_N - \rho_2 W)^{-1}\varepsilon. \end{aligned}$$

We now note something about spatial models which may be somewhat unexpected. The solution of the model in (2.1.2), given in (2.1.1.1), involves the elements of the $N \times N$ matrices $(I_N - \rho_1 W)^{-1}$ and $(I_N - \rho_2 W)^{-1}$. These elements will generally depend upon the size of the sample. Since, via (2.1.1.1), the elements of the dependent vector y depend upon these inverses, the implication is that each of the elements of the vector y will generally change as the sample size changes even though the model remains the same. In other words, the first value of y when $N = 5$ will not necessarily be the same as when $N = 6$. For this reason, in a formal analysis, the elements of the dependent vector would have two indices: one denoting the observation number, and the other denoting the sample size. For example, $y_{i,j}$ would denote the ith element of y when the sample size is j, and in general, $y_{i,j} \neq y_{i,s}$ if $j \neq s$. Since all of the elements of the dependent vector would be subscripted with the sample size, the dependent vector itself would be so subscripted, y_N. If these data are plotted, a triangular appearance, such as that in Fig. 2.1.1, is revealed.

3. Many applied works also include the square of the age variable to capture a "vintage" effect.

Because of this triangular appearance, the values of the dependent variable will be described as a triangular array.

Here lies an important difference between spatial and time series data. In a time series study based on annual data, the sample increases as additional years pass. The implication is that data corresponding to earlier years do not change as data on later years become available except, perhaps, for error corrections, e.g., the unemployment rate in 2005 does not change when the data for 2006 becomes available. As will become evident in latter discussions, inference in many spatial models relates to results obtained from large sample theory. This means that one typically determines estimation results for the limiting case in which $N \to \infty$, and then assumes that those results are a reasonable approximation for the finite sample which is available. In this case, the sample size is often viewed as "increasing" with (hypothetically) increasingly larger random samples. In such a scenario, each observation on the elements of the regressor matrix, X, would also be expected to change in a triangular array fashion. For example, if the first value of a regressor is the income level of the first observed family, that "first" value need not be the same when $N = 20$ as when $N = 30$. For instance, if random samples are taken, the first family observed when $N = 20$ may not even be in the random sample taken when $N = 30$. Therefore, in formal studies, the regressor matrix would also be subscripted with the sample size, e.g., X_N.

At this point we do not index the variables in the model for simplicity of notation. We will, however, account for the triangular nature of the sample in spatial models.

2.1.2 Geršgorin's Theorem[4] and Weighting Matrices

As suggested in (2.1.1.1), the model in (2.1.2) is complete in that it can be solved for the dependent vector y in terms of X, WX, and ε **if** the matrix $(I_N - aW)$ is nonsingular for all $|a| < 1$. Consistent with this, the parameter space for ρ_1 and ρ_2 are often taken as $|\rho_1| < 1$ and $|\rho_2| < 1$. Note that this parameter space is continuous for both ρ_1 and ρ_2 in a known region. Below we show that, under very reasonable conditions, the weighting matrix can always be normalized in such a way that $(I_N - aW)$ is nonsingular for all $|a| < 1$. Furthermore, the normalization will not effect the size, sign, or significance of the model parameters. These "normalization" results are important because, under the very reasonable conditions, one can always work with a spatial model for which $(I_N - aW)^{-1}$ exists for all $|a| < 1$. This is important for a number of reasons. First, in many spatial models inference is based on large sample properties of the estimators

4. A formal statement of this theorem is given in Horn and Johnson (1985, pp. 344–346). See also Kelejian and Prucha (2010a).

which depend upon the inverse of $(I_N - aW)$ in a continuous and known region for a, among other things. Second, important measures of spatial model spillovers, described in detail in Chapter 3, depend upon the existence of the inverse of $(I_N - aW)$ in a continuous interval for a. Third, many spatial models are estimated by procedures which would encounter considerable "complications" if the space for a for which $(I_N - aW)^{-1}$ exists is not continuous.

We now consider conditions for the nonsingularity of a matrix $(I_N - aW)$, where a is a constant.

Note 1. If W is row normalized, $(I_N - aW)$ is singular at $a = 1$.

Indeed, let $e_N = (1, 1, ..., 1)'_{N\times 1}$. Then

$$(I_N - W)e_N - e_N - We_N = e_N - e_N = 0. \tag{2.1.2.1}$$

This is why in (2.1.1) the parameter space for ρ_1 and ρ_2 does not include 1.

Note 2. If W is row normalized, then $(I_N - aW)^{-1}$ exits for all $|a| < 1$.

Proof. We prove this by relying on the theorem by Geršgorin and a matrix result concerning characteristic roots by Ord (1975). Let $A_{N\times N}$ have elements a_{ij}. Let $R_i, i = 1, ..., N$ be the sum of the absolute values of the elements in the ith row of A with the exception of its diagonal elements; similarly, let C_j, $j = 1, ..., N$ be the sum of the absolute values in the jth column of A, again with the exception of the diagonal elements:

$$R_i = \sum_{j=1, j\neq i}^{N} |a_{ij}|, \quad C_j = \sum_{i=1, i\neq j}^{N} |a_{ij}|. \tag{2.1.2.2}$$

Then Geršgorin's theorem implies that each eigenvalue, λ_i, of A satisfies at least one of the inequalities relating to the row sums:

$$|\lambda - a_{ii}| \leq R_i, \quad i = 1, ..., N. \tag{2.1.2.3}$$

Furthermore, each root satisfies at least one of the inequalities relating to the column sums:

$$|\lambda - a_{jj}| \leq C_j, \quad j = 1, ..., N. \tag{2.1.2.4}$$

Let us now apply this statement to a weighting matrix W with diagonal elements $w_{ii} = 0$. Let

$$\begin{aligned} r &= \max_i \textstyle\sum_j |w_{ij}| & c &= \max_j \textstyle\sum_i |w_{ij}| \\ &= \max_i R_i, & &= \max_j C_j. \end{aligned} \tag{2.1.2.5}$$

Given (2.1.2.2)–(2.1.2.5), the roots of W must satisfy the conditions

$$|\lambda_i| \leq r, |\lambda_i| \leq c, \quad i = 1, ..., N. \tag{2.1.2.6}$$

If W is row normalized, $r = 1$. From (2.1.2.6) it then follows that when W is row normalized $|\lambda_i| \leq 1, i = 1, ..., N$.

Now let Q be the matrix that triangularizes W, i.e.,

$$QWQ^{-1} = D_\lambda, \quad D_\lambda = \begin{bmatrix} \lambda_1 & & \lambda_{ij} \\ & \ddots & \\ 0 & & \lambda_N \end{bmatrix}. \tag{2.1.2.7}$$

Thus, applying the result suggested by Ord (1975), $|D_\lambda| = \lambda_1 \ldots \lambda_N$ and we have[5]

$$\begin{aligned} |I_N - aW| &= \left| QQ^{-1}(I_N - aW) \right| \\ &= \left| Q(I_N - aW)Q^{-1} \right| \\ &= |I_N - aD_\lambda| = (1 - a\lambda_1)\ldots(1 - a\lambda_N) \\ &\neq 0 \end{aligned} \tag{2.1.2.8}$$

if $|a| < 1$, then $|a\lambda_i| \leq |a| < 1$. Thus, $(I_N - aW)$ is nonsingular if $|a| < 1$.

Note 3. Finally, we note one more point, which appears in the literature, and corresponds to a special case; see Anselin (1988). Let W again be a weighting matrix, with $w_{ii} = 0$, $i = 1, \ldots, N$, and assume that all of the roots of W are real,[6] and that W is not row normalized. Let $\lambda_{\max}$ and $\lambda_{\min}$ be the largest and smallest roots of W, respectively. Assume, as will typically be the case if all of the roots are real, that $\lambda_{\max} > 0$ and $\lambda_{\min} < 0$. Then $(I_N - aW)$ is nonsingular for all

$$\lambda_{\min}^{-1} < a < \lambda_{\max}^{-1}. \tag{2.1.2.9}$$

Proof. First note that $(I_N - aW)$ is nonsingular for $a = 0$. If $a \neq 0$, we have as before

$$\begin{aligned} |I_N - aW| &= |I_N - aD_\lambda| \\ &= (1 - a\lambda_1)(1 - a\lambda_2)\cdots(1 - a\lambda_N) \end{aligned} \tag{2.1.2.10}$$

so $I_N - aW$ is nonsingular unless a is equal to the inverse of a root, i.e., $\lambda_1^{-1}, \ldots, \lambda_N^{-1}$, or a^{-1} is equal to a root $\lambda_1, \ldots, \lambda_N$.

---

5. Recall that if A and B are two $N \times N$ matrices, then $|AB| = |A||B|$.
6. This is a very strong assumption which will be evident from the results below.

Thus if

$$a^{-1} < \lambda_{\min}$$

or if

$$a^{-1} > \lambda_{\max}$$

then

$$(I_N - aW) \quad \text{is nonsingular.}$$

But

$$\begin{aligned} &\text{if } a^{-1} > \lambda_{\max} \text{ then } a < \lambda_{\max}^{-1}; \\ &\text{if } a^{-1} < \lambda_{\min} \text{ then } a > \lambda_{\min}^{-1}, \end{aligned} \tag{2.1.2.11}$$

and so (2.1.2.9) holds.

Although this result appears in various parts of the literature, it is of limited importance because the roots of a nonsymmetric matrix will typically not all be real, e.g., some will be complex. Complex numbers are not ordered and so the maximum and minimum roots cannot be identified. For example, let $i = (-1)^{1/2}$. Then one cannot say that $5i > 4i$ since multiplying across by i yields $-5 > -4$, which is not true. If multiplication by i reverses the inequality, then multiplying $5i > 4i$ across by i repeatedly yields $5 < 4$, which is also not true.[7]

2.1.3 Normalization to Ensure a Continuous Parameter Space

The discussion above indicates that if W is row normalized, the parameter space for ρ_1 and ρ_2 specified in (2.1.1) is such that the inverses in (2.1.1.1) exist. If W is *not* row normalized $(I_N - aW)$ will generally be singular for certain values of $|a| < 1$. As shown in Kelejian and Prucha (2010a), in this case the model can be easily transformed to obtain a reparameterized form of the weighting matrix W, say W^*, such that $(I_N - aW^*)$ is nonsingular for all $|a| < 1$. This transformed model is such that the interpretations, and estimated statistical significance of the regression parameters are not effected. This is demonstrated below. Thus for purposes of analysis, one need not consider the case for which the model has a weighting matrix, say W^+, which is such that $(I_N - aW^+)$ is singular for certain values of $|a| < 1$.

---

7. Although one cannot say that $a + bi$ is greater than or less than $c + di$, one could order complex roots by their absolute values, $(a^2 + b^2)^{1/2}$ and $(c^2 + d^2)^{1/2}$. However, the above proof would not go through.

Let $\alpha = \min(r, c)$, where r and c are defined in (2.1.2.5) with respect to W above. Then, assuming that the elements of W are nonnegative we will first show that

$$(I_N - aW) \text{ is nonsingular for all } |a| < 1/\alpha. \tag{2.1.3.1}$$

Given (2.1.3.1), the parameter space for ρ_1 and ρ_2 could be taken as $|\rho_1| < 1/\alpha$ and $|\rho_2| < 1/\alpha$.

Proof. As we mentioned earlier, if $a = 0$, then $(I_N - aW)$ is nonsingular. Consider now the case in which $a \neq 0$. In this case $|I_N - aW| = 0$ implies

$$\begin{aligned} &\left|\left(\frac{1}{a}\right) I_N - W\right| = 0 \text{ or} \\ &\left|W - \left(\frac{1}{a}\right) I_N\right| = 0. \end{aligned} \tag{2.1.3.2}$$

Therefore, $(I_N - aW)$ is singular if $\left(\frac{1}{a}\right)$ is equal to a root of W. In addition, observe that since the roots of W are such that

$$|\lambda_i| \leq r, \quad |\lambda_i| \leq c, \tag{2.1.3.3}$$

then

$$|\lambda_i| \leq \min(r, c) = \alpha. \tag{2.1.3.4}$$

As a result,

$$\begin{aligned} &|I_N - aW| \neq 0 \text{ if} \\ &\left|\frac{1}{a}\right| > \min(r, c) = \alpha \text{ or} \\ &|a| < \frac{1}{\alpha}. \end{aligned} \tag{2.1.3.5}$$

The result in (2.1.3.1) follows.

This is an important result because a model which has a weighting matrix which is not row normalized can always be normalized in such a way that the inverse needed to solve the model will exist in an easily established region. For example, suppose W is not row normalized. Then the model[8]

$$\begin{aligned} y &= ae_N + XB + \rho_1 Wy + \varepsilon \\ &= ae_N + XB + (\rho_1 \alpha)\left(\frac{W}{\alpha}\right) y + \varepsilon \end{aligned} \tag{2.1.3.6}$$

8. Note that α below will depend on N and hence so will ρ_1^* and W^*. For ease of notation, we do not indicate this dependence. We note, however, that for many models, α would be a known finite constant for all sample sizes N.

or

$$y = ae_N + XB + \rho_1^* W^* y + \varepsilon \tag{2.1.3.7}$$

$$\text{where } \rho_1^* = \rho_1 \alpha \ , \ \ W^* = \frac{W}{\alpha}, \text{ and}$$

$$\alpha = \min(c, r) : c = \max_j \sum_i |w_{ij}|; \quad r = \max_i \sum_j |w_{ij}|,$$

where α, c, and r relate to W. Note that α is easily determined. Also note that the maximum sum of the absolute values of the elements in the rows and columns of $(1/\alpha)W$ are $(1/\alpha)r$ and $(1/\alpha)c$, respectively. Thus, given (2.1.3.1),

$$|I_N - \rho_1^* W^*| \neq 0$$

since

$$\begin{aligned} |\rho_1^*| &< \frac{1}{\min\left(\frac{c}{\alpha}, \frac{r}{\alpha}\right)} \\ &< \frac{1}{\left(\frac{1}{\alpha}\right)\min(c, r)} = 1. \end{aligned}$$

Hence if the model is renormalized as

$$y = ae_N + XB + \rho_1^* W^* y + \varepsilon \tag{2.1.3.8}$$

and ρ_1^* is taken to be the parameter, the inverse exists for all $|\rho_1^*| < 1$. One would then estimate ρ_1^*, and since $\rho_1^* = \rho_1 \alpha$, it is easy to estimate ρ_1 from

$$|\hat{\rho}_1| = \hat{\rho}_1^* / \alpha. \tag{2.1.3.9}$$

2.1.4 An Important Condition in Large Sample Analysis

The general model in (2.1.1) involves the parameters ρ_1 and ρ_2. Clearly, the estimation of this general model has to account for both of these parameters in some way. In the next sections we argue that, unless $\rho_2 = 0$, the disturbance terms are spatially correlated as well as heteroskedastic. Additionally, unless $\rho_1 = 0$, the model contains an endogeneity that must be accounted for. There are two ways of coping with these issues. One can use either maximum likelihood procedures or an instrumental variables procedure (IV). Hypothesis tests based on these procedures are based on large sample results. These large sample results typically rely on certain widely used matrix assumptions which may not be obvious to all readers and so they are discussed in this section. As we will indicate, these assumptions rule out certain models.

1. We will say that the row and column sums of an $N \times N$ matrix, A, are uniformly bounded in absolute value if

$$\max_i \sum_{j=1}^{N} |a_{ij}| \le c_a, \qquad (2.1.4.1)$$
$$\max_j \sum_{i=1}^{N} |a_{ij}| \le c_a,$$

for all $N \ge 1$ where c_a is a finite constant which does not depend on N.[9] We will also, on occasion, abbreviate reference to a matrix such as A by saying that it is "absolutely summable." Note for future reference that a given column, say column j in the matrix A above, **cannot** satisfy the condition in (2.1.4.1) if the elements of that column are such that $|a_{ij}| > d \ge 0$ for all $i = 1, ..., N$ and $N \ge 1$. In this case the jth unit would be a central unit to which all units relate. Among other things, a unit could be central because of financial issues.

2. If A and B are $N \times N$ absolutely summable matrices, then so is $D = AB$. Because the proof of this statement is instructive it is given below.

Proof. The (i, j)th element of D is, using evident notation,

$$d_{ij} = \sum_{r=1}^{N} a_{ir} b_{rj}. \qquad (2.1.4.2)$$

Given (2.1.4.2), let r_i be the ith row sum and note that

$$\begin{aligned} r_i &= \sum_{j=1}^{N} |d_{ij}| \le \sum_{j=1}^{N} \sum_{r=1}^{N} |a_{ir}| |b_{rj}| \qquad (2.1.4.3) \\ &= \sum_{r=1}^{N} \sum_{j=1}^{N} |a_{ir}| |b_{rj}| \\ &= \sum_{r=1}^{N} |a_{ir}| \sum_{j=1}^{N} |b_{rj}| \\ &\le c_a c_b, \text{ for all } i = 1, ..., N \text{ and } N \ge 1. \end{aligned}$$

A similar demonstration will reveal that

$$\sum_{i=1}^{N} |d_{ij}| \le c_a c_b, \text{ for all } j = 1, ..., N \text{ and } N \ge 1. \qquad (2.1.4.4)$$

9. As an illustration, if the maximum of the row and column sums are, respectively, 5 and 7 then they are both less than 7.

3. If A is absolutely summable, its elements are bounded. This should be obvious.

4. If A is absolutely summable and $Z_{N\times K}$ has **uniformly** bounded elements, then the elements of $Z'AZ$ are at most of order N, e.g., $O(N)$ see Section A.14 in Appendix A, which deals with large sample theory.

Proof. Let Z_{ij} be the (i, j)th element of Z, and let $|Z_{ij}| \leq c_z$ for all i, j and $N \geq 1$. Now consider the (i, j)th element of $Z'AZ$, say δ_{ij},

$$\delta_{ij} = \sum_{r=1}^{N}\sum_{s=1}^{N} Z_{si}a_{sr}Z_{rj}, \tag{2.1.4.5}$$

$$\begin{aligned} \left|\delta_{ij}\right| &\leq \sum_{r=1}^{N}\sum_{s=1}^{N} |Z_{si}|\,|a_{sr}|\,Z_{rj}| \\ &\leq c_z^2 \sum_{r=1}^{N}\sum_{s=1}^{N} |a_{sr}| \\ &\leq c_z^2 \sum_{r=1}^{N} c_a \\ &\leq c_z^2 c_a N = 0(N). \end{aligned}$$

2.2 ESTIMATION: VARIOUS SPECIAL CASES

In this section we turn to the estimation of various special cases of the general model presented above. For convenience, rewrite the model in (2.1.2) as

$$\begin{aligned} y &= ae_N + XB_1 + \rho_1 Wy + (WX)\,B_2 + u, \\ u &= \rho_2\,(Wu) + \varepsilon, \quad |\rho_1| < 1, \; |\rho_2| < 1. \end{aligned} \tag{2.2.1}$$

Assume $(I_N - aW)^{-1}$ exits for $|a| < 1$. As we showed in the previous section, this is not a restrictive assumption since a model can always be normalized to ensure this condition.

2.2.1 Estimation When $\rho_1 = \rho_2 = 0$

In this case the model reduces to

$$\begin{aligned} y &= ae_N + XB_1 + (WX)\,B_2 + \varepsilon \\ &= Z\gamma + \varepsilon, \\ Z &= (e_N, X, WX), \quad \gamma' = (a, B_1', B_2') \end{aligned} \tag{2.2.1.1}$$

where X is $N \times k$, and we are assuming that the rank $(e_N, X, WX) = 2K + 1$ in order to rule out perfect multicolinearity. Clearly, in this framework X does not include the constant term. Recall that in (2.1.1) that ε_i are i.i.d. $\left(0, \sigma_\varepsilon^2\right)$ so that $\varepsilon \sim \left(0, \sigma_\varepsilon^2 I_N\right)$ and that X and W are nonstochastic. Note, however, that we have not assumed any particular distribution for ε, e.g., the normal.

Given the model in (2.2.1.1) the least squares estimator of γ is

$$
\begin{aligned}
\hat{\gamma} &= (Z'Z)^{-1}Z'y \\
&= \gamma + (Z'Z)^{-1}Z'\varepsilon.
\end{aligned}
\tag{2.2.1.2}
$$

Using (2.2.1.2) it follows that

$$
\begin{aligned}
E(\hat{\gamma}) &= \gamma + E\left[(Z'Z)^{-1}Z'\varepsilon\right] \\
&= \gamma + (Z'Z)^{-1}Z'E(\varepsilon) \\
&= \gamma
\end{aligned}
\tag{2.2.1.3}
$$

so that $\hat{\gamma}$ is unbiased. Analogously, the variance–covariance matrix of $\hat{\gamma}$ is $VC_{\hat{\gamma}}$ where

$$
\begin{aligned}
VC_{\hat{\gamma}} &= E(\hat{\gamma} - \gamma)(\hat{\gamma} - \gamma)' \\
&= (Z'Z)^{-1}Z'E[\varepsilon\varepsilon']Z(Z'Z)^{-1} \\
&= (Z'Z)^{-1}Z'\sigma_\varepsilon^2 I_N Z(Z'Z)^{-1} \\
&= \sigma_\varepsilon^2(Z'Z)^{-1}.
\end{aligned}
\tag{2.2.1.4}
$$

However, the mean and variance covariance matrices given in (2.2.1.3) and (2.2.1.4) are not enough to test hypotheses concerning γ because the distribution of $\hat{\gamma}$ is not known. Of course, in this simple model if one assumes that ε is normally distributed, $\varepsilon \sim N(0, \sigma_\varepsilon^2 I_N)$, and also recalls that linear combinations of jointly normal variables are also normal, then via (2.2.1.2) $\hat{\gamma} \sim N(\gamma, \sigma_\varepsilon^2(Z'Z)^{-1})$. However, since σ_ε^2 will typically not be known, this result is still not enough to test hypotheses.

A typical unbiased estimator of σ_ε^2 is $\hat{\sigma}_\varepsilon^2 = (y - Z\hat{\gamma})'(y - Z\hat{\gamma})/(N - 2K - 1)$. Given this, and the normality assumption, tests of hypotheses can then be based on the usual t-ratio, or F tests. For example, let $\hat{\gamma}_i$ be the ith element of $\hat{\gamma}$, and let $\hat{\sigma}_{\hat{\gamma}_i}^2$ be the ith diagonal element of $\widehat{VC}_{\hat{\gamma}} = \hat{\sigma}_\varepsilon^2(Z'Z)^{-1}$. Then, e.g., using evident notation the variable corresponding to $\hat{\gamma}_i$ would be significant at the (two tail) 5% level if

$$
|\hat{\gamma}_i / \hat{\sigma}_{\hat{\gamma}_i}| > t_{N-2K-1}(0.975) \doteq 1.96,
$$

where $t_{N-2K-1}(0.975)$ would be taken from a table of values on the t distribution. Similarly, using evident notation, the joint hypothesis $H_0: R\gamma = r$ against $H_1: R\gamma \neq r$, where R is a known $q \times 2K+1$ matrix, $q < 2K+1$, and r is a known $q \times 1$ vector would be accepted at the 5% level if

$$(R\hat{\gamma} - r)[R\widehat{VC}_{\hat{\gamma}_i} R']^{-1}(R\hat{\gamma} - r) > F_{q,N-2K-1}(0.95).$$

In more realistic and complex models, the normality of the disturbance term will not be enough to determine the distribution of $\hat{\gamma}$. For this reason we give a simple illustration of the large sample approach. Specifically, we determine the large sample distribution of $\hat{\gamma}$ which, in turn, suggests an approximation to the small (or finite) sample distribution of $\hat{\gamma}$. Hypotheses can then be tested in terms of this small sample approximation. In the more complex models considered below, and in later chapters, the large sample procedures are essentially the same.

A complete set of formal assumptions for the general model in (2.2.1) is given in a later section. At this point we note that two of these assumptions, applied to (2.2.1.1), are that the elements of Z are uniformly bounded in absolute value, and $N^{-1}Z'Z \to Q_{zz}$ where Q_{zz} is a finite nonsingular matrix. In the analysis below recall that the elements in the error term in (2.2.1.1) are i.i.d. $(0, \sigma_\varepsilon^2)$.

The least squares estimator of γ in (2.2.1.2) can be expressed as

$$N^{1/2}(\hat{\gamma} - \gamma) = N(Z'Z)^{-1}[N^{-1/2}Z'\varepsilon]. \tag{2.2.1.5}$$

Given the assumption that $N(Z'Z)^{-1} \to Q_{zz}^{-1}$, the central limit theorem given in Section A.15 of Appendix A yields

$$N^{-1/2}Z'\varepsilon \xrightarrow{D} N(0, \sigma_\varepsilon^2 Q_{zz}). \tag{2.2.1.6}$$

Given (2.2.1.5) and (2.2.1.6), and the result in (A.10.3) in Appendix A, it then follows that

$$\begin{aligned} N^{1/2}(\hat{\gamma} - \gamma) &\xrightarrow{D} N(0, \sigma_\varepsilon^2 Q_{zz}^{-1} Q_{zz} Q_{zz}^{-1}) \\ &= N(0, \sigma_\varepsilon^2 Q_{zz}^{-1}). \end{aligned} \tag{2.2.1.7}$$

Using the results in Section A.12 of Appendix A, small sample inference, and tests of hypotheses can be based on the approximation

$$\hat{\gamma} \simeq N[\gamma, \hat{\sigma}_\varepsilon^2 (Z'Z)^{-1}] \tag{2.2.1.8}$$

where $\hat{\sigma}_\varepsilon^2 = (y - Z\hat{\gamma})'(y - Z\hat{\gamma})/(N - \tau)$ and τ can be taken to be $(2K+1)$, or zero. In both cases typical modeling assumptions will imply that $\hat{\sigma}_\varepsilon^2$ is consistent for σ_ε^2 since consistency is a large sample property. Note that the large sample distribution obtained in (2.2.1.7) does not require an assumed distribution of the random term ε.

In passing we note that the results above imply that $\hat{\gamma}$ is consistent. For example, (2.2.1.3) implies that $\hat{\gamma}$ is unbiased and its variance–covariance matrix in (2.2.1.4) is such that $\sigma_\varepsilon^2(Z'Z)^{-1} = \sigma_\varepsilon^2 N^{-1}[N(Z'Z)^{-1}] \to 0$ since $N(Z'Z)^{-1} \to Q_{ZZ}^{-1}$ which is a finite matrix. It then follows from Chebyshev's inequality in Section A.3 of Appendix A that $\hat{\gamma} \xrightarrow{P} \gamma$. This consistency result can also be obtained from (2.2.1.7) since $\hat{\gamma} - \gamma = N^{-1/2}[N^{1/2}(\hat{\gamma} - \gamma)] = N^{-1/2}0_P(1) \to 0$; see the discussion of orders in probability in Section A.14 of Appendix A.

Illustration 2.2.1.1: House value and its determinants

The data set used in this example is very well known among researchers in spatial econometrics since it has served as an example for many scientific contributions (see, e.g., Gilley and Pace, 1996, among others).[10] We estimate a model relating the logarithm of the median housing price in 506 Boston area communities (*price*) to various house and location characteristics such as the average number of *rooms*; the logarithm of the weighted distance (*dist*) of the community from five employment centers; a measure of per-capita crime in the community (*crime*); the concentration of nitrogen oxide (*nox*) in the air measured in parts per million; and a variable (*stratio*) measuring the average student–teacher ratio of schools in the community. Finally, we also include in the model the spatial lag of crime in neighboring communities (*wcrime*). The intuition is that being close to neighboring communities that have high level of crime reduces the median house value.

The OLS results from the estimated model are reported below:

$$\begin{aligned}\widehat{\log(price)} = {} & 2.049(0.159) - 0.875(0.101)\log(nox) - 0.272(0.039)\log(dist) \\ & - 0.036(0.005)\, stratio + 0.244(0.016)\, rooms \\ & - 0.009(0.002)\, crime - 0.016(0.002)\, wcrime\end{aligned}$$

where standard errors are in the parentheses.

The slope estimates all have the expected sign and are significantly different from zero. The coefficient estimate of the spatial lag of the crime variable is negative and statistically significant. It measures the semielasticity of price with respect to the per-capita crime in the neighboring communities.

10. For simplicity, we only consider some of the variables generally included in the empirical specification.

Illustration 2.2.1.2: A model of the murder rate

In the following example,[11] we relate the number of murders per 100,000 people (*mrdrte*) in each of the US 49 continental states to the state unemployment rate (*unem*) and the state total number of prisoners' executions over the past three years (*exec*). We also include the spatial lag of executions (*wexec*) in bordering states over the past three years. We are interested in seeing whether there is evidence for a deterrent effect of capital punishment. Our expectation on the coefficients is the following: The number of state executions should have a negative effect, and the unemployment rate should have a positive effect on the murder rate. We expect the coefficient of (*wexec*) to be negative. For example, the higher the number of executions in neighboring states, the lower the incentive to commit crime within the boundaries of those states.

The OLS results from the estimated model are reported below:

$$\begin{aligned}\widehat{mrdrte} = {} & -6.030(7.039) + 0.071(0.298)\ exec \\ & + 2.384(1.061)\ unem - 0.182(0.529)\ wexec\end{aligned}$$

where standard deviations are in the parentheses.

We start by saying that the only significant variable is the rate of unemployment, and, therefore, the regression does not provide any evidence that capital punishment acts as a deterrent for murderers. Likewise, spatial effects play no roles when the spatial lag of the executions is included. The R-squared of the model is only 0.115. The lesson to be learned from this illustration is that "true model" for the murder rate is more complex.

Illustration 2.2.1.3: A model of DUI arrests

The data in this example were used by Drukker et al. (2013c,d) in a series of papers to explain the spatial functions available from STATA. The same data set was also used by Bivand and Piras (2015) for a comparison of the implementation of spatial econometrics model estimation techniques across different software packages.[12] The simulated US Driving Under the Influence (DUI) county data set covers 3109 counties (omitting Alaska, Hawaii, and US territories), and uses simulations from variables used by Powers and Wilson (2004).[13] The dependent variable, *dui,* is defined as the alcohol-related arrest rate per 100,000

11. The dataset has been taken from Wooldridge (2013). The original dataset is a panel data on 51 US states (including Alaska and Hawaii), but we only consider the most recent year (1993). Additionally, to create the row-standardized weighting matrix (with the queen criterion), we used a shape file that was obtained from the following address: http://www.arcgis.com/home/item.html?id=f7f805eb65eb4ab787a0a3e1116ca7e5.

12. In particular, they focus on R, Stata, Matlab, and PySAL.

13. The counties are taken from an ESRI Shapefile downloaded from the US Census.

daily vehicle miles traveled (DVMT). The explanatory variables include *police* (number of sworn officers per 100,000 DVMT); *nondui* (non-alcohol-related arrests per 100,000 DVMT); *vehicles* (number of registered vehicles per 1000 residents), and *dry* (a dummy for counties that prohibit alcohol sale within their borders, about 10% of counties). We also consider *wpolice,* which is the spatial lag of the number of officers in neighboring counties. Powers and Wilson (2004, p. 331) found that "there is no significant relationship between prohibition status and the DUI arrest rate when controlling for the proportionate number of sworn officers and the non-DUI arrest rate per officer" when examining data for 75 counties in Arkansas.

The OLS results from the estimated model are reported below:

$$\begin{aligned}\widehat{dui} &= -6.474(0.541) + 0.599(0.015)\ police + 0.000(0.001)\ nondui \\ &\quad + 0.016(0.001)\ vehicles + 0.107(0.035)\ dry + 0.034(0.016)\ wpolice.\end{aligned}$$

In this extended formulation of the model, there is some evidence, *ceteris paribus*, of the relationship between prohibition and arrest rate. Additionally, the number of officer in neighboring counties significantly affects the arrest rate. The simulated data has a higher R^2 value of 0.850, and the explanatory variables with the exception of *nondui* are all significant.

2.2.2 Estimation When $\rho_1 = 0$ and $\rho_2 \neq 0$

As a one step generalization, consider now the case in which the error terms are directly interrelated but the dependent variable is not:

$$\begin{aligned}y &= Z\gamma + u, \\ u &= \rho_2 W u + \varepsilon\end{aligned} \tag{2.2.2.1}$$

where again Z and γ are defined in (2.2.1.1). This model is often referred to as the spatial error model. In this case parameter γ should be estimated by a GLS procedure which accounts for the specification of the disturbance terms.

Properties of u

Since

$$u = (I_N - \rho_2 W)^{-1} \varepsilon \tag{2.2.2.2}$$

and $\varepsilon \sim \left(0, \sigma_\varepsilon^2 I_N\right)$, it follows that

$$\begin{aligned}E\left(u\right) &= (I_N - \rho_2 W)^{-1} E(\varepsilon) = 0, \\ E\left(uu'\right) &= (I_N - \rho_2 W)^{-1} E[\varepsilon\varepsilon'] \left(I_N - \rho_2 W'\right)^{-1}\end{aligned} \tag{2.2.2.3}$$

$$\begin{aligned} &= \sigma_\varepsilon^2 (I_N - \rho_2 W)^{-1} \left(I_N - \rho_2 W'\right)^{-1} \\ &= \sigma_\varepsilon^2 \Omega_u, \\ \Omega_u &= (I_N - \rho_2 W)^{-1} \left(I_N - \rho_2 W'\right)^{-1}. \end{aligned}$$

For most weighting matrices, the elements of u will be both spatially correlated and heteroskedastic.

Assume for the moment that ρ_2 is known. Then, the GLS estimator of γ is

$$\hat{\gamma}_{GLS} = \left(Z'\Omega_u^{-1}Z\right)^{-1} Z'\Omega_u^{-1}y. \tag{2.2.2.4}$$

Substituting y from (2.2.1.1) into (2.2.2.4) it follows that

$$\hat{\gamma}_{GLS} = \gamma + \left(Z'\Omega_u^{-1}Z\right)^{-1} Z'\Omega_u^{-1}u. \tag{2.2.2.5}$$

Therefore, as easily shown,

$$\begin{aligned} E(\hat{\gamma}_{GLS}) &= \gamma, \\ VC_{\hat{\gamma}_{GLS}} &= E(\hat{\gamma}_{GLS} - \gamma)(\hat{\gamma}_{GLS} - \gamma) \\ &= \sigma^2 \left(Z'\Omega_u^{-1}Z\right)^{-1}. \end{aligned} \tag{2.2.2.6}$$

In general, ρ_2 will not be known and so the GLS estimator in (2.2.2.4) is not feasible. There are, however, two feasible procedures. The first one, which we are going to see next, is based on maximum likelihood. The second procedure (discussed in a later section) is based on a generalized moments estimator of ρ_2.

2.2.2.1 Maximum Likelihood Estimation: $\rho_1 = 0$, $\rho_2 \neq 0$[14]

Typically, maximum likelihood estimation is based on the normality assumption, $\varepsilon \sim N\left(0, \sigma_\varepsilon^2 I_N\right)$.[15] Assuming normality of ε, it follows from (2.2.2.2) that

14. There is a large body of literature which focuses on the maximum likelihood procedure, and procedures associated with it; see, e.g., Anselin (1988), Baltagi and Li (2004), Beron and Vijverberg (2004), Bolduc et al. (1995), Burridge (2012), Case (1991), Case et al. (1993), Dubin (1995), Florax and de Graaff (2004), Mur and Angulo (2006), Lee (2004), Lee and Yu (2012b), Yu et al. (2008).

15. Let Ψ be a random $r \times 1$ vector with mean μ and nonsingular (and therefore positive definite) VC matrix $\sigma^2\Omega$. Then, if Ψ is multivariate normal its density is

$$f(\psi) = \frac{e^{-\frac{1}{2\sigma^2}(\psi-\mu)'\Omega^{-1}(\psi-\mu)}}{(2\pi)^{r/2}(\sigma^2)^{r/2}\,|\Omega|_+^{1/2}}, \qquad -\infty < \psi < \infty$$

where $|\Omega|_+^{1/2}$ is the positive square root of $|\Omega|$, and $-\infty < \psi < \infty$ is meant to hold for each of the r elements of ψ.

$$u \sim N\left(0, \sigma_\varepsilon^2 \Omega_u\right), \tag{2.2.2.1.1}$$
$$\Omega_u = \sigma_\varepsilon^2 \left(I_N - \rho_2 W\right)^{-1} \left(I_N - \rho_2 W'\right)^{-1},$$

and then from (2.2.2.1) we get

$$y \sim N\left(Z\gamma, \sigma_\varepsilon^2 \Omega_u\right). \tag{2.2.2.1.2}$$

Since the likelihood function is the joint distribution of the dependent variable,

$$L = \frac{e^{-\frac{1}{2\sigma_\varepsilon^2}[y - Z\gamma]' \Omega_u^{-1} [y - Z\gamma]}}{\left(\sigma_\varepsilon^2\right)^{\frac{N}{2}} \sqrt{2\pi}^N \left|I_N - \rho_2 W\right|_+^{-1}}. \tag{2.2.2.1.3}$$

Typically, it is easier to maximize the logarithm of the likelihood than the likelihood itself. The logarithm of L defined in (2.2.2.1.3) can be expressed and simplified as follows:

$$\begin{aligned}
\ln(L) = &-\frac{1}{2\sigma_\varepsilon^2} \left[y - Z\gamma\right]' \left[I_N - \rho_2 W'\right] \left[I_N - \rho_2 W\right] \left[y - Z\gamma\right] \\
&- \frac{N}{2} \ln\left(\sigma_\varepsilon^2\right) + \ln\left|I_N - \rho_2 W\right|_+ - N \ln\left(\sqrt{2\pi}\right) \\
= &-\frac{1}{2\sigma_\varepsilon^2} \left(\left[I_N - \rho_2 W\right]\left[y - Z\gamma\right]\right)' \left(\left[I_N - \rho_2 W\right]\left[y - Z\gamma\right]\right) \\
&- \frac{N}{2} \ln\left(\sigma_\varepsilon^2\right) + \ln\left(\left|I_N - \rho_2 W\right|_+\right) - N \ln\left(\sqrt{2\pi}\right) \\
= &-\frac{1}{2\sigma_\varepsilon^2} \left(y^*(\rho_2) - Z^*(\rho_2)\gamma\right)' \left(y^*(\rho_2) - Z^*(\rho_2)\gamma\right) \\
&- \frac{N}{2} \ln\left(\sigma_\varepsilon^2\right) + \ln\left(\left|I_N - \rho_2 W\right|_+\right) - N \ln\left(\sqrt{2\pi}\right)
\end{aligned} \tag{2.2.2.1.4}$$

where

$$y^*(\rho_2) = y - \rho_2 W y, \tag{2.2.2.1.5}$$

For future reference note that, in general, since Ω is positive definite, there exists a matrix V such that $V'\Omega V = I_r$ where V is nonsingular. Therefore, $\Omega = (V')^{-1} V^{-1}$, and so in the density above

$$\begin{aligned}
|\Omega|_+^{1/2} &= |\sigma^2 (V')^{-1} V^{-1}|^{1/2} \\
&= (\sigma^2)^{r/2} |V^{-1}|_+.
\end{aligned}$$

Note that in (2.2.2.1.3) the VC matrix has this "decomposition".
Also for future reference, we note that the marginal distributions of a multivariate normal, say of Ψ above, are themselves normal. The means and VC matrices of these marginal distributions are given by the respective elements of μ and $\sigma^2\Omega$, e.g., the mean and variance of the first element of Ψ are respectively the first element of μ and the first diagonal element of $\sigma^2\Omega$.

$$Z^*(\rho_2) = Z - \rho_2 W Z.$$

Note $y^*(\rho_2)$ and $Z^*(\rho_2)$ are spatial counterparts to the Cochrane–Orcutt transformation; see Cochrane and Orcutt (1949).

At this point we note a potentially serious problem in maximizing $\ln(L)$. This problem relates to the term $\ln\left(|I_N - \rho_2 W|_+\right)$ In fact, this term must:

(a) Be evaluated repeatedly for each trial value of ρ_2. If N is large this will indeed be "tedious" for certain weighting matrices. For example, cross-sectional units could relate to counties, and there are over 3000 counties in the US. In other cross-sectional studies, the number of cross-sectional units could be families and so it could be the case that N gets large very easily.

(b) Using Ord's (1975) suggestion for evaluating the determinant in terms of its characteristic roots, we have

$$\ln|I_N - \rho_2 W|_+ = \ln[(1-\rho_2\lambda_1)\cdots(1-\rho_2\lambda_N)] \qquad (2.2.2.1.6)$$
$$= \sum_{i=1}^{N} \ln(1-\rho_2\lambda_i).$$

If the roots can be accurately evaluated, $\ln|1 - \rho_2 W|_+$ can be evaluated in terms of the sum for each trial value of ρ_2. This will be far simpler than the method proposed in (a). The problem is that if $N \geq 450$ both (a) and (b) could involve computational accuracy problems. For example, Kelejian and Prucha (1999) found that the calculation of roots for even a 400×400 non-symmetric matrix involved accuracy problems. Despite this, many other solutions have been proposed, both exact (e.g., Cholesky decomposition for symmetric matrices) and approximated such as the Chebyshev decomposition (Pace and LeSage, 2004) or the Monte Carlo approach (Barry and Pace, 1999). A complete treatment of these alternative methods is beyond the scope of our book and it can be found, for example, in LeSage and Pace (2009). Here we just want to mention that most of the methods generally used to approximate the log-Jacobian term (or simply speed up its computations) are both very efficient and reliable particularly when the sample size is large and the weighting matrix is particularly sparse.[16]

(c) Another problem with the maximum likelihood procedure itself is that many models considered in practice are such that the regressor matrix X contains some regressors which are endogenous. In this case the maximum likelihood procedure cannot be implemented unless the joint distribution of those endogenous regressors and the model dependent variable is known.

---

16. Modern spatial econometrics software, such as R or Matlab, has the capability of dealing with many of those methods.

This will typically not be the case, and so other procedures are suggested below!

The Form of the MLE for γ and σ_ε^2

Based on (2.2.2.1.4), we have

$$\frac{\partial \ln L}{\partial \gamma} = -\frac{1}{2\sigma_\varepsilon^2}\left(-2Z^*(\rho_2)' y^*(\rho_2) + 2Z^*(\rho_2)' Z^*(\rho_2)\gamma\right), \tag{2.2.2.1.7}$$
$$\frac{\partial \ln L}{\partial \sigma_\varepsilon^2} = \frac{1}{2\sigma_\varepsilon^4}\left[y^*(\rho_2) - Z^*(\rho_2)\gamma\right]'\left[y^*(\rho_2) - Z^*(\rho_2)\gamma\right] - \frac{N}{2\sigma_\varepsilon^2}.$$

It follows that

$$\hat{\gamma}_{ML} = \left[Z^*(\hat{\rho}_2)' Z^*(\hat{\rho}_2)\right]^{-1} Z^*(\hat{\rho}_2)' y^*(\hat{\rho}_2), \tag{2.2.2.1.8}$$
$$\hat{\sigma}_\varepsilon^2 = \frac{1}{N}\left[y^*(\hat{\rho}_2) - Z^*(\hat{\rho}_2)\hat{\gamma}_{ML}\right]'\left[y^*(\hat{\rho}_2) - Z^*(\hat{\rho}_2)\hat{\gamma}_{ML}\right].$$

The interpretation of the MLEs is straightforward. Premultiplying (2.2.2.1) by $(I_N - \rho_2 W)$ yields

$$y^*(\rho_2) = Z^*(\rho_2)\gamma + \varepsilon, \quad \varepsilon \sim N\left(0, \sigma^2 I_N\right). \tag{2.2.2.1.9}$$

If ρ_2 were known, the model in (2.2.2.1.9) would be a standard linear regression model with a disturbance term that is normally distributed. The efficient estimator of γ would be the least squares estimator defined in (2.2.2.1.8) with $\hat{\rho}_2$ replaced by ρ_2, e.g., the MLE is just the feasible counterpart to that estimator.

In an important article, Lee (2004) gave a formal demonstration of conditions that ensure consistency and asymptotic normality of the ML estimators for the general spatial model considered. In applied studies, dealing with a variety of regression models, it is (almost) always assumed that the usual results hold. For the model at hand, we have

$$\sqrt{N}\left(\hat{P} - P\right) \xrightarrow{D} N(0, V), \tag{2.2.2.1.10}$$
$$V^{-1} = -\lim E\left[N^{-1}\left(\frac{\partial^2 \ln L}{\partial P \partial P'}\right)\right], \quad P = \begin{bmatrix} \gamma \\ \rho_2 \\ \sigma_\varepsilon^2 \end{bmatrix}.$$

The matrix $-E\left(\frac{\partial^2 \ln L}{\partial P \partial P'}\right)$ is referred to as the information matrix, denoted by $I(P)$, and

$$I(P) = -E\left(\frac{\partial^2 \ln L}{\partial P \partial P'}\right) = E\left(\frac{\partial \ln(L)}{\partial P}\right)\left(\frac{\partial \ln(L)}{\partial P}\right)'. \tag{2.2.2.1.11}$$

Small sample inference is typically based on the approximations

$$\hat{P} = \begin{bmatrix} \hat{\gamma}_{ML} \\ \hat{\rho}_{2,ML} \\ \hat{\sigma}^2_{\varepsilon,ML} \end{bmatrix}, \quad \hat{P} \dot{\sim} N\left(P, -\frac{\hat{V}}{N}\right), \tag{2.2.2.1.12}$$

$$\frac{\hat{V}}{N} = \left[\frac{\partial^2 \ln L}{\partial P \partial P'}\right]^{-1}_{\hat{P}}.$$

A Computational Note on ML

The estimators in (2.2.2.1.8) are functions of $\hat{\rho}_2$. Computationally, a concentrated likelihood approach is generally taken. The idea is to concentrate out of the likelihood function both γ and σ^2_ε. The resulting function only depends on the parameter ρ_2. Then, from a computational perspective, the following steps are undertaken:

1. A simple linear regression model of y over Z allows the computation of an initial set of OLS residuals.

2. Using these residuals, one can maximize the concentrated likelihood and find an initial estimate of ρ_2.

3. Next, a feasible GLS procedure can be implemented to estimate γ, and another set of GLS residuals can be computed.

4. Finally, one should iterate back and forth between FGLS and ML until a convergence criterion is met.

Virtually all the available software use a procedure like the one described above.

Illustration 2.2.2.1.1: House value, air pollution, and crime in Boston

Let us consider again the housing price dataset in Boston. There are many additional variables that were not included in the original specification that might well be spatially correlated. In this illustration we account for these "left-out" variables in terms of a disturbance term that follows a spatial autoregressive model of order one.[17]

17. We use the expression "spatial autoregressive model of order one" to indicate that we only consider the first spatial lag. However, other models could be specified including more than one lag (or even lags including different spatial weighting matrix). The estimation theory for these models was considered by Lee and Liu (2010) and Badinger and Egger (2011), among others. Evident estimators should be suggested by problems 1–3 at the end of this chapter.

The results from the estimated model that include an autocorrelated disturbance term are reported below:

$$\begin{aligned}\widehat{\log(price)} &= 2.306(0.170) - 0.588(0.132)\log(nox) - 0.151(0.058)\log(dist)\\ &\quad - 0.032(0.006)\, stratio + 0.193(0.013)\, rooms\\ &\quad - 0.008(0.001)\, crime - 0.014(0.002)\, wcrime.\end{aligned}$$

The model was estimated by ML using the Ord (1975) procedure to calculate the Jacobian term. The value of ρ_2 is equal to 0.681 and is statistically significant at the 1% level (with an asymptotic standard error of 0.034). The coefficient measuring the elasticity of price with respect to the level of pollution is lower than the one estimated in Examples 2.2.1.1. This can be interpreted as a sign of misspecification of the simple OLS model without the spatially autocorrelated error term.

Let us now consider the same model estimated by ML but using a different method for the computation of the Jacobian term.[18] The results from this model are reported below[19]:

$$\begin{aligned}\widehat{\log(price)} &= 2.305(0.170) - 0.589(0.132)\log(nox) - 0.151(0.058)\log(dist)\\ &\quad - 0.032(0.006)\, stratio + 0.193(0.013)\, rooms\\ &\quad - 0.008(0.001)\, crime - 0.014(0.0025)\, wcrime\end{aligned}$$

with $\rho_2 = 0.680$ again strongly significant. As can be noted, there is virtually no difference between the exact and approximated computation of the log-Jacobian term on this data.

2.2.3 Assumptions of the General Model

Before considering the development of an IV procedure put forth by Kelejian and Prucha (1998, 1999) for the general model in (2.2.1), we review and interpret its basic assumptions.

18. Of the various methods available, we choose the Monte Carlo approach (Barry and Pace, 1999, LeSage and Pace, 2009). This method is based on the simple intuition: Since the matrix logarithm has a simple infinite series expansion in terms of the powers of W and that the trace is a linear operator, the log-determinant can be expressed as a weighted series of traces of the powers of W:

$$\ln|I_N - \rho_2 W| = -\sum_{i=1}^{\infty} \frac{\rho_2^i Tr(W^i)}{i} = -\sum_{i=1}^{k} \frac{\rho_2^i Tr(W^i)}{i} - R.$$

For small R, the expression above can be used to approximate the log-determinant.

19. Note that the Monte Carlo approach is an approximated method therefore the results are subject to change (slightly) over different trials.

First note that the general model in (2.2.1) can be expressed as

$$y = Z\beta + u, \qquad (2.2.3.1)$$
$$u = \rho_2 (Wu) + \varepsilon, \quad |\rho_1| < 1, \ |\rho_2| < 1,$$

where

$$Z = (e_N, X, Wy, WX),$$
$$\beta = (a, B_1', \rho_1, B_2').$$

As we already observed in previous sections of this chapter, the presence of Wy introduces an endogeneity into the model. Therefore, the model needs to be estimated by a procedure which accounts for this endogeneity. In this section we discuss an instrumental variable procedure.

As shown in Kelejian and Prucha (1998), the ideal instruments are simply $E(Wy)$. Assume that the characteristic roots of the weighting matrix W are less than or equal to 1 in absolute value, which they would be if W is row normalized. In this case

$$(I_N - \rho_1 W)^{-1} = I_N + \rho_1 W + \rho_1^2 W^2 + \dots . \qquad (2.2.3.2)$$

Given this inverse, the solution of the model for y as described in (2.2.3.1) is

$$y = (I_N - \rho_1 W)^{-1} [ae_N + XB_1 + WXB_2 + u] \qquad (2.2.3.3)$$
$$= [I_N + \rho_1 W + \rho_1^2 W^2 + \dots][ae_N + XB_1 + WXB_2 + u].$$

Since $E(u) = 0$, it follows from (2.2.3.3) that the mean of y is linear in $e_N, We_N, W^2 e_N, \dots, X, WX, W^2 X, \dots$.

Our instrument matrix for this model is H, where H is an $N \times k_H$ nonstochastic matrix which consists of the linearly independent (LI) columns of $(e_N, X, We_N, WX, W^2 e_N, W^2 X, \dots, W^r X)$ and is denoted as

$$H = (e_N, X, We_N, WX, W^2 e_N, W^2 X, \dots, W^r X)_{LI} \qquad (2.2.3.4)$$

where r is a finite constant. In many cases the weighting matrix is row normalized and so the terms $We_N, W^2 e_N, \dots$ are not considered. The reason for this is that $We_N = e_N$, $W^2 e_N = We_N = e_N$, and so on, by repeated substitution $W^r e_N = e_N$. For estimation, researchers often take $r = 2$.[20]

20. For further details, see, e.g., Kelejian and Prucha (1999), Lee (2003, 2007), Kelejian et al. (2004), and Das et al. (2003), among others.

For the error term in (2.2.3.1), let $\bar{u} = Wu$, $\bar{\bar{u}} = W^2 u$, and $\bar{\varepsilon} = W\varepsilon$, and let

$$g = \frac{1}{N}\begin{bmatrix} u'u \\ \bar{u}'\bar{u} \\ u'\bar{u} \end{bmatrix}, \quad G = \frac{1}{N}\begin{bmatrix} -\bar{u}'\bar{u} & 2u'\bar{u} & N \\ -\bar{\bar{u}}'\bar{\bar{u}} & 2\bar{\bar{u}}'\bar{u} & Tr(W'W) \\ -\bar{u}'\bar{\bar{u}} & u'\bar{\bar{u}} + \bar{u}'\bar{u} & 0 \end{bmatrix}. \quad (2.2.3.5)$$

Using this notation, the assumptions for the general model are given below. Their interpretations follow.

Assumption 2.1. The elements of the innovation vector ε are independent and identically distributed with mean zero and variance σ_ε^2, and have finite fourth moments. That is, ε_i is i.i.d. $\left(0, \sigma_\varepsilon^2\right)$, $E\left(\varepsilon_i^4\right) < \infty$.[21]

Assumption 2.2. $|\rho_1| < 1$, $|\rho_2| < 1$.

Assumption 2.3. Let $P_{(a)} = (I_N - aW)$. Then $P_{(a)}$ is nonsingular for all $|a| < 1$.

Assumption 2.4. The diagonal elements of the spatial weighting matrix W are set to zero: $w_{ii} = 0, i = 1, \ldots, N$.

Assumption 2.5. The row and column sums of W and $P_{(a)}^{-1}$ are uniformly bounded in absolute value for all $|a| < 1$.

Assumption 2.6. (a) $g \xrightarrow{P} g^*$ where the elements of g^* are finite; (b) $G \xrightarrow{P} G^*$ where G^* is a finite nonsingular matrix.

Assumption 2.7. The matrix of regressors X and the matrix of instruments H are nonstochastic matrices whose elements are uniformly bounded in absolute value.

Assumption 2.8. (a) The matrix of the exogenous regressors has full column rank: $rank(e_N, X, WX) = 2k + 1$; (b) The instrument matrix H has full column rank and contains at least the columns (e_N, X, WX, W^2X) and $rank(H) \geq 2 + 2k$.

Assumption 2.9. The following matrix products are such that:

$$(A)\ p\lim_{N\to\infty} N^{-1}H'Z = Q_{HZ},$$

$$(B)\ p\lim_{N\to\infty} N^{-1}H'WZ = Q_{HWZ},$$

21. This statement of the assumption does not allow for triangular arrays. A more formal statement of the assumption which does allow for triangular arrays is the central limit theorem in Section A.15 of the appendix.

$$(C)\ p \lim_{N\to\infty} N^{-1}H'H = Q_{HH}$$

where Q_{HZ}, Q_{HWZ}, Q_{HH}, and $(Q_{HZ} - \rho_2 HWZ)$ are finite full column rank matrices, and so Q_{HH} is positive definite.

Interpretations of Assumptions

On an intuitive level, Assumption 2.1 indicates that the elements of ε are independent and identically distributed with zero mean and finite fourth moments. As stated, this assumption does not account for triangular arrays which (most) spatial models imply. The assumption is given in this simple form for ease of presentation and interpretation. A formal version of this assumption which accounts for triangular arrays is given in Section A.15 of the appendix on large sample theory. In that formal version the dependence of the disturbance vector ε and its elements on the sample size is denoted as ε_N and ε_{iN}, respectively.

Note that in the formal assumption in Section A.15, for each given value of $N \geq 1$, the terms $\varepsilon_{1,N}, \varepsilon_{2,N}, ..., \varepsilon_{N,N}$ are assumed to be identically and jointly independently distributed. It does **not** say, e.g., that $\varepsilon_{5,N}$ is independent of ε_{5,N^*} if $N^* \neq N$. These two terms may, or may not, be independent; indeed, they may not even relate to the same unit; see the discussion in Section 2.1.1.

Assumptions 2.2 and 2.3 imply that the general model in (2.2.1) is complete in that it can be solved for the dependent vector y in terms of the exogenous variables, the weighting matrix, and the stochastic term ε. In particular, as in (2.1.1.1),

$$y = (I_N - \rho_1 W)^{-1}[ae_N + XB_1 + (WX)\,B_2 + (I_N - \rho_2 W)^{-1}\varepsilon]. \quad (2.2.3.6)$$

Assumption 2.4 is typical in that it is virtually assumed in all applied works. It states that the diagonal elements of W are taken to be zero. This simply implies that no unit is viewed as its own neighbor.

Although Assumption 2.5 is typically made in formal large sample analysis,[22] it does place restrictions which may not hold in certain models. For example, in a spatial framework if one unit, say the fifth unit, is central in that all other units relate to it in a nonnegligible fashion, then the sum of the absolute values of the elements in the fifth column of W would be expected to diverge as $N \to \infty$. Thus, Assumption 2.5 rules out models which have a "central" unit which all units are related to with weights that are bounded away from zero.

Parts (a) and (b) of Assumption 2.6 relate to the consistency of one of our suggested estimators of ρ_2 described below. This is demonstrated in the appendix. The consistency of our second suggested estimator of ρ_2, also described

22. See, e.g., Kelejian and Prucha (1998, 1999, 2004), Lee (2004, 2007), and Kelejian and Piras (2011), among others.

below, then follows on an intuitive level. A formal, but tedious proof of consistency for the second suggested estimator is given in Kelejian and Prucha (1999).

Given Assumptions 2.3 and 2.5, we give results in Section 2.2.4 below, which demonstrate how to easily determine the probability limits described in Assumption 2.6.

Assumption 2.7 and part (a) of Assumption 2.8 rule out perfect multicolinearity. Part (b) of Assumption 2.8 implies that the number of linearly independent instruments is at least as large as the number of parameters to be estimated in the model. Assumption 2.9 is standard in large sample analysis and will, along with our other assumptions, ensure consistency and asymptotic normality of our regression parameter estimator.[23]

2.2.4 A Generalized Moments Estimator of ρ_2

The IV estimation of our general model in (2.2.3.1) which accounts for the spatial correlation requires an estimator of ρ_2. In this section we suggest two generalized moments estimators (GMM) given in Kelejian and Prucha (1999) for ρ_2. The first one of these two estimators is linear, and the second one is nonlinear. In the appendix to this chapter we give a somewhat high-level proof that the linear estimator is consistent under very reasonable conditions. That proof will strongly suggest that the nonlinear estimator is also consistent. Our high-level proof is not overly tedious, is straightforward, and instructive in that its format can be applied in other situations. A more complex low-level proof that both of our estimators are consistent is given by Kelejian and Prucha (1999).

As one might expect, our estimator of ρ_2 will be based on an estimated disturbance vector, u, which in turn requires an initial estimator of the regression parameters, β. In this section we also describe this estimator.

A Preliminary Result on Limits of Stochastic Quadratic Forms

Let S be an $N \times N$ nonstochastic matrix whose row and column sums are uniformly bounded in absolute value. Let $\nu' = (\nu_1, \ldots, \nu_N)$ where ν_i are i.i.d. $\left(0, \sigma_\nu^2\right)$ and $E\left(\nu_i^4\right) = \mu_4 < \infty$. Then,

$$\frac{\nu' S \nu}{N} - E(\frac{\nu' S \nu}{N}) \xrightarrow{P} 0 \qquad (2.2.4.1)$$

where, of course,

$$E(\frac{\nu' S \nu}{N}) = \sigma_\nu^2 \frac{Tr\,(S)}{N}.$$

23. For example, assumptions similar to our Assumption 2.8 have been used in various frameworks, see, e.g., Kelejian and Prucha (1998, 2004), Kapoor et al. (2007), Kelejian and Piras (2011), and Lee (2004).

If the limit of $Tr\,(S)\,/N$ exists, and is given by

$$\lim_{N\to\infty} \frac{Tr\,(S)}{N} = S^*, \tag{2.2.4.2}$$

then from (2.2.4.1) we have

$$\frac{\nu' S \nu}{N} \xrightarrow{P} \sigma_\nu^2 S^*. \tag{2.2.4.3}$$

The proof of (2.2.4.1) is given in the appendix to this chapter.

The result in (2.2.4.1) is important, and somewhat general, and will be used at various points in this book. As a simple application of (2.2.4.1)–(2.2.4.3), the reader should convince himself/herself that

$$(\frac{\nu' I_N \nu}{N}) = (\frac{\nu'\nu}{N}) \xrightarrow{P} \sigma_\nu^2. \tag{2.2.4.4}$$

Consider again Assumption 2.6 which relates to the probability limits of g and G. Since $\bar{u} = Wu$ and $\bar{\bar{u}} = W^2 u$, every element of g and G, except for those in the third column of G, can be expressed as a quadratic form in the disturbance vector u. Since $u = (I_N - \rho_2 W)^{-1}\varepsilon$ and $\bar{\varepsilon} = W\varepsilon$, these terms can also be expressed as quadratic forms in the innovation vector ε. Finally, note that the matrices in these quadratic forms in ε involve products of W and $(I_N - \rho_2 W)^{-1}$. Since $|\rho_2| < 1$, Assumption 2.5 implies that the row and column sums of W and $(I_N - \rho_2 W)^{-1}$ are uniformly bounded in absolute value. Furthermore, since the row and column sums of the product of such matrices are also uniformly bounded in absolute value, each term in g and all the terms in G, other than the constants in the third column, can be expressed as $\varepsilon' S \varepsilon$ where, again, S is a matrix whose rows and column sums are uniformly bounded in absolute value.[24] The probability limits in Assumption 2.6 can be determined using the result in (2.2.4.3).

A Preliminary, but Consistent Estimator of β

Our preliminary consistent estimator of β is the two stage least squares (henceforth, 2SLS) estimator using the instrument matrix H given in (2.2.3.4). Specifically, let $\tilde{Z} = H(H'H)^{-1}H'Z$; then our preliminary estimators of β in (2.2.3.1) and of the disturbance vector u are

$$\tilde{\beta} = (\tilde{Z}'\tilde{Z})^{-1}\tilde{Z}'y, \tag{2.2.4.5}$$
$$\hat{u} = y - Z\tilde{\beta}.$$

24. Let a and b be any two finite constants. Then the row and column sums of $aS + bS$ are clearly also uniformly bounded in absolute value, i.e., $aS + bS = S$.

To see the consistency of $\tilde{\beta}$, first note that $H(H'H)^{-1}H'$ is symmetric idempotent and so $\tilde{Z}'Z = \tilde{Z}'\tilde{Z}$. Thus, replacing y by its expression in (2.2.3.1) we have

$$\begin{aligned}\tilde{\beta} &= \beta + (\tilde{Z}'\tilde{Z})^{-1}\tilde{Z}'u \qquad (2.2.4.6)\\ &= \beta + \left([N^{-1}Z'H][N(H'H)^{-1}][N^{-1}H'Z]\right)^{-1} * \\ &[N^{-1}Z'H][N^{-1}H'H]^{-1}[N^{-1}H'u].\end{aligned}$$

Assumptions 2.9 and 2.6 imply that

$$(\tilde{\beta} - \beta) - (Q'_{HZ}Q^{-1}_{HH}Q_{HZ})^{-1}Q'_{HZ}Q^{-1}_{HH}[N^{-1}H'u] \xrightarrow{P} 0. \qquad (2.2.4.7)$$

Since, by Assumption 2.9, $(Q'_{HZ}Q^{-1}_{HH}Q_{HZ})^{-1}Q'_{HZ}Q^{-1}_{HH}$ is a finite matrix, it should be clear from (2.2.4.7) that $\tilde{\beta}$ is consistent: $\tilde{\beta} \xrightarrow{P} \beta$ if $N^{-1}H'u \xrightarrow{P} 0$. This follows from Chebyshev's inequality. To see that this is the case, let $\phi = N^{-1}H'u$, and note that $E(\phi) = 0$ and $E(\phi\phi') = \sigma_\varepsilon^2 N^{-2}H'\Omega H$, where $\Omega = (I_N - \rho_2 W)^{-1}(I_N - \rho_2 W')^{-1}$. Assumption 2.5 implies that the row and column sums of Ω are uniformly bounded in absolute value; it then follows from statement 4 following (2.1.4.4) that $N^{-2}H'\Omega H \to 0$. Therefore, by Chebyshev's inequality $N^{-1}H'u \xrightarrow{P} 0$ and so $\tilde{\beta} \xrightarrow{P} \beta$.

Development of the GMM of ρ_2

We now develop a GMM estimator for ρ_2. This GMM estimator will be based on $\tilde{\beta}$ and $\hat{u}$ in (2.2.4.5).

First note from (2.2.3.1) that

$$u - \rho_2 Wu = \varepsilon. \qquad (2.2.4.8)$$

Premultiplying across by W yields

$$Wu - \rho_2 W^2 u = W\varepsilon. \qquad (2.2.4.9)$$

Again, let $\bar{u} = Wu$, $\bar{\bar{u}} = W^2u$, $\bar{\varepsilon} = W\varepsilon$, and denote their ith elements by $\bar{u}_i$, $\bar{\bar{u}}_i$, and $\bar{\varepsilon}_i$, respectively. Then

$$\begin{aligned} u_i - \rho_2 \bar{u}_i &= \varepsilon_i, \qquad (2.2.4.10)\\ \bar{u}_i - \rho_2 \bar{\bar{u}}_i &= \bar{\varepsilon}_i, \quad i = 1, \ldots, N.\end{aligned}$$

Square the first line in (2.2.4.10), then sum and divide by N to get

$$\frac{\sum u_i^2}{N} + \rho_2^2 \frac{\sum \bar{u}_i^2}{N} - 2\rho_2 \frac{\sum u_i \bar{u}_i}{N} = \frac{\sum \varepsilon_i^2}{N}. \qquad (2.2.4.11)$$

Square the second line in (2.2.4.10), then sum and divide by N to get

$$\frac{\sum \bar{u}_i^2}{N} + \rho_2^2 \frac{\sum \bar{\bar{u}}_i^2}{N} - 2\rho_2 \frac{\sum \bar{u}_i \bar{\bar{u}}_i}{N} = \frac{\sum \bar{\varepsilon}_i^2}{N}. \tag{2.2.4.12}$$

Finally, multiply the first line in (2.2.4.10) by the second line in (2.2.4.10), then sum and divide by N to get

$$\frac{\sum u_i \bar{u}_i}{N} + \rho_2^2 \frac{\sum \bar{u}_i \bar{\bar{u}}_i}{N} - \rho_2 \left[\frac{\sum u_i \bar{\bar{u}}_i}{N} + \frac{\sum \bar{u}_i^2}{N} \right] = \frac{\sum \varepsilon_i \bar{\varepsilon}_i}{N}. \tag{2.2.4.13}$$

Now consider the right-hand sides of (2.2.4.11)–(2.2.4.13). Since ε_i are i.i.d. $\left(0, \sigma_\varepsilon^2\right)$ and $E\left(\varepsilon_i^4\right) < \infty$, it follows from (2.2.4.1)–(2.2.4.3) that the right-hand side term in (2.2.4.11) is such that

$$\frac{\sum \varepsilon_i^2}{N} = \sigma_\varepsilon^2 + \delta_1 \text{ where } \delta_1 \xrightarrow{P} 0. \tag{2.2.4.14}$$

Now consider the right-hand side term in (2.2.4.12) and note that

$$\frac{\sum \bar{\varepsilon}_i^2}{N} = \frac{\varepsilon' W' W \varepsilon}{N}. \tag{2.2.4.15}$$

Since, by Assumption 2.5, the row and column sums of W are uniformly bounded in absolute value, the row and column sums of WW' are also bounded in absolute value. It then follows from (2.2.4.1) that

$$\frac{\sum \bar{\varepsilon}_i^2}{N} - \sigma_\varepsilon^2 \frac{Tr\left(W'W\right)}{N} \xrightarrow{P} 0. \tag{2.2.4.16}$$

Assumption 2.6 implies that the limit of $Tr\left(W'W\right)/N$ exits, and so we will express (2.2.4.16) as

$$\frac{\sum \bar{\varepsilon}_i^2}{N} = \sigma_\varepsilon^2 \frac{Tr\left(W'W\right)}{N} + \delta_2 \text{ where } \delta_2 \xrightarrow{P} 0. \tag{2.2.4.17}$$

Finally, the term on the right-hand side of (2.2.4.13) can be expressed as

$$\frac{\sum \varepsilon_i \bar{\varepsilon}_i}{N} = \frac{\varepsilon' W \varepsilon}{N}. \tag{2.2.4.18}$$

By Assumption 2.4, the diagonal elements of W are zero. Given this, it follows that

$$\begin{aligned} E(\varepsilon' W \varepsilon / N) &= \frac{1}{N} \sum_{i=1}^{N} E[\varepsilon_i^2] w_{ii} + \frac{1}{N} \sum_{i=1}^{N} \sum_{\substack{i=1 \\ i \neq j}}^{N} E[\varepsilon_i \varepsilon_j] \\ &= 0 \end{aligned} \tag{2.2.4.19}$$

since w_{ii} is zero and $E(\varepsilon_i\varepsilon_j)$ equal zero if $i \neq j$. Since the row and column sums of W are uniformly bounded in absolute value, it follows from (2.2.4.1)–(2.2.4.3) that

$$\frac{\varepsilon' W' \varepsilon}{N} \xrightarrow{P} 0. \tag{2.2.4.20}$$

For consistency of notation, we express $\varepsilon' W' \varepsilon / N$ as

$$\frac{\varepsilon' W' \varepsilon}{N} = \delta_3 \text{ where } \delta_3 \xrightarrow{P} 0. \tag{2.2.4.21}$$

At this point we bring together the three equations which will be used to estimate ρ_2. These equations are (2.2.4.11), (2.2.4.12), and (2.2.4.13) with the right-hand side terms involving ε_i, $i = 1, ..., N$ replaced by their expressions in (2.2.4.14), (2.2.4.17), and (2.2.4.21):

$$\begin{aligned} \frac{\sum u_i^2}{N} + \rho_2^2 \frac{\sum \bar{u}_i^2}{N} - 2\rho_2 \frac{\sum u_i \bar{u}_i}{N} &= \sigma_\varepsilon^2 + \delta_1, \\ \frac{\sum \bar{u}_i^2}{N} + \rho_2^2 \frac{\sum \bar{\bar{u}}_i^2}{N} - 2\rho_2 \frac{\sum \bar{u}_i \bar{\bar{u}}_i}{N} &= \sigma_\varepsilon^2 \frac{Tr\left(W'W\right)}{N} + \delta_2, \\ \frac{\sum u_i \bar{u}_i}{N} + \rho_2^2 \frac{\sum \bar{u}_i \bar{\bar{u}}_i}{N} - \rho_2 \left[\frac{\sum u_i \bar{\bar{u}}_i}{N} + \frac{\sum \bar{u}_i^2}{N} \right] &= \delta_3. \end{aligned} \tag{2.2.4.22}$$

For the moment, we reparameterize these three equations by replacing ρ_2^2 by a "new" parameter, say η, i.e., $\eta = \rho_2^2$. In this case, the three equations in (2.2.4.22) can be viewed as a regression model with three parameters, η, ρ_2, and σ_ε^2, and three observations, i.e., the information that $\eta = \rho_2^2$ is ignored. To see this, let $\zeta' = \left[\eta, \rho_2, \sigma_\varepsilon^2\right]$ and $\delta' = [\delta_1, \delta_2, \delta_3]$. Note that the left-most terms in these three equations do not involve one of the three parameters, and all the other terms do, with the exception of the error terms δ_1, δ_2, and δ_3.

Let

$$y_* = \begin{bmatrix} \frac{\sum u_i^2}{N} \\ \frac{\sum \bar{u}_i^2}{N} \\ \frac{\sum u_i \bar{u}_i}{N} \end{bmatrix}, \quad X_* = \begin{bmatrix} -\frac{\sum \bar{u}_i^2}{N} & 2\frac{\sum u_i \bar{u}_i}{N} & 1 \\ -\frac{\sum \bar{\bar{u}}_i^2}{N} & 2\frac{\sum \bar{u}_i \bar{\bar{u}}_i}{N} & \frac{Tr(W'W)}{N} \\ -\frac{\sum \bar{u}_i \bar{\bar{u}}_i}{N} & \left[\frac{\sum u_i \bar{\bar{u}}_i}{N} + \frac{\sum \bar{u}_i^2}{N}\right] & 0 \end{bmatrix}. \tag{2.2.4.23}$$

Given this notation, the three equations in (2.2.4.22) can be expressed as

$$y_* = X_* \zeta + \delta, \quad \delta \xrightarrow{P} 0, \tag{2.2.4.24}$$

$$\delta' = (\delta_1, \delta_2, \delta_3).$$

Finally, let $\hat{y}_*$ and $\hat{X}_*$ be respectively identical to y_* and X_* except that u in (2.2.4.23) is replaced everywhere by $\hat{u}$ in (2.2.4.5). Defining $\hat{\delta} = \hat{y}_* - \hat{X}_*\zeta$, the three equations in (2.2.4.22), with u replaced by $\hat{u}$, can be expressed as

$$\hat{y}_* = \hat{X}_*\zeta + \hat{\delta}. \tag{2.2.4.25}$$

Note that $\hat{y}_*$ and $\hat{X}_*$ are observable and are respectively a 3×1 vector and a 3×3 matrix. The model in (2.2.4.25) can be viewed as a regression model.

The linear generalized moments estimator given in Kelejian and Prucha (1999) for ρ_2 is the least squares estimator of ρ_2 based on (2.2.4.25), i.e., the second element of $\hat{\zeta}$ is

$$\hat{\zeta} = \hat{X}_*^{-1}\hat{y}_*. \tag{2.2.4.26}$$

The nonlinear generalized moments estimator in Kelejian and Prucha (1999) for ρ_2 is also based on the model in (2.2.4.25) except that η is replaced by ρ_2^2 and then nonlinear least squares is applied, i.e., $\hat{\delta}'\hat{\delta}$ is minimized with respect to the remaining parameters, namely ρ_2 and σ_ε^2. It should be clear that the linear estimator of ρ_2 will be inefficient relative to the nonlinear estimator which uses the information that $\eta = \rho_2^2$. Results given in Kelejian and Prucha (1999) suggest that this is indeed the case.

In the appendix to this chapter the linear estimator $\hat{\zeta}$ in (2.2.4.26) is shown to be consistent. In addition, an argument is given which strongly suggests that the nonlinear estimator is also consistent. A more complex and tedious low-level proof that both the linear and nonlinear estimators are consistent is given in Kelejian and Prucha (1999).

A Note on the Spatial Error Model

In the spatial error model $\rho_1 = 0$ and $\rho_2 \neq 0$ and so the general solution for y in (2.2.3.3) reduces to

$$\begin{aligned} y &= ae_N + XB_1 + WXB_2 + u \\ &= MC + u \end{aligned} \tag{2.2.4.27}$$

where $M = (e_N, X, WX)$ and $C' = (a, B_1', B_2')$. In this case there is no endogeneity, and so the above GMM estimator of ρ_2 would be based on

$$\begin{aligned} \tilde{u} &= y - M\hat{C}, \\ \hat{C} &= (M'M)^{-1}M'y. \end{aligned} \tag{2.2.4.28}$$

2.3 IV ESTIMATION OF THE GENERAL MODEL

We are now ready to develop the IV estimation for the general model. As a preview, there are two complications that must be considered when estimating this model. The first complication is that Wy is endogenous since it is correlated with the error term. This should be evident since y depends directly on the error term, u. The second problem is that the error term is spatially correlated as well as heteroskedastic; see (2.2.2.3). If this second complication is not accounted for, the resulting regression parameter estimator will not be efficient.

Consider again the general model as expressed in (2.2.1), namely

$$y = ae_N + XB_1 + \rho_1 Wy + (WX)B_2 + u, \quad (2.3.1)$$
$$u = \rho_2(Wu) + \varepsilon, \quad |\rho_1| < 1, \, |\rho_2| < 1,$$

and its more compact expression in (2.2.3.1), namely

$$y = Z\beta + u, \quad (2.3.2)$$
$$Z = (e_N, X, Wy, WX),$$
$$\beta = (a, B_1', \rho_1, B_2').$$

In our estimation procedure we first use the GMM procedure to estimate ρ_2, and then transform the model in a way that is similar to the Cochrane–Orcutt (1946) procedure. Finally, we estimate the transformed model by an IV procedure, namely two stage least squares. The procedure was first suggested by Kelejian and Prucha (1998), and is called general spatial two stage least squares, henceforth abbreviated a GS2SLS.

The IV Estimator

Note first that since $\hat{\rho}_2$ is consistent it can be expressed as

$$\hat{\rho}_2 = (\rho_2 + \Delta_{1,N}), \quad \Delta_{1,N} \xrightarrow{P} 0. \quad (2.3.3)$$

Therefore, from (2.2.3.1) it follows that

$$\begin{aligned}(I_N - \hat{\rho}_2 W)u &= (I_N - (\rho_2 + \Delta_{1,N})W)u \\ &= (I_N - \rho_2 W)u - \Delta_{1,N} Wu \\ &= \varepsilon - \Delta_{1,N} Wu.\end{aligned} \quad (2.3.4)$$

Therefore, in a manner somewhat similar to the time series Cochrane–Orcutt (1946) approach, if (2.3.1) or its more stacked form in (2.3.2) is multiplied across by $(I_N - \hat{\rho}_2 W)$, we have

$$(I_N - \hat{\rho}_2 W)y = (I_N - \hat{\rho}_2 W)Z\beta + \varepsilon - \Delta_{1,N} Wu. \quad (2.3.5)$$

We will show that the transformed model in (2.3.5) accounts for spatial correlation in the sense that the term $\Delta_{1,N}Wu$ is asymptotically negligible in the IV estimation. However, since Wy is one of the regressors in Z, there is still an endogenous regressor problem. The IV approach we take to estimate (2.3.5) is 2SLS. The instruments we use in our empirical illustrations below are the columns of H in (2.2.3.4) with $r = 2$. This accounts for the endogeneity, as well as for the exogenous variables in the model.

Let

$$\begin{aligned} y(\hat{\rho}_2) &= (I_N - \hat{\rho}_2 W)y, \\ Z(\hat{\rho}_2) &= (I_N - \hat{\rho}_2 W)Z, \\ \hat{Z}(\hat{\rho}_2) &= H(H'H)^{-1}H'Z(\hat{\rho}_2) \end{aligned} \tag{2.3.6}$$

where we have indicated the dependence of the expressions on the estimator $\hat{\rho}_2$. Then our IV estimator of β is

$$\hat{\beta}(\hat{\rho}_2) = [\hat{Z}'(\hat{\rho}_2)\hat{Z}(\hat{\rho}_2)]^{-1}\hat{Z}'(\hat{\rho}_2)y(\hat{\rho}_2). \tag{2.3.7}$$

In the appendix to this chapter we show

$$N^{1/2}[\hat{\beta}(\hat{\rho}_2) - \beta] \xrightarrow{D} N(0, \sigma_\varepsilon^2 p\lim N([\hat{Z}'(\rho_2)\hat{Z}(\rho_2)]^{-1}) \tag{2.3.8}$$

where

$$p\lim[N^{-1}\hat{Z}'(\hat{\rho}_2)\hat{Z}(\hat{\rho}_2)] = (Q'_{HZ} - \rho_2 Q'_{HWZ})Q_{HH}^{-1}(Q_{HZ} - \rho_2 Q_{HWZ}). \tag{2.3.9}$$

Following the procedure in Sections A.2 and A.12 of Appendix A, our small sample approximation to the distribution of $\hat{\beta}(\hat{\rho}_2)$ is

$$\hat{\beta}(\hat{\rho}_2) \simeq N(\beta, \hat{\sigma}_\varepsilon^2[\hat{Z}'(\hat{\rho}_2)\hat{Z}(\hat{\rho}_2)]^{-1}) \tag{2.3.10}$$

where

$$\hat{\sigma}_\varepsilon^2 = \frac{1}{N-\delta}[y(\hat{\rho}_2) - Z(\rho_2)\hat{\beta}(\hat{\rho}_2)]'[y(\hat{\rho}_2) - Z(\rho_2)\hat{\beta}(\hat{\rho}_2)]$$

and δ can be taken to be zero or **any** finite constant because, asymptotically, $\frac{N}{N-\delta} \to 1$. Some researchers take δ as the number of regression parameters in the model, which in this case is $(2k+2)$.

As an illustration, suppose one wanted to test hypothesis H_0 that $R\beta = q$, where R is a known $\varphi \times 2k+2$ matrix with rank of $\varphi < 2k+2$, and q is a known $\varphi \times 1$ vector. This test could be carried out in terms of $R\hat{\beta}(\hat{\rho}_2)$. For example, given H_0, the approximate small sample distribution of $R\hat{\beta}(\rho_2)$ suggested by (2.3.10) would be

$$R\hat{\beta}(\rho_2) \simeq N(q, R\,\hat{\sigma}_{\varepsilon}^2[\hat{Z}'(\rho_2)\hat{Z}(\rho_2)]^{-1}R'). \tag{2.3.11}$$

Hypothesis H_0 would be rejected at the 5% level if

$$[R\hat{\beta}(\rho_2) - q]' \left[R\,\hat{\sigma}_{\varepsilon}^2[\hat{Z}'(\rho_2)\hat{Z}(\rho_2)]^{-1}R'\right]^{-1} [R\hat{\beta}(\rho_2) - q] > \chi_{\varphi}^2(0.95). \tag{2.3.12}$$

Illustration 2.3.1: A larger model of housing prices

We again consider the Boston dataset, but now we fit two models to the data. In the first model the error term is taken to be spatially correlated, $\rho_2 \neq 0$, and in the other model it is not, $\rho_2 = 0$.

In real estate markets, it is good practice for realtors always to look at comparable houses not too far from the property they are looking at with their clients. In our context, something like this would correspond to adding a spatial lag of the price variable based on neighboring houses.

The results from the 2SLS estimator for the model in which $\rho_2 = 0$ are reported below. Standard deviations are in the parentheses:

$$\begin{aligned}\widehat{\log(price)} = {} & 0.603(0.189) - 0.457(0.089)\log(nox) - 0.145(0.030)\log(dist) \\ & - 0.021(0.004)\,stratio + 0.181(0.014)\,rooms \\ & - 0.008(0.001)\,crime + 0.526(0.053)\,w\log(price).\end{aligned}$$

All the variables have the expected sign and are strongly significant. The significance of the estimator of ρ_1 suggests that housing prices indeed partially depend on neighboring house prices. There are interesting spillover effects associated with this coefficient, which will be discussed in Chapter 3.

The results for the model in which $\rho_2 \neq 0$ are

$$\begin{aligned}\widehat{\log(price)} = {} & 0.571(0.203) - 0.448(0.098)\log(nox) - 0.140(0.034)\log(dist) \\ & - 0.022(0.005)\,stratio + 0.185(0.014)\,rooms \\ & - 0.007(0.001)\,crime + 0.532(0.055)\,w\log(price);\ \hat{\rho}_2 = 0.198.\end{aligned}$$

In this case the results are quite similar. Specifically, all of the signs of the estimated coefficients are the same, their magnitudes are similar, and they are all significant. This similarity is not always the case!

Illustration 2.3.2: A larger model of DUI arrests

In Illustration 2.2.1.3 we used the simulated US driving under the influence data from Drukker et al. (2013c). In the present example we will consider a variation of that model with the same data set but we estimate the full model. In this model we assume spatial correlation of the error term, and consider the spatial lag of the dependent variable, but do not consider the spatial lag of the police variable. The results are reported below:

$$\widehat{dui} = -6.410(0.418) + 0.598(0.015)\ police + 0.000(0.001)\ nondui$$
$$+ 0.016(0.000)\ venichles + 0.106(0.035)\ dry + 0.047(0.017)\ wdui.$$

The evidence is consistent with our earlier example described in Illustration 2.2.1.3. The explanatory variables, with the exception of *nondui*, are all significant. The results also highlight that the coefficient relating to the variable *wdui* is positive and statistically significant. Finally, the estimated value of $\rho_2 = 0.0009$. This suggests that the true value of ρ_2 may be zero, and hence the absence of spatial correlation. Formal tests for spatial correlation are given in Chapter 11.

2.4 MAXIMUM LIKELIHOOD ESTIMATION OF THE GENERAL MODEL

Consider again the general model in (2.2.3.1), or (2.2.1),

$$\begin{aligned} y &= ae_N + XB_1 + \rho_1 Wy + (WX)\,B_2 + u, \\ u &= \rho_2\,(Wu) + \varepsilon, \quad |\rho_1| < 1,\ |\rho_2| < 1, \end{aligned} \tag{2.4.1}$$

but now assume normality, $\varepsilon \sim N(0, \sigma_\varepsilon^2 I_N)$. Let $X_+ = (e_N, X, WX)$ and $\gamma' = (a, B_1', B_2')$. Then the model in (2.4.1) can be expressed as

$$y = X_+\gamma + \rho_1 Wy + u. \tag{2.4.2}$$

Again, assuming the inverses exist, the solution for y in terms of X_+ and ε is

$$y = (I_N - \rho_1 W)^{-1}\,X_+\gamma + (I_N - \rho_1 W)^{-1}\,(I_N - \rho_2 W)^{-1}\,\varepsilon. \tag{2.4.3}$$

It follows that

$$\begin{aligned} y &\sim N(\mu_y, \sigma_\varepsilon^2 V_y), \\ \mu_y &= (I_N - \rho_1 W)^{-1}\,X_+\gamma, \\ V_y &= G^{-1}G^{-1\prime}, \\ G &= (I_N - \rho_2 W)\,(I_N - \rho_1 W). \end{aligned} \tag{2.4.4}$$

The likelihood function is therefore

$$L = \frac{e^{-\frac{1}{2\sigma_\varepsilon^2}[y-\mu_y]'G'G[y-\mu_y]}}{(2\pi)^{N/2}(\sigma_\varepsilon^2)^{N/2}|V_y|_+^{1/2}} \tag{2.4.5}$$

where $|V_y|_+^{1/2}$ is the positive square root of $|V_y|$. Since the determinant of the product of square matrices is equal to the product of the determinants, $|V_y|_+^{1/2} = [|G^{-1}||G^{-1}|]_+^{1/2} = |G|_+^{-1}$, given the likelihood in (2.4.5),[25] the log-likelihood is

$$\begin{aligned}\ln(L) & \qquad (2.4.6)\\ &= -\frac{1}{2\sigma_\varepsilon^2}[y-\mu_y]'G'G[y-\mu_y] - \frac{N}{2}\ln(2\pi) - \frac{N}{2}\ln(\sigma_\varepsilon^2) + \ln(|G|_+)\\ &= -\frac{1}{2\sigma_\varepsilon^2}[Gy-G\mu_y]'[Gy-G\mu_y] - \frac{N}{2}\ln(2\pi) - \frac{N}{2}\ln(\sigma_\varepsilon^2) + \ln(|G|_+).\end{aligned}$$

The MLEs of a, B_1, ρ_1, B_2, and σ_ε^2 are obtained by maximizing the log-likelihood in (2.4.6). Again, one would base inferences on asymptotic normality of those estimators, and the small sample approximations as was done in Section 2.2.2.1. Recall that computational difficulties may be involved.

The form of the maximum likelihood estimators of γ and σ_ε^2 have an intuitive appeal. For example, let $\hat{\Psi} = (\hat{a}, \hat{B}_1', \hat{\rho}_1, \hat{B}_2', \hat{\rho}_2, \hat{\sigma}_\varepsilon^2)'$ be the vector of maximum likelihood estimators. Note that $G(I_N - \rho_1 W)^{-1} = (I_N - \rho_2 W)$. Then the first order condition corresponding to γ is

$$\frac{\partial \ln(L)}{\partial \gamma}|_{\hat{\Psi}} = 0,$$

or

$$\begin{aligned}X_+'(I_N - \hat{\rho}_2 W)'(I_N - \hat{\rho}_2 W)(I_N - \hat{\rho}_1 W)y = \\ X_+'(I_N - \hat{\rho}_2 W)'(I_N - \hat{\rho}_2 W)X_+'\hat{\gamma}.\end{aligned} \tag{2.4.7}$$

25. We obtained the likelihood directly in terms of the joint density of y. Another way to determine the likelihood is to obtain the joint density of ε, say $f_\varepsilon(\varepsilon)$, and then the joint density of y, say $f_y(y)$, as

$$f_y(y) = f_\varepsilon(\varepsilon)\,|\frac{\partial \varepsilon}{\partial y}|_+$$

where ε is replaced by its expression in y, which in our case is obtained by solving (2.4.3) for ε in terms of y. Recalling that $\varepsilon \sim N(0, \sigma_\varepsilon^2 I_N)$, and noting that $|\frac{\partial \varepsilon}{\partial y}|_+ = |G|_+$, we leave it to the reader to demonstrate that the result is identical to (2.4.5).

Let $X_{+}(\hat{\rho}_2) = (I_N - \hat{\rho}_2 W)X_{+}$ and $y(\hat{\rho}_2) = (I_N - \hat{\rho}_2 W)y$. Then, it follows from (2.4.7) that the maximum likelihood estimator of γ is

$$\hat{\gamma} = [X_{+}(\hat{\rho}_2)' X_{+}(\hat{\rho}_2)]^{-1} X_{+}(\hat{\rho}_2)'(I_N - \hat{\rho}_2 W)(I_N - \hat{\rho}_1 W)y. \tag{2.4.8}$$

There is a straightforward interpretation of $\hat{\gamma}$. For example, the model in (2.4.2) implies that

$$(I_N - \rho_1 W)y = X_{+}\gamma + u. \tag{2.4.9}$$

The implication is that if ρ_1 were known, the model in (2.4.2) could be transformed so that the only regressors are those in the exogenous matrix X_{+}. If ρ_2 were also known, (2.4.9) could be multiplied across by $(I_N - \rho_2 W)$ to obtain

$$(I_N - \rho_2 W)(I_N - \rho_1 W)y = (I_N - \rho_2 W)X_{+}\gamma + \varepsilon. \tag{2.4.10}$$

The model in (2.4.10) does not have an endogeneity problem or a spatially correlated error term. Clearly, γ would be estimated by least squares. Using evident notation,

$$\tilde{\gamma} = [X_{+}(\rho_2)' X_{+}(\rho_2)]^{-1} X_{+}(\rho_2)'(I_N - \rho_2 W)(I_N - \rho_1 W)y. \tag{2.4.11}$$

Comparing (2.4.8) to (2.4.11), the maximum likelihood estimator of γ is just the feasible counterpart to $\tilde{\gamma}$ in (2.4.11).

In a similar light, the first order condition corresponding to σ_ε^2 is

$$\begin{aligned}\frac{\partial \ln(L)}{\partial \sigma_\varepsilon^2}|_{\hat{\Psi}} &= 0 \qquad (2.4.12)\\ &= \frac{1}{2\hat{\sigma}_\varepsilon^4}[\hat{G}y - \hat{G}\hat{\mu}_y]'[\hat{G}y - \hat{G}\hat{\mu}_y] - \frac{N}{2\hat{\sigma}_\varepsilon^2} = 0\end{aligned}$$

where $\hat{G} = \left(I_N - \hat{\rho}_2 W\right)\left(I_N - \hat{\rho}_1 W\right)$ and $\hat{\mu}_y = \left(I_N - \hat{\rho}_1 W\right)^{-1} X_{+}\hat{\gamma}$. The result in (2.4.12) implies

$$\hat{\sigma}_\varepsilon^2 = \frac{[\hat{G}(y - \hat{\mu}_y)]'[\hat{G}(y - \hat{\mu}_y)]}{N}. \tag{2.4.13}$$

For purposes of interpretation, note that if $\hat{\rho}_2$, $\hat{\rho}_1$, and $\hat{\gamma}$ were replaced by ρ_2, ρ_1, and γ, respectively, the MLE $\hat{\sigma}_\varepsilon^2$ would reduce to

$$\hat{\sigma}_\varepsilon^2 = \varepsilon'\varepsilon/N.$$

Illustration 2.4.1: House values and crime in Boston: MLE

Let us consider the same model as in Illustration 2.3.1, but now consider the results obtained by ML. Those results are shown in the following equation:

$$\begin{aligned}\widehat{\log(price)} &= 0.449(0.202) - 0.412(0.094)\log(nox) - 0.138(0.031)\log(dist) \\ &\quad - 0.019(0.005)\, stratio + 0.178(0.016)\, rooms \\ &\quad - 0.007(0.001)\, crime + 0.578(0.061)\, w\log(price)\end{aligned}$$

with $\rho_2 = 0.098$ having standard error of 0.112. An interesting issue here is that the results obtained by ML are very close to those that we highlighted in Illustration 2.3.1. This is even more surprising if one considers that the sample size of the Boston data set is only 506.

2.5 AN IDENTIFICATION FALLACY

Consider the model

$$\begin{aligned} y &= X\beta + \rho_1 Wy + u, \\ u &= \rho_2 Mu + \varepsilon \end{aligned} \tag{2.5.1}$$

where X is exogenous, $\varepsilon \sim N(0, \sigma^2 I_N)$, and W and M are two weighting matrices. Now consider a special case of this model in which $\beta = 0$ and $W = M$. Assuming both inverses exist, in this case

$$\begin{aligned} &y \sim N(0, \sigma^2\Omega), \\ &\Omega = (I_N - \rho_1 W)^{-1}(I_N - \rho_2 W)^{-1}(I_N - \rho_2 W')^{-1}(I_N - \rho_1 W')^{-1} \end{aligned} \tag{2.5.2}$$

and so

$$\begin{aligned} \Omega^{-1} &= (I_N - \rho_1 W')(I_N - \rho_2 W')(I_N - \rho_2 W)(I_N - \rho_1 W) \\ &= GG', \\ G &= [I_N - (\rho_1 + \rho_2)W' + \rho_1\rho_2 W'W']. \end{aligned} \tag{2.5.3}$$

It should be clear from (2.5.3) that the likelihood is perfectly symmetric in ρ_1 and ρ_2, and so these two parameters are not identified under the stated conditions. This is a known result in the literature. Note carefully what we have stated. If in (2.5.1) $\beta = 0$ and $W = M$, there is an identification problem concerning ρ_1 and ρ_2.

In practice it is typically assumed that in a model such as (2.5.1) $W = M$. However, models in which $\beta = 0$ are not typically considered in practice. Results given below will demonstrate that if in a model such as (2.5.1), $\beta \neq 0$ there is no identification problem concerning the parameters of the model even if $W = M$. This is important to note, and unfortunately has not been noted by all researchers. For instance, as we have previously noted, if $\rho_1 = 0$, the model in (2.5.1) is often referred to as the spatial error model; if in (2.5.1) $\rho_1 \neq 0$ but

$\rho_2 = 0$, the model is often referred to as the spatial lag model. There have been quite a number of studies in which researchers (still) tried to determine whether the true model is a spatial error model, or a spatial lag model because it has been assumed that the identification condition restricts the consideration of the general model in (2.5.1) in which neither ρ_1 nor ρ_2 are zero. This is unfortunate because the spatial patterns implied by the more general model in which $\rho_1 \neq 0$ and $\rho_2 \neq 0$ are "richer" in their correlation patterns than that implied by either the spatial error model or the spatial lag model.

2.6 TIME SERIES PROCEDURES DO NOT ALWAYS CARRY OVER

In this section we illustrate that certain time series procedures should not be used in a spatial framework. We consider this issue because some time series procedures have been suggested to estimate spatial models.

In order to avoid unnecessary complications, consider the simple model

$$y = X\beta + u, \qquad (2.6.1)$$
$$u = \rho_2 W u + \varepsilon$$

where X is an $N \times k$ exogenous regressor matrix, and $\varepsilon \sim N(0, \sigma^2 I_N)$. Following a time series approach, replace u by $(y - X\beta)$ in the second line in (2.6.1) to get

$$\begin{aligned} y &= X\beta + \rho_2 W(y - X\beta) + \varepsilon \\ &= X\beta + \rho_2 W y + W X\gamma + \varepsilon, \quad \gamma = -\beta\rho_2. \end{aligned} \qquad (2.6.2)$$

If the information that $\gamma = -\beta\rho_2$ is not recognized, the model on the second line of (2.6.2) is overparameterized. Its apparent benefit is that its error term is not spatially correlated. Since the model contains the endogenous variable Wy, it cannot be consistently estimated by ordinary least squares. One might therefore attempt to estimate the model by an IV procedure, namely 2SLS.

Suppose D is **any** $N \times s$, $s \geq 2k + 1$ nonstochastic instrument matrix, e.g., D could be, among other things, $(X, WX, W^2X, W^3X, ..., W^rX)_{LI}$, where r is any finite constant such that $s \geq 2k + 1$. The resulting 2SLS estimator of the model's $2k + 1$ parameters, namely $(\beta', \rho_2, \gamma')$, will **not** be consistent. The reason for this is that $E(Wy) = WX\beta$, and (2.6.2) already contains WX as a regressor matrix; therefore there will be no "informative" instrument for Wy. For example, in (2.6.2), let Z be the $2k + 1$ regressor matrix $Z = (X, Wy, WX)$. Then, under typical conditions and notation such as that in Section 2.2.3,

$$p \lim_{N\to\infty} N^{-1} D'Z = p \lim_{N\to\infty} N^{-1} D'Z \qquad (2.6.3)$$

$$= p \lim_{N\to\infty} N^{-1}(D'X, D'WX\beta, D'WX)$$
$$\equiv \Psi.$$

Since $D'WX\beta$ is linear in the columns of $D'WX$, the rank of Ψ will be less than $2k+1$, which is the number of its columns. The implication of (2.6.3) is that the second stage regressor matrix will be singular in large samples and so the 2SLS estimator will not be consistent or defined in the large sample. To see this, let the second stage regressor matrix in the 2SLS procedure be

$$\hat{Z} = D(D'D)^{-1}D'Z.$$

Then, using evident notation,

$$p \lim_{N\to\infty} N^{-1}\hat{Z}'\hat{Z} = p \lim_{N\to\infty} [N^{-1}Z'D]\,[N(D'D)^{-1}]\,[N^{-1}D'Z] \tag{2.6.4}$$
$$= \Psi' Q_{DD}^{-1}\Psi$$

and note that the rank of the $2k+1 \times 2k+1$ matrix $\Psi' Q_{DD}^{-1}\Psi$ will be less than $2k+1$.

One would think that (2.6.2) can be consistently estimated by nonlinear 2SLS, using the instruments D described above. In this procedure the restriction $\gamma = -\beta\rho_2$ would be used and so the only parameters would be β and ρ_2. Unfortunately, this procedure is also not consistent. The reason for this is similar to that given above. To see the issue involved rewrite (2.6.2) as

$$y_{N\times 1} = P_{N\times 1} + \varepsilon_{N\times 1}, \tag{2.6.5}$$
$$P_{N\times 2k+1} = X\beta + \rho_2 Wy - WX\rho_2\beta.$$

Suppose we again use the instrument matrix D. Then, a condition given by Amemiya (1985, pages 110 and 246) for consistency of the nonlinear 2SLS estimator is that

$$p \lim_{N\to\infty} N^{-1}D'\left(\frac{\partial P}{\partial(\rho_2, \beta')}\right) = L \tag{2.6.6}$$

where L has full column rank. Now

$$\frac{\partial P}{\partial(\rho_2, \beta')} = \left[Wy - WX\beta,\ X - \rho_2 WX\right] \tag{2.6.7}$$
$$= \left[W(y - X\beta),\ X - \rho_2 WX\right]$$
$$= [Wu,\ X - \rho_2 WX].$$

The reader should be able to demonstrate that the first column of

$$p \lim_{N\to\infty}\left[N^{-1}D'\frac{\partial P}{\partial(\rho_2, \beta')}\right]$$

is a column of zeros if, as is typically assumed,

$$N^{-1}D'D \rightarrow Q_{DD}$$

where Q_{DD} is a finite invertible matrix. It follows that Amemiya's condition will not hold.

On a simpler scale, to see that "something is wrong" note that

$$\begin{aligned} E[P] &= X\beta + \rho_2 WX\beta - \rho_2 WX\beta \\ &= X\beta \end{aligned} \tag{2.6.8}$$

only involves K variables which can be used as instruments. However, the nonlinear model in (2.6.5) has $K+1$ parameters. It follows that, at least for the spatial error model, the considered times series procedure does not lead to consistent estimators.

APPENDIX A2 PROOFS FOR CHAPTER 2

Proof of (2.2.4.1)

Let the (i, j)th element of S be s_{ij}. Note that

$$\frac{v'Sv}{N} = \frac{\sum_{i=1}^{N} v_i^2 s_{ii}}{N} + \frac{\sum_{i<j=2}^{N} v_i v_j \left[s_{ij} + s_{ji}\right]}{N}. \tag{A2.1}$$

Note that $E\left(v_i^2 v_r v_s\right) = 0$, unless $r = s$ which is ruled out in (A2.1). Therefore every term in the double sum in (A2.1) is uncorrelated with every squared term. Also all the squared terms are uncorrelated with each other, as are all of the cross-product terms since $E\left[v_i v_j v_r v_s\right] = 0$ unless $i = j$ and $r = s$, or $i = r$ and $j = s$, or $i = j = r = s$. All of these conditions are ruled out. Thus since $E\left(v_i v_j\right)^2 = E\left(v_i^2\right) E\left(v_j^2\right) = \sigma_v^4$, if $i \neq j$, we have from (A2.1)

$$\begin{aligned} Var\left(\frac{v'Sv}{N}\right) &= \frac{1}{N^2}\left[\sum_{i=1}^{N} s_{ii}^2 Var\left(v_i^2\right) + \sum_{i<j=2}^{N} \sigma_v^4 \left[s_{ij} + s_{ji}\right]^2\right] \\ &\leq \frac{1}{N^2}\left[\sum_{i=1}^{N} s_{ii}^2 h + \sigma_v^4 \sum_{i<j=2}^{N} \left[\left|s_{ij}\right| + \left|s_{ji}\right|\right]^2\right] \end{aligned} \tag{A2.2}$$

where $h = E\left(v_i^4\right) - \sigma_v^4$. Let c_s be the bound on the row and column sums of the absolute values of the elements of S, and therefore also on the absolute values of the elements of S. It then follows from (A2.2) that

$$Var\left(\frac{v'Sv}{N}\right) \leq \frac{1}{N^2}\sum_{i=1}^{N} s_{ii}^2 h + \frac{\sigma_v^4}{N^2}\sum_{i=1}^{N}\sum_{j=1}^{N}[|s_{ij}|^2 + |s_{ji}|^2 + 2|s_{ij}s_{ji}|] \quad \text{(A2.3)}$$

$$\leq \frac{c_s}{N^2}\sum_{i=1}^{N}|s_{ii}|h + \frac{\sigma_v^4 c_s}{N^2}\sum_{i=1}^{N}\sum_{j=1}^{N}[|s_{ij}| + |s_{ji}| + 2|s_{ij}|]$$

$$\leq \frac{hc_s}{N^2}\sum_{i=1}^{N}|s_{ii}| + \frac{\sigma_v^4 c_s}{N^2}\sum_{i=1}^{N}\left(\sum_{j=1}^{N}[|s_{ij}| + |s_{ji}| + 2|s_{ij}|]\right)$$

$$\leq \frac{hc_s}{N} + \frac{\sigma_v^4 c_s}{N^2}\sum_{i=1}^{N} 4c_s$$

$$\leq \frac{hc_s}{N} + \frac{4\sigma_v^4 c_s^2}{N} \to 0.$$

Therefore $Var\left(\frac{v'Sv}{N}\right) \to 0$ as $N \to \infty$, and the result in (2.2.4.1) follows from Chebyshev's inequality.

The Generalized Moments Estimator of ρ_2. Proof of Consistency

Our proof has two parts. First we prove consistency of the estimator of ρ_2 if the disturbance vector u is observed. We then show that u can be replaced in the generalized moments estimator for ρ_2 by $\hat{u}$ described in Section 2.2.4.

If u were observed, the estimation of ζ would be based on (2.2.4.24) in the text. In this case both y_* and X_* are observed. Note that

$$u = (I_N - \rho_2 W)^{-1}\varepsilon, \quad \text{(A2.4)}$$
$$\bar{u} = W(I_N - W)^{-1}\varepsilon,$$
$$\bar{\bar{u}} = WW(I_N - \rho_2 W)^{-1}\varepsilon.$$

If $u, \bar{u}$, and $\bar{\bar{u}}$ are replaced in (2.2.4.23) by their expressions in (A2.4), X_* turns out to be identical to G in (2.2.4.5). Therefore, by part (b) of Assumption 2.6, X_* is nonsingular for N large enough. In addition, by part (b) of Assumption 2.6 and (2.2.4.1)–(2.2.4.3),

$$p\lim_{N\to\infty} X_* = G^*. \quad \text{(A2.5)}$$

Also taking probability limits across in (2.2.4.24) yields

$$p\lim_{N\to\infty} y_* = p\lim_{N\to\infty} X_*\zeta \quad \text{(A2.6)}$$
$$= G^*\zeta.$$

Given this, and if, preliminarily, the disturbance vector u were observed, the linear GMM of ρ_2, say $\tilde{\rho}_2$, would just be the second element of the least squares estimator of ζ based on (2.2.4.24), namely

$$\begin{aligned}\tilde{\zeta} &= (X_*'X_*)^{-1}X_*'y_* \\ &= X_*^{-1}y_*\end{aligned} \tag{A2.7}$$

since X_* is a 3×3 matrix which is nonsingular.

Taking probability limits across (A2.7) and using (A2.5)–(A2.6) implies

$$p \lim_{N \to \infty} (\tilde{\zeta}) = \zeta. \tag{A2.8}$$

Thus, if the disturbance vector u were observed, the linear estimator would be consistent

$$\tilde{\rho}_2 \xrightarrow{P} \zeta. \tag{A2.9}$$

Now consider the estimator of ζ based on $\hat{u}$ as given by the second element of $\hat{\zeta}$ in (2.2.4.26). Since the estimator of β in (2.2.4.5) is consistent, it can be expressed as

$$\tilde{\beta} = \beta + \Delta_N, \quad \Delta_N \xrightarrow{P} 0. \tag{A2.10}$$

Given the model in (2.2.3.1), the estimator of u is

$$\begin{aligned}\hat{u} &= y - Z(\beta + \Delta_N) \\ &= u - Z\Delta_N.\end{aligned} \tag{A2.11}$$

Recall (A2.4) and that the row and column sums of W and $(I_N - \rho_2 W)^{-1}$ are uniformly bounded in absolute value. As suggested in the text, and should be clear from (2.2.4.23), with the exception of the constants in the third column of X_*, every element of X_* and y_* can be expressed as a quadratic of the form $\varepsilon' S\varepsilon/N$ where S is an $N \times N$ matrix whose row and column sums are uniformly bounded in absolute value. Given (A2.11),

$$\frac{\hat{u}'S\hat{u}}{N} = \frac{u'Su}{N} - \frac{2\Delta_N' Z' Su}{N} + \frac{\Delta_N' Z' SZ\Delta_N}{N}. \tag{A2.12}$$

We will show that

$$\frac{\Delta_N' Z' Su}{N} \xrightarrow{P} 0, \quad \frac{\Delta_N' Z' SZ\Delta_N}{N} \xrightarrow{P} 0, \tag{A2.13}$$

and so

$$\frac{\hat{u}'S\hat{u}}{N} - \frac{u'Su}{N} \xrightarrow{P} 0. \tag{A2.14}$$

Given (A2.13),

$$\hat{y}_* - y_* \xrightarrow{P} 0, \quad \hat{X}_* - X_* \xrightarrow{P} 0, \tag{A2.15}$$

and so, by (A2.5) and (A2.6),

$$\hat{y}_* \xrightarrow{P} G^* \zeta, \quad \hat{X}_* \xrightarrow{P} G^*. \tag{A2.16}$$

The consistency of $\hat{\zeta}$ then follows from (A2.5), (A2.6), and (A2.16).

The Limits of $\Delta_N' Z' Su/N$ and $\Delta_N' Z' SZ\Delta_N/N$

Consider first $\Delta_N' Z' Su/N$ and recall that $Z = (e_N; X; Wy; WX)$. Recalling from (A2.10) that $\Delta_N \xrightarrow{P} 0$, the result in (A2.13) relating to $\Delta_N' Z' Su/N$ will hold if $Z' Su/N$ is $0_P(1)$, i.e., if $Z' Su/N^{1+\delta} \xrightarrow{P} 0$, for all $\delta > 0$.

Again, let matrix S denote any $N \times N$ matrix whose row and column sums are uniformly bounded in absolute value. This is the only property of S that is assumed. As an example, given Assumption 2.5,

$$(I_N - \rho_2 W) = S,$$
$$W(I_N - \rho_1 W)^{-1}(I_N - \rho_1 W') = S, \text{ etc.}$$

Given this notation, and the solution of the model for y in (2.2.3.6) can be expressed as

$$\begin{aligned} y &= S[ae_N + XB_1 + (WX)B_2 + (I_N - \rho_2 W)^{-1}\varepsilon] \\ &= aSe_N + SXB_1 + SXB_2 + S\varepsilon. \end{aligned} \tag{A2.17}$$

Note that Wy is also expressible as

$$Wy = aSe_N + SXB_1 + SXB_2 + S\varepsilon. \tag{A2.18}$$

It follows that

$$Z' Su/N = \begin{bmatrix} e_N' S\varepsilon/N \\ X' S\varepsilon/N \\ y' S\varepsilon/N \\ X' S\varepsilon/N \end{bmatrix}. \tag{A2.19}$$

Using Chebyshev's inequality, the reader should have no difficulty in showing that

$$p \lim_{N\to\infty} e_N' S\varepsilon/N = 0 \quad \text{and} \quad p \lim_{N\to\infty} X_N' S\varepsilon/N = 0. \tag{A2.20}$$

Consider the remaining term, namely $y'S\varepsilon/N$, in (A2.19). Given (A2.17) and (A2.20), $Z'Su/N$ is $0_P(1)$ if $\varepsilon'S\varepsilon/N$ is $0_P(1)$; see Section A.14 in the appendix on large sample theory. Given Assumptions 2.1–2.5, and (2.2.4.1)–(2.2.4.3)

$$[\varepsilon'S\varepsilon/N - \sigma_\varepsilon^2 Tr(S)/N] \xrightarrow{P} 0. \tag{A2.21}$$

Since the elements of S are all uniformly bounded in absolute value, so is $Tr(S)/N$ and hence $\varepsilon'S\varepsilon/N = 0_P(1)$. The result in (A2.13) relating to $\Delta_N' Z'Su/N$ follows. Using similar manipulations, the result in (A2.13) that relates to $\Delta_N' Z'SZ\Delta_N/N$ is left as an exercise.

The consistency of the nonlinear GMM should be evident. It is based on the same model, namely (2.2.4.25), except that it imposes the true condition $\eta = \rho_2^2$. A formal, and tedious proof of consistency is given in Kelejian and Prucha (1999).

Derivation of the Large Sample Result in (2.3.8)

Let $\hat{\rho}_2$ be any consistent estimator of ρ_2. Premultiplying the model in (2.2.3.1) by $(I_N - \hat{\rho}_2 W)$, we have

$$\begin{aligned} y(\hat{\rho}_2) &= Z(\hat{\rho}_2)\beta + (I_N - \hat{\rho}_2 W)u \\ &= Z(\hat{\rho}_2)\beta + \varepsilon - \Delta_N W u. \end{aligned} \tag{A2.22}$$

Since $H(H'H)^{-1}H'$ is idempotent, it should be clear that $\hat{Z}'(\hat{\rho}_2)Z(\hat{\rho}_2) = \hat{Z}'(\hat{\rho}_2)\hat{Z}(\hat{\rho}_2)$ in (2.3.7). Thus, substituting (A2.22) into (2.3.7), we have

$$\hat{\beta}(\hat{\rho}_2) = \beta + [\hat{Z}'(\hat{\rho}_2)\hat{Z}(\hat{\rho}_2)]^{-1}\hat{Z}'(\hat{\rho}_2)[\varepsilon - \Delta_N W u], \tag{A2.23}$$

or

$$N^{1/2}[\hat{\beta}(\hat{\rho}_2) - \beta] = [N^{-1}\hat{Z}'(\hat{\rho}_2)\hat{Z}(\hat{\rho}_2)]^{-1} N^{-1/2}\hat{Z}'(\hat{\rho}_2)[\varepsilon - \Delta_N W u]. \tag{A2.24}$$

We now consider each of the components in (A2.24) in turn. Recalling that $H(H'H)^{-1}H'$ is idempotent, we have from Assumption 2.9 that

$$\begin{aligned} &N^{-1}\hat{Z}'(\hat{\rho}_2)\hat{Z}(\hat{\rho}_2) \\ &= N^{-1}Z'(\hat{\rho}_2)H(H'H)^{-1}H'Z'(\hat{\rho}_2) \\ &= N^{-1}[Z'(I_N - \hat{\rho}_2 W')H][N(H'H)^{-1}][N^{-1}H'(I_N - \hat{\rho}_2 W)Z] \\ &\xrightarrow{P} (Q_{HZ}' - \rho_2 Q_{HWZ}')Q_{HH}^{-1}(Q_{HZ} - \rho_2 Q_{HWZ}). \end{aligned} \tag{A2.25}$$

Now consider the next term in (A2.24), namely $N^{-1/2}\hat{Z}'(\hat{\rho}_2)\varepsilon$. Given (2.3.6), the consistency of $\hat{\rho}_2$, and Assumption 2.9, we have

$$N^{-1/2}\hat{Z}'(\hat{\rho}_2)\varepsilon = N^{-1}[Z'(I_N - \hat{\rho}_2 W')H]\,[N(H'H)^{-1}]\,N^{-1/2}H'\varepsilon \tag{A2.26}$$

and so

$$N^{-1/2}\hat{Z}'(\hat{\rho}_2)\varepsilon - [Q'_{HZ} - \rho_2 Q'_{HWZ}]Q_{HH}^{-1}[N^{-1/2}H'\varepsilon] \xrightarrow{P} 0. \tag{A2.27}$$

By Assumptions 2.7 and 2.9, the elements of H are uniformly bounded in absolute value and $p\lim_{N\to\infty} N^{-1}H'H = Q_{HH}$ which is nonsingular. Therefore by Assumption 2.1 and the central limit theorem in Section A.15 of the large sample theory appendix,

$$N^{-1/2}H'\varepsilon \xrightarrow{D} N(0, \sigma_\varepsilon^2 Q_{HH}). \tag{A2.28}$$

Thus, by (A2.27), (A2.28), and the continuous mapping result in (A.10.3) in the large sample theory appendix,

$$N^{-1/2}\hat{Z}'(\hat{\rho}_2)\varepsilon \xrightarrow{D} N(0, \sigma_\varepsilon^2[Q'_{HZ} - \rho_2 Q'_{HWZ}]Q_{HH}^{-1}[Q_{HZ} - \rho_2 Q_{HWZ}]). \tag{A2.29}$$

For the moment, assume the absence of the term in (A2.24) involving Δ_N. In this case the results in (2.3.8) and (2.3.9) follow from (A2.24), (A2.25), (A2.29), and the continuous mapping result given in (A.10.3) in the large sample theory appendix.

We now show that the term involving Δ_N in (A2.24) can be ignored since its probability limit is zero. In (A2.24) let $F = N^{-1/2}\hat{Z}'(\hat{\rho}_2)\Delta_N Wu$. Again, given (2.3.6) and noting that Δ_N is a scalar,

$$F = \Delta_N[N^{-1}[Z'(I_N - \hat{\rho}_2 W')H]\,[N(H'H)^{-1}]\,N^{-1/2}H'Wu], \tag{A2.30}$$

or

$$F - \Delta_N[Q'_{HZ} - \rho_2 Q_{HWZ}]Q_{HH}^{-1}[N^{-1/2}H'Wu] \xrightarrow{P} 0.$$

Let $F_1 = N^{-1/2}H'Wu$. Then

$$\begin{aligned} E(F_1) &= 0, \\ E(F_1F_1') &= \sigma_\varepsilon^2 N^{-1}H'W\Omega_u W'H \\ &= \sigma_\varepsilon^2 N^{-1}H'SH \end{aligned} \tag{A2.31}$$

where $\Omega_u = (I_N - \rho_2 W)^{-1}\left(I_N - \rho_2 W'\right)^{-1}$, and S is again a matrix whose row and column sums are uniformly bounded in absolute value. It then follows from (2.1.4.5) that the elements of the product $N^{-1}H'SH$ are $0(1)$, i.e., are uniformly bounded in absolute value. Given this, it follows from Chebyshev's inequality that $F_1 = 0_P(1)$ and so, since $\Delta_N \to 0$, we have $F \xrightarrow{P} 0$ because

$$\Delta_N[Q'_{HZ} - \rho_2 Q_{HWZ}]Q_{HH}^{-1}[N^{-1/2}H'Wu] \xrightarrow{P} 0. \tag{A2.32}$$

SUGGESTED PROBLEMS

1. For a sample size N, consider the spatial moving average model for the error term

$$(P.1) \quad u = \varepsilon + \rho W \varepsilon, \ |\rho| < 1$$

where ε has mean and VC matrix of 0 and $\sigma^2 I_N$, respectively.
Determine the VC matrix of u, and then determine equations for a GMM approach you would use to estimate ρ and σ^2.

2. Consider the spatial model for the error term

$$(P.2) \quad u = \rho W u + \varepsilon + \lambda W \varepsilon$$

where ε has mean and VC matrix of 0 and $\sigma^2 I_N$, respectively.
Determine equations which could be used in a GMM approach to estimate ρ, λ, and σ^2.

3. Consider the model

$$(P.3) \quad y = X\beta + \lambda_1 W_1 y + \lambda_2 W_2 y + u,$$
$$u = \rho M u + \varepsilon$$

where ε has mean and VC matrix of 0 and $\sigma^2 I_N$, respectively, and W_1, W_2, and M are observed exogenous weighting matrices.

   (a) Suggest an instrumental variable estimation procedure for this model which accounts for the endogeneity of $W_1 y$ and $W_2 y$, as well as for the spatially correlated error term.

   (b) Let $\gamma = (\beta', \lambda_1, \lambda_2)$. If $\rho = 0$ in the above model $(P.3)$, describe the large sample distribution of your instrumental variable estimator given in part (a).

4. Assuming $\rho \neq 0$ in $(P.3)$, obtain the likelihood function, and then determine the first order conditions for β.

5. Consider the model

$$(P.4) \quad y = X\beta + \lambda_1 W_1 y + \lambda_2 W y + \varepsilon$$

where W_1 and W_2 are row normalized. Give a condition which is sufficient for the model $(P.4)$ to be solved for y in terms of X and ε.

6. Consider the model

$$(P.5) \quad y = X\beta + \lambda W y + u,$$
$$u = \varepsilon + \rho W \varepsilon,$$

and assume the elements of ε are i.i.d. with mean and variance of 0 and σ^2, respectively, as well as satisfying the remaining conditions in Section 2.2.4. Suggest an instrumental variable estimator and determine whether or not it is consistent.

Chapter 3

Spillover Effects in Spatial Models*

In this chapter we present and discuss various types of spatial spillovers. The usual interpretation of β as the effect of a one unit change in x on y, *ceteris paribus*, is no longer valid in spatial models when ρ_1 in (3.1.1) below is different from zero. In the next section we define the spatial effects emanating from a given unit. Specifically, we specify three types of effects: a direct effect, an emanating effect, and an own spillover effect. In Section 3.2 we look at these effects from a different angle, and we define a vulnerability index. This index relates to the sensitivity of a unit to changes in its environment.

3.1 EFFECTS EMANATING FROM A GIVEN UNIT

With evident notation, consider the model

$$y = X\beta + \rho_1 Wy + u \tag{3.1.1}$$

where X is matrix of only exogenous variables, and $E(u) = 0$. Since in this chapter we do not consider issues of parameter estimation, we do not focus on particular properties of the error term such as spatial correlation.[1]

The solution of the model in (3.1.1) for the dependent variable y is

$$y = (I_N - \rho_1 W)^{-1}[X\beta + u] \tag{3.1.2}$$

and so

$$E(y) = (I_N - \rho_1 W)^{-1} X\beta. \tag{3.1.3}$$

---

* As one might expect, the specification, estimation, and indexing of spatial spillovers are of prime importance in spatial modeling. Some references which relate to the material in this chapter are Easterly and Levine (1998), Fujita et al. (1999), Persson and Tabellini (2009), LeSage and Fischer (2008), LeSage and Pace (2009), Autant-Bernard and LeSage (2011), Kim et al. (2003), Abreu et al. (2005), and Halleck Vega and Elhorst (2015).

1. As an aside, the particular pattern of spatial correlation of the error term does not affect the interpretation of β. Therefore, the fact that we are not considering any particular structure for the error term should not be viewed as a limitation in the present context.

Spatial Econometrics. http://dx.doi.org/10.1016/B978-0-12-813387-3.00003-2

We will now consider interpretations of the model that are based on (3.1.2) and (3.1.3). For ease of presentation, at first suppose X is an $N \times 1$ vector so that there is only one exogenous variable. Let x_1 be the first element of X. The extension of our analysis to the case in which X is an $N \times k$ matrix is considered below.

If there were no spatial effects in the sense that $\rho_1 = 0$, the effect of a one unit change in x_1 on either y_1 or on its mean, $E(y_1)$, would be β, which in this particular case would be a scalar. In the context of a spatial model, this effect can be thought of as a **direct effect** of x_1 on y_1 in the sense that it does not account for spatial spillovers which would take place if $\rho_1 \neq 0$. Clearly, if $\rho_1 = 0$ a change in x_1 would not have an effect on any of the other values of y_j, $j = 2, ..., N$.

Consider now the case in which $\rho_1 \neq 0$. Let

$$G = (I_N - \rho_1 W)^{-1} \tag{3.1.4}$$

and let G_{ji} be the (j, i)th element of G. From (3.1.3) it should be clear that the expected effect of a change in x_1 on all of the other elements of $E(y)$ can be expressed as

$$\frac{\partial E(y_j)}{\partial x_1} = G_{j1}\beta, \ j = 2, ..., N. \tag{3.1.5}$$

Two things should be noted here. For most weighting matrices, the effects described in (3.1.5) would not all be the same. The second remark is less obvious but, nonetheless, important. Suppose units 1 and j are not neighbors and so $w_{1j} = 0$. Despite this, for most weighting matrices it will still be the case that $\frac{\partial E(y_j)}{\partial x_1} \neq 0$. On an intuitive level, the reason for this is that, e.g., unit 1 may be a neighbor to some units which are neighbors to the jth unit. Therefore, a change in x_1 would be expected to effect its neighboring units, which in turn would effect the jth unit.

The effects described in (3.1.5) have been referred to in the literature as **emanating effects** (see, e.g., Hondroyiannis et al., 2009).[2] These effects describe how a change in a regressor relating to a given unit, in our illustration unit 1, "fan out" to all the units. This is illustrated in Fig. 3.1.1.

Of course, these emanating effects can also be described in terms of elasticities. Using evident notation, the elasticity corresponding to (3.1.5) can be expressed as

$$\eta_{j1} = G_{j1}\beta\frac{x_1}{y_j}, \ j = 2, ..., N. \tag{3.1.6}$$

2. Other authors refer to the same issue as indirect effects (e.g., LeSage and Pace, 2009).

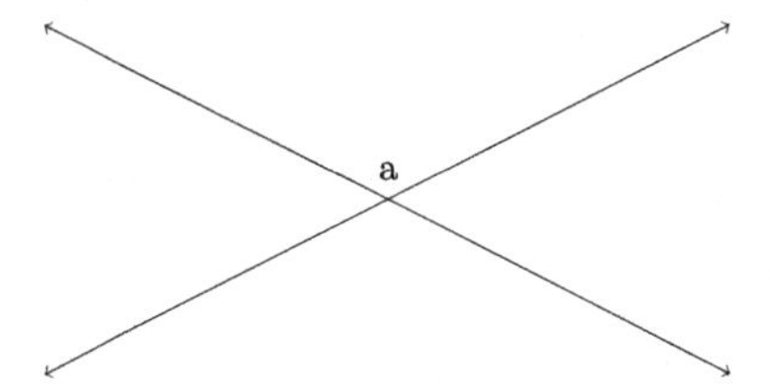

FIGURE 3.1.1 The emanating effect

A final comment may be evident. If N is large, one would not typically give tables describing the emanating effect of each unit on all the other units. In such cases a researcher would typically describe a selection of emanating effects that may be of particular importance, or selected measures (e.g., averages) of effects.

A closely related concept is that of an "**own spillover effect**." This relates to a situation where a change in a regressor (e.g., corresponding to unit one) results in a change in the dependent variables corresponding to the other units. In turn, those changes in other units "feed back" via (3.1.3) to the dependent variable in unit one. We indicated above that in the absence of spillovers, the effect of a change in x_1 on $E(y_1)$ is just β. In the presence of spillovers, that effect is

$$\frac{\partial E(y_1)}{\partial x_1} = G_{11}\beta. \tag{3.1.7}$$

Therefore, a measure of the effect of a change in x_1 on y_1, above and beyond the direct effect of x_1 on y_1, called the "**own spillover effect**", is from (3.1.5) and (3.1.7) given by

$$(G_{11} - 1)\beta. \tag{3.1.8}$$

Of course, this effect can also be expressed in terms of elasticities.

In passing we note that the above discussion relates to the effect of a change in a single regressor corresponding to a given unit, i.e., the first unit. Of course, one can also calculate the effects on each given unit of a change in a subset of the regressors corresponding to that given unit, as well as to one or more of the other units. For example, consider the model in (3.1.1) and assume now that X is an $N \times k$ matrix. Then, the change in $E(y)$ as given in (3.1.3) in response to a change in a subset of the variables in X is

$$\Delta E(y) = (I_N - \rho_1 W)^{-1}[X^H - X^0]\beta \tag{3.1.9}$$

where X^H is the hypothesized value of the regressor matrix in response to a change in one or more of the elements of X, and X^0 is the value of the regressor matrix, X, before the change. One application of this is given in

Kelejian et al. (2013) in their study relating to spillovers which are involved in institutional development, i.e., how institutions in one country are influenced by corresponding levels in neighboring countries. Another study dealing with similar issues is Seldadyo et al. (2010).

Illustration 3.1.1: The murder rate: Own spillover effects

Let us consider again a slightly modified version of the murder rate model in Illustration 2.2.1.2, where we add a spatial lag of the dependent variable, but we delete the spatial lag of the execution variable, *wexec*. We are going to use this model to compute the own spillover effects as described in (3.1.8). The first step towards the calculation of these effects consists in estimating the model to obtain an estimate of the coefficients. Recall that the spatial lag of the dependent variable is endogenous. Using two stages least squares, the estimate of ρ_1 turns out to be 0.273, while the slope corresponding to the execution variable turns out to be 0.121. The second step is using the estimate of ρ_1 to estimate $G = (I_N - \rho_1 W)^{-1}$. The own spillover effect of a change in prisoners executions on the murder rate for Alabama (i.e., the first observation in the data) turns out to be 0.0020. The average of the own spillover effects over all the 49 US States is 0.0023, which is quite similar to that for Alabama. In this case these own spillover effects are quite small, but still positive.

3.2 EMANATING EFFECTS OF A UNIFORM WORSENING OF FUNDAMENTALS

In their study, Kelejian et al. (2006) used a spatial model to study contagion problems in foreign exchange markets. In this scenario, the currency of a given country experiences a "run" and it depreciates due to speculative activity. Depreciations then fan out to other related countries in the system. Hondroyiannis et al. (2009) considered a variant of the emanating effects described above. In particular, instead of calculating the effect of a given variable (or a set of variables) in one country on the other countries, they considered a "uniform worsening" of the exogenous variables of that originating country on the other countries involved.

In more detail, let X be an $N \times k$ regressor matrix, and let X_i be its ith column, e.g., X_i is the $N \times 1$ vector of N values of the ith regressor for the N countries. Write X as $X = (X_1, ..., X_k)$. Given this notation, express the conditional mean in (3.1.3) as, using evident notation,

$$\begin{aligned} E(y) &= (I - \rho_1 W)^{-1} X\beta \\ &= G[X_1\beta_1 + ... + X_k\beta_k] \end{aligned} \tag{3.2.1}$$

where $\beta' = (\beta_1, ..., \beta_k)$. Suppose that high values of the dependent variable are associated with more severe exchange problems. In this case if the coefficient of a regressor is negative, a worsening of the corresponding variable in the originating country would relate to a decrease in that variable, i.e., the change in that variable multiplied by the corresponding coefficient is positive. Similarly, if a coefficient of a regressor is positive, a worsening of that variable would be an increase in the value of the corresponding regressor and so again the product would be positive.

Let the first value of X_i be $x_{1,i}$, $i = 1, ..., k$, and, in order to avoid unnecessary tediousness, assume that the values of all of the regressors are positive. The implication of the above is that the response of $E(y_j)$, $j = 2, ..., N$ with respect to a worsening of all k of the regressors of country 1 would be

$$\begin{aligned} \Delta E(y_j) &= G_{j1}(\Delta x_{1,1}\beta_1) + ... + G_{j1}(\Delta x_{1,k}\beta_k) \\ &= G_{j1}|\Delta x_{1,1}\beta_1| + ... + G_{j1}|\Delta x_{1,k}\beta_k|, \ j = 2, ..., N \end{aligned} \tag{3.2.2}$$

or, if a uniform **percentage** worsening is considered,

$$\begin{aligned} \Delta E(y_j) &= G_{j1}\frac{|\Delta x_{1,1}\beta_1|x_{1,1}}{x_{1,1}} + ... + G_{j1}\frac{|\Delta x_{1,k}\beta_k|x_{1,k}}{x_{1,k}} \\ &= G_{j1}|\beta_1|\ x_{1,1}\alpha + ... + G_{j1}|\beta_k|\ x_{1,k}\alpha \end{aligned} \tag{3.2.3}$$

where $\alpha = |\Delta x_{1,i}|/x_{1,i} > 0$ is the uniform percentage worsening, $i = 1, ..., k$. Similarly, one can calculate the emanating percentage change of $E(y_j)$ with respect to the uniform percentage worsening of all of the regressors in the originating country as

$$\frac{\Delta E(y_j)}{\alpha y_j} = G_{j1}\left[\frac{x_{1,1}}{y_j}|\beta_1| + ... + \frac{x_{1,k}}{y_j}|\beta_k|\right]\alpha. \tag{3.2.4}$$

Of course, an alternative to (3.2.4) would be to replace y_j in the denominator of (3.2.4) by $E(y_j)$ which can be estimated from (3.1.5). Incidentally, we note that this sort of analysis can easily be applied to other models, such as spatial labor market models, housing market models, and government quality indices models, just to name a few.[3] As an aside, we note that these emanating effects have been generalized to a dynamic panel framework in Kelejian and Mukerji (2011). Additionally, they have also been considered by LeSage and Fischer (2008), and LeSage and Pace (2009).

3. See LeSage and Pace (2009), or Bivand and Piras (2015) for details relating to a Monte Carlo approach to some of these issues.

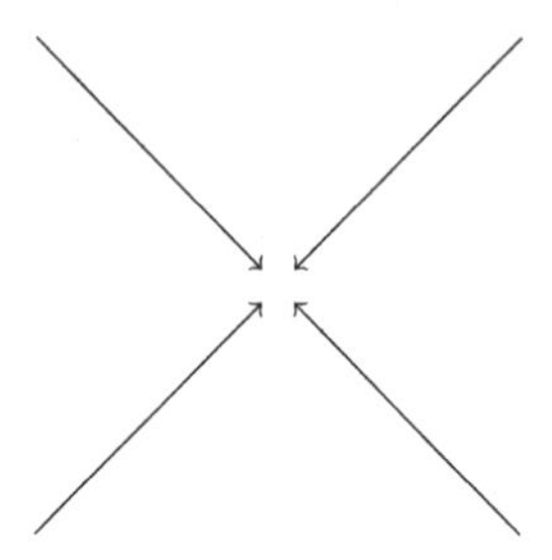

FIGURE 3.3.1 The vulnerability effect

3.3 VULNERABILITY OF A GIVEN UNIT TO SPILLOVERS

The emanating effect describes how events in one unit spill over to other units due to spatial interactions. As an example, the emanating effect would correspond to the effect that the smoking habits of a teenager might have on the smoking habits of his/her peers. Sometimes it is interesting to consider the reverse situation that we call "vulnerability." The vulnerability effect is the reverse of the emanating effect in that it describes the response of a given unit to events in neighboring units. In the teenager smoking example, the issue would be how the smoking habits of a given teenager are affected by the smoking habits of his/her peers. This index was introduced by Kelejian and Mukerji (2011), and is illustrated by Fig. 3.3.1.

More formally consider again the model in (3.1.1)

$$y = X\beta + \rho_1 Wy + u$$

where X is an $N \times 1$ vector whose ith element is x_i, $G = (I_N - \rho_1 W)^{-1}$, and $E(y) = GX\beta$. Again note that in this case β is a scalar. For ease of interpretation, suppose the units are countries, X is a vector of GDPs, and y is a vector of exports. For purposes of illustration, suppose $\beta > 0$.

It should be clear that the expected effect of a change in the GDPs in all countries other than the first, namely changes in $x_2, ..., x_N$, on the exports of the first country is V_1 where

$$\begin{aligned} V_1 &= \sum_{j=2}^{N} \frac{\partial E(y_1)}{\partial x_j} \\ &= \sum_{j=2}^{N} G_{1j}\beta \end{aligned} \tag{3.3.1}$$

The index V_1 is an example of the vulnerability effect. It illustrates the extent of vulnerability of country's exports to changes in the GDPs of all other countries.

The discrete counterpart to (3.3.1) is

$$\Delta y_1 = \sum_{j=2}^{N} G_{1j} \Delta x_j \beta$$

Consider the vulnerability of country ones exports to a uniform worsening (decrease) in the GDPs of the other countries. In this case $\Delta x_j < 0$, for all $j = 2, ..., N$ and since $\beta > 0$, $\Delta x_j \beta < 0$. Therefore the vulnerability of the first country's exports in this case would be

$$\begin{aligned} y_1 &= \sum_{j=2}^{N} G_{1j} \Delta x_j \beta \\ &= \sum_{j=2}^{N} G_{1j} \frac{\Delta x_j}{x_j} \beta x_j \\ &= \sum_{j=2}^{N} G_{1j} \beta x_j \alpha \end{aligned}$$

where $\alpha = \frac{\Delta x_j}{x_j} < 0$.

Illustration 3.3.1: The murder rate: The vulnerability effect

In this illustration we calculate the vulnerability effect based on the results which were obtained for the model that was used in Illustration 3.1.1. The vulnerability of the murder rate in Alabama to changes in executions in all of the other US States turns out to be 0.0435. This figure is only given for illustrative purposes concerning the calculations involved because the estimated coefficient of the execution variable, upon which it is based, is not significant. Therefore, one would not conclude that the murder rate in Alabama would increase in response to an increase in executions in other states. All of this suggests that the model's specification may not be correct. One possible specification error is that the execution variable was treated as exogenous in the estimation of the model, but it may, in fact, be endogenous. This endogeneity may arise because of a simultaneous relationship between these two variables: executions may indeed have a negative effect on the murder rate, but the crime of murder is, sometimes, punishable by execution. That suggests that if one were to explain the number of executions, one of the explanatory variables would be the number of murders, and its coefficient would be expected to be positive. The proper estimation of models some of whose explanatory variables are endogenous is explained in Chapter 6.

An Illustration of the Vulnerability Effect

Again, assume that high values of the dependent variable are associated with more severe problems, and suppose now that X is an $N \times 2$ matrix and let the jth row of X be $x_{j.}$. Let the two variables of X be a credit variable, $Credit$, and a national debt variable, $NatD$, so, that using evident notation, $x_{j.} = (Credit_j, NatD_j)$ and $\beta_0' = (\beta_{CR}, \beta_{ND})$. Let $\Delta Credit_j$ and $\Delta NatD_j$ be the hypothesized changes in the credit and national debt variables. Then, the vulnerability effect index with respect to country one can be expressed as

$$\Delta y_1 = \sum_{j=2}^{N} G_{1j}[\Delta Credit_j \beta_{CR} + \Delta NatD_j \beta_{ND}] \tag{3.3.2}$$

or, in percentage terms,

$$\upsilon_{y_1} = \sum_{j=2}^{N} G_{1j}[\upsilon_{j,CR}\frac{Credit_j}{y_1}\beta_{CR} + \upsilon_{j,ND}\frac{NatD_j}{y_1}\beta_{ND}]$$

where

$$\upsilon_{j,CR} = 100\frac{\Delta Credit_j}{Credit_j}, \quad \upsilon_{ND} = 100\frac{\Delta NatD_j}{NatD_j}, \tag{3.3.3}$$

$$\upsilon_{y_1} = 100\frac{\Delta y_1}{y_1}.$$

Clearly, it could be of interest to apply this index to markets of labor, housing, exchange, etc.

SUGGESTED PROBLEMS

1. Consider the model

$$(P.1) \quad y = X\beta + \rho_1 W_1 y + \rho_2 W_2 y + u$$

where W_1 and W_2 are weighting matrices. Assuming typical conditions, give expressions for the emanating and vulnerability effects that relate to unit 1.

2. Consider the model

$$(P.2) \quad y_1 = X_1\beta_1 + \lambda_1 W_1 y_1 + y_2\alpha_1 + u_1,$$
$$y_2 = X_2\beta_2 + y_1\alpha_2 + u_2$$

where y_1 and y_2 are $N \times 1$ vectors on dependent variables (e.g., wages and productivity), and the remaining notation should be evident. To simplify notation assume that X_1 and X_2 are $N \times 1$ vectors. Give expressions for the emanating and vulnerability effects as they relate to the first unit of y_1.

3. Consider the model

$$(P.3) \quad y = X\beta_1 + WX\beta_2 + u$$

where the notation should be evident. Describe the emanating and vulnerability effects for this model as they relate to unit 1. Again, assume that X is an $N \times 1$ vector.

4. Consider the model $(P.1)$ above. Suppose X is an $N \times k$ matrix, and large values of the elements of y are not desired. Give and expression for the emanating effect of a uniform percentage worsening of the exogenous variables in unit 1.

Chapter 4

Predictors in Spatial Models

An important application of spatial and other models is prediction. In this chapter we discuss some of the basic issues involved in prediction. In particular, we focus on conditional means and their relation to minimum mean squared prediction errors. In doing this, we point out a condition that is typically overlooked but is necessary for certain properties of conditional mean predictors. We also discuss the importance of information sets that underlie conditional mean predictors.

In Section 4.1 we describe results concerning expectations which may not be evident to all readers. Section 4.2 considers four different predictors based on different information sets. The first predictor is simply based on the model solution, while the second and third predictors are based on larger information sets. The last predictor is an intuitive predictor that assumes that the researcher ignores the correlations of endogenous regressors with the disturbance term. Finally, in Section 4.3 we give the explicit expressions for the mean squared errors of the predictors.

4.1 PRELIMINARIES ON EXPECTATIONS[1]

Let $\mathbf{m}$ and $\mathbf{v}$ be scalar random variables. For ease of presentation, suppose that the possible values of $\mathbf{v}$ are $v_1, ..., v_L$ and that $\Pr(\mathbf{v} = v_J) = p_J$, $J = 1, ..., L$. Assuming that the means exist, the expectation of $\mathbf{m}$ conditional on $\mathbf{v} = v_J$ can be expressed as

$$E(\mathbf{m}|\mathbf{v} = v_J), \quad J = 1, ..., L. \tag{4.1.1}$$

Generalizing, it should be somewhat evident that the **unconditional** mean of $\mathbf{m}$ can be obtained by averaging these conditional means over all possible values

1. There is a large body of literature that relates to various issues of prediction which are discussed in this chapter. References concerning conditional expectations are Judge et al. (1985), Brockwell and Davis (1991), Greene (2003), and Cameron and Trivedi (2005). An early and widely cited study relating to best linear unbiased predictions in linear models is Goldberger (1962). Issues relating to optimal prediction in spatial models are discussed in Cressie (1993). Banerjee et al. (2003) discuss methods used in spatial models to form predictions. Other studies which involve prediction are Anselin (1988), Haining (1990), Lenze (2000), Bivand (2002), Baltagi and Li (2006), Kelejian and Prucha (2007b), Pace and LeSage (2008), Elhorst (2009), Baltagi et al. (2012), and Baltagi et al. (2014b), among others.

Spatial Econometrics. http://dx.doi.org/10.1016/B978-0-12-813387-3.00004-4

TABLE 4.1.1 Illustration of Eqs. (4.1.1) and (4.1.2)

v	m	z	$E(\mathbf{m}\vert\mathbf{v}=v_J)$	$E(\mathbf{m}\vert\mathbf{v}=v_J,\mathbf{z}=1)$	$E(\mathbf{m}\vert\mathbf{v}=v_J,\mathbf{z}=0)$
	73	1			
1	70	0	59	73	52
	34	0			
	69	1			
	66	0			
2	68	0	57	53.5	59.33
	38	1			
	44	0			
3	74	1	73	74	72
	72	0			
	$E(\mathbf{m})=60.8$		$\sum_{J=1}^{L} p_J\ E(\mathbf{m}\vert\mathbf{v}=v_J)=60.8$		

of **v** as

$$E(\mathbf{m})=\sum_{J=1}^{L} p_J\ E(\mathbf{m}|\mathbf{v}=v_J). \tag{4.1.2}$$

The result in (4.1.2) indicates that if the mean of **m** is obtained for every possible value of **v**, and then these conditional means are averaged over all possible values of **v** using probabilities weights, the result will be the unconditional mean of **m**.

As an illustration, consider the situation depicted in Table 4.1.1. Suppose there is a building which has 3 rooms, each containing a certain number of people. Let **m** be the height of a person in inches who is chosen at random, and let **v** be the room chosen at random. Let $\mathbf{z}=1$ if the chosen person is male, and let $\mathbf{z}=0$ if that person is female.

Consider first the result in (4.1.2). The average height of the people in the building can be obtained by taking a straight average of the heights of all the people in the building. This is given in the bottom row of the second column of Table 4.1.1, namely 60.8. This corresponds to the left-hand side of (4.1.2), namely $E(\mathbf{m})$. Alternatively, one could obtain the average height of the people in each room, and then take a weighted average of the room averages. The weights for each room would be the number of people in the room divided by the number of people in the building. This corresponds to the right-hand side of (4.1.2) and is given in the fourth column of Table 4.1.1.

Note that (4.1.2) entails two components. One is in terms of the conditional distribution of **m** on **v**, and the other is in terms of the distribution of **v**, which determines the probability weights.

The result in (4.1.2) can be written in more general form as

$$\begin{aligned} E(\mathbf{m}) &= E_{\mathbf{v}}\ [E(\mathbf{m}|\mathbf{v})] \\ &= E_{\mathbf{v}}\ \left[E_{\mathbf{m}|\mathbf{v}}(\mathbf{m})\right]. \end{aligned} \tag{4.1.3}$$

The term within the brackets is the expectation of $\mathbf{m}$ conditional on $\mathbf{v}$ which is randomly chosen from its possible values. Since the expectation of $\mathbf{m}$ conditional on $\mathbf{v}$ generally depends on the chosen value of $\mathbf{v}$, the conditional expectation $E(\mathbf{m}|\mathbf{v})$ can be viewed as a function of $\mathbf{v}$, $E(\mathbf{m}|\mathbf{v}) = S(\mathbf{v})$. That is why the outer expectation on the right-hand side of (4.1.3) is with respect to the distribution of $\mathbf{v}$, denoted as $E_{\mathbf{v}}$. That is, in the second line in (4.1.3)

$$E_{\mathbf{v}}\ \left[E_{\mathbf{m}|\mathbf{v}}(\mathbf{m})\right] = E_{\mathbf{v}}\ [S(\mathbf{v})],$$

which can also be written as

$$E(\mathbf{m}) = E[E(\mathbf{m}|\mathbf{v})]$$

since it is understood that $E(\mathbf{m}|\mathbf{v})$ is a function of $\mathbf{v}$ and so the outer expectation is with respect to the distribution of $\mathbf{v}$.

Using evident notation, the result in (4.1.3) can be generalized. For example, recalling that $\mathbf{z} = 1$ if the chosen person is male, and $\mathbf{z} = 0$ if female, and again assuming only that the means exist,

$$E(\mathbf{m}|\mathbf{v}, \mathbf{z}) = S_1(\mathbf{v}, \mathbf{z}) \tag{4.1.4}$$

where $S_1(\mathbf{v}, \mathbf{z})$ is a function of $\mathbf{v}$ and $\mathbf{z}$, which are jointly and randomly chosen. At least on an intuitive level, if $\mathbf{z}$ were averaged out while $\mathbf{v}$ was held fixed, the result would be $E(\mathbf{m}|\mathbf{v})$:

$$\begin{aligned} E(\mathbf{m}|\mathbf{v}) &= E_{\mathbf{z}|\mathbf{v}}\ [S_1(\mathbf{v}, \mathbf{z})] \\ &= E_{\mathbf{z}|\mathbf{v}}\ [E(\mathbf{m}|\mathbf{v}, \mathbf{z})] \\ &= E_{\mathbf{z}|\mathbf{v}}\ \left[E_{\mathbf{m}|\mathbf{v},\mathbf{z}}(\mathbf{m})\right] \end{aligned} \tag{4.1.5}$$

where we have indicated that the outer expectation in (4.1.5) is with respect to the conditional distribution of $\mathbf{z}$ given $\mathbf{v}$. Alternatively, once an expression for $E_{\mathbf{m}|\mathbf{v},\mathbf{z}}(\mathbf{m})$ is determined, which is $S_1(\mathbf{v}, \mathbf{z})$ in (4.1.5), one then takes the expectation of that expression using the distribution of $\mathbf{z}$ conditional on $\mathbf{v}$ in order to obtain $\mathbf{E}(\mathbf{m}|\mathbf{v})$. This observation will become important in our development below.

Again, the result in (4.1.5) can be written as

$$E(\mathbf{m}|\mathbf{v}) = E[E(\mathbf{m}|\mathbf{v}, \mathbf{z})|\mathbf{v}]$$

where it is understood that the outer expectation is with respect to the conditional distribution of **z** on **v** since $E(\mathbf{m}|\mathbf{v}, \mathbf{z})$ is a function of **v** and **z**.

For illustrative purposes, consider again the situation depicted in Table 4.1.1. There are at least two ways to obtain the average height of people in a given room, say room 2. One way would be to just obtain the average height of all the people in room 2. Using evident notation, this corresponds to $E(\mathbf{m}|\mathbf{v}=2)$ (i.e., 57 in the fourth column of Table 4.1.1). Another way would be to obtain the average height of the males, and then the average height of the females in room 2, and then average these averages by the proportions of males and females in room 2. In this case $E(\mathbf{m}|\mathbf{v}=2, \mathbf{z}=1)$ corresponds to the average height of males in room 2 (i.e., 53.5 in the fifth column of Table 4.1.1), and $E(\mathbf{m}|\mathbf{v}=2, \mathbf{z}=0)$ corresponds to the average height of females in room 2 (i.e., 59.33 in the sixth column of Table 4.1.1). Clearly, taking a weighted average of $E(\mathbf{m}|\mathbf{v}=2, \mathbf{z}=1)$ and $E(\mathbf{m}|\mathbf{v}=2, \mathbf{z}=0)$ corresponds to $E(\mathbf{m}|\mathbf{v}=2)$. We leave it as an exercise for the reader to demonstrate that the numbers in Table 4.1.1 are all consistent.

Conditional means are important because, under their given conditions, they correspond to minimum mean squared error (MMSE) predictors. For example, in (4.1.4), if **v** and **z** were realized and known to be 3 and 17, respectively, the corresponding MMSE predictor of **m** when $\mathbf{v}=3$ and $\mathbf{z}=17$ would be $S_1(3, 17)$. However, there is an implicit assumption behind this statement. Specifically, the conditional mean in (4.1.4) typically involves the parameters of the conditional distribution of **m** on **v** and **z**. Let $\gamma_{m|v,z}$ be this vector of parameters. Then, a full statement of (4.1.4) is

$$E(\mathbf{m}|\mathbf{v}, \mathbf{z}) = S_2(\mathbf{v}, \mathbf{z}, \gamma_{v,z}). \tag{4.1.6}$$

In many cases, S_2 will be nonlinear in $\mathbf{v}, \mathbf{z}$, and $\boldsymbol{\gamma}_{v,z}$. As in the above example, given the realization that $\mathbf{v}=3$ and $\mathbf{z}=17$, the MMSE predictor of **m** is $S_2(3, 17, \gamma_{v,z})$. For this to be useful, $\gamma_{v,z}$ must be known. In practice, $\gamma_{v,z}$ is not known and so has to be estimated as, say $\hat{\gamma}_{v,z}$, and the predictor of **m**, say $\mathbf{m}^P$, is taken as

$$\mathbf{m}^P = S_2(3, 17, \hat{\gamma}_{v,z}). \tag{4.1.7}$$

However, even if $\hat{\gamma}_{v,z}$ is the maximum likelihood estimator of $\gamma_{v,z}$, the predictor in (4.1.7) need not be the MMSE predictor of **m**. More generally, given $\mathbf{v}=v_j$ and $\mathbf{z}=z_j$, $S_2(v_j, z_j, \hat{\gamma}_{v,z})$ need not be the MMSE predictor of **m**. Despite this, $S_2(v_j, z_j, \hat{\gamma}_{v,z})$ is typically used as the predictor because, especially for nonlinear models relating **m** to **v** and **z**, the MMSE predictor of **m** corresponding to the conditions $\mathbf{v}=v_j$, $\mathbf{z}=z_j$, and $\hat{\gamma}_{v,z}$ is difficult to determine. For example, given $\mathbf{v} = v_j$, $\mathbf{z} = z_j$, and $\hat{\gamma}_{v,z}$, the MMSE would be $\mathbf{m}^+$ where

$$\begin{aligned} \mathbf{m}^+ &= E(\mathbf{m}|\mathbf{v} = v_j, \mathbf{z} = z_j, \hat{\gamma}_{v,z}) \\ &\neq E(\mathbf{m}|\mathbf{v} = v_j, \mathbf{z} = z_j, \gamma_{v,z}). \end{aligned} \tag{4.1.8}$$

4.2 INFORMATION SETS AND PREDICTORS OF THE DEPENDENT VARIABLE

As another preliminary, we note the following result for the convenience of the reader. Using evident notation, let the vectors Z_1 and Z_2 be jointly normally distributed column vectors, $(Z_1, Z_2) \sim N(\mu, V)$, where

$$\mu' = (\mu_1', \mu_2'), \; V = \{V_{ij}\}, i, j = 1, 2.$$

Then the distribution of Z_1 conditional on a particular value of Z_2, say z_2, is normal, and its mean and VC matrix are

$$\begin{aligned} E(Z_1 \mid Z_2 = z_2) &= \mu_1 + V_{12}V_{22}^{-1}(z_2 - \mu_2), \\ VC(Z_1 \mid Z_2 = z_2) &= V_{11} - V_{12}V_{22}^{-1}V_{21}; \end{aligned} \tag{4.2.1}$$

see, e.g., Greene (2003, p. 872). In light of the discussion in Section 4.1, the mean and VC matrix of Z_1 conditional on any value of Z_2, which may be randomly chosen, are

$$\begin{aligned} E(Z_1 \mid Z_2) &= \mu_1 + V_{12}V_{22}^{-1}(Z_2 - \mu_2), \\ VC(Z_1 \mid Z_2) &= V_{11} - V_{12}V_{22}^{-1}V_{21}. \end{aligned} \tag{4.2.2}$$

As expected, it follows from the first line in (4.2.2) and (4.1.3) that

$$\begin{aligned} E(Z_1) = E[E(Z_1 \mid Z_2)] &= \mu_1 + V_{12}V_{22}^{-1}[E(Z_2) - \mu_2] \\ &= \mu_1 + V_{12}V_{22}^{-1}[\mu_2 - \mu_2] \\ &= \mu_1. \end{aligned}$$

The minimum mean squared error predictor of Z_1 based on a given value of Z_2 is the conditional mean given in (4.2.1). Results relating to Z_2 conditional on Z_1 can be obtained from (4.2.1) by reversing the subscripts.

As an illustration of (4.2.1), suppose Z_1 and Z_2 are scalars so that $V_{11} = \sigma_1^2$, $V_{22} = \sigma_2^2$, and $V_{12} = \sigma_{12}$. Then, using evident notation, (4.2.1) implies

$$Z_1 = \mu_1 + \frac{\sigma_{12}}{\sigma_2^2}(z_2 - \mu_2) + \eta$$

where $\eta = Z_1 - E(Z_1|Z_2 = z_2)$ and so

$$E(\eta|Z_2 = z_2) = 0$$

and

$$\begin{aligned} E(\eta^2|Z_2 = z_2) &= \sigma_1^2 - \frac{\sigma_{12}^2}{\sigma_2^2} \\ &= \sigma_1^2[1 - \frac{\sigma_{12}^2}{\sigma_2^2\sigma_1^2}] \\ &= \sigma_1^2[1 - R^2]. \end{aligned}$$

Predictors Based on Known Parameter Values

The results obtained below concerning the efficiency of predictors are primarily based on results obtained by Kelejian and Prucha (2007b). These results are based on the assumption that the model parameters are known. Of course, in practice the model parameters are not known, and so feasible predictors which are based on estimated parameter values would be considered. As Kelejian and Prucha (2007b) note, if feasible predictors are considered, an analysis of their efficiency would have to account for a variety of sample sizes, regressor and error term specifications, as well as the covariances involved. The reason for this is that these characteristics of a model affect the efficiency of parameter estimators and this, in turn, affects the efficiency of predictors. Indeed, one can imagine that for different combinations of sample sizes, regressor and error term specifications, etc., different feasible predictors might even "take turns" at being best in the sense of having the lowest mean squared prediction errors. By focusing the discussion on predictors based on the true values of the parameters, we do not have to consider such specification issues. Our interpretation of the results is that they relate to the **limits** of efficiency, e.g., conditional mean predictors based on true values of the parameters are efficient!

The Predictor Based on the Spatial Model Solution

Consider the model

$$\begin{aligned} y &= \rho_1 Wy + X\beta + u, \\ u &= \rho_2 Wu + \varepsilon, \end{aligned} \tag{4.2.3}$$

where y is an $N \times 1$ vector of values of the dependent variable, X and W are respectively an $N \times k$ exogenous regressor matrix and an $N \times N$ exogenous weighting matrix, and the remaining notation should be evident. Assuming the inverse exists, the solution of the model for y is

$$\begin{aligned} y &= (I_N - \rho_1 W)^{-1} X\beta + (I_N - \rho_1 W)^{-1} u \\ &= (I_N - \rho_1 W)^{-1} X\beta + (I_N - \rho_1 W)^{-1} (I_N - \rho_2 W)^{-1} \varepsilon. \end{aligned} \tag{4.2.4}$$

We assume that $\varepsilon \sim N(0, \sigma_\varepsilon^2 I_N)$. Let λ denote the parameters of the model in (4.2.3). Then, we also assume X, W, and λ are known, as well as the first $N-1$ values of y. The issue relates to the prediction of the last, and out-of-sample element of y, namely y_N. One scenario which fits into these specifications relates to the prediction of the sale price of a new house in a given area. In such a case, the prices (or values) of other related properties as well as the hedonic characteristics of the new house would be known. In addition, distances of the new house to the other relevant houses would be known, and might be taken as the corresponding elements of the weighting matrix.

Let $(I_N - \rho_1 W)_{N.}^{-1}$ be the Nth row of $(I_N - \rho_1 W)^{-1}$. Given this notation, the result in (4.2.4) implies that the element of y to be predicted, y_N, is determined as

$$y_N = (I_N - \rho_1 W)_{N.}^{-1} X\beta + (I_N - \rho_1 W)_{N.}^{-1} u. \tag{4.2.5}$$

For future reference, another expression for y_N is given by the right-hand side of the model in (4.2.3), namely

$$\begin{aligned} y_N &= x_{N.}\beta + \rho_1 w_{N.} y + u_N, \\ u_N &= \rho_2 w_{N.} u_N + \varepsilon_N \end{aligned} \tag{4.2.6}$$

where $x_{N.}$ is the Nth row of X, and $w_{N.}$ is the Nth row of W, etc.

One predictor of y_N that has been considered in the literature is the conditional mean of y_N based on the model solution given in (4.2.5); see, e.g., Dubin (2004) and Kelejian and Yuzefovich (2004). This predictor, given as $y_N^{[1]}$ in (4.2.7) below, is suggested by mean squared error issues and equals

$$\begin{aligned} y_N^{[1]} &= E(y_N | X, W, \lambda) \\ &= (I - \rho_1 W)_{N.}^{-1} X\beta. \end{aligned} \tag{4.2.7}$$

At certain points we will refer to the information set (X, W, λ) as $\Psi_1 = (X, W, \lambda)$. Also, researchers often do not reference the set Ψ_1 because it does not involve random elements. Therefore, $E(y_N | \Psi_1)$ would typically be written in simpler notation as just $E(y_N)$. Our presentation below is based on this simplification of notation. As an example, in the development below $E(w_{N.} y | \Psi_1)$ is written as $E(w_{N.} y)$, etc.

A Predictor Based on a Larger Information Set

The efficiency of a predictor can often be increased by increasing the information set. The right-hand side of the first line of (4.2.6) involves $w_{N.}y$ and so it is reasonable to expand Ψ_1 to include $w_{N.}y$. Let $\Psi_2 = (X, W, \lambda, w_{N.}y)$. Recalling (4.2.2) and (4.2.6), the conditional mean of y_N based on Ψ_2 is $y_N^{[2]}$ given by

$$\begin{aligned} y_N^{[2]} &= E(y_N|\Psi_2) \\ &= \rho_1 w_{N.}y + x_{N.}\beta + E(u_N|\Psi_2) \\ &= \rho_1 w_{N.}y + x_{N.}\beta + \\ & \frac{cov(u_N, w_{N.}y)}{var(w_{N.}y)}\left[w_{N.}y - E(w_{N.}y)\right]. \end{aligned} \tag{4.2.8}$$

The predictor $y_N^{[2]}$ was considered in Kelejian and Prucha (2007b), and accounts for the correlation of the regressor $w_{N.}y$ with u_N. This predictor depends on $w_{N.}y$ but since the diagonal elements of a weighting matrix are all zero, $w_{N.}y$ does not involve the variable being predicted, y_N.

The terms involved in (4.2.8) are straightforward to determine. For example, consider $cov(u_N, w_{N.}y)$. Since $u = (I_N - \rho_2 W)^{-1}\varepsilon$, it follows that

$$u_N = (I_N - \rho_2 W)_{N.}^{-1}\varepsilon \tag{4.2.9}$$

and so $u_N \sim N(0, \sigma_\varepsilon^2 (I_N - \rho_2 W)_{N.}^{-1}(I_N - \rho_2 W)_N^{-1\prime})$. It should also be clear that

$$\begin{aligned} w_{N.}y = {} & w_{N.}(I_N - \rho_1 W)^{-1}X\beta + \\ & w_{N.}(I_N - \rho_1 W)^{-1}(I_N - \rho_2 W)^{-1}\varepsilon \end{aligned} \tag{4.2.10}$$

so that from (4.2.9) and (4.2.10)

$$\begin{aligned} cov(u_N, w_{N.}y) &= E[u_N(w_{N.}y)'] \\ &= \sigma_\varepsilon^2 (I_N - \rho_2 W)_{N.}^{-1}(I_N - \rho_2 W')^{-1}(I_N - \rho_1 W')^{-1}w'_{N.}. \end{aligned} \tag{4.2.11}$$

The remaining terms to be determined on the third line of (4.2.8) are $var(w_{N.}y)$ and $E(w_{N.}y)$. Their calculation is left as exercises at the end of this chapter. Clearly, the empirical counterpart to the predictor $y_N^{[2]}$ in (4.2.8) requires the estimation of β, ρ_1, ρ_2, and σ_ε^2, which can be obtained by maximum likelihood, or by the IV procedures described in Sections 2.3 and 2.4 of Chapter 2.

The Full Information Predictor

The predictors, $y_N^{[1]}$ and $y_N^{[2]}$ of y_N do not use all of the available information. For example, the model in (4.2.3) implies an interrelationships between all of the elements of y. Therefore, a predictor of y_N could involve all $N-1$ observed values of y and not just the single linear combination $w_{N.}y$. Let y_{-N} be identical to y except that y_N is deleted, i.e., y_{-N} is an $N-1 \times 1$ vector. Given the model in (4.2.3), and the values of the parameters, namely λ, there is no information beyond that given by the set (X, W, λ, y_{-N}) that would be useful for purposes of predicting y_N.

Let $\Psi_3 = (X, W, \lambda, y_{-N})$. The full information predictor of y_N, which was also considered in Kelejian and Prucha (2007b), is given by the conditional mean

$$\begin{aligned} y_N^{[3]} &= E(y_N|\Psi_3) \\ &= \rho_1 w_{N.}y + x_{N.}\beta + E(u_N|\Psi_3) \\ &= \rho_1 w_{N.}y + x_{N.}\beta + \\ &\quad cov(u_N, y_{-N})\left[VC(y_{-N})\right]^{-1}\left[y_{-N} - E(y_{-N})\right] \end{aligned} \tag{4.2.12}$$

where we have again used (4.2.2).

In order to determine the terms on the fourth line of (4.2.12), let $I_{-N,N}$ be identical to the identity matrix of order N except that the Nth row is deleted. Then $y_{-N} = I_{-N,N}y$. Therefore, from (4.2.4)

$$y_{-N} = I_{-N,N}[(I-\rho_1 W)^{-1}X\beta + (I-\rho_1 W)^{-1}(I-\rho_2 W)^{-1}\varepsilon] \tag{4.2.13}$$

and so, again not referencing Ψ_1,

$$\begin{aligned} E(y_{-N}) &= I_{-N,N}[(I-\rho_1 W)^{-1}X\beta], \\ VC(y_{-N}) &= \sigma_\varepsilon^2 I_{-N,N}AA'I'_{-N,N} \\ A &= (I-\rho_1 W)^{-1}(I-\rho_2 W)^{-1}. \end{aligned} \tag{4.2.14}$$

The term $cov(u_N, y_{-N})$ can be obtained from (4.2.9) and (4.2.13), and is left as an exercise. Again, this predictor is not feasible but its feasible counterpart can easily be obtained from the estimation of (4.2.3).

The Intuitive Predictor

If a researcher ignores the correlations of endogenous regressors with the disturbance term, that researcher might predict y_N from just the right-hand side of the equation determining it, namely the first line in (4.2.6)

$$y_N^{[4]} = x_{N.}\beta + \rho_1 w_{N.}y. \tag{4.2.15}$$

This predictor is biased because it is based on the information set $\Psi_2 = (X, W, \lambda, w_{N.}y)$ but does not account for the correlation between $w_{N.}y_N$

and u_N. Recalling that, based on Ψ_2, $y_N^{[2]}$ is unbiased, it follows from (4.2.8) and (4.2.15) that the bias in $y_N^{[4]}$ is

$$\begin{aligned} bias_N^{[4]} &= y_N^{[2]} - y_N^{[4]} \\ &= \frac{cov(u_N, w_{N.}y)}{var(w_{N.}y)} \left[w_{N.}y - E(w_{N.}y) \right]. \end{aligned} \tag{4.2.16}$$

One motive for using $y_N^{[4]}$ is that, although it is biased, it is intuitive and easily calculated. For future reference, note that its information set is larger than that of $y_N^{[1]}$ in that it involves $w_{N.}y$.

Illustration 4.2.1: Prediction with a spatial model

The first step needed to calculate the feasible counterparts to the predictors $y_N^{[j]}$, $j = 1, ..., 4$ presented in Section 4.2 consists of estimating the complete model either by maximum likelihood or by the IV procedure to obtain sample estimates of ρ_1, ρ_2, β, and σ_ε^2. To simplify things, we assume that all of the observations on the dependent variable are observed so that our prediction will be in-sample. Also, the model we specify relates the median house price from the Boston data set to crime, age, and average number of rooms. The model is estimated by the IV procedure. We obtain the following relationship:

$$\begin{aligned} \widehat{\log(price)} &= -21.879(2.465) - 0.089(0.029)crime \\ &\quad - 0.042(0.011)age + 6.041(0.360)rooms \end{aligned}$$

where again standard errors are in the parentheses. Additionally, $\rho_1 = 0.426$ (with a standard error equal to 0.068) is statistically significant; and $\rho_2 = 0.421$. The value of $\sigma_\varepsilon^2 = \frac{\sum_{i=1}^N \hat{u}_i^2}{N-k-1} = 18.513$.

The predictors for the 25th observation in the sample are: $y_{25}^{[1]} = 17.126$, $y_{25}^{[2]} = 15.416$, $y_{25}^{[3]} = 15.621$, and $y_{25}^{[4]} = 16.383$. The observed value of the 25th sample observation is 15.6.

4.3 MEAN SQUARED ERRORS OF THE PREDICTORS

Mean squared errors are often expressed as the sum of the squared bias plus the variance. The predictors $y_N^{[1]}$, $y_N^{[2]}$, and $y_N^{[3]}$ are unbiased since they are conditional means and so their prediction mean squared errors are just their predictor variances conditional on the information set. The predictor $y_N^{[4]}$ is not a conditional mean and so its mean squared error will involve the square of its prediction bias, as well as a variance term.

The Mean Squared Error of $y_N^{[1]}$

Given the expression for $y_N^{[1]}$ in (4.2.7) and the expression for y_N in (4.2.5), the error in its prediction is $y_N - y_N^{[1]} = (I_N - \rho_1 W)_{N.}^{-1} u$. Clearly, $E[(I_N - \rho_1 W)_{N.}^{-1} u] = 0$, and so the mean squared error, or its prediction error variance, is

$$MSE(y_N^{[1]}) = \sigma_\varepsilon^2 (I - \rho_1 W)_{N.}^{-1} \Omega_u (I - \rho_1 W)_{N.}^{-1\prime} \qquad (4.3.1)$$

where $\Omega_u = (I - \rho_1 W)^{-1}(I - \rho_1 W')^{-1}$.

The Mean Squared Error of $y_N^{[2]}$

The predictor $y_N^{[2]}$ is based on the information set Ψ_2, which includes $w_{N.}y$. Thus, to calculate the mean squared prediction error of $y_N^{[2]}$ conditional on Ψ_2, we first express u_N and y_N conditional on Ψ_2.

The error term u_N can be expressed as

$$u_N = E(u_N|\Psi_2) + v_N \qquad (4.3.2)$$

where v_N is the difference between u_N and its mean, and so $E(v_N|\Psi_2) = 0$. The expression in (4.2.2) implies

$$E(u_N|\Psi_2) = \frac{cov(u_N, w_{N.}y)}{var(w_{N.}y)} \left[w_{N.}y - E(w_{N.}y) \right]. \qquad (4.3.3)$$

Also, since $E(u_N|\Psi_2)$ is conditional on Ψ_2, under Ψ_2, $w_{N.}y$ is a constant and so from (4.3.2)

$$var(u_N|\Psi_2) = var(v_N|\Psi_2). \qquad (4.3.4)$$

Now consider y_N conditional on Ψ_2. Given (4.3.2), (4.3.3), and y_N in (4.2.6)

$$\begin{aligned} y_N &= x_{N.}\beta + \rho_1 w_{N.}y + E(u_N|\Psi_2) + v_N \qquad (4.3.5) \\ &= x_{N.}\beta + \rho_1 w_{N.}y + \frac{cov(u_N, w_{N.}y)}{var(w_{N.}y)} \left[w_{N.}y - E(w_{N.}y) \right] + v_N. \end{aligned}$$

The prediction mean squared error of $y_N^{[2]}$ conditional on Ψ_2 may now be evident. Given the expression for $y_N^{[2]}$ in (4.2.8) and the expression y_N in (4.3.5), it follows that $y_N - y_N^{[2]} = v_N$. The variance expressions in (4.2.2) and (4.3.4) then imply

$$\begin{aligned} MSE(y_N^{[2]}) &= var(v_N|\Psi_2) = var(u_N|\Psi_2) \qquad (4.3.6) \\ &= \sigma_\varepsilon^2 \Omega_u^{N,N} - \frac{cov(u_N, w_{N.}y)^2}{var(w_{N.}y)} \end{aligned}$$

where $\Omega_u^{N,N}$ is the Nth diagonal element of $(I_N - \rho_1 W)^{-1}(I_N - \rho_1 W')^{-1}$, and so $\sigma_\varepsilon^2 \Omega_u^{N,N}$ is the variance of u_N.

The Mean Squared Error of $y_N^{[3]}$

This predictor is based on the information set Ψ_3 which involves y_{-N}. In a manner similar to the development leading to (4.3.5), y_N conditional on Ψ_3 can be expressed as

$$\begin{aligned} y_N &= x_{N.}\beta + \rho_1 w_{N.}y + E(u_N|\Psi_3) + q_N & (4.3.7) \\ &= x_{N.}\beta + \rho_1 w_{N.}y + cov(u_N, y_{-N})\left[VC(y_{-N})\right]^{-1}\left[y_{-N} - E(y_{-N})\right] + q_N \end{aligned}$$

where $E(q_N|\Psi_3) = 0$. Using the variance expression in (4.2.2),

$$\begin{aligned} var(q_N|\Psi_3) &= var(u_N|\Psi_3) & (4.3.8) \\ &= \sigma_\varepsilon^2 \Omega_u^{N,N} - cov(u_N, y_{-N})VC(y_{-N})^{-1}cov(u_N, y_{-N})'. \end{aligned}$$

Now consider the prediction mean squared error of $y_N^{[3]}$ conditional on Ψ_3. Given the expression for $y_N^{[3]}$ (4.2.12) and the expression y_N in (4.3.5), it follows that $y_N - y_N^{[3]} = q_N$ and so the variance expression in (4.2.2) then implies

$$\begin{aligned} MSE(y_N^{[3]}) &= var(u_N|\Psi_3) & (4.3.9) \\ &= \sigma_\varepsilon^2 \Omega_u^{N,N} - cov(u_N, y_{-N})VC(y_{-N})^{-1}cov(u_N, y_{-N})' \end{aligned}$$

since $var(u_N|\Psi_3) = var(q_N|\Psi_3)$ – see the development leading to (4.3.4). The similarity of (4.3.9) and (4.3.6) is evident.

The Mean Squared Error of $y_N^{[4]}$

This predictor is based on the information set Ψ_2 and is biased because it does not account for the correlation of $w_{N.}y$ and the error term, u. The expression for $y_N^{[4]}$ in (4.2.15) and the expression for y_N in (4.3.5) imply

$$\begin{aligned} y_N - y_N^{[4]} &= \frac{cov(u_N, w_{N.}y)}{var(w_{N.}y)}\left[w_{N.}y - E(w_{N.}y)\right] + v_N & (4.3.10) \\ &= bias^{[4]} + v_N, \quad E(v_N|\Psi_2) = 0, \end{aligned}$$

where the bias involved in the use of the predictor $y_N^{[4]}$ is

$$bias^{[4]} = \frac{cov(u_N, w_{N.}y)}{var(w_{N.}y)}\left[w_{N.}y - E(w_{N.}y)\right]. \tag{4.3.11}$$

Note that, under Ψ_2, $bias^{[4]}$ can be viewed as a constant because it only depends on the model parameters, W, and $w_{N.}y$, all of which are given and therefore constant **under** Ψ_2. Using this notation and (4.3.4), (4.3.6), and (4.3.10), the mean squared prediction error of the intuitive "naive" predictor $y_N^{[4]}$ is

$$\begin{aligned} MSE(y_N^{[4]}) &= E[(y_N - y_N^{[4]})^2|\Psi_2] \\ &= bias^2 + E(u_N^2|\Psi_2) \\ &= (bias^{[4]})^2 + \sigma_\varepsilon^2\Omega_u^{N,N} - \frac{cov(u_N, w_{N.}y)^2}{var(w_{N.}y)} \\ &= (bias^{[4]})^2 + MSE(y_N^{[2]}). \end{aligned} \tag{4.3.12}$$

The second line in (4.3.12) is based upon the observation that the cross-product which results from the squaring in the first line of (4.3.12) has an expectation of zero since $E(bias^{[4]}v_N|\Psi_2) = bias^{[4]}E(v_N|\Psi_2) = 0$.

Avoiding a Subtle Error

A naive and incorrect approach to the determination of the mean squared error of $y_N^{[4]}$ would be to simply compare y_N in (4.2.6) to $y_N^{[4]}$ in (4.2.15), and then take expectations of the squared difference conditional on Ψ_2. For example, in this case one would calculate, using the variance expression in (4.2.2),

$$\begin{aligned} E[(y_N - y_N^{[4]})^2|\Psi_2] &= E[u_N^2|\Psi_2] \\ &= \sigma_\varepsilon^2\Omega_u^{N,N} - \frac{cov(u_N, w_{N.}y)^2}{var(w_{N.}y)}. \end{aligned} \tag{4.3.13}$$

The expression in (4.3.13) does not account for bias which results from the use of the predictor $y_N^{[4]}$, and is therefore **incorrect**! The error in this procedure is that u_N in (4.2.6) is not conditionalized on Ψ_2, as it is in (4.3.2) and (4.3.3). The lesson is that to calculate a mean squared error of a predictor, one should condition the variable being predicted on the predictor's information set before making comparisons.

Putting Prediction Mean Squared Errors on an Equal Footing

The $MSE(y_N^{[4]})$ involves $bias_N^{[4]}$, which involves $w_{N.}y$, and so its value will depend upon the realization of the error term, u. This implies that the quality of the predictor $y_N^{[4]}$ will vary over the realizations of the error term, u. The mean squared errors of $y_N^{[1]}$, $y_N^{[2]}$, and $y_N^{[3]}$, given in (4.3.1), (4.3.6), and (4.3.9), respectively, only involve the elements of the model parameters and W, which are nonstochastic. Therefore these mean squared errors do not depend upon particular realizations of the error term. In order to meaningfully compare the mean squared error of $y_N^{[4]}$ to that of the other three predictors, one should "average"

$MSE(y_N^{[4]})$ over the realizations of u. This can be done quite simply by just taking the expectation of $MSE(y_N^{[4]})$ as given in (4.3.12). As will become apparent, this expectation will result in an expression which only depends upon the model parameters and W. As indicated, the mean squared errors of $y_N^{[1]}$, $y_N^{[2]}$, and $y_N^{[3]}$ also only involve the model parameters and W so these mean squared errors are comparable.

Given (4.3.6) and (4.3.12), it follows that[2]

$$\begin{aligned} E[MSE(y_N^{[4]})] &= E[(bias^{[4]})^2 + MSE(y_N^{[4]})] \\ &= E[(bias^{[4]})^2 + \sigma_\varepsilon^2 \Omega_u^{N,N} - \frac{cov(u_N, w_{N.}y)^2}{var(w_{N.}y)}]. \end{aligned} \tag{4.3.14}$$

It then follows from (4.3.11) that unconditionally

$$\begin{aligned} E(bias^{[4]}) &= \frac{cov(u_N, w_{N.}y)}{var(w_{N.}y)} \left[E(w_{N.}y) - E(w_{N.}y) \right] \\ &= 0. \end{aligned} \tag{4.3.15}$$

Therefore $E(bias^{[4]})^2$ in (4.3.14) is the variance of $bias^{[4]}$. Since the only random term in $bias^{[4]}$ is $w_{N.}y$, the variance of $bias^{[4]}$ is (see (4.3.11))

$$\begin{aligned} var(bias^{[4]}) &= \left[\frac{cov(u_N, w_{N.}y)}{var(w_{N.}y)} \right]^2 var(w_{N.}y) \\ &= \frac{[cov(u_N, w_{N.}y)]^2}{var(w_{N.}y)}. \end{aligned} \tag{4.3.16}$$

From (4.3.14)–(4.3.16)

$$\begin{aligned} &E[MSE(y_N^{[4]})] \\ &= \frac{[cov(u_N, w_{N.}y)]^2}{var(w_{N.}y)} + \sigma_\varepsilon^2 \Omega_u^{N,N} - \frac{[cov(u_N, w_{N.}y)]^2}{var(w_{N.}y)} \\ &= \sigma_\varepsilon^2 \Omega_u^{N,N}. \end{aligned} \tag{4.3.17}$$

Comparing Prediction Mean Squared Errors

It is typically the case that mean squared errors of conditional mean predictors will **never** increase, and will typically decrease if the information set underlying that predictor is increased. Intuitively, if the new information is irrelevant,

2. On a more formal level, the expectation in (4.3.14) is $E[MSE(y_N^{[4]})|\Psi_1]$. This expectation is averaging over $w_{N.}y$. For a still more formal development in terms of iterated expectations, see the development in (4.1.3)–(4.1.5), and the illustration following (4.1.5).

a conditional mean predictor will not involve that new information, i.e., it will have a zero weight! On the other hand, if the new information is relevant, a conditional mean predictor will give it a nonzero weight, and so the prediction mean squared error will decrease.

The predictors $y_N^{[1]}$, $y_N^{[2]}$, and $y_N^{[3]}$ are based on the information sets Ψ_1, $\Psi_2 = (\Psi_1, w_{N.}y)$, and $\Psi_3 = (\Psi_1, y_{-N})$, respectively. Since $w_{N.}y$ is just one linear combination of y_{-N} which does not involve y_N, and Ψ_3 contains both W and y_{-N}, it also contains $w_{N.}y$, as well as other elements of the vector y_{-N}. Therefore Ψ_1, Ψ_2, and Ψ_3 are increasing sets:

$$\Psi_1 \subset \Psi_2 \subset \Psi_3. \tag{4.3.18}$$

Using a result in Mood et al. (1974, p. 159), it can be shown that

$$\begin{aligned} &MSE(y_N^{[1]}|X, W) \geq MSE(y_N^{[2]}|X, W) \geq MSE(y_N^{[3]}|X, W), \\ &MSE(y_N^{[4]}|X, W) \geq MSE(y_N^{[2]}|X, W). \end{aligned} \tag{4.3.19}$$

The first line in (4.3.19) relates directly to (4.3.18). The second line is based on (4.3.12) or (4.3.14).

As indicated, the results above are based on known parameter values. Using Monte Carlo techniques, Kelejian and Prucha (2007b) evaluated the mean squares errors over a wide range of model parameter values. Their numerical results are revealing. On average, the ratio of the mean squared errors of $y_N^{[J]}$, $J = 1, 2, 4$ to that of the efficient predictor, $y_N^{[3]}$, were found to be:

$$\begin{aligned} &\bar{y}_N^{[1]} : 16.6, \\ &\bar{y}_N^{[2]} : 1.07, \\ &\bar{y}_N^{[4]} : 2.2. \end{aligned} \tag{4.3.20}$$

Perhaps contrary to what one might expect, the predictor based on the reduced form, namely $y_N^{[1]}$, is, on average, **by far** the worst of the four predictors. Recalling that $y_N^{[1]}$ is a conditional mean predictor which is therefore unbiased, while $y_N^{[4]}$ is biased, the results in (4.3.20) quite strongly indicate the importance of the size of the information set underlying predictors. In this case, the resulting increase in prediction accuracy resulting from the use of a larger information underlying $y_N^{[4]}$ more than compensates for its loss of prediction accuracy due to its bias. Also note that the loss of efficiency due to the use of $y_N^{[2]}$ instead of $y_N^{[3]}$ is only 7%. At least for the predictors considered, the suggestion is that the information set has a much greater effect on the precision of the predictor, than does accounting of correlations of regressors with the error term.

SUGGESTED PROBLEMS

1. Using the notation of this chapter, assume the model in (4.2.6), i.e.,

$$y_N = x_{N.}\beta + \rho_1 w_{N.}y + u_N,$$
$$u_N = \rho_2 w_{N.}u_N + \varepsilon_N.$$

(a) Determine the variance $var(w_{N.}y)$ which appears in (4.2.8).
(b) Determine the expected value $E(w_{N.}y)$ which appears in (4.2.8).
(c) Determine the covariance $cov(u_N, y_{-N})$ which appears in (4.2.12).

2. Consider the model

$$y = X\beta + \lambda_1 W_1 y + \lambda_2 W_2 y + \varepsilon$$

where the elements of ε are i.i.d. $N(0, \sigma^2)$, and W_1 and W_2 are weighting matrices which, along with X, are exogenous. Assume $(I_N - \lambda_1 W_1 - \lambda_2 W_2)$ is nonsingular. Let y_N be the Nth value of y.
Determine $E(y_N|X, W_1 y, W_2 y)$.

3. Using evident notation, consider the model

$$y = X\beta + \lambda W y + u,$$
$$u = \varepsilon + W\varepsilon$$

where ε is defined in problem 2. Again let y_N be the Nth value of y.
Determine $E(E(y_N|X, Wy))$.

Chapter 5

Problems in Estimating Weighting Matrices

The weighting matrix is typically an important feature of a spatial econometric model. As suggested in Chapter 1, there are quite a few possible specifications of this matrix. Still further illustrations and discussions of weighting matrices are given in Anselin (1988), Corrado and Fingleton (2012), Cressie (1993), Bavaud (1998), Seldadyo et al. (2010), Smith (2014), and Stakhovych and Bijmolt (2009).

In some cases a researcher may not be sure of the correct specification of the weighting matrix and may therefore "experiment" with different formulations. This experimentation can take many forms. One of these relates to the fit of the model as described by the R^2 statistic. That is, the weighting matrix selected for the study might be the one which produces the highest R^2 statistic. In this chapter we suggest that this procedure should not be used. Another procedure that might be considered for the selection of the weighting matrix is to take the one which leads to empirical results which are the "most" consistent with theoretical notions. In Chapter 8 we point out a number of problems which are associated with this procedure. They also relate to cases in which the weighting matrix is first estimated based on empirical hypotheses, and then assumed in the full spatial model. This will become clear from the discussion in Chapter 8. On a more positive note, as described in Chapter 12, if a researcher feels confident in a particular weighting matrix, but is willing to consider one or more alternatives to it, that researcher can formally reject those alternatives at a certain level of significance, typically 5%. This can be done using the J-test, which is described in Chapter 12.

5.1 THE SPATIAL MODEL

A demonstration that selection based on the R^2 criterion is "problematic" is based on results obtained by Kelejian et al. (2006).

Consider the model

$$y = \alpha e_N + X\beta + \rho_1 W y + u \tag{5.1.1}$$

Spatial Econometrics. http://dx.doi.org/10.1016/B978-0-12-813387-3.00005-6

where e_N is the $N \times 1$ vector of unit elements, α is a scalar parameter, y is an $N \times 1$ vector of observations on the dependent variable, X is an $N \times k$ exogenous regressor matrix which does not include the constant term, and the remaining notation should be evident. Assume that all of the nondiagonal elements of W are the same. Since the sample size is N, this common value could – but need not – be a function of N, say c_N. Let W be

$$W = \begin{bmatrix} 0 & c_N & c_N & . & . & c_N \\ c_N & 0 & c_N & . & . & c_N \\ c_N & c_N & . & c_N & & . \\ . & . & . & . & c_N & . \\ . & . & . & & . & c_N \\ c_N & . & . & . & c_N & 0 \end{bmatrix}. \tag{5.1.2}$$

Assume that (e_N, X) has full column rank. The error term in u need not be specified because the results below do not depend on its specification. The results below also do not depend on a particular specification of c_N.

5.2 SHORTCOMINGS OF SELECTION BASED ON R^2

Let $y' = (y_1, ..., y_N)$, and let the ith row of W be $w_{i.}$. Then, given the specification in (5.1.2),

$$\begin{aligned} w_{i.}y &= \sum_{i=1}^{N} c_N y_i - c_N y_i \\ &= N c_N \bar{y} - c_N y_i; \; \bar{y} = N^{-1}\sum_{i=1}^{N} y_i. \end{aligned} \tag{5.2.1}$$

It then follows from (5.2.1) that

$$Wy = (N c_N \bar{y}) e_N - c_N y. \tag{5.2.2}$$

Substituting (5.2.2) into (5.1.1), we have

$$y = \alpha e_N + X\beta + \rho_1[e_N(c_N N\, \bar{y}) - c_N y] + u. \tag{5.2.3}$$

Suppose (5.1.1) is estimated by a procedure which minimizes a quadratic form of the residuals, where the matrix of the quadratic is at least positive semidefinite. Note that both the least squares and two stage least squares estimators fall into this category, as well as a lot of other estimators. Let the estimated values of α, β, and ρ_1 be $\hat{\alpha}$, $\hat{\beta}$, and $\hat{\rho}_1$, respectively. Then, as shown by Kelejian et al. (2004),

$$\hat{\rho}_1 = -1/c_N, \; \hat{\alpha} = N\bar{y}, \; \hat{\beta} = 0. \tag{5.2.4}$$

The demonstration of (5.2.4) is not difficult and, for instructive purposes, is given below. Note that the model in (5.1.1) is a typical linear spatial model, except that its weighting matrix has uniform elements. The result in (5.2.4) clearly implies that such a model is not useful. If estimated by typical procedures, the estimates obtained will not be meaningful – they will be as given in (5.2.4) – and so totally unrelated to the theoretical meaning of the model!

The proof of (5.2.4) is straightforward. Let $\hat{u} = y - \hat{y}$ be the estimated residual vector corresponding to the model in (5.1.1). Then, given (5.1.2) and (5.2.3), it follows that

$$\begin{aligned}\hat{u} &= y - (\hat{\alpha} + \hat{\rho}_1 N c_N \bar{y})e_N - X\hat{\beta} + \hat{\rho}_1 c_N y \\ &= y(1 + \hat{\rho}_1 c_N) - (\hat{\alpha} + \hat{\rho}_1 N c_N \bar{y})e_N - X\hat{\beta},\end{aligned} \tag{5.2.5}$$

which in turn implies that

$$\begin{aligned}&\hat{u} = 0 \text{ if} \\ &\hat{\rho}_1 = -1/c_N, \ \hat{\alpha} = N\bar{y}, \ \hat{\beta} = 0.\end{aligned} \tag{5.2.6}$$

Thus, a quadratic form such as $\hat{u}'D\hat{u}$, where D is any positive semidefinite matrix, can always be reduced to zero

$$\hat{u}'D\hat{u} = 0$$

by taking the parameter estimates as in (5.2.4). Clearly, the least squares procedure corresponds to $D = I_N$, and the two stage least squares procedure corresponds to $D = H(H'H)^{-1}H'$ where H is a matrix of instruments with full column rank.

Now consider the implications of (5.2.6) for selecting a weighting matrix based on the R^2 statistic. If various weighting matrices are considered and judged on the bases of the R^2 statistic, there will be a bias towards selecting the matrix whose elements are the most uniform. Clearly, the interpretation of the resulting parameter estimates should be "called into question."

Illustration 5.2.1: Equal weights and estimation – One panel

The data used in this example are available in R with the library spdep.[1] The data consist of house sales prices and characteristics for a spatial hedonic regression in Baltimore, MD which refer to 1978 (Dubin, 1992). The dependent variable is the (log) price, while among the set of explanatory variables we consider only house characteristics such as age, lot size, square footage, and the number of

1. See Appendix B.

rooms. There are 211 observations in the data set, and so we set $c_N = 1/211$ and construct the spatial weighting matrix accordingly. The two stage least squares estimate of the spatial model that includes a spatially lagged dependent variable is:

$$\begin{aligned}\widehat{\log(price)} &= 770.5606(3.37e^{-11}) + 8.19e^{-15}(1.03e^{-15})age \\ &\quad - 6.77e^{-16}(3.01e^{-16})lotsz - 1.74e^{-15}(3.14e^{-15})sqft \\ &\quad - 3.96e^{-14}(2.14e^{-14})rooms - 211(2.14e^{-14})W\log(price).\end{aligned}$$

Looking at (5.2.6), these results are not surprising, e.g., $\hat{\rho}_1 = -1/c_N = -1/(1/211) = -211$, $\hat{\alpha} = N\bar{y} = 211 \times 3.651946 = 770.5606$, and the elements of the vector $\hat{\beta}$ are virtually all zeros.

5.3 AN EXTENSION TO NONLINEAR SPATIAL MODELS

The results in Section 5.2 relate to a linear spatial model. However, comparable results relate to nonlinear spatial models, too. For example, consider a generalization of the model in (5.1.1) in which the elements of the weighting matrix are parameterized. As one example, suppose the model is

$$y = \alpha e_N + X\beta + \rho_1 W^* y + u \tag{5.3.1}$$

where the (i, j)th element of W^* is

$$w_{ij}^* = \exp(-[a_1|z_{ij}| + a_2|s_{ij}|]) \tag{5.3.2}$$

where z_{ij} and s_{ij} are distance measures between units i and j, $a_1 \geq 0$ and $a_2 \geq 0$ are scalar parameters.

Suppose the parameters of (5.3.1) are estimated by minimizing a quadratic in the residuals where the matrix of the quadratic is positive semidefinite. Among others, nonlinear two stage least squares falls into this category. Then from the results in Section 5.2, especially (5.2.4), it should be clear that the quadratic will be minimized at zero if

$$\hat{a}_1 = 0,\ \hat{a}_2 = 0,\ \hat{\rho}_1 = -1/c_N,\ \hat{\alpha} = N\bar{y},\ \hat{\beta} = 0 \tag{5.3.3}$$

since if $a_1 = a_2 = 0$ the weights are uniform, i.e., $c_N = 1$.

The results in (5.3.3) relate to the weighting matrix whose elements are given in (5.3.2). However, it should be clear that comparable results hold for any weighting matrix whose elements are parameterized in such a way that uniform weights result as a special case. Again, the conclusion is that if there is uncertainty concerning a weighting matrix, that matrix should not be chosen on the basis of the R^2 statistic.

5.4 R^2 SELECTION IN THE MULTIPLE PANEL CASE

The results above relate to a single panel, e.g., one village, one school, one time period, etc. The results in the multiple panel case are not so straightforward. Unlike for the single panel model, in some cases described below the model is useful even if the weighting matrix has uniform weights. In other cases such a model is not useful. However, we still suggest that in all cases, the weighting matrix should not be selected on the bases of the R^2 statistic.

For example, suppose a researcher's study involves more than one village. In this framework, consider the case of farmers and the extent of fertilizer they use. Assume that within a village all farmers "learn" from each other, but there is no interaction between villages. Suppose also that the researcher knows the village the farmer is in, but within that village there is no available measure of "learning" distance between farmers. Finally, assume that there are G villages and the number of farmers in village J is N_J, $J = 1, ..., G$.

Let y_J be the $N_J \times 1$ vector of observations on the dependent variable in the Jth village, and consider the model

$$y_J = e_{N_J}\alpha + X_J\beta + \rho_1 W_J y_J + u_J, \ J = 1, ..., G \tag{5.4.1}$$

where e_J is an $N_J \times 1$ vector of unit elements, X_J is an $N_J \times k$ matrix of observations on exogenous regressors which do not include the constant term, W_J is the corresponding $N_J \times N_J$ exogenous weighting matrix, and the remainder of the notation should be evident. Assuming there is a different number of farmers in each village, assume

$$W_J = \begin{bmatrix} 0 & c_{N_J} & c_{N_J} & . & . & c_{N_J} \\ c_{N_J} & 0 & c_{N_J} & . & . & c_{N_J} \\ c_{N_J} & c_{N_J} & . & c_{N_J} & & . \\ . & . & . & . & c_{N_J} & . \\ . & . & . & & 0 & c_{N_J} \\ c_{N_J} & . & . & . & c_{N_J} & 0 \end{bmatrix}_{N_J \times N_J}, \ J = 1, ..., G. \tag{5.4.2}$$

Let $N = N_1 + ... + N_G$, and let the stacked version of (5.4.1) be

$$y = e_N\alpha + X\beta + \rho_1 W y + u \tag{5.4.3}$$

where

$$\begin{aligned} y' &= (y_1', ..., y_G'), \\ X' &= (X_1', ..., X_G'), \\ W &= diag_{J=1}^{G}(W_J), \end{aligned}$$

$$u' = (u'_1, ..., u'_G).$$

Let the ith element of y_J be $y_{i,J}$, $i = 1, ..., N_J$. Using calculations which are identical to those used in (5.2.1) and (5.2.2) yields

$$Wy = \begin{bmatrix} (N_1 c_{N_1} \bar{y}_1) e_{N_1} - c_{N_1} y_1 \\ \vdots \\ (N_G c_{N_G} \bar{y}_G) e_{N_G} - c_{N_G} y_G \end{bmatrix} \tag{5.4.4}$$

where $\bar{y}_J = \sum_{i=1}^{N_J} y_{i,J}/N_J$. Therefore (5.4.3) can be expressed as

$$\begin{bmatrix} y_1 \\ \vdots \\ y_G \end{bmatrix} = \alpha \begin{bmatrix} e_{N_1} \\ \vdots \\ e_{N_G} \end{bmatrix} + \begin{bmatrix} X_1 \\ \vdots \\ X_G \end{bmatrix} \beta \tag{5.4.5}$$
$$+ \rho_1 \begin{bmatrix} (N_1 c_{N_1} \bar{y}_1) e_{N_1} - c_{N_1} y_1 \\ \vdots \\ (N_G c_{N_G} \bar{y}_G) e_{N_G} - c_{N_G} y_G \end{bmatrix} + \begin{bmatrix} u_1 \\ \vdots \\ u_G \end{bmatrix}.$$

Again let the estimated values of α, β, and ρ_1 be $\hat{\alpha}$, $\hat{\beta}$, and $\hat{\rho}_1$, respectively, and let $\hat{y} = e_N \hat{\alpha} + X\hat{\beta} + \hat{\rho}_1 Wy$. Then the estimated residuals $\hat{u} = y - \hat{y}$ are

$$\begin{bmatrix} \hat{u}_1 \\ \vdots \\ \hat{u}_G \end{bmatrix} = \begin{bmatrix} y_1 \\ \vdots \\ y_G \end{bmatrix} - \hat{\alpha} \begin{bmatrix} e_{N_1} \\ \vdots \\ e_{N_G} \end{bmatrix} - \begin{bmatrix} X_1 \\ \vdots \\ X_G \end{bmatrix} \hat{\beta} \tag{5.4.6}$$
$$- \hat{\rho}_1 \begin{bmatrix} (N_1 c_{N_1} \bar{y}_1) e_{N_1} \\ \vdots \\ (N_G c_{N_G} \bar{y}_G) e_{N_G} \end{bmatrix} + \hat{\rho}_1 \begin{bmatrix} c_{N_1} y_1 \\ \vdots \\ c_{N_G} y_G \end{bmatrix}.$$

Unlike for the results in Section 5.2, in the absence of further conditions, if $G > 1$ the result in (5.4.6) cannot be factored in a manner comparable to that in (5.2.5). Therefore, there are no values of $\hat{\alpha}$, $\hat{\beta}$, and $\hat{\rho}_1$ which will make $\hat{u} = [\hat{u}_1, ..., \hat{u}_G]' = 0$. Thus, the model in (5.4.1) does not have the same estimation problems as that in (5.1.1) and (5.1.2), i.e., it is useful. For this model, if a weighting matrix is selected on the basis of an R^2 statistic, there will not be a bias in the direction of uniform weights. However, as described in Chapter 8, there will be other problems in such a selection procedure.

There are conditions which will render the model in (5.4.1) useless and these conditions will hold in some cases. For example, generally when confronted with a panel data model such as (5.4.1), researchers often allow the intercept to be different in each group, i.e., to vary over $J = 1, ..., G$. Let the intercept in the Jth panel be α_J, where α_J is nonstochastic, $J = 1, ..., G$. These are typically referred to as fixed effects. Also, assume that the panels are balanced in that there are the same number of units in each panel, e.g., $N_J = S$, $J = 1, ..., G$ and so $N = SG$. This would typically be the case if the panels relate to time periods and the observations relate to the same units over time. Let c_S be the constant in the weighting matrix – in (5.4.2) $c_{N_J} = c_S$, $J = 1, ..., G$.

In this case the model in (5.4.1) becomes

$$y_J = e_S\alpha_J + X_J\beta + \rho_1 W_J y_J + u_J, \quad J = 1, ..., G. \tag{5.4.7}$$

Let $\hat{\alpha}_J, \hat{\beta}$, and $\hat{\rho}_1$ be the estimated values of α_J, β_J, and ρ_1, $J = 1, ..., G$. In this case (5.4.6) reduces to

$$\begin{bmatrix} \hat{u}_1 \\ \vdots \\ \hat{u}_G \end{bmatrix} = \begin{bmatrix} y_1 \\ \vdots \\ y_G \end{bmatrix} - \begin{bmatrix} e_S\hat{\alpha}_1 \\ \vdots \\ e_S\hat{\alpha}_G \end{bmatrix} - \begin{bmatrix} X_1 \\ \vdots \\ X_G \end{bmatrix} \hat{\beta} \tag{5.4.8}$$
$$- \hat{\rho}_1 \begin{bmatrix} (Sc_S\bar{y}_1)e_S \\ \vdots \\ (Sc_S\bar{y}_G)e_S \end{bmatrix} + \hat{\rho}_1 \begin{bmatrix} c_S y_1 \\ \vdots \\ c_S y_G \end{bmatrix}$$
$$= \begin{bmatrix} y_1(1+\hat{\rho}_1 c_S) \\ \vdots \\ y_G(1+\hat{\rho}_1 c_S) \end{bmatrix} - \begin{bmatrix} e_S(\hat{\alpha}_1 + \hat{\rho}_1 Sc_S\bar{y}_1) \\ \vdots \\ e_S(\hat{\alpha}_G + \hat{\rho}_1 Sc_S\bar{y}_G) \end{bmatrix} - \begin{bmatrix} X_1 \\ \vdots \\ X_G \end{bmatrix} \hat{\beta}.$$

Clearly, $\hat{u} = 0$ if $\hat{\rho}_1 = -1/c_S$, $\hat{\alpha}_J = S\bar{y}_J$, and $\hat{\beta} = 0$, $J = 1, ..., G$. Therefore, balanced panel data models which have fixed effects and weighting matrices with uniform elements are not useful. Again the implication is that if a weighting matrix is selected in a fixed effects balanced panel data model on the bases of the R^2 statistic, there will be a bias favoring matrices whose weights are the most uniform.

In passing we note that panel data models which relate to schools, villages, etc., will typically not be balanced and so they will not have such problems.

Illustration 5.4.1: Equal weights – Multiple panels

Let us consider again the model for the murder rate that was considered in Illustration 2.2.1.2. There is a variable in this data set that relates to each state in a region within the US. The region considered are: East North Central, East

South Central, Middle Atlantic, Mountain, New England, Pacific, South Atlantic, West North Central, and West South Central. We are assuming that the murder rate does not spill over between regions but only within regions. After sorting the data by subregions, this situation corresponds to a block diagonal spatial weighting matrix. The elements on each block are taken as c_{N_J}, where c_{N_J} is the reciprocal of the number of states in each region. Specifically, there are three states in the Middle Atlantic and Pacific regions; four in the East South Central and West South Central regions; the East North Central region has five states, six states are in New England, seven are in the West North Central region, the Mountain region consists of eight states, and the remaining nine are classified as South Atlantic.

With a weighting matrix defined in this fashion, the results of the model are meaningful:

$$\widehat{mrdrte} = -14.335(11.519) + 0.067(0.322)exec \\ + 2.724(1.170)unem + 0.830(0.980)wmrdrte.$$

SUGGESTED PROBLEMS

1. Consider the model

$$(P.1) \quad y = X\beta + \lambda W y + u, \quad u = \rho W u + \varepsilon$$

where the (i, j)th element of the weighting matrix is

$$(P.2) \quad w_{ij} = \exp(-\alpha d_{ij}), \alpha \geq 0$$

where d_{ij} is a distance measure, and the remaining notation should be evident.

(a) Discuss possible estimation problems.

(b) Suppose the (i, j)th element of W is

$$(P.3) \quad w_{ij} = \exp(-d_{ij}).$$

Are there the same issues relating to estimation as in part (a)?

(c) Suppose the specification of w_{ij} in $(P.2)$ were changed to

$$(P.4) \quad w_{ij} = \exp(-\alpha d_{ij}), \quad \text{if } d_{ij} < d, \ \alpha \geq 0; \quad w_{ij} = 0, \quad \text{if } d_{ij} \geq d,$$

where d is known and is viewed as an upper bound distance defining neighbors.

Are the estimation issues the same as for the case in which w_{ij} is defined in $(P.2)$?

2. Is the model in (5.4.1) and (5.4.2) likely to be useful if the panels relate to students in various schools?

Chapter 6

Additional Endogenous Variables: Possible Nonlinearities*

In this chapter we deal with spatial models which have additional endogenous regressors. Since most economic variables are determined in an economy-wide system, additional endogenous regressors will often arise. As will typically be the case, we assume that the system determining these additional regressors is not known. Despite this, the researcher may know some of the exogenous variables that are in the unknown system. This is often the case considered in many applied studies.

Section 6.1 contains some introductory comments, while Section 6.2 analyzes identification and estimation issues in a linear system. In Section 6.3 we introduce notation for a nonlinear structural equation model, and in Section 6.4 we consider its estimation. Sections 6.5 and 6.6 are somewhat technical and deal with large sample issues. Finally, in Section 6.7 we consider some applications to spatial models. Section 6.8 concludes this chapter with a discussion of maximum likelihood that highlights some of the problems with that approach.

6.1 INTRODUCTORY COMMENTS

As should appear evident at this point, this book is primarily concerned with linear spatial models. Despite this, possible issues relating to nonlinear systems may still arise! For example, the models considered in this section relate to typical spatial models which are linear in the parameters but have additional endogenous regressors. As an example, using evident notation, one such model would be of the form

$$y = XB + \rho_1 Wy + Y\gamma + u \tag{6.1.1}$$

---

* Spatial models involving additional endogenous variables were considered, among others, by Anselin (2011), Drukker et al. (2013c,d), Fingleton and Le Gallo (2008), Kelejian and Piras (2014), and Kelejian and Prucha (2007a). Useful references relating to issues involving nonlinearities which are discussed in this chapter are Amemiya (1985), Cameron and Trivedi (2005), Greene (2003), Kelejian (1971), and Pötscher and Prucha (1997, 2000).

Spatial Econometrics. http://dx.doi.org/10.1016/B978-0-12-813387-3.00006-8

where y is a vector of observations on the demand for labor in certain regional areas, X is a corresponding matrix of observations on exogenous variables, and Y is a matrix of observations on corresponding wage rates, productivity measures, etc. One would typically view wage rates and productivity measures as endogenous in a model for labor demand.

As will typically be the case, we assume that the system determining these additional endogenous regressors is not known. On the other hand, the researcher may know one or more of the exogenous variables that are in that unknown system. Actually, this is the typical framework of general spatial two- and three-stage least squares procedure. However, in this chapter we allow for the possibility that the "unknown system" determining the additional endogenous regressors in the model to be estimated may contain nonlinearities. Under certain conditions, in this case the researcher does not need to know any of the exogenous variables in that unknown system but yet may still be able to obtain a consistent estimator of the model parameters.

We develop our results in terms of a sequence of simple models which contain one or more nonlinearities. We then generalize those results to more "realistic models."[1]

6.2 IDENTIFICATION AND ESTIMATION: A LINEAR SYSTEM

Many properties and estimation procedures of nonlinear systems are quite different than the corresponding procedures of linear systems. For example, first consider a simple two equation linear model

$$y_{i1} = a_1 + a_2 y_{i2} + a_3 x_i + \varepsilon_{i1}, i = 1, ..., N, \quad (6.2.1)$$

$$y_{i2} = b_1 + b_2 x_i + \varepsilon_{i2}, i = 1, ..., N \quad (6.2.2)$$

where x_i is a nonstochastic scalar, and for ease of presentation, assume that $(\varepsilon_{i1}, \varepsilon_{i2})$ is i.i.d. $N(0, \Sigma_\varepsilon)$ where

$$\Sigma_\varepsilon = \{\sigma_{ij}\}, i, j = 1, 2, \quad (6.2.3)$$
$$\sigma_{12} \neq 0.$$

The order condition for identification of an equation in a linear system is that the number of endogenous regressors appearing in the equation must be less than

1. For future reference in this chapter, the following will be needed. Let $\phi \sim N(\mu, \sigma^2)$. Then

$$E[e^{\phi}] = e^{\mu+\sigma^2/2}$$

and

$$var[e^{\phi}] = (e^{\sigma^2} - 1)e^{2\mu+\sigma^2}.$$

or equal to the number of predetermined variables which are excluded from the equation but are in the system. This condition is obviously not satisfied in (6.2.1) because y_{i2} is endogenous due to the correlation of the error terms, and there are no excluded predetermined variables. Therefore the parameters of (6.2.1) are not identified and so cannot be consistently estimated.

Anticipating a comparison with nonlinear models, suppose the 2SLS procedure is applied to (6.2.1). In this case one would regress y_{i2} on the exogenous variables in the system (i.e., the constant term and x_i) and obtain, using evident notation, the predicted value, $\hat{y}_{i2} = \hat{b}_1 + \hat{b}_2 x_i$. The so-called second stage regressor matrix would then be $\widehat{Z}_1$ given by

$$\widehat{Z}_1 = \begin{bmatrix} 1 & \hat{y}_{12} & x_1 \\ \vdots & \vdots & \vdots \\ 1 & \hat{y}_{N2} & x_N \end{bmatrix}. \tag{6.2.4}$$

Unfortunately, $rank(\widehat{Z}_1) = 2$ because the second column is linear in the first and third. Consequently, the rank of $\widehat{Z}_1'\widehat{Z}_1$ is also two, and $\widehat{Z}_1'\widehat{Z}_1$ is singular; therefore 2SLS cannot even be implemented.

Still anticipating a comparison with nonlinear models, a determined researcher might try to overcome this singularity problem by first regressing y_{i2} on the constant term, x_i, and x_i^2 to obtain the predicted value of y_{i2}. In this case, the predicted value of y_{i2} would be $\hat{y}_{i2} = \hat{b}_1 + \hat{b}_2 x_i + \hat{b}_3 x_i^2$. The rank of the second stage regressor matrix would be three and hence 2SLS could be **implemented**! However, as we will show, it turns out that under typical specifications, the resulting estimators are not consistent because $\hat{b}_3 \xrightarrow{P} 0$. This means that, on an intuitive level, in large samples $rank(\widehat{Z}_1) = 2$ and so $\widehat{Z}_1'\widehat{Z}_1$ would be singular.

More formally, let $x_{i,2} = (1, x_i, x_i^2)$ and let the $N \times 3$ matrix of observations on $x_{i,2}$ be $X_2' = [x_{1,2}', ..., x_{N,2}']$. Let $\widehat{Z}_2$ be identical to $\widehat{Z}_1$ in (6.2.4) except that its second column is $\hat{y}_{i2} = \hat{b}_1 + \hat{b}_2 x_i + \hat{b}_3 x_i^2, i = 1, ..., N$. Note, in this case $\widehat{Z}_2$ can be expressed as

$$\widehat{Z}_2 = \begin{bmatrix} 1 & x_1 & x_1^2 \\ \vdots & \vdots & \vdots \\ 1 & x_N & x_N^2 \end{bmatrix} \begin{bmatrix} 1 & \hat{b}_1 & 0 \\ 0 & \hat{b}_2 & 1 \\ 0 & \hat{b}_3 & 0 \end{bmatrix} \tag{6.2.5}$$

$$\equiv X_2 \hat{B}$$

where

$$X_2 = \begin{bmatrix} 1 & x_1 & x_1^2 \\ \vdots & \vdots & \vdots \\ 1 & x_N & x_N^2 \end{bmatrix}, \quad \hat{B} = \begin{bmatrix} 1 & \hat{b}_1 & 0 \\ 0 & \hat{b}_2 & 1 \\ 0 & \hat{b}_3 & 0 \end{bmatrix}.$$

We make the following two assumptions:

Assumption 6.1. The elements of X_2 are uniformly bounded in absolute value.

Assumption 6.2. $N^{-1}X_2'X_2 \rightarrow Q_2$, where Q_2^{-1} exists.

To show that $\hat{b}_3 \xrightarrow{P} 0$, first note that the regression of y_{i2} on the constant, x_i, and x_i^2 corresponds to an expanded version of (6.2.2), namely

$$y_{i2} = b_1 + b_2 x_i + b_3 x_i^2 + \varepsilon_{i2}, \; i = 1, ..., N \tag{6.2.6}$$

where the true value of $b_3 = 0$. In matrix terms, this would be equal to

$$\begin{aligned} y_2 &= X_2\beta + \varepsilon, \\ \beta' &= (b_1, b_2, 0). \end{aligned} \tag{6.2.7}$$

Let $\hat{\beta}' = (\hat{b}_1, \hat{b}_2, \hat{b}_3)$ be the OLS estimator of β based on (6.2.7). We leave it as an exercise to show that $\hat{\beta} \xrightarrow{P} \beta$ and

$$p\lim N^{-1}\widehat{Z}_2'\widehat{Z}_2 = Q_{3\times 3}$$

where Q is a singular matrix.

6.3 A CORRESPONDING NONLINEAR MODEL

Now consider the model

$$y_{i1} = a_1 + a_2(e^{y_{i2}}) + a_3 x_i + \varepsilon_{i1}, \tag{6.3.1}$$

$$y_{i2} = b_1 + b_2 x_i + \varepsilon_{i2}. \tag{6.3.2}$$

These equations are identical to (6.2.1) and (6.2.2) except that y_{i2} in (6.2.1) is replaced in (6.3.1) by $e^{y_{i2}}$. Substituting (6.3.2) into (6.3.1) yields the solution of the model for y_{i1}, namely

$$\begin{aligned} y_{i1} &= a_1 + a_2(e^{b_1 + b_2 x_i + \varepsilon_{i2}}) + a_3 x_i + \varepsilon_{i1} \\ &= a_1 + a_2(e^{b_1 + b_2 x_i})e^{\varepsilon_{i2}} + a_3 x_i + \varepsilon_{i1}. \end{aligned} \tag{6.3.3}$$

Note that the solution of the model for y_{i1} is not linear in ε_{i2}. Also note that since $\varepsilon_{i2} \sim N(0, \sigma_{22})$, it follows that $E(e^{\varepsilon_{i2}}) = K$, where $K = e^{\sigma_{22}/2}$. Therefore, the mean value of y_{i1} exists and can be obtained by taking expectations across (6.3.3), namely

$$\begin{aligned} E[y_{i1}] &= a_1 + a_2 e^{b_1 + b_2 x_i} E e^{\varepsilon_{i2}} + a_3 x_i \\ &= a_1 + a_2 e^{b_1 + b_2 x_i} K + a_3 x_i . \end{aligned} \tag{6.3.4}$$

It follows by comparing (6.3.3) to (6.3.4) that the mean of y_{i1}, which would be its minimum mean squared error predictor, cannot be obtained by simply solving the model and replacing the error terms by zero.

A Generalization of the Nonlinear System in (6.3.1) and (6.3.2)

Before proceeding to estimation issues associated with (6.3.1), it might be useful to see the results obtained thus far in a more general framework. Ironically, the issues obtained thus far are more transparent in the more general nonlinear framework.

Let a G equation nonlinear system containing a $G \times 1$ endogenous vector $y_i = (y_{i,1}, ..., y_{i,G})'$, a $G \times 1$ disturbance vector $\varepsilon_i = (\varepsilon_{i1}, ..., \varepsilon_{iG})'$, and an $L \times 1$ nonstochastic vector X_i be

$$\begin{bmatrix} f_1(y_i, X_i, \varepsilon_{i1}) = 0 \\ \vdots \\ f_G(y_i, X_i, \varepsilon_{iG}) = 0 \end{bmatrix}. \tag{6.3.5}$$

A system of equation such as the one illustrated in (6.3.5) is generally named a structural equation model. As in (6.3.1) and (6.3.2), some, or none, of the G structural equations in (6.3.5) may be linear. The model in (6.3.5) can be expressed in more compact notation as

$$F(y_i, X_i, \varepsilon_i) = 0_{G \times 1} \tag{6.3.6}$$

where $F(y_i, X_i, \varepsilon_i)$ is the $G \times 1$ vector of functions described in (6.3.5).

Assuming the model has a solution, the solution of the model for y_i in (6.3.6) can be expressed as

$$y_i = S(X_i, \varepsilon_i) \tag{6.3.7}$$

where, again, $S(X_i, \varepsilon_i)$ is $G \times 1$ vector of functions. On an intuitive level, if a model containing y_i, X_i, and ε_i is solved for y_i, the solution must be a function of the remaining elements of that model!

Since at least some of the equations in (6.3.6) are nonlinear, the reduced form equations in (6.3.7) will generally be nonlinear in the elements of the disturbance vector, ε_i. Therefore, the conditional mean prediction equations cannot be obtained by setting the disturbance vector equal to zero, and then solving the resulting system for y_i, e.g.,

$$\begin{aligned} E(y_i) &= E\left[S\left(X_i, \varepsilon_i\right)\right] \\ &\neq S(X_i, E\left(\varepsilon_i\right)) = S\left(X_i, 0\right). \end{aligned} \tag{6.3.8}$$

6.4 ESTIMATION IN THE NONLINEAR MODEL

Let us now go back to the system in (6.3.1) and (6.3.2). If we assume that $\sigma_{12} \neq 0$, then $e^{y_{i2}}$ is an endogenous regressor in (6.3.1). As a consequence of this, the parameters of (6.3.1) cannot be consistently estimated by OLS. We will now show that, unlike for the corresponding linear system, the parameters of (6.3.1) can be consistently estimated by 2SLS using the matrix of instruments X_2 as described in (6.2.5).

First note from (6.3.2) that

$$\begin{aligned} e^{y_{i2}} &= e^{[b_1 + b_2 x_i + \varepsilon_{i2}]} \\ &= e^{[b_1 + b_2 x_i]} e^{\varepsilon_{i2}}. \end{aligned} \tag{6.4.1}$$

Since $E[e^{\varepsilon_{i2}}] = e^{\sigma_{22}/2} = K$ it follows that

$$\begin{aligned} e^{\varepsilon_{i2}} &= K + q_i, \\ E(q_i) &= 0. \end{aligned} \tag{6.4.2}$$

Since ε_{i2} are i.i.d. $N(0, \sigma_{22})$, q_i are *i.i.d.* and their variance is

$$\begin{aligned} \sigma_{q_i}^2 &= E(q_i^2) - K^2, \\ E(q_i^2) &= E(e^{2\varepsilon_{i2}}) \\ &= e^{2\sigma_{22}}. \end{aligned} \tag{6.4.3}$$

From (6.4.1) and (6.4.2)

$$\begin{aligned} e^{y_{i2}} &= K e^{[b_1 + b_2 x_i]} + e^{[b_1 + b_2 x_i]} q_i \\ &= f(x_i) + w_i \end{aligned} \tag{6.4.4}$$

where

$$f(x_i) = K e^{[b_1 + b_2 x_i]}, \tag{6.4.5}$$

$$w_i = e^{[b_1 + b_2 x_i]} q_i,$$
$$E(w_i) = 0, i = 1, ..., N.$$

Finally, since ε_{i2} is independently distributed over $i = 1, ..., N$ and x_i is nonstochastic, w_i is also independently distributed and its variance, say $\sigma^2_{w_i}$, is

$$\sigma^2_{w_i} = e^{2[b_1 + b_2 x_i]} \sigma^2_{q_i}, i = 1, ..., N. \tag{6.4.6}$$

For future reference, note that the variance of w_i is uniformly bounded because the elements of X_2, by Assumption 6.1, are uniformly bounded in absolute value.

If $e^{y_{i2}}$ is regressed on the constant, x_i, and x_i^2, the predicted value of $e^{y_{i2}}$ would be, using evident notation,

$$\widehat{e^{y_{i2}}} = \hat{c}_1 + \hat{c}_2 x_i + \hat{c}_3 x_i^2, i = 1, ..., N. \tag{6.4.7}$$

Let $e^{y(2)}$ be the $N \times 1$ vector whose ith element is $e^{y_{i2}}, i = 1, ..., N$. Then the predicted values described in (6.4.7) can be expressed as

$$\widehat{e^{y(2)}} = X_2 \hat{C}, \tag{6.4.8}$$
$$\hat{C}' = (\hat{c}_1, \hat{c}_2, \hat{c}_3)$$

and so the second stage regressor matrix, say $\hat{M}$, can be expressed as

$$\hat{M} = \begin{bmatrix} 1 & \widehat{e^{y_{12}}} & x_1 \\ \vdots & \vdots & \vdots \\ 1 & \widehat{e^{y_{N2}}} & x_N \end{bmatrix}, \tag{6.4.9}$$

or

$$\hat{M} = \begin{bmatrix} 1 & x_1 & x_1^2 \\ \vdots & \vdots & \vdots \\ 1 & x_N & x_N^2 \end{bmatrix} \begin{bmatrix} 1 & \hat{c}_1 & 0 \\ 0 & \hat{c}_2 & 1 \\ 0 & \hat{c}_3 & 0 \end{bmatrix} \tag{6.4.10}$$
$$= X_2 \hat{\mathbf{C}}$$

where

$$\hat{\mathbf{C}} = \begin{bmatrix} 1 & \hat{c}_1 & 0 \\ 0 & \hat{c}_2 & 1 \\ 0 & \hat{c}_3 & 0 \end{bmatrix}.$$

Recall that for the **linear** model in (6.2.1) and (6.2.2), the estimator of b_3, namely $\hat{b}_3$ in (6.2.5), had a probability limit of zero, $\hat{b}_3 \rightarrow 0$, and so in the limit, the second stage regressor matrix would have a rank of two. Hence, in the linear case, the 2SLS procedure based on the use of the instruments including the constant term, x_i, and x_i^2 is not consistent. We now show that the parameters of (6.3.1) can be consistently estimated by 2SLS using those same instruments. We first show that $p\lim \hat{c}_3 \neq 0$.

Using evident notation, the matrix form of (6.4.4) is via (6.4.5)

$$e^{y(2)} = f(x) + w \tag{6.4.11}$$

where $E(w_i) = 0, i = 1, ..., N$. Since $\hat{C}$ in (6.4.8) is determined by the OLS regression of $e^{y(2)}$ on X_2,

$$\begin{aligned} \hat{C} &= (X_2'X_2)^{-1}X_2'e^{y(2)} \\ &= (X_2'X_2)^{-1}X_2'f(x) + (X_2'X_2)^{-1}X_2'w. \end{aligned} \tag{6.4.12}$$

Let $\xi = (X_2'X_2)^{-1}X_2'w$. Then, since $E(w_i) = 0, i = 1, ..., N$ and since w_i is independently distributed,

$$\begin{aligned} &E(\xi) = 0, \\ &E[\xi\xi'] = (X_2'X_2)^{-1}X_2'\Omega_w X_2(X_2'X_2)^{-1} \end{aligned} \tag{6.4.13}$$

where Ω_w is a diagonal matrix whose ith diagonal element is $\sigma_{w_i}^2$. Assumption 6.1 and (6.4.6) imply that the diagonal elements of Ω_w are uniformly bounded. Therefore, from (6.4.13) and Assumption 6.2,

$$\begin{aligned} E[\xi\xi'] &= \frac{1}{N}(N^{-1}X_2'X_2)^{-1}N^{-1}[X_2'\Omega_w X_2](N^{-1}X_2'X_2)^{-1} \\ &\rightarrow \frac{1}{N}Q_2^{-1}\lim N^{-1}[X_2'\Omega_w X_2]Q_2^{-1} \\ &\rightarrow 0 \end{aligned} \tag{6.4.14}$$

because the elements of X_2 and Ω_w are uniformly bounded in absolute value, and therefore the elements of $N^{-1}[X_2'\Omega_w X_2]$ are uniformly bounded in absolute value. We leave the proof of this statement as an exercise. It follows from Chebyshev's inequality, (6.4.13) and (6.4.14) that

$$\begin{aligned} \xi &= (X_2'X_2)^{-1}X_2'w \\ &\xrightarrow{P} 0. \end{aligned} \tag{6.4.15}$$

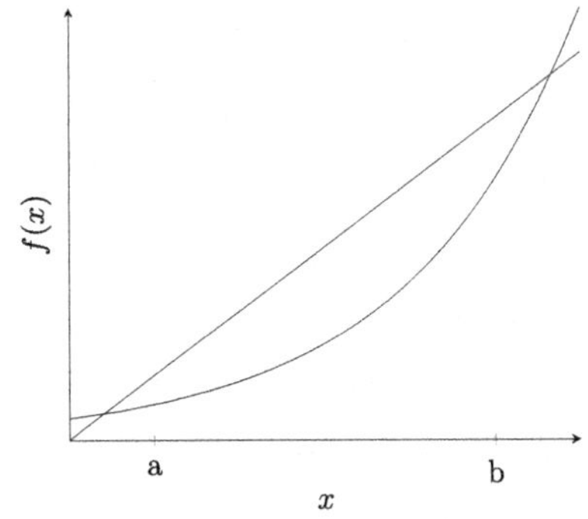

FIGURE 6.4.1 A linear approximation to an exponential

Therefore from (6.4.12)

$$\hat{C} - (X_2'X_2)^{-1}X_2'f(x) \xrightarrow{P} 0. \tag{6.4.16}$$

Assuming quite reasonably that the limit of $(X_2'X_2)^{-1}X_2'f(x)$ exists,[2] it follows that

$$\begin{aligned} p\lim \hat{C} &= \lim (X_2'X_2)^{-1}X_2'f(x) \\ &= (c_1, c_2, c_3)' \end{aligned} \tag{6.4.17}$$

where c_1, c_2, and c_3 are finite constants.

In (6.4.17) the probability limit of $\hat{C}$ is in terms of the OLS regression of $f(x)$ on X_2. Since the elements of $f(x)$ are nonlinear functions of x_i, namely $f(x_i) = Ke^{[b_1+b_2x_i]}$, if the probability limit of $\hat{c}_3 = 0$, the best fitting polynomial of degree 2 to the nonlinear function $f(x_i)$ would be linear! As Fig. 6.4.1 suggests, this is clearly not going to be the case. The figure is based on the assumption that b_1 and b_2 are positive, and the range of values for x is between the two finite constants a and b. Clearly, a quadratic would improve the approximation. It follows from (6.4.10), that if $p\lim \hat{c}_3 \neq 0$ the singularity problem encountered in the linear model case would not arise! Furthermore, as we now show, the 2SLS estimator of the parameters of the model (6.3.1) is consistent!

To see this consistency, first express the model in (6.3.1) in matrix terms as

$$y_1 = MA + \varepsilon_1 \tag{6.4.18}$$

2. Assumption 6.1 above implies that $(X_2'X_2)^{-1}X_2'f(x) = 0(1)$. Unless the sequence of values of x_i is extremely peculiar, it is reasonable to assume its limit exits. One example of a "peculiar" sequence of x_i would be

$$1, 2, 2, 3, 3, 3, 1, 1, 1, 1, 2, 2, 2, 2, 2, \ldots.$$

For such a sequence, the average $\Sigma_{i=1}^{N}(x_i/N)$ would not stabilize.

where $A' = (a_1, a_2, a_3)$ and M is identical to $\hat{M}$ in (6.4.9) except that its second column contains the values of $\exp(y_{i2})$. Now note that the second stage regressor matrix in (6.4.9) and (6.4.10) can also be expressed in more typical fashion as

$$\hat{M} = X_2(X_2'X_2)^{-1}X_2'M. \tag{6.4.19}$$

Because X_2 contains the column vector of ones, e_N, and the vector of observations on x_i, say x, $X_2(X_2'X_2)^{-1}X_2'e_N = e_N$ and $X_2(X_2'X_2)^{-1}X_2'x = x$. Therefore the second column of $\hat{M}$ is just $X_2(X_2'X_2)^{-1}X_2'e^{y(2)} = \widehat{e^{y(2)}}$.

The 2SLS estimator of A in (6.4.18) is

$$\hat{A} = (\hat{M}'\hat{M})^{-1}\hat{M}'y_1. \tag{6.4.20}$$

Given (6.4.19) and noting that $X_2(X_2'X_2)^{-1}X_2'$ is symmetric idempotent, it follows that $\hat{M}'M = \hat{M}'\hat{M}$. Therefore, replacing y_1 in (6.4.20) by its expression in (6.4.18),

$$\begin{aligned}\hat{A} &= A + (\hat{M}'\hat{M})^{-1}\hat{M}'\varepsilon_1 \\ &= A + \left(\hat{\mathbf{C}}'N^{-1}X_2'X_2\hat{\mathbf{C}}\right)^{-1}\hat{\mathbf{C}}'N^{-1}X_2'\varepsilon_1\end{aligned} \tag{6.4.21}$$

where the second line in (6.4.21) follows from (6.4.10). Given (6.4.17) and Assumption 6.2,

$$\hat{\mathbf{C}} \to \mathbf{C}, \tag{6.4.22}$$

$$\mathbf{C} = \begin{bmatrix} 1 & c_1 & 0 \\ 0 & c_2 & 1 \\ 0 & c_3 & 0 \end{bmatrix}$$

where $\mathbf{C}$ has rank 3 since $c_3 \neq 0$. Finally, in (6.4.21), by Assumption 6.2, $N^{-1}X_2'X_2 \to Q_2$ where Q_2 is nonsingular, and $N^{-1}X_2'\varepsilon_1 \to 0$, whose proof we leave as an exercise. It then follows from (6.4.21) and (6.4.22) that

$$\hat{A} \xrightarrow{P} A \tag{6.4.23}$$

so that the 2SLS estimator of the parameters in (6.3.1), or its matrix form in (6.4.18), is consistent!

6.5 LARGE SAMPLE AND RELATED ISSUES

It follows from (6.4.21) and (6.4.22) that

$$N^{1/2}(\hat{A} - A) = (N^{-1}\hat{M}'\hat{M})^{-1}\hat{\mathbf{C}}'[N^{-1/2}X_2'\varepsilon_1]. \tag{6.5.1}$$

By Assumptions 6.1 and 6.2 in Section 6.2, and the central limit theorem in Section A.15 of the appendix, we have

$$[N^{-1}\hat{M}'\hat{M}]^{-1} \xrightarrow{P} [\mathbf{C}'Q_2\mathbf{C}]^{-1}, \tag{6.5.2}$$
$$N^{-1/2}X_2'\varepsilon_1 \xrightarrow{D} N(0, \sigma_{11}Q_2).$$

It then follows from the continuous mapping theorem in (A.10.3) of Appendix A that

$$\begin{aligned} N^{1/2}(\hat{A}-A) &\xrightarrow{D} N(0, \sigma_{11}[\mathbf{C}'Q_2\mathbf{C}]^{-1}) \\ &= N(0, \sigma_{11}p\lim[N^{-1}\hat{M}'\hat{M}]^{-1}) \\ &= N(0, \sigma_{11}p\lim[N^{-1}M'X_2(X_2'X_2)^{-1}X_2'M]^{-1}). \end{aligned} \tag{6.5.3}$$

The last line of (6.5.3) follows from (6.4.19). Of course, consistent with (6.4.23) and (6.5.3) is that $\hat{A} \xrightarrow{P} A$.[3] Before generalizing our results, we demonstrate an important property of the VC matrix in (6.5.3). These results should shed light on the efficiency of estimators, as well as conflicts relating to small versus large sample properties of estimators.

The $N \times 3$ regressor matrix corresponding to the model in (6.3.1) is

$$M = [e_N, e^{y(2)}, x], \tag{6.5.4}$$

and so from (6.4.11) the mean of this regressor matrix is

$$E[M] = [e_N, f(x), x]. \tag{6.5.5}$$

The VC matrix on the third line of (6.5.3), say $VC_{\hat{A}}$, can be expressed as

$$VC_{\hat{A}} = \sigma_{11}p\lim[\ (N^{-1}M'X_2)\ N(X_2'X_2)^{-1}\ (N^{-1}X_2'M)\ ]^{-1}. \tag{6.5.6}$$

Consider the term $(N^{-1}X_2'M)$. Using (6.4.11) and the properties of w_i as described in (6.4.5) and (6.4.6), the reader should be able to show that

$$p\lim N^{-1}X_2'e^{y(2)} = p\lim N^{-1}X_2'f(x), \tag{6.5.7}$$

and so from (6.5.4) and (6.5.5)

$$p\lim N^{-1}X_2'M = p\lim N^{-1}X_2'E[M]. \tag{6.5.8}$$

---

3. This follows because $N^{1/2}(\hat{A}-A) = 0_P(1)$, and so

$$\begin{aligned} (\hat{A}-A) &= N^{-1/2}N^{1/2}(\hat{A}-A) \\ &= 0_P(N^{-1/2}) \\ &\xrightarrow{P} 0. \end{aligned}$$

Therefore $VC_{\hat{A}}$ in (6.5.3) can be expressed as

$$VC_{\hat{A}} = \sigma_{11} p\lim[N^{-1}E(M)'[P]E(M)]^{-1} \tag{6.5.9}$$

where $P = X_2(X_2'X_2)^{-1}X_2'$.

6.6 GENERALIZATIONS AND SPECIAL POINTS TO NOTE

The Nature of Instruments

The issues discussed in this section are important, and relate to identification, the efficiency of estimation, and conflicts between large and small sample properties of estimators. It will become apparent that certain procedures which lead to an increase in asymptotic efficiency may lead to a decrease in small (finite) sample efficiency.

In the linear system (6.2.1) and (6.2.2), the parameters of (6.2.1) cannot be estimated because there is an endogenous regressor but there are no omitted exogenous variables from that equation that are in the system. The order condition for identification is therefore not satisfied. On the other hand, the nonlinear system in (6.3.1) and (6.3.2) has the same structure as the linear system except that in (6.3.1) the endogenous regressor has a nonlinearity while in (6.2.1) there is no nonlinearity. On a somewhat more general plane, the difference is that in linear systems the mean of an endogenous variable can, at most, be only dependent on the predetermined variables **in the system**. Therefore, if an equation in a linear system has, say φ, endogenous regressors, the order condition for identification requires that there are at least φ predetermined variables which appear in the system but are excluded from the equation being estimated. That is why equation (6.2.1) cannot be consistently estimated. On the other hand, in nonlinear systems the mean of an endogenous variable can depend on all of the predetermined variables that are in the system, as well as nonlinear functions of those predetermined variables. That is why the parameters of (6.3.1) can be estimated. It is as if the endogenous regressor in (6.3.1), namely $e^{y_{i2}}$, created its own instrument because its mean did not appear in the original system and is linearly independent of the exogenous variables that do appear!

As an obvious and simple illustration, consider the following extension of the model in (6.3.1) and (6.3.2)

$$y_{i1} = a_1 + a_2(e^{y_{i2}}) + a_3x_i + a_4y_{i2}^2 + \varepsilon_{i1}, \tag{6.6.1}$$

$$y_{i2} = b_1 + b_2x_i + \varepsilon_{i2}. \tag{6.6.2}$$

Given all of the assumptions underlying (6.3.1) and (6.3.2), the reader should have no difficulty convincing himself/herself that the parameters of (6.6.1) can be consistently estimated using as instruments the constant term, $x_i, x_i^2, ..., x_i^r$ where $r \geq 3$. Essentially, (6.6.1) has four regressors, and so to estimate it by instrumental variables there must be at least four instruments that are linearly independent that can be used. In addition to the constant term and x_i, which are in (6.6.1), two more instruments are needed. One is x_i^2 which arises because the mean of y_{i2}^2 involves x_i^2. A fourth instrument is x_i^3 since the mean of $e^{y_{i2}}$ involves an exponential in x_i whose power series expansion involves powers of x_i beyond the second. Clearly, the instrument set could also include x_i^4, x_i^5, etc. Below we discuss issues that relate to the use of higher powers of x_i in the instrument set.

Now consider the model

$$y_{i1} = a_1 + a_2(e^{y_{i2}}) + a_3 x_i + a_4 y_{i2}^2 + a_5(x_i y_{i2}) + \varepsilon_{i1}, \quad (6.6.3)$$
$$y_{i2} = b_1 + b_2 x_i + \varepsilon_{i2}. \quad (6.6.4)$$

Eq. (6.6.3) involves five parameters and so at least five instruments are needed. In addition to the constant term and x_i which appear in (6.6.3), three more instruments are needed. The mean of y_{i2}^2 involves x_i^2 and so only two more instruments are needed. The mean of $x_i y_{i2}$ involves x_i and x_i^2. However, both of these instruments are already accounted for. One might think that the two additional instruments can be taken as x_i^3 and x_i^4 since these would be involved in the power series expansion of the mean of $e^{y_{i2}}$. This, however, is not the case. The model in (6.6.3) is not identified. Essentially, the regressor $x_i y_{i2}$ does not produce an instrument which is linearly independent of the instruments produced by the other regressors.

As an illustration, consider the extreme case in which $\varepsilon_{i1} = \varepsilon_{i2} = 0$, $i = 1, ..., N$ and b_1 and b_2 are known. In this case

$$e^{y_{i2}} = e^{b_1 + b_2 x_i} \equiv h(x_i), \quad (6.6.5)$$
$$y_{i2}^2 = b_1^2 + b_2^2 x_i^2 + 2 b_1 b_2 x_i,$$
$$x_i y_{i2} = b_1 x_i + b_2 x_i^2$$

and so the model in (6.6.3) reduces to

$$y_{i1} = \alpha_1 + \alpha_2 h(x_i) + \alpha_3 x_i + \alpha_4 x_i^2, i = 1, ..., N \quad (6.6.6)$$

where

$$\alpha_1 = a_1 + a_4 b_1^2, \quad (6.6.7)$$
$$\alpha_2 = a_2,$$
$$\alpha_3 = a_3 + 2a_4 b_1 b_2 + b_1 a_5,$$

$$\alpha_4 = a_4 b_2^2 + a_5 b_2.$$

Notice that the model in (6.6.6) has only four regressors, and four parameters to be estimated but those four parameters, $\alpha_1, ..., \alpha_4$ involve all five parameters in (6.6.1), $a_1, ..., a_5$, as well as the two parameters in (6.6.2), b_1 and b_2. It should be clear that even if b_1 and b_2 are known, the basic model parameters, $a_1, ..., a_5$ cannot be deduced from the four parameters in (6.6.6). To conclude this illustration, let G be the $N \times 4$ regressor matrix defined by (6.6.6), and $\alpha' = (\alpha_1, \alpha_2, \alpha_3, \alpha_4)$. The matrix form of (6.6.6) is

$$y_1 = G\alpha. \tag{6.6.8}$$

Since the rank of G is four, the estimate of α based on (6.6.6) is

$$\begin{aligned} \hat{\alpha} &= (G'G)^{-1}G'y_1 \\ &= (G'G)^{-1}G'G\alpha \\ &= \alpha. \end{aligned} \tag{6.6.9}$$

In more general systems the various endogenous variables would be interrelated directly, as well as via the error terms, e.g., y_{i1} would be a regressors in (6.6.4), etc. Unless there are parameter restrictions, the basic principle involved in IV estimation is the following. Let Z be the regressor matrix in a model which may, or may not, involve nonlinearities. Suppose Z has q columns. Then the **necessary** condition for identification is the $rank(E[Z]) = q$.

The Minimum VC Matrix

In this section we will use the following result. Let B be a symmetric positive definite matrix, and let C be symmetric, and at least a positive semidefinite matrix. Let

$$A = B + C. \tag{6.6.10}$$

Then A is positive definite and

$$B^{-1} - A^{-1} = D \tag{6.6.11}$$

where D is at least positive semidefinite. As a simple illustration, if A and B are scalars, say $A = 5$ and $B = 2$, then $B^{-1} - A^{-1} = 0.5 - 0.2 = 0.3$.

Now consider the matrix being inverted in the VC expression in (6.5.9), namely $E(M)'[P]E(M)$, where $P = X_2(X_2'X_2)^{-1}X_2'$. Since $P' = P$ and $PP = P$, the matrix P is positive semidefinite. For example, let c be a constant $N \times 1$ column vector. Then $c'Pc = c'P'Pc = (Pc)'(Pc) = d'd \geq 0$ where d is the column vector, $d = Pc$.

The matrix $E(M)'E(M)$ is positive definite[4] and relates to $E(M)'[P]E(M)$ in the same manner as the matrices in (6.6.10), namely

$$E(M)'E(M) = E(M)'[P]E(M) + E(M)'[I_N - P]\, E(M) \tag{6.6.12}$$

since $E(M)'[I_N - P]\, E(M)$ is positive semidefinite because $[I_N - P]' = [I_N - P]$ and $[I_N - P]^2 = [I_N - P]$. Therefore, from (6.6.10) and (6.6.11), we have

$$[E(M)'PE(M)]^{-1} = [E(M)'E(M)]^{-1} + PSD \tag{6.6.13}$$

where PSD is a positive semidefinite matrix. Among other things, this implies that the diagonal elements of PSD are greater than or equal to zero.

The results in (6.5.9) and (6.6.13) imply that the lower bound of $VC_{\hat{A}}$, say $VC_{\hat{A}}^{\min}$, is

$$VC_{\hat{A}}^{\min} = \sigma_{11} p\lim[N^{-1}E(M)'E(M)]^{-1}. \tag{6.6.14}$$

The interpretation behind (6.6.14) is important. Recall that the matrix $E(M)$ is defined in (6.5.5) as

$$E(M) = [e_N, f(x), x] \tag{6.6.15}$$

and that $P = X_2(X_2'X_2)^{-1}X_2'$, where $X_2 = [e_N, x, x^{(2)}]$, where the ith element of the $N \times 1$ vector $x^{(2)}$ is x_i^2. Since X_2 contains the intercept term and the vector x, it follows that $P[e_N, x] = [e_N, x]$, since the predicted value of a variable from the OLS regression on itself and other variables is itself. Therefore

$$PE(M) = [e_N, \widehat{f(x)}, x] \tag{6.6.16}$$

where $\widehat{f(x)}$ is the predicted value of $f(x)$ from the OLS regression of itself on X_2. For purposes of generalization, we will express $\widehat{f(x)}$ as $\widehat{f(x)_2}$ to indicate that the predicted value of $f(x)$ in (6.6.16), which is $Pf(x)$, is based on the hypothetical OLS regression of $f(x)$ on a polynomial of degree 2 in x.

Suppose now that instead of the instrument matrix X_2, the estimation procedure is based on the instrument matrix X_r, $r \geq 2$ where, e.g., the ith row of X_r is $[1, x_i, x_i^2, ..., x_i^r]$. In this case, the second column of the second stage regressor matrix would be the column of observations of the predicted values of $e^{y_{i2}}$ from the OLS regression of $e^{y_{i2}}$ on $[1, x_i, x_i^2, ..., x_i^r]$. Using evident notation, instead

4. Since $E(M)$ has full column rank, it follows that $z = E(M)c \neq 0$. Therefore

$$\begin{aligned} c'[E(M)'E(M)]c &= [E(M)c]'[E(M)c] \\ &= z'z > 0. \end{aligned}$$

of (6.4.10), the second stage regressor matrix would be

$$\hat{M}_r = \begin{bmatrix} 1 & x_1 & x_1^2 & \dots & x_1^r \\ \vdots & \vdots & \vdots & \ddots & \vdots \\ 1 & x_N & x_N^2 & \dots & x_N^r \end{bmatrix} \begin{bmatrix} 1 & \hat{c}_0 & 0 \\ 0 & \hat{c}_1 & 1 \\ . & \hat{c}_2 & 0 \\ \vdots & \vdots & \vdots \\ 0 & \hat{c}_r & 0 \end{bmatrix}, \tag{6.6.17}$$

e.g., the second column of $\hat{M}_r$ in (6.6.17) would be $\widehat{e_r^{y(2)}}$. Let $P_r = X_r(X_r'X_r)^{-1}X_r'$. In this case the large sample VC matrix in (6.5.9) would be

$$VC_{\hat{A}} = \sigma_{11} p \lim[N^{-1} E(M)'[P_r]E(M)]^{-1} \tag{6.6.18}$$

and the minimum VC matrix would still be given by (6.6.14). However, now in (6.6.18)

$$P_r E(M) = [e_N, \ \widehat{f(x)_r}, x] \tag{6.6.19}$$

where $\widehat{f(x)_r}$ is the predicted value of $f(x)$ from the hypothetical regression of $f(x)$ and X_r. Compare now (6.6.16), which is based on the instruments X_2 and so its second column is $\widehat{f(x)_2}$ to (6.6.19). The only difference is their second columns which both differ from the second column of $E(M)$ which is the matrix involved in the minimum VC matrix. One would assume that very high values of r should be used in the estimation because the polynomial approximation $\widehat{f(x)_r}$ to $f(x)$ should be better than one based on $\widehat{f(x)_q}$ if $q < r$.

Taken by itself, the argument above suggests that "very" high values of r should be used.[5] However, as we will see below, the use of high values of r leads to small sample/large sample issues.

Large Sample/Small Sample Issues

Large sample distributions are based on $N \to \infty$. However, in practice the sample size is finite! This discrepancy causes problems. For example, suppose the regressor matrix in a model is the $N \times k$ matrix S, and because there are endogenous regressors, the model is estimated by an IV technique, say 2SLS. Let

5. It can be "tediously" shown that, in general,

$$E(M)'[P_r]E(M) = E(M)'[P_s]E(M) + PSD$$

where $r \leq s$ and PSD denotes a positive semidefinite matrix.

the instrument matrix be the $N \times q$ matrix Z. Then, the second stage regressor matrix would be

$$\hat{S} = Z(Z'Z)^{-1}Z'S. \tag{6.6.20}$$

To see the conflicts involved, suppose the researcher selected $q = N$, e.g., the same number of instruments as the sample size. In the nonlinear models above, this would be equivalent to selecting a polynomial of degree $N - 1$ so that, with the intercept, the number of instruments would be N.

In this case Z in (6.6.20) would be $N \times N$ and since instruments are to be linearly independent, Z is nonsingular. Thus

$$\begin{aligned} \hat{S} &= Z(Z'Z)^{-1}Z'S \\ &= Z^{-1}ZZ'^{-1}Z'S \\ &= S. \end{aligned} \tag{6.6.21}$$

Thus the 2SLS procedure would reduce to the OLS procedure which is not consistent! Thus, in the case of nonlinear models, which are linear in the parameters, as researchers attempt to better approximate the mean of the regressor by choosing higher and higher powers of the polynomial, the results become more and more like that of OLS. Since statistical estimation is essentially based on averaging, it is suggested that the difference between the sample size and the number of instruments be at least 40. This number is not based on any formal result but only on our own experience and knowledge of system estimation of spatial models. Research concerning the optimal number of instruments used in estimating spatial models would be welcome.

6.7 APPLICATIONS TO SPATIAL MODELS

As indicated above, spatial researchers often consider models which may have additional endogenous regressors. One possible example of such models, which was given in Section 6.1, is explaining the demand for labor in terms of wage rates and productivity measures. Another such model would be in an international finance framework explaining national bond rate differential in terms of differentials in national debts, deficits, GDP growth rates, among other variables. Some of these variables would surely be considered endogenous.

In this section we apply the results obtained in Sections 6.1–6.6 to the estimation of a spatial model which is linear in the model parameters, but contains additional endogenous variables. We explicitly consider the case in which the system determining the additional endogenous variables is completely linear; we also consider the case in which that unknown system contains nonlinearities. As will become evident these issues relate to the selection of instruments.

Consider the model

$$y = X_1\beta_1 + \rho_1 W_1 y + Y\beta_2 + u, \tag{6.7.1}$$
$$u = \rho_2 W_1 u + \varepsilon, \ |\rho_i| < 1, i = 1, 2$$

where X_1 is an $N \times k_1$ exogenous regressor matrix, W_1 is an $N \times N$ weighting matrix, Y is an $N \times q$ matrix of observations on q variables which are endogenous, u is the disturbance term, and ε is an $N \times 1$ vector of innovations whose elements are i.i.d. $(0, \sigma_\varepsilon^2)$. Also assume that the model in (6.7.1) is complete in the sense that $(I_N - aW_1)$ is nonsingular for all $|a| < 1$.

We will consider a sequence of cases below. In all cases in which the model is identified, the estimation procedure will be GS2SLS. The only difference between these cases will be the set of instruments used. For future reference note that the solution of (6.7.1) for y in terms of X_1, W_1, Y, and u is

$$y = [I_N - \rho_1 W_1]^{-1}[X_1\beta_1 + Y\beta_2 + u]. \tag{6.7.2}$$

Also note that the model in (6.7.1) cannot be estimated by maximum likelihood unless all of the equations determining y and Y are known. In practice, they will typically not be known.

Case A: The Completely Linear System

Assume that the full system determining y and the q endogenous variables in Y is not known.[6] Assume that this system is linear and contains the exogenous matrices X_1 and X_2, where X_2 is $N \times k_2$, and X_1 and X_2 do not have any elements in common. In this case, X_2 represents all the exogenous variables in the system that do not appear in the model in (6.7.1). In addition, assume that the full m equation system contains the weighting matrices $W = (W_1, ..., Wq)$, but only W_1 is known to the researcher. Finally, assume that the researcher has observations on a subset of the variables in X_2, say X_{2*}, where X_{2*} is $N \times s$, $s \leq k_2$.

Under reasonable assumptions, the linear system determining y and Y can be solved, and the solution will be linear in X_1, X_2, disturbance vectors in the system, as well as spatial lags and compound spatial lags of these variables involving the matrices W.[7] Under very reasonable further assumptions,

---

6. That system may actually contain more than $1 + q$ equations if it contains endogenous variables in addition to y and Y. However, this issue is ignored in the discussion below, but does not effect the given analysis in any way.

7. A compound spatial lag of, say X_1, would be a premultiplication of X_1 by more than one term involving weighting matrices. As one example,

$$W_1(I_N - \rho W_3)^{-1}X_1.$$

the expected value of each of the q variables in $Y_{N\times q}$ will exist, and be linear in X_1 and X_2, and the spatial and compound spatial lags of X_1 and X_2. Let $\Gamma = (X_1, X_2, W)$. Then, since the expected value of a matrix is the expected value of each element of the matrix, the expected value of Y can be expressed as

$$E(Y) = G(\Gamma) \tag{6.7.3}$$

where G is an $N \times q$ matrix of linear functions of the elements of Γ where the (i, j)th element of $G(\Gamma)$ is the expected value of the (i, j)th element of Y.

To estimate (6.7.1) by GS2SLS, we need instruments. Since the only exogenous variables we have data for are X_1, X_{2*}, and W_1, our instruments can be based on these terms. Specifically, we suggest the instrument set

$$H_L = (X_1, W_1X_1, ..., W_1^rX_1, X_{2*}, W_1X_{2*}, ..., W_1^rX_{2*})_{LI} \tag{6.7.4}$$

where, typically, $r = 2$, and the subscript LI indicates the linearly independent columns of the matrix in parentheses. Spatial lags in X_{2*} involving W_1 are considered because they would be involved in the approximation to the mean value of the Y given in (6.7.3). Since the model in (6.7.1) has $k_1 + q + 1$ regression parameters, the number of linearly independent columns of H_L must be at least $k_1 + q + 1$. Taking $r = 2$ in (6.7.4), H_L can be an adequate, although weak, instrument matrix even if $s < q$ as long as $3k_1 + 3s \geq k_1 + q + 1$. The reason for this is that the exogenous variables economists deal with are typically correlated, and so the instruments described in (6.7.4) would also correlate with some of the systems variables for which data are not available. However, we stress that the correlations may be weak and so the asymptotic variances could be somewhat "large."

Express the model in (6.7.1) as

$$\begin{aligned} y &= M\gamma + u, \\ u &= \rho_2 W_1 u + \varepsilon \end{aligned} \tag{6.7.5}$$

where $M = (X_1, W_1y, Y)$ and $\gamma = (\beta_1', \rho_1, \beta_2')$. Let $\hat{M} = P_{H_L}M$ where $P_{H_L} = H_L(H_L'H_L)^{-1}H_L'$. Then the estimation procedure is:

1. Estimate γ as $\hat{\gamma} = (\hat{M}\hat{M})^{-1}\hat{M}'y$.
2. Obtain $\hat{u} = y - M\hat{\gamma}$.
3. Using $\hat{u}$, use the GMM procedure in Section 2.2.4 to estimate ρ_2 as $\hat{\rho}_2$.
4. Transform the terms in the first line of (6.7.5) as $y(\hat{\rho}_2) = y - \hat{\rho}_2 Wy$, $M(\hat{\rho}_2) = M - \hat{\rho}_2 WM$.

5. Reestimate γ as

$$\tilde{\gamma} = [\tilde{M}(\hat{\rho}_2)'\tilde{M}(\hat{\rho}_2)]^{-1}\tilde{M}(\hat{\rho}_2)'y(\hat{\rho}_2) \tag{6.7.6}$$

where $\tilde{M}(\hat{\rho}_2) = H_L(H_L'H_L)^{-1}H_L'M(\hat{\rho}_2)$.

6. Then estimate σ_ε^2 as

$$\tilde{\sigma}_\varepsilon^2 = [y(\hat{\rho}_2) - M(\hat{\rho}_2)\tilde{\gamma}]'[y(\hat{\rho}_2) - M(\hat{\rho}_2)\tilde{\gamma}]/(N-\delta) \tag{6.7.7}$$

where $\delta \geq 0$ is a constant which typically would be taken to be zero, or $k+q+1$, which is the number of parameters in (6.7.1). The asymptotic results underlying (6.7.8) below are not effected by the selection of δ as long as its a finite constant.

7. Finally, inferences could be based on the small sample approximation to the large sample distribution

$$\tilde{\gamma} \doteq N(\gamma, \tilde{\sigma}_\varepsilon^2[\tilde{M}(\hat{\rho}_2)'\tilde{M}(\hat{\rho}_2)]^{-1}). \tag{6.7.8}$$

Case B: When Nonlinearities Are Involved

Assume again the model in (6.7.1) and the conditions under Case A above relating to the m equation system for y, Y, and $m-1-q$ additional endogenous variables in an unknown system except that now we allow for nonlinearities. Also, assume again that the researcher has observations on a subset of the variables in X_2, say X_{2+} where X_{2+} is $N \times s$, $s \leq k_2$, and s could be $s \leq q$ or $s \geq q$.

One form of nonlinearity would be the case in which one or more of the endogenous regressors in Y in (6.7.1) are nonlinear in one or more endogenous variables in the full system. Examples of this were given in Sections 6.3 and 6.4, e.g., $e^{y_{i2}}$. In this case the model could still be linear in the parameters. Another case would be the one in which some of the equations in the system are not linear in the parameters of the model, and contain other non-linearities as well.

Given the results in Sections 6.3–6.6, the selection of instruments can now be viewed in a more expanded framework. For example, let $\Gamma_{NL} = (X_1, X_2, W)$ where again W is the set of all weighting matrices in the system. Then, assuming the expected value of Y exists, we would generally have

$$E(Y) = G_{NL}(\Gamma_{NL}) \tag{6.7.9}$$

where G_{NL} is an $N \times q$ matrix of functions of the elements of Γ_{NL}. In this case, however, these functions would generally be nonlinear. Taking note of

Sections 6.3–6.6, the parameters in the model in (6.7.1) can still be consistently estimated, under very reasonable conditions, using the instruments

$$H_{NL} = (X_1, X_1^2, W_1X_1, W_1X_1^2, W_1^2X_1, W_1^2X_1^2, \\ X_{2+}, X_{2+}^2, W_1X_{2+}, W_1X_{2+}^2, W_1^2X_{2+}, W_1^2X_{2+}^2)_{LI}$$

where, for ease of presentation, we have only indicated up to the second power, and where X_1^J and X_{2+}^J are respectively the $N \times k_1$ and $N \times s$ matrices of observations on the k_1 variables in X_1 and the s variables in X_{2+} where each element of X_1 and X_{2+} is raised to the Jth power. Let h_{NL} be the number of linearly independent columns of H_{NL}. Then a necessary condition for consistency of an IV procedure is $h_{NL} \geq k_1 + q + 1$. Since the selection of instruments involves powers of the observable variables beyond the first, this necessary condition will be easier to satisfy in the nonlinear case than in the linear case. Also, recalling our discussion in Sections 6.3–6.6, large sample efficiency suggests taking higher and higher powers of the indicated variables because the resulting approximation to (6.7.9) in the estimation procedure will be better. However, this may conflict with small sample efficiency because the use of higher and higher powers of the indicated variables results in an IV estimator that is closer to ordinary least squares, which is not consistent.

Illustration 6.7.1: Consequences of ignoring endogeneity

Consider again the model for DUI arrest where the alcohol related arrest rate is associated with the number of sworn police officers, non-alcohol related arrest, the number of registered vehicles, and a dummy variables for counties that prohibit alcohol. The results for the spatial lag model when the number of police officers is taken as exogenous are reported below:

$$\widehat{dui} = -6.410(0.418) + 0.598(0.015)police + 0.000(0.001)nondui \\ = 0.016(0.001)vehicles + 0.106(0.035)dry + 0.047(0.017)wdui$$

where standard errors are in the parentheses.

However, the size of the police force may be seen as endogenous in that a high crime rate, in this case DUI, may induce an increase in the police force. For purposes of comparison we reestimate the model treating the police variable as endogenous. Drukker et al. (2013d) suggest that a valid instrument for the size of the police force is a dummy variable equal one if a county government faces an election and zero otherwise. The results of this model based on the 2SLS procedure, taking the police variable as endogenous, are[8]

$$\begin{aligned}\widehat{dui} &= -11.508(1.686) - 1.348(0.141)police + -0.000(0.003)nondui \\ &= 0.092(0.006)vehicles + 0.397(0.091)dry + 0.196(0.046)wdui\end{aligned}$$

where standard errors are given in the parentheses.

The results are clearly different when the endogeneity of the police variable is accounted for. Perhaps a most notable difference is the coefficient of the police variable. When this variable is treated as endogenous, its coefficient is negative; if this endogeneity is not considered, it is positive. The negative coefficient seems more reasonable in that, *ceteris paribus*, a greater police presence should lead to a reduction in DUIs.

Illustration 6.7.2: Nonlinearities and efficiencies: A Monte Carlo illustration

The results in Section 6.6 suggest that estimation efficiency can be improved if nonlinear forms of the instruments are considered when the system determining the variables of the model contains nonlinearities. The purpose of this example is to illustrate the efficiency gain. This is done in terms of a simple Monte Carlo experiment.

Specifically, we generate the dependent variable y_1 from the first line of (6.2.1) as, say

$$(A) \quad y_1 = \alpha_0 + \alpha_1 e^{y_2} + \alpha_2 x_1 + \rho_1 W y_1 + \varepsilon_1$$

while y_2 is generated from

$$(B) \quad y_2 = \beta_0 + \beta_1 x_1 + \beta_2 x_2 + \varepsilon_2.$$

We consider three sets of data corresponding to three regular grids of dimension 10×10, 20×20, and 25×25, leading to sample sizes of $N = 100$, $N = 400$, and $N = 625$, respectively. For each sample size, we construct a spatial weighting matrix based on a queen contiguity criteria.

The two regressors x_1 and x_2 are normalized versions of income per capita and the proportion of housing units that are rental units in 1980, in 760 counties in Midwestern United States.[9] The data are normalized by subtracting from each observation its sample average, and then dividing that result by its sample standard deviation. The first N values of these normalized variables were used in our Monte Carlo. The regressors x_1 and x_2 are held constant over all of the

8. The instruments used are the intercept, all the exogenous variables included the dummy for the elections, and the spatial lags (up to the second order) of all these exogenous variables.
9. These data were taken from Kelejian and Robinson (1995).

TABLE 6.7.1 MSE results. The upper part of the table report results based on H_1, while the bottom part refer to results based on H_2

Results based on H_1						
ρ	N	σ_{12}	α_0	α_1	α_2	ρ_1
$\rho = 0.5$	100	0.2	2.4154	0.2013	0.0852	1.7356
	100	0.8	7.1009	0.3334	0.2814	3.5754
	400	0.2	4.1259	0.1304	0.0351	3.2578
	400	0.8	1.7843	0.1122	0.0242	1.5548
	900	0.2	1.1191	0.0709	0.0161	0.9397
	900	0.8	1.4600	0.1175	0.0266	1.0095
Average			3.0009	0.1609	0.0781	2.0122
Results based on H_2						
ρ	N	σ_{12}	α_0	α_1	α_2	ρ_1
$\rho = 0.5$	100	0.2	0.4074	0.0267	0.0243	0.3358
	100	0.8	0.4330	0.0296	0.0231	0.2971
	400	0.2	0.2859	0.0206	0.0102	0.2781
	400	0.8	0.2778	0.0178	0.0095	0.2321
	900	0.2	0.2568	0.0157	0.0065	0.2424
	900	0.8	0.2400	0.0170	0.0081	0.2306
Average			0.3168	0.0213	0.0136	0.2694

Monte Carlo runs. The model parameters α_0, α_1, α_2, β_0, β_1, and β_2 are set to 0.1, while ρ_1 is fixed to 0.5. The innovation vectors ε_1 and ε_2 are generated from a multivariate normal distribution, where both variances are set to 2, and two different values for σ_{12} are considered, namely 0.4, and 0.8.

Given this data generating process, the parameters of (A) above are estimated by 2SLS in two ways. One is in terms of the instrument matrix $H_1 = (e_N, x_1, x_2, Wx_1, Wx_2)$ and the other is in terms of the instrument matrix $H_2 = (e_N, x_1, x_2, Wx_1, Wx_2, Wx_1^2$ and $Wx_2^2)$, where e_N is an $N \times 1$ vector of unit elements. Clearly, the use of H_1 corresponds to the classic case in which 2SLS is based on an instrument matrix which does not account for nonlinearities. The use of H_2 relates to the case in which nonlinearities are recognized. The number of Monte Carlo samples is set to 2000.

Mean squared errors are reported in Table 6.7.1 for these two cases. Note that the results relating to H_2 are completely consistent with prior notions. For example, for a fixed level of correlation, as the sample size increases, the MSEs in every case decrease. In addition, the MSEs relating to the use of H_2 are, in each and every case, less than the corresponding ones relating to the use of H_1.

Furthermore, the gain in efficiency due to the use of the nonlinear instruments is considerable. For example, on average, the MSEs relating to the use of H_1 are roughly more than seven times larger than the corresponding MSEs relating to the use of H_2.

Note that the MSEs relating to H_1 do not all decrease as the sample size increases. Perhaps this reflects the weak nature of those instruments. As an overview, these results strongly suggest that the existence of possible nonlinearities and their consequent effect on the instrument set should be considered.

6.8 PROBLEMS WITH MLE

There are problems in trying to estimate the parameters of (6.7.1) by maximum likelihood. The reason for this is that the q variables in Y are endogenous and so the likelihood must involve either the joint density of the $q + 1$ variables, y and Y, or the conditional density of y on Y. In a limited information framework, the joint density and this conditional density would not be known! If the model is estimated by assuming that Y is exogenous, when in fact it is endogenous, the estimators will be inconsistent. Note that IV procedures are straightforward whenever Y is endogenous or not. Because of this, IV procedures have been generally suggested in this text. Classically, economists have used a limited information approach when estimating a model which contains additional endogenous variables; see, e.g., classic econometrics texts Schmidt (1976), Dhrymes (1978), Amemiya (1985), Judge et al. (1985), Kmenta (1986), and Greene (2003). For a similar approach, in a spatial framework, see Fingleton and Le Gallo (2008).

SUGGESTED PROBLEMS

1. Consider, again the model

$$y_{i1} = a_1 + a_2 y_{i2} + a_3 x_i + \varepsilon_{i1},$$
$$y_{i2} = b_1 + b_2 x_i + \varepsilon_{i2}, i = 1, ..., N$$

where $(\varepsilon_{i1}, \varepsilon_{i2})$ are i.i.d. $N(0, \Sigma)$ where Σ is a 2×2 nonsingular matrix. Show that if the researcher attempts to estimate the first equation by using the instruments (the constant, x_i, x_i^2, and x_i^3), the two stage least squares estimator will not be consistent.

2. Consider the model

$$(1)\ y_{i1} = a_1 + a_2 y_{i2} y_{i3} + a_3 x_i + \varepsilon_{i1},$$
$$(2)\ y_{i2} = b_1 + b_2 x_i + \varepsilon_{i2},$$
$$(3)\ y_{i3} = c_1 + c_2 \exp(x_i) + \varepsilon_{i3}, i = 1, ..., N$$

with the same assumptions for equations (1) and (2) as those that were made for exercise 1. Let $\varepsilon_i' = (\varepsilon_{i1}, \varepsilon_{i2}, \varepsilon_{i3})$ and assume that ε_i are i.i.d. $(0, \Sigma)$ where

$$\Sigma = (\sigma_{ij}), ij, = 1, 2, 3.$$

What instruments would you use to estimate (1)?

3. Consider the model that was considered in the text, namely

$$y_{i1} = a_1 + a_2(e^{y_{i2}}) + a_3 x_i + \varepsilon_{i1},$$
$$y_{i2} = b_1 + b_2 x_i + \varepsilon_{i2}.$$

Suppose the parameters are known. Also, suppose the researcher predicts y_{i1} by solving the model, and setting $\varepsilon_{i1} = \varepsilon_{i2} = 0$:

$$y_{i1}^{(P)} = a_1 + a_2 \exp(b_1 + b_2 x_i) + a_3 x_i.$$

(a) Discuss biases that are in this procedure.
(b) Will these biases be related to the value of x_i?

Chapter 7

Bayesian Analysis*

The Bayesian framework is a fascinating and convincing theory of learning. As will become apparent, it is difficult not to be a Bayesian, but it is also difficult to implement the Bayesian procedure in many cases. Essentially, there are two fundamental principles involved: One is the concept of subjective probability. The second is a method for combining new information with prior beliefs. Perhaps the concept of subjective probability may seem strange to some researchers, and so we will discuss it first. The combining of new information with prior beliefs will be discussed in later sections. After some examples on the linear regression model, we show how the Bayesian framework can be extended to deal with spatial models.

7.1 INTRODUCTORY COMMENTS

In Bayesian analysis, a researcher takes what we see, e.g., a sample, as given, and what we wish to learn about, perhaps the value of a parameter, as unknown in a random setting. For example, in economics there is a parameter, say b, in the consumption function which is called the marginal propensity to consume. This parameter describes the extent to which a consumer will increase his consumer expenditures in response to an increase in income. "Most" of us do not know the exact value of this parameter, but might guess its value. For purposes of illustration, suppose that guess is 0.85. If pressed, one might go on to say that the chances (probabilities) are higher that it is between 0.85 ± 0.03 than between 0.90 ± 0.03, or 0.80 ± 0.03; one might also state that the "chances" are roughly the same, due to symmetry issues, that it is between 0.90 ± 0.03 or between 0.80 ± 0.03. Such statements concerning the "chances" that b lies in certain regions reflect a subjective distribution that one may have concerning the value of b which would be based on prior experiences, samples, etc.

* Three fundamental studies in Bayesian analysis are Zellner (1971), Jeffreys (1961), and Lindley (1965). There are a series of more recent books such as Lancaster (2004), Geweke (2005), and Koop (2003). See also LeSage (1999) for MATLAB programs relating to certain Bayesian models.

Spatial Econometrics. http://dx.doi.org/10.1016/B978-0-12-813387-3.00007-X

Actually, many of us have, on many occasions, relied on subjective probability in forming our beliefs. For example, one may wonder what the "chances" are that one's spouse is not "being honorable in some way" even if that spouse has never been known to be involved in "dishonorable" activities. As another example, a parent may wonder what the "chances" are that his/her child will be happy or successful as an adult. Such statements are subjective in nature and are often evaluated in terms of subjective probabilities.

In classical statistics (non-Bayesian) the parameter is viewed as fixed, and the sample is viewed in a random setting in the sense that it is one of "many" possible samples that could have been observed. Based on that particular sample that is observed, the parameter is estimated in terms of an estimator (a formula) which is a function of the observed sample data. Using the data in the sample, the estimator produces an estimate of the parameter, which is a particular numerical value. In classical statistics, hypotheses relating to the true value of the parameter are based on a distribution theory that relates to the possible numerical values that would be obtained corresponding to the possible samples that could have been observed.

7.2 FUNDAMENTALS OF THE BAYESIAN APPROACH

Let $f(x, \eta)$ be the joint density of an observable variable and the parameter η. Then $f(x, \eta)$ can be factored into marginals and conditionals in two ways, namely

$$\begin{aligned} f(x, \eta) &= f_x(x) f_{\eta|x}(\eta|x) \\ &= f_\eta(\eta) f_{x|\eta}(x|\eta) \end{aligned} \tag{7.2.1}$$

where $f_x(x)$ and $f_\eta(\eta)$ are the marginals of x and η, and $f_{\eta|x}(\eta|x)$ and $f_{x|\eta}(x|\eta)$ are the corresponding conditional densities. Equating the two expressions for $f(x, \eta)$, we have

$$P_{\eta|x}(\eta|x) = \frac{f_\eta(\eta) f_{x|\eta}(x|\eta)}{f_x(x)} \tag{7.2.2}$$

where $P_{\eta|x}(\eta|x) \equiv f_{\eta|x}(\eta|x)$. The rational for the change in notation will become evident!

In a Bayesian framework, the terms in (7.2.2) have the following interpretation. Consider the terms on the right-hand side of (7.2.2). The term $f_{x|\eta}(x|\eta)$ is the distribution of the observable variable x conditional on the parameter η. It is the likelihood function. The term $f_\eta(\eta)$ is called the prior distribution of the parameter η. It reflects the researcher's prior beliefs about the parameter η before a sample on the related variable x is available. In other words, before a sample is available, if the researcher were to gamble on the values of η, his selections of η would be based on $f_\eta(\eta)$.

The term in the denominator of (7.2.2) is the (unconditional) marginal density of x, and $1/f_x(x)$ is just a normalizing constant for $P_{\eta|x}(\eta|x)$. To see this, note that (7.2.2) can be rewritten in more standard form as

$$P_{\eta|x}(\eta|x) = \frac{f(x,\eta)}{f_x(x)}, \tag{7.2.3}$$

and so

$$\begin{aligned} \int_\eta P_{\eta|x}(\eta|x)d\eta &= \frac{1}{f_x(x)}\int_\eta f(x,\eta)d\eta \\ &= \frac{1}{f_x(x)} f_x(x) = 1. \end{aligned} \tag{7.2.4}$$

Finally, the term $P_{\eta|x}(\eta|x)$ on the left-hand side of (7.2.2) is called the posterior distribution of η given the sample on x. It reflects the researcher's beliefs about η given the sample on x, and his prior beliefs about η.

In passing we note that because $1/f_x(x)$ is just a normalizing constant of integration, which does not depend on η, in many cases the posterior in (7.2.2) is written as

$$P_{\eta|x}(\eta|x) \propto f_\eta(\eta) f_{x|\eta}(x|\eta) \tag{7.2.5}$$

where $\propto$ denotes proportionality. One reason for the expression in (7.2.5) is that in some Bayesian studies the posterior is determined by a number of calculations and the most tedious part of these calculations often relates to the exact determination of the normalizing constant of integration. Instead of analytically determining this constant, researchers typically determine it by numerical integration. In other cases the constant of integration becomes obvious because the numerator in (7.2.2) often relates to a recognizable density for which the normalizing constant is evident. Illustrations relating to these cases are given below. The point of all this is that in many Bayesian studies constants are often "put into" the proportionality factor!

7.3 LEARNING AND PREJUDGMENT ISSUES

The Bayesian approach can be applied in an evolutionary framework in time. For example, let x_t, $t = 1, .., T$ be an observable random vector at time t, and let η be the parameter of interest. Assume that at time t the available data is $Z_t = (x_1, ..., x_t)$. Using evident notation, at time $t = 1$ the posterior distribution of η is

$$P_{\eta|Z_1}(\eta|Z_1) = \frac{f_\eta(\eta) f_{Z_1|\eta}(Z_1|\eta)}{f_{Z_1}(Z_1)}. \tag{7.3.1}$$

In (7.3.1) $f_\eta(\eta)$ is the prior distribution of η before the first sample is available at period $t = 1$. As will be discussed in more detail below, it is often assumed that before samples relating to η are available, the researcher does not have "much" information about η, and so the variance of η defined by the prior would typically be "large."

The posterior in period $t = 2$ reflects learning in the sense that the prior in period $t = 2$ can be taken as the posterior obtained in period $t = 1$. Specifically,

$$P_{\eta|Z_2}(\eta|Z_2) = \frac{P_{\eta|Z_1}(\eta|Z_1)\ f_{Z_2|\eta}(Z_2|\eta)}{f_{Z_2}(Z_2)} \tag{7.3.2}$$

where $f_{Z_2}(Z_2)$ is the joint density of Z_2. Note that in period $t = 2$, the researcher is building on previous information in that the posterior of the previous period is taken as the prior for the current period. It should be evident that this procedure would be maintained in periods beyond $t = 2$. Specifically, using evident notation, the posterior distributions in periods $t = 3, ..., T$ are

$$P_{\eta|Z_t}(\eta|Z_t) = \frac{P_{\eta|Z_{t-1}}(\eta|Z_{t-1})\ f_{Z_t|\eta}(Z_t|\eta)}{f_{Z_t}(Z_t)}, \quad t = 3, ..., T. \tag{7.3.3}$$

The results in (7.3.1)–(7.3.3) reflect a theory of learning, as well as insights into prejudice. For example, consider again the posterior distribution in (7.3.1). As suggested, before the first sample is available, the researcher may only have vague information, or none at all, about η. This is sometimes taken to mean that the values of η are equally likely to be in any area of the interval $\pm m$ where m is taken to be a **very** large number. In this case the prior could be taken as $f_\eta(\eta) = 1/(2m)$; and $-m < \eta < m$. Such a prior is uninformative and often simply described as a uniform prior. Given that the prior is constant over the possible values of η and $1/f_{Z_1}(Z_1)$ is a constant of integration, the posterior in (7.3.1) can be expressed as

$$P_{\eta|Z_1}(\eta|Z_1) \propto f_{Z_1|\eta}(Z_1|\eta). \tag{7.3.4}$$

That is, if the prior is "vague" the posterior is effectively determined by the sample as given by the likelihood. Recall, however, that in the Bayesian framework, the parameter η is viewed as random and the sample is viewed as given. For example, suppose in (7.3.4) that

$$f_{Z_1|\eta}(Z_1|\eta) \propto \exp[-\frac{1}{2}(\eta - \mu)^2]. \tag{7.3.5}$$

In this case, the expression in (7.3.5) describes a normal distribution in which η is normal with a mean of μ and a variance of 1. Therefore the constant of integration must be $(2\pi)^{-1/2}$. Also note that in this case inferences about η would be based entirely on the available sample.

Now consider the case in which the researcher has very strong prior beliefs concerning η. As an example, suppose in (7.3.1) the prior is

$$f_\eta(\eta) = 0.2, \ (0.2 - 10^{-25}) < \eta < (0.2 + 10^{-25}). \qquad (7.3.6)$$

In this case the prior is so sharp that over the range 0.2 ± 10^{-25} one would expect the likelihood in (7.3.1) to be virtually constant. This implies that the posterior is completely determined by the prior. In this case prior beliefs are held so strongly that the researcher will not be influenced by new sample information. An illustration of this is given below.

To a Bayesian, unless one has never experienced any related events, one always prejudges via the posterior. This could be viewed as a form of prejudice. In the Bayesian framework, these issues of prejudice relate to the prior. As suggested above, the sharper the prior, the less useful, and the less used, will the new sample information be. Thus, in a sense, there are degrees of prejudice that relate to the sharpness of the prior. On an intuitive level, issues of discrimination and prejudice should focus on the prior. This is to say: what must the prior be for an economic agent to act in the way he/she is acting? Such an analysis could take place in a profit maximizing or cost minimizing framework, among others. This would be preferable to "yes/no" type results that are based on the use of (0, 1) dummy variables. Similar comments were made in Kelejian (2016).

7.4 COMMENTS ON UNINFORMED PRIORS

In the illustration above we specified a uniform prior of η as $f(\eta) = 1/(2m)$; $-m < \eta < m$. In some cases an (uninformative) uniform prior would be taken as

$$f(\eta) \propto c, \quad -\infty < \eta < \infty \qquad (7.4.1)$$

where c is a constant. Although considered,[1] the prior in (7.4.1) is also recognized by researchers not to be a proper one because it does not integrate to 1. There are "involved" discussions relating to the prior in (7.4.1) (see, e.g., Zellner, 1971 and Jeffreys, 1961), but, at the same time, there are also straightforward interpretations. One such interpretation is that the density beyond a certain point, e.g., $\pm m$, is very low and converges to zero quickly and so can

1. Among others, see Zellner (1971, Chapter 2), LeSage (1999, Chapter 4), Hepple (2004).

be ignored. Still another interpretation of the uniform prior is that it is just an approximation to a normal with a very large variance. For example, if we took

$$f(\eta) \propto \exp[-\frac{1}{2\sigma^2}(\eta-\mu)^2], \quad -\infty < \eta < \infty \tag{7.4.2}$$

where σ^2 is "very" large, and $\mu = 0$, $f(\eta)$ would be very similar to a uniform in that it would be virtually flat, but unlike the uniform over $\pm\infty$ it would integrate to 1.

One of the parameters in a spatial as well as in other models is the standard deviation of the error term, say σ. Unlike some parameters for which prior information may not be available, there is information about σ, namely that $\sigma > 0$. Given this information, one cannot assume a uniform prior over the interval from $-\infty$ to $+\infty$ for σ. However, researchers often assume a uniform prior not for σ but for $z = \ln(\sigma)$. For example, as $\sigma \to \infty$, $z \to \infty$ and as $\sigma \to 0$, $z \to -\infty$. Let $f_z(z)$ be the density of z. Then,

$$\begin{aligned} f_z(z) &= f(\sigma)\frac{d\sigma}{dz}, \\ f(\sigma) &= f_z(z)\frac{dz}{d\sigma}. \end{aligned} \tag{7.4.3}$$

If we assume that $f_z(z)$ is uniform, $f_z(z) \propto c$, then the implied prior for σ is

$$f(\sigma) \propto \frac{1}{\sigma} \tag{7.4.4}$$

since

$$\frac{dz}{d\sigma} = \frac{1}{\sigma}. \tag{7.4.5}$$

Let β be the regression parameter vector in a regression model, and assume that, along with z, the researcher has no information about their values. In this case a joint uninformative prior is needed. A specification made by Zellner (1971), Hepple (2004) and (many) others is that σ and β are independent and so the joint (uniform) prior is often taken as

$$\begin{aligned} F_{\sigma,\beta}(\sigma,\beta) &= f_\sigma(\sigma) f_\beta(\beta) \\ &\propto 1/\sigma. \end{aligned} \tag{7.4.6}$$

In passing we note that the prior is sometimes taken to be a function that combines "conveniently" with the likelihood in the posterior. An example of this is given in the next section. Such priors are sometimes called natural conjugate priors; see, e.g., Zellner (1971, Chapter 2).

7.5 APPLICATIONS AND LIMITING CASES[2]

Completing a Quadratic

Let Z be an $N \times 1$ vector, A be an $N \times N$ symmetric nonsingular matrix, and B be an $N \times 1$ vector. Then, as a preliminary, the quadratic/linear expression $Z'AZ - 2B'Z$ can be expressed as

$$Z'AZ - 2B'Z = (Z - A^{-1}B)'A(Z - A^{-1}B) - B'A^{-1}B. \qquad (7.5.1)$$

The result in (7.5.1) is easily checked. It is obviously a generalization of "completing the square" in scalar algebra. The usefulness of (7.5.1) will become apparent.

An Illustration: A Linear Model With Known σ

In the Bayesian framework, consider the model

$$y = X\beta + \varepsilon \qquad (7.5.2)$$

where y is $N \times 1$, X is an $N \times k$ nonstochastic matrix, β is $k \times 1$, and $\varepsilon \sim N(0, \sigma^2 I_N)$. In this model we will assume that σ^2 is known and so the only parameter is β. Let σ_*^2 be the known value of σ^2. In this illustration, we assume a natural conjugate prior for β, namely $\beta \sim N(\beta_0, \sigma_0^2 I_k)$. Since β_0 and σ_0^2 are parameters of the prior, their values are known. Clearly, the value of σ_0^2 reflects the precision of the prior: the larger the σ_0^2, the less precise the prior information. On the other hand, σ_*^2 is the known value of the variance of the error term in the regression model: the larger the σ_*^2, the less information there is in the sample concerning β.

The posterior for β in the model (7.5.2) is

$$P(\beta|data) \qquad (7.5.3)$$
$$\propto \exp[-\frac{1}{2\sigma_*^2}(y - X\beta)'(y - X\beta)]\exp[-\frac{1}{2\sigma_0^2}(\beta - \beta_0)'(\beta - \beta_0)].$$

Let $\hat{\beta} = (X'X)^{-1}X'y$ and $\hat{\varepsilon} = (y - X\hat{\beta})$. Then, $(y - X\beta)$ can be expressed as $[(y - X\hat{\beta}) + (X\hat{\beta} - X\beta)] = [\hat{\varepsilon} + X(\hat{\beta} - \beta)]$. Therefore, recalling that $\hat{\varepsilon}'X = 0$, the likelihood component of the posterior in (7.5.3) can be expressed as

$$L \propto \exp[-\frac{1}{2\sigma_*^2}(\hat{\varepsilon}'\hat{\varepsilon} + (\hat{\beta} - \beta)'X'X(\hat{\beta} - \beta))] \qquad (7.5.4)$$

2. For further discussions and implications of the issues below, see Zellner (1971) and Kelejian (2016).

$$\propto \exp[-\frac{1}{2\sigma_*^2}\hat{\varepsilon}'\hat{\varepsilon}]\exp[-\frac{1}{2\sigma_*^2}(\hat{\beta}-\beta)'X'X(\hat{\beta}-\beta)]$$
$$\propto \exp[-\frac{1}{2\sigma_*^2}(\hat{\beta}-\beta)'X'X(\hat{\beta}-\beta)]$$

where $\exp[-\frac{1}{2\sigma_*^2}\hat{\varepsilon}'\hat{\varepsilon}]$ has been incorporated into the proportionality factor since σ_*^2 is known, and $\hat{\varepsilon}$ only depends on sample data.

The issue now is to express the posterior in such a way that (7.5.1) can be implemented. In light of (7.5.4), the posterior in (7.5.3) can be expressed as

$$P(\beta|data) \propto \exp[-\frac{1}{2\sigma_*^2}(\hat{\beta}'X'X\hat{\beta}-2\hat{\beta}'X'X\beta+\beta'X'X\beta) \quad (7.5.5)$$
$$-\frac{1}{2\sigma_0^2}(\beta'\beta-2\beta_0'\beta+\beta_0'\beta_0)]$$
$$\propto \exp[-\frac{1}{2}(\beta'A_1\beta-2A_2\beta)]\exp[-\frac{1}{2\sigma_*^2}\hat{\beta}'X'X\hat{\beta}-\frac{1}{2\sigma_0^2}\beta_0'\beta_0]$$
$$\propto \exp[-\frac{1}{2}(\beta'A_1\beta-2A_2'\beta)]$$

where

$$A_1 = [\frac{1}{\sigma_*^2}X'X+\frac{1}{\sigma_0^2}I_k], \quad (7.5.6)$$
$$A_2 = [\frac{1}{\sigma_*^2}X'X\hat{\beta}+\frac{1}{\sigma_0^2}\beta_0].$$

Thus, applying (7.5.1) to (7.5.5), and noting that the term corresponding to $B'A^{-1}B$ in (7.5.1) does not involve β and so is accounted for by the proportionality factor, the posterior is

$$P(\beta|data) \propto \exp[-\frac{1}{2}(\beta-A_1^{-1}A_2)'A_1(\beta-A_1^{-1}A_2)], \quad (7.5.7)$$

which implies that the posterior for β is multivariate normal with mean and VC matrix given by

$$E(\beta|data) = A_1^{-1}A_2, \quad (7.5.8)$$
$$VC_{\beta|data} = A_1^{-1}.$$

Prior and Likelihood Limiting Cases

To see how the posterior merges prior information with sample information, consider some limiting cases. In the first the prior distribution on β is completely uninformative, e.g., $\sigma_0^2 \to \infty$. In this case

$$A_1 \to \frac{1}{\sigma_*^2} X'X. \tag{7.5.9}$$

Also,

$$A_2 \to \frac{1}{\sigma_*^2} X'X\hat{\beta}. \tag{7.5.10}$$

Therefore, in this limiting case of no prior information on β, the mean and VC matrix of β are:

$$\begin{aligned} E(\beta|data) &\to \hat{\beta}, \\ VC_{\beta|data} &\to \sigma_*^2 (X'X)^{-1} \end{aligned} \tag{7.5.11}$$

which is what one would obtain based entirely on the likelihood – there is no prior information.

Now consider the case in which the prior information on β is extremely sharp, e.g., $\sigma_0^2 \to 0$. In this case note that A_1^{-1} can be written as

$$A_1^{-1} = \sigma_0^2 [\frac{\sigma_0^2}{\sigma_*^2} X'X + I_k]^{-1} \tag{7.5.12}$$

so that

$$\begin{aligned} A_1^{-1} A_2 &= [\frac{\sigma_0^2}{\sigma_*^2} X'X + I_k]^{-1} [\frac{\sigma_0^2}{\sigma_*^2} X'X\hat{\beta} + \beta_0] \\ &\to \beta_0. \end{aligned} \tag{7.5.13}$$

Thus, in this limiting case of an extremely sharp prior, the mean of β as determined by the posterior is just the mean of the prior: $E(\beta|data) \to \beta_0$. There is no learning! Also, as one would expect, if $\sigma_0^2 \to 0$, the variance–covariance matrix of β, given by A_1^{-1} in (7.5.8), is just a matrix of zeros, signifying that there is no uncertainly. To see this, recall from (7.5.8) that the VC matrix of β is A_1^{-1}. If $\sigma_0^2 \to 0$, (7.5.12) implies

$$A_1^{-1} = \sigma_0^2 [\frac{\sigma_0^2}{\sigma_*^2} X'X + I_k]^{-1} \to 0. \tag{7.5.14}$$

Now consider the opposite case in which the sample information is extremely sharp, namely $\sigma_*^2 \to 0$. From (7.5.8) and (7.5.6), the mean of β can be expressed as

$$E(\beta) = [X'X + \frac{\sigma_*^2}{\sigma_0^2} I_k]^{-1} [X'X\hat{\beta} + \frac{\sigma_*^2}{\sigma_0^2} \beta_0] \tag{7.5.15}$$

$$\rightarrow \hat{\beta} \text{ as } \sigma_*^2 \rightarrow 0.$$

Thus, in this case the sample information completely dominates prior information.

Now consider the VC matrix of β, namely A_1^{-1}, for this case. Again from (7.5.6), as $\sigma_*^2 \rightarrow 0$ we get

$$\begin{aligned} VC_\beta &= A_1^{-1} \qquad (7.5.16) \\ &= \sigma_*^2[X'X + \frac{\sigma_*^2}{\sigma_0^2} I_k]^{-1} \rightarrow 0. \end{aligned}$$

Thus the posterior for β is such that its value is known with certainty.

There is another case in which the sample completely dominates the prior. Specifically, consider the more typical case in which if $\sigma_0^2 > 0$, $\sigma_*^2 > 0$, but $N \rightarrow \infty$. We leave it as an exercise for the reader to show that, under typical assumptions for X,

$$E(\beta|data) \rightarrow \hat{\beta} \text{ as } N \rightarrow \infty. \qquad (7.5.17)$$

That is, asymptotically, the sample completely dominates the prior and so the mean of β is determined entirely by the likelihood. The reader should also be able to show, again under typical assumptions, that if $\sigma_0^2 > 0$, $\sigma_*^2 > 0$ but $N \rightarrow \infty$,

$$VC_\beta \rightarrow 0. \qquad (7.5.18)$$

In summary, the mean and VC matrix of β in the posterior depend on the precision parameters σ_*^2 and σ_0^2, as well as the sample size N. These parameters determine the weights given to the sample and prior information in the posterior.

Illustration 7.5.1: A computer illustration of the limiting cases

To demonstrate the prior and likelihood limiting cases, we design a brief computer illustration. Specifically, we generate $N = 100$ observations from the linear regression model

$$y_i = \beta_0 + \beta_1 x_{i,1} + u_i, i = 1, ..., N$$

where $\beta_0 = \beta_1 = 2$, the regressors $x_{1,i}$ are i.i.d. $N(0, 1)$, and the error terms u_i are i.i.d. $N(0, \sigma_*^2)$, where σ_*^2 is known. In the experiments reported below two values are considered for σ_*^2, namely 0.0001 and 1.243. The priors for the parameters β_0 and β_1 are normal with means $E(\beta_0) = E(\beta_1) = 1.5$, variance σ_0^2, and a covariance of zero, so that, given normality, β_0 and β_1 are independent. Two values are considered for σ_0^2, namely 1.0 and 0.0001. In the experiments

TABLE 7.5.1 Limiting Bayesian results

σ_*^2	σ_0^2	$E(\beta_0)$	$E(\beta_1)$
0.0001	1	2.240	2.115
1.243	0.0001	1.506	1.505

the value of $\sigma_*^2 = 0.0001$ corresponds to an extremely sharp likelihood, and $\sigma_0^2 = 0.0001$ corresponds to an extremely sharp prior. Finally, the results in the table above require the calculation of the OLS estimates of β_0 and β_1 when $\sigma_*^2 = 0.0001$. For our particular sample, these values turn out to be $\hat{\beta}_0 = 2.240$ and $\hat{\beta}_1 = 2.115$.

The Bayesian results based on the simulated data are described in Table 7.5.1. The results in the first line of the table are consistent with the theoretical development, when σ_*^2 is close to zero, the mean $E(\beta) \doteq \hat{\beta}$; see (7.5.15). On the other hand, as should be clear from the second line of the table, when the prior variance σ_0^2 is close to zero, $E(\beta)$ is close to the priors for β_0 and β_1; see (7.5.13).

A Joint Posterior of β and σ^2

Consider the model

$$y = X\beta + \varepsilon \tag{7.5.19}$$

where y is an $N \times 1$, X is an $N \times k$ exogenous regressor, and $\varepsilon \sim N(0, \sigma^2 I_N)$. We assume that the joint prior for β and σ^2 is, as in (7.4.6), $F_{\sigma,\beta}(\sigma, \beta) \propto 1/\sigma$. Thus, in light of (7.5.4), the posterior is

$$\begin{aligned} P(\sigma, \beta|data) &\propto \frac{1}{\sigma^{N+1}} \exp(-\frac{1}{2}[y - X\beta]'[y - X\beta]) \\ &\propto \frac{1}{\sigma^{N+1}} \exp(-\frac{1}{2\sigma^2}[\hat{\varepsilon}'\hat{\varepsilon} + (\beta - \hat{\beta})'X'X(\beta - \hat{\beta})]) \end{aligned} \tag{7.5.20}$$

where $\hat{\beta} = (X'X)^{-1}X'y$ and $\hat{\varepsilon} = (y - X\hat{\beta})$.

The posterior in (7.5.20) is expressible as

$$\begin{aligned} P(\sigma, \beta|data) &\propto g_1(\sigma|data) g_2(\sigma, \beta|data), \\ g_1(\sigma|data) &= \frac{1}{\sigma^{N+1-k}} \exp[-\frac{1}{2\sigma^2}\hat{\varepsilon}'\hat{\varepsilon}], \\ g_2(\sigma, \beta|data) &= \frac{1}{\sigma^k} \exp[-\frac{1}{2\sigma^2}[(\beta - \hat{\beta})'X'X(\beta - \hat{\beta})]]. \end{aligned} \tag{7.5.21}$$

Note that, given the data, $g_1(\sigma|data)$ is a function of σ that does not include β, and $g_2(\sigma, \beta|data)$ is a function of both σ and β. Since the posterior is the joint density of σ and β conditional on the data, $g_1(\sigma|data)$ is proportional to the marginal posterior of σ, and $g_2(\sigma, \beta|data)$ is proportional to the conditional posterior of β given σ. Clearly, the conditional posterior of β given σ is the normal distribution: $\beta \simeq N[\hat{\beta}, \sigma^2(X'X)^{-1}]$. Note that in the Bayesian approach β is random and the data are fixed. Therefore, $E(\beta|\sigma, data) = \hat{\beta}$ and $VC_{\beta|\sigma} = \sigma^2(X'X)^{-1}$. In the classical approach, one would have $E(\hat{\beta}|data) = \beta$ and $VC_{\hat{\beta}|data} = \sigma^2(X'X)^{-1}$.

Since the conditional posterior of β given σ involves σ, which is not known, this distribution is not useful for making inferences about β. For this purpose we need the marginal posterior distribution of β. This can be obtained by integrating the joint posterior in (7.5.20) over σ.

Let

$$A = [\hat{\varepsilon}'\hat{\varepsilon} + (\beta - \hat{\beta})]'X'X(\beta - \hat{\beta})] \tag{7.5.22}$$

so that

$$P(\beta|data) \propto \int_0^\infty \frac{1}{\sigma^{N+1}} \exp[-\frac{A}{2\sigma^2}]d\sigma. \tag{7.5.23}$$

In (7.5.23) let

$$z = \frac{A}{2\sigma^2} \tag{7.5.24}$$

so that

$$\sigma = \frac{A^{1/2}}{2^{1/2}} z^{-1/2} \tag{7.5.25}$$

and

$$d\sigma = -\frac{A^{1/2}}{2^{3/2}} z^{-3/2}.$$

Note that the limits on z corresponding to $(0, \infty)$ for σ are $(\infty, 0)$.

Transforming the integral in (7.5.23) from σ to z, and factoring constants, which are all terms not involving σ or β, into the proportionality factor, it follows that

$$\begin{aligned} P(\beta|data) &\propto \int_0^\infty A^{-N/2} z^{(N/2-1)} \exp(-z)dz \\ &\propto A^{-N/2} \int_0^\infty z^{(N/2-1)} \exp(-z)dz \\ &\propto A^{-N/2} \end{aligned} \tag{7.5.26}$$

since the integral in (7.5.26) integrates to a constant which does not involve β.

In order to get a better understanding of the distribution in (7.5.26), note first that $\hat{\varepsilon}'\hat{\varepsilon}$ is just part of the data and so it is a constant. Therefore, $\hat{\varepsilon}'\hat{\varepsilon}$, and then

$(N-k)$ can be factored out of A which leads to

$$A^{-N/2} \propto \left[(N-k) + \frac{(\beta-\hat{\beta})'X'X(\beta-\hat{\beta})}{\hat{\varepsilon}'\hat{\varepsilon}/(N-k)}\right]^{-\frac{N}{2}} \tag{7.5.27}$$

$$\propto \left[(N-k) + \frac{(\beta-\hat{\beta})'X'X(\beta-\hat{\beta})}{\hat{\varepsilon}'\hat{\varepsilon}/(N-k)}\right]^{-\frac{(k+N-k)}{2}}.$$

Bringing results together, we have the marginal posterior of β as

$$P(\beta|data) \propto \left[(N-k) + \frac{(\beta-\hat{\beta})'X'X(\beta-\hat{\beta})}{\hat{\varepsilon}'\hat{\varepsilon}/(N-k)}\right]^{-\frac{(k+N-k)}{2}}. \tag{7.5.28}$$

In this form the posterior is seen to be a multivariate t-distribution with $N-k$ degrees of freedom. The normalizing constant is given below in (7.6.1). As will be clear from the general description below

$$\begin{aligned} E(\beta|data) &= \hat{\beta} \text{ if } N-k>1, \\ E[(\beta-\hat{\beta})(\beta-\hat{\beta})'|data] &= \hat{\sigma}^2(X'X)^{-1} \text{ if } N-k>2, \\ \hat{\sigma}^2 &= \hat{\varepsilon}'\hat{\varepsilon}/(N-k-2). \end{aligned} \tag{7.5.29}$$

The marginal distribution of σ can be obtained in the following way. One should first integrate the joint distribution in (7.5.20) over β

$$P(\sigma|data) \propto \int_{\infty}^{\infty} \frac{1}{\sigma^{N+1}} \exp[-\frac{1}{2\sigma^2}(\hat{\varepsilon}'\hat{\varepsilon} + (\beta-\hat{\beta})'X'X(\beta-\hat{\beta}))]d\beta \tag{7.5.30}$$

$$\propto \frac{1}{\sigma^{N+1-k}} \exp[-\frac{1}{2\sigma^2}(\hat{\varepsilon}'\hat{\varepsilon})]*$$

$$\int_{-\infty}^{\infty} \frac{1}{(2\pi)^{k/2}\sigma^k} \exp[-\frac{1}{2\sigma^2}((\beta-\hat{\beta})'X'X(\beta-\hat{\beta}))]d\beta$$

$$\propto \frac{1}{\sigma^{N+1-k}} \exp[-\frac{1}{2\sigma^2}(\hat{\varepsilon}'\hat{\varepsilon})]$$

since σ is constant with respect to the integration, and since the normal density integrates to 1:

$$\int_{-\infty}^{\infty} \frac{1}{(2\pi)^{k/2}\sigma^k} \exp[-\frac{1}{2\sigma^2}((\beta-\hat{\beta})'X'X(\beta-\hat{\beta}))]d\beta = 1.$$

Also note that the integral is equal to 1 since it relates to a multivariate normal whose mean and variance covariance matrix are $\hat{\beta}$ and $\sigma^2(X'X)^{-1}$, respectively.

Finally, the result obtained for $P(\sigma|data)$ is an inverted gamma; see, e.g., Zellner (1971, p. 371). In particular,

$$P(\sigma|data) = c\,\frac{\exp(-\frac{\hat{\varepsilon}'\hat{\varepsilon}}{2}\sigma^2)}{\sigma^{N-k+1}}, \tag{7.5.31}$$
$$c = \frac{(\hat{\varepsilon}'\hat{\varepsilon})^{(N-k)/2}}{\Gamma(\frac{N-k}{2})2^{[(N-k)/2]-1}}.$$

Comments on Hypothesis Testing

Consider again the posterior in (7.5.7), which is a multivariate normal. This posterior is useful for inferring probabilities concerning possible values of β. As an illustration, suppose β is a scalar and in the context of a consumption function, it is the marginal propensity to consume. For certain macroeconomic fiscal policies, the value of β would be of interest since multipliers relate to it. In such a setting, one might be interested in the hypothesis that $\beta > 0.9$ because large values of β imply large values of the multiplier. For purposes of illustration, suppose as typically assumed, a type I error of 0.05 is considered. Then, if the posterior in (7.5.7) indicates that $\Pr(\beta > 0.9) < 0.05$, the hypothesis that $\beta > 0.9$ would be rejected.

As our discussion below relating to loss functions will indicate, in some cases a point estimate of β may be of interest. Based on the posterior in (7.5.7), in such cases one would typically take that point estimate as the mean of β, namely $E(\beta|data) = A_1^{-1}A_2$, as given in (7.5.8).

Suppose again that β is a scalar, and relates to a variable of interest in the regression model. In such setting, one might be interested in the hypothesis H_0 : $\beta = \beta_0$, e.g., typically $\beta_0 = 0$. Assume that if $\beta \neq \beta_0$ the researcher does not have any prior information as to the value of β, that is to say, whether $\beta > \beta_0$ or $\beta < \beta_0$. Let σ_β be the standard deviation of the scalar β based on (7.5.7) and (7.5.8). In such a case, $H_0 : \beta = \beta_0$ would be rejected if the 95% confidence interval

$$\Pr[A_1^{-1}A_2 - 1.96\sigma_\beta < \beta < A_1^{-1}A_2 + 1.96\sigma_\beta] = 0.95, \tag{7.5.32}$$

which is based on (7.5.7), does **not** contain β_0. Alternatively, rearranging terms in (7.5.32), $H_0 : \beta = \beta_0$ would be rejected if

$$|(\beta_0 - A_1^{-1}A_2)/\sigma_\beta| > 1.96. \tag{7.5.33}$$

The expression in (7.5.33) is the usual t-ratio that frequently appears in classical statistics. However, the interpretation of (7.5.33) in the Bayesian framework is quite different. Specifically, in classical statistics, one views the confidence interval as random in the sense that if a "large" number of hypothetical

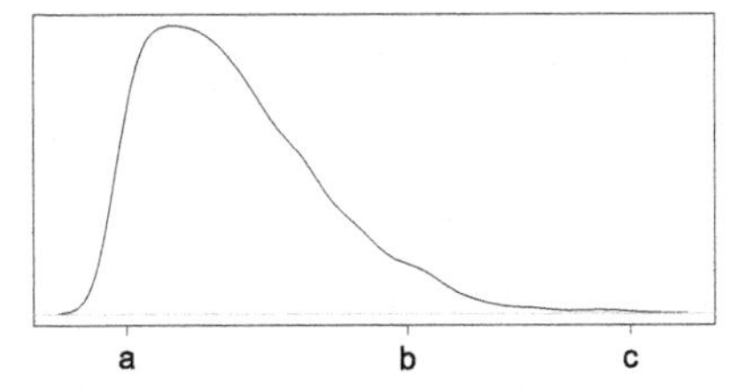

FIGURE 7.5.1 A nonsymmetric posterior

samples were to be drawn, and in each case a confidence interval constructed, 95% of them would be expected to cover the hypothesized value if it were true. In the Bayesian framework, the confidence interval relates to the available and **fixed** sample, and the probability statement underlying the confidence interval relates to the random parameter β, i.e., in (7.5.32) β is the random variable.[3]

Now consider the posterior for the $k \times 1$ vector β in (7.5.28). In our more general discussion of the multivariate t-distribution in Section 7.6, we point out that the marginal distributions, as well as linear combinations of multivariate t variables are again multivariate t with the same degrees of freedom, say v. If $v > 2$, the mean and VC matrix of a subset of elements of β, or of a linear combination of those elements, can easily be obtained by standard methods from the mean and variance formulas given in (7.5.29). As an example, in (7.5.29) let $\hat{\beta}_1$ be the first element of $\hat{\beta}$, and let $\sigma^2_{\hat{\beta}_1}$ be the first diagonal element of $\hat{\sigma}^2(X'X)^{-1}$. If $v = N - k > 2$ in (7.5.28), the mean of the first element of β, say β_1, is $\hat{\beta}_1$ and the variance of β_1 is $\sigma^2_{\hat{\beta}_1}$. Since a linear combination of multivariate t variables is again a t variable with the same degrees of freedom, $(\beta_1 - \hat{\beta}_1)/\sigma^2_{\hat{\beta}_1}$ has a t distribution with mean and variance of 0 and 1, respectively, which we denote as $t_{v,0,1}$. Consider the hypothesis H_0: $\beta_1 := \beta_1^0$. In this case H_0 would be rejected at the 5% level if the confidence interval

$$\Pr(t_{v,0,1}(0.025) < (\beta_1 - \hat{\beta}_1)/\sigma^2_{\hat{\beta}_1} < t_{v,0,1}(0.975)) = 0.95 \tag{7.5.34}$$

does not contain β_1^0, where, in general, $t_{v,0,1}(\alpha)$ is obtained from the t table with v degrees of freedom as the value such that $\Pr[t_{v,0,1} < t_{v,0,1}(\alpha)] = \alpha$.

In passing we note that the distribution of $t_{v,0,1}$ is bell-shaped and closely resembles the $N(0, 1)$ except that its tails are "thicker." Therefore the t-distribution, as the normal, is symmetric and peaks at only one point, namely the mean. This implies that all other 95% confidence intervals corresponding to (7.5.32) and (7.5.34) would be wider. To see the importance of this, consider the posterior distribution of a parameter, say η, as in Fig. 7.5.1.

3. There are subtleties relating to hypothesis testing in the Bayesian framework; see, e.g., Lindley (1961, 1965) and Zellner (1971, Chapter 10).

Suppose the hypothesis is $H_0 : \eta = c$. In this case if the shortest 95% confidence interval is between a and b, the hypothesized value of $\eta = c$ would be rejected. If, on the other hand, one used a 95% interval starting at a point near b and extending to the right of that point, the hypothesized value of $\eta = c$ would surely be accepted. The issue, or rule, is that to be accepted, the hypothesized value should be where the posterior is "high"; the use of the shortest 95% interval is consistent with that rule.

To summarize, if the hypothesized value of a parameter, say ζ, does not fall between s_1 and s_2 in (7.5.35) below, and if $|s_2 - s_1|$ is less than the distance between the endpoints of any other 95% confidence interval relating to ζ, that hypothesis should be rejected:

$$P(s_1 < \zeta < s_2) = 0.95. \tag{7.5.35}$$

7.6 PROPERTIES OF THE MULTIVARIATE t

An $m \times 1$ random vector X has a multivariate t-distribution with v degrees of freedom if its density has the form[4]

$$f(x) = \frac{v^{v/2}\Gamma[(v+m)/2]|V|^{1/2}}{\pi^{m/2}\Gamma(v/2)}[v + (x-\theta)'V(x-\theta)]^{-[m+v]/2} \tag{7.6.1}$$
$$-\infty < x < \infty, \; v > 0$$

where $\Gamma(\cdot)$ is the gamma function:

$$\Gamma(r) = \int_0^\infty x^{r-1}\exp(-x)dx, \; 0 < r < \infty, \tag{7.6.2}$$
$$\Gamma(1/2) = \pi^{1/2}.$$

Given (7.6.1),

$$E(X) = \theta \text{ if } v > 1, \tag{7.6.3}$$
$$E(X-\theta)(X-\theta)' = \frac{v}{v-2}V^{-1} \text{ if } v > 2.$$

For ease of exposition in this section, we describe the distribution of the $m \times 1$ vector X described in (7.6.1) as $t_{m,v,\theta,V}$. If $m = 1$, we will omit reference to m and simply denote $t_{m,v,\theta,V}$ as $t_{v,\theta,V}$ as we did above.

The multivariate t has certain properties that are similar to those of the multivariate normal; see, e.g., the development in Zellner (1971, pp. 383–389). For

4. An excellent presentation of the multivariate t as well as other distributions is given in Raiffa and Schlaifer (1961, Chapter 7), and in Zellner (1971, Appendix B.2).

example, the marginal distributions of a multivariate t with v degrees of freedom are again multivariate t with v degrees of freedom. In particular, let the first q elements of the $m \times 1$ random vector $X \sim t_{m,v,\theta,V}$ be X_1, the first q elements of θ be θ_1, and let $v > 2$. Let V be correspondingly partitioned as

$$V = \begin{bmatrix} V_{11} & V_{12} \\ V_{21} & V_{22} \end{bmatrix}. \tag{7.6.4}$$

Then, if $q < m$, then $X_1 \sim t_{q,v,\theta_1,V_1}$ where $V_1 = (V_{11} - V_{12}V_{22}^{-1}V_{21})$, e.g.,

$$E(X_1) = \theta_1,$$
$$E(X_1 - \theta_1)(X_1 - \theta_1)' = \frac{v}{(v-2)}(V_{11} - V_{12}V_{22}^{-1}V_{21})^{-1}.$$

Note that the variance–covariance matrix of X_1 follows from (7.6.1) and (7.6.3) by partitioned matrix inversion.

Another result which is similar to that of the multivariate normal is that conditional distributions of a multivariate t are also multivariate t, although the degrees of freedom parameter is different. Still another property that corresponds to the multivariate normal is that linear combinations of multivariate t variables are again multivariate t with the same degrees of freedom. Specifically, let $Z = DX$, where $X \sim t_{m,v,\theta,V}$, $v > 2$, and D is a constant $m \times m$ nonsingular matrix. Then, $X = D^{-1}Z$ and the Jacobian from X to Z is $|D|^{-1}$, which is a constant. Express the density in (7.6.1) as

$$f(x) \propto [v + (x - \theta)'V(x - \theta)]^{-[m+v]/2}. \tag{7.6.5}$$

Using evident notation, the density of Z is

$$\begin{aligned} f_z(z) &\propto [v + (D^{-1}z - \theta)'V(D^{-1}z - \theta)]^{-[m+v]/2} \\ &\propto \left[v + (D^{-1}[z - D\theta])'V\ (D^{-1}[z - D\theta])\right]^{-[m+v]/2} \\ &\propto \left[v + [z - D\theta]'\ [D^{-1\prime}V\ D^{-1}]\ [z - D\theta]\right]^{-[m+v]/2}. \end{aligned} \tag{7.6.6}$$

It follows from (7.6.6) that $Z \sim t_{m,v,D\theta,D^{-1\prime}VD^{-1}}$ and so

$$E(Z) = D\theta \text{ if } v > 1, \tag{7.6.7}$$
$$E(Z - D\theta)(Z - D\theta)' = \frac{v}{v-2}DV^{-1}D' \text{ if } v > 2.$$

Note that the force of (7.6.6) is that Z is a multivariate t; the mean and VC matrix of Z follow by obvious manipulations.

In a somewhat similar light, let $h = \alpha' X$, where α' is a $1 \times m$ constant row vector, and again let $X \sim t_{m,v,\theta,V}$, $v > 2$. Note that $E(h) = \alpha'\theta$ and $E(h - \alpha'\theta)(h - \alpha'\theta)' = \frac{v}{v-2}\alpha' V^{-1}\alpha$. It follows that h is a scalar t variable: $h \sim t_{1,v,\alpha'\theta,(\alpha' V^{-1}\alpha)^{-1}}$. As one example of the usefulness of this result, consider the hypotheses $H_0 : h = 10$ against the two tail alternative $H_1 : h \neq 10$. Let $\sigma_h^2 = \frac{v}{v-2}\alpha' V^{-1}\alpha$. Then, with a type I error of 0.05, $H_0 : h = 10$ would be rejected in the Bayesian framework if

$$\left| \frac{10 - \alpha'\theta}{\sigma_h} \right| > t_{1,v,0,1}(0.975) \tag{7.6.8}$$

where

$$\Pr(|t_{1,v,0,1}| > t_{1,v,0,1}(0.975)) = 0.05. \tag{7.6.9}$$

7.7 USEFUL SAMPLING PROCEDURES IN BAYESIAN ANALYSIS

As will become evident shortly, Bayesian analysis of many spatial econometric models often results in complicated joint posteriors which are not "standard" distributions. Because of this, the marginal posteriors are difficult to determine analytically. These marginal posteriors are important because inference concerning parameter values are typically based on them. Given the analytical difficulties involved, researchers often rely upon sampling methods to determine the marginal posteriors, or their properties. At this point we illustrate a few of these sampling methods.[5]

Monte Carlo Sampling Integration

In research one is sometimes faced with the problem of evaluating an integral. This can be challenging because in some cases the evaluation can not be done analytically. In such cases, numerical methods are often considered. Some of these methods are based on sampling procedures.

For example, consider the integral

$$G = \int_a^b g(x)dx \tag{7.7.1}$$

and suppose that analytical integration is "difficult." Let $f(x) > 0$ be a density on the interval (a, b). Then, G can always be expressed as

5. Very useful overviews are given in Casella and George (1992), Resnik and Hardisty (2010), Walsh (2004), and Song (2011). More detailed presentations are given in LeSage (1999), Geweke (2005), Koopman et al. (2009), and Douc et al., 2007. LeSage (1999) also gives useful MATLAB programs.

$$G = \int_a^b [\frac{g(x)}{f(x)}] f(x) dx \tag{7.7.2}$$
$$= \int_a^b [q(x)] f(x) dx$$

where $q(x) = g(x)/f(x)$. Let X be a random variable whose density is $f(x)$. The result in (7.7.2) implies that G can be viewed as the expected value of $q(X)$ with respect to the density $f(x)$.[6] Given this, G in (7.7.2) can be expressed as

$$G = E_f[q(X)]. \tag{7.7.3}$$

The Monte Carlo sampling integration method is based on (7.7.2) and (7.7.3). As an example, let $X_1, ..., X_N$ be a random sample from $f(x)$. Then a sampling approach to the estimation of G in (7.7.2) would be

$$\hat{G} = N^{-1} \sum_{i=1}^{N} q(X_i). \tag{7.7.4}$$

The estimator of G is consistent. Since $X_1, ..., X_N$ is a random sample from $f(x)$, and recalling (7.7.3),

$$E_f[\hat{G}] = N^{-1} \sum_{i=1}^{N} E_f[q(X_i)] \tag{7.7.5}$$
$$= G.$$

Since in (7.7.4) $\hat{G}$ is the sum of N independent identically distributed random variables, its variance, with respect to $f(x)$, is

$$var_f[\hat{G}] = N^{-1} var_f[q(X)] \to 0. \tag{7.7.6}$$

Therefore, by Chebyshev's inequality given in Section A.3 of the appendix on large sample theory, $\hat{G}$ is consistent, i.e.,

$$\hat{G} \xrightarrow{P} G \text{ as } N \to \infty. \tag{7.7.7}$$

In this case one could also appeal to Khinchine's Theorem in Section A.4 of that appendix for the consistency of $\hat{G}$. Khinchine's Theorem does not require the variance to even exist!

6. On a formal level, in this illustration we are assuming that the first two moments of $q(X)$ exist with respect to the density $f(x)$.

The Ideal Selection of $f(x)$

Clearly, some selections of $f(x)$ will lead to more efficient estimation of G. The ideal case is the one in which

$$g(x) = Kf(x) \tag{7.7.8}$$

where K is a constant. In this case G in (7.7.2) is

$$G = \int_a^b Kf(x)dx = K. \tag{7.7.9}$$

Similarly, since $q(x) = g(x)/f(x) = K$, $\hat{G}$ in (7.7.4) reduces to $\hat{G} = K$ and its variance is zero!

One suggestion is that, if possible, $f(x)$ should be roughly proportional to $g(x)$, or at least have the same general shape. If $-a$ and b are infinite, in some cases one might take $f(x)$ as the normal $N(c, \sigma^2)$, where c is roughly near the midpoint or peak of $g(x)$, and σ^2 is such that the tails of $f(x)$ decrease in a manner similar to the tails of $g(x)$. Similar comments relate to the use of other standard distributions such as the chi-squared, etc. If $-a$ and b are finite, there may be cases in which the uniform defined on (a, b) might be a reasonable approximation to $g(x)$.

However, in many cases standard distributions may not offer good approximations to $g(x)$. In these cases nonstandard distributions may be considered for which there may not be any available computer sampling programs. Fortunately, there is a fairly simple solution which is based upon the following steps. Let Z be a random variable whose density is $h(z)$, and whose CDF is

$$(A) \quad H(z) = \int_{-\infty}^{z} h(r)dr.$$

For future reference, note that

$$(B) \quad \frac{dH(z)}{dz} = h(z).$$

Let $M = H(Z)$. Then the density of M is the uniform based on $(0, 1)$.[7] The solution for Z in terms of M involves the inverse function $H^{-1}(\cdot)$, namely

7. To see this, let $v(m)$ be the density of M. Note that m is in the interval $(0, 1)$. Then,

$$v(m)dm = h(z)dz$$

and so

$$\begin{aligned} v(m) &= h(z)\frac{dz}{dm} \\ &= h(z)\frac{1}{dm/dz} \end{aligned}$$

$$(C) \quad Z = H^{-1}(M).$$

The implication of (C) is that $H^{-1}(M)$ has the same distribution as Z. More importantly for Monte Carlo sampling integration, suppose we want a random sample from the density $h(x)$. This can be obtained as follows. Generate a random sample of size N from the uniform (0, 1), say $p_1, ..., p_N$, and transform these observations as $H^{-1}(p_1), ..., H^{-1}(p_N)$. Then, this transformed sample can be viewed as a random sample from the density $h(\cdot)$.

An illustration may be useful. Suppose in (7.7.1), $a = 0$, $b = 5$, and $g(x) = \exp(-x)$. Of course, in this case we know that $G = 1 - \exp(-5) = 0.9933$. However, to illustrate the procedure in (7.7.1)–(7.7.7), suppose we use the density $f(x)$ to approximate the density $g(x)$:

$$(D) \quad f(x) = \frac{c}{1+x}, \quad 0 < x < 5,$$
$$c = 1/\ln(6).$$

The density $f(x)$ clearly has a shape that is similar to that of $g(x)$. The density $f(x)$ is not a standard one. In this case the CDF corresponding to $f(x)$ is

$$F(x) = \int_0^x \frac{c}{1+u} du$$
$$= c\ln(1+x).$$

Let $m = c\ln(1+x)$. The inverse function is obtained by solving for x in terms of m, namely

$$x = \exp(m/c) - 1.$$

Thus, if a random sample of size N is taken from the uniform density (0, 1), say $m_1, ..., m_N$, the transformed sample $[\exp(m_1/c) - 1], ..., [\exp(m_N/c) - 1]$ can be viewed as a random sample from $f(x)$.

Therefore, in light of (7.7.1) and (7.7.2), in this case the integral

$$G = \int_0^5 e^{-x} dx$$
$$= \int_0^5 [\frac{e^{-x}}{c/(1+x)}] \frac{c}{1+x} dx$$
$$= \int_0^5 [e^{-x}(1+x)\ln(6)] \frac{c}{1+x} dx$$

$$= h(z)/h(z) = 1.$$

Thus, $v(m) = 1$ on (0, 1).

TABLE 7.7.1 Numerical integration accuracy and sample size

N	$\hat{G}$
100	0.9675
1000	0.9637
10,000	0.9973
100,000	0.9935

can be approximated by

$$\hat{G} = \sum_{i-1}^{N} e^{-x_i}(1 + x_i)\ln(6)$$

where $x_i = \exp(m_i/c) - 1$ and $m_1, \ldots, m_N$ is a random sample taken from a uniform distribution over (0, 1).

Clearly, for larger N the approximation should become more accurate. As an example, in the illustration above $g(x) = \exp(-x)$, $G = 1 - \exp(-5) = 0.9933$, and $f(x) = c(1+x)^{-1}$, $0 < x < 5$. The estimates of G obtained following the procedure described above are reported in Table 7.7.1. As the sample size increases, the estimates get closer to 0.9933.

A Quality Measure for the Selected Function $f(x)$

One quality measure of the function $f(x)$ is based on the difference between $g(x)$ and $f(x)$. Let $g(x) - f(x) = r(x)$ so that

$$g(x) = f(x) + r(x). \tag{7.7.10}$$

Recalling that $f(x)$ is a density, in this case G in (7.7.2) is

$$\begin{aligned} G &= \int_a^b [\frac{f(x) + r(x)}{f(x)}] f(x) dx \\ &= 1 + \int_a^b [\frac{r(x)}{f(x)}] f(x) dx. \end{aligned} \tag{7.7.11}$$

Let $p(x) = r(x)/f(x)$. Then

$$G = 1 + E_f[p(X)]. \tag{7.7.12}$$

Again, let $X_1, ..., X_N$ be a random sample from $f(x)$. Then the estimator of G is

$$\hat{G} = 1 + N^{-1} \sum_{i=1}^{N} p(X_i). \tag{7.7.13}$$

An analysis that is identical to that in (7.7.4)–(7.7.6) implies that

$$E_f[\hat{G}] = G, \qquad (7.7.14)$$
$$var_f[\hat{G}] = N^{-1} var_f[p(X_i)].$$

Thus, one measure of the quality of the selected function $f(x)$ is the variance it leads to, namely $N^{-1} var_f[p(X_i)]$. The reader can easily show that if $g(x)/f(x) = K$, then

$$p(x) = (K - 1) \qquad (7.7.15)$$

and so $var_f[p(X_i)] = 0$.

Importance Sampling

Consider now the estimation of the mean of a function, say $s(X)$, with respect to the density $h(x)$ defined on the interval (a, b),

$$E_h[s(X)] = \int_a^b s(x)h(x)dx, \qquad (7.7.16)$$

but now assume that, in addition to integration difficulties, the normalizing constant, say c, of the density $h(x)$ is not known, and is "difficult" to calculate. Thus, a random sample cannot be taken from $h(x)$.

It is clear that (7.7.16) can be expressed as

$$E_h[s(X)] = \int_a^b [s(x)\frac{h(x)}{q(x)}]q(x)dx \qquad (7.7.17)$$

where $q(x) > 0$ is a density defined on (a, b), which is known and "easy" to sample from. Given this, $E_h[s(X)]$ as defined in (7.7.16), or in (7.7.17), can be viewed as the expected value of $s(X)[h(X)/q(X)]$ with respect to the density $q(x)$.

Again, assuming the expected value exists, let $X_1, ..., X_N$ be a random sample from $q(x)$. Also, let

$$r^*(X_i) = \frac{h_1(X_i)}{q(X_i)}, i = 1, ..., N \qquad (7.7.18)$$

where $h_1(x)$ is the kernel of $h(x)$ which is assumed to be known, $h(x) = ch_1(x)$. Then, in importance sampling, $E_h[s(X)]$ in (7.7.16) would be estimated as

$$\widehat{E_h[s(X)]} = \frac{\sum_{i=1}^{N} r^*(X_i)s(X_i)}{\sum_{i=1}^{N} r^*(X_i)}. \qquad (7.7.19)$$

Note that since $h_1(x)$ is known, the expression in (7.7.19) is feasible. We will now show that the estimator $\widehat{E_h[s(X)]}$ in (7.7.19) is a consistent estimator for $E_h[s(X)]$ in (7.7.16).

Note first that $r^*(X_i) = \frac{1}{c}h(X_i)/q(X_i)$, and $r^*(X_i)$ appears in both the numerator and denominator of (7.7.19). Therefore, the constant c cancels and so (7.7.19) can be written as

$$\widehat{E_h[s(X)]} = \frac{\sum_{i=1}^{N} r(X_i)s(X_i)}{\sum_{i=1}^{N} r(X_i)} \tag{7.7.20}$$
$$= \frac{N^{-1}\sum_{i=1}^{N} r(X_i)s(X_i)}{N^{-1}\sum_{i=1}^{N} r(X_i)}$$

where $r(X_i) = h(X_i)/q(X_i)$.

The numerator of the ratio on the second line of (7.7.20) is

$$N^{-1}\sum_{i=1}^{N} r(X_i)s(X_i) = N^{-1}\sum_{i=1}^{N} \frac{h(X_i)}{q(X_i)}s(X_i) \tag{7.7.21}$$

which is based on a random sample from $q(x)$. Then, by Khinchine's Theorem and (7.7.16),

$$N^{-1}\sum_{i=1}^{N} \frac{h(X_i)}{q(X_i)}s(X_i) \xrightarrow{P} E_q[\frac{h(x)}{q(x)}s(x)] \tag{7.7.22}$$
$$= \int_a^b \frac{h(x)}{q(x)}s(x)q(x)dx$$
$$= \int_a^b s(x)h(x)dx$$
$$= E_h[s(X)].$$

Recalling that $r(X_i) = h(X_i)/q(X_i)$, now consider the denominator on the second line in (7.7.20), namely

$$N^{-1}\sum_{i=1}^{N} r(X_i) = N^{-1}\sum_{i=1}^{N} \frac{h(X_i)}{q(X_i)} \tag{7.7.23}$$

where again the sample is from $q(x)$. It follows from Khinchine's Theorem that

$$N^{-1}\sum_{i=1}^{N} r(X_i) \xrightarrow{P} E_q[\frac{h(x)}{q(x)}] \tag{7.7.24}$$
$$= \int_a^b \frac{h(x)}{q(x)}q(x)dx$$

$$= \int_a^b h(x)dx$$

$$= 1$$

since $h(x)$ is a density. Finally, from (7.7.20), (7.7.22), and (7.7.24),

$$\widehat{E_h[s(X)]} \xrightarrow{P} E_h[s(X)]. \quad (7.7.25)$$

An Application: Obtaining a Marginal Posterior

Under certain conditions, sampling methods can be used to determine marginal, or joint marginal posteriors. To see this, let $P_{z,x}(z, x|data)$ be the posterior of Z and X, which is known up to a normalizing constant, and suppose that, given the data, the marginal posterior of Z, say $P_z(z|data)$, is to be estimated.[8] In this illustration Z and X can be scalars or vectors. If Z is a vector then $P_z(z|data)$ is the joint marginal of Z.

The marginal of Z relates to the joint of Z and X as

$$P_z(z|data) = \int_a^b P_{z,x}(z, x|data)dx. \quad (7.7.26)$$

Suppose, $P_{z,x}(z, x|data)$ can be expressed as the product of two functions, one containing only x and one containing z and x:

$$P_{z,x}(z, x|data) = g(z, x|data)\ f(x|data). \quad (7.7.27)$$

Also, suppose that by proper normalization, $f^*(x|data) = cf(x|data)$ is a density defined on (a, b), where c is the normalizing constant. In this case the result in (7.7.26) can be expressed as

$$P_z(z|data) = \int_a^b \frac{1}{c} g(z, x|data)\ f^*(x|data)dx. \quad (7.7.28)$$

In (7.7.28), $P_z(z|data)$ can be viewed as the expected value of $c^{-1}g(Z, X|data)$ with respect to the density $f^*(x|data)$. For evident reasons, assume that this expected value exits. Also note that in (7.7.28) z is constant with respect to the integration. It should then be evident that $P_z(z|data)$ can be estimated using sampling methods. For example, let $X_1, ..., X_N$ be a random sample from $f^*(x|data)$. Then at a point, say z_J, $P_z(z_J|data)$ can be estimated as $\widehat{P_z(z_J|data)}$ where

$$\widehat{P_z(z_J|data)} = N^{-1}c^{-1}\sum_{i=1}^{N} g(z_J, X_i|data). \quad (7.7.29)$$

8. Z and X are random variables; z and x denote the values they take.

Again, by Khinchine's Theorem,

$$\widehat{P_z(z_J|data)} \xrightarrow{P} P_z(z_J|data). \tag{7.7.30}$$

The estimate in (7.7.29) is only an estimate of the posterior $P_z(z|data)$ at the point z_J. If (7.7.29) is repeated for various values of z, say $z_1, ..., z_S$, a histogram of the posterior $P_z(z|data)$ can be constructed. Probability statements concerning Z can be approximated with this estimated posterior.

The Metropolis–Hastings Sampling Algorithm[9]

This sampling procedure can be used, among other things, to obtain samples on distributions which are not completely determined. It can also be used to evaluate integrals which have certain difficulties. However, it is different from the procedures discussed above because in this case, each point which is drawn to be part of a sample is actually a potential sample point in the sense that there is a probability of accepting or rejecting that point. In one case, the potential sample point is drawn from a static distribution in the sense that the distribution does not depend on earlier sample values. In another case, the potential sample point is drawn from a dynamic distribution which does depend on earlier sample values.

Again in a Bayesian framework, let ψ be an $r \times 1$ parameter of interest and let $p(\psi)$ be its density. Suppose we want to obtain a sample from $p(\psi)$ but its normalizing constant, say k, is not known and difficult to determine. Let $p(\psi) = kf(\psi)$ where the kernel $f(\psi)$ is known.

A Static Framework

Let $q(\psi) > 0$ be a density which is an approximation to $p(\psi)$. In some cases the researcher may estimate a model containing ψ by maximum likelihood and obtain the MLEs, $\hat{\psi}_{ML}$ and $VC_{\hat{\psi}_{ML}}$. Then, $q(\psi)$ can be taken as $N(\hat{\psi}_{ML}, VC_{\hat{\psi}_{ML}})$:

$$q(\psi) = \frac{1}{(2\pi)^{r/2}|VC_{\hat{\psi}_{ML}}|^{1/2}} \exp[(\psi - \hat{\psi}_{ML})'[VC_{\hat{\psi}_{ML}}]^{-1}(\psi - \hat{\psi}_{ML})]. \tag{7.7.31}$$

The jth potential sample point, say ψ_j^*, would be drawn from (7.7.31). If that point is accepted, by the procedure described below, it would then be relabeled

9. Very useful lecture notes on the procedures described below are given in Song (2011) and Walsh (2004). A useful presentation is also given in Wikipedia.

as ψ_J. If it is rejected, the Jth sample point would then be taken as ψ_{J-1} which is the preceding accepted sample point. In passing we note that, in general,

$$q(\psi_J^*) \neq q(\psi_{J-1}). \tag{7.7.32}$$

A Dynamic Framework

In this case one might determine the dynamic density as follows. Draw the Jth potential sample point, ψ_J^*, from the normal density

$$q(\psi_J^*|\psi_{J-1}) = \frac{1}{(2\pi)^{r/2}|VC_{\hat{\psi}_{ML}}|^{1/2}} \exp[(\psi_J^* - \psi_{J-1})'[VC_{\hat{\psi}_{ML}}]^{-1}(\psi_J^* - \psi_{J-1})]. \tag{7.7.33}$$

For future reference note that the distribution in (7.7.33) is symmetric: $q(\psi_J^*|\psi_{J-1}) = q(\psi_{J-1}|\psi_J^*)$.

Details of the Procedure

M1. Chose an initial value of ψ, say ψ_0, such that $f(\psi_0) > 0$.

M2. If the static case is chosen, draw from the approximating distribution $q(\psi)$ in (7.7.31) and obtain a potential sample point, say ψ_1^*.

M3. Calculated α where

$$\alpha = \min[\frac{f(\psi_1^*)}{f(\psi_0)} \frac{q(\psi_0)}{q(\psi_1^*)}, 1]. \tag{7.7.34}$$

If $\alpha = 1$, the point ψ_1^* is kept as part of the sample, and is relabeled as ψ_1, and one returns to **M2** to continue the process but now taking ψ_1 as the initial value, etc. If $\alpha < 1$, ψ_1^* is kept with probability α, and rejected with probability $1-\alpha$. One way to implement this is to randomly draw a value from the uniform distribution on (0, 1). If that value is less than or equal to α, the sample point ψ_1^* is accepted and relabeled ψ_1; if that value exceeds α, ψ_1^* is rejected, i.e., ψ_1 is taken as ψ_0, and one returns to **M2** to generate a sample of size N. In this procedure the sample points relating to $\alpha = 1$ will mostly relate to the high part of the kernel (and therefore the density) which is where most of the points in a random sample on the density $p(x)$ would be expected. Those points in the sample relating to $\alpha < 1$ occur with lower probability and relate to the "tails" of $p(x)$.

If the dynamic case is considered, the procedure is the same as that described above except in **M2** the draws would be from $q(\psi_J^*|\psi_{J-1})$ in (7.7.33), and α

would just be

$$\alpha = \min[\frac{f(\psi_1^*)}{f(\psi_0)}, 1] \tag{7.7.35}$$

because $q(\psi_J^*|\psi_{J-1}) = q(\psi_{J-1}|\psi_J^*)$, $J = 1, ..., N$.

In the Metropolis–Hastings sampling procedure there is typically a burn-in where a certain number of sample points are discarded before the sample is viewed as coming from $p(\psi)$. This is further discussed below. Note that in both the static and dynamic case the sample that is generated is not a random sample because each accepted sample point is, in part, dependent upon its earlier values. Thus, the sample points are autocorrelated.

The Gibbs Sampler

Suppose there is a joint distribution, say $f(\psi_1, ..., \psi_k)$, and we want to obtain the marginal densities, say $f_i(\psi_i)$, $i = 1, ..., k$. Again, suppose that these marginal densities cannot be determined by integrating the joint distribution due to complications. Another way to obtain estimates of these marginal densities is with the Gibbs sampling technique.

For ease of presentation, first consider a bivariate joint density of the parameters λ and ϕ, say $g(\lambda, \phi)$. Using evident notation, this joint density can be factored into the marginals and conditionals as

$$\begin{aligned} g(\lambda, \phi) &= g_1(\lambda) g_2(\phi|\lambda) \\ &= g_3(\phi) g_4(\lambda|\phi). \end{aligned} \tag{7.7.36}$$

Then, the Gibbs sampling procedure is as follows:

G1. First select an initial value of λ, say λ_0.

G2. Given this initial value of λ, randomly select a value of ϕ, say ϕ_0, from $g_2(\phi|\lambda = \lambda_0)$.

G3. Using the value ϕ_0, randomly select a value of λ, say λ_1, from $g_4(\lambda|\phi = \phi_0)$.

G4. Using λ_1, randomly select a value of ϕ, say ϕ_1, from $g_2(\phi|\lambda = \lambda_1)$.

G5. Continue this process to obtain the sample (λ_j, ϕ_j), $j = 1, ..., N$.

Let F_j be the cumulative distribution function (CDF) for the sample pair (λ_j, ϕ_j), $j = 1, ..., N$. Let G be the CDF of λ and ϕ corresponding to (7.7.36). Then, it can be shown that as $N \to \infty$, F_N converges to an equilibrium CDF, say F, which is **independent** of the initial values λ_0 and ϕ_0. In addition, $F = G$; see, e.g., Gelfand and Smith (1990). Thus, the sample constructed from the conditional distributions leads to a sample which can be viewed as being drawn from the joint distribution. This procedure is generalized below.

On a formal level, note that the convergence result relates to the CDF and not the density. As described in earlier chapters, the reason for this is that for continuous variables there are an infinite number of densities corresponding to a given CDF. As a review, let Z be a normal variable $Z \sim N(\mu, \sigma^2)$, and let $n(z)$ be its density. Consider now another density, say $n_1(z)$, which is identical to $n(z)$ except at the point 1. At that point, $n_1(1) = n(1) + 0.5$. Since $\Pr(Z = 1) = 0$, and since a CDF relates to probability statements, these two densities have the same CDF. Clearly, there are an infinite number of such "discontinuous" densities that have the same CDF as $N(\mu, \sigma^2)$. Of course, in practice one would assume the density is $n(z)$, and not one of the "discontinuous" densities.

Burn-In Samples and Autocorrelation

In practice, a sample on λ and ϕ, say of size S, can be obtained by generating a sample of size $S_* + S$ and then discarding the first "burn-in" sample points S_* in order to "eliminate" the effect of the initial values (λ_0, ϕ_0). However, because the sample point (λ_j, ϕ_j) depends on its earlier value $(\lambda_{j-1}, \phi_{j-1})$, there is autocorrelation, and so the sample produced by the Gibbs procedure is not a random sample. Call these Type 1 samples: the effect of the initial condition has been eliminated but there is still autocorrelation. This autocorrelation can be "reduced", after the first S_* burn-in points, by only taking every other nth point in the sample where n is relatively large. In this case if the obtained sample is of size Q the total number of points generated would be $S_* + nQ$. Call these Type 2 samples. Note that in both Type 1 and Type 2 samples there should be correlation between λ_j and ϕ_j, $cov(\lambda_j, \phi_j) \neq 0$.

Given a Type 1 sample of size S beyond the burn-in point S_*, one can estimate various properties of the marginals. For example, for a sample of size S beyond the burn-in points, (λ_j, ϕ_j), $j = 1, ..., S$, let $\lambda_{(S)} = (\lambda_1, ..., \lambda_S)'$ and $\phi_{(S)} = (\phi_1, ..., \phi_S)'$. Let e_S be the $S \times 1$ vector of unit elements. Then, the means of λ and ϕ can be estimated as

$$\hat{\mu}_\lambda = S^{-1} \sum_{j=1}^{S} \lambda_j = S^{-1} e_S' \lambda_{(S)}, \tag{7.7.37}$$
$$\hat{\mu}_\phi = S^{-1} \sum_{j=1}^{S} \phi_j = S^{-1} e_S' \phi_{(S)}.$$

Note that the marginals can also be described in terms of histograms, which can in turn be used to make probability statements about λ or ϕ.

Consider now the end point of the burn in sample. Suppose S_* is large enough to eliminate the effect of the initial values. Then, the sample points beyond S_* should all come from the same given distribution. One way to check for this is by comparing sample moments in different subsamples of S; see, e.g.,

Geweke (1992). As an example, suppose we break S into three segments, say $S = S_1 + S_2 + S_3$, where S_1 and S_3 each contain 25% of the sample, and S_2 contains the remaining 50%. Assume that this 50% separation between the S_1 and S_3 is large enough so that the sample points in S_1 are independent of those in S_3. Using the notation corresponding to (7.7.37), let

$$\hat{\mu}_1 = \sum_{j=1}^{S_1} \lambda_j / S_1 = S_1^{-1} e'_{S_1} \lambda_{(S_1)}, \tag{7.7.38}$$

$$\hat{\mu}_3 = \sum_{j=S_1+S_2+1}^{S_1+S_2+S_3} \lambda_j / S_3 = S_3^{-1} e'_{S_3} \lambda_{(S_3)},$$

$$\lambda_{(S_3)} = (\lambda_{S_1+S_2+1}, ..., \lambda_{S_1+S_2+S_3})'.$$

Then, $\hat{\mu}_1$ and $\hat{\mu}_3$ should be "close", and one could test for this to see if S_* is "big enough." A similar comparison of averages relating to ϕ should also be considered.

Let $\hat{\sigma}_{\hat{\mu}_1}$ and $\hat{\sigma}_{\hat{\mu}_3}$ be the estimated standard deviations of $\hat{\mu}_1$ and $\hat{\mu}_3$. These estimators are described below. At this point, one would reject the hypothesis that S_* is "big enough" if

$$\left| \frac{\hat{\mu}_1 - \hat{\mu}_3}{\hat{\sigma}_{\hat{\mu}_1} + \hat{\sigma}_{\hat{\mu}_3}} \right| > 1.96. \tag{7.7.39}$$

This is "user friendly" but it is not efficient because a joint test should be considered which accounts for the nonzero covariance between λ_j and ϕ_j.

Consider now the estimators $\hat{\sigma}_{\hat{\mu}_1}$ and $\hat{\sigma}_{\hat{\mu}_3}$. Because the Gibbs sample contains autocorrelation, and the exact specification of that autocorrelation is not known, $\sigma_{\hat{\mu}_1}$ and $\sigma_{\hat{\mu}_3}$ cannot be estimated in the usual way. Instead, $\hat{\sigma}_{\hat{\mu}_1}$ and $\hat{\sigma}_{\hat{\mu}_3}$ should be estimated as the square root of their corresponding estimated variances by procedures which are robust to unknown patterns of autocorrelations. A more complete discussion of such robust procedures is given in Chapter 9. At this point we illustrate one such procedure.

Consider first the estimation of $\sigma^2_{\hat{\mu}_1}$. Using evident notation, the first line in (7.7.38) implies

$$\sigma^2_{\hat{\mu}_1} = S_1^{-2} e'_{S_1} VC_{\lambda_{(S_1)}} e_{S_1}. \tag{7.7.40}$$

Let the (i, j)th element of $VC_{\lambda_{(S_1)}}$ be $\sigma_{i,j}$. Then

$$\sigma^2_{\hat{\mu}_1} = S_1^{-2} \sum_{i=1}^{S_1} \sum_{j=1}^{S_1} \sigma_{i,j}. \tag{7.7.41}$$

In a Gibbs sample one would assume that the correlation between λ_i and λ_j decreases as the distance $d_{ij} = |i - j|$ between them increases. In the limit that correlation should be zero.

Let

$$(\lambda - \hat{\mu}_1)'_{S_1} = [(\lambda_1 - \hat{\mu}_1), (\lambda_2 - \hat{\mu}_1), ..., (\lambda_{S_1} - \hat{\mu}_1)] \tag{7.7.42}$$

and note that $(\lambda - \hat{\mu}_1)'_{S_1}$ is observed since $\lambda_1, ..., \lambda_{S_1}$ are the observed generated sample of values corresponding to λ. Then, one robust estimator of $\sigma^2_{\hat{\mu}_1}$ would be of the form

$$\begin{aligned}\sigma^2_{\hat{\mu}_1} &= S_1^{-2} \sum_{i=1}^{S_1} \sum_{j=1}^{S_1} (\lambda_i - \hat{\mu}_1)(\lambda_j - \hat{\mu}_1)\, k[d_{ij}, G_{S_1}] \\ &= S_1^{-2} (\lambda - \hat{\mu}_1)'_{S_1} K\, (\lambda - \hat{\mu}_1)_{S_1}\end{aligned} \tag{7.7.43}$$

where K is the $S_1 \times S_1$ matrix whose (i, j)th element is $k[d_{ij}, G_{S_1}]$. The function $k(\cdot)$ is called a kernel function, and its values are taken to decrease as the distance d_{ij} increases, and beyond a certain point, $d_{ij} > G_{S_1} + 1$, are taken to be zero. There are a number of such kernel functions, some of which are described in Chapter 9. The cut-off G_{S_1} is sometimes taken as the nearest integer to S_1^{θ}, $\theta < 1/3$, so that it will satisfy a limiting theoretical condition relating to such robust estimators, namely

$$\frac{G_{S_1}}{S_1^{1/3}} \to 0, \text{ as } S_1 \to \infty \text{ and } G_{S_1} \to \infty. \tag{7.7.44}$$

One widely referenced procedure was suggested by Newey and West (1987). To illustrate their procedure, suppose $S_1 = 125$, and take $S_1^{1/4} \simeq 3.34$ so that the nearest integer is 3.0. The kernel function would be taken as $k[d_{ij}, G_{S_1}]$

$$\begin{aligned}k[d_{ij}, 3] &= 1 - \frac{|i - j|}{3 + 1}, \\ k[d_{ij}, 3] &= 0 \text{ if } |i - j| > 4.\end{aligned} \tag{7.7.45}$$

For example, for $i = 1$,

$$\begin{aligned}k[d_{11}, 3] &= 1, \\ k[d_{12}, 3] &= 1 - 1/4 = 3/4, \\ k[d_{13}, 3] &= 1 - 2/4 = 2/4, \\ k[d_{14}, 3] &= 1 - 3/4 = 1/4, \\ k[d_{1j}, 3] &= 0 \text{ for all } j > 4.\end{aligned} \tag{7.7.46}$$

7.8 THE SPATIAL LAG MODEL AND GIBBS SAMPLING

Consider the Bayesian model

$$y = X\beta + \rho_1 Wy + \varepsilon, \ |\rho_1| < 1 \tag{7.8.1}$$

where y is the $N \times 1$ dependent vector, X is an $N \times k$ exogenous regressor matrix, W is a constant row normalized weighting matrix, and ε is an $N \times 1$ innovations vector which is normally distributed with mean and VC matrix $(0, \sigma^2 I_N)$. The assumption that W is row normalized implies that $(I_N - aW)$ is nonsingular for all $|a| < 1$. Let $M_{\rho_1} = (I_N - \rho_1 W)^{-1}$. Conditional on β, ρ_1, and σ^2, our specifications imply that y is normally distributed, $y \sim N(M_{\rho_1} X\beta, \sigma^2 M_{\rho_1} M'_{\rho_1})$.

The parameters of the model are β, ρ_1, and σ^2, and we are assuming independence of the joint prior of β, ρ_1, and σ, that is,

$$F(\beta, \rho_1, \sigma) = f_1(\beta) f_2(\rho_1) f_3(\sigma). \tag{7.8.2}$$

The value of ρ_1 is restricted to the open interval $(-1, 1)$ so that the model is complete in the sense that it can be solved for y in terms of X and ε. The value of σ is restricted to the open interval $(0, \infty)$. In the interval $(-1, 1)$ assume a uniform prior of ρ_1, and assume that the prior for σ is $f_3(\sigma) \propto 1/\sigma$. The prior for β is the uniform $f_1(\beta) \propto$ constant.

The posterior for the model in (7.8.1) is

$$\begin{aligned} &P(\beta, \rho_1, \sigma | data) \\ &\propto \frac{|I_N - \rho_1 W|}{\sigma^{N+1}} * \\ &\exp\left[-\frac{1}{2\sigma^2}\left[(y - M_{\rho_1} X\beta)'(I_N - \rho_1 W')(I_N - \rho_1 W)(y - M_{\rho_1} X\beta)\right]\right]. \end{aligned} \tag{7.8.3}$$

The posterior in (7.8.3) is clearly not a standard form, and the marginal posteriors of β, ρ_1, and σ are not "obvious." One way to describe these marginal posteriors is by using the Gibbs sampling procedure, along with the Metropolis sampling algorithm; see Section 7.7.

Specifically, first consider the posterior of β conditional on ρ_1 and σ. Since $(y - M_{\rho_1} X\beta) = M_{\rho_1}(M_{\rho_1}^{-1} y - X\beta)$, the conditional posterior of β reduces to

$$\begin{aligned} &P(\beta | \rho_1, \sigma, data) \\ &\propto \exp\left[-\frac{1}{2\sigma^2}\left[(M_{\rho_1}^{-1} y - X\beta)'(M_{\rho_1}^{-1} y - X\beta)\right]\right] \\ &\propto \exp\left[-\frac{1}{2\sigma^2}\left[(M_{\rho_1}^{-1} y - X\hat{\beta}_{\rho_1} + X\hat{\beta}_{\rho_1} - X\beta)' * \right.\right. \end{aligned} \tag{7.8.4}$$

$$(M_{\rho_1}^{-1}y - X\hat{\beta}_{\rho_1} + X\hat{\beta}_{\rho_1} - X\beta)\Big]\Big]$$

$$\propto \exp\left[-\frac{1}{2\sigma^2}\left[(\hat{\varepsilon}_{\rho_1} + X(\hat{\beta}_{\rho_1} - \beta))'(\hat{\varepsilon}_{\rho_1} + X(\hat{\beta}_{\rho_1} - \beta))\right]\right]$$

where $\hat{\beta}_{\rho_1} = (X'X)^{-1}X'M_{\rho_1}^{-1}y = (X'X)^{-1}X'(I_N - \rho_1 W)y$, $\hat{\varepsilon}_{\rho_1} = M_{\rho_1}^{-1}y - X\hat{\beta}_{\rho_1}$, and all terms not involving β are absorbed by the proportionality factor. Note that

$$\begin{aligned}(\hat{\beta}_{\rho_1} - \beta)'X'\hat{\varepsilon}_{\rho_1} &= (\hat{\beta}_{\rho_1} - \beta)'X'[M_{\rho_1}^{-1}y - X\hat{\beta}_{\rho_1}] \\ &= (\hat{\beta}_{\rho_1} - \beta)'X'[M_{\rho_1}^{-1}y - X(X'X)^{-1}X'M_{\rho_1}^{-1}y] \\ &= (\hat{\beta}_{\rho_1} - \beta)'[X'M_{\rho_1}^{-1}y - X'M_{\rho_1}^{-1}y] \\ &= 0.\end{aligned}$$

Therefore the posterior of β conditional on ρ_1 and σ is

$$\begin{aligned}P(\beta|\rho_1, \sigma, data) &\propto \exp\left[-\frac{1}{2\sigma^2}\left[(X(\hat{\beta}_{\rho_1} - \beta))'(X(\hat{\beta}_{\rho_1} - \beta))\right]\right] \\ &\propto \exp\left[-\frac{1}{2\sigma^2}\left[(\beta - \hat{\beta}_{\rho_1})'X'X(\beta - \hat{\beta}_{\rho_1})\right]\right],\end{aligned} \tag{7.8.5}$$

or the conditional in (7.8.4) is the multivariate normal, i.e.,

$$P(\beta|\rho_1, \sigma, data) = N(\hat{\beta}_{\rho_1}, \sigma^2(X'X)^{-1}) \tag{7.8.6}$$

Recall that the marginal and the conditional distributions of a multivariate normal are themselves normal; their means and VC matrices were given in Section 4.2. These results will be needed below.

Now consider the posterior of σ conditional on β and ρ_1. From (7.8.3)–(7.8.5),

$$\begin{aligned}&P(\sigma|\beta, \rho_1, data) \\ &\propto \frac{1}{\sigma^{N+1}}\exp\left[-\frac{1}{2\sigma^2}\left[(\hat{\varepsilon}_{\rho_1} + X(\hat{\beta}_{\rho_1} - \beta))'(\hat{\varepsilon}_{\rho_1} + X(\hat{\beta}_{\rho_1} - \beta))\right]\right] \\ &\propto \frac{1}{\sigma^{N+1}}\exp\left[-\frac{1}{2\sigma^2}\left[\hat{\varepsilon}_{\rho_1}'\hat{\varepsilon}_{\rho_1} + (\hat{\beta}_{\rho_1} - \beta)'X'X(\hat{\beta}_{\rho_1} - \beta)\right]\right] \\ &\propto \frac{1}{\sigma^{N+1}}\exp[-\frac{1}{2\sigma^2}A]\end{aligned} \tag{7.8.7}$$

where

$$A = \left[\hat{\varepsilon}_{\rho_1}'\hat{\varepsilon}_{\rho_1} + (\hat{\beta}_{\rho_1} - \beta)'X'X(\hat{\beta}_{\rho_1} - \beta)\right].$$

The distribution in (7.8.7) is an inverted gamma – again, see Zellner (1971, p. 371).

Finally, consider the posterior distribution of ρ_1 conditional on β and σ. From (7.8.3) and (7.8.4), this distribution is

$$\begin{aligned} &P(\rho_1|\beta,\sigma,data) \\ &\propto |I_N-\rho_1 W| \exp\left[-\frac{1}{2\sigma^2}\left[(\hat{\varepsilon}_{\rho_1}+X(\hat{\beta}_{\rho_1}-\beta))'(\hat{\varepsilon}_{\rho_1}+X(\hat{\beta}_{\rho_1}-\beta))\right]\right] \\ &\propto |I_N-\rho_1 W| \exp\left[-\frac{1}{2\sigma^2}\left[\hat{\varepsilon}'_{\rho_1}\hat{\varepsilon}_{\rho_1}+(\hat{\beta}_{\rho_1}-\beta)'X'X(\hat{\beta}_{\rho_1}-\beta)\right]\right]. \end{aligned} \tag{7.8.8}$$

Recall that both $\hat{\varepsilon}_{\rho_1}$ and $\hat{\beta}_{\rho_1}$ depend on ρ_1 and so these terms in the exponent in (7.8.8) cannot be ignored. Clearly, the conditional posterior in (7.8.8) is not in a standard form and so a sampling procedure should be useful.

Applying the Gibbs and Metropolis Sampling Procedures

For purposes of illustration, denote the conditional distributions relating to β and σ as

$$\begin{bmatrix} f_\beta(\beta|\sigma,\rho_1,data) \\ f_\sigma(\sigma|\beta,\rho_1,data) \end{bmatrix}. \tag{7.8.9}$$

Recall from (7.8.6) that the posterior of β conditional on ρ_1 and σ is normal. Also, the posterior of σ conditional on β and ρ_1 is an inverted gamma as given in (7.8.7).

To start the procedure, let β^0, σ^0, and ρ_1^0 be the initial values of β, σ and ρ_1, respectively. Let $q(\rho_1)$ be the approximating distribution for ρ_1 as in (7.7.31). Then the sampling procedure can be summarized as follows:

For $j=0, ..., S$, (7.8.10)

1. Draw from $f_\beta(\beta|\sigma^j,\rho_1^j,data)$ to get β^{j+1}.
2. Draw from $f_\sigma(\sigma|\beta^{j+1},\rho_1^j,data)$ to get σ^{j+1}.
3. Use the Metropolis sampling procedures to get ρ_1^{j+1}.
4. To do this, get the next potential value of ρ_1, say $\rho^*_{1_{j+1}}$ from $q(\rho_1)$

   and determine α as $\alpha=\min[\frac{f(\rho^*_{1_{j+1}})}{f(\rho_{1_j})}, 1]$ where the kernel is

   $f(\rho_1)=|I_N-\rho_1 W|*$

   $\exp[-\frac{1}{2\sigma^2_{j+1}}\left[\hat{\varepsilon}'_{\rho_1}\hat{\varepsilon}_{\rho_1}+(\hat{\beta}_{\rho_1}-\beta_{j+1})'X'X(\hat{\beta}_{\rho_1}-\beta_{j+1})\right].$

TABLE 7.8.1 Comparison of spatial lag models: Bayesian sampling procedure vs. maximum likelihood

	Bayesian mean $\hat{\beta}$	ML $\hat{\beta}$
Intercept	−0.0094	−0.0093
	(−0.0980)	(−0.1015)
CRIME	−0.0062	−0.0062
	(−6.089)	(−6.353)
AGE	−0.0009	−0.0009
	(−2.907)	(−2.831)
ROOMS	0.1776	0.1775
	(14.801)	(14.212)
WPRICE	0.6619	0.6620
	(25.280)	(25.190)
σ	0.1680	0.1676

Dependent variable: Log-price

5. If $\alpha > 1$, keep $\rho^*_{1_{j+1}}$ and relabel it as $\rho_{1_{j+1}}$ then go to step 1.
6. If $\alpha < 1$ take a random draw from the uniform distribution on (0, 1).
7. If that draw is less than α, keep $\rho^*_{1_{j+1}}$, relabel it as $\rho_{1_{j+1}}$, and go to step 1.
8. If that draw is greater than α, take $\rho_{1_{j+1}} = \rho_{1_j}$ and go back to step 1.

Illustration 7.8.1: A Bayesian model for a house price

In this example we consider again the Boston data and formulate a model that relates the median house price to the level of crime, the age of the construction, and the number of rooms. We will compare the Bayesian sampling procedure to the ML approach and show that the two methodologies produce very similar estimates. As for the Bayesian sampling procedure, we follow the steps described above. We run 25,000 samples and discard the first 5000. Table 7.8.1 summarizes the results obtained in comparison with the maximum likelihood method.

The numbers in parenthesis are the t values. For the Bayesian model, these statistics are calculated as the ratio of the average values of β (obtained from the Monte Carlo draws) and the standard deviation of β (also obtained from the Monte Carlo draws). From the table, we can observe that the Bayesian sampling procedure produces results that are almost identical to those obtained by the maximum likelihood method.

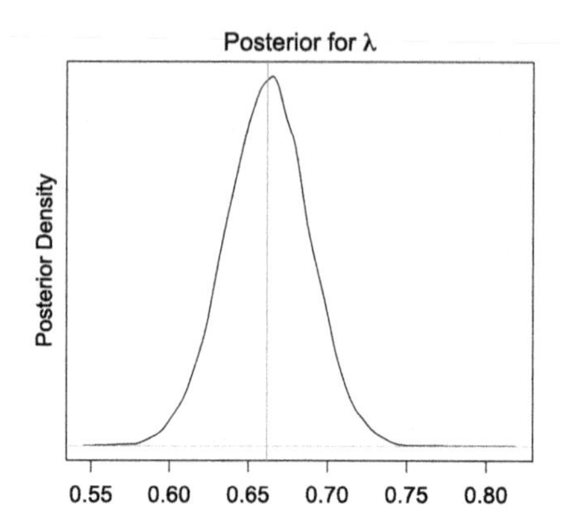

FIGURE 7.8.1 Kernel density estimates of the posterior distribution for ρ_1

Additionally, in Fig. 7.8.1 we report the kernel density estimates of the posterior distribution for ρ_1.

7.9 BAYESIAN POSTERIOR ODDS AND MODEL SELECTION

Suppose we are interested in a certain variable, say y_t, and we have two hypotheses, H_0 and H_1, concerning its generation. For example, if we are interested in consumer expenditures, H_0 might be Friedman's permanent income hypothesis, and H_1 might be the hypothesis that consumer expenditures are related to current income. In this case H_0 and H_1 relate to different models. In other cases H_0 and H_1 might relate to the same model but impose different parameter values. As an example, H_0 might be nested in H_1 in the sense that if a certain parameter or set of parameters are zero, H_1 reduces to H_0.

Let $y' = (y_1, ..., y_T)$ be the data and denote the distribution of y conditional on H_0 and on H_1 as $f_0(y|H_0, data)$ and $f_1(y|H_1, data)$, respectively. Let

$$\begin{aligned} w &= 0 \text{ if } H_0 \text{ is true,} \\ w &= 1 \text{ if } H_1 \text{ is true.} \end{aligned} \tag{7.9.1}$$

Suppose we have our prior probabilities as

$$\begin{aligned} \Pr(w = 0) &= p_0, \\ \Pr(w = 1) &= p_1. \end{aligned} \tag{7.9.2}$$

Then our prior odds ratio in favor of H_0 is p_0/p_1, e.g., if $p_0/p_1 = 2$ then based on priors, and hence before looking at the data, we feel that H_0 is twice as likely to be true.

Using evident notation, the joint distribution of w and y can be expressed as

$$h(y, w|data) = f_w(w|data) f_{y|w}(y|w, data) \quad (7.9.3)$$
$$= f_y(y|data) f_{w|y}(w|y, data)$$

where $f_{w|y}(w|y, data)$ is the posterior of w given y and the data.

Note that if H_0 is given then $w = 0$; if H_1 is given then $w = 1$. Noting this, along with (7.9.1)–(7.9.3), once the data is given, we can evaluate these posterior probabilities as

$$\Pr(w = 0|y, data) = \frac{1}{f_y(y|data)} p_0 f_{y|w}(y|H_0, data), \quad (7.9.4)$$
$$\Pr(w = 1|y, data) = \frac{1}{f_y(y|data)} p_1 f_{y|w}(y|H_1, data)$$

where $f_{y|w}(y|H_0, data)$ and $f_{y|w}(y|H_1, data)$ are likelihood functions. Evaluating (7.9.4) we determine the posterior odds in favor of H_0 as the ratio of the two probabilities in (7.9.4)

$$odds(H_0) = \frac{p_0}{p_1} \frac{f_{y|w}(y|H_0, data)}{f_{y|w}(y|H_1, data)}, \quad (7.9.5)$$

so that the posterior odds ratio in favor of H_0 is the product of the prior odds and the ratio of the likelihoods. As an illustration, in the above example the prior odds were 2. Suppose the ratio of the likelihoods turn out to be 0.7. In this case we would still accept H_0 even though the data are more consistent with H_1.

A more complete analysis would involve loss functions. Let $L(H_0|H_1)$ be the loss in a return of some sort that is due to a suboptimal action that is taken which is based on the assumption that H_0 is true when in fact H_1 is true. This loss could be the difference between the return under the optimal action taken under H_1 and the action taken under H_0. In a similar light, we define $L(H_1|H_0)$. We also note that $L(H_0|H_0) = 0$ and $L(H_1|H_1) = 0$.

Given this, a rational way to select one hypothesis over the other is to minimize the expected loss involved in each selection. Let

$$p_0 = P(w = 0|y, data), \quad (7.9.6)$$
$$p_1 = P(w = 1|y, data)$$

where these posterior probabilities are given in (7.9.4). Then, the expected loss associated with the selection of H_0 can be viewed as

$$E_w[L(H_0|w, data)] \quad (7.9.7)$$
$$= L(H_0|w = 0, data) * p_0 + L(H_0|w = 1, data) * p_1$$

$$= L(H_0|w = 1, data) * p_1$$

since $L(H_0|w = 0, data) = L(H_0|H_0) = 0$. Similarly, the expected loss associated with the selection of H_1 is

$$E_w[L(H_1|w, data)] = L(H_1|w = 0, data) * p_0. \quad (7.9.8)$$

Clearly, H_0 should be selected if $E_w[L(H_0|w = 1, data)]p_1 < E_w[L(H_1|w = 0, data)]p_0$.

7.10 PROBLEMS WITH THE BAYESIAN APPROACH

In Chapter 6 we discussed issues relating to models which have additional endogenous variables. In an instrumental variable framework the estimation of such models is reasonably straightforward. The reason is that the researcher only has to know a subset of exogenous variables that appear in that larger system. The researcher does not even have to know the way those variables appear in that larger system! However, in a Bayesian framework "solutions" are not so straightforward. Actually, the problems are similar to those of the maximum likelihood procedure. For example, consider again the model in Chapter 6, namely

$$y = X_1\beta_1 + \rho_1 W_1 y + Y\beta_2 + u, \quad (7.10.1)$$
$$u = \rho_2 W_1 u + \varepsilon, \; |\rho_i| < 1, i = 1, 2$$

where Y is an $N \times q$ matrix of observations on endogenous variables, etc. Recall that the likelihood is a component of the posterior. Since the matrix Y contains endogenous variables, in order to obtain the posterior distribution of the parameters, one must specify the joint distribution of the $q + 1$ endogenous variables in (7.10.1), namely (y, Y). Typically, this joint distribution will not be known because, among other things, all the equations of the larger system will not be known. Therefore, unless very strong and unusual conditions are imposed, the Bayesian approach cannot be implemented.

SUGGESTED PROBLEMS

1. Consider the model

$$y_i = a + bx_i^2 + \varepsilon_i,\ i = 1, ..., N$$
$$\varepsilon_i \text{ are i.i.d. } N(0, \sigma^2).$$

Assume σ^2 is known to be 3, and the prior for $c' = (a, b)$ is $p(c) \propto const.$

(a) Obtain the posterior for c, and give an interpretation.

(b) Suppose σ^2 is not known and the joint prior for c and σ is $p(c, \sigma) \propto 1/\sigma$. Obtain the conditional posterior of c given σ, and the posterior of σ.

2. Consider the model

$$y_i = a + b\exp(\lambda x_i) + \varepsilon_i,\ i = 1, ..., N$$
$$\varepsilon_i \text{ are i.i.d. } N(0, \sigma^2).$$

(a) Let $c' = (a, b)$. Obtain the posterior of c given that σ and λ are known.

(b) Now assume that λ and σ are not known, and the joint prior for $\gamma' = (c, \sigma, \lambda)$ is $p(\gamma) \propto 1/\sigma$. Obtain the joint posterior for (c, λ) conditional only on the data.

3. Using evident notation, consider the model

$$y = X\beta + \varepsilon,$$
$$\varepsilon = \rho(I_N + W)u$$

where u is $N(0, I_N)$.

(a) Explain why the restriction $\sigma^2 = 1$ is not really restrictive in this model.

(b) Assuming the prior $p(\beta, \rho) \propto const$, obtain the posterior of (β, ρ).

(c) Obtain the posterior for ρ.

4. Consider the quadratic $X'(Q'Q)X + 8FX$ where Q and F do not involve X. Complete the quadratic.

5. Consider the integral

$$G = \int_0^{25} g(x)dx,$$
$$g(x) = \ln(50 + x^{1/2}).$$

Suggest a sampling method for estimating this integral.

Chapter 8

Pretest and Sample Selection Issues in Spatial Analysis

8.1 INTRODUCTORY COMMENTS[1]

Pretest procedures abound in applied economic work. These procedures entail statistical problems which are typically ignored. An illustration of one such procedure is the following. Assume that a researcher estimates a model but the empirical results are not consistent with prior expectations. In many cases that researcher would formulate a modified version of the model which will then be estimated as if it had been considered from the start. These modified versions often entail dropping certain variables, adding others, taking logs of some of the variables, changing the sample size, etc. These reformulations of the model typically continue until the empirical results obtained are consistent with prior beliefs, i.e., all the coefficients have the expected signs, etc. The results are then presented as if the final model was the only model that was considered. Note that each model involved in the sequence leading to the final model has been considered because the previous model has been found (tested) to be lacking in some way. Obviously, there is an element of circular reasoning involved in such a procedure. Because of this, in the sections below we show that such procedures entail statistical "complications." It will also be clear that these complications will arise in virtually all cases in which a model is specified, or considered on the basis of earlier empirical calculations based on the same data which are used to estimate the model.

8.2 A PRELIMINARY RESULT

Let Z be a **discrete** random variable with density

$$f(z_i) = p_i, \ i = 1, ..., N, \tag{8.2.1}$$

1. There is a large literature relating to pretest issues; see, e.g., Wallace (1977), Judge and Bock (1978), Judge and Yancey (1986), Baltagi et al. (2008), Piras and Prucha (2014), and the references cited therein. For reviews see Judge et al. (1985), Anselin (1988), and Greene (2003). Also, portions of this chapter are an elaboration and extension of results given in Kelejian (2016).

Spatial Econometrics. http://dx.doi.org/10.1016/B978-0-12-813387-3.00008-1

$$p_i \geq 0, \ \sum_{i=1}^{N} p_i = 1.$$

Let X be a continuous random variable with density $f(x)$. Let $h(X)$ be a function of X such that

$$E(h(X)) = \int_{-\infty}^{\infty} h(x) f(x) dx = \alpha \tag{8.2.2}$$

where α is a finite constant. Then

$$E[Zh(X)] = \sum_{i=1}^{N} z_i p_i E[h(X)|Z = z_i] \tag{8.2.3}$$

The interpretation of (8.2.3) is straightforward. The expected value of the product of a continuous random variable, in this case $h(X)$, with a discrete variable is a weighted sum of the conditional expectations. The weights are the products of the values the discrete variable takes on, and the probabilities for taking on those values.

The proof of (8.2.3) is based on iterated expectations. Specifically,

$$\begin{aligned} E[Zh(X)] &= E\ \{E[Z\, h(X)|Z]\ \} \\ &= E\ \{Z\,[E(h(X)|Z]\} \\ &= \sum_{i=1}^{N} z_i p_i E[h(X)|Z = z_i]. \end{aligned} \tag{8.2.4}$$

In going from the first line of (8.2.4) to the second, $E[Zh(X)|Z] = ZE[h(X)|Z]$ since Z is constant with respect to the conditional distribution of X given Z.

8.3 ILLUSTRATIONS

Biases

Suppose the following model is **a** true model:

$$(M1) \quad y = X_1 \beta_1 + \varepsilon \tag{8.3.1}$$

where X_1 is an $N \times k$ exogenous regressor matrix with full column rank, and $\varepsilon \sim N(0, \sigma^2 I_N)$. Suppose now that the model the researcher considers is $(M2)$ where

$$(M2) \quad y = X_1 \beta_1 + X_2 \beta_2 + \varepsilon \tag{8.3.2}$$

where X_2 is an $N \times r$ exogenous regressor matrix. The model $(M2)$ would be considered if the researcher does not known whether or not X_2 is important in the determination of y, i.e., the researcher does not know whether or not $\beta_2 = 0$. Note, however, that **both** $(M1)$ and $(M2)$ are true models. Clearly, specifications of $(M2)$ are true because β_2 is specified to be a vector of constants, and it is indeed a vector of constants, namely zeroes. The difference between $(M1)$ and $(M2)$ is that $(M1)$ contains more information, e.g., the information that $\beta_2 = 0$. It is for this reason that we did **not** say that $M1$ is **the** true model – actually, there are clearly many true models!

Assume that $rank(X_1, X_2) = k + r$. The following pretest procedure might be considered by the researcher:

(1) Estimate $(M2)$ and test the hypothesis $H_0 : \beta_2 = 0$ against $H_1 : \beta_2 \neq 0$ at the 5% level. Suppose this testing procedure is based on the F statistic, $F_{k_2, n-k_1-k_2}$. In this setup the researcher does not question the importance of X_1.

(2) If H_0 is accepted, then estimate β_1 via $(M1)$. The reason for doing this is, typically, to reduce variances.

(3) On the other hand, if H_0 is rejected then take the estimate of β_1 as obtained from $(M2)$.

Let $\hat{\beta}_{1,1}$ be the estimator of β_1 from $(M1)$, and let $\hat{\beta}_{1,2}$ be the estimator of β_1 from $(M2)$. Let

$$\lambda = \begin{cases} 1 & \text{if } H_0 \text{ is accepted,} \\ 0 & \text{if } H_0 \text{ is rejected.} \end{cases} \tag{8.3.3}$$

Since both $(M1)$ and $(M2)$ are true models, under typical specifications,

$$E(\hat{\beta}_{1,1}) = E(\hat{\beta}_{1,2}) = \beta. \tag{8.3.4}$$

Also note that since our test of H_0 is at the 5% level, and that $(M2)$ is a true model

$$\begin{aligned} \Pr(\lambda = 1) &= 0.95, \\ \Pr(\lambda = 0) &= 0.05. \end{aligned} \tag{8.3.5}$$

Let $\tilde{\beta}_1$ be the estimator of β_1 that results from this procedure. Then,

$$\begin{aligned} \tilde{\beta}_1 &= \lambda \hat{\beta}_{1,1} + (1 - \lambda)\hat{\beta}_{1,2} \\ &= \hat{\beta}_{1,2} + \lambda(\hat{\beta}_{1,1} - \hat{\beta}_{1,2}). \end{aligned} \tag{8.3.6}$$

One would think that because the final estimator of β_1 is either $\hat{\beta}_{1,1}$ or $\hat{\beta}_{1,2}$ and both of these estimators are unbiased, that $\tilde{\beta}_1$ is also unbiased. This, however, is not the case. On a somewhat intuitive level, the reason for this is that λ

is an endogenous variable since it depends on the error term ε because of the testing procedure. The estimators $\hat{\beta}_{1,1}$ and $\hat{\beta}_{1,2}$ also depend upon ε. Therefore, λ and $\hat{\beta}_{1,i}, i=1,2$ are not independent and so, in (8.3.6), $E[\lambda(\hat{\beta}_{1,1}-\hat{\beta}_{1,2})] \neq E[\lambda]E(\hat{\beta}_{1,1}-\hat{\beta}_{1,2})=0$. More formally, in light of (8.2.3) and (8.3.6), and recalling that the only two values that λ takes on are 1 and 0,

$$\begin{aligned} E(\tilde{\beta}_1) &= E[\hat{\beta}_{1,2}] + E[\lambda(\hat{\beta}_{1,1}-\hat{\beta}_{1,2})] \\ &= \beta_1 + \Pr(\lambda=1)\ E[\ (\hat{\beta}_{1,1}-\hat{\beta}_{1,2})|\lambda=1] \\ &= \beta_1 + 0.95\ E[\ (\hat{\beta}_{1,1}-\hat{\beta}_{1,2})|F_{k_2,N-k_1-k_2} < F^{0.95}_{k_2,N-k_1-k_2}] \end{aligned} \tag{8.3.7}$$

since, given our assumptions, $\Pr(\lambda=1)=0.95$. Perhaps somewhat surprisingly, although the unconditional mean $E(\hat{\beta}_{1,1}-\hat{\beta}_{1,2})=0$, the conditional mean in (8.3.7) is not zero. Thus, $E(\tilde{\beta}_1) \neq \beta_1$.

A word of caution. The result that $\tilde{\beta}_1$ is biased does **not** imply that, generally, multistep procedures are biased. The value of $\tilde{\beta}_1$ is randomly determined to be either $\hat{\beta}_{1,1}$ or $\hat{\beta}_{1,2}$. That determination is endogenous because λ involves ε via the estimation of $(M2)$. Now consider the 2SLS estimator. In this procedure a predicted value of the endogenous regressor is estimated, and then **always** used to obtain the final estimator. There is no branching point: one does not say if the predicted value of the endogenous regressor is "A" do "B", but if it is "C" do "D."

Another Illustration

The illustration below involves a probability result that may also be useful in other scenarios. It should also reinforce the results given above.

Using evident notation, consider the classical linear regression model

$$\begin{aligned} y_i &= a_0 + a_1 x_{1,i} + a_2 x_{2,i} + \varepsilon_i, \\ \varepsilon_i &\ \text{ is i.i.d. } (0,\sigma^2), i=1,...,N. \end{aligned} \tag{8.3.8}$$

Let $\hat{a}_j,\ j=0,1,2$ be the least squares estimators of the regression parameters in (8.3.8). Note that since (8.3.8) is a classic linear regression model, $E(\hat{a}_j)=a_j,\ j=0,1,2$. For purposes of illustration, suppose the true value of $a_1=0$.

First, consider the scenario in which the researcher believes that a_1 should be positive. If $\hat{a}_1$ turns out to be negative, $\hat{a}_1$ is taken to be zero and, consequently, $x_{1,i}$ is dropped. If $\hat{a}_1>0$, it is accepted as is, and $x_{1,i}$ is maintained. We will focus our attention on the bias involved in the final estimator of a_1.

The case described above is only considered for illustrative purposes. Clearly, the scenario involved is a simplification of what might take place in practice. For example, the researcher might believe that the only reason for

$\hat{a}_1 < 0$ is that $x_{1,i}$ must be reflecting the influence of one (or more) variables that are important, and are omitted from the model. In that case the researcher might begin searching for these "important other" variables to expand the model. In such a case, there would probably be issues concerning whether or not each new variable has an estimated coefficient that is consistent with theory, is statistically significant, etc. As will become evident, such procedures will add to the pretest issues involved.

For our considered case, let

$$\tilde{a}_1 = \delta \hat{a}_1 + (1-\delta)0 \tag{8.3.9}$$

where

$$\delta = \begin{cases} 1 & \text{if } \hat{a}_1 \geq 0, \\ 0 & \text{if } \hat{a}_1 < 0. \end{cases}$$

Since the only values of δ are 0 and 1, it follows from (8.2.3) that

$$\begin{aligned} E(\tilde{a}_1) &= E(\hat{a}_1 | \delta = 1) \Pr(\delta = 1) \\ &= E(\hat{a}_1 | \hat{a}_1 \geq 0) \Pr(\hat{a}_1 \geq 0) \\ &\neq E(\hat{a}_1) = a_1. \end{aligned} \tag{8.3.10}$$

As might be evident, $E(\tilde{a}_1) > a_1 = 0$ since only the positive values of $\hat{a}_1$ are being considered. This can be demonstrated using the following probability result:

Let Z be a random variable whose density is $f(z)$. Then[2]

$$\begin{aligned} E(Z) &= \int_{-\infty}^{\infty} z f(z) dz \\ &= \Pr(Z<0) \int_{-\infty}^{0} \frac{z f(z) dz}{\Pr(Z<0)} + \Pr(Z \geq 0) \int_{0}^{\infty} \frac{z f(z) dz}{\Pr(Z \geq 0)} \\ &= \Pr(Z<0)\ E(Z|Z<0) + \Pr(Z \geq 0)\ E(Z|Z \geq 0). \end{aligned} \tag{8.3.11}$$

Note that the second line of (8.3.10) corresponds, using (8.3.11), to

$$\Pr(Z \geq 0)\, E(Z|Z \geq 0) = E(Z) - \Pr(Z<0)\, E(Z|Z<0). \tag{8.3.12}$$

Finally, note that $\Pr(Z < 0)$ is obviously nonnegative and $E(Z|Z<0) < 0$, and so from (8.3.12)

$$\Pr(Z \geq 0)\, E(Z|Z \geq 0) > E(Z). \tag{8.3.13}$$

2. We are using the following. If $f(z)$ is the unconditional density of Z, the conditional density of Z given that Z is in the region R is

$$\frac{f(z)}{\Pr(Z \in R)}, \quad z \in R.$$

Same Scenario but Different Method – Same Answer

From (8.3.9) we have $\tilde{a}_1 = \delta\hat{a}_1$, where δ is a function of $\hat{a}_1$. Let the density of $\hat{a}_1$ be $g(z)$. Since both δ and $\tilde{a}_1$ are functions of $\hat{a}_1$, and $\delta = 1$ if $\hat{a}_1 \geq 0$, and zero otherwise, we have

$$\begin{aligned} E(\tilde{a}_1) &= E(\delta\hat{a}_1) \\ &= \int_0^\infty zg(z)dz \\ &= \Pr(\hat{a}_1 \geq 0)\int_0^\infty \frac{zg(z)dz}{\Pr(\hat{a}_1 \geq 0)} \\ &= \Pr(\hat{a}_1 \geq 0)E(\hat{a}_1|\hat{a}_1 \geq 0). \end{aligned} \tag{8.3.14}$$

The result in (8.3.14) is the same as that in (8.3.10).

8.4 MEAN SQUARED ERRORS

The results above imply that, in general, a pretest estimator will be biased. Somewhat surprisingly though, in some cases the mean squared error (MSE) of a pretest estimator may be smaller than the MSE of the corresponding non-pretest estimator. In this section we elaborate on a simple illustration of this.[3] Further details relating to mean squared errors are given in Judge et al. (1985, Chapter 3).

Consider the classical linear regression model

$$y = X\beta + Z\gamma + u \tag{8.4.1}$$

where X is $N \times k$, Z is $N \times r$, X and Z are exogenous, $rank(X, Z) = k + r$, $E(u) = 0$, and $E(uu') = \sigma^2 I_N$. Consider the hypothesis $H_0 : \beta = \beta_0$ against $H_1 : \beta \neq \beta_0$. Let

$$\delta = \begin{cases} 1 & \text{if } H_0 \text{ is accepted via an } F \text{ test,} \\ 0 & \text{otherwise.} \end{cases} \tag{8.4.2}$$

Assume that if H_0 is accepted then the estimator of β is taken to be β_0; if H_0 is rejected then the estimator of β is taken as the OLS estimator based on (8.4.1), namely $\hat{\beta}$.

The pretest estimator of β is

$$\tilde{\beta} = \delta\beta_0 + (1 - \delta)\hat{\beta}. \tag{8.4.3}$$

3. The illustration was suggested by Ingmar Prucha.

Subtracting β from both sides of (8.4.3) yields

$$\begin{aligned}\tilde{\beta} - \beta &= \delta\beta_0 - \beta + (1-\delta)(\hat{\beta} - \beta + \beta) \\ &= (1-\delta)(\hat{\beta} - \beta) + \delta(\beta_0 - \beta),\end{aligned} \tag{8.4.4}$$

and so

$$\begin{aligned}(\tilde{\beta} - \beta)'(\tilde{\beta} - \beta) &= (1-\delta)^2(\hat{\beta} - \beta)'(\hat{\beta} - \beta) + \delta^2(\beta_0 - \beta)'(\beta_0 - \beta) \\ &= (1-\delta)(\hat{\beta} - \beta)'(\hat{\beta} - \beta) + \delta(\beta_0 - \beta)'(\beta_0 - \beta)\end{aligned} \tag{8.4.5}$$

since, by (8.4.2), $\delta(1-\delta) = 0$, $\delta^2 = \delta$, and $(1-\delta)^2 = (1-\delta)$ since $\delta = 0$ or 1.

Observe that, since the only two values of δ and $(1-\delta)$ are 0 and 1, it also holds that

$$\delta(\beta_0 - \beta)'(\beta_0 - \beta) \leq (\beta_0 - \beta)'(\beta_0 - \beta), \tag{8.4.6}$$

and so from (8.4.5)

$$\begin{aligned}(\tilde{\beta} - \beta)'(\tilde{\beta} - \beta) &\leq (1-\delta)(\hat{\beta} - \beta)'(\hat{\beta} - \beta) + (\beta_0 - \beta)'(\beta_0 - \beta) \\ &\leq (\hat{\beta} - \beta)'(\hat{\beta} - \beta) + (\beta_0 - \beta)'(\beta_0 - \beta).\end{aligned} \tag{8.4.7}$$

Taking expectations across (8.4.7) gives

$$MSE(\tilde{\beta}) \leq MSE(\hat{\beta}) + (\beta_0 - \beta)'(\beta_0 - \beta). \tag{8.4.8}$$

It follows that if $\beta_0 = \beta$,

$$MSE(\tilde{\beta}) \leq MSE(\hat{\beta}). \tag{8.4.9}$$

The result in (8.4.9) suggests that for small values of $(\beta_0 - \beta)'(\beta_0 - \beta)$, the mean squared error of the pretest estimator $\tilde{\beta}$ will be less than that of the estimator $\hat{\beta}$. Essentially, for values of β_0 close to β, the reduction in the variance of the pretest estimator more than compensates for its bias. Of course, large differences between β_0 and the true value of β would be less favorable to the pretest estimator.

8.5 PRETESTING IN SPATIAL MODELS: LARGE SAMPLE ISSUES

Consider the spatial model

$$(M1) \quad y = X_1\beta_1 + X_2\beta_2 + \rho_1 Wy + u, \; |\lambda| < 1 \tag{8.5.1}$$

where X_1 and X_2 are $N \times k_1$ and $N \times k_2$ exogenous regressor matrices, W is a weighting matrix, $E(u) = 0$, and $E(uu') = \sigma^2 I_N$, etc. Suppose the researcher is primarily interested in the spatial coefficient ρ_1, but is unsure about the significance of X_2. A procedure that has "probably" often been considered is the following:

1. First estimate $(M1)$ and test $H_0 : \beta_2 = 0$ against $H_1 : \beta_2 \neq 0$.
2. If H_0 is rejected, the estimator of ρ_1, say $\hat{\rho}_{1,1}$, is taken from $(M1)$.

   If H_0 is accepted, the researcher estimates

$$(M2) \quad y = X_1\beta_1 + \rho_1 W y + u \tag{8.5.2}$$

and takes his estimate of ρ_1 from $(M2)$ as $\hat{\rho}_{1,2}$. Note that because of the endogeneity of Wy, the expected values of $\hat{\rho}_{1,1}$ and $\hat{\rho}_{1,2}$ are not known and so we resort to large sample theory.

Basic Estimators: Their Large Sample Properties

Assume $(I_N - \rho_1 W)$ is nonsingular for all $|\rho_1| < 1$. Since Wy is endogenous, assume the researcher estimates $(M1)$ by an IV procedure based on the instrument matrix[4]

$$IV_1 = (X_1, X_2, WX_1, W^2X_1, WX_2, W^2X_2). \tag{8.5.3}$$

As we have seen in Chapter 2, under typical conditions, the IV estimator of the parameters in a model such as $(M1)$ is consistent and asymptotically normal. That is, based on $(M1)$, let $\gamma' = (\beta_1', \beta_2', \rho_1)$ and let $\hat{\gamma}$ be its IV estimator. Then, under typical conditions,[5]

$$N^{1/2}(\hat{\gamma} - \gamma) \xrightarrow{D} N(0, V_\gamma) \tag{8.5.4}$$

where V_γ is finite and positive definite since (under typical assumptions) it is a nonsingular VC matrix. Among other things, (8.5.4) implies that $\hat{\gamma} \xrightarrow{P} \gamma$ and so $\hat{\rho}_{1,1} \xrightarrow{P} \rho_1$. Note that the asymptotic result in (8.5.4) holds under both H_0 and H_1 since $(M1)$ is a true model under both H_0 and H_1.

Let $V_{\gamma,22}$ be the part of V_γ that relates to the IV estimator of β_2, namely $\hat{\beta}_2$, i.e., the $(2, 2)$ diagonal $k_2 \times k_2$ block of V_γ. Then, under **both** H_0 and H_1,

$$N^{1/2}(\hat{\beta}_2 - \beta_2) \xrightarrow{D} N(0, V_{\gamma,22}) \tag{8.5.5}$$

---

4. Observe that the notation of the instrument matrix was changed from previous chapters to avoid confusion with the alternative hypothesis H_1.
5. For further details about the large sample conditions, see Kelejian and Prucha (1998, 2004). See also Kelejian (2016) whose results on large sample issues relating to pretest estimators form the basis for the results given in this section.

where $V_{\gamma,22}$ is also positive definite. Let $\hat{V}_{\gamma,22}$ be a consistent estimator of $V_{\gamma,22}$. Then, given (8.5.5), the hypothesis $H_0 : \beta_2 = 0$ would be rejected at the 5% level if

$$N\,(\hat{\beta}_2'\,\hat{V}_{\gamma,22}^{-1}\,\hat{\beta}_2) > \chi_{k_2}^2(0.95) \tag{8.5.6}$$

where N denotes the sample size. For future reference, we note the following. In (8.5.6) if H_0 is true, $\hat{\beta}_2 \rightarrow 0$ and $\hat{V}_{\gamma,22}^{-1} \xrightarrow{P} V_{\gamma,22}^{-1}$, which is positive definite. Given this, the test statistic in (8.5.6) converges to a chi-squared variable with k_2 degrees of freedom, i.e.,

$$(\text{Given } H_0) \quad N\,(\hat{\beta}_2'\,\hat{V}_{\gamma,22}^{-1}\,\hat{\beta}_2) \xrightarrow{D} \chi_{k_2}^2. \tag{8.5.7}$$

On the other hand, if H_1 is true, $\hat{\beta}_2 \rightarrow \beta_2 \neq 0$, but we still have $\hat{V}_{\gamma,22}^{-1} \xrightarrow{P} V_{\gamma,22}^{-1}$ which is positive definite and so

$$(\text{Given } H_1) \quad N\,(\hat{\beta}_2'\,\hat{V}_{\gamma,22}^{-1}\,\hat{\beta}_2) \rightarrow \infty. \tag{8.5.8}$$

Now consider $(M2)$, let $\psi = (\beta_1', \rho_1)'$, and let $\hat{\psi}$ be its IV estimator based on the instruments

$$IV_2 = (X_1, WX_1, W^2X_1). \tag{8.5.9}$$

If H_0 is true,

$$N^{1/2}(\hat{\psi} - \psi) \xrightarrow{D} N(0, V_\psi), \tag{8.5.10}$$

and so $\hat{\psi}$ is consistent, i.e., $\hat{\psi} \xrightarrow{P} \psi$, and hence under H_0, $\hat{\rho}_{1,2} \xrightarrow{P} \rho_1$. On the other hand, if H_1 is true, under general conditions, $\hat{\psi} \xrightarrow{P} c \neq \psi$, and $\hat{\rho}_{1,2} \xrightarrow{P} \rho_1^* \neq \rho_1$ where c is a $(k_1 + 1) \times 1$ vector with finite elements, and ρ_1^* is a finite constant.

The Pretest Estimator and Its Properties

Let

$$\delta_N = \begin{cases} 1 & \text{if } H_0 \text{ is accepted,} \\ 0 & \text{if } H_0 \text{ is rejected,} \end{cases} \tag{8.5.11}$$

where we have indicated the sample size (i.e., N) the "dummy" variable is based on. In this case our final estimator of ρ_1 is

$$\begin{aligned} \tilde{\rho}_1 &= \delta_N \hat{\rho}_{1,2} + (1 - \delta_N)\hat{\rho}_{1,1} \\ &= \delta_N(\hat{\rho}_{1,2} - \hat{\rho}_{1,1}) + \hat{\rho}_{1,1}. \end{aligned} \tag{8.5.12}$$

Small sample analysis in terms of expectations cannot be undertaken because of the endogeneity of Wy, i.e., $E(\hat{\rho}_{1,i}), i = 1, 2$ is not known. Hence, we again resort to large sample analysis. First, recall that

$$\begin{aligned} p\lim \hat{\rho}_{1,1} &= \rho_1, \text{ under both } H_0 \text{ and } H_1; \\ p\lim \hat{\rho}_{1,2} &= \rho_1, \text{ under } H_0; \\ p\lim \hat{\rho}_{1,2} &= \rho_1^* \neq \rho_1, \text{ under } H_1. \end{aligned} \tag{8.5.13}$$

From (8.5.6), (8.5.8), and (8.5.11), it follows that in the limiting case $N \to \infty$,

$$\begin{aligned} \text{If } H_0 \text{ is true then } \Pr(\delta_N = 1) &\to 0.95, \\ \Pr(\delta_N = 0) &\to 0.05, \end{aligned} \tag{8.5.14}$$

and

$$\begin{aligned} \text{If } H_1 \text{ is true then } \Pr(\delta_N = 1) &\to 0, \\ \Pr(\delta_N = 0) &\to 1. \end{aligned} \tag{8.5.15}$$

For future reference, note that (8.5.15) implies

$$\text{If } H_1 \text{ is true then } p \lim_{N\to\infty} \delta_N = 0, \tag{8.5.16}$$

so that asymptotically, if H_1 is true, H_0 will not be accepted!

Consider now the large sample properties of the pretest estimator $\tilde{\rho}_1$. First consider the case in which H_0 is true. From (8.5.11)–(8.5.14) we have

$$\text{If } H_0 \text{ is true then } p \lim_{N\to\infty} \tilde{\rho}_1 = \rho_1, \tag{8.5.17}$$

and so $\tilde{\rho}_1$ is consistent. However, its large sample distribution is not the typical one that would be assumed.

For example, consider the large sample distribution:

$$\begin{aligned} \text{If } H_0 \text{ is true then } & N^{1/2}(\tilde{\rho}_1 - \rho_1) \\ &= \delta_N[N^{1/2}(\hat{\rho}_{1,2} - \hat{\rho}_{1,1})] + N^{1/2}(\hat{\rho}_{1,1} - \rho_1). \end{aligned} \tag{8.5.18}$$

Note the complexities involved in determining the large sample distribution of $\tilde{\rho}_1$. First, nonlinearities are involved because of the multiplication of δ_N with $N^{1/2}(\hat{\rho}_{1,2} - \hat{\rho}_{1,1})$. Another complication is that δ_N is not independent of $(\hat{\rho}_{1,2} - \hat{\rho}_{1,1})$ because they both depend on the error vector u. Still another complication is that in the limiting case $N \to \infty$, δ_N converges to a dichotomous discrete variable which has nonzero probabilities; see (8.5.14). Given all this, it should be clear that, under H_0, the large sample distribution of $\tilde{\rho}_1$ is not in the standard form.

Now consider the large sample properties of the pretest estimator $\tilde{\rho}_1$ when H_1 is true. From (8.5.12), (8.5.13), and (8.5.16),

$$\begin{aligned}\text{If } H_1 \text{ is true then } & p\lim_{N\to\infty} \tilde{\rho}_1 \\ &= (p\lim_{N\to\infty} \delta_N)\, p\lim_{N\to\infty} (\hat{\rho}_{1,2}-\hat{\rho}_{1,1}) + p\lim_{N\to\infty} \hat{\rho}_{1,1} \\ &= \rho_1,\end{aligned} \tag{8.5.19}$$

and so the pretest estimator is again consistent.

Now consider the large sample distribution of $\tilde{\rho}_1$ under H_1. As a preliminary, consider the variable $\Delta_N = N^{1/2}\delta_N$ and note from (8.5.11) that

$$\begin{aligned}\Delta_N &= N^{1/2} \text{ if } H_0 \text{ is accepted,} \\ \Delta_N &= 0 \text{ if } H_0 \text{ is rejected.}\end{aligned} \tag{8.5.20}$$

Then, from (8.5.8), (8.5.15), and (8.5.20), it should be clear that

$$\text{If } H_1 \text{ is true then} \Pr(|\Delta_N| \neq 0) = \Pr(\delta_N = 1) \to 0, \tag{8.5.21}$$

and therefore

$$\text{If } H_1 \text{ is true then } p\lim_{N\to\infty} \Delta_N = 0. \tag{8.5.22}$$

Now consider the large sample distribution of the pretest estimator $\tilde{\rho}_1$ under H_1:

$$\begin{aligned}\text{If } H_1 \text{ is true then } & N^{1/2}(\tilde{\rho}_1 - \rho_1) \\ &= \delta_N N^{1/2}(\hat{\rho}_{1,2}-\hat{\rho}_{1,1}) + N^{1/2}(\hat{\rho}_{1,1}-\rho_1) \\ &= \Delta_N(\hat{\rho}_{1,2}-\hat{\rho}_{1,1}) + N^{1/2}(\hat{\rho}_{1,1}-\rho_1).\end{aligned} \tag{8.5.23}$$

By (8.5.13) and (8.5.22),

$$\begin{aligned}\text{If } H_1 \text{ is true then } p\lim \Delta_N &= 0, \\ p\lim \hat{\rho}_{1,2} &= \rho_1^*, \\ p\lim \hat{\rho}_{1,1} &= \rho_1.\end{aligned} \tag{8.5.24}$$

It follows from (8.5.23) that

$$\text{If } H_1 \text{ is true then } N^{1/2}(\tilde{\rho}_1 - \rho_1) - N^{1/2}(\hat{\rho}_{1,1}-\rho_1) \xrightarrow{P} 0, \tag{8.5.25}$$

and so asymptotically, under H_1, the large sample distributions of the pretest estimator, $N^{1/2}(\tilde{\rho}_1 - \rho_1)$, and the estimator, $N^{1/2}(\hat{\rho}_{1,1}-\rho_1)$, based on the full model $(M1)$, have the same distribution![6]

6. Recall from Section A.10 in Appendix A that convergence in probability implies convergence in distribution.

At first this result may seem puzzling. However, its rationale is straightforward on an intuitive level. Under H_1, $\beta_2 \neq 0$, and so in the large sample case, the probability of accepting H_0 is zero. The implication is that the alternative model ($M2$) will never be considered, i.e., the pretest estimator will always be based on the full model ($M1$).

As a summary, the pretest estimator $\tilde{\rho}_1$ is consistent under both H_0 and H_1, but its large sample distribution under H_0 is complex and generally will not be in a standard form. Under H_1, its large sample distribution is, under typical conditions, straightforward to determine and is identical to the standard estimator based on the full model. In practice, we typically will not know whether H_0 or H_1 is true and so all we can assume is consistency. Based on this, the suggestion is **not** to use pretest estimators.

Illustration 8.5.1: Small sample properties of a pretest estimator

The results in Section 8.5 suggest that the pretest estimator $\tilde{\rho}_1$ is consistent under both H_0 and H_1. In this illustration we explore the small sample properties of the pretest estimator in the context of a small Monte Carlo experiment. Specifically, we generate the dependent variable from (8.5.1) as

$$y = \beta_0 + x_1\beta_1 + x_2\beta_2 + \rho_1 Wy + u.$$

We consider three sets of data corresponding to three regular grids of dimension 5×5, 7×7, and 10×10, leading to sample sizes of $N = 25$, $N = 49$, and $N = 100$, respectively. For each sample size, we construct a spatial weighting matrix based on a queen contiguity criterion.

The two regressors are the same as used in Illustration 6.7.2. They are normalized versions of income per capita and the proportion of housing units that are rental units in 1980, in 760 counties in Midwestern United States. The first N values of these normalized variables were used in the Monte Carlo study.

The model parameters β_0 and β_1 are fixed to 1, while β_2 is either 0 or 1. Parameter ρ_1 takes three different values, namely 0, 0.3, and 0.6. Finally, the innovation vector u is generated from a normal distribution with mean 0 and standard deviation 2.

The Monte Carlo results presented in Table 8.5.1 are based on the three-step procedure described above. In particular, for each Monte Carlo sample, we estimate the "full" model (the intercept, x_1, x_2, and Wy) and test for the significance of β_2. If the null hypothesis that β_2 is equal to zero is rejected, we take the pretest estimator as the estimator of ρ_1 from this "full" model, and record it. If the null hypothesis is accepted, the value of the pretest estimator of ρ_1 is taken from the truncated model obtained by dropping x_2. This result is also recorded. The table reports the MSE for this pretest estimator of ρ_1, and for the estimator

TABLE 8.5.1 MSE for the pretest and nonpretest estimators based on 10,000 Monte Carlo samples

β_2	ρ_1	N	Pretest MSE	Nonpretest MSE
$\beta_2 = 0$	$\rho_1 = 0$	N = 25	0.1786	0.1984
		N = 49	0.1642	0.1578
		N = 100	0.0955	0.0919
$\beta_2 = 0$	$\rho_1 = 0.3$	N = 25	0.1785	0.1847
		N = 49	0.1569	0.1304
		N = 100	0.0806	0.0700
$\beta_2 = 0$	$\rho_1 = 0.6$	N = 25	0.1770	0.1596
		N = 49	0.1393	0.0962
		N = 100	0.0449	0.0363
$\beta_2 = 1$	$\rho_1 = 0$	N = 25	0.2454	0.1904
		N = 49	0.1747	0.1711
		N = 100	0.2075	0.1483
$\beta_2 = 1$	$\rho_1 = 0.3$	N = 25	0.3697	0.1984
		N = 49	0.2135	0.1858
		N = 100	0.2317	0.1597
$\beta_2 = 1$	$\rho_1 = 0.6$	N = 25	0.4864	0.2093
		N = 49	0.2259	0.1705
		N = 100	0.2019	0.1327

of ρ_1 which is always based on the "full" model. This "full" model estimator of ρ_1 is referred to in the table as the nonpretest estimator.

While analyzing the results, we should keep in mind the discussion in Section 8.4, where we showed that if the null hypothesis is true, the MSE of the pretest estimator could be smaller than the estimator which is always based on the "full model." In Table 8.5.1, the MSE of the pretest estimator when $\beta_2 = 1$ is consistently higher than the MSE of the nonpretest estimator. However, when the null hypothesis is true (i.e., $\beta_2 = 0$), the situation is mixed, and there are cases in which the MSE is lower for the pretest estimator and cases in which the MSE is higher. Furthermore, in almost every experiment the MSE decreases as the sample size increases. Finally, the results do not seem to be influenced by the particular values of ρ_1 in our small sample experiment.

8.6 FINAL COMMENTS ON PRETESTING

It should be noted that pretest procedures are often more involved than that described above. For instance, researchers sometimes specify a "simple" model and then sequentially test for a number of complications. These complications may relate to the existence of spatial correlation, a spatial lag in one or more variables, the significance of certain additional regressors, etc. If a complication is found to be significant, the model is expanded to incorporate that complication, and the possible significance of the next complication is determined, etc. The final model is arrived at in this way. This might be referred to as a bottom-up procedure. Another procedure can be referred to as a top-down procedure. In this case, a full model containing various complications is specified, and then the significance of each complication is tested. If a complication is not significant, the model is simplified by dropping that complication. If it is found to be significant, it is maintained in the model, and then the significance of the next complication is determined, etc. There are also still other pretest procedures, some of which are mixtures of the bottom-up and the top-down procedures.[7]

Our results described above strongly indicate that these "bottom-up" or "top-down" procedures may involve biases, inconsistencies, their large sample distributions may depend upon the truth of a particular hypothesis which is not known with certainty, etc. In some cases the biases involved can be quite large; see, e.g., the study by Piras and Prucha (2014) who use Monte Carlo methods to evaluate a bottom-up procedure.

The comments above are quite negative concerning the use of pretest estimators. However, there are other points of view concerning these estimators. For example, advocates of pretesting strategies generally argue that economics is a social science, and as such, is different from an exact discipline, e.g., mathematics. Therefore it relates to the world, and we learn about that world by observing it and forming hypotheses. However, since the data we have also relate to the world, we should use that data to learn, and reformulate our hypotheses. For example, to take an extreme case, if one assumed, theoretically, that interest rates respond to the number of jelly fish on the Maryland shore, one suspects that our data would strongly indicate that this hypothesis is not true. It would certainly then be reasonable to modify our hypothesis regarding interest rates!

As another example, suppose there are two researchers who wish to explain the level of steel production. One of these researchers spends years reading what he feels is the relevant literature, then formulates a model and estimates it. The other researcher is in a hurry! He quickly formulates a preliminary model, estimates it, and, given the results, reformulates that model, and continues this process until his final model is arrived at. The question then relates to whether or not these two researchers arrive at the same model?

A major problem with the pretest procedure of the researcher who is in a hurry, described above, is that the final model "typically" confirms the researcher's prior beliefs! That is, the search process **stops** when the results confirm prior beliefs. If final models are arrived at in this manner, hypotheses would

7. For a further discussion see the discussion in Florax et al. (2003).

never be rejected. That indeed is a major issue. A science should not advance in this manner.

Credibility of Results: An Illustration

The result that pretest procedures may lead to hypotheses always being accepted clearly suggests credibility issues concerning our accepted hypotheses! An illustration may reinforce this point.

Suppose a researcher has a beautiful mathematical theory relating to interest rates, and the theory predicts that a certain variable has a significant and positive effect on interest rates. Suppose that the researcher then gets data and estimates his model, but his variable is not significant. That researchers then drops some variables, adds others, perhaps changes the sample size and then reestimates his model. If his variable is still not significant, this process continues until his variable is significant and has an estimated positive coefficient. The researcher then writes a paper describing his beautiful mathematical theory, and gives the empirical results relating to the last estimation which is consistent with the theory. However, the researcher says nothing about the process leading to that last estimation. Clearly, credibility issues arise!

The comments above, and the results in this chapter are meant to point out "issues." The reader can arrive at his own conclusions.

8.7 A RELATED ISSUE: DATA SELECTION

A somewhat different but related issue discussed in this section concerns data selection procedures. Before estimating their models, researchers sometimes adjust their samples by discarding certain data points because, for example, one or more of the data points are too large or too small with respect to the average for a particular variable, or a set of variables. They then estimate their models with the modified data set. Generally, no attempt is made to account for the procedure used for discarding certain data points. The assumption, typically made implicitly, is that the discarded data points may not satisfy the model assumptions. Often, the section of the data points to be discarded is on an *ad hoc* basis.

In a sense, such data selection procedures prior to the estimation of the model are similar to the pretest procedures described above. Consider the following example. In the above pretest procedures, the estimated parameters assume one value if, e.g., $\delta_N = 0$, is observed, and something else if $\delta_N = 1$. Of course, the estimated value of that statistic, δ_N, is based on the same sample used to estimate the model parameters. In the data selection procedure, the estimated values of the models parameters will be different if the entire original sample is used, or if a subset of that sample is used. Again, the decision to use a subset of the original sample is made by the researcher after looking at the data, e.g., he is preselecting the data to be used to estimate the model. Below we describe in more detail some of these issues.

In partial defense of data selection procedures, there may be cases in which the value of a model variable is clearly in error. As a somewhat obvious illustration, the unemployment rate is, by definition between 0% and 100%. If a value of this variable is recorded as 897%, then there is obviously an error. The solution may be to either drop the observation, attempt to modify it by statistical means, or to investigate why such a value was arrived at, and then attempt to correct it.

Our analysis in the sections below will describe data selection issues when the criteria for selection is endogenous, and when it is exogenous. On a somewhat intuitive level, the problems described above mostly relate to data selection issues when the criterion for selection is endogenous; a different set of issues arise when the selection is exogenous.

8.8 ENDOGENOUS DATA SELECTION ISSUES

Suppose the model is

$$y_i = x_{i1}\alpha_1 + x_{i2}\alpha_2 + \varepsilon_i, i = 1, ..., N \tag{8.8.1}$$

where ε_i are i.i.d. $(0, \sigma^2)$ and the regressors are exogenous. If the model in (8.8.1) were estimated by OLS using the full data set, the estimators would be unbiased and consistent under typical assumptions.

Suppose, however, that the researcher were to only use the ith observation if $y_i < y^0$, where y^0 is a value of the dependent variable the researcher believes is "too high" for whatever reason. Then the model which, in fact, is being considered is

$$y_i = x_{i1}\alpha_1 + x_{i2}\alpha_2 + \varepsilon_i \text{ only if } y_i < y^0. \tag{8.8.2}$$

In this case the properties of the error term will be affected because of the conditioning statement in (8.8.2). For example, the error term would have the property

$$\begin{aligned} E(\varepsilon_i | y_i < y^0) &= E(\varepsilon_i | \varepsilon_i < y^0 - x_{i1}\alpha_1 - x_{i2}\alpha_2) \\ &= g(y^0 - x_{i1}\alpha_1 - x_{i2}\alpha_2) \\ &\neq 0 \end{aligned} \tag{8.8.3}$$

where $g(\cdot)$ is a function which depends upon the particular distribution assumed for ε_i – more on this later. The result in (8.8.3) implies that the model corresponding to the restricted sample has an error term which does not even have a mean of zero and, furthermore, its mean varies from unit to unit because x_{i1} and x_{i2} vary over the units. Clearly, OLS type estimators would be biased.

If the distribution of ε_i is not specified, the function $g(\cdot)$ in (8.8.3) will not be known. In this case, other than approximations, exact adjustments for the nonzero mean of ε_i would not be available. If, however, normality is assumed, that is, if ε_i are i.i.d. $N(0, \sigma^2)$, then $g(\cdot)$ is identified.

To see further details of the issues involved in reference to (8.8.3), note, in general, the following. Let $f(z)$, $-\infty < z < \infty$ be the density of some variable Z, and let $f_1(z|z \in A)$ be the conditional density of Z given that Z is in the region A.[8] Then, that conditional density is

$$f_1(z|z \in A) = \frac{f(z)}{\Pr(z \in A)}, \quad z \in A. \tag{8.8.4}$$

Now suppose in (8.8.3) that ε_i is i.i.d. $N\left(0, \sigma^2\right)$. To calculate the conditional mean in (8.8.3), we need the conditional density of ε_i given that $\varepsilon_i < c$, where $c = y^0 - x_{i1}\alpha_1 - x_{i2}\alpha_2$. Applying (8.8.4) we have

$$\begin{aligned} f_1(\varepsilon_i|\varepsilon_i < c_i) &= K^{-1}\exp(-\frac{{\varepsilon_i}^2}{2\sigma^2}), \quad \varepsilon_i < c_i, \\ K &= \sqrt{2\pi}\sigma \Pr(\varepsilon_i \in A). \end{aligned} \tag{8.8.5}$$

Denote the density and the CDF of the standard normal variable $N(0, 1)$ as

$$\begin{aligned} \varphi(q) &= \frac{1}{\sqrt{2\pi}}\exp(-\frac{q^2}{2}), \\ \Phi(q) &= \int_{-\infty}^{q} \varphi(u)du. \end{aligned} \tag{8.8.6}$$

Now consider (8.8.3) and note that ε_i/σ is a standard normal variable. Also, note that the expectation in (8.8.3), with $c_i = y^0 - x_{i1}\alpha_1 - x_{i2}\alpha_2$, can be expressed as

$$E(\varepsilon_i|\varepsilon_i < c_i) = \sigma E(\frac{\varepsilon_i}{\sigma}|\frac{\varepsilon_i}{\sigma} < \frac{c_i}{\sigma}) \tag{8.8.7}$$

where ε_i/σ is a standard normal variable.

Maddala (1983, pp. 365–371) gives a number of expressions for conditional expectations relating to the standard normal variable. One of these directly re-

8. To avoid confusion in our notation, the random variable is Z; z denotes the values it takes. For example, if a coin is tossed, we might define $Z = 1$ if heads results, and $Z = 0$ if tails results. In this case $z = 0, 1$.

lates to (8.8.7). In particular,

$$E(\frac{\varepsilon_i}{\sigma}|\frac{\varepsilon_i}{\sigma} < \frac{c_i}{\sigma}) = -\frac{\phi(c_i/\sigma)}{\Phi(c_i/\sigma)}, \tag{8.8.8}$$

and so, from (8.8.7) and (8.8.8),

$$E(\varepsilon_i|\varepsilon_i < c) = -\sigma\frac{\phi(c_i/\sigma)}{\Phi(c_i/\sigma)}. \tag{8.8.9}$$

The proof of (8.8.8) is left as an exercise at the end of this chapter – hints are given.

In general, let Q be a standard normal variable and as in the above, denote its density and CDF as $\phi(\cdot)$ and $\Phi(\cdot)$, respectively. Then, the following are useful expressions for various conditional expectations relating to Q which are given in Maddala (1983, pp. 365–371):

$$\begin{aligned} E(Q|Q \geq C_1) &= \frac{\phi(C_1)}{1-\Phi(C_1)} = M_1, \\ Var(Q|Q \geq C_1) &= 1 - M_1(M_1 - C_1), \\ E(Q|Q \leq C_2) &= \frac{-\phi(C_2)}{\Phi(C_2)} = M_2, \\ Var(Q|Q \leq C_2) &= 1 - M_2(M_2 - C_2), \\ E(Q|C_1 \leq Q \leq C_2) &= \frac{\phi(C_1)-\phi(C_2)}{\Phi(C_2)-\Phi(C_1)} = M, \\ Var(Q|C_1 \leq Q \leq C_2) &= 1 - M^2 + \frac{C_1\phi(C_1) - C_2\phi(C_2)}{\Phi(C_2)-\Phi(C_1)}. \end{aligned} \tag{8.8.10}$$

8.9 EXOGENOUS DATA SELECTION ISSUES

As we saw above, if a data selection procedure is endogenous in that it affects the properties of the error term, estimation problems will arise. Thus, for example, if data selection relates to values of a spatially lagged dependent variable, or some additional endogenous variable in the model, biases will result. However, such biases will not arise if the data selection procedure is exogenous in that it does not affect the properties of the error term. Unfortunately, other issues do arise.

Again consider the model (8.8.1) which is recalled here for the convenience of the reader

$$y_i = x_{i1}\alpha_1 + x_{i2}\alpha_2 + \varepsilon_i, i = 1, ..., N.$$

Assume the regressors x_{i1} and x_{i2} are exogenous and therefore independent of the error terms $\varepsilon_i, i = 1, ..., N$. Suppose now that the ith observation is used only if $x_{i1} < \alpha$ where α is some constant. In this case

$$E(\varepsilon_i |\, x_{i1} < \alpha) = E(\varepsilon_i) = 0, \qquad (8.9.1)$$
$$E(\varepsilon_i^2 |\, x_{i1} < \alpha) = E(\varepsilon_i^2) = \sigma^2.$$

More generally, restricting the sample with an exogenous data selection procedure will not affect the properties of the error term. However, it will affect the properties of the estimators. For example, the sample size will be smaller. Secondly, the variance of an estimator generally is smaller the larger the variation in the regressors. Restricting the sample by throwing out all observations for which the value of a regressor is viewed, for example, as "large" reduces the variation of that regressor and consequently increases the variance of the estimator of the parameters.

The discussion above suggests that data selection procedures should not be used on an *ad hoc* basis. There are consequences to both endogenous and exogenous data selection procedures.

SUGGESTED PROBLEMS

1. Let X have the density $f(x) = 1/2, x = 1, 2$ and let $Z \sim N(\mu, \sigma^2)$. Let

$$h = XZ.$$

Give an expression for $E(XZ)$.

2. Consider the model

$$(M_1) \quad y_i = a_0 + a_1 x_i + a_2 z_i + \varepsilon_i, \; i = 1, ..., N,$$

under typical conditions. Let $\hat{a}_i, i = 1, 2, 3$ be the OLS estimators of $a_i, i = 1, 2, 3$. Suppose the researcher believes in the null hypothesis $H_0 : a_1 + a_2 \leq 0.9$ and so estimates $A = a_1 + a_2$ as

$$\hat{A} = \hat{a}_1 + \hat{a}_2 \text{ if } \hat{a}_1 + \hat{a}_2 \leq 0.9,$$
$$\hat{A} = 0.9 \text{ if } \hat{a}_1 + \hat{a}_2 > 0.9.$$

(a) Give an expression for $E(\hat{A})$.

(b) As above, let $H_0 : a_1 + a_2 \leq 0.9$ and let H_1: $a + b > 0.9$. Suppose now that $\hat{A} = \hat{a}_1 + \hat{a}_2$ if the H_0 is accepted at the 5% level, and $\hat{A} = 0.9$ if H_0 is rejected. Determine $p\lim(\hat{A}|H_1)$, i.e., under H_1.

3. Under typical specifications, consider the model

$$(M_1) \quad y = X\beta + \lambda_1 W_1 y + \lambda_2 W_2 y + \varepsilon.$$

Consider the hypothesis $H_0 : \lambda_1 = 0$ against the alternative $H_1 : \lambda_1 \neq 0$. Consider the following estimation procedure. First (M_1) is estimated and H_0 is tested at the 5% level against H_1. If H_0 is rejected, the estimator of λ_2, say $\hat{\lambda}_{2,1}$, is taken from (M_1). If H_0 is accepted, the researcher estimates λ_2 as, say $\hat{\lambda}_{2,2}$, from the model

$$(M_2) \quad y = X\beta + \lambda_2 W_2 y + \varepsilon.$$

Let $\tilde{\lambda}_2$ be the pretest estimator of λ_2.

(a) Assuming typical conditions, determine $p\lim(\tilde{\lambda}_2|H_1)$.

(b) Again assuming typical conditions, give an expression for $p\lim(\tilde{\lambda}_2|H_0)$. Is $\tilde{\lambda}_2$ consistent?

4. Consider the model

$$(M_1) \quad y = X\beta + \lambda W y + \varepsilon$$

and assume that the researcher does not know W. He/she therefore first uses the data on y and X to estimate W as, say $\hat{W}$, and then estimates the model

$$(M_2) \quad y = X\beta + \lambda \hat{W} y + \varepsilon.$$

Discuss any problems, pretest or otherwise, that may result from this procedure.

5. Consider the model

$$(M_1) \quad y_i = x_i b + z_i c + \varepsilon_i, i = 1, ..., N_1, N_1 + 1, ..., N_1 + N_2.$$

Assume that ε_i is i.i.d. $(0, \sigma^2)$. Suppose the researcher estimates this model using only the data for $i = 1, ..., N_1$ and tests the hypothesis $H_0 : c = 0$ against $H_1 : c \neq 0$. If H_0 is rejected, the estimator of b is taken from (M_1) using that data $i = N_1 + 1, ..., N_1 + N_2$. If H_0 is accepted, the estimator of b is taken from

$$(M_2) \quad y_i = x_i b + \varepsilon_i, i = N_1 + 1, ..., N_1 + N_2$$

again using the data $N_1 + 1, ..., N_1 + N_2$. Let $\tilde{b}$ be the pretest estimator of b. Determine $E(\tilde{b}|H_0)$.

Chapter 9

HAC Estimation of VC Matrices*

9.1 INTRODUCTORY COMMENTS ON HETEROSKEDASTICITY

In spatial econometric models the error terms may be spatially correlated and heteroskedastic. These two "complications" are often considered by spatial researchers. Historically, in the absence of spatial correlation, heteroskedasticity used to be accounted for in certain *ad hoc* ways which involved the exact specification of the heteroskedasticity. After the seminal paper by White (1980), a robust approach to deal with heteroskedasticity became usual practice. In this robust approach heteroskedasticity was assumed to possibly exist, but be unspecified. A corresponding robust approach relating to spatial correlation is only sometimes taken by spatial researchers.

In this chapter we discuss heteroskedastic and autocorrelation consistent (henceforth HAC) estimators of variance–covariance matrices which may involve both heteroskedasticity and autocorrelation. These estimators are nonparametric and robust, and are a natural extension of the procedure suggested by White (1980).

The "Old Way" of Handling Heteroskedasticity

Consider a standard linear model whose error terms are heteroskedastic:

$$
\begin{aligned}
y_i &= x_i\beta + u_i, i = 1, ..., N, \qquad (9.1.1)\\
E(u_i) &= 0, \;\; E(u_i u_j) = 0, \;\; i \neq j,\\
E(u_i^2) &= \sigma_i^2, \;\; i = 1, ..., N
\end{aligned}
$$

where x_i is the ith observation on a $1 \times k$ vector of exogenous variables, β is a corresponding parameter vector, and u_i is the ith disturbance term. In (9.1.1) it is assumed that the disturbance term is normally distributed, is not autocorrelated, but is also heteroskedastic.

---

* Some important studies relating to the nonparametric estimation of VC matrices are White (1980), Newey and West (1987), Gallant and White (1988), Andrews (1991), Pötscher and Prucha (1997, Chapter 12), and de Jong and Davidson (2000). Contributions directly dealing with spatial issues are Driscoll and Kraay (1998), Pinkse et al. (2002), Conley and Dupor (2003), Kelejian and Prucha (2007a), and Kim and Sun (2011). Applications can be found in Anselin and Lozano-Gracia (2008), Fingleton and Le Gallo (2008), Piras et al. (2012), and Kelejian and Piras (2014), among many others.

Spatial Econometrics. http://dx.doi.org/10.1016/B978-0-12-813387-3.00009-3

The model in (9.1.1) can be expressed as

$$y = X\beta + u, \qquad (9.1.2)$$
$$E(uu') = D$$

where $D = diag_{i=1}^{N}(\sigma_i^2)$ and X is the $N \times k$ matrix whose ith row is x_i. The expression for the least squares estimator of β is the usual one, that is,

$$\hat{\beta} = (X'X)^{-1}X'y \qquad (9.1.3)$$

which can easily be shown to be unbiased. However, its variance–covariance matrix has a complication due to the heteroskedasticity. In particular, it is straightforward to show that the variance–covariance matrix of $\hat{\beta}$ is $V_{\hat{\beta}}$ where

$$\begin{aligned} V_{\hat{\beta}} &= E(\hat{\beta} - \beta)(\hat{\beta} - \beta)' \\ &= (X'X)^{-1}X'DX(X'X)^{-1}. \end{aligned} \qquad (9.1.4)$$

If D and therefore $V_{\hat{\beta}}$ were known, hypotheses could, under typical conditions, be tested in terms of

$$\hat{\beta} \simeq N(\beta, V_{\hat{\beta}}). \qquad (9.1.5)$$

However, in practice D and $V_{\hat{\beta}}$ are not known. Before an important paper, and then a book by Halbert White (1980, 1984), the complication confronting researchers was that $V_{\hat{\beta}}$, via D, involved N unknown variances, σ_i^2, which along with the k unknown elements of β, exceeded the sample size, N. In an attempt to overcome this "degrees of freedom" problem, researchers typically specified the variances, σ_i^2, parametrically.[1] In practice it was often assumed that

$$\sigma_i^2 = f(z_i, \gamma), \ i = 1, ..., N \qquad (9.1.6)$$

where $f(\cdot)$ was a well-behaved function, z_i were usually taken to be a subset of x_i, and γ were corresponding parameters. For example, the variance, σ_i^2, might be assumed to be related to the size of the ith unit, and so one or more of the regressors which describe that size might be taken to be the elements of z_i.

Given the model in (9.1.1) and (9.1.6), and assuming normality of the error term, there were two methods that typically were considered – again see Kmenta (1986) and White (1980). The first method was maximum likelihood where the function is

$$L(\beta, \gamma) = \frac{\exp[-\frac{1}{2}(y - X\beta)'D^{-1}(y - X\beta)]}{(2\pi)^{N/2}|D|^{1/2}} \qquad (9.1.7)$$

1. See the very clear discussion of this in the text by Kmenta (1986, Section 8.2).

$$= \frac{\exp[\sum_{i=1}^{N} -\frac{1}{2f_i}(y_i - x_i\beta)'(y_i - x_i\beta)]}{(2\pi)^{N/2}[f_1 ... f_N]^{1/2}}$$

with $f_i = f(z_i, \gamma)$. In this approach $L(\beta, \gamma)$ would then be maximized with respect to β and γ, etc.

The second method used to estimate the model was a two-step procedure where one would first estimate γ and then account for the heteroskedasticity by division. In particular, let $\hat{u}_i = y_i - x_i\hat{\beta}$. Note that, given (9.1.6), $E(u_i^2) = f(z_i, \gamma)$ and so

$$u_i^2 = f(z_i, \gamma) + \delta_i, \; i = 1, ..., N \tag{9.1.8}$$

where $E(\delta_i) = 0$. Then γ in (9.1.8) can be estimated, under reasonable conditions, in terms of the nonlinear least squares regression model

$$\hat{u}_i^2 \simeq f(z_i, \gamma) + \delta_i, \; i = 1, ..., N. \tag{9.1.9}$$

Let $\hat{\gamma}$ be the resulting estimator of γ and let $\hat{f}_i = f(z_i, \hat{\gamma})$. Then, the heteroskedasticity problem was solved by dividing (9.1.1) across by $\hat{f}_i^{0.5}$, namely

$$(1/\hat{f}_i^{0.5})y_i = (1/\hat{f}_i^{0.5})x_i\beta + (1/\hat{f}_i^{0.5})u_i, \; i = 1, ..., N \tag{9.1.10}$$

and then estimating (9.1.10) by taking $(1/\hat{f}_i^{0.5})u_i$ as i.i.d. with mean and variance one.

The Modern Way of Handling Heteroskedasticity

In a very influential paper, White (1980) suggested that modeling the error term's variance as in (9.1.6) and then estimating the model by either maximum likelihood or by dividing across by $(1/\hat{f}_i^{0.5})$ may lead to biases of various sorts. In addition, it was pointed out that theoretical hypotheses typically relate to the variables of the regression model, and not to the error term. The error terms are the **unknown** parts of the model. A transformation such as that in (9.1.10) is, typically, completely *ad hoc*. Instead of such an approach, White (1980) noted that in order to estimate $V_{\hat{\beta}}$, it is not necessary to estimate each element of D. Specifically, the estimation of $V_{\hat{\beta}}$ only requires the estimation of $X'DX$; see (9.1.4). This was a tremendous insight and simplification. For example, in the limiting case in which $k = 1$, so that X is an $N \times 1$ vector, $X'DX$ is just a scalar. Consequently, the degrees of freedom problem is no longer an issue!

The procedure for estimating $V_{\hat{\beta}}$ in (9.1.4) that White suggested is straightforward. In particular, let

$$\hat{D} = diag_{i=1}^{N}[\hat{u}_i^2] \tag{9.1.11}$$

where, again, $\hat{u}_i = y_i - x_i\hat{\beta}$. Then our estimator of $V_{\hat{\beta}}$ is $\hat{V}_{\hat{\beta}}$ where

$$\hat{V}_{\hat{\beta}} = (X'X)^{-1}[X'\hat{D}X]\,(X'X)^{-1}. \tag{9.1.12}$$

Inference can then be undertaken by replacing $V_{\hat{\beta}}$ in (9.1.5) by $\hat{V}_{\hat{\beta}}$ in (9.1.12).

On a formal level, assume that the elements of X and the variances σ_i^2 are uniformly bounded in absolute value, that $N^{-1}X'X \to Q_{xx}$, $N^{-1}X'DX \to Q_{xDx}$, where Q_{xx} and Q_{xDx} are nonsingular, and u_i is independently distributed over $i = 1, ..., N$. Then, among other things, White (1980) showed that

$$N^{1/2}(\hat{\beta} - \beta) \xrightarrow{D} N(0, V_{\hat{\beta}}) \tag{9.1.13}$$

where

$$\begin{aligned} V_{\hat{\beta}} &= \lim_{N\to\infty} [N(X'X)^{-1}]\,[N^{-1}X'DX]\,[N(X'X)^{-1}] \\ &= Q_{xx}^{-1} Q_{xDx} Q_{xx}^{-1}. \end{aligned} \tag{9.1.14}$$

In light of (9.1.13) and (9.1.14), it should be clear that $\hat{V}_{\hat{\beta}}$ is a consistent estimator of $V_{\hat{\beta}}$ in the sense that

$$p \lim N\hat{V}_{\hat{\beta}} = V_{\hat{\beta}}. \tag{9.1.15}$$

Given (9.1.13) and (9.1.15), hypotheses can be tested in terms of

$$\hat{\beta} \simeq N(\beta, N^{-1}\hat{V}_{\hat{\beta}}). \tag{9.1.16}$$

In passing we stress one more thing. Each element of $\hat{D}$ in (9.1.11) is **not** a consistent estimator of the corresponding element in D. We leave the proof of this as an exercise for the reader by hinting the following: Demonstrate that $\hat{\beta} \xrightarrow{P} \beta$ and note

$$\begin{aligned} \hat{u}_i &= y_i - x_i(\beta + \hat{\beta} - \beta) \\ &= u_i - x_i(\hat{\beta} - \beta) \end{aligned} \tag{9.1.17}$$

as well as

$$p \lim_{N\to\infty} (\hat{\beta} - \beta) = 0.$$

Then show that

$$\hat{u}_i^2 \xrightarrow{P} u_i^2 \neq \sigma_i^2. \tag{9.1.18}$$

9.2 SPATIALLY CORRELATED ERRORS: ILLUSTRATIONS

The Traditional Approach

Spatial econometric models are often assumed to have spatially correlated error terms. Spatial correlation is often specified in terms of three models: the spatial autoregressive model (SAR), the spatial moving average model (SMA), and the spatial error correction model (SEC). More formally, the expression for each of these models, using evident notation, is

$$\begin{aligned} (SAR(s)) \quad & u = \rho_1 W_1 u + ... + \rho_s W_s u + \varepsilon, \ \ 1 \le s \le G, \\ (SMA(g)) \quad & u = \psi + \rho_1 W_1 \psi + ... + \rho_g W_g \psi, \ \ 1 \le g \le G, \\ (SEC) \quad & u = \phi + W^* \eta, \ \ W^* = I_N + W \end{aligned} \tag{9.2.1}$$

where u is an $N \times 1$ disturbance vector and G is a finite constant. We briefly consider each of these in turn.

$SAR(s)$ is a spatial autoregressive model of order s, where the innovation term ε has mean and VC matrix of 0 and $\sigma_\varepsilon^2 I_N$, respectively. The case in which $s = 1$ was discussed in Chapter 2. Assume that the values of the elements of the s weighting matrices are all nonnegative. Let $\max(i)$ be the maximum of the row sums of $W_i, i = 1, ..., s$. Then a **sufficient** condition for u to be solved for in terms of ε is [2]

$$\sum_{i=1}^{s} |\rho_i \max(i)| < 1. \tag{9.2.2}$$

Of course, if the weighting matrices are all row normalized, the condition in (9.2.2) simplifies to

$$\sum_{i=1}^{s} |\rho_i| < 1. \tag{9.2.3}$$

In this model the weighting matrices sometimes relate to distances. These distances could relate to geography, to the extent of economic interactions between units, etc. As an illustration, consider the case of geographical distances. In this case, the ith row of W_1 might select neighbors which are less than 15 miles from the ith unit, $i = 1, ..., N$; the ith row of W_2 might select neighbors which are between 15 miles and 30 miles from the ith unit, etc.

Let the ith row of W_j be $W_{j,i.}$, $j = 1, ..., s$. Then, relative to the ith unit, because a neighboring unit cannot be in more than one neighboring group,

$$W_{j,i.} W'_{q,i.} = 0, \ \text{for all } j \neq q. \tag{9.2.4}$$

2. This result follows from Geršgorin's theorem discussed in Section 2.1.2 of Chapter 2. For more on parameter space in higher order spatial models, see also Elhorst et al. (2012).

In other cases the weighting matrices may relate to different channels of transmission. For example, W_1 may relate to geographical distances between units, W_2 could relate to various economics differences between units such as income, W_3 could relate to government quality differences between units, etc.

Given the $SAR(s)$ model in (9.2.1), and the condition in (9.2.2), $u = (I_N - \rho_1 W_1 - ... - \rho_s W_s)^{-1}\varepsilon$, and so the variance–covariance matrix of u in this model is

$$VC_{u|SAR(s)} = \sigma_\varepsilon^2 (I_N - \rho_1 W_1 - ... - \rho_s W_s)^{-1} (I_N - \rho_1 W_1' - ... - \rho_s W_s')^{-1}. \tag{9.2.5}$$

Clearly, the expression in (9.2.5) suggests that u is both spatially correlated and heteroskedastic. More on this is said below.

With similar interpretations of the weighting matrices, consider the spatial moving average model $SMA(g)$. Assume that the mean and VC matrix of the innovation term ψ are 0 and $\sigma_\psi^2 I_N$, respectively. In this case the variance–covariance matrix of u is

$$VC_{u|SMA(g)} = \sigma_\psi^2 (I_N + \rho_1 W_1 + ... + \rho_g W_g)(I_N + \rho_1 W_1' + ... + \rho_g W_g'). \tag{9.2.6}$$

Again, the VC matrix in (9.2.6) suggests both spatial correlation and heteroskedasticity.

Finally, consider the spatial error component model, SEC, and assume that the innovation vectors ϕ and η are both $N \times 1$ random vectors which are independent and have means 0 and VC matrices $\sigma_\phi^2 I_N$ and $\sigma_\eta^2 I_N$, respectively. Given this, the VC matrix of u is

$$VC_{u|SEC} = \sigma_\phi^2 I_N + \sigma_\eta^2 W^* W^{*\prime} \tag{9.2.7}$$

where $W^* = (I_N + W)$. For purposes of interpretation, let the units be states. One interpretation of the spatial error component model is that in each state two types of disturbance materialize: In the first, the elements of ϕ do not have effects which spill over into other states; In the second, the elements of η have effects which do spill over. The reason that the matrix $W^* = (I_N + W)$ is used in the specification of the SEC process is that the diagonal elements of a weighting matrix W are zero. Therefore an SEC process specified in terms of a weighting matrix W instead of W^* would imply that a random disturbance materializing within each state only has spillover effects to other states, but has no effects in the originating state. In general, the elements of u are again spatially correlated and heteroskedastic.

There is an important difference between $VC_{u|SAR(s)}$ in (9.2.5) and $VC_{u|SMA(g)}$ and $VC_{u|SEC}$ in (9.2.6) and (9.2.7), respectively. Specifically, because of the inverse matrix involved, the (i, j)th element of $VC_{u|SAR(s)}$ need not be zero even if the weighting matrices $W_1, ..., W_s$ in (9.2.1) all have zero elements for units that are far enough apart. On the other hand, if the matrices corresponding to the $SMA(g)$ and SEC models have zero elements for units that are far enough apart, both $VC_{u|SMA(g)}$ and $VC_{u|SEC}$ will have zero elements. In this sense, the $SMA(g)$ and SEC models can be viewed as local correlation models, unlike the $SAR(g)$ model.

Spatial researchers often assume that their error terms are spatially correlated by a process, such as those given in (9.2.1). Given this, their spatial regression models are estimated by procedures which account for the structure of the error terms. Just as for the case of heteroskedasticity, if the assumed structure of the error terms is not correct, biases of various sorts result, and obtained results can be very misleading. Again, the suggestion is to assume that the error terms are generated in a robust, or nonparametric, structure and then estimate the model accordingly. We now turn to such procedures.

HAC Estimation: An Illustration of the New Approach

Using evident notation, consider the simple illustrative model

$$y_i = x_i \beta + u_i, \ i = 1, ..., N, \tag{9.2.8}$$

where $E(u_i) = 0$ and

$$\begin{aligned} E(u_i^2) &= \sigma_i^2, \\ E(u_i u_{i+1}) &= \sigma_{i,i+1}, \ i = 1, ..., N-1, \\ E(u_i u_s) &= 0 \ \text{ if } |s-i| > 1, \end{aligned} \tag{9.2.9}$$

so u_i is only correlated with u_j if the distance between them, $d_{ij} = |i - j| \le 1$.

Let $y' = (y_1, ..., y_N)$, $X' = (x_1', ..., x_N')$, and $u' = (u_1, ..., u_N)$, so that the model in (9.2.8) can be written as

$$y = XC + u. \tag{9.2.10}$$

Noting that $\sigma_{i,j} = \sigma_{j,i}$, in this case the VC matrix of u is

$$G = \begin{bmatrix} \sigma_{1,1}^2 & \sigma_{1,2} & 0 & . & . & . & . & 0 \\ \sigma_{1,2} & \sigma_{2,2}^2 & \sigma_{2,3} & 0 & . & . & . & 0 \\ 0 & \sigma_{2,3} & \sigma_{3,3}^2 & \sigma_{3,4} & & & & \\ . & & . & . & . & & & \\ . & & & . & . & . & & \\ . & & & & . & . & . & 0 \\ . & & & & & \sigma_{N-2,N-1} & . & \sigma_{N-1,N} \\ 0 & 0 & . & . & . & \sigma_{N-1,N} & & \sigma_{N,N}^2 \end{bmatrix}. \tag{9.2.11}$$

The least squares estimator of C is $\hat{C} = (X'X)^{-1}X'y$ and its variance–covariance matrix is $V_{\hat{C}}$ where

$$V_{\hat{C}} = (X'X)^{-1}X'GX(X'X)^{-1}. \tag{9.2.12}$$

Note that $V_{\hat{C}}$ depends on G, where G implies that the error terms are both heteroskedastic and spatially correlated. Also note that the number of parameters determining $V_{\hat{\beta}}$ clearly exceeds the sample size.

An estimator of $V_{\hat{C}}$, which is a direct extension of the one in (9.1.12), and which is heteroskedastic and autocorrelation consistent (HAC) in the sense of (9.1.13) and (9.1.14) is

$$\hat{V}_{\hat{C}} = (X'X)^{-1}X'\hat{G}X(X'X)^{-1} \tag{9.2.13}$$

where

$$\hat{G} = \begin{bmatrix} \hat{u}_1^2 & \hat{u}_1\hat{u}_2 & 0 & . & . & . & . & 0 \\ \hat{u}_1\hat{u}_2 & \hat{u}_2^2 & \hat{u}_2\hat{u}_3 & 0 & . & . & . & 0 \\ 0 & \hat{u}_2\hat{u}_3 & \hat{u}_3^2 & \hat{u}_3\hat{u}_4 & & & & \\ . & 0 & . & . & . & & & \\ . & . & 0 & . & . & . & & \\ . & . & . & 0 & . & . & . & 0 \\ . & . & . & . & 0 & \hat{u}_{N-2}\hat{u}_{N-1} & \hat{u}_{N-1}^2 & \hat{u}_{N-1}\hat{u}_N \\ 0 & 0 & 0 & 0 & . & 0 & \hat{u}_{N-1}\hat{u}_N & \hat{u}_N^2 \end{bmatrix}. \tag{9.2.14}$$

It is tedious but straightforward to show that, under standard conditions, $\hat{V}_{\hat{C}}$ in (9.2.13) is a consistent estimator of $V_{\hat{C}}$ in (9.2.12) in the sense that

$$(N\hat{V}_{\hat{C}} - NV_{\hat{C}}) \xrightarrow{P} 0. \tag{9.2.15}$$

Again, in small samples, inferences can be based on

$$\hat{C} \simeq N(\beta, N^{-1}\hat{V}_{\hat{C}}). \tag{9.2.16}$$

For purposes of generalization, we will express $N^{-1}X'\hat{G}X$ in a different way. Specifically, let $x_{.i} = (x_{1,i}, ..., x_{N,i})'$ be the ith column of X, $i = 1, ..., N$. Now let $\hat{G}_{ij}$ be the (i, j)th element of $\hat{G}$ in (9.2.14). Then, the (i, j)th element of $N^{-1}X'\hat{G}X$, say $\hat{\delta}_{ij}$, is

$$\hat{\delta}_{ij} = N^{-1}\sum_{q=1}^{N}\sum_{r=1}^{N} x_{r,i}x_{q,j}\hat{G}_{rq}, \; i, j = 1, ..., N. \tag{9.2.17}$$

Because $\hat{G}_{rq}$ is zero if the distance between the r and q units, namely $d_{rq} = |r - q| > 1$, and **if** $\hat{G}_{rq}$ is not zero, then $\hat{G}_{rq} = \hat{u}_r \hat{u}_q$, another way to express $\hat{\delta}_{ij}$ is

$$\hat{\delta}_{ij} = N^{-1} \sum_{q=1}^{N} \sum_{r=1}^{N} x_{r,i} x_{q,j} \hat{u}_r \hat{u}_q K(d_{r,q}/d_N) \tag{9.2.18}$$

where, in this case, $d_N = 1$, and $K(d_{r,q}/d_N)$ is a kernel function such that

$$K(d_{r,q}/d_N) = \begin{cases} 1 & \text{if } d_{r,q}/d_N \leq 1, \\ 0 & \text{if } d_{r,q}/d_N > 1. \end{cases} \tag{9.2.19}$$

In (9.2.19) d_N can be viewed as a cutoff in the sense that if the distance between units r and q is greater than d_N, namely if $d_{rq} > d_N$, then $K(d_{r,q}/d_N) = 0$.

The kernel in (9.2.19) is a variation of what is called a rectangular kernel, which is further discussed below. It is chosen in this case because we are assuming a known pattern of correlations of the error terms. Although the use of the rectangular kernel, under typical assumptions, leads to consistent HAC estimation, in more complex spatial correlation patterns, it is typically not used because it is inefficient. In the next section we will consider more general specifications of the error term, and suggest other kernels which have been used in the literature.

9.3 ASSUMPTIONS AND HAC ESTIMATION

In this section we consider more general specifications of the error term, and account for that generalization with an HAC estimator of the variance–covariance matrix. Our estimator is a generalization of the one described in (9.2.13) and (9.2.14).

Consider the model

$$\begin{aligned} y &= X\beta + \rho_1 W y + u \\ &= Z\gamma + u, \\ u &= R\varepsilon \end{aligned} \tag{9.3.1}$$

where y is the $N \times 1$ vector of observations on the dependent variable, X is an $N \times k$ exogenous matrix, W is the $N \times N$ exogenous weighting matrix, u is the corresponding error term specified in the third line of (9.3.1) where R is an $N \times N$ **unknown** matrix of constants, $Z = (X, Wy)$, $\gamma = (\beta', \rho_1)'$, and where ε is an $N \times 1$ random vector such that $E(\varepsilon\varepsilon') = (0, I_N)$. Further assumptions relating to ε are given below. At this point we only assume that R is nonsingular. Again, further assumptions are given below.

The specification in (9.3.1) implies $E(uu') = V_u$ where

$$V_u = RR'. \tag{9.3.2}$$

The specification in (9.3.2) is very general in that it allows for general patterns of both spatial correlation and heteroskedasticity. As just one example, consider the spatial autoregressive model[3]

$$\varphi = \rho_2 W\varphi + \eta \tag{9.3.3}$$

where $E(\eta) = 0$ and $E(\eta\eta') = D_\eta$ where $D_\eta = diag_{i=1}^N(\sigma_i^2)$, i.e., the elements of η are heteroskedastic. Assuming that the inverse exits,

$$\varphi = (I_N - \rho_2 W)^{-1}\eta, \tag{9.3.4}$$

which in turn implies

$$V_\varphi = (I_N - \rho_2 W)^{-1} D_\eta (I_N - \rho_2 W')^{-1}. \tag{9.3.5}$$

Since $\sigma_i^2 \geq 0$, D_η can be expressed as

$$D_\eta = D_\eta^{1/2} D_\eta^{1/2}, \tag{9.3.6}$$
$$D_\eta^{1/2} = diag_{i=1}^N(\sigma_i),$$

and so in this case

$$\begin{aligned} V_\varphi &= (I_N - \rho_2 W)^{-1} D_\eta^{1/2} D_\eta^{1/2} (I_N - \rho_2 W')^{-1} \\ &= RR' \end{aligned} \tag{9.3.7}$$

where $R = (I_N - \rho_2 W)^{-1} D_\eta^{1/2}$.

Assumptions for the Model (9.3.1)

Because the spatial lag variable is endogenous, we will estimate the model by 2SLS and determine the VC matrix of the estimator by an HAC procedure. Note that the error term specification rules out maximum likelihood estimation.

Our instrument matrix is the $N \times q$ matrix $H = (X, WX, W^2X)_{LI}$ where LI denotes the linearly independent columns of the matrix (X, WX, W^2X), with $q \geq k + 1$. Clearly, since R is not known, a transformation that will render the error term free of spatial correlation and heteroskedasticity is not available.

For sample size N, assume the researcher can select a distance measure d_N such that $d_N \to \infty$, as $N \to \infty$. Also assume that for each sample size N,

---

3. The change of notation in the spatial autoregressive model is meant to avoid confusion with model (9.3.1).

the researcher knows the distance between all units. For the sample size N denote the distance between the ith and jth units as $d_{i,j,N}$ Then, suppose the jth unit is viewed as a neighbor to the ith unit if $d_{i,j,N} \leq d_N$, i.e., d_N is a cutoff which determines the number of neighbors each unit has. This cutoff measure is sometimes called bandwidth and it can be either fixed (i.e., same for all the observations in the sample) or variable (i.e., observation specific). For sample size N, let $J_{i,N}$ be the number of neighbors the ith unit has. Let $J_N = \max_i(J_{i,N})$, i.e., for sample size N, no unit has more than J_N neighbors. Finally, let ω_{ij} be the covariance between the ith and jth element of u, i.e., ω_{ij} is the (i, j)th element of $V_u = RR'$ in (9.3.2). Recall that the elements of ε are i.i.d. (0, 1) and have a finite fourth moment. Given these definitions, our list of assumptions are given below.[4,5]

Assumption 9.1. The regressor matrix X is an $N \times k$ exogenous matrix which has full column rank for N large enough.

Assumption 9.2. **(a)** The $N \times N$ weighting matrix W is exogenous and its diagonal elements are all zero. **(b)** $(I_N - aW)$ is nonsingular for all $|a| < 1$. **(c)** The row and column sums of W and $(I - aW)^{-1}$ are uniformly bounded in absolute value for all $|a| < 1$.

Assumption 9.3. The matrices R and R^{-1} are unknown nonstochastic $N \times N$ nonsingular matrices whose rows and columns sums are uniformly bounded in absolute value.

Assumption 9.4. The elements of H are uniformly bounded in absolute value and $rank(H) = q \geq k + 1$. In addition,

$$\begin{aligned}
(A) \quad & p \lim_{N\to\infty} N^{-1} H'Z = Q_{HZ}, \qquad (9.3.8)\\
(B) \quad & p \lim_{N\to\infty} N^{-1} H'H = Q_{HH},\\
(C) \quad & p \lim_{N\to\infty} N^{-1} H'RR'H = Q_{HRRH}\\
& = p \lim_{N\to\infty} N^{-1} H'E[uu']H
\end{aligned}$$

where Q_{HZ} is a full column rank matrix, and Q_{HH} and Q_{HRRH} are finite nonsingular matrices. The second line in part (C) follows from (9.3.2) and facilitates the development of the HAC estimator below.

4. For a more general list of assumptions see Kelejian and Prucha (2007a).
5. The matrices X, W, R, H, and Z, as well as the innovation vector ε, depend on the sample size, N. We do not indicate this dependence in order to avoid "tedious" notation.

Assumption 9.5. For each $N > 1$, the elements of ε, say ε_i are i.i.d. with mean and variance of 0 and 1, respectively, and have a finite fourth moment $E(\varepsilon_i^4) < c_\varepsilon < \infty$, $i = 1, ..., N$.[6]

Assumption 9.6. The maximum number of neighbors any unit has for sample size N is $J_N = o(N^\alpha)$, where $\alpha = 1/3$.[7]

Assumption 9.7. $\sum_{j=1}^{N} |\omega_{ij,N}| d_{ij,N}^{\rho_s} < c_s < \infty$, for some $\rho_s \geq 1$ and c_s is non-negative and finite, for all $i = 1, ..., N$ and $N \geq 1$.

Interpretation of Assumptions 9.6 and 9.7

Assumptions 9.1–9.5 are straightforward and they were interpreted at various places in the book. Therefore we focus on the interpretation of Assumptions 9.6 and 9.7. On a formal level, Assumption 9.6 implies $J_N/N^{1/3} \to 0$, as $N \to \infty$. That is, d_N is selected in such a way that as the sample size increases, the number of neighbors the ith unit has, defined by $d_{i,j,N} \leq d_N$, can not increase as fast as $N^{1/3}$, $i = 1, ..., N$. Note that the number of neighbors **need not** increase at all with the sample size! For example, Assumption 9.6 is typically satisfied in practice because in many studies researchers specify their model in such a way that each unit has only a finite number of neighbors, regardless of the sample size. For example, recalling Fig. 1.4.1 in Chapter 1, in a rook pattern the maximum number of neighbors a unit can have is 4; in the queen pattern that maximum is 8, and in the double queen pattern it is 24.

Before we turn to Assumption 9.7, we note the following. Our assumptions involving the sample size and the number of neighbors are conceptual. In practice the researcher typically only has one sample, and therefore given values of N and J_N. If J_N is large relative to N, e.g., if $J_N = 170$ and $N = 200$, one should not assume that the large sample results offer a "reasonable" approximation to the small sample properties of the estimator. Alternatively, the large sample distribution should be a better approximation to the small sample distribution if, say, $J_N = 5$ and $N = 200$ than if $J_N = 170$ and $N = 200$. As one example, if the units in a spatial study were US counties, which number over 3000,[8] and if the neighbors to a county are defined as counties that are contiguous, then no county in the US would have more than 10 neighbors. In this case $J_N = 10$ and $N \simeq 3000$ and one might assume that the large sample results are a reasonable approximation to the small sample results.

6. This is a somewhat intuitive specification in that it does not account for triangular arrays. The more formal specification which accounts for triangular arrays is given in Section A.15 in Appendix A.
7. For a discussion of orders of magnitude see Section A.13 in the appendix on large sample theory.
8. In 2013 there were 3007 counties. In addition there were 137 county equivalents.

Now consider Assumption 9.7. This assumption implies that the covariances, ω_{ij}, decrease with distance fast enough to ensure that the sum remains bounded as $N \to \infty$. Assumptions of this sort also occur in time series analysis. For example, corresponding to $\rho_s = 1$, and using evident notation, consider the time series model

$$\begin{aligned} y_t &= x_t b + u_t, \\ u_t &= \rho u_{t-1} + \varepsilon_t \end{aligned} \tag{9.3.9}$$

where $|\rho| < 1$ and ε_t are i.i.d. $(0, \sigma^2)$. Solving (9.3.9) for u_t in terms of u_{t-i} we have

$$u_t = \rho^i u_{t-i} + \rho^{i-1}\varepsilon_{t-i+1} + ... + \varepsilon_t. \tag{9.3.10}$$

Therefore the covariance between u_t and u_{t-i} is

$$\begin{aligned} E(u_t u_{t-i}) &= \rho^i E(u_{t-i}^2) + E(u_{t-i}[\rho^{i-1}\varepsilon_{t-i+1} + ...\varepsilon_t]) \\ &= \rho^i \sigma_u^2 \end{aligned} \tag{9.3.11}$$

since u_{t-i} only involves $[\varepsilon_{t-i}, \varepsilon_{t-i-1}, ...]$, $E(\varepsilon_t \varepsilon_s) = 0$, if $t \neq s$, and where $\sigma_u^2 = \sigma_\varepsilon^2/(1-\rho^2)$.

Note that the distance between u_t and u_{t-i} is i, and their covariance is $\rho^i\sigma^2$. Therefore, the model for the error term in (9.3.9) satisfies Assumption 9.7 because[9]

$$\begin{aligned} \sum_{i=1}^{N} |\rho^i| i &= |\rho| \sum_{i=1}^{N} |\rho^{i-1}|\, i, \\ & |\rho| \frac{1}{[1-|\rho|]^2} < const < \infty. \end{aligned} \tag{9.3.12}$$

Large Sample Distribution of the Parameter Estimator

Rewrite (9.3.1) as

$$y = Z\gamma + u \tag{9.3.13}$$

---

9. As a bit of background concerning the result in (9.3.12), note that if $|x| < 1$, then

$$\begin{aligned} z &= \frac{1}{1-x} \\ &= 1 + x + x^2 + ... \end{aligned}$$

Therefore,

$$\begin{aligned} \frac{dz}{dx} &= \frac{1}{(1-x)^2} \\ &= 1 + 2x + 3x^2 + ... \end{aligned}$$

where $Z = (X, Wy)$. Let $\hat{Z} = H(H'H)^{-1}H'Z$. Then, the 2SLS estimator of γ is

$$\hat{\gamma} = (\hat{Z}'\hat{Z})^{-1}\hat{Z}'y. \tag{9.3.14}$$

Replacing y by the right-hand side of (9.3.1) and simplifying yields

$$\begin{aligned} N^{1/2}(\hat{\gamma} - \gamma) &= N(\hat{Z}'\hat{Z})^{-1}[N^{-1}Z'H][N(H'H)^{-1}][N^{-1/2}H'u] \\ &= [N^{-1}Z'H\, N(H'H)^{-1}N^{-1}H'Z]^{-1} * \\ &\quad N^{-1}Z'\, H\, N(H'H)^{-1}\, N^{-1/2}H'R\varepsilon. \end{aligned} \tag{9.3.15}$$

Assumption 9.4 implies

$$p \lim_{N\to\infty} \left[N^{1/2}(\hat{\gamma} - \gamma) - A_1^{-1}A_2\, N^{-1/2}H'R\varepsilon \right] = 0 \tag{9.3.16}$$

where

$$\begin{aligned} A_1^{-1} &= p \lim_{N\to\infty} N(\hat{Z}'\hat{Z})^{-1} \\ &= [Q'_{HZ}Q_{HH}^{-1}Q_{HZ}]^{-1}, \\ A_2 &= p \lim_{N\to\infty} N^{-1}Z'\, H\, N(H'H)^{-1} \\ &= Q'_{HZ}Q_{HH}^{-1}. \end{aligned} \tag{9.3.17}$$

The central limit theorem in Section A.15 of Appendix A implies

$$N^{-1/2}H'R\varepsilon \xrightarrow{D} N(0, Q_{HRRH}). \tag{9.3.18}$$

Thus, from (9.3.15)–(9.3.18),

$$N^{1/2}(\hat{\gamma} - \gamma) \xrightarrow{D} N(0, A_1^{-1}A_2 Q_{HRRH} A'_2 A_1^{-1}),$$

and so finite sample small inferences would be based on the approximation

$$\hat{\gamma} \simeq N(\gamma, N^{-1}\hat{A}_1^{-1}\hat{A}_2\hat{Q}_{HRRH}\hat{A}'_2\hat{A}_1^{-1}) \tag{9.3.19}$$

where

$$\begin{aligned} \hat{A}_1^{-1} &= N(\hat{Z}'\hat{Z})^{-1}, \\ \hat{A}_2 &= Z'\, H\, (H'H)^{-1}, \end{aligned} \tag{9.3.20}$$

and $\hat{Q}_{HRRH}$ is an estimator of Q_{HRRH} which will be determined by an HAC procedure described below.

The HAC Estimator

Consider now the estimator of Q_{HRRH}. Let the (i, j)th element of Q_{HRRH} be $Q_{i,j}$, the ith element of u be u_i, and the (i, j)th element of H be h_{ij}. Given this notation, it follows from the fourth line in (9.3.8) that

$$\begin{aligned} Q_{r,s} &= p \lim_{N\to\infty} N^{-1} \sum_{j=1}^{N} \sum_{i=1}^{N} h_{ir} h_{js} E[u_i u_j] \\ &= p \lim_{N\to\infty} N^{-1} \sum_{j=1}^{N} \sum_{i=1}^{N} h_{ir} h_{js} \omega_{ij,N}. \end{aligned} \tag{9.3.21}$$

Assumption 9.7 implies that as distances between units increase beyond limit, $d_{ij,N} \to \infty$, the corresponding covariances vanish, $\omega_{ij,N} \to 0$. The suggestion is that the terms in (9.3.21) relating to smaller distances between units are more significant in the determination of $Q_{r,s}$ than are the terms which corresponding to units whose distances are large.

In a manner similar to (9.2.19), let $K(\frac{d_{ij,N}}{d_N})$ be a kernel function (described in detail below), and again assume that $d_N \to \infty$, as $N \to \infty$. Then, the HAC estimator of the (r, s)th element of Q_{HRRH}, namely $Q_{r,s}$, is

$$\hat{Q}_{r,s} = \sum_{j=1}^{N} \sum_{i=1}^{N} h_{ir} h_{js} \hat{u}_i \hat{u}_j K(\frac{d_{ij,N}}{d_N}) \tag{9.3.22}$$

where $\hat{u}_i$ and $\hat{u}_j$ are the ith and jth elements of $\hat{u} = y - X\hat{\beta} - \hat{\rho}_1 W y$, $i, j = 1, ..., N$. Let $\hat{Q}_{HRRH}$ be the estimator of Q_{HRRH}, i.e., its (r, s)th element is $\hat{Q}_{r,s}$. Then a more "macro" expression for $\hat{Q}_{HRRH}$ is

$$\hat{Q}_{HRRH} = N^{-1} H' \bar{K} H \tag{9.3.23}$$

where $\bar{K}$ is the $N \times N$ matrix whose (i, j)th element is $\hat{u}_i \hat{u}_j K(\frac{d_{ij,N}}{d_N})$.

Kernel Functions

Clearly, for (9.3.22) to be operable, the kernel function must be specified. Unlike for times series, in a spatial framework distances between units are always defined to be positive and so the kernel function will be defined on the interval $[0, 1]$.

Assumption 9.8. For the kernel function $K(x)$ assume

$$\begin{aligned} &K(0) = 1, \\ &K(x) = 0 \text{ if } x > 1, \\ &|K(x) - 1| \le c_K \, x^{b_K} \text{ if } 0 \le x \le 1, \end{aligned} \tag{9.3.24}$$

where $0 < c_K < \infty$ is a finite constant and $b_K \geq 1$.

Given the specifications in (9.3.24), for each u_i in the sum in (9.3.22) defining $\hat{Q}_{r,s}$, d_N clearly limits the number of cross-products involving u_i, i.e., d_N determines the maximum distance a unit can be from the ith unit and still be a neighbor to the ith unit, and hence appear in the sum. In (9.3.22) the number of cross-products involving u_i is the number of neighbors to the ith unit. In this sense d_N can be viewed as a bandwidth parameter in the time series literature; see Cameron and Trivedi (2005, pp. 302–304), Pötscher and Prucha (1997), and Lambert et al. (2008). Note that although Assumption 9.6 limits the maximum number of neighbors a unit can have, it does not imply that all units have the same number of neighbors. Therefore, the number of cross-products relating to each unit in (9.3.22) can be different.

The results in Kelejian and Prucha (2007a)[10] imply that, given Assumptions 9.1–9.7, and if the kernel in (9.3.22) satisfies (9.3.24), then $\hat{Q}_{HRRH}$ is consistent for Q_{HRRH}:

$$\hat{Q}_{HRRH} \xrightarrow{P} Q_{HRRH}. \tag{9.3.25}$$

9.4 KERNEL FUNCTIONS THAT SATISFY ASSUMPTION 9.8

The rectangular kernel

$$K(x) = \begin{cases} 1 & \text{if } 0 \le x \le 1, \\ 0 & \text{if } x > 1; \end{cases} \tag{9.4.1}$$

The triangular or Bartlett kernel

$$K(x) = \begin{cases} 1 - x & \text{if } 0 \le x \le 1, \\ 0 & \text{if } x > 1; \end{cases} \tag{9.4.2}$$

The Epanechnikov kernel

$$K(x) = \begin{cases} 1 - x^2 & \text{if } 0 \le x \le 1, \\ 0 & \text{if } x > 1; \end{cases} \tag{9.4.3}$$

The Parzen kernel

$$K(x) = \begin{cases} 1 - 6x^2 + 6x^3 & \text{if } 0 \le x \le 1/2, \\ 2(1 - x)^3 & \text{if } 1/2 \le x \le 1, \\ 0 & \text{if } x > 1; \end{cases} \tag{9.4.4}$$

10. The results in Kelejian and Prucha (2007a) were extended to a panel framework by Kim and Sun (2011).

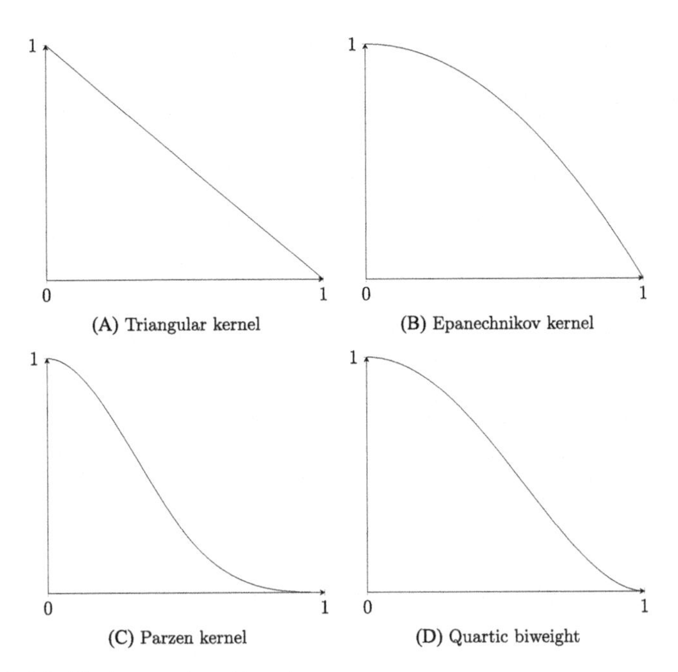

FIGURE 9.4.1 The four considered kernels

The quartic biweight kernel

$$K(x) = \begin{cases} (1-x^2)^2 & \text{if } 0 \leq x \leq 1, \\ 0 & \text{if } x > 1. \end{cases} \tag{9.4.5}$$

We leave it to the reader to demonstrate that the five kernel functions above satisfy Assumption 9.8. For a further discussion of kernel functions, see Brockwell and Davis (1991, Section 10.3), Cameron and Trivedi (2005, Section 9.3), and Pötscher and Prucha (1997, Chapter 12).

We suggested above that the rectangular kernel may not be efficient. One reason for this is illustrated below by comparing it to the other four kernels described above. First note that in an HAC estimator such as that in (9.3.22), the weight given to estimated error term cross-products $\hat{u}_i \hat{u}_j$ is determined by the kernel function $K(d_{ij,N}/d_N)$ which is such that $K(d_{ij,N}/d_N) = 0$ if $d_{ij,N} > d_N$. This implies that cross-products which correspond to large distances between units, $d_{ij,N} > d_N$, will not be included in the sum. This reflects the assumption that covariances of the error terms decrease as their corresponding distances increase. Except for the rectangular kernel, the kernels described in Fig. 9.4.1 are such that they continuously decrease to zero as the argument increases towards 1, which in the case of (9.3.22) corresponds to $d_{ij,N} \to d_N$. Because they

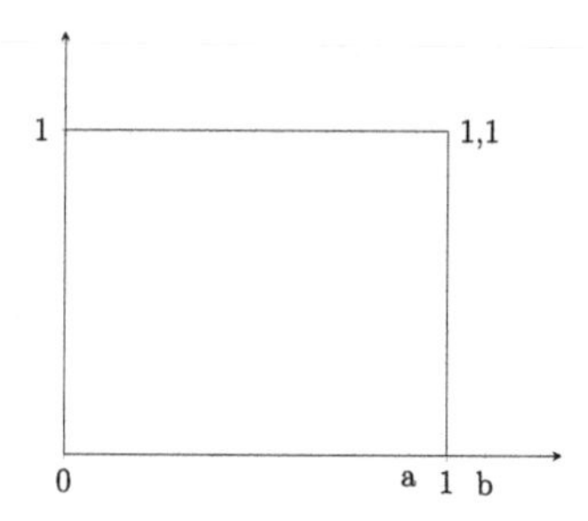

FIGURE 9.4.2 The rectangular kernel

decrease as $d_{ij,N}$ increases, the weight given to a cross-product such as $\hat{u}_i\hat{u}_j$ decreases as their distance increases.

Now consider the rectangular kernel in Fig. 9.4.2. The value of this kernel is 1 for all $0 \leq x \leq 1$. This means that for all unit pairs (i, j), such that their distance is $d_{ij,N} \leq d_N$, the weight given to error term cross-products, $\hat{u}_i\hat{u}_j$, is the same. There is no "discounting" for distance. The rectangular kernel also implies that the weight corresponding to the distance $a = d_N - 0.0001$ is 1 while the weight corresponding to $b = d_N + 0.0001$ is zero. In the other four kernels considered in Fig. 9.4.1, this knife-edge phenomenon is absent; the weights in these two "extreme" cases would be virtually the same.

A Positive Semidefinite VC Matrix

The HAC estimator, $\hat{Q}_{HRRH}$, is consistent but it may not be positive semidefinite in finite samples, except in some cases. One case in which it will be positive semidefinite in finite samples is the following. Suppose the distance between units, $d_{ij,N}$, is in terms of a Euclidean distance based on p attributes in each unit, e.g., differences in unemployment rates, income levels, etc. Using evident notation, let this distance measure be

$$d_{ij,N} = [(z_{i,1} - z_{j,1})^2 + ... + (z_{i,p} - z_{j,p})^2]^{1/p}. \tag{9.4.6}$$

Let $d_N^* = d_N^{2/p}$ and suppose that j is a neighbor to the ith unit and so $d_{ij,N} < d_N^*$. Of course, this implies that j is a neighbor to i if $d_{ij,N} < d_N^{2/p}$ and so d_N would be chosen to satisfy Assumptions 9.6 and 9.7 in terms of d_N^*. In this case

$$\begin{aligned}\frac{d_{ij,N}}{d_N^*} &= \left(\left[\frac{z_{i,1} - z_{j,1}}{d_N}\right]^2 + ... + \left[\frac{z_{i,p} - z_{j,p}}{d_N}\right]^2\right)^{1/p} \\ &= [(z_{i,1}^* - z_{j,1}^*)^2 + ... + (z_{i,p}^* - z_{j,p}^*)^2]^{1/p}\end{aligned} \tag{9.4.7}$$

where $z^*_{i,r} = z_{i,r}/d_N$ and $z^*_{j,r} = z_{jr}/d_N$, $r = 1, ..., p$. Again, let $x = d_{ij,N}/d^*_N$. Suppose also that the considered kernel is

$$K_\eta(x) = (1-x)^\eta, \text{ for } 0 \le x \le 1, \qquad (9.4.8)$$
$$K_\eta(x) = 0, \text{ for } x \ge 1,$$

where $\eta \ge (p + 1)/2$. Then, the HAC estimator $\hat{Q}_{HRRH}$ will be positive semidefinite in finite samples; see Golubov (1981), and Kelejian and Prucha (2007a) for further details.

As an illustration, if in (9.3.22) $\hat{Q}_{r,s}$ is taken as

$$\hat{Q}_{r,s} = \sum_{j=1}^{N}\sum_{i=1}^{N} h_{ir}h_{js}\hat{u}_i\hat{u}_j K(\frac{d_{ij,N}}{d^*_N}) \qquad (9.4.9)$$

where $\frac{d_{ij,N}}{d^*_N}$ is taken as in (9.4.7) and

$$K(\frac{d_{ij,N}}{d^*_N}) = \begin{cases} \left(1 - \frac{d_{ij,N}}{d^*_N}\right)^3 & \text{if } 0 \le \frac{d_{ij,N}}{d^*_N} \le 1, \\ 0 & \text{if } \frac{d_{ij,N}}{d^*_N} \ge 1, \end{cases} \qquad (9.4.10)$$

then $\hat{Q}_{r,s} \xrightarrow{P} Q_{r,s}$ for all $r, s = 1, ..., q$ and $\hat{Q}_{HRRH} \xrightarrow{P} Q_{HRRH}$ where Q_{HRRH} is positive semidefinite.

There is still another way to obtain a consistent estimator of Q_{HRRH} that is positive semidefinite in finite samples. In particular, consider again the estimator given in (9.3.22), $\hat{Q}_{HRRH}$, which may be based on any of the kernels described in Fig. 9.4.1 and whose distance measure satisfies Assumptions 9.6 and 9.7. Given that $\hat{Q}_{HRRH} \to Q_{HRRH}$, part (C) of Assumption 9.4 implies that Q_{HRRH} is positive definite. As a positive definite matrix all of its characteristic roots are positive. Let D be the diagonal $q \times q$ matrix whose elements are the roots of Q_{HRRH}. Then, assuming the distance measure is symmetric, it follows that $\hat{Q}_{HRRH}$ is symmetric. Therefore there exists an orthogonal $q \times q$ matrix, say F_N,[11] such that $F'_N F_N = I_q$ and

$$F'_N \hat{Q}_{HRRH} F_N = D_N \qquad (9.4.11)$$

where D_N is a diagonal matrix whose elements are the roots of $\hat{Q}_{HRRH}$. It follows that

$$\hat{Q}_{HRRH} = F_N D_N F'_N. \qquad (9.4.12)$$

11. To avoid confusion concerning the following statements, we indicate the sample size that this orthogonal matrix is based on.

TABLE 9.4.1 Comparison of various robust estimator for the Boston data in terms of their standard error

Variables	2SLS	Tri	Epa	Par	Qua	Rec
Intercept	0.1896	0.2428	0.2506	0.2330	0.2405	0.2750
$\log(nox)$	0.0889	0.1231	0.1307	0.1147	0.1228	0.1519
$\log(dis)$	0.0296	0.0468	0.0505	0.0427	0.0467	0.0608
stratio	0.0045	0.0043	0.0043	0.0043	0.0043	0.0043
rooms	0.0138	0.0271	0.0289	0.0258	0.0276	0.0327
crime	0.0012	0.0016	0.0016	0.0015	0.0016	0.0018
$w\log(price)$	0.0533	0.0882	0.0921	0.0850	0.0893	0.0994

Since $\hat{Q}_{HRRH} \xrightarrow{P} Q_{HRRH}$ and q is fixed and finite, $D_N \xrightarrow{P} D$. The following estimator of Q_{HRRH} is suggested. Let D_N^* be identical to D_N except that all diagonal elements of D_N which are negative are replaced by zero. Then a consistent positive semidefinite estimator of Q_{HRRH} is

$$\hat{Q}_{HRRH} = F_N D_N^* F_N'. \tag{9.4.13}$$

In practice, researchers often obtain "usable" results without ensuring that their estimator of Q_{HRRH} is positive semidefinite. In particular, they typically use an estimator such as the one given in (9.3.21), $\hat{Q}_{HRRH}$, which is based on one of the kernels described in Fig. 9.4.1, and the maximum number of neighbors any unit has is "small" relative to the sample size.

Illustration 9.4.1: Robust estimation of the Boston data

To illustrate the various typologies of kernels, we use again the Boston data and, particularly, the same specification as in Illustration 2.3.1. The columns of Table 9.4.1 report the standard errors for the estimated coefficients corresponding to each variable. Specifically, the first column (2SLS) reports the "classical" two stage least squares estimated standard errors. These would be consistent if the elements of the error term were uncorrelated and homoskedastic. The remaining five columns correspond to HAC estimation using the five kernels described above. These HAC estimators are consistent under far more general assumptions concerning the error term; see (9.3.1). In the table, Tri stands for Triangular, Epa for Epanechnikov, Par for Parzen, Qua for Quartic biweight, and Rec for rectangular.[12] For all five HAC estimators we considered a variable bandwidth (a different cutoff) based on the distance to the six nearest neighbors.[13] That is,

12. Since the estimated coefficient values are the same as those reported in Illustration 2.3.1, we do not report them here.

13. The distance function used is the Euclidean distance.

for each observation we choose a different bandwidth that ensures that each unit relates to exactly six neighbors.

The results in Table 9.4.1 suggest that the assumptions underlying the consistency of the 2SLS standard error estimations are not satisfied for the considered model. That is, if these assumptions were satisfied, the estimated standard errors based on the 2SLS procedure, as well as the HAC procedures, would all be consistent and so should all be quite similar. However, reading across the rows of Table 9.4.1, except for that corresponding to the *stratio* variable, the estimated standard errors based on the 2SLS procedure are always less than those based on the HAC procedures which are similar. We noted above that the HAC procedure based on the rectangular kernel is less efficient than HAC procedures based on other kernels. This is also revealed in Table 9.4.1. In particular, with the exception of the *stratio* variable, standard error estimates in Table 9.4.1 based on the rectangular kernel are always higher than those based on the other four kernels which are all quite similar. In the literature it is often the case that researchers find estimated standard errors based on kernels other than the rectangular to be similar; see, e.g., Anselin and Lozano-Gracia (2008) and Piras et al. (2012), among others.

Before concluding, we need to say something about the choice of the bandwidth which is often important in HAC estimation. Unfortunately, this issue has not been discussed much in the spatial literature and is beyond the intended scope of this text. Data driven procedures have been used for the selection of the bandwidth (see, e.g., Kim and Sun, 2011), but none of the available software implementations use those procedures.

9.5 HAC ESTIMATION WITH MULTIPLE DISTANCES

In most cases there are a number of meaningful "distances" between units, e.g., units may differ in the percentage of rental housing units, unemployment rates, etc. Instead of a measure such as that in (9.4.6), which gives equal weight to all variables, one may want to weight each difference differently. Fortunately, we can allow for this possibility in the HAC procedure.

First, on an intuitive level suppose there are G variables whose difference between units is important. Suppose also that for each of these G variables the researcher has a distance measure which relates to the difference between these variables among the units. Then the jth unit is viewed as a neighbor to the ith unit if at least one of the G variables in the jth unit is "close" to the corresponding variable in the ith unit.

On a more formal level, suppose again that there are G variables whose comparison between units may be of interest. Let $d_{ij,r,N}$ be the distance measure between the ith and jth units in the rth variable, $r = 1, ..., G$. For the rth variable, let $d_{r,N}$ be the cutoff distance that the researcher selects such that the jth unit is viewed as close to the ith unit with respect to the rth variable if $d_{ij,r,N} \le d_{r,N}$. Let the number of units which are viewed as neighbors to the ith unit be $L_{i,N}$, where $L_{i,N}$ is equal to the number of units which are close, in the above sense, to the ith in at least one of the variables. Given the distance measures, let L_N be the maximum number of neighbors any unit has

$$L_N = \max_{i=1,\dots,N} [L_{i,N}] \tag{9.5.1}$$

and assume that $L_N = o(N^{1/3})$. Finally, assume that the covariances in V_u decay fast enough so that the following holds for at least one measure, which for purposes of presentation is taken to be the first

$$\sum_{j=1}^{N} \sum_{j=1}^{N} |\omega_{ij,N}| d_{ij,1,N}^{\rho_s} \le c_s < \infty \tag{9.5.2}$$

for some $\rho_s \ge 1$, where c_s is a finite constant and $N \ge 1$.

The spatial HAC estimator, sometimes called the SHAC estimator of the (r, s)th element of Q_{HRRH} in this case is

$$\hat{Q}_{r,s} = N^{-1} \sum_{j=1}^{N} \sum_{i=1}^{N} h_{ir} h_{js} \hat{u}_i \hat{u}_j K\left(\min_{r=1,\dots,G} \left\{ \frac{d_{ij,r,N}}{d_{r,N}} \right\} \right) \tag{9.5.3}$$

where the kernel in (9.5.3) satisfies (9.3.24). Note, for two units, say i and j, if $d_{ij,r,N} > d_{r,N}$, for all $r = 1, \dots, G$, then the summation in (9.5.3) will not include the cross-product $\hat{u}_i \hat{u}_j$ since $\min_{r=1,\dots,G} \left\{ \frac{d_{ij,r,N}}{d_{r,N}} \right\}$ will exceed 1 and $K(x) = 0$ if $x > 1$. Alternatively, cross-products involving $\hat{u}_i \hat{u}_j$ will only appear if units i and j are close in at least one of the G distances.

Given Assumptions 9.1–9.8, as modified by the distance measures in this section, Kelejian and Prucha (2007a) show that

$$\hat{Q}_{r,s} \xrightarrow{P} Q_{r,s}, \; r, s = 1, \dots, q. \tag{9.5.4}$$

9.6 NONPARAMETRIC ERROR TERMS AND MAXIMUM LIKELIHOOD: SERIOUS PROBLEMS

If the error terms are nonparametrically specified as in (9.3.1), the maximum likelihood procedure, as typically considered, cannot be implemented. To see this, consider the spatial model

$$y = X\beta + \rho_1 W y + R\varepsilon \tag{9.6.1}$$

where X and W are an exogenous regressor matrix and a weighting matrix, which are both observed, and R is an unknown nonstochastic matrix which allows for general patterns of spatial correlation and heteroskedasticity. Assume $\varepsilon \sim N(0, \sigma^2 I_N)$. Let $M = (I_N - \rho_1 W)^{-1}$. Then, in this case $y \sim N(MX\beta, MRR'M')$ and so the log-likelihood is

$$\begin{aligned}\ln(L) &= -\frac{1}{2}\left[(y - MX\beta)'(MRR'M')^{-1}(y - MX\beta)\right] \\ &\quad + \ln(|I_N - \rho_1 W|) + c, \\ c &= -\frac{N}{2}\ln(2\pi) - \ln(|RR'|).\end{aligned} \tag{9.6.2}$$

The first partial derivative with respect to β is

$$\frac{\partial \ln(L)}{\partial \beta} = -X'M'(MRR'M')^{-1}y + X'M'(MRR'M')^{-1}MX\beta. \tag{9.6.3}$$

Setting the derivative in (9.6.3) to zero yields

$$\hat{\beta} = [X'M'(MRR'M')^{-1}MX]^{-1}X'M'(MRR'M')^{-1}y. \tag{9.6.4}$$

Since $(MRR'M')^{-1} = M'^{-1}(RR')^{-1}M^{-1}$ and $M^{-1} = (I_N - \rho_1 W)$, the expression for $\hat{\beta}$ simplifies to

$$\hat{\beta} = [X'(RR')^{-1}X]^{-1}X'(RR')^{-1}[y - \hat{\rho}_1 W]. \tag{9.6.5}$$

Thus, without further very restrictive assumptions, even if ρ_1 were known, $\hat{\beta}$ could not be calculated because RR' is not known. Furthermore, RR' cannot be incorporated into the maximum likelihood procedure because, in general, it contains $N(N+1)/2$ unknown elements. In the IV procedure, a term such as RR' arose in a "sandwich" form. That is, if H is the instrument matrix, one only had to estimate, in the large sample distribution, $Q = \lim_{N\to\infty} N^{-1}H'RR'H$. All of this suggests that with a general nonparametric specification of the error term, the maximum likelihood procedure, as typically described, is not "useful." Similar comments relate to Bayesian methods.

SUGGESTED PROBLEMS

1. Model (9.1.1) is reported below:

$$y_i = x_i \beta + u_i, \ i = 1, ..., N,$$
$$E(u_i) = 0, \ E(u_i u_j) = 0, \ i \neq j,$$
$$E(u_i^2) = \sigma_i^2 < const, \ i = 1, ..., N.$$

Let $X' = (x_1', ..., x_N')'$ and $D = diag_{i=1}^N(\sigma_i^2)$. Assume that the elements of X and D are uniformly bounded in absolute value.

(a) Demonstrate that the elements of $N^{-1}X'DX$ remain bounded for all $N > 1$.

(b) Demonstrate that despite the result above, the elements of $N^{-1}X'DX$ need not converge.

(c) Again, suppose x_i is a scalar. Let $\hat{\beta}$ be the OLS estimator of β, $\hat{u}_i = y_i - x_i\hat{\beta}$, and $\hat{D} = diag_{i=1}^N(\hat{u}_i)$. Using evident notation, demonstrate that

$$[N^{-1}X'\hat{D}X - N^{-1}X'DX] \xrightarrow{P} 0$$

so that if $N^{-1}X'DX$ converges, then $N^{-1}X'\hat{D}X$ converges to the same limit. (**Hint**) Let $\Delta_N = \beta - \hat{\beta}$ and note that $\Delta_N \xrightarrow{P} 0$. Then note that $\hat{u}_i^2 = u_i^2 + x_i^2\Delta_N^2 - 2x_i u_i \Delta_N$.

2. For the $SAR(s)$ model in (9.2.1) demonstrate that the result in (9.2.2) is sufficient for u to be solved for in terms of ε.

3. For the model in (9.2.8) and (9.2.9) in the text, suppose

$$E(u_i u_j) \neq 0 \text{ if } |i - j| \leq 2.$$

Describe the corresponding change in G given in (9.2.11) that you would consider.

4. Consider the model, with evident notation,

$$y = X\beta + \rho_1 W y + \varepsilon$$

where the (i, j)th element of W is the trade share of country i with country j. Give an illustration in which this model may not satisfy the typical assumption that the rows and column sums of W are uniformly bounded in absolute value.

5. Do the kernels in (9.4.1)–(9.4.5) satisfy (9.3.24)? Illustrate this for the Epanechnikov kernel.

Chapter 10

Missing Data and Edge Issues*

10.1 INTRODUCTORY COMMENTS

Unfortunately, in many cases there are problems with the data set used to estimate a model. A typical problem relates to "holes" in the data, i.e., the data set is incomplete because of missing observations. These observations may relate to one or more of the regressors, as well as to the dependent variable.

In some cases observations may simply be unavailable; in other cases certain observations may be available but their quality may be doubtful and, therefore, researchers may be reluctant to use them. As an example, the GDP of a country may be overstated because of "political" issues occurring in that country. Other examples might relate to measures of air pollution, quality measures of the government, and so on. However, we are not interested in exploring all the possible causes of missing data, but simply in reviewing different techniques how researchers cope with these issues.

There are a variety of ways researchers deal with missing observations when estimating their models. In some cases the "holes" in the data are simply ignored. As we will see in more detail later in the chapter, this case might arise when the model has a spatial lag in a variable but the values of that variable are not available for certain edge units and the spatial lag is calculated implicitly by taking those values as zeros. In other cases the missing values are estimated, or predicted, using the available data and then used as if they were true values. Examples of such situations relate to the use of sample means, predictions based on various correlation methods, interpolations, and so on. In some cases assumptions are made about the consequences of missing values. In other cases it is implicitly assumed that there are no consequences. These are some of the issues considered in this chapter.

---

* There is a large literature dealing with the issues discussed in this chapter; see, e.g., Afifi and Elashoff (1966, 1967), Kelejian (1969), Griffith and Amrhein (1983), Griffith (1983, 1985), Anselin (1988, 2002), Besag et al. (1991), Little (1992), Borcard and Legendre (2002), LeSage and Pace (2004), Kelejian and Prucha (2010b), Kelejian et al. (2013), Wang and Lee (2013), and the references cited therein.

Spatial Econometrics. http://dx.doi.org/10.1016/B978-0-12-813387-3.00010-X

10.2 A SIMPLE MODEL AND LIMITS OF INFORMATION

Consider the model

$$y_i = ax_i + z_i\beta + \varepsilon_i, \ i = 1, ..., N_1 + N_2 \tag{10.2.1}$$

where x_i is the ith value of a scalar independent variable, and z_i is a $1 \times p$ vector of independent variables. Assume that observations on x_i are only available for $i = 1, ..., N_1$, while observations on y_i and z_i are available for all $i = 1, ..., N_1 + N_2$. Also assume that x_i and z_i are jointly normally distributed with zero means and are i.i.d., $i = 1, ..., N_1 + N_2$.[1]

Let $N = N_1 + N_2$, $X' = (x_1, ..., x_N)$, and $Z' = (z_1, ..., z_N)$. Assume that X and Z are independent of $\varepsilon' = (\varepsilon_1, ..., \varepsilon_N)$, which is also normally distributed as $N(0, \sigma_\varepsilon^2 I_N)$. These assumptions are strong and, one would think, "ideal" concerning the handling of the missing observations on x_i in the estimation of the model in (10.2.1). As we shall see later, in an important way these assumptions are not ideal!

One way to handle the missing observations relating to x_i is to predict its values using the observations on z_i. Recalling (4.2.1) and (4.2.2) in Section 4.2, the joint normality of (x_i, z_i) implies that the conditional mean of x_i given z_i is linear in z_i:

$$E(x_i|z_i) = z_i\gamma, \ i = 1, ..., N_1 + N_2 \tag{10.2.2}$$

where γ is a $p \times 1$ constant vector. The result in (10.2.2), together with the i.i.d. normality assumption, implies that

$$x_i = z_i\gamma + \delta_i, \ i = 1, ..., N_1 + N_2 \tag{10.2.3}$$

where

$$\begin{aligned} &E(\delta_i|z_i) = 0, \\ &E(\delta_i^2|z_i) = \sigma_\delta^2, \ i = 1, ..., N_1 + N_2, \end{aligned} \tag{10.2.4}$$

with δ_i being a variance whose value is independent of z_i; see, e.g., (4.2.2).

Substituting (10.2.3) into (10.2.1) and combining results, the essentials of the model can be expressed as

$$\begin{aligned} (A) \quad & y_i = ax_i + z_i\beta + \varepsilon_i, \\ (B) \quad & y_i = z_i\mu + w_i, \\ (C) \quad & w_i = a\delta_i + \varepsilon_i, \end{aligned} \tag{10.2.5}$$

1. Results are the same for the case in which the means of x_i and z_i are not zero, and the proof of this is left as an exercise.

$$(D) \quad x_i = z_i\gamma + \delta_i$$

where $\mu = a\gamma + \beta$. Since ε and (X, Z) are independent, and using (10.2.4), we get

$$E(w_i|z_i) = 0, \tag{10.2.6}$$
$$E(w_i^2|z_i) = a^2\sigma_\delta^2 + \sigma_\varepsilon^2, \; i = 1, ..., N_1 + N_2.$$

Note first that the incomplete portion of the sample relates to part (B) in (10.2.5), with $i = N_1 + 1, ..., N_1 + N_2$.

The Limiting Case in Which Both γ and μ Are Known

In this case there would be no information relating to parts (B), (C), or (D) of (10.2.5) concerning the estimation of $c' = (a, \beta')$. Specifically, **if** μ and γ are known, an efficient estimator of c is just the least squares estimator of c based on part (A) in (10.2.5) for $i = 1, ..., N_1$ subject to the restriction that $\mu = a\gamma + \beta$.

There are at least two ways of estimating the model in (A) of (10.2.5) subject to the restriction $\mu = a\gamma + \beta$. One way would be to note that since μ and γ are known, one could substitute $\beta = \mu - a\gamma$ into (A) of (10.2.5) to obtain $(y_i - z_i\mu) = a(x_i - z_i\gamma) + \varepsilon_i$ and then estimate a as $\hat{a}$ by the OLS regression of $y_i - z_i\mu$ on $(x_i - z_i\gamma)$. The variance of $\hat{a}$ would then be $var(\hat{a}) = \sigma_\varepsilon^2[(X - Z\gamma)'(X - Z\gamma)]^{-1}$. The estimator of β would then be $\hat{\beta} = \mu - \gamma\hat{a}$ and so its VC matrix would be $VC_{\hat{\beta}} = \gamma[var(\hat{a})]\gamma' = var(\hat{a})\gamma\gamma'$. This restricted least squares procedure for estimating a and β is computationally straightforward, and efficient relative to the OLS estimator of a and β which is based only on (A) of (10.2.5) which does not use the restriction $\mu = a\gamma + \beta$. However, a formal demonstration of this efficiency is quite tedious when a and β are estimated in this fashion.

In the above procedure the parameter a and β are estimated by least squares after the restriction is substituted into the model. Another way to account for the restriction is to use the Lagrangian method. In this procedure the objective function would be

$$\min_{a,\beta,\lambda}(L) = (y - Xa - Z\beta)'(y - Xa - Z\beta) - \lambda(\mu - a\gamma - \beta)$$

where λ is a Lagrangian multiplier, and the minimization is with respect to a, β, and λ. The estimators of a and β given below are obtained by solving the first order conditions and are equivalent to the ones above using the "substitution out" method. However, the expressions are such that efficiency comparisons of the restricted least squares estimator and the ordinary least squares estimator are straightforward. They can also be easily extended to the case in which the parameters μ and γ are unknown but can be estimated. Finally, neither the restricted nor the unrestricted estimators are consistent essentially because the sample size N_1 is finite.

In somewhat more detail, let $m_i = (x_i, z_i)$ and

$$y'_{(1)} = (y_1, ..., y_{N_1}), \qquad (10.2.7)$$
$$M'_{(1)} = (m'_1, ..., m_{N_1})'$$

where $M_{(1)}$ has full column rank, namely $1 + p$. Let $\hat{c}_{OLS}$ be the ordinary least squares estimator of $c = (a, \beta')'$ based on (A) in (10.2.5) which is based on the sample $i = 1, ..., N_1$, $\hat{c}_{OLS} = [M'_{(1)} M_{(1)}]^{-1} M'_{(1)} y_{(1)}$. For purposes of generalization, let $\varphi' = (x_1, ..., x_{N_1}, z'_1, ..., z'_{N_1+N_2})$. Then, since φ is independent of the disturbance vector $\varepsilon = (\varepsilon_1, ..., \varepsilon_{N_1+N_2})'$, standard manipulations imply $E(\hat{c}_{OLS}|\varphi) = E(\hat{c}_{OLS}) = c$. Note that μ can be expressed as $\mu = [\gamma, I_p]c$ where, in this case, both μ and γ are known. Let $R = [\gamma, I_p]$. Then the efficient restricted estimator of c, based on known values of γ and μ, is $\hat{c}_r$ where[2]

$$\hat{c}_r = \hat{c}_{OLS} - [M'_{(1)} M_{(1)}]^{-1} R' \left\{ R[M'_{(1)} M_{(1)}]^{-1} R' \right\}^{-1} [R\hat{c}_{OLS} - \mu]. \qquad (10.2.8)$$

Conditional on φ, all terms in (10.2.8) are constant except for $\hat{c}_{OLS}$, and $E(\hat{c}_{OLS}|\varphi) = E(\hat{c}_{OLS}) = c$. It follows from (10.2.8) that $\hat{c}_r$ is unbiased, i.e., $E(\hat{c}_r|\varphi) = E(\hat{c}_r) = c$, since $E((R\hat{c}_{OLS} - \mu)|\varphi) = R\ E(\hat{c}_{OLS}|\varphi) - \mu = Rc - \mu = 0$. Conditional on φ, the variance–covariance of $\hat{c}_r$ is easily shown to be (see, e.g., Greene, 2003, pp. 99–100):

$$VC_{\hat{c}_r} = VC_{OLS} - \sigma_\varepsilon^2 [M'_{(1)} M_{(1)}]^{-1} R' * \qquad (10.2.9)$$
$$\left\{ R[M'_{(1)} M_{(1)}]^{-1} R' \right\}^{-1} R[M'_{(1)} M_{(1)}]^{-1},$$
$$VC_{OLS} = \sigma_\varepsilon^2 [M'_{(1)} M_{(1)}]^{-1}.$$

If c was estimated entirely in terms of the complete portion of the sample, namely (A) in (10.2.5), for $i = 1, ..., N_1$, the efficient estimator of c, under normality, would be the least squares estimator $\hat{c}_{OLS}$. Therefore, in this case a measure of the value of the information relating to the incomplete portion of the sample is, due to (10.2.9),

$$VC_{OLS} - VC_{\hat{c}_r} \qquad (10.2.10)$$
$$= \sigma_\varepsilon^2 [M'_{(1)} M_{(1)}]^{-1} R' \left\{ R[M'_{(1)} M_{(1)}]^{-1} R' \right\}^{-1} R[M'_{(1)} M_{(1)}]^{-1}.$$

2. For details on the restricted least squares estimator see Amemiya (1985, pp. 20–23) and Greene (2003, pp. 99–100).

Under typical assumptions concerning the regressors, the difference of matrices in (10.2.10) is positive definite. The proof of this is left as an exercise. The hint given is to first note that $[M'_{(1)}M_{(1)}]$ is positive definite and so its inverse is positive definite. The rank of R is clearly p and so the matrix $R[M'_{(1)}M_{(1)}]^{-1}R'$ is positive definite. Finally, the rank of the matrix $R[M'_{(1)}M_{(1)}]^{-1}$ is p. The positive definiteness of $VC_{OLS} - VC_{\hat{c}_r}$ (10.2.10) then follows since $\sigma_\varepsilon^2 > 0$. Among other things, since all the diagonal elements of a positive definite matrix are positive, all the variances of the elements of c_{OLS} are larger than the corresponding variances of the elements of $\hat{c}_r$.

Since $VC_{OLS} - VC_{\hat{c}_r}$ is positive definite, there is obviously a gain in efficiency due to the use of the restriction $\mu = a\gamma + \beta$ which appears in (10.2.5). However, recall that $\hat{c}_r$ is not consistent, e.g., it is not based on a sample size which increases beyond limit. Therefore, generalizing in an obvious manner, if in addition to the missing values of x_i, observations on one or more of the elements of z_i were also missing, resulting estimators of c will not be consistent.

The Case in Which γ and μ Are Not Known

If γ and μ are not known, they can be estimated, and then a feasible form of $\hat{c}_r$, say $\tilde{c}_r$, can be easily constructed. The parameter γ would be estimated by OLS as, say $\hat{\gamma}$, based on (D) of (10.2.5) for $i = 1, ..., N_1$. For future reference, we note that $E(\hat{\gamma}) = \gamma$ in light of (10.2.2)–(10.2.4). The estimator of μ would be the OLS based on (B) of (10.2.5), for $i = 1, ..., N_1 + N_2$. In light of (B) of (10.2.5), and (10.2.6), $E(\hat{\mu}) = \mu$.

Another alternative to $\hat{c}_r$ would be to estimate, or predict, the values of x_i for $i = N_1 + 1, ..., N_1 + N_2$ as $z_i\hat{\gamma}$ and then estimate $c = (a, \beta)$ by OLS in terms of a completed sample corresponding to (10.2.1).

We consider each of these two methods in turn. Obviously, if the efficient estimator c_r is **not** consistent when both γ and μ are known then, since $\hat{c}_r$ and $\tilde{c}_r$ are based on estimated values of these parameters, they will also not be consistent.

The Feasible Form of $\hat{c}_r$ Is Biased

The feasible counterpart to $\hat{c}_r$ in (10.2.8) is

$$\tilde{c}_r = \hat{c}_{OLS} - [M'_{(1)}M_{(1)}]^{-1}\hat{R}' \left\{\hat{R}[M'_{(1)}M_{(1)}]^{-1}\hat{R}'\right\}^{-1} [\hat{R}\hat{c}_{OLS} - \hat{\mu}] \quad (10.2.11)$$

where $\hat{R} = [\hat{\gamma}, I_p]$. First note that conditional on φ every term except for $\hat{c}_{OLS}$ on the right-hand side of (10.2.11) is nonstochastic. Let $\varphi_1 = (z'_1, ..., z'_{N_1+N'_2})$. Then from (10.2.3), (10.2.4), and (D) of (10.2.5), $E(\hat{R}|\varphi_1) = R$ and so $E(\hat{R}) = R$. Similarly, from (B) of (10.2.5), $E(\hat{\mu}|\varphi_1) = E(\hat{\mu}) = \mu$.

Although $\hat{R}$ and $\hat{\mu}$ are unbiased, $\tilde{c}_r$ is biased. Recall that $E(\hat{c}_{OLS}|\varphi) = E(\hat{c}_{OLS}) = c$ and $Rc = \mu$. Given all this, and using iterated expectations,[3] it follows from (10.2.11) that

$$\begin{aligned} E(\tilde{c}_r) &= E(E(\tilde{c}_r|\varphi)) \\ &= E\{E(\hat{c}_{OLS}) - [M'_{(1)}M_{(1)}]^{-1}\hat{R}' * \\ &\left\{\hat{R}[M'_{(1)}M_{(1)}]^{-1}\hat{R}'\right\}^{-1}[\hat{R}E(\hat{c}_{OLS}) - \hat{\mu}]\} \\ &= E\{c - [M'_{(1)}M_{(1)}]^{-1}\hat{R}'\left\{\hat{R}[M'_{(1)}M_{(1)}]^{-1}\hat{R}'\right\}^{-1}[\hat{R}c - \hat{\mu}]\} \\ &\neq c - [M'_{(1)}M_{(1)}]^{-1}R'\left\{R[M'_{(1)}M_{(1)}]^{-1}R'\right\}^{-1}[Rc - \mu] \\ &= c. \end{aligned} \tag{10.2.12}$$

The reason the fifth line in (10.2.12) is not equal to the fourth is as follows: Let $S = [M'_{(1)}M_{(1)}]^{-1}\hat{R}'\left\{\hat{R}[M'_{(1)}M_{(1)}]^{-1}\hat{R}'\right\}^{-1}$. Then, from (10.2.12) we get

$$\begin{aligned} E(\tilde{c}_r) &= c - E[S(\hat{R}c - \mu)] \\ &\neq c - E(S)[E(\hat{R})c - \mu] \\ &= c - E(S)[Rc - \mu] \\ &= c \end{aligned} \tag{10.2.13}$$

since S involves $\hat{R}$, and so $E(S\hat{R}) \neq E(S)E(R)$.

An Estimator Based on the Complete Sample

Now consider the least squares estimator of c based on the complete sample $i = 1, ..., N_1 + N_2$. Let the predicted value of x_i over the period $i = N_1 + 1, ..., N_1 + N_2$ be $\hat{x}_i = z_i\hat{\gamma}$. Let

$$\begin{aligned} y_{(2)} &= (y_{N_1+1}, ..., y_{N_1+N_2}), \\ z'_{(1)} &= (z'_1, ..., z'_{N_1}), \\ z'_{(2)} &= (z'_{N_1+1}, ..., z'_{N_1+N_2}), \\ x'_{(1)} &= (x_1, ..., x_{N_1}), \\ \hat{x}_{(2)} &= z_{(2)}\hat{\gamma}, \\ x'_{(2)} &= (x_{N_1+1}, ..., x_{N_1+N_2}) \end{aligned} \tag{10.2.14}$$

3. See Sections 4.1 and 4.2 for a presentation of iterated expectations.

where, of course, $x_{(2)}$ is not observed. Let the $(N_1+N_2)\times(p+1)$ true regressor matrix be G, and estimated regressor matrix be $\hat{G}$ where

$$G=\begin{bmatrix} x_{(1)} & z_{(1)} \\ x_{(2)} & z_{(2)} \end{bmatrix},\ \hat{G}=\begin{bmatrix} x_{(1)} & z_{(1)} \\ \hat{x}_{(2)} & z_{(2)} \end{bmatrix}. \tag{10.2.15}$$

Note that $rank(\hat{G})=p+1$ since its first N_1 rows are linearly independent, i.e., the rank of $M_{(1)}$ in (10.2.7) is $1+p$.

The true model relating y_i to the regressors over the period $i=1,\ldots,N_1+N_2$ is, using evident notation,

$$y_{(1)}=x_{(1)}a+z_{(1)}\beta+\varepsilon_{(1)},$$
$$y_{(2)}=x_{(2)}a+z_{(2)}\beta+\varepsilon_{(2)},$$

or

$$Y=Gc+\varepsilon, \tag{10.2.16}$$

where $Y'=(y'_{(1)},y'_{(2)})$ and $\varepsilon'=(\varepsilon_1,\ldots,\varepsilon_{N_1+N_2})$. Let $x_{(2)}-\hat{x}_{(2)}=\delta_{(2)}$, so that $x_{(2)}=\hat{x}_{(2)}+\delta_{(2)}$. Note that both $\hat{x}_{(2)}$ and $\delta_{(2)}$ only relate to values of the exogenous regressors. Then since $G=\hat{G}+H$ where

$$H=\begin{bmatrix} 0 & 0 \\ \delta_{(2)} & 0 \end{bmatrix},$$

the model relating Y to $\hat{G}$ is

$$Y=\hat{G}c+[Hc+\varepsilon] \tag{10.2.17}$$

where the term in brackets can be viewed as an error term. The corresponding least squares estimator of c is

$$\begin{aligned}\hat{c}&=(\hat{G}'\hat{G})^{-1}\hat{G}'Y \\ &=c+(\hat{G}'\hat{G})^{-1}\hat{G}'Hc+(\hat{G}'\hat{G})^{-1}\hat{G}'\varepsilon.\end{aligned} \tag{10.2.18}$$

Note that $\hat{G}$ and H both involve $(x_{(1)},z_{(1)},z_{(2)})$ and so they are not independent. Also recall that x_i and z_i both have zero means and are i.i.d. Since $\hat{x}_{(2)}=z_{(2)}\hat{\gamma}$, where $\hat{\gamma}$ only depends upon $x_{(1)}$ and $z_{(1)}$, it follows that $\hat{\gamma}$ is independent of $z_{(2)}$. Thus, $E(\hat{x}_{(2)})=E[z_{(2)}]E[\hat{\gamma}]=0$. Therefore, $E(\delta_{(2)})=E[x_{(2)}]-E[\hat{x}_{(2)}]=E[z_{(2)}]\gamma]-E[\hat{x}_{(2)}]=0$, and so $E(H)=0$.

Now consider the expected value of $\hat{c}$:

$$E(\hat{c})=c+E[(\hat{G}'\hat{G})^{-1}\hat{G}'H]c+E[(\hat{G}'\hat{G})^{-1}\hat{G}'H]E(\varepsilon) \tag{10.2.19}$$

$$
\begin{aligned}
&c+E[(\hat{G}'\hat{G})^{-1}\hat{G}'H]c\\
&\neq c+E[(\hat{G}'\hat{G})^{-1}\hat{G}']\,E[H]c\\
&=c.
\end{aligned}
$$

Therefore, again, the estimator is inconsistent as well as biased.

A Nonnormal Distribution Relating x_i to z_i – Consistency

Consider again the simple model in (10.2.1) and again assume that observations on x_i are not available for $i = N_1 + 1, ..., N_1 + N_2$. Suppose now, however, that the joint distribution of (x_i, z_i) is **not** normal, but they are still i.i.d. and independent of ε_i, which are also i.i.d. Again, assume that ε_i has a mean and variance of 0 and σ_ε^2, respectively. Also assume that the conditional mean $E(x_i|z_i) = g(z_i, \lambda)$, where $g(\cdot,\cdot)$ is a smooth nonlinear continuous function which is bounded, has continuous first two derivatives, and is known. Then instead of (D) of (10.2.5) we would have

$$
\begin{aligned}
x_i &= g(z_i,\lambda)+\psi_i, \\
E(\psi_i|z_i) &= 0,\\
E(\psi_i^2|z_i) &= q(z_i)\\
&\equiv \sigma_i^2,\ i=N_1,...,N_1+N_2
\end{aligned}
\tag{10.2.20}
$$

where the variance of the error term on the first line of (10.2.20) will generally be a function of z_i, i.e., $q(z_i)$. For purposes of generality, we assume that $q(\cdot)$ is not known and so we simply denote that variance of ψ_i as σ_i^2.

In this case the model in (10.2.1) implies

$$
\begin{aligned}
y_i &= x_i a + z_i\beta+\varepsilon_i,\ i=1,...,N_1,\\
y_i &= g(z_i,\lambda)a+z_i\beta+r_i,\\
r_i &= [\varepsilon_i + a\psi_i],\ i=N_1+1,...,N_1+N_2
\end{aligned}
\tag{10.2.21}
$$

where ε_i and ψ_i are independent, and so $E(r_i^2)=\sigma_\varepsilon^2+a^2\sigma_i^2\equiv\sigma_{r,i}^2$.

Using evident notation, the model in (10.2.21) can be expressed as

$$
\begin{aligned}
Y &= S(c,\lambda)+\delta,\\
S(c,\lambda) &= F(\lambda)c
\end{aligned}
\tag{10.2.22}
$$

where as above $Y' = (y_1, ..., y_{N_1+N_2})$ and, using evident notation,

$$
F(\lambda)=\begin{bmatrix} x_{(1)} & z_{(1)}\\ g(z_{(2)},\lambda) & z_{(2)}\end{bmatrix},\quad \delta=\begin{bmatrix}\varepsilon_{(1)}\\ \varepsilon_{(2)}+a\psi_{(2)}\end{bmatrix}.
\tag{10.2.23}
$$

Note that δ is heteroskedastic, but not autocorrelated.

Under reasonable assumptions, the original parameter vector $c' = (a, \beta')$, as well as λ, in (10.2.21) and (10.2.22), can be **consistently** estimated by nonlinear least squares (NLLS) if the incomplete portion of the sample $N_2 \to \infty$, regardless of whether N_1 remains finite, or tends to infinity. If $N_1 \to \infty$ while N_2 remains finite, c can be consistently estimated even if N_2 remains finite. Thus, while at times convenient, the assumption of normality, which implies linear conditional means, rules out consistency, unless the **complete** portion of the sample size $N_1 \to \infty$. Under normality and linear conditional means, the information contained in the incomplete portion of the sample only relates to a linear restriction on the parameters; see, e.g., the discussion leading to (10.2.8). As a point of information, many nonnormal distributions imply nonlinear conditional means.

Technical issues and results relating to the NLLS estimator are described in Amemiya (1985, Section 4.3), Cameron and Trivedi (2005, Sections 5.8 and 5.9), and Judge et al. (1985, Chapter 6), among others. For the convenience of the reader, the NLLS is described below. The model considered in the illustration is more general than the one in (10.2.22).

The NLLS Procedure

Consider the model

$$y_i = f(\xi_i, \beta) + u_i, \; i = 1, ..., N \tag{10.2.24}$$

where $f(\xi_i, \beta)$ is the regression function which is nonlinear in the $k \times 1$ parameter vector β. In the framework of a nonlinear model, the regressor vector, ξ_i, need not have k elements.[4] Using evident notation, the model in (10.2.24) can be expressed as

$$y = F + u. \tag{10.2.25}$$

Assume that some of the elements of the regressor vector ξ_i are endogenous – it may contain a spatial lag of the dependent variable. Also assume that the disturbance vector u is determined as

$$u = R\varepsilon \tag{10.2.26}$$

where the elements of ε are i.i.d. with mean and variance of 0 and 1, respectively, and have a finite fourth moment. Assume that the $N \times N$ matrix R is nonsingular, its elements are unknown constants, and its row and column sums

4. For example, let $\xi_{i,1}$ be one of the elements in the regressor vector ξ_i. Then the model could contain $b_0 \xi_{i,1}^{b_1 \xi_{i,1}}$.

are uniformly bounded in absolute value. In this case the VC matrix of u is $V_u = RR'$.

Let H be an $N \times s$ matrix of instruments, $s \geq k$ with the usual properties, and let $P_H = H(H'H)^{-1}H'$. The NLLS estimator of β which accounts for the endogeneity of some of the components of ξ_i is determined by minimizing the quadratic Q where

$$Q = \min_{\beta}(y - F)'H(H'H)^{-1}H'(y - F). \tag{10.2.27}$$

Let $\hat{\beta}$ be the minimizing value of β. Then, assuming the technical conditions in Amemiya (1985, Chapters 4 and 8), a minor extension of those results implies[5]

$$\begin{aligned} N^{1/2}(\hat{\beta} - \beta) &\xrightarrow{D} N(0, p\lim VC_{\hat{\beta}}), \qquad (10.2.28)\\ VC_{\hat{\beta}} &= C(N^{-1}H'RR'H)C', \\ C &= N\left[\frac{\partial F'}{\partial \beta}P_H\frac{\partial F}{\partial \beta}\right]^{-1}\left[[N^{-1}\frac{\partial F'}{\partial \beta}H][(N(H'H)^{-1})]\right] \end{aligned}$$

where $\frac{\partial F}{\partial \beta}$ is an $N \times k$ matrix whose ith row is

$$\frac{\partial f(\xi_i, \beta)}{\partial \beta} = [\frac{\partial f(\xi_i, \beta)}{\partial \beta_1}, \ldots, \frac{\partial f(\xi_i, \beta)}{\partial \beta_k}]. \tag{10.2.29}$$

Small sample inference can be based on

$$\hat{\beta} \simeq N(\beta, N^{-1}\widehat{VC}_{\hat{\beta}}) \tag{10.2.30}$$

where $\widehat{VC}_{\hat{\beta}}$ is identical to $VC_{\hat{\beta}}$ except that β is replaced everywhere by $\hat{\beta}$ and $\left[N^{-1}H'RR'H\right]$ is replaced by its HAC estimator.

10.3 INCOMPLETE SAMPLES AND EXTERNAL DATA

In some cases the researcher may predict the missing values of a regressor not only in terms of the other regressors but also in terms of exogenous variables which are not in the model. It should be clear that the results relating to the incomplete portion of the sample will again be just a linear restriction on the regression parameters if linear conditional means are involved. For example, consider again the model in (10.2.1) but now assume that in addition to z_i the researcher has s additional variables, say φ_i, which are not included in (10.2.1). As in Section 10.2, assume that the observations on x_i are only available for

5. Amemiya (1985), Judge et al. (1985), and Cameron and Trivedi (2005) did not consider the error specification $u = R\varepsilon$, but the results for this case easily follow from the results they give.

$i = 1, ..., N_1$, but those of z_i and φ_i are available for $i = 1, ..., N_1 + N_2$. For ease of presentation, also assume that (x_i, z_i, φ_i) are i.i.d. over $i = 1, ..., N_1 + N_2$ and are independent of the error term ε_i. In this case, an analysis virtually identical to that given above will demonstrate that the incomplete portion of the sample, at best, only leads to a linear restriction on the regression parameters. If N_1 is finite, the regression parameters will not be consistently estimated.

If the conditional mean of x_i given z_i and φ_i is not known, and only estimated in an *ad hoc* way, then biases, as well as inconsistencies, would result. For example, suppose the predicted value of x_i is $\hat{x}_i = g(z_i, \varphi_i)$. Let $v_i = x_i - \hat{x}_i$ so that $x_i = \hat{x}_i + v_i$. Given that $g(z_i, \varphi_i)$ is not the conditional mean, and v_i is the error in the approximation, it would not even have a zero mean. Thus the incomplete portion of the sample using $\hat{x}_i$ as the predictor of x_i would be

$$y_i = \hat{x}_i a + z\beta + [\varepsilon_i + v_i a], \; i = N_1 + 1, ..., N_1 + N_2. \tag{10.3.1}$$

The error term in brackets involves v_i, which therefore leads to a missing variable problem.

The conclusion is that one should be very careful before completing a sample!

10.4 THE SPATIAL ERROR MODEL: IV AND ML WITH MISSING DATA

Consider the model

$$\begin{aligned} y &= X\beta + u, \\ u &= \rho_2 W u + \varepsilon \end{aligned} \tag{10.4.1}$$

where $y' = (y_1, ..., y_{N_1}, y_{N_1+1}, ..., y_{N_1+N_2}) = (y'_{(1)}, y'_{(2)})$ is a $1 \times (N_1 + N_2)$ vector, $X' = (X'_{(1)}, X'_{(2)})$, X is exogenous, etc. Assume that $y_{(1)}$ is observed but $y_{(2)}$ is not. Also assume that the elements of ε are i.i.d. $(0, \sigma_\varepsilon^2)$ and have a finite fourth moment.

With evident notation, the weighting matrix W can be partitioned as

$$W = \begin{bmatrix} W_{11} & W_{12} \\ W_{21} & W_{22} \end{bmatrix}. \tag{10.4.2}$$

There are a number of procedures for handling the estimation of (10.4.1) which account for spatial correlation. We will describe some of these procedures and indicate certain problems with some of them.

A Typical Approach

As we have seen in Chapter 2, a standard way to estimate this model is to somehow estimate ρ_2 as, say $\hat{\rho}_2$, take a spatial Cochrane–Orcutt transform of the data, and estimate the resulting model by least squares. This method would be based on the model relating to $y_{(1)}$ which is

$$\begin{aligned} y_{(1)} &= X_{(1)}\beta + u_{(1)}, \\ u_{(1)} &= \rho_2[W_{11}, W_{12}]u + \varepsilon_1 \end{aligned} \tag{10.4.3}$$

where $u = [u_{(1)}, u_{(2)}]$.

Two problem arise. One is that $u_{(2)}$ cannot be estimated because observations on $y_{(2)}$ are not available. Therefore the spatial Cochrane–Orcutt transform involving u_1 would not be equal to $\varepsilon_{(1)}$ but instead would be

$$(I_{N_1} - \rho_2 W_{11})u_{(1)} = \rho_2 W_{12}u_{(2)} + \varepsilon_{(1)}. \tag{10.4.4}$$

This transform involves the term $\rho_2 W_{12}u_{(2)}$. Therefore, without further conditions, the GMM approach cannot be implemented to obtain a consistent estimator of ρ_2.

Asymptotically, one condition under which the term $\rho_2 W_{12}u_{(2)}$ can be ignored in the GMM procedure relates to the size of that part of the sample relating to $y_{(2)}$, namely N_2. Specifically, if N_2 is "small" relative to N_1 in the sense that $N_2/N_1 \to 0$, as $N_1 \to \infty$, the term $\rho_2 W_{12}u_{(2)}$ in (10.4.4) turns out to be asymptotically negligible and so it can be dropped in (10.4.4). The value of N_2 can, but need not, remain finite as the sample size increases as long as $N_2/N_1 \to 0$. This was noted in Kelejian et al. (2013). A proof of this is given in the appendix to this chapter.

Given $N_2/N_1 \to 0$, one can estimate ρ_2 consistently as, say $\hat{\rho}_2$, and use the spatial Cochrane–Orcutt transformation to obtain

$$\begin{aligned} y_{(1)}(\hat{\rho}_2) &= (I_{N_1} - \hat{\rho}_2 W_{11})y_{(1)}, \\ X_{(1)}(\hat{\rho}_2) &= (I_{N_1} - \hat{\rho}_2 W_{11})X_{(1)}, \end{aligned} \tag{10.4.5}$$

and then estimate β as

$$\hat{\beta} = [X'_{(1)}(\hat{\rho}_2)X_{(1)}(\hat{\rho}_2)]^{-1}X'_{(1)}(\hat{\rho}_2)y_{(1)}(\hat{\rho}_2). \tag{10.4.6}$$

Inferences would be based on

$$\hat{\beta} \simeq N(\beta, \hat{\sigma}_\varepsilon^2[X'_{(1)}(\hat{\rho}_2)X_{(1)}(\hat{\rho}_2)]^{-1}) \tag{10.4.7}$$

where $\hat{\sigma}_\varepsilon^2 = [y_{(1)}(\hat{\rho}_2) - X_{(1)}(\hat{\rho}_2)\hat{\beta}]'[y_{(1)}(\hat{\rho}_2) - X_{(1)}(\hat{\rho}_2)\hat{\beta}]/N_1$.

Maximum Likelihood

The maximum likelihood approach can also be considered. For instance, from the second line of (10.4.3) and from (10.4.1) we obtain

$$u_{(1)} = \rho_2[W_{11}, W_{12}](I_{N_1+N_2} - \rho_2 W)^{-1}\varepsilon + \varepsilon_{(1)} \tag{10.4.8}$$

which can be expressed as

$$\begin{aligned} u_{(1)} &= \rho_2[W_{11}, W_{12}](I_{N_1+N_2} - \rho_2 W)^{-1}\varepsilon + [I_{N_1}, 0_{N_1\times N_2}]\varepsilon \\ &= \left\{\rho_2[W_{11}, W_{12}](I_{N_1+N_2} - \rho_2 W)^{-1} + [I_{N_1}, 0_{N_1\times N_2}]\right\}\varepsilon \\ &= M\varepsilon \end{aligned} \tag{10.4.9}$$

where $M = \left\{\rho_2[W_{11}, W_{12}](I_{N_1+N_2} - \rho_2 W)^{-1} + [I_{N_1}, 0_{N_1\times N_2}]\right\}$. It follows that the variance–covariance matrix of $u_{(1)}$ is $\Omega_{(1)}$ where

$$\Omega_{(1)} = \sigma_\varepsilon^2 MM'. \tag{10.4.10}$$

The matrix $\Omega_{(1)}$ is a bit complex and contains W_{21} and W_{22} which relate to the borders. However, it does not involve $X_{(2)}$. If W_{21} and W_{22} are known, the likelihood will be

$$L = \frac{\exp[-\frac{1}{2}(y_{(1)} - X_{(1)}\beta)'\Omega_{(1)}^{-1}(y_{(1)} - X_{(1)}\beta)]}{(2\pi)^{N_1}\,|\Omega_{(1)}|^{1/2}},$$

which, if maximized, will lead to the estimators $\hat{\beta}_{ML}, \hat{\sigma}^2_{\varepsilon,ML}$, and $\hat{\rho}_{2,ML}$, etc. However, as suggested, this approach **cannot** be implemented unless W_{21} and W_{22} are known.

10.5 A MORE GENERAL SPATIAL MODEL[6]

In Section 10.4 above, the considered model contained a spatially lagged error term. This required the estimation of the autoregressive parameter ρ_2 in order to account for spatial correlation, or the maximization of a likelihood involving a rather complicated variance–covariance matrix. As suggested in Chapter 9, researchers may **assume** their error terms are of a certain form but, typically, have no basis for doing so. Also, estimation results are often very sensitive to assumed specifications of the error term.

6. This section is based on formal results given in Kelejian and Prucha (2010b). The model considered in Kelejian and Prucha (2010b) is more general than the one we consider here, but that increase in generality would typically not be considered in practice. Furthermore, it would also unnecessarily complicates notation.

In this section we consider a spatial model which has a spatial lag in the dependent variable. The error term is specified nonparametrically and allows for very general patterns of spatial correlation; see, e.g., Chapter 9. We consider missing observations which relate to the dependent variable, as well as to the exogenous regressors corresponding to those missing on the dependent variable. This pattern of missing observations precludes the use of maximum likelihood estimation, and so IV estimation is considered.

In this section we give formal asymptotic results. This is important because in many cases researchers "fill in" missing observations in an *ad hoc* way, or in some cases simply ignore them. Empirical results based upon such "processes" are given as if there are no data problems.

The model considered by Kelejian and Prucha (2010b) is

$$\begin{bmatrix} y_1 \\ y_2 \\ y_3 \end{bmatrix} = \begin{bmatrix} X_1 \\ X_2 \\ X_3 \end{bmatrix} \beta + \rho_1 \begin{bmatrix} W_{11} & W_{12} & 0 \\ W_{21} & W_{22} & W_{23} \\ W_{31} & W_{32} & W_{33} \end{bmatrix} \begin{bmatrix} y_1 \\ y_2 \\ y_3 \end{bmatrix} + \begin{bmatrix} u_1 \\ u_2 \\ u_3 \end{bmatrix}, \tag{10.5.1}$$

$$\begin{bmatrix} u_1 \\ u_2 \\ u_3 \end{bmatrix} = \begin{bmatrix} P_{11} & P_{12} & P_{13} \\ P_{21} & P_{22} & P_{23} \\ P_{31} & P_{32} & P_{33} \end{bmatrix} \begin{bmatrix} \varepsilon_1 \\ \varepsilon_2 \\ \varepsilon_3 \end{bmatrix}$$

where y_i is an $N_i \times 1, i = 1, 2, 3$ vector of values of the dependent variable, X_i is an $N_i \times k$ matrix of values of k exogenous variables, $W_{ij}, i, j = 1, 2, 3$ with $W_{13} = 0$ are correspondingly defined components of a weighting matrix. We assume that y_1, y_2, X_1, and X_2 are observed, but y_3 and X_3 are not. We also assume that all of the components of weighting matrix are known.

The model in (10.5.1) can be written in more compact notation as

$$\begin{aligned} y &= X\beta + \rho_1 Wy + u, \\ u &= P\varepsilon \end{aligned} \tag{10.5.2}$$

where $y' = (y_1, y_2, y_3)$, $X' = (X_1', X_2', X_3')$, W is the $(N_1 + N_2 + N_3) \times (N_1 + N_2 + N_3)$ weighting matrix, P is the $(N_1 + N_2 + N_3) \times (N_1 + N_2 + N_3)$ matrix multiplying $\varepsilon' = (\varepsilon_1', \varepsilon_2', \varepsilon_3')$ on the second line of (10.5.1).

The assumptions concerning the missing values and the specification in (10.5.1) are quite reasonable. Typically, in spatial models all units are not neighbors to all other units. In (10.5.1) the units corresponding to y_3 are not neighbors to those of y_1. On the other hand, the model in (10.5.1) allows the units defining y_1 to be neighbors of the units defining y_3. This asymmetric dependence does not affect any of the results. Given that y_2 and X_1 are observed, all of the regressors for the model relating to y_1 are observed. On the other hand, since y_3 is not observed, all of the regressors for the model corresponding to y_2 are not available because the spatial lag involves y_3.

Kelejian and Prucha (2010b) considered three cases concerning the size of the samples, N_1, N_2, and N_3. Specifically,

Case 1. $N_1 \to \infty$.

Case 2. $N_1 \to \infty$ and $\frac{N_3}{(N_1+N_2)^{1/2}} \to 0$.

Case 3. $N_1 \to \infty$ and $\frac{N_3}{(N_1+N_2)^{1/2}} \to c > 0$.

In Case 1, there are no assumptions concerning N_2 and N_3. For example, they could both remain finite, or tend to infinity at any rate. As an illustration, both $N_2/N_1 \to \infty$ and $N_3/N_1 \to \infty$ are possible. In Case 2, N_3 may remain finite, or increase beyond limit but at a rate less than that of $(N_1 + N_2)^{1/2}$. This allows for the possibility that both N_2 and N_3 could increase faster than N_1. If so, Case 2 requires that $N_3/N_2^{1/2} \to 0$. In Case 3, N_3 is assumed to increase at the same rate as that of $(N_1 + N_2)^{1/2}$. Clearly, if N_3 does not increase beyond limit, Case 3 would reduce to Case 2.

Asymptotic distributions corresponding to the three cases described above were determined by Kelejian and Prucha (2010b), and are described below. Before applying those asymptotic results for purposes of hypothesis testing in the three cases, the researcher should at least check the conditions of the case. For example, if empirical results are obtained corresponding to Case 2 and $N_1 = 400$, $N_2 = 300$, and $N_3 = 80$, one should be hesitant before applying the asymptotic results for purposes of hypothesis testing, e.g., $80/(700)^{1/2} \simeq 3$.

Kelejian and Prucha (2010b) focused their attention on asymptotic distributions. Those distributions imply consistency of the corresponding parameters estimators. However, if one were only to focus on consistency, the conditions described in Cases 2 and 3 would be too strong. For example, the estimator described corresponding to Cases 2 and 3 can easily be shown to be consistent, under typical assumptions, if $N_3/(N_1 + N_2) \to 0$. We give Monte Carlo results below which are consistent with this claim.

The Model and Estimation Under Case 1

In this case, the considered model is

$$\begin{aligned} y_1 &= X_1\beta + \rho_1 W_{11,12} y_{1,2} + u_1 \quad |\rho_1| < 1, \\ &= Z_1\gamma + u_1, \\ u_1 &= P_1\varepsilon \end{aligned} \tag{10.5.3}$$

where

$$
\begin{aligned}
W_{11,12} &= (W_{11}, W_{12}),\\
y_{1,2}' &= (y_1', y_2'),\\
Z_1 &= (X_1, W_{11,12}y_{1,2}),\\
\gamma' &= (\beta', \lambda),\\
P_1 &= [P_{11}, P_{12}, P_{13}],
\end{aligned}
$$

and where it should be noted that $W_{11,12}$ is an $N_1 \times (N_1 + N_2)$ matrix.[7]

Since the spatially lagged dependent variable is endogenous, the model is estimated by instrumental variables. Note that the maximum likelihood approach would entail a many "difficulties." The reason for this is that y_1 and y_2, which both explicitly appear in (10.5.3), are jointly determined with y_3. The ML approach would therefore be based on the joint distribution of (y_1, y_2, y_3) which would, among other things, involve X_3 which is also not observed.

The instruments for this model are

$$H_1 = (X_1, W_{11}X_1, ..., W_{11}^r X_1)_{LI} \tag{10.5.4}$$

where, in general, the subscript LI denotes the linearly independent columns of the corresponding matrix and, typically, $r = 2$. The assumptions for this model are first presented and then discussed.

Assumption 10.1. The elements of ε are i.i.d. (0, 1), where $\varepsilon' = (\varepsilon_1', \varepsilon_2', \varepsilon_3')$. In addition, they have a finite fourth moment.[8]

Assumption 10.2. The row and column sums of W, $(I_N - aW)^{-1}$, and P are uniformly bounded in absolute value for all $|a| < 1$.

Assumption 10.3. The elements of the instrument matrix H_1 are uniformly bounded in absolute value and, for N_1 large enough, H_1 has full column rank.

Assumption 10.4.

$$
\begin{aligned}
&(A) \quad \lim_{N_1\to\infty} N^{-1} H_1' H_1 = Q_{H_1H_1},\\
&(B) \quad \lim_{N_1\to\infty} N^{-1} H_1' P_1 P_1' H_1 = Q_{H_1P_1P_1H_1},\\
&(C) \quad p\lim_{N_1\to\infty} N_1^{-1} H_1' Z_1 = Q_{H_1Z_1}
\end{aligned}
$$

7. Recall from Section 2.4 that the model can always be renormalized to insure $|\rho_1| < 1$.
8. This statement of the assumption does not allow for triangular arrays. A more formal statement of the assumption which does allow for triangular arrays is the central limit theorem in Section A.15 of the appendix.

where $Q_{H_1H_1}$ and $Q_{H_1P_1P_1H_1}$ are positive definite, and $Q_{H_1Z_1}$ has full column rank.

Assumption 10.1 does not account for triangular arrays. It is given because it is intuitive. A formal version of Assumption 10.1 is given in Section A.15 of the appendix on large sample theory. Assumptions 10.2 and 10.3 are standard, as is Assumption 10.4, except for a subtlety. In particular, one component of the limit in (C) of Assumption 10.4 is $p\lim_{N_1\to\infty} N_1^{-1}H_1'W_{11,12}y_{1,2}$. The term $y_{1,2}$ is an $(N_1+N_2)\times 1$ vector, and in Case 1 one allowed configuration is that $N_2/N_1\to\infty$ but the deflator in (C) of Assumption 10.4 is only N_1^{-1}. The reason that the elements of $H_1'W_{11,12}y_{1,2}$ are only of order N_1 and not (N_1+N_2) is that the rows and columns sums of $W_{11,12}$ are uniformly bounded in absolute value. As an illustration, suppose $N_1=1$ and $N_2\to\infty$. In this case $W_{11,12}$ would be an $1\times(1+N_2)$ matrix. Let e_{1+N_2} be an $(1+N_2)\times 1$ vector all of whose elements are 1. In this case $W_{11,12}e_{1+2N}=\alpha$, where α is a finite constant, i.e., $N_1=1$ and there is only one finite constant. If $N_2=2$, $W_{11,12}e_{1+2N}$ would be a 2×1 vector of **finite** constants, etc.

Let $\hat{Z}_1=H_1(H_1'H_1)^{-1}H_1'Z_1$ and let

$$\hat{\gamma}_1=(\hat{Z}_1'\hat{Z}_1)^{-1}\hat{Z}_1'y_1. \tag{10.5.5}$$

Then, given the model in (10.5.3), H_1 in (10.5.4), and Assumptions 10.1–10.4, Kelejian and Prucha (2010b) prove the following theorem.

Theorem 1.

$$\begin{aligned}
N_1^{1/2}(\hat{\gamma}_1-\gamma)&\to N(0,V_{\hat{\gamma}_1}),\\
V_{\hat{\gamma}_1}&=G_1[Q_{H_1P_{1.}P_{1.}H_1}]G_1',\\
G_1&=(Q_{H_1Z_1}'Q_{H_1H_1}^{-1}Q_{H_1Z_1})^{-1}Q_{H_1Z_1}'Q_{H_1H_1}^{-1}.
\end{aligned} \tag{10.5.6}$$

Small sample inference can be based on the approximation

$$\begin{aligned}
\hat{\gamma}_1&\simeq N(\gamma,N_1^{-1}\hat{V}_{\hat{\gamma}_1}),\\
\hat{V}_{\hat{\gamma}_1}&=\hat{G}_1\hat{Q}_{H_1P_{1.}P_{1.}'H_1}\hat{G}_1',\\
\hat{G}_1&=N_1(\hat{Z}_1'\hat{Z}_1)^{-1}H_1'Z_1(H_1'H_1)^{-1}
\end{aligned} \tag{10.5.7}$$

where $\hat{Q}_{H_1P_{1.}P_{1.}'H_1}$ is the HAC estimator of $Q_{H_1P_{1.}P_{1.}'H_1}$ as described in Chapter 9.

In passing we note that the proof of Theorem 1 is quite standard. No difficulties arise due to the sample size N_2 because the elements of $H_1'W_{11,12}y_{1,2}$ are of order N_1 regardless of the magnitude of N_2.

Model and Estimation Under Case 2

In Case 2, N_3 is "small" relative to $(N_1+N_2)^{1/2}$. The regressors determining y_1 are observed. All of the regressors determining y_2 are observable except for the spatial lag of the dependent variable because $W_{23}y_3$ is not observed. Since N_3 is "relatively" small, the suggestion is to base the estimation of γ on the model determining both y_1 and y_2.

Let $y'_{1+2}=(y'_1, y'_2)$ and $X'_{1+2}=(X'_1, X'_2)$. Then the considered model under Case 2 is

$$\begin{aligned} y_{1+2} &= X_{1+2}\beta+\rho_1 W_{1+2}y_{1+2}+\left\{P_{1+2}\varepsilon+\rho_1\begin{bmatrix}0\\ W_{23}y_3\end{bmatrix}\right\} \\ &= Z_2\gamma+\left\{P_{1+2}\varepsilon+\rho_1\begin{bmatrix}0\\ W_{23}y_3\end{bmatrix}\right\}\end{aligned} \tag{10.5.8}$$

where the terms in the braces can be seen as error terms, and

$$\begin{aligned} Z_2 &= (X_{1+2}, W_{1+2}y_{1+2}), \\ W_{1+2} &= \begin{bmatrix} W_{11} & W_{12} \\ W_{21} & W_{22}\end{bmatrix}, \\ P_{1+2} &= \begin{bmatrix} P_{11} & P_{12} & P_{13} \\ P_{21} & P_{22} & P_{23}\end{bmatrix}. \end{aligned}$$

The instrument matrix for estimating this model is

$$\begin{aligned} H_2 &= (X_{1+2}, W_{1+2}X_{1+2}, \ldots, W^r_{1+2}X_{1+2}) \\ &= (H'_{2.1}, H'_{2.2})' \end{aligned} \tag{10.5.9}$$

where $H_{2.1}$ denotes the first N_1 rows of H_2, $H_{2.2}$ denotes the last N_2 rows of H_2, and where typically $r=2$.

In addition to Assumptions 10.1 and 10.2, we need additional assumptions to derive the asymptotic properties for this case. Those assumptions are listed below:

Assumption 10.5. The elements of the instrument matrix H_2 are uniformly bounded in absolute value, and for N_1 large enough, H_2 has full column rank.

Assumption 10.6.

$$(A) \quad \lim_{N_1\to\infty} N^{-1}H'_2H_2 = Q_{H_2H_2},$$

$$(B) \quad \lim_{N_1\to\infty} N^{-1}H'_2P_2P'_2H_2 = Q_{H_2P_2P_2H_2},$$

$$(C) \quad p\lim_{N_1\to\infty} N_1^{-1} H_2' Z_2 = Q_{H_2 Z_2}$$

where $Q_{H_2H_2}$ and $Q_{H_2P_2P_2H_2}$ are positive definite, and $Q_{H_2Z_2}$ has full column rank.

Notice that nothing is said about the term $\rho_1 \begin{bmatrix} 0' & (W_{23}y_3)' \end{bmatrix}'$ in (10.5.8). The reason for this is that this term is asymptotically negligible and therefore can be ignored in the IV estimation of (10.5.8). This will become evident from our "instructive" proof given in the appendix to this chapter.

Let $\hat{Z}_2 = H_2(H_2'H_2)^{-1}H_2'Z_2$. Then, the IV estimator of γ is

$$\hat{\gamma}_2 = (\hat{Z}_2 \hat{Z}_2)^{-1} \hat{Z}_2' y_{1+2}. \tag{10.5.10}$$

Given the model in (10.5.8), and Assumptions 10.1, 10.2, 10.5, 10.6 and the limits described in Case 2, Kelejian and Prucha prove the following theorem.

Theorem 2.

$$\begin{aligned} &(N_1 + N_2)^{1/2}(\hat{\gamma}_2 - \gamma) \xrightarrow{D} N(0, V_{\hat{\gamma}_2}), \qquad (10.5.11)\\ &V_{\hat{\gamma}_2} = G_2[Q_{H_2P_2.P_2.H_2}]G_2',\\ &G_2 = (Q_{H_2Z_2}' Q_{H_2H_2}^{-1} Q_{H_2Z_2})^{-1} Q_{H_2Z_2}' Q_{H_2H_2}^{-1}. \end{aligned}$$

In practice inferences can be based on the approximation

$$\begin{aligned} &\hat{\gamma}_2 \simeq N(\gamma, (N_1 + N_2)^{-1}\hat{V}_{\hat{\gamma}_2}),\\ &\hat{V}_{\hat{\gamma}_2} = \hat{G}_2 \hat{Q}_{H_2P_2.P_2.H_2} \hat{G}_2',\\ &\hat{G}_2 = (N_1 + N_2)(\hat{Z}_2\hat{Z}_2)^{-1} Z_2' H_2 (H_2'H_2)^{-1} \end{aligned}$$

where again $\hat{Q}_{H_2P_2.P_2.H_2}$ would be obtained by an HAC estimator as described in Chapter 9.

Model and Estimation Under Case 3

Under Case 3, the model and estimator of γ in (10.5.10) is the same. Kelejian and Prucha show that under Case 3, $\hat{\gamma}_2$ is consistent. However, the mean of the corresponding large sample is not zero and involves X_3. If X_3 is not observed, as we have assumed and would be typical in practice, the large sample distribution relating to $\hat{\gamma}_2$ is not "overly" useful.[9]

9. It may be confusing that an estimator is consistent, yet the mean of its normalized large sample distribution is not zero. An example may clarify the situation.

Illustration 10.5.1: A Monte Carlo experiment under Case 1 and Case 2

In order to analyze the small sample performance of the estimators under Cases 1 and 2, we set up a Monte Carlo experiment. Our data generating process is a special case of the model in (10.5.2), namely

$$y = \beta_0 + \beta_1 x_1 + \beta_2 x_2 + \lambda W y + \varepsilon$$

where the matrix P that appeared in (10.5.2) is taken to be an identity matrix. The two regressors (x_1 and x_2) have been used in various illustrations in the book. In particular, x_1 is a normalized version of income per capita in 1980 and x_2 represents the proportion of housing units that are rental units in the same year. The sample observations refer to 760 counties in the Midwestern United States. The parameters β_0, β_1, and β_2 are set to one, and we consider only one value for λ, namely 0.3. Finally, we generate ε from a normal distribution with mean zero and standard deviation equal to two.

We set up two experiments for Case 1 and two different experiments for Case 2. The difference between those experiments relates to the dimension of the three subsamples. For the first experiment related to Case 1, we set $N_1 = 400$, $N_2 = 16$, and $N_3 = 49$, while for the second experiment we pick $N_1 = 400$, $N_2 = 625$, and $N_3 = 144$. Recall that in Case 1 the values of N_2 and N_3 are irrelevant. For the first experiment related to Case 2, we set $N_1 = 400$, $N_2 = 625$, and $N_3 = 20$, while for the second experiment we set $N_1 = 400$, $N_2 = 625$, and $N_3 = 100$. In this second experiment for Case 2, $100/(1025)^{1/2} \simeq 3$, and so one might be hesitant to apply the asymptotic results for purposes of hypothesis testing. However, since $100/(1025) \simeq 0.098$, one would assume consistency and so expect biases and mean squared error to be somewhat small.

As for the spatial weight matrix, we follow the structure in (10.5.1) where the elements of W_{13} are set to zero, and we consider two different spatial weighting matrix both based on a circular world. The first one takes as neighbors the six ahead and six behind spatial units (ab = 6), and the second one considers the 20 ahead and 20 behind spatial units (ab = 20).

Using evident notation, let $\hat{\beta}$ be an estimator of β, and suppose its large sample distribution is

$$N^{1/2}(\hat{\beta} - \beta) \xrightarrow{D} N(\alpha, V)$$

where the mean and VC matrix are finite. Then,

$$(\hat{\beta} - \beta) = [N^{-1/2}]N^{1/2}(\hat{\beta} - \beta) \xrightarrow{D} N(0, 0)$$

and so $\hat{\beta} \xrightarrow{P} \beta$; see (A.10.1) and (A.10.2) in the appendix on large sample theory.

TABLE 10.5.1 Bias and MSE for the estimator in Case 1 under different sample size combinations and weighting matrices

	BIAS Model in Case 1			
	β_0	β_1	β_2	λ
$N_1=400$, $N_2=16$, $N_3=49$, ab = 6	−0.0085	−0.0066	−0.0041	0.0050
$N_1=400$, $N_2=625$, $N_3=49$, ab = 6	−0.0089	−0.0060	−0.0029	0.0046
$N_1=400$, $N_2=16$, $N_3=49$, ab = 20	−0.0142	−0.0074	−0.0044	0.0085
$N_1=400$, $N_2=625$, $N_3=49$, ab = 20	−0.0164	−0.0071	−0.0033	0.0094
	MSE **Model in Case 1**			
	β_0	β_1	β_2	λ
$N_1=400$, $N_2=16$, $N_3=49$, ab = 6	0.0370	0.0123	0.0131	0.0118
$N_1=400$, $N_2=625$, $N_3=49$, ab = 6	0.0372	0.0127	0.0128	0.0117
$N_1=400$, $N_2=16$, $N_3=49$, ab = 20	0.0478	0.0125	0.0131	0.0164
$N_1=400$, $N_2=625$, $N_3=49$, ab = 20	0.0472	0.0128	0.0128	0.0160

TABLE 10.5.2 Bias and MSE for the estimator in Case 2 under different sample size combinations and weighting matrices

	BIAS Model in Case 2			
	β_0	β_1	β_2	λ
$N_1=400$, $N_2=625$, $N_3=20$, ab = 6	−0.0042	−0.0033	−0.0028	0.0023
$N_1=400$, $N_2=625$, $N_3=100$, ab = 6	−0.0057	−0.0026	−0.0028	0.0029
$N_1=400$, $N_2=625$, $N_3=20$, ab = 20	−0.0068	−0.0033	−0.0030	0.0044
$N_1=400$, $N_2=625$, $N_3=100$, ab = 20	−0.0097	−0.0030	−0.0030	0.0058
	MSE **Model in Case 2**			
	β_0	β_1	β_2	λ
$N_1=400$, $N_2=625$, $N_3=20$, ab = 6	0.0161	0.0043	0.0041	0.0048
$N_1=400$, $N_2=625$, $N_3=100$, ab = 6	0.0156	0.0045	0.0043	0.0047
$N_1=400$, $N_2=625$, $N_3=20$, ab = 20	0.0213	0.0044	0.0041	0.0070
$N_1=400$, $N_2=625$, $N_3=100$, ab = 20	0.0208	0.0045	0.0043	0.0068

Results from these experiments are reported in Tables 10.5.1 and 10.5.2 and are based on 10,000 Monte Carlo samples. Specifically, Table 10.5.1 displays the results for Case 1 under different sample size combinations and weighting matrices. The upper part of the table reports on the bias, while the bottom part shows the mean squared error. The results for Case 2 are presented in Table 10.5.2 following the same format.

While looking at Table 10.5.1, we should keep in mind that in Case 1 there are no assumptions concerning the magnitudes of N_2 and N_3, and, in a sense, asymptotically only N_1 matters. So we expect the bias and MSE results for the two sample configurations to be very similar. A glance at Table 10.5.1 reveals that this theoretical expectation is confirmed in the Monte Carlo results in that the bias figures are all very small. Specifically, given the spatial weighting matrix, an increase in the sample size for N_2 does not seem to affect the bias very much. The use of a less sparse spatial weighting matrix (second two rows of the table) seems to affect the bias even if this effect is still very mild. The same considerations can be made about the MSE.

We now turn our attention to Table 10.5.2. As for the bias, the figures are again consistently very small. This is true both if we use a different weighting matrix and if we select a larger sample size for N_3. Additionally, as can be observed from the bottom part of the table and consistently with the theoretical expectation, the mean squared errors are very small despite the selection of N_3.

10.6 SPATIAL ERROR MODELS: BE CAREFUL WHAT YOU DO

Consider the spatial error model

$$
\begin{aligned}
y_i &= X_i\beta + u_i, \ i = 1, 2, \qquad (10.6.1)\\
u &= \rho_2 W u + \varepsilon,\\
u' &= \begin{bmatrix} u_1', & u_2' \end{bmatrix}, \ \varepsilon' = \begin{bmatrix} \varepsilon_1' & \varepsilon_2' \end{bmatrix},\\
W &= \begin{bmatrix} W_{11} & W_{12} \\ W_{21} & W_{22} \end{bmatrix},\\
\varepsilon &\sim N(0, \sigma^2 I_N), \ N = N_1 + N_2
\end{aligned}
$$

where y_1 is an $N_1 \times 1$ vector of dependent variables which are observed, y_2 is an $N_2 \times 1$ vector of dependent variables which are **not** observed, X_1 and X_2 are correspondingly defined observed nonstochastic matrices, etc. This scenario might be consistent with models of housing prices where the hedonic characteristics of new houses are known but the price of those new houses is not yet known. Assume the usual conditions. The problem is to determine the value of the second equation in the estimation of β. That is, because of the spatially lagged error terms, the vectors y_1 and y_2 are obviously dependent. Thus, one might try to "fill in" the missing values of y_2 in terms of their predictions based on y_1, and then use the completed sample to estimate β; see, e.g., LeSage and Pace (2004) and references cited therein. In this section we show that there is no value in completing the sample concerning the estimation of β.

Noting that $u = (I_N - \rho_2 W)^{-1}\varepsilon$, the variance–covariance matrix of u is $\Sigma_u = \sigma^2(I_N - \rho_2 W)^{-1}(I_N - \rho_2 W')^{-1}$. Partition Σ_u as

$$\Sigma_u = \begin{bmatrix} \Sigma_{1,1} & \Sigma_{1,2} \\ \Sigma_{2,1} & \Sigma_{2,2} \end{bmatrix}$$

and, given the normality assumption, obtain

$$E(y_2|y_1) = X_2\beta + \Sigma_{2,1}\Sigma_{1,1}^{-1}(y_1 - X_1\beta). \tag{10.6.2}$$

Therefore

$$y_2 = X_2\beta + \Sigma_{2,1}\Sigma_{1,1}^{-1}(y_1 - X_1\beta) + \eta_2 \tag{10.6.3}$$

where

$$E(\eta_2|y_1) = 0. \tag{10.6.4}$$

Given (10.6.3), the equation in (10.6.1) relating to y_2 can be written as

$$X_2\beta + \Sigma_{2,1}\Sigma_{1,1}^{-1}(y_1 - X_1\beta) + \eta_2 = X_2\beta + u_2, \tag{10.6.5}$$

or after simplifying as

$$\Sigma_{2,1}\Sigma_{1,1}^{-1}y_1 = \Sigma_{2,1}\Sigma_{1,1}^{-1}X_1\beta + [u_2 - \eta_2]. \tag{10.6.6}$$

Multiplying the equation in (10.6.1) relating to y_1 across by $\Sigma_{2,1}\Sigma_{1,1}^{-1}$ yields

$$\Sigma_{2,1}\Sigma_{1,1}^{-1}y_1 = \Sigma_{2,1}\Sigma_{1,1}^{-1}X_1\beta + \Sigma_{2,1}\Sigma_{1,1}^{-1}u_1. \tag{10.6.7}$$

The results in (10.6.6) and (10.6.7) imply

$$\eta_2 = u_2 - \Sigma_{2,1}\Sigma_{1,1}^{-1}u_1 \tag{10.6.8}$$

so that, even though there is spatial correlation, there is no value in (10.6.6), i.e., it's just a linear combination of the equations in (10.6.1) relating to y_1. Alternatively, there is no information in the equation of (10.6.1) relating to y_2!

In a sense, all of this can easily be seen by considering the likelihood function of y_1. Given the normality assumption and (10.6.1),

$$y_1 \sim N(X_1\beta, \sigma^2 V_{11}) \tag{10.6.9}$$

where V_{11} is the upper $N_1 \times N_1$ block of $(I - \rho_2 W)^{-1}(I - \rho_2 W')^{-1}$. Therefore the likelihood only contains $\beta, \sigma^2, \rho_2, X_1$, and W. It does not contain X_2.

There are at least three ways of estimating the parameters in (10.6.9). One is maximum likelihood. In this case a computational difficulty relates to the matrix V_{11}. If $N_2/N_1 \to 0$, a second way to estimate β, σ^2, and ρ_2 is to use the procedure described in Section 10.4 which estimates the parameter ρ_2, then transforms the data via the spatial Cochrane–Orcutt method, and then estimates the resulting model by least squares.

A third method is to express the model in (10.6.1) relating to y_1 as

$$\begin{aligned} y_1 &= X_1\beta + u_1, \\ E(u_1 u_1') &= S \end{aligned} \tag{10.6.10}$$

where the information that $u = \rho_2 W u + \varepsilon$ is ignored, and so S is just taken as the variance–covariance matrix of u_1. In this case the least squares estimator of β based on (10.6.10) is

$$\hat{\beta} = (X_1'X_1)^{-1}X_1'y_1. \tag{10.6.11}$$

Then, assuming typical conditions, it is left as an exercise for the reader to show that

$$N_1^{1/2}(\hat{\beta} - \beta) \xrightarrow{D} N(0, Q_{x_1x_1}^{-1} Q_{X_1SX_1} Q_{x_1x_1}^{-1}) \tag{10.6.12}$$

where $Q_{x_1x_1} = \lim_{N_1\to\infty} N_1^{-1}(X_1'X_1)$ and $Q_{X_1SX_1} = \lim_{N_1\to\infty} N_1^{-1}X_1'SX_1$. In practice inferences can be based on

$$\hat{\beta} \simeq N(\beta, N_1(X_1'X_1)^{-1}\hat{Q}_{X_1SX_1}(X_1'X_1)^{-1} \tag{10.6.13}$$

where $\hat{Q}_{X_1SX_1}$ is the HAC estimator of $Q_{X_1SX_1}$.

APPENDIX A10 PROOFS FOR CHAPTER 10

Asymptotic Negligibility of $\rho_2 \mathbf{W}_{12}\mathbf{u}_{(2)}$ in GMM Estimator of ρ_2

From (10.4.4) we have $u_{(1)} - \rho_2 W_{11} u_{(1)} = \rho_2 W_{12} u_{(2)} + \varepsilon_{(1)}$ and so the first equation underlying the GMM procedure is

$$\begin{aligned} &N_1^{-1}[u_{(1)} - \rho_2 W_{11}u_{(1)}]'[u_{(1)} - \rho_2 W_{11}u_{(1)}] \\ &= \rho_2^2 N_1^{-1} u_{(2)}' W_{12}' W_{12} u_{(2)} \\ &+ N_1^{-1}\varepsilon_{(1)}'\varepsilon_{(1)} + 2\rho_2 N_1^{-1}\varepsilon_{(1)}' W_{12}u_{(2)}. \end{aligned} \tag{A10.1}$$

Let $\delta = N_1^{-1}u_{(2)}' W_{12}' W_{12} u_{(2)}$ and $\Omega_2 = E(u_{(2)}u_{(2)}')$. Given typical assumptions, the row and column sums of $(I_N - \rho_2 W)^{-1}$ are uniformly bounded in absolute value, and so are the row and column sums of $(I_N - \rho_2 W)^{-1}(I_N - \rho_2 W')^{-1}$. It follows that that the row and column sums of Ω_2 are also uniformly bounded in absolute value. Now note that

$$\begin{aligned} E(\delta) &= N_1^{-1} E(u'_{(2)} W'_{12} W_{12} u_{(2)}) \\ &= N_1^{-1} Tr(E[u_{(2)})u'_{(2)} W'_{12} W_{12}]) \\ &= N_1^{-1} Tr(\Omega_2 W'_{12} W_{12}) \end{aligned} \tag{A10.2}$$

where the row and column sums of the $N_2 \times N_2$ matrix $\Omega_2 W'_{12} W_{12}$ are also uniformly bounded in absolute value since both Ω_2 and $W'_{12} W_{12}$ are such. It follows that $Tr(\Omega_2 W'_{12} W_{12}) = 0(N_2)$. Therefore, since $N_2/N_1 \to 0$,

$$\begin{aligned} E(\delta) &= N_1^{-1} Tr(\Omega_2 W'_{12} W_{12}) \\ &= N_1^{-1}\, 0(N_2) \to 0. \end{aligned} \tag{A10.3}$$

Now recall that the elements of ε are i.i.d. with finite fourth moments. Note that each element of $u_{(2)}$ is linear in ε with weights that relate to the rows of W. It follows that the elements of $u_{(2)}$ also have finite fourth moments.

Let $S = W'_{12} W_{12}$ and let its (i, j)th element be s_{ij}. Let the ith element of $u_{(2)}$ be $u_{2,i}$. Then

$$\begin{aligned} E(\delta^2) &= N_1^{-2} E\,[u'_{(2)} S\, u_{(2)}]^2 \\ &= N_1^{-2}\, E \left[\sum_{i=1}^{N_2} \sum_{j=1}^{N_2} u_{2,i} u_{2,j} s_{ij} \right]^2 \\ &= N_1^{-2}\, E[\sum_{i=1}^{N_2} \sum_{j=1}^{N_2} \sum_{r=1}^{N_2} \sum_{q=1}^{N_2} u_{2,i} u_{2,j} u_{2,r} u_{2,q} s_{ij} s_{rq}] \\ &= N_1^{-2} \sum_{i=1}^{N_2} \sum_{j=1}^{N_2} \sum_{r=1}^{N_2} \sum_{q=1}^{N_2} E[u_{2,i} u_{2,j} u_{2,r} u_{2,q}] s_{ij} s_{rq} \\ &\le N_1^{-2} \sum_{i=1}^{N_2} \sum_{j=1}^{N_2} \sum_{r=1}^{N_2} \sum_{q=1}^{N_2} E|u_{2,i} u_{2,j} u_{2,r} u_{2,q}|\, |s_{ij}|\, |s_{rq}| \\ &\le c_4 N_1^{-2} \sum_{i=1}^{N_2} \sum_{j=1}^{N_2} |s_{ij}| \sum_{r=1}^{N_2} \sum_{q=1}^{N_2} |s_{rq}| \\ &\le c_4 c_s^2 N_1^{-2} \sum_{i=1}^{N_2} \sum_{r=1}^{N_2} \\ &\le c_4 c_s^2 N_2^2 / N_1^2 \to 0 \end{aligned} \tag{A10.4}$$

where $c_4 = \max_{i,j,r,q} E|u_{2,i}u_{2,j}u_{2,r}u_{2,q}|$, and c_s is a finite constant such that $\sum_{j=1}^{N_2} |s_{ij}| < c_s$ and $\sum_{q=1}^{N_2} |s_{rq}| < c_s$. Since $var(\delta) = E(\delta^2) - [E(\delta)]^2$, it follows from (A10.3), (A10.4), and Chebyshev's inequality that

$$\begin{aligned}\delta &= N_1^{-1} u'_{(2)} W'_{12} W_{12} u_{(2)} \\ &\xrightarrow{P} 0.\end{aligned}$$

Using similar manipulations, it is not difficult to show that in (A10.1) the term $2\rho_2 N_1^{-1} \varepsilon'_{(1)} W_{12} u_{(2)} \xrightarrow{P} 0$. It follows that the term $\rho_2 W_{12} u_{(2)}$ can be ignored in the GMM procedure.

SUGGESTED PROBLEMS

1. The model in (10.5.8) and the result in (10.5.11) imply that the term involving $W_{23}y_3$ is asymptotically negligible in the estimation of $\hat{\gamma}_2$ in (10.5.10). Demonstrate this. (**Hint**) First express

$$H_2 = (H'_{2.1}, H'_{2.2})'$$

where $H_{2.1}$ and $H_{2.2}$ are respectively the first N_1 and last N_2 rows of H_2. Then note that $W_{23}y_3$ will be asymptotically negligible in the estimation of $\hat{\gamma}_2$ if

$$(N_1 + N_2)^{-1/2} H'_{2.2} W_{23} y_3 \xrightarrow{P} 0$$

as $N_1 \to \infty$ and $\frac{N_3}{(N_1+N_2)^{1/2}} \to 0$.

2. For $\hat{c}_r$ in (10.2.8), show that $E(\hat{c}_r|\varphi) = c$, and so unconditionally $E(\hat{c}_r) = c$.
3. Derive the expression for $VC_{\hat{c}_r}$ in (10.2.9).
4. For the model in (10.2.22), explain why it is stated that the normality assumption may not always be ideal!
5. Consider the model

$$y_i = a\exp(\lambda x_i) + \varepsilon_i, \; i = 1, ..., N$$

where ε_i are i.i.d. $(0, \sigma^2)$. Let $F = [a\exp(\lambda x_1), ..., a\exp(\lambda x_N)]'$ and $\gamma = (a, \lambda)'$. Evaluate the expression $\frac{\partial F}{\partial \gamma}$; see, e.g., (10.2.29).
6. Although not necessary for the suggested procedure, what exactly is γ in (10.2.2)?

Chapter 11

Tests for Spatial Correlation

11.1 INTRODUCTORY COMMENTS: OCCAM'S RAZOR[1]

Perhaps one of the oldest, and most widely and implicitly accepted principles in scientific research is Occam's razor. Simply put, the principle states that if there are two models which explain a given event, one should prefer the model with the fewest assumptions, i.e., cut away unnecessary variables! Intuitively, assume that an individual sees an object at position X (Fig. 11.1.1). At a later point the individual observes the same object at position Y, but he/she does not know how the object moved from X to Y. According to the Occam's razor principle, the individual would assume that the object traveled by the path labeled A and not by the path labeled B.

To put things in perspective, Occam's razor was the principle that led to the acceptance of the hypothesis that the sun is the central body in our solar system, and not the earth! An implication of Occam's razor is that one should only accept a more complex model if the available evidence (i.e., the data) "forces" you to do so. For example, the estimation of linear models with spatially correlated error terms is more complex than models with i.i.d. error terms. Thus, in testing between such models, the null, or maintained hypothesis would be that the error terms are i.i.d. Indeed, in model testing procedures, unless there are strong rea-

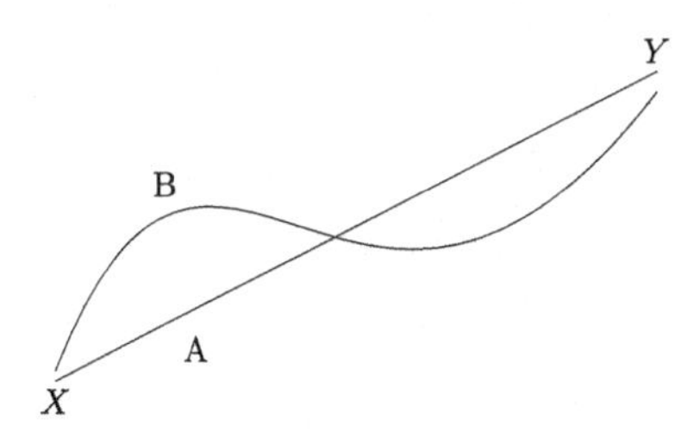

FIGURE 11.1.1 A comparison of two models

1. Classic references relating to tests for spatial correlation in a single panel framework are Moran (1950), Cliff and Ord (1972, 1973, 1981), Burridge (1980), and Anselin (1988). Other interesting studies are Bartels and Hordijk (1977), King (1981), Anselin and Rey (1991), Anselin (2001), Anselin and Moreno (2003), Kelejian and Prucha (2001), Anselin and Florax (1995a), Florax and de Graaff (2004), Pinkse (2004), and Kelejian and Robinson (2004).

Spatial Econometrics. http://dx.doi.org/10.1016/B978-0-12-813387-3.00011-1

sons to believe otherwise, the simpler model is always the null, or maintained model.

The above discussion relates to a general principle in scientific research. However, there are more immediate reasons why tests for spatial correlation are of the essence. For example, if error terms are spatially correlated, and this is not accounted for in the estimation procedure, tests of hypotheses as well as the efficiency of parameter estimation will be affected. Clearly, the issue of spatially correlated error terms should not be ignored.

We note, however, a caveat. Sometimes researchers consider testing for the spatial correlation of a variable, say y, that might typically be viewed as a dependent variable in a spatial model. In a standard linear spatial model containing exogenous regressors, as well as a spatially lagged dependent variable there are many reasons for y to be spatially correlated. For example, the exogenous variables themselves are often spatially correlated, the spatial lag in the dependent variable induces spatial correlation, and, of course, the error terms can be spatially correlated. However, in the present chapter we only focus on the possible spatial correlation of the error terms. In fact, as we stated in Chapter 2, spatial correlation of other explanatory variables in a spatial model are often of no concern!

Below we present tests for spatial correlation of the error terms under various conditions. These tests are described in a single panel framework.

11.2 SOME PRELIMINARY ISSUES ON A QUADRATIC FORM

Consider the quadratic form Q

$$Q = v'Av \tag{11.2.1}$$

where $A = A'$ is an $N \times N$ constant matrix, $v' = (v_1, ..., v_N)$, and v has mean and VC matrix of 0 and Σ, respectively, where Σ is nonsingular. Let the (i, j)th element of A be a_{ij}, and let $P'\Sigma P = I_N$ so that $\Sigma = (P')^{-1}P^{-1}$. Let $\varepsilon = P'v = (\varepsilon_1, ..., \varepsilon_n)'$ so that $E(\varepsilon) = 0$ and $E(\varepsilon\varepsilon') = P'\Sigma P = I_N$. Given its mean and variance, assume also that ε_i, $i = 1, ..., N$ are i.i.d. and

$$E|\varepsilon_i^3| = \mu_3 < \infty, \tag{11.2.2}$$
$$E(\varepsilon_i^4) = \mu_4 < \infty.$$

Finally, let

$$A^* = P^{-1}A(P')^{-1}. \tag{11.2.3}$$

Since A is symmetric, A^* is also symmetric. For future reference note that

$$Tr(A^*) = Tr[P^{-1}A(P')^{-1}] \tag{11.2.4}$$

$$= Tr[(P')^{-1}P^{-1}A]$$
$$= Tr[\Sigma A].$$

Note that $v = (P')^{-1}\varepsilon$, and so from (11.2.1) and (11.2.3)

$$Q = \varepsilon' P^{-1} A (P')^{-1} \varepsilon \quad (11.2.5)$$
$$= \varepsilon' A^* \varepsilon.$$

Given the above assumptions, and recalling that the elements of ε are i.i.d. (0, 1), the following results are a special case of results given in Kelejian and Prucha (2001):

$$E(Q) = Tr(A^*) \quad (11.2.6)$$
$$var(Q) = 4\sum_{i=1}^{N}\sum_{j=1}^{i-1}(a_{ij}^*)^2 + \sum_{i=1}^{N}(a_{ii}^*)^2[\mu_4 - 1]$$

where a_{ij}^* is the (i, j)th element of A^* and $\mu_4 = E(\varepsilon_i^4)$.[2]

For future reference, if $\varepsilon \sim N(0, I_N)$, and $A^{*\prime} = A^*$ the variance formula in (11.2.6) can be shown to reduce to

$$var(Q) = 2Tr(A^* A^*) \quad (11.2.7)$$

If, in addition $A^* = (W + W')/2$

$$Tr(A^* A^*) = \frac{1}{4}Tr(WW + WW' + W'W + W'W') \quad (11.2.8)$$
$$= \frac{1}{4}Tr(2WW + 2WW')$$
$$= \frac{1}{2}Tr(WW + WW')$$

since $Tr(W'W') = Tr(WW)$ and $Tr(WW') = Tr(W'W)$. Therefore, in this case via (11.2.7) and (11.2.8), the variance of Q reduces to

$$var(Q) = Tr(WW + WW') \quad (11.2.9)$$

An Additional Comment

Let D be any $N \times N$ matrix. Then, since $v'Dv = v'D'v$,

$$v'Dv = v'[\frac{D + D'}{2}]v \quad (11.2.10)$$

2. In Kelejian and Prucha (2001), their term $\sigma_{i,N}^4$ is the square of the variance of the ith element of their random vector. In our case, since ε_i are i.i.d. (0, 1), $E(\varepsilon_i^2) = 1$ and so the squared variance is also 1.

where $\frac{1}{2}(D + D')$ is obviously symmetric. Thus, the restriction that A is symmetric is not binding, e.g., in (11.2.1) just replace A by $(A + A')/2$.

11.3 THE MORAN *I* TEST: A BASIC MODEL

There is a class of tests which are often referred to as Moran I tests, where "I" denotes the name of the test statistic. These tests are based on pioneering studies by Moran (1950), and by Cliff and Ord (1972, 1973, 1981). Some of these tests differ in their level of generality, and some relate to different types of models. This will become apparent from our discussion below. In a sense, the unifying theme of these tests is that they are all based on a statistic which is a variation of the original "I" statistic suggested for the standard regression model and which is given in (11.3.3) below. We will first describe the Moran I test for the OLS model, and then some of its "variations".

Consider the model

$$y = X\beta + u, \qquad (11.3.1)$$
$$u = \rho_2 W u + \varepsilon$$

where X is an $N \times k$ exogenous regressor matrix which has full column rank for N large enough, W is a weighting matrix, and $(I_N - aW)$ is nonsingular for all $|a| < 1$. We will assume that the elements of X are uniformly bounded in absolute value, $N^{-1}X'X \to Q_x$ where Q_x is nonsingular, and the row and column sums of W and $(I_N - \rho_2 W)^{-1}$ are uniformly bounded in absolute value. In addition, the elements of the innovation vector ε are i.i.d. $N(0, \sigma_\varepsilon^2)$.

Clearly, if $\rho_2 = 0$ then $u = \varepsilon$, and so the disturbance vector u is not spatially correlated. Thus, consider the hypotheses

$$H_0 : \rho_2 = 0 \text{ against } H_1 : \rho_2 \neq 0. \qquad (11.3.2)$$

For the model in (11.3.1), the Moran I statistic for testing H_0 against H_1 is

$$I = \frac{\hat{u}' W \hat{u}}{N^{-1}\hat{u}'\hat{u}[Tr(W'W + WW)]^{1/2}}, \qquad (11.3.3)$$
$$\hat{u} = y - X\hat{\beta},\ \hat{\beta} = (X'X)^{-1}X'y.$$

Note that the I statistic is feasible, and can be calculated because it does not involve any unknown parameters. Given the above assumptions, results given in Kelejian and Prucha (2001) imply

$$I \xrightarrow{D} N(0, 1). \qquad (11.3.4)$$

Therefore, based on the Moran I procedure, H_0 would be rejected in favor of H_1 at the 5% level if

$$|\, I \,| > 1.96. \tag{11.3.5}$$

In a number of studies the Moran I test for spatial correlation had been shown to be quite powerful, e.g., see King (1981), Anselin and Rey (1991), and Florax and de Graaff (2004). Below we give an illustration which relates to the finite sample property of the Moran I test. Of course, our results will confirm the results published in this large body of literature.

Let the (i, j)th element of W be w_{ij}. Then, we note that the expression for the Moran I statistic given in Cliff and Ord (1981, p. 201) and in Anselin (1988, p. 101), say I^*, differs from the one in (11.3.3) in that $[Tr(W'W + WW)]^{1/2}$ in our (11.3.3) is replaced by $S = \Sigma_{j=1}^{N}\Sigma_{i=1}^{N} w_{ij}$. In general, $S \neq [Tr(W'W + WW)]^{1/2}$ and so their suggested Moran I statistics are not the same as ours in (11.3.3). However, their test for spatial correlation is based on a transformed or normalized version of I^* which converges in distribution to $N(0, 1)$. Therefore, tests for spatial correlation based on the normalized version of I^* are proper. Interestingly, in that normalization, the term S cancels, suggesting that reference to the term S is somewhat unnecessary.

In passing we note that, given (11.3.1), Burridge (1980) showed that, under normality, the Lagrangian multiplier test of H_0 against H_1 is based on the square of the I statistic in (11.3.3). Recall that the square of a normal (0, 1) variable has a χ_1^2 distribution. Therefore, the Lagrangian multiplier test of H_0 against H_1 is in terms of the χ_1^2 distribution, e.g., at the 5% level reject H_0 if $I^2 > \chi_1^2(0.95)$. Thus, the Lagrangian multiplier test is equivalent to this version of the Moran I test.

An Interpretation of the Moran I Statistic

Under H_0, $u = \varepsilon$, and the term $N^{-1}\hat{u}'\hat{u}$ in the denominator of the I statistic in (11.3.3) is a consistent estimator of σ_ε^2. Similarly, $\hat{\beta}$ is a consistent estimator of β. For purposes of interpretation, consider a variant of the I statistic in (11.3.3) which is based on σ_ε^2 and $u = y - X\beta$ instead of their estimated values counterparts

$$\tilde{I} = \frac{u'Wu}{\sigma_\varepsilon^2[Tr(W'W + WW)]^{1/2}}. \tag{11.3.6}$$

Note that under H_0

$$\begin{aligned} E(\tilde{I}) &= \frac{1}{\sigma_\varepsilon^2[Tr(W'W + WW)]^{1/2}} E(u'Wu) \\ &= \frac{1}{\sigma_\varepsilon^2[Tr(W'W + WW)]^{1/2}} Tr(uu'W) \end{aligned} \tag{11.3.7}$$

$$= \frac{\sigma_\varepsilon^2}{\sigma_\varepsilon^2[Tr(W'W + WW)]^{1/2}} Tr(W)$$
$$= 0,$$

since the diagonal elements of a weighting matrix are zeroes.

Again under H_0, consider now the variance of $\tilde{I}$. Noting that in general W will not be symmetric, the variance of $\tilde{I}$ can be expressed as

$$\begin{aligned} var(\tilde{I}) &= c^2 var(u'Wu) \\ &= c^2 var(u'Gu), \\ G &= [\frac{W + W'}{2}], \; c = \frac{1}{\sigma_\varepsilon^2[Tr(W'W + WW)]^{1/2}}, \end{aligned} \tag{11.3.8}$$

and so in light of (11.2.9) $var(u'Wu)$ is

$$var(u'Wu) = var(u'Gu) = \sigma_\varepsilon^4 Tr(WW + W'W). \tag{11.3.9}$$

It follows from (11.3.6)–(11.3.9) that the mean and variance of $\tilde{I}$ are 0 and 1, respectively. Thus, the Moran I statistic in (11.3.3) is an estimated version of $\tilde{I}$ in (11.3.6).

A Small Sample Version of the Moran I Test

There is a small sample version of the Moran I test of H_0 against H_1 which is based on the assumption that under H_0, $\varepsilon \sim N(0, \sigma_\varepsilon^2)$. The assumption of normality facilitates the calculation of the mean and variance of the I statistic in (11.3.3). Specifically, let $M_x = I - P_x$ where $P_x = X\left(X'X\right)^{-1}X'$. Then, given H_0, $u = \varepsilon \sim N\left(0, \sigma_\varepsilon^2 I\right)$. The mean and variance of the Moran I statistic are

$$\begin{aligned} E(I) &= c_1 Tr(P_x W), \\ var(I) &= c_2 \left\{Tr(M_x W M_x W') + Tr(M_x W M_x W) + [Tr(M_x W)]^2\right\} - [E(I)]^2 \\ c_1 &= \frac{-N}{(N-k)\,[Tr(W'W + WW)]^{1/2}}, \\ c_2 &= \frac{N^2}{(N-k)(N-k+2)\; Tr(W'W + WW)}. \end{aligned} \tag{11.3.10}$$

If the normalizations S in Anselin (1988, p. 102), and S_0 in Cliff and Ord (1981, pp. 202–203) are replaced by $[Tr(W'W + WW)]^{1/2}$, their expressions for the mean and variance of their I statistics are equivalent to those given in (11.3.10).

Note that the mean and variance of I do not involve any unknown parameters and so their calculation is feasible. Given (11.3.10), it follows that

$$\frac{I - E(I)}{var(I)^{1/2}} \sim (0, 1). \tag{11.3.11}$$

It is not difficult to show that as $N \to \infty$,

$$\begin{aligned} E(I) &\to 0, \\ var(I) &\to 1. \end{aligned} \tag{11.3.12}$$

Since $I \xrightarrow{D} N(0, 1)$, the results in (11.3.12) imply

$$\frac{I - E(I)}{var(I)^{1/2}} \xrightarrow{D} N(0, 1). \tag{11.3.13}$$

Based on the "small sample version" of the Moran I test, H_0 would be rejected if

$$\left| \frac{I - E(I)}{var(I)^{1/2}} \right| > 1.96. \tag{11.3.14}$$

Although the small sample mean and variance formulas are based on the normality assumption, the test does very well even in the absence of normality; see, e.g., Anselin and Rey (1991).

Illustration 11.3.1: A Monte Carlo experiment for the Moran I test under a basic model

In this illustration we investigate the finite sample property of the Moran's I test statistic in the simple context of an OLS model using a number of simulated data sets. We generate data on regular lattice structure. In particular, we consider five different regular grids of dimension 7×7 ($N = 49$), 10×10 ($N = 100$), 15×15 ($N = 225$), 20×20 ($N = 400$), and 30×30 ($N = 900$). We consider five values for the spatial coefficient ρ_2, namely, 0, 0.2, 0.4, 0.6, and 0.8. The spatial weighting matrix are based on the queen row normalized contiguity criterion.

Under the null hypothesis of no spatial dependence, the model is specified as a simple linear regression model

$$y = \beta_0 + \beta_1 x_1 + u$$

where β_0 and β_1 are both taken to be one, x_1 is generated from a uniform distribution over the interval $(2, 6)$, and $u_i \sim N(0, 1)$.

The models under the alternative are obtained from the reduced form of (11.3.1) as

$$y = \beta_0 + \beta_1 x_1 + (I - \rho_2 W)^{-1} u$$

TABLE 11.3.1 Frequencies of rejection of the null hypothesis based on Eq. (11.3.3)

N	49	100	225	400	900
$\rho_2 = 0$	0.0377	0.0410	**0.0489**	**0.0457**	**0.0467**
$\rho_2 = 0.2$	0.0985	0.1780	0.3842	0.5842	0.8946
$\rho_2 = 0.4$	0.3423	0.6172	0.9277	0.9937	1.0000
$\rho_2 = 0.6$	0.7066	0.9481	0.9996	1.0000	1.0000
$\rho_2 = 0.8$	0.9451	0.9992	1.0000	1.0000	1.0000

where all variables have already been defined. Each Monte Carlo experiment consists of 10,000 replications.[3]

Table 11.3.1 present the results for the Moran I statistics based on Eq. (11.3.3). The first column reports the different sample sizes, while the first row displays the values for ρ_2. The figures in the table are frequencies of rejection of the null hypothesis based on the Monte Carlo samples. A value of $\rho_2 = 0$ corresponds to an estimate of the size of the test. Values of $\rho_2 \neq 0$ are estimates of the power of the test.

First note the results in Table 11.3.1 in terms of the size of the test. We highlighted in bold the values within two standard deviations of 0.05. For larger sample sizes the rejection frequencies are very close to the theoretical 5% level and fall within the interval [0.0456, 0.0544]. Now consider the rejection frequencies for the test statistic under the alternative hypothesis. The results strongly suggest that the power of the test increases both with the level of spatial autocorrelation and the sample size. For example, when the sample size is small ($N = 49$) and the value of ($\rho_2 = 0.2$), the power of the test is very low, namely 0.0985. However, even when the sample is as small as $N = 49$, when $\rho_2 = 0.8$ the power is very close to 1! Consistent with theoretical expectations, when the sample size is large ($N = 900$), the power is quite high for all of the values of ρ_2 considered.

Table 11.3.2 displays the results for the small sample version of the Moran I statistics based on Eqs. (11.3.10)–(11.3.13). The size of the test is much closer to the 5% value in all experimental situations. There is also a decent increase in power with respect to the numbers in Table 11.3.1, which suggests the use of the small sample version of the Moran I test.

3. This is roughly the number of replication needed to obtain a 95% confidence interval of length 0.0087 on the size of a test statistic. Therefore, an estimate of the size is viewed as being significantly different from the 0.05 theoretical level if it is not within the interval [0.0456, 0.0544].

TABLE 11.3.2 Frequencies of rejection of the null hypothesis based on Eqs. (11.3.10)–(11.3.13)

N	49	100	225	400	900
$\rho_2 = 0$	**0.0492**	**0.0469**	**0.0513**	**0.0476**	**0.0481**
$\rho_2 = 0.2$	0.1630	0.2411	0.4311	0.6238	0.9063
$\rho_2 = 0.4$	0.4567	0.6958	0.9423	0.9946	1.0000
$\rho_2 = 0.6$	0.7919	0.9656	0.9997	1.0000	1.0000
$\rho_2 = 0.8$	0.9668	0.9996	1.0000	1.0000	1.0000

11.4 AN IMPORTANT INDEPENDENCE RESULT

In this section we present an independence result which is due to Koopmans (1942). It is also given in Cliff and Ord (1981, p. 43). This result enables the exact small sample calculation of the mean and variance of the Moran I statistic in (11.3.3). The calculations involved, however, are tedious.

The Independence Result

Let ε_i be i.i.d. $N(0, 1)$, $i = 1, \ldots, N$, and let $h(\varepsilon_1, \ldots, \varepsilon_N)$ be a scale-free function in the sense that $h(\lambda\varepsilon_1, \ldots, \lambda\varepsilon_N) = h(\varepsilon_1, \ldots, \varepsilon_N)$. Then

$$h(\varepsilon_1, \ldots, \varepsilon_N) \text{ and } Q = \sum_{i=1}^{N} \varepsilon_i^2 \text{ are independent.} \tag{11.4.1}$$

Proof.[4] Using evident notation, consider the joint moment generating function (MGF)

$$\begin{aligned}
\phi(t_1, t_2) &= E\left(e^{t_1 h(\varepsilon_1,\ldots,\varepsilon_N)+t_2 Q}\right) \\
&= \int \frac{e^{t_1 h(\varepsilon_1,\ldots,\varepsilon_N)}}{\sqrt{2\pi}^N} e^{t_2 \sum_{i=1}^N \varepsilon_i^2} e^{-\frac{1}{2}\sum_{i=1}^N \varepsilon_i^2} d\underline{\varepsilon} \\
&= \int \frac{e^{t_1 h(\varepsilon_1,\ldots,\varepsilon_N)}}{\sqrt{2\pi}^N} e^{-\frac{1}{2}[1-2t_2]\sum_{i=1}^N \varepsilon_i^2} d\underline{\varepsilon}
\end{aligned} \tag{11.4.2}$$

where we are using the notation

$$d\underline{\varepsilon} = d\varepsilon_1 \ldots d\varepsilon_N.$$

4. This proof is an elaboration of that given in Cliff and Ord (1981).

Let $z_i = (1-2t_2)^{\frac{1}{2}}\,\varepsilon_i$ in (11.4.2). Then, since $h(\varepsilon_1,\ldots,\varepsilon_N)$ is scale free, $h\left(\frac{z_1}{(1-2t_2)},\ldots,\frac{z_N}{(1-2t_2)}\right) = h(z_1,...,z_N)$ and so

$$\begin{aligned}\phi(t_1,t_2) &= \frac{1}{(1-2t_2)^{\frac{N}{2}}}\int e^{t_1 h(z_1,\ldots,z_N)}\, e^{-\frac{1}{2}\sum z_i^2}\, d\underline{z} \\ &= \frac{1}{(1-2t_2)^{\frac{N}{2}}}\int e^{t_1 h(\varepsilon_1,\ldots,\varepsilon_N)} e^{-\frac{1}{2}\sum \varepsilon_i^2} d\underline{\varepsilon} \\ &= \frac{1}{(1-2t_2)^{\frac{N}{2}}} E\left(e^{t_1 h(\varepsilon_1,\ldots,\varepsilon_N)}\right) \\ &= g_1(t_1)\, g_2(t_2)\end{aligned} \tag{11.4.3}$$

where we have again used the notation

$$d\underline{z} = dz_1 \ldots dz_N.$$

Thus $h(\varepsilon_1,\ldots,\varepsilon_N)$ and Q are independent since their joint MGF factors.

Three things are worth noticing:

1. The second line in (11.4.3) is simply a change of notation.
2. The above can be carried out in terms of the joint characteristic function, and so the MGF need not exist for the independence result to hold.
3. It should be clear that the result concerning independence holds if ε_i are i.i.d. $N(0,\sigma_\varepsilon^2)$.

11.5 APPLICATION: THE MOMENTS OF THE MORAN *I*

Given the assumption of normality H_0: $u = \varepsilon \sim N\left(0, \sigma_\varepsilon^2 I\right)$, we show below that the above independence result implies that the Moran I statistic in (11.3.3) is independent of $\left(\hat{u}'\hat{u}\right)$ in its denominator. Therefore, multiplying (11.3.3) across by $\hat{u}'\hat{u}$ and raising I to the Jth power yields

$$I^J\ (\hat{u}'\hat{u})^J = \frac{N^J\ (\hat{u}'W\hat{u})^J}{[Tr(W'W+WW)]^{J/2}}. \tag{11.5.1}$$

Given the independence of I and $\hat{u}'\hat{u}$, taking expectations across (11.5.1) yields

$$E(I^J)\ E[(\hat{u}'\hat{u})^J] = \frac{N^J\ E[(\hat{u}'W\hat{u})^J]}{[Tr(W'W+WW)]^{J/2}} \tag{11.5.2}$$

and so

$$E(I^J) = \frac{N^J\ E[(\hat{u}'W\hat{u})^J]}{E[(\hat{u}'\hat{u})^J]\ [Tr(W'W+WW)]^{J/2}}. \tag{11.5.3}$$

Thus, the moments of I can be determined in terms of the moments of $\hat{u}'M_x\hat{u}$ and $\hat{u}'\hat{u}$.

Proof that I is Independent of $\hat{u}'\hat{u}$

First note that $M_x = (I_N - P_x)$ is symmetric and idempotent, and so its characteristic roots are either 0 or 1. The number of nonzero roots is equal to the rank of M_x which is equal to its trace, namely $Tr(M_x) = Tr(I_N - X(X'X)^{-1}X') = N - Tr(X'X(X'X)^{-1}) = N - k$.

Let $\psi = G'\hat{u} = G'M_x u$, where G is such that $G'G = GG' = I_N$ and

$$G'(I_N - P_x)G = D = \begin{bmatrix} I_{N-k} & 0 \\ 0 & 0 \end{bmatrix}. \tag{11.5.4}$$

Under H_0, $u = \varepsilon \sim N\left(0, \sigma_\varepsilon^2 I\right)$, and so $\psi = N(0, \sigma_\varepsilon^2 G'M_x G) = N(0, \sigma_\varepsilon^2 D)$. Consider the partition $\psi' = (\psi_1', \psi_2')$ where ψ_1 is $(N-k) \times 1$ and ψ_2' is $k \times 1$. Then, since $\psi \sim N(0, \sigma_\varepsilon^2 D)$ it follows that

$$\psi = \begin{bmatrix} \psi_1 \\ 0 \end{bmatrix}, \; \psi_1 \sim N\left(0, \sigma_\varepsilon^2 I_{N-k}\right). \tag{11.5.5}$$

Finally note that the Moran I statistic in (11.3.3) can be expressed as

$$\begin{aligned} I &= \frac{N}{[Tr(W'W + WW)]^{1/2}} \frac{[\hat{u}'G]\, G'WG\, [G'\hat{u}]}{\hat{u}'GG'\hat{u}} \\ &= \frac{N}{[Tr(W'W + WW)]^{J/2}} \frac{\psi_1' A_{11} \psi_1}{\psi_1'\psi_1} \end{aligned} \tag{11.5.6}$$

where A_{11} is the $(N-k) \times (N-k)$ upper diagonal matrix of $A = G'WG$.

Let the ith element of ψ_1 be $\psi_{1,i}$, $i = 1, ..., N-k$. Clearly, I is scale free, the elements of ψ_1 are i.i.d. $N(0, \sigma_\varepsilon^2)$, and $\psi_1'\psi_1 = \Sigma_{i=1}^{N-k} \psi_{1,i}^2$. It follows from (11.4.1) that I is independent of the stochastic term in its denominator, namely $\psi_1'\psi_1 = \hat{u}'\hat{u}$, and therefore, as claimed,

$$E\left(I\, \hat{u}'\hat{u}\right) = E(I)\, E\left(\hat{u}'\hat{u}\right). \tag{11.5.7}$$

11.6 GENERALIZED MORAN I TESTS: QUALITATIVE MODELS AND SPATIALLY LAGGED DEPENDENT VARIABLE MODELS

The above Moran I test for spatial correlation relates to the model in (11.3.1). Unfortunately, the model in (11.3.1) is linear and so the Moran I test based on it cannot be applied to models which have qualitative dependent variables.

The model in (11.3.3) also does not have a spatially lagged dependent variable, and so the Moran I test based on it cannot be applied to models which contain spatially lagged dependent variables. These are severe restrictions. The purpose of this section is to present results which can be applied in such cases. These results were derived by Kelejian and Prucha (2001).

A Needed Preliminary Result

Consider the (possibly) nonlinear model

$$y_i = f(x_i, z_i, \beta) + \varepsilon_i, \ i = 1, ..., N \tag{11.6.1}$$

where x_i is a $1 \times k$ vector of exogenous variables, z_i is a vector of endogenous variables, and ε_i is the disturbance term. Assume, under H_0, that ε_i, $i = 1, ..., N$ are independently distributed with mean and variance of 0 and σ_i^2, respectively, and $\sup_i E|\varepsilon_i|^{4+\delta} < \infty$ for some $\delta > 0$. Note, ε_i is assumed to be (possibly) heteroskedastic and therefore not i.i.d.

Assume that the variance, σ_i^2, is a function of x_i, say

$$\sigma_i^2 = h(x_i, \beta). \tag{11.6.2}$$

Also, assume that the expected value of $f(\cdot)$, and also of its first two continuous derivatives with respect to β are uniformly bounded in absolute value. Assume that $h(\cdot)$ and its first derivatives with respect to the elements of β are uniformly bounded in absolute value. Finally, assume that a consistent estimator for β exists, say $\hat{\beta}$, and $N^{1/2}(\hat{\beta} - \beta) = O_p(1)$. For a formal and complete list of assumptions needed for the asymptotic result described below, see Kelejian and Prucha (2001).

Note that the above assumptions are quite reasonable. Typically, concerning $f(\cdot)$, researchers do not consider models whose moments diverge. As one example, if x_i and β are scalars, a model such as $f(x_i, z_i, \beta) = \beta / x_i$, where $x_i > 0$ is ruled out.

Consider now the hypotheses

$$H_0 : \varepsilon_i \text{ is independently distributed,}$$
$$H_1 : \varepsilon_i \text{ is spatially correlated.}$$

Suppose that under H_1 the researcher considers the weighting matrix W, where the diagonal elements of W are zero, $w_{ii} = 0$, and its row and column sums are uniformly bounded in absolute value. Suppose also that

$$N^{-1} \Sigma_{i=1}^{N} \Sigma_{j=1}^{N} (w_{ij} + w_{ji})^2 \geq c_w > 0, \ N > N^*. \tag{11.6.3}$$

A sufficient condition for (11.6.3) is that the elements of W are nonnegative, each row has at least one positive element, and the positive elements are bounded away from zero.

Let $\hat{\varepsilon}' = (\hat{\varepsilon}_1, ..., \hat{\varepsilon}_n)$, where $\hat{\varepsilon}_i = y_i - f(x_i, \hat{\beta})$, and consider a variation of the Moran I test statistic

$$I = \frac{Q}{\hat{\sigma}_Q}, \quad Q = \hat{\varepsilon}' W \hat{\varepsilon} \tag{11.6.4}$$

where

$$\begin{aligned} \hat{\sigma}_Q^2 &= \frac{1}{2} \Sigma_{i=1}^N \Sigma_{j=1}^N (w_{ij} + w_{ji})^2 \hat{\sigma}_i^2 \hat{\sigma}_j^2 \\ &= Tr(W \hat{\Sigma} W \hat{\Sigma} + W' \hat{\Sigma} W \hat{\Sigma}), \\ \hat{\Sigma} &= diag_i^N (\hat{\sigma}_i^2), \ \hat{\sigma}_i^2 = h(x_i, \hat{\beta}). \end{aligned} \tag{11.6.5}$$

Then, under their reasonable further conditions, Kelejian and Prucha (2001) show, under H_0,

$$\frac{Q}{\hat{\sigma}_Q} \to N(0, 1). \tag{11.6.6}$$

Applications

The Tobit Model

Consider the model

$$\begin{aligned} &(A) \quad y_i^* = x_i \beta + \eta_i, \\ &(B) \quad y_i = y_i^* \text{ if } y_i^* \geq c, \\ &(C) \quad y_i = 0 \text{ otherwise} \end{aligned} \tag{11.6.7}$$

where y_i^* is a latent variable which is not observed, c is a constant threshold value which need not be known, and could be zero, x_i is a row vector of regressors which includes the constant term. Examples of Tobit models are durable good purchases, length of a worker's "down" time due to injury, length of unemployment, etc. For instance, in the case of a durable good purchase, (A) in (11.6.7) would relate to the extent of desired purchases, c in (B) would be the least expensive of that durable good, and y_i would indicate that the extent of the actual purchase, which would be equal to the desired purchase, y_i^*, if the desired purchase is at least as high as the least expensive durable. Clearly, if the purchase is not made $y_i = 0$ as in (C).

As a technicality, given that the constant term is one of the regressors in x_i, and for purposes of illustration, let $x_i \beta = b + z_i \gamma$ where z_i is an observed regressor vector. Then, in this case the inequality condition in (B), $y_i^* \geq c$ would be $b_0 + z_i\gamma + \eta_i \geq 0$, where $b_0 = (b - c)$. It follows that the original intercept b cannot be estimated unless the threshold c is known. However, this is not typically a concern because interest usually only focuses on the coefficients of the regressors, namely γ in this formulation of the model.

Assume, under H_0, that η_i are i.i.d. $N(0, \sigma_\eta^2)$, and assume that the model satisfies the typical regularity assumptions. Also, express the inequality restriction in (11.6.7) as

$$y_i = 0 \text{ if } \eta_i < -x_i\beta_1 \tag{11.6.8}$$

where β_1 is identical to β except for the intercept, i.e., unless $c = 0$. Since the normal density with zero mean is symmetric about zero,

$$\begin{aligned} \Pr(\eta_i < -x_i\beta_1) &= \Pr\left(\frac{\eta_i}{\sigma_\eta} < \frac{-x_i\beta_1}{\sigma_\eta}\right) \\ &= 1 - F\left(\frac{x_i\beta_1}{\sigma_\eta}\right) \end{aligned} \tag{11.6.9}$$

where $F(\cdot)$ is the cumulative distribution function (CDF) of the standard normal variable, $N(0, 1)$. Under H_0, the likelihood for the model in (11.6.7) is

$$L = \prod_{i \in T_0}\left[1 - F\left(\frac{x_i\beta_1}{\sigma_\eta}\right)\right] * \prod_{i \in T_1}\left(\frac{1}{\sigma_\eta}\right) f\left(\frac{y_i - x_i\beta_1}{\sigma_\eta}\right) \tag{11.6.10}$$

where $f(\cdot)$ is the standard normal density, T_0 is the set of values of i for which $y_i = 0$, and T_1 is the set of values for which $y_i > 0$; see, e.g., Judge et al. (1985, p. 781).

Results given in Amemiya (1985, pp. 370–371) imply

$$\begin{aligned} E(y_i) &= f(x_i, \beta_1, \sigma_\eta^2), \\ f(x_i, \beta_1, \sigma_\eta^2) &= \sigma_\eta F\left[\frac{x_i\beta_1}{\sigma_\eta}\right]\left[\frac{x_i\beta_1}{\sigma_\eta} + \frac{f(\frac{x_i\beta_1}{\sigma_\eta})}{F\left[\frac{x_i\beta_1}{\sigma_\eta}\right]}\right]. \end{aligned} \tag{11.6.11}$$

Amemiya's results also imply that

$$\begin{aligned} y_i &= f(x_i, \beta_1, \sigma_\eta^2) + \varepsilon_i, \\ E(\varepsilon_i) &= 0, \ var(\varepsilon_i) = \sigma_i^2, \\ \sigma_i^2 &= \sigma_\eta^2 F\left[\frac{x_i\beta_1}{\sigma_\eta}\right]\left[(\frac{x_i\beta_1}{\sigma_\eta})^2 + 1 + (\frac{x_i\beta_1}{\sigma_\eta})\frac{f(\frac{x_i\beta_1}{\sigma_\eta})}{F(\frac{x_i\beta_1}{\sigma_\eta})}\right] - [f(x_i, \beta_1, \sigma_\eta^2)]^2 \\ &\equiv h_i(\beta_1, \sigma_\eta^2). \end{aligned} \tag{11.6.12}$$

A test for spatial correlation, namely H_0: η_i are i.i.d. $N(0, \sigma_\eta^2)$, against H_1: η_i are spatially correlated can be based on (11.6.4)–(11.6.6). In particular, for this Tobit model let

$$\hat{\varepsilon}_i = y_i - f(x_i, \hat{\beta}_1, \hat{\sigma}_\eta^2), \qquad (11.6.13)$$
$$\hat{\sigma}_i^2 = h_i(\hat{\beta}_1, \hat{\sigma}_\eta^2)$$

where $\hat{\beta}_1$ and $\hat{\sigma}_\eta^2$ are the maximum likelihood estimators of β_1 and σ_η^2. Let Q and $\hat{\sigma}_Q^2$ in (11.6.4) and (11.6.5) be based on $\hat{\varepsilon}_i$ and $\hat{\sigma}_i^2$ in (11.6.13), and an assumed weighting matrix, W. Then, at the 5% level, H_0 would be rejected if

$$\left| \frac{Q}{\hat{\sigma}_Q} \right| > 1.96. \qquad (11.6.14)$$

Illustration 11.6.1: A Monte Carlo experiment for the Moran I test in Tobit models

Amaral and Anselin (2014) investigated the finite sample properties of the Moran I test in Tobit models. Their main findings are that the test has the correct size and good power even for data sets corresponding to a medium number of observations. This suggests a certain robustness of the test. In our illustration we reproduce some of their results. The setup of the Monte Carlo is pretty simple and in many aspects similar to the one adopted by Amaral and Anselin.

First of all, we generate data on regular lattice structure and consider the same sample sizes of Illustration 11.3.1. We also consider the same five values for the spatial coefficient. The spatial weighting matrix is based on the row normalized queen contiguity criterion.

The model under the null is the one in (11.6.7) with

$$y^* = \beta_0 + \beta_1 x_1 + \eta$$

in which β_0 and β_1 are taken to be 1 and 0.5, respectively, the elements of x_1 are generated from a uniform distribution over the interval $(-7, 3)$, and $\eta_i \sim N(0, 1)$. As in Amaral and Anselin (2014), these values were taken to guarantee that the average of y^* is approximately zero.

The models under the alternative are

$$y^* = \beta_0 + \beta_1 x_1 + u,$$
$$u = \rho_2 W u + \eta,$$

and so the data on y^* were obtained from

$$y^* = \beta_0 + \beta_1 x_1 + (I - \rho_2 W)^{-1} \eta$$

TABLE 11.6.1 Frequencies of rejection of the null hypothesis based on a Tobit model

N	49	100	225	400	900
$\rho_2 = 0$	0.0382	0.0447	**0.0481**	**0.0502**	**0.0482**
$\rho_2 = 0.2$	0.0622	0.0994	0.1499	0.2862	0.5236
$\rho_2 = 0.4$	0.1769	0.3297	0.5489	0.8519	0.9933
$\rho_2 = 0.6$	0.4275	0.7225	0.9407	0.9989	1.0000
$\rho_2 = 0.8$	0.7702	0.9630	0.9993	1.0000	1.0000

where, again, all variables have already been defined. Each Monte Carlo experiment consisted of 10,000 replications. The test is based on (11.6.14).

Table 11.6.1 summarizes the main findings. Except for the smallest sample size, the size of the test is extremely close to the theoretical 5% level. Not surprisingly, this is true also for small sample sizes as shown in Amaral and Anselin (2014). The rejection frequencies for the statistic under the alternative ranges between 6% (for $N = 49$ and $\rho_2 = 0.2$) and 100%. As expected, the power increases with the sample size and with the intensity of the spatial correlation. It is worth noticing that when the sample size is $N = 900$, the power is close to one even when $\rho_2 = 0.4$. These results are in line with previous findings.

A Dichotomous Dependent Variable Model: The Probit

Consider the model

$$\begin{aligned} y_i^* &= x_i\beta + \eta_i, i = 1, ..., N, \\ y_i &= 1 \text{ if } y_i^* \geq 0, \\ y_i &= 0 \text{ otherwise,} \end{aligned} \tag{11.6.15}$$

where under H_0, η_i are i.i.d. $N(0, 1)$. The model in (11.6.15) is essentially a special case of the Tobit model in that if the event takes place, the researcher only knows that it took place, e.g., the durable was purchased! The extent of that purchase is not known.

Again let $F(\cdot)$ be the CDF of the standard normal. In this case it turns out that[5]

$$y_i = F(x_i\beta) + \varepsilon_i, \tag{11.6.16}$$

5. Note that $\Pr(y_i = 1) = \Pr(\eta_i > -x_i\beta)$, and because the normal distribution has a symmetric density, $\Pr(y_i = 1) = \Pr(\eta_i < x_i\beta)$. Since the only values of y_i are zero and one, $E(y_i) = F(x_i\beta)$. The variance of y_i is equal to that of η_i and is

$$E(y_i^2) - [E(y_i)]^2 = F(x_i\beta) - [F(x_i\beta)]^2.$$

TABLE 11.6.2 Frequencies of rejection of the null hypothesis based on a Probit model

N	49	100	225	400	900
$\rho_2 = 0$	0.0399	0.0434	0.0437	**0.0487**	**0.0499**
$\rho_2 = 0.2$	0.0461	0.0693	0.0894	0.1275	0.2311
$\rho_2 = 0.4$	0.0811	0.1731	0.2706	0.4763	0.7981
$\rho_2 = 0.6$	0.1916	0.4369	0.6987	0.9293	0.9992
$\rho_2 = 0.8$	0.4850	0.8538	0.9881	0.9999	1.0000

$$E(\varepsilon_i) = 0, \; var(\varepsilon_i) = \sigma_i^2,$$
$$\sigma_i^2 = F(x_i\beta)[1 - F(x_i\beta)].$$

Let $\hat{\beta}$ be the MLE of β, and let

$$\hat{\sigma}_i^2 = F(x_i\hat{\beta})[1 - F(x_i\hat{\beta})], \qquad (11.6.17)$$
$$\hat{\varepsilon}_i = y_i - F(x_i\hat{\beta}).$$

Then, given a weighting matrix, say W, describing spatial correlation under H_1, and calculating Q and $\hat{\sigma}_Q$ in (11.6.4) and (11.6.5) in terms of $\hat{\sigma}_i^2$ and $\hat{\varepsilon}_i$ in (11.6.17), the null hypothesis H_0 would be rejected at the 5% level if

$$\left|\frac{Q}{\hat{\sigma}_Q}\right| > 1.96. \qquad (11.6.18)$$

Illustration 11.6.2: A Monte Carlo experiment for the Moran *I* test in Probit models

Amaral et al. (2013) conducted an extensive Monte Carlo experiment to compare three test statistics suggested in the literature to test for the presence of spatial autocorrelation in the context of a Probit model. The test statistic that proved to behave the best among the three is the Moran I proposed in Kelejian and Prucha (2001) and presented above. Also in this illustration we reproduce some of their results that are summarized in Table 11.6.2. The setup of the Monte Carlo is identical to the one described for the Tobit model and, therefore, we do not repeat the description.

Except for the smallest sample size, the size of the test is close to the theoretical 5% level. Estimates of the size for $N = 400$ and $N = 900$ are not statistically different from the theoretical level. The estimates of the power of the test are in line with the theoretical expectations that the figures should increase both with the sample size and with the level of correlation in the error term. The evidence reported in Amaral et al. (2013) is also quite close to the one in these experiments.

A Sample Selection Model

Consider now a typical sample selection model[6] of the form

$$\begin{aligned} y_{1i}^* &= x_{1i}\beta_1 + \eta_{1i}, \\ y_{2i}^* &= x_{2i}\beta_2 + \eta_{2i}, \\ y_{2i} &= y_{2i}^* \text{ if } y_{1i}^* \geq 0, \\ y_{2i} &= 0 \text{ otherwise.} \end{aligned} \tag{11.6.19}$$

Under the null hypothesis (η_{1i}, η_{2i}) are i.i.d. $N(0, \Sigma)$, where $\Sigma = (\sigma_{ij})$. In this model the observed sample is x_{1i} for all i, x_{2i} and y_{2i} when $y_{1i}^* \geq 0$, and the sign of y_{1i}^*. Since only the sign of y_{1i}^* is observed, σ_{11} is not identified and so the model is typically normalized on $\sigma_{11} = 1$.

One example of a sample selection model is due to Heckman (1979). In his model y_{1i}^* would relate to the perceived benefits of migrating to a "higher wage" country, and y_{2i}^* would relate to the earnings of workers in that higher wage country who in fact migrated.

Amemiya (1985, p. 386) gives the likelihood for the model in (11.6.19), namely

$$L = \prod_{y_{1i}^* \leq 0} [1 - F(x_{1i}\beta_1] \prod_{y_{1i}^* > 0} A\ (1/\sigma_2)\ f[\sigma_2^{-1}(y_{2i} - x_{2i}\beta_2)], \tag{11.6.20}$$

$$A = F\{[x_{1i}\beta_1 + \frac{\sigma_{12}}{\sigma_2^2}(y_{2i} - x_{2i}\beta_2)][1 - \frac{\sigma_{12}^2}{\sigma_2^2}]^{-1/2}\}.$$

Let $\alpha = (\beta_1, \beta_2, \sigma_{22}, \sigma_{12})$ and let the MLE of α based on (11.6.19) be $\hat{\alpha}$. Results given in Amemiya (1985, pp. 385–387) imply

$$\begin{aligned} y_{2i} &= f(x_{1i}, x_{2i}, \alpha) + \varepsilon_i, \\ E(\varepsilon_i) &= 0,\ var(\varepsilon_i) = \sigma_i^2 \end{aligned} \tag{11.6.21}$$

where

$$\begin{aligned} f(x_{1i}, x_{2i}, \alpha) &= x_{2i}\beta_2 + \sigma_{12}\frac{\phi(x_{1i}\beta_1)}{\Phi(x_{1i}\beta_1)}, \\ \sigma_i^2 &= \sigma_{22} - \sigma_{12}^2\left[x_{1i}\beta_1\frac{\phi(x_{1i}\beta_1)}{\Phi(x_{1i}\beta_1)} + \left[\frac{\phi(x_{1i}\beta_1)}{\Phi(x_{1i}\beta_1)}\right]^2\right] \\ &\equiv H_i(\alpha). \end{aligned} \tag{11.6.22}$$

6. Amemiya (1985, p. 385) calls this model the type 2 Tobit model and shows how various models are connected.

In this case

$$\hat{\varepsilon}_i = y_{2i} - f(x_{1i}, x_{2i}, \hat{\alpha}), \qquad (11.6.23)$$
$$\hat{\sigma}_i^2 = H_i(\hat{\alpha}).$$

Again, H_0 can be tested against the hypothesis of spatial correlation in terms of the large sample distribution given in (11.6.6). In this case Q in (11.6.4) and $\hat{\sigma}_Q$ in (11.6.5) would be based on (11.6.23).

A Polychotomous Model

Consider the model

$$\Pr(y_i = j) = P_j(x_i, \gamma), \; j = 1, ..., k, \; \; i = 1, ..., N \qquad (11.6.24)$$

where x_i is $1 \times k$ and γ is $1 \times q$, and generally $q > k$. This formulation is consistent with both ordered and unordered models.

The ordered model is an intensity model. For example, y_i could be the medal won by the ith Olympian. In this case the values of y_i might be 3 if a gold medal is won, 2 if a silver medal is won, 1 if a bronze medal is won, and 0 if no medal is won. The vector x_i might describe the hours in training, financial support received, etc. As another example, suppose we wish to explain the extent that a person smokes cigarettes. In this case we could have $y_i = 0$ if that person does not smoke, $y_i = 1$ if the person smokes, but smokes less than a pack/day, and $y_i = 2$ if more than two packs/day are smoked. Let $F(z)$ be the CDF of the (0, 1) normal distribution, and consider the ordered model for the case of the Olympian described above. Recall that in the dichotomous variable model, $\Pr(y_i = 1) = F(x_i\beta) = \Pr(y_i \leq x_i\beta)$, and $\Pr(y_i = 0) = 1 - F(x_i\beta) = \Pr(y_i \geq x_i\beta)$. The interpretation of this is that if $x_i\beta$ is small, then the event will have a low chance of taking place. A suggested probability specification for the Olympian ordered model described above is given in Maddala (1983, p. 47):

$$\begin{aligned}
\Pr(y_i = 3) &= F(x_i\beta), \qquad (11.6.25)\\
\Pr(y_i = 2) &= F(x_i\beta + \alpha_1) - F(x_i\beta),\\
\Pr(y_i = 1) &= F(x_i\beta + \alpha_1 + \alpha_2) - F(x_i\beta + \alpha_1),\\
\Pr(y_i = 0) &= 1 - F(x_i\beta + \alpha_1 + \alpha_2).
\end{aligned}$$

It is not difficult to show that $\sum_{j=0}^{3} \Pr(y_i = j) = 1$.

The unordered polychotomous model is not an intensity model. For example, in a study of travel mode between cities, the values of y_i might indicate how the ith person traveled. For instance, if by car, $y_i = 1$, if by air, $y_i = 2$, if by train, $y_i = 3$, and $y_i = 4$ otherwise. Other examples might relate to occupational choice, residential choice, choice of energy form, etc. The probabilities involved can be given by the logit, probit, or other specifications. One specification of the probabilities is the logit specification given in Maddala (1983, pp. 34–35). For the travel mode illustration described above, that specification would be

$$\Pr(y_i = J) = \frac{\exp(x_i\beta_J)}{D_i}, \quad J = 1, 2, 3, \tag{11.6.26}$$
$$\Pr(y_i = 4) = \frac{1}{D_i},$$
$$D_i = 1 + \exp(x_i\beta_1) + \exp(x_i\beta_2) + \exp(x_i\beta_3).$$

For further details see Maddala (1983).

Consider now the test for spatial correlation in terms of the general specification given in (11.6.24). Given (11.6.24), we have

$$y_i = f(x_i, \beta) + \varepsilon_i \tag{11.6.27}$$

where

$$f(x_i, \beta) = \Sigma_{j=1}^{k} j P_j(x_i, \beta), \tag{11.6.28}$$
$$E(\varepsilon_i) = 0, \ var(\varepsilon_i) = \sigma_i^2,$$
$$\sigma_i^2 = \Sigma_{j=1}^{k} j^2 P_j(x_i, \beta) - \left[\Sigma_{j=1}^{k} j P_j(x_i, \beta)\right]^2.$$

The hypothesis that ε_i are not spatially correlated against the alternative that they are can again be tested by (11.6.6). Let $\hat{\beta}$ be the MLE of β based on (11.6.24). Then, in this case

$$\hat{\varepsilon}_i = y_i - f(x_i, \hat{\beta}), \tag{11.6.29}$$
$$\hat{\sigma}_i^2 = \Sigma_{j=1}^{k} j^2 P_j(x_i, \hat{\beta}) - \left[\Sigma_{j=1}^{k} j P_j(x_i, \hat{\beta})\right]^2.$$

A Model With a Spatially Lagged Dependent Variable

Finally, consider the model

$$y = X\beta + \rho_1 M y + u, \tag{11.6.30}$$
$$u = \rho_2 W u + \varepsilon$$

with the usual assumptions of Section 2.2.3. The matrix W is the matrix which describes the spatial patterns assumed by the researcher. It could be the same as M. Clearly, the power of the test will depend upon how well W captures the spatial interactions of the error terms – provided that they exist at all!

The issue is to test the hypothesis $H_0 : \rho_2 = 0$ against $H_1 : \rho_2 \neq 0$. Under H_0, $u = \varepsilon$ and the elements of ε are assumed to be i.i.d. $(0, \sigma_\varepsilon^2)$, and $E(\varepsilon_i^4) < \infty$. Note that since the spatial lag in the dependent variable cannot be assumed exogenous, the standard Moran I test described above is not appropriate.

To test H_0 against H_1, first rewrite the model in (11.6.30) under H_0 as

$$\begin{aligned} y &= Z\theta + \varepsilon, \\ Z &= (X, My), \ \theta' = (\beta', \rho_1). \end{aligned} \tag{11.6.31}$$

The two-stage least squares estimator of θ is

$$\begin{aligned} \hat{\theta} &= (\hat{Z}'\hat{Z})^{-1}\hat{Z}'y, \\ \hat{Z} &= H(H'H)^{-1}H'Z \end{aligned} \tag{11.6.32}$$

where H is the instrument matrix

$$H = (X, MX, ..., M^r X), \tag{11.6.33}$$

and typically $r = 2$. Let $\hat{\varepsilon} = y - Z\hat{\theta}$. In this case the test statistic is

$$I_{SL} = \frac{\hat{\varepsilon}' W \hat{\varepsilon}}{\hat{\sigma}_Q}, \tag{11.6.34}$$

but because of the endogeneity of My, the normalization factor $\hat{\sigma}_Q$ is in this case

$$\hat{\sigma}_Q^2 = \hat{\sigma}_\varepsilon^4 Tr(WW + W'W) + \hat{\sigma}_\varepsilon^2 \hat{b}'\hat{b} \tag{11.6.35}$$

where

$$\begin{aligned} \hat{\sigma}_\varepsilon^2 &= n^{-1}\hat{\varepsilon}'\hat{\varepsilon}, \\ \hat{b}' &= -\hat{d}'PH', \\ P &= N(\hat{Z}'\hat{Z})^{-1}Z'H(H'H)^{-1}, \\ \hat{d}' &= N^{-1}\hat{\varepsilon}'(W + W')Z. \end{aligned} \tag{11.6.36}$$

Under additional (reasonable) conditions, Kelejian and Prucha (2001) show that, under $H_0 : \rho_2 = 0$,

$$I_{SL} \to N(0, 1). \tag{11.6.37}$$

Therefore, at the two-tail 5% level, one would reject H_0 if

$$|I_{SL}| > 1.96. \tag{11.6.38}$$

Illustration 11.6.3: A Monte Carlo experiment for the Moran I test in a model with a spatially lagged dependent variable

In this illustration we study the small sample properties of the Moran I test in the context of a model with a spatially lagged dependent variable. Also, in this case we generate data on regular lattice that gives rise to five sample sizes. The spatial weighting matrix adopted is based on the row normalized queen contiguity criterion.

The data are generated from the following model:

$$y = \beta_0 + \beta_1 x_1 + \rho_1 W y + u,$$
$$u = \rho_2 W u + \varepsilon$$

where β_0 and β_1 are both set to 1, and x_1 is generated from an uniform distribution over the interval $(2, 6)$. Finally, ρ_1 takes three different values, namely 0, 0.4, and 0.8; and ρ_2 takes five different values, namely 0, 0.2, 0.4, 0.6, and 0.8. The number of Monte Carlo samples is 10,000.

Results are reported in Table 11.6.3 where each panel of the table corresponds to a different sample size and different combinations of the values of the spatial parameters. The evidence can be summarized as follows: For small sample sizes ($N = 49$ and $N = 100$) the size of the test is consistently lower than 5%. The power of the test is very low (at most 4%!). For larger sample sizes ($N = 225$, $N = 400$, and $N = 900$), the size of the test is close to 5% and also the power is reasonably good. There is clearly an impressive difference between the sample size of 100 and 225 observations. Therefore, we also performed two additional experiments (that we decided not to report in the table) with sample sizes of $N = 144$ and $N = 196$ observations, respectively. These experiments confirm that the power increases with the sample size.

For larger sample sizes, the power increases with ρ_2, as it should because the larger the ρ_2, the stronger the spatial correlation, and hence, the more easily it can be detected. The power also decreases when ρ_1 increases. At first, this last result may seem a little counterintuitive. However, the reason for this is that, as ρ_1 increases, the variance of the dependent variable increases, leading to a less informative sample. Consistent with this, the increase in the variance produces a decrease in the power of the test, as documented in the table.

11.7 LAGRANGIAN MULTIPLIER TESTS

Some Basics

Lagrangian multiplier procedures are often used in general econometric applications, as well as in spatial econometrics, to test for spatial correlation. The

TABLE 11.6.3 Frequencies of rejection of the null hypothesis based on a model with a spatially lagged dependent variable

N = 49		$\rho_1 = 0$	$\rho_1 = 0.4$	$\rho_1 = 0.8$
	$\rho_2 = 0$	0.0304	0.0374	0.0394
	$\rho_2 = 0.2$	0.0161	0.0144	0.0132
	$\rho_2 = 0.4$	0.0132	0.0054	0.0037
	$\rho_2 = 0.6$	0.0098	0.0024	0.0018
	$\rho_2 = 0.8$	0.0043	0.0010	0.0059
N = 100		$\rho_1 = 0$	$\rho_1 = 0.4$	$\rho_1 = 0.8$
	$\rho_2 = 0$	0.0368	0.0400	0.0384
	$\rho_2 = 0.2$	0.0286	0.0113	0.0076
	$\rho_2 = 0.4$	0.0421	0.0051	0.0023
	$\rho_2 = 0.6$	0.0391	0.0042	0.0086
	$\rho_2 = 0.8$	0.0171	0.0033	0.0716
N = 225		$\rho_1 = 0$	$\rho_1 = 0.4$	$\rho_1 = 0.8$
	$\rho_2 = 0$	0.0438	0.0430	0.0455
	$\rho_2 = 0.2$	0.1339	0.1126	0.0921
	$\rho_2 = 0.4$	0.4642	0.4486	0.3815
	$\rho_2 = 0.6$	0.8258	0.7894	0.6576
	$\rho_2 = 0.8$	0.8865	0.7112	0.4606
N = 400		$\rho_1 = 0$	$\rho_1 = 0.4$	$\rho_1 = 0.8$
	$\rho_2 = 0$	0.0463	0.0433	0.0441
	$\rho_2 = 0.2$	0.1920	0.1441	0.0888
	$\rho_2 = 0.4$	0.6510	0.5628	0.4096
	$\rho_2 = 0.6$	0.9460	0.8949	0.6633
	$\rho_2 = 0.8$	0.9809	0.8093	0.5008
N = 900		$\rho_1 = 0$	$\rho_1 = 0.4$	$\rho_1 = 0.8$
	$\rho_2 = 0$	0.0478	0.0489	0.0480
	$\rho_2 = 0.2$	0.4713	0.4503	0.4671
	$\rho_2 = 0.4$	0.9682	0.9661	0.9783
	$\rho_2 = 0.6$	1.0000	1.0000	0.9999
	$\rho_2 = 0.8$	1.0000	0.9990	0.9153

general principles of the test are described quite nicely in Judge et al. (1985, pp. 182–187) and Cameron and Trivedi (2005, pp. 233–241). Anselin (1988) gives results relating to a number of Lagrangian multiplier tests that spatial researchers would consider.

The test is based on maximizing a likelihood, **subject** to the restriction being considered under a null hypothesis. It is therefore based on restricted maximum likelihood estimator. These estimators can also be obtained by substituting the restrictions directly into the model and then maximizing the resulting restricted likelihood function. For example, if $L(a, b)$ is the likelihood function, a and b are the parameters, and the null is $H_0 : b = 0$, then the restricted likelihood is $L(a, 0)$. Because the likelihood is typically simpler under the restrictions of the null, the statistic used in the Lagrangian method is generally simpler to calculate than corresponding statistics which are based on unrestricted maximum likelihood estimators. The Wald test is one such test based on unrestricted maximum likelihood estimators. The Wald test is described in Section 11.8.

As an overview, let $L(\gamma)$ be the log-likelihood of the model being considered where γ is a $k \times 1$ parameter vector, and let the sample size be N. Let $\hat{\gamma}_u$ be the unrestricted MLE of γ. Then, under the regularity conditions, described in Judge et al. (1985), Theil (1971), and others,[7]

$$N^{1/2}(\hat{\gamma}_u - \gamma) \xrightarrow{D} N(0, p \lim_{N\to\infty} [N^{-1} I(\gamma)]^{-1}, \tag{11.7.1}$$

$$I(\gamma) = -E(\frac{\partial^2 L(\gamma)}{\partial\gamma\partial\gamma'}) = E(\frac{\partial L}{\partial\gamma})(\frac{\partial L}{\partial\gamma})'.$$

The matrix $I(\gamma)$ is the information matrix. For ease of notation, denote the limiting VC matrix in (11.7.1) as

$$\overline{I(\gamma)} = p \lim_{N\to\infty} [N^{-1} I(\gamma)]^{-1} \tag{11.7.2}$$

so that (11.7.1) can be written as

$$N^{1/2}(\hat{\gamma}_u - \gamma) \xrightarrow{D} N(0, \overline{I(\gamma)}). \tag{11.7.3}$$

Suppose now that there are $h < k$ parameter restrictions under H_0, which are expressed as $G(\gamma) = 0$ where $G(\gamma)$ is an $h \times 1$ vector of functions of γ. Then, the Lagrangian is defined as the log-likelihood, subject to the restriction $G(\gamma) = 0$, namely

$$\pounds = L(\gamma) - \lambda' G(\gamma), \tag{11.7.4}$$

7. There are two matrix differentiation formulas used in this section which we review here. Let $M = a'x$ where a and x are $k \times 1$ vectors. Then

$$\frac{\partial M}{\partial x} = a.$$

Let $Q = (q_1, ..., q_p)'$ be a $p \times 1$ vector whose elements may be functions of x. Then $\partial Q'/\partial x$ is an $k \times p$ matrix whose ith row is $Q_{i.}$ where

$$Q_{i.} = [\frac{\partial q_1}{\partial x_i}, \frac{\partial q_2}{\partial x_i}, ..., \frac{\partial q_p}{\partial x_i}], \ i = 1, ..., k.$$

For a nice review of matrix differentiation, see Dhrymes (1978, Appendix A.4).

where λ' is a $1 \times h$ vector of Lagrangian multipliers and $L(\gamma)$ is the log-likelihood.

The first order conditions for a maximum are

$$\left[\frac{\partial L(\gamma)}{\partial \gamma}\right]_{\hat{\gamma}_R,\hat{\lambda}_R} - \left[\frac{\partial \lambda' G(\gamma)}{\partial \gamma}\right]_{\hat{\gamma}_R,\hat{\lambda}_R} = 0, \qquad (11.7.5)$$
$$G(\hat{\gamma}_R) = 0,$$

which can be expressed as

$$\left[\frac{\partial L(\gamma)}{\partial \gamma}\right]_{\gamma=\hat{\gamma}_R} = \left[\frac{\partial G(\gamma)'}{\partial \gamma}\right]_{\gamma=\hat{\gamma}_R} \hat{\lambda}_R, \qquad (11.7.6)$$
$$G(\hat{\gamma}_R) = 0,$$

where $\hat{\gamma}_R$ is the restricted maximum likelihood estimator of γ, and $\hat{\lambda}_R$ is the solution value of λ based on (11.7.5). Note that in (11.7.6) $\frac{\partial G(\gamma)'}{\partial \gamma}$ is a $k \times h$ matrix.

Let

$$L_R = \left[\frac{\partial L(\gamma)}{\partial \gamma}\right]_{\hat{\gamma}_R}, \quad G'_R = \left[\frac{\partial G(\gamma)'}{\partial \gamma}\right]_{\hat{\gamma}_R}. \qquad (11.7.7)$$

If H_0 is true, we would expect $\hat{\gamma}_R$ and $\hat{\gamma}_u$ to be "close", and $\hat{\lambda}_R \simeq 0$. Under H_0, and reasonable regularity conditions, it can be shown that

$$L'_R[\, I(\hat{\gamma}_R)]^{-1} L_R \xrightarrow{D} \chi^2_h \qquad (11.7.8)$$

where $I(\hat{\gamma}_R)$ is the information matrix evaluated at the restricted estimator, $\hat{\gamma}_R$. Therefore, the suggested test of H_0 would be to reject H_0 at the 5% level if

$$L'_R[\, I(\hat{\gamma}_R)]^{-1} L_R > \chi^2_h(0.95). \qquad (11.7.9)$$

The test based on (11.7.9) is referred to as a Lagrangian multiplier test. One reason for this is that (11.7.5)–(11.7.7) imply that $L_R = G'_R\hat{\lambda}_R$, and so the test statistic in (11.7.9) can be expressed in terms of the Lagrangian multipliers

$$\hat{\lambda}'_R G'_R[\, I(\hat{\gamma}_R)]^{-1} G_R \hat{\lambda}_R > \chi^2_h(0.95). \qquad (11.7.10)$$

One of the problems in the problem set to this chapter relates to the determination of a particular Lagrangian multiplier test. The reader is strongly advised to do that problem. Of course, the answer to the problem is given in the answer manual at the end of this book. As will become apparent, details associated with the construction of a Lagrangian multiplier test are not trivial even if the model is simple. That many Lagrangian tests are not trivial to construct will also become apparent by the results described below relating to the classic Lagrangian test for spatial correlation determined by Burridge (1980). This may be one reason that researchers often use the Wald principle, described in Section 11.8 below, to test many hypotheses instead of using the Lagrangian principle despite its use of simpler restricted estimators.

An Illustration: The Classic Result of Burridge (1980)[8]

We illustrate the Lagrangian multiplier procedure outlined above by filling in some of the details in the proof given by Burridge (1980) that the square of the Moran I test statistic in (11.3.3) is identical to the corresponding Lagrangian multiplier test statistic.

Some Preliminaries[9]

(1) Let A be an $N \times N$ matrix with characteristic roots, $\lambda_1, ..., \lambda_N$. Let J be a finite integer, positive or negative. Then

$$|A^J| = |A|^J = \lambda_1^J ... \lambda_N^J. \tag{11.7.11}$$

(2) For the matrix A in (1)

$$Tr(A^J) = \sum_{i=1}^{N} \lambda_i^J. \tag{11.7.12}$$

(3) Suppose the elements of the nonsingular matrix A are functions of the scalar α. Then

$$\frac{\partial |A|}{\partial \alpha} = |A| \, Tr(A^{-1} \frac{\partial |A|}{\partial \alpha}). \tag{11.7.13}$$

From (11.7.13) it follows that

$$\frac{\partial \ln(|A|)}{\partial \alpha} = Tr(A^{-1} \frac{\partial |A|}{\partial \alpha}). \tag{11.7.14}$$

Burridge's Lagrangian Statistic[10]

Let us again consider the model

$$y = X\beta + u, \tag{11.7.15}$$

8. Although instructive, this subsection is a bit tedious and can be omitted without harm.
9. The matrix results below, and many more, are nicely given in Dhrymes (1978).
10. This discussion can be skipped without harm. It is given only because it contains a variety of manipulations which should be instructive and, perhaps, useful to the reader in his/her future research.

$$u = \rho_2 W u + \varepsilon$$

where y is $N \times 1$, X is $N \times k$, $\varepsilon \sim N(0, \sigma^2 I_N)$, etc. Let $M = (I_N - \rho_2 W)^{-1}$. For this model consider the Lagrangian multiplier test of $H_0 : \rho_2 = 0$ against $H_1 : \rho_2 \neq 0$.

The log-likelihood for this model is

$$L = c - \frac{1}{2\sigma^2}[(y - X\beta)'[MM']^{-1}(y - X\beta)] - \ln(|I_N - \rho_2 W|) \quad (11.7.16)$$

where $c = -[N/2]\ln(2\pi)$. The Lagrangian is

$$\pounds = c - \frac{1}{2\sigma}[(y - X\beta)'[MM']^{-1}(y - X\beta)] - \ln(|I_N - \rho_2 W|) - \lambda\rho_2. \quad (11.7.17)$$

Let $\gamma = (\sigma^2, \beta', \rho)'$. Then, via (11.7.6)–(11.7.9), the components of the Lagrangian multiplier statistic are $\partial L/\partial\gamma = [\partial L/\partial\sigma^2, \partial L/\partial\beta', \partial L/\partial\rho]'$ and the information matrix is $I(\gamma)$, which are all evaluated at the restricted maximum likelihood estimator, $\hat{\gamma}_R$.

In the context of the model in (11.7.15),

$$G_R' = \begin{bmatrix} 0 \\ 0_{k\times 1} \\ 1 \end{bmatrix}_{k+2\times 1} . \quad (11.7.18)$$

Also note that

$$[MM']^{-1} = (I_N - \rho_2 W')(I_N - \rho_2 W) = I_N - \rho_2(W' + W) + \rho_2^2 W'W \quad (11.7.19)$$

and so

$$\frac{\partial[MM']^{-1}}{\partial\rho_2} = -(W' + W) + 2\rho_2 W'W. \quad (11.7.20)$$

The first order conditions are given in (11.7.5) and (11.7.6). Given the Lagrangian in (11.7.17), using (11.7.14), and the log-likelihood in (11.7.16), the first order derivatives are

$$\partial L/\partial\sigma^2 = \partial\pounds/\partial\sigma^2 = \frac{1}{2\sigma^4}(y - X\beta)'[MM']^{-1}(y - X\beta) - \frac{N}{2\sigma^2}, \quad (11.7.21)$$

$$\partial L/\partial\beta = \partial\pounds/\partial\beta = -\frac{1}{2\sigma^2}[2X'[MM']^{-1}X\beta - 2X'[MM']^{-1}y],$$

$$\partial\pounds/\partial\rho_2 = \partial L/\partial\rho_2 - \lambda,$$

$$\partial L/\partial\rho_2 = -\frac{1}{2\sigma^2}[(y - X\beta)'\{-(W' + W) + 2\rho_2 W'W\}(y - X\beta)]$$
$$- Tr([I_N - \rho_2 W]^{-1}W),$$
$$\frac{\partial \pounds}{\partial\lambda} = -\rho_2.$$

Setting $\partial L/\partial\beta = 0$ and imposing $\rho_2 = 0$ yields

$$\hat{\beta} = (X'X)^{-1}X'y, \tag{11.7.22}$$

and so the restricted estimator of β is just the least squares estimator. Given this, and setting $\partial L/\partial\sigma^2 = 0 = \rho_2$ yields

$$\hat{\sigma}^2 = (y - X\hat{\beta})'(y - X\hat{\beta})'/N, \tag{11.7.23}$$

so that the restricted estimator of σ^2 is just N^{-1} times the residual sum of squares based on the least squares estimator of β. Now consider the solution value of λ. Setting $\partial\pounds/\partial\rho_2 = 0$ and imposing $\rho_2 = 0$ yields

$$\begin{aligned}\hat{\lambda} &= \frac{1}{2\hat{\sigma}^2}[(y - X\hat{\beta})'\{W' + W\}(y - X\hat{\beta}) \\ &= \frac{1}{\hat{\sigma}^2}[(y - X\hat{\beta})'W(y - X\hat{\beta})\end{aligned} \tag{11.7.24}$$

since $Tr(W) = 0$ and $(y - X\hat{\beta})'W'(y - X\hat{\beta}) = (y - X\hat{\beta})'W(y - X\hat{\beta})$.

The Lagrangian statistic in (11.7.9), or (11.7.10), requires the calculation of the information matrix, $I(\hat{\gamma}_R)$, as described in (11.7.1). Let $A = [MM']^{-1}$. Then, given (11.7.21), it is straightforward to show that

$$\begin{aligned}-E\left[\frac{\partial^2 L}{\partial\sigma^2, \partial\beta}\right] &= -\frac{1}{2\sigma^2}[-2X'AE(y) + 2X'AX\beta] \\ &= 0,\end{aligned} \tag{11.7.25}$$

since $E(y) = X\beta$.

Now consider the cross-product derivative of $\partial L/\partial\sigma^2$ with respect to ρ_2. From (11.7.20) and (11.7.21) and setting $\rho_2 = 0$, we obtain

$$\begin{aligned}&\partial^2 L/(\partial\sigma^2, \partial\rho_2) \\ &= \frac{1}{2\sigma^4}(y - X\beta)'[-(W' + W) + 2\rho_2 W'W](y - X\beta) \\ &= \frac{1}{2\sigma^4}(y - X\beta)'[-(W' + W)](y - X\beta).\end{aligned} \tag{11.7.26}$$

Thus,

$$-E\left[\partial^2 L/(\partial\sigma^2, \partial\rho_2)\right] \tag{11.7.27}$$

$$
\begin{aligned}
&= \frac{1}{2\sigma^4} E\left[Tr\left[(y - X\beta)'[-(W' + W)](y - X\beta)\right]\right] \\
&= \frac{1}{2\sigma^4} E\left[Tr\left[(y - X\beta)(y - X\beta)'[-(W' + W)]\right]\right] \\
&= \frac{\sigma^2}{2\sigma^4} Tr[-(W' + W)] = 0.
\end{aligned}
$$

Finally, consider the cross-product of $\frac{\partial^2 L}{\partial\beta, \partial\rho_2}$. Using similar manipulations

$$
\partial^2 L/(\partial\beta, \partial\rho_2) = -\frac{1}{2\sigma^2}\left[\begin{array}{c} 2X'[-(W' + W) + 2\rho_2 W'W]X\beta - 2X'* \\ [-(W' + W) + 2\rho_2 W'W]y \end{array}\right]. \tag{11.7.28}
$$

Setting $\rho_2 = 0$ yields

$$
\begin{aligned}
&- E\left[\partial^2 L/(\partial\beta, \partial\rho_2)\right] \qquad (11.7.29) \\
&= -\frac{1}{2\sigma^2}\left[2X'[-(W' + W)]X\beta - 2X'[-(W' + W)]E(y)\right] \\
&= 0,
\end{aligned}
$$

since $E(y) = X\beta$.

The results in (11.7.25)–(11.7.29) imply that the information matrix is diagonal. Let $\hat{I}_{R,\rho_2,\rho_2}$ be the last diagonal element of the information matrix. Then, for the model in (11.7.15), with G_R' in (11.7.18), and $\hat{\lambda}$ given in (11.7.24), the Lagrangian statistic described in (11.7.10) is just $\hat{\lambda}^2 \hat{I}_{R,\rho_2,\rho_2}^{-1}$. Thus, consider the calculation of $\hat{I}_{R,\rho_2,\rho_2}$.

Let S be the matrix that diagonalizes W, i.e., $SWS^{-1} = D_r = diag_{i=1}^{N}(r_i)$, where $r_1, \ldots, r_N$ are the roots of W. Then

$$
SWS^{-1} = S^{-1} D_r S, \tag{11.7.30}
$$

and so using (11.7.11),

$$
(I_N - \rho_2 W)^{-1} = S^{-1}[I_N - \rho_2 D_r]^{-1} S. \tag{11.7.31}
$$

Recalling that for any two matrices such that their product is a square matrix, $Tr(AB) = Tr(BA)$, the expression for $\partial L/\partial\rho_2$ in (11.7.21) can be expressed as

$$
\begin{aligned}
\partial L/\partial\rho_2 = &-\frac{1}{2\sigma^2}[(y - X\beta)'\left[-(W' + W) + 2\rho_2 W'W\right](y - X\beta)] \qquad (11.7.32) \\
&- Tr(S^{-1}[I_N - \rho_2 D_r]^{-1} S\, S^{-1} D_r S).
\end{aligned}
$$

Let $\Psi = -\frac{1}{2\sigma^2}[(y - X\beta)'\left[-(W' + W) + 2\rho_2 W'W\right](y - X\beta)]$. Then

$$\begin{aligned} \partial L/\partial \rho_2 &= \Psi - Tr([I_N - \rho_2 D_r]^{-1} D_r) \\ &= \Psi - \sum_{i=1}^{N}(1 - \rho_2 r_i)^{-1} r_i. \end{aligned} \tag{11.7.33}$$

Therefore

$$\begin{aligned} &-E\left[\partial^2 L/\partial \rho_2^2\right]_{\rho_2=0} \\ &= \frac{1}{2\sigma^2} E[(y - X\beta)'(2W'W)(y - X\beta)] + \sum_{i=1}^{N} r_i^2 \\ &= \frac{1}{\sigma^2} Tr(W'W) E[(y - X\beta)(y - X\beta)'] + Tr(W^2) \\ &= Tr\{W'W + W^2\}. \end{aligned} \tag{11.7.34}$$

Therefore, the Lagrangian multiplier statistic (LM) is, from (11.7.24) and (11.7.34), just the square of the Moran I statistic for the same model, namely

$$LM = \left[\frac{(y - X\hat{\beta})'W(y - X\hat{\beta})}{\hat{\sigma}^2[Tr(W'W + W^2)]^{1/2}}\right]^2. \tag{11.7.35}$$

11.8 THE WALD TEST

Consider the general linear spatial model

$$\begin{aligned} y &= X\beta + \rho_1 W y + u, \\ u &= \rho_2 W u + \varepsilon, \ |\lambda| < 1, \ |\rho| < 1, \end{aligned} \tag{11.8.1}$$

where X is an $N \times k$ exogenous regressor matrix, W is an $N \times N$ exogenous weighting matrix, $(I_N - aW)$ is nonsingular for all $|a| < 1$, $\varepsilon \sim N(0, \sigma_\varepsilon^2 I_N)$, etc. The issue is to test the hypothesis $H_0 : \rho_2 = 0$ against $H_1 : \rho_2 \neq 0$.

Let $\gamma' = (\beta', \rho_1, \rho_2, \sigma_\varepsilon^2)$. In the Wald procedure the model would be estimated by maximum likelihood; see Sections 2.2.2.1 and 2.4. Let $\hat{\gamma}$ be the maximum likelihood estimator of γ. Then, small sample inference would be based on classical results relating to maximum likelihood estimation:

$$\hat{\gamma} \simeq N(\gamma, \hat{V}), \tag{11.8.2}$$

$$\hat{V} = \left[\frac{\partial^2 \ln L}{\partial \gamma \partial \gamma'}\right]_{\hat{\gamma}}^{-1}. \tag{11.8.3}$$

Let $\hat{\sigma}^2_{\hat{\rho}_2}$ be the diagonal element of $\hat{V}$ corresponding to ρ_2. Then the Wald test for spatial correlation in this model would be to reject H_0 if

$$|\frac{\hat{\rho}_2}{\hat{\sigma}_{\hat{\rho}_2}}| > 1.96. \tag{11.8.4}$$

Note that the Wald test requires calculation of the unrestricted maximum likelihood estimators of the model parameters. As we have already noted, these are typically more complex than the corresponding restricted maximum likelihood estimators which are involved in the Lagrangian test procedure.

The Wald Test: A More Typical Case

Let $\hat{\beta}$ be an estimator of β based on a sample of size N. The model containing β may, or may not, be linear. Suppose there is an hypothesis of interest, namely $H_0 : R\beta = r$ against $H_1 : R\beta \neq r$. In the Wald framework, the estimator $\hat{\beta}$ is typically the unrestricted estimator of β. If $\hat{\beta}$ is the maximum likelihood estimator, the calculations determining $\hat{\beta}$ could be "quite" challenging.

Suppose it is determined that

$$N^{1/2}(\hat{\beta} - \beta) \xrightarrow{D} N(0, V) \tag{11.8.5}$$

and the variance–covariance matrix V is estimated as $\hat{V}$. In this case, finite sample inferences would be based on the approximation

$$\hat{\beta} \simeq N(\beta,\ N^{-1}\hat{V}). \tag{11.8.6}$$

The Wald test of H_0 against H_1 would be based on the following. Given (11.8.6), one would assume

$$\begin{aligned} R\hat{\beta} &\simeq N(R\beta, R\,[N^{-1}\hat{V}]\,R') \\ &= N(r, R\,[N^{-1}\hat{V}]\,R'). \end{aligned} \tag{11.8.7}$$

Therefore based on the Wald procedure, one would reject H_0 at the 5% level if

$$(R\hat{\beta} - r)'[R\,[N^{-1}\hat{V}]\,R']^{-1}(R\hat{\beta} - r) > \chi^2_h(0.95). \tag{11.8.8}$$

11.9 SPATIAL CORRELATION TESTS: COMMENTS AND CAVEATS

General Comments: A Caveat

The parameters of primary interest in a model are typically those that relate to the regression coefficients. In many cases the reason for this is that the specifications of the regression model are typically based on theoretical notions.

Therefore comparisons of the signs and significance of estimated parameters with those theoretical notions are of interest. On the other hand, the error terms are typically the unexplained components of the model. Our theoretical notions usually do not relate to error terms. That is, we may have reason to feel that spatial correlation and/or heteroskedasticity may be involved, but a formal structural model describing those complications involved in the error terms is not within our theoretical construct.

One reason that tests for spatial correlation and/or heteroskedasticity are considered is that the results of those tests may lead the researcher to specify a simpler model. For example, if the null hypothesis, say H_0, relates to the absence of spatial correlation, the acceptance of H_0 might lead the researcher to specify a model which does not have spatial correlation.

We offer two suggestions. The first is that spatial correlation and/or heteroskedasticity may be present and should be specified nonparametrically along with HAC procedures as described in Chapter 9. This way these issues are accounted for without biasing the estimation of the regression parameters due to, possibly, misspecified error term specifications; see Section 9.1. Our second suggestion is that models should not be revised on the basis of prior estimations because of pretest problems which were described in Chapter 8.

Spatial Correlation Tests and Specification Errors

In general, tests for spatial correlation will be biased in one direction or another if the model being considered is misspecified. In some cases, however, in which the test is based on estimated error terms, and the misspecification is that a spatial lag of a variable (exogenous or endogenous) is omitted from the model, the direction but not the extent, of bias may be predictable. We close this section by giving an illustration of this.

As an example, consider the models

$$\begin{aligned} &(A) \quad y = X\beta + \varepsilon, \\ &(B) \quad y = X\beta + \rho_1 W y + \varepsilon. \end{aligned} \tag{11.9.1}$$

In testing for spatial correlation, suppose the researcher's considered model is (A) in (11.9.1) but the true model is (B). Under typical assumptions, the researcher would estimate β by OLS, say $\hat{\beta} = (X'X)^{-1}X'y$. Since the model (B) in (11.9.1) is the true model, $\hat{\beta} = \beta + (X'X)^{-1}[\rho_1 W y + \varepsilon]$. Therefore the estimated error is

$$\begin{aligned} \hat{\varepsilon} &= y - X\hat{\beta} \\ &= -\rho_1 P_x W y + (I_N - P_x)\varepsilon \end{aligned} \tag{11.9.2}$$

where $P_x = X(X'X)^{-1}X'$. Because of the specification error, e.g., $\rho_1 \neq 0$, $\hat{\varepsilon}$ involves the term $\rho_1(I_N - P_x)Wy$. Asymptotically, this term will not be negligible in the test for spatial correlation. Since this term involves a spatial lag, it will generally be spatially interdependent. This spatial interdependence should lead to type one errors which are larger than the theoretical values even if components of ε are i.i.d. $(0, \sigma^2)$. On an intuitive level, a test for spatial correlation based on (A) would focus on whether or not $y - X\beta$ is spatially correlated. If the model in (B) is the true model, then $y - X\beta = u$, where $u = \rho_1 Wy + \varepsilon$ and components of u are spatially correlated due to the (omitted) spatial lag of the dependent variable. A similar analysis would suggest that type one errors may also be higher than the theoretical values if the researchers model is (A) in (11.9.1) but the true model is

$$(C) \quad y = X\beta + WX\beta_1 + \varepsilon. \tag{11.9.3}$$

SUGGESTED PROBLEMS

1. Show that the result in (11.4.1) holds if ε_i are i.i.d. $N(0, \sigma^2)$.
2. Demonstrate that the limiting result relating to $E(I)$ described in (11.3.12) holds under very reasonable conditions.
3. Suppose β in (11.6.2) is a scalar, and $h(\cdot, \cdot)$ is a step function in β. Will the given assumptions relating to $h(\cdot, \cdot)$ hold?
4. Consider the model

$$y = X\beta + \varepsilon$$

where y is the $N \times 1$ vector on the dependent variable, X is an $N \times k$ matrix of exogenous variables, and $\varepsilon \sim N(0, \sigma^2 I_N)$, etc.

(a) Determine the restricted least squares estimator of β subject to $R\beta = r$ where $R_{h \times k}$ and $r_{h \times 1}$ are known.

(b) Determine the Lagrangian multiplier test for $H_0 : R\beta = r$ against $H_1 : R\beta \neq r$.

Chapter 12

Nonnested Models and the *J*-Test

12.1 INTRODUCTORY COMMENTS

In this chapter we discuss a well-known procedure, called the J-test, that is used to test nonnested alternatives.[1] The test was originally developed in a nonspatial framework. Anselin (1986) suggested its extension to a spatial framework, and Kelejian (2008) provided the formal development.[2]

In a nutshell, the J-test can be used to test a null model against one or more nonnested alternatives. These models may differ in their sets of regressors, in their weighting matrices, or both. Essentially, the test is based on whether or not predictions based on the alternative models are jointly statistically significant when added to the null model. Under typical conditions, the test has good power even if the null model and its alternatives only differ in their weighting matrices. As described in earlier chapters, the weighting matrix is often used to specify spatial correlation of the error term, as well as spillover effects such as the emanating and vulnerability effects described in Chapter 3. It should therefore be evident that tests relating to its specification are important.

---

1. As an example, consider a null model and only one alternative. In particular, assume that the null is specified, using obvious notation, as

$$y_i = \beta_0 + \beta_1 x_{1i} + \beta_2 x_{2i} + \beta_3 x_{3i} + \varepsilon_i.$$

Suppose the alternative model is

$$y_i = \gamma_0 + \gamma_1 x_{1i} + \gamma_2 x_{4i} + \eta_i.$$

Clearly, these two models are nonnested in the sense that neither of them can be considered as a "special" case of the other. It should also be evident that standard techniques for model comparison cannot be used in this case.

2. A few important studies are Pesaran (1974, 1982), Pesaran and Deaton (1978), Davidson and MacKinnon (1981), MacKinnon et al. (1983), Godfrey (1983), and Dastoor (1983) See also the reviews in Greene (2003), Kmenta (1986), and Anselin (1986). For a review of related issues, namely nonnested models, see Pesaran and Weeks (2001).

Spatial Econometrics. http://dx.doi.org/10.1016/B978-0-12-813387-3.00012-3

12.2 THE NULL MODEL: NONPARAMETRIC ERROR TERMS

Consider the null model

$$\begin{aligned} &H_0: \\ &y = X\beta_1 + \rho_1 Wy + Y\beta_2 + u, \\ &u = R\varepsilon \end{aligned} \tag{12.2.1}$$

where y is an $N \times 1$ dependent vector, X is an $N \times k$ exogenous regressor matrix, W is an $N \times N$ exogenous weighting matrix, Y is an $N \times h$ matrix of observations on h endogenous variables, u is the disturbance vector, R is an $N \times N$ constant non-singular unknown matrix whose row and column sums are uniformly bounded in absolute value, and where the elements of ε are i.i.d. with mean and variance of 0 and 1, respectively.

Assume that $(I_N - aW)$ is nonsingular for all $|a| < 1$ so that y can be expressed as

$$y = (I_N - \rho_1 W)^{-1}[X\beta_1 + Y\beta_2 + u], \; |\rho_1| < 1. \tag{12.2.2}$$

It is reasonable to assume that the researcher has observations on s exogenous variables that are in the system generating the h variables in Y but are not contained in X. Assume that $s \geq h$.[3] Let S be the $N \times s$ matrix of observations on these s variables, and let

$$\Phi = (X, S, WX, WS, ..., W^r X, W^r S)_{LI}. \tag{12.2.3}$$

The subscript LI denotes the linearly independent columns of the indicated matrix, where typically $r = 2$. Given the value of r, it is assumed that $rank(\Phi) \geq k + 1 + h$.

As described in Chapter 6, the null model cannot be estimated by maximum likelihood unless the joint distribution of all of the endogenous variables is known. This is also the case even if $h = 0$ since R in (12.2.1) is not known. Also note, as in Chapter 9, that the error term specification in (12.2.1) allows for general patterns of heteroskedasticity, as well as spatial correlation.

12.3 THE ALTERNATIVE MODELS

Suppose the researcher considers the alternative to (12.2.1) to be one of G models. That is, if (12.2.1) is rejected, the researcher only knows that the true model is one of the G models; he does not know which of the G models is the true model.

3. As discussed in Chapter 6, in IV estimation, the model could be estimated even if $s < h$ but the instruments may be weak.

In particular, suppose the alternative hypothesis is

$$H_1: \qquad (12.3.1)$$
$$y = M_J\beta_{1,J} + \rho_{1,J}W_J\, y + Y_J\beta_{2,J} + v_J, \;\; J = 1, ..., G$$

where M_J and W_J are respectively the exogenous regressor and weighting matrices that the researchers considers in the Jth alternative model. Similarly, Y_J is an $N \times h_J$ matrix of observations on h_J endogenous variables that appear in the Jth model, and v_J is the disturbance vector. As for the null model, suppose the researcher has observations on $s_J \geq h_J$ exogenous variables which appear in the system determining the h_J endogenous variables in Y_J. Let S_J be the $N \times h_J$ matrix of observations on these exogenous variables.

Under the specifications of the Jth model, the researcher specifies the error terms either structurally as, e.g., an SAR process, or nonparametrically. In either case it is assumed by the researcher that $E(v_J) = 0$ and $E(v_J v_J') = \Omega_J$ where Ω_J is a positive definite matrix whose row and column sums are uniformly bounded in absolute value. It turns out that the exact specifications of the Ω_J are asymptotically irrelevant.

The Jth model in (12.3.1) is assumed to be estimated by instrumental variables which could be based on the instrument matrix

$$\Phi_J = (M_J, S_J, W_J M_J, W_J S_J, ..., W_J^r M_J, W_J^r S_J)_{LI}, \;\; J = 1, ..., G \qquad (12.3.2)$$

where typically $r = 2$. As in the case of the null model, there are obstacles to estimating the models in (12.3.1) by maximum likelihood.

Assume that $(I_N - aW_J)$ is nonsingular for all $|a| < 1$. Given this, we note for future reference that the solution of (12.3.1) for y in terms of M_J, Y_J, and v_J is

$$y = (I_N - \rho_{1,J}W_J)^{-1}(M_J\beta_J + Y_J\beta_{2,J} + v_J), \;\; J = 1, ..., G. \qquad (12.3.3)$$

Once more, we would like to emphasize that the specification in (12.3.1) is only meant to imply that **if** H_0 is not true, the true model is one of the models specified in (12.3.1); the researcher, however, does not know which of these models is true if H_0 is not true.

We will develop results for the specifications in H_0 and H_1. Results for the more classic spatial autoregressive error term (e.g., $u = \rho_2 Wu + \varepsilon$) will also be given below.

12.4 TWO PREDICTORS

In this section we introduce two predictors. Under the specifications given in Sections 12.2 and 12.3, the researcher is assumed to estimate the parameters of each of the alternative models, $\beta_{1,J}$, $\rho_{1,J}$, and $\beta_{2,J}$, $J = 1, ..., G$. Let $\hat{\beta}_{1,J}$, $\hat{\rho}_{1,J}$, and $\hat{\beta}_{2,J}$ be the estimators obtained, $J = 1, ..., G$. Note that one way of estimating the parameters of each of the alternative models might be just 2SLS. The crucial assumption made about these predictors is that, under H_0, these converge in probability to finite constants:

$$(\hat{\beta}_{1,J}, \hat{\rho}_{1J}, \hat{\beta}_{2,J}) \xrightarrow{P} (a_{1,J}, a_{2,J}, a_{3,J}), \ \ J = 1, ..., G. \tag{12.4.1}$$

Two predictors of y are considered for each of the alternative G models under H_1. These predictors are

$$\begin{aligned} \hat{y}_J^{(A)} &= M_J \hat{\beta}_{1,J} + \hat{\rho}_{1J} W_J \ y + Y_J \hat{\beta}_{2,J}, \\ \hat{y}_J^{(B)} &= (I_N - \hat{\rho}_{1J} W_J)^{-1} (M_J \hat{\beta}_{1,J} + Y \hat{\beta}_{2,J}). \end{aligned} \tag{12.4.2}$$

Note that $\hat{y}_J^{(A)}$ is the estimated right hand side of (12.3.1), while $\hat{y}_J^{(B)}$ is the estimated solution value for y in terms of M_J and Y_J. The predictor $\hat{y}_J^{(A)}$ that was also introduced in Chapter 4, has been called a "naive" predictor by Kelejian and Prucha (2007b) because it does not account for the correlation of the endogenous regressors, $W_J y$ and Y, with the error term.[4] In the context of the power of the J-test, this correlation can be shown, under typical assumptions, to be asymptotically negligible and so it can be ignored. It can also be shown that if the Jth model is the only alternative to the null, $\hat{y}_J^{(A)}$ and $\hat{y}_J^{(B)}$ are asymptotically equivalent in terms of the power of the J-test.[5] Since $y_J^{(A)}$ does not require the calculation of an inverse matrix, we suggest its use. The development below is in terms of $\hat{y}_J^{(A)}$; the corresponding development in terms of $\hat{y}_J^{(B)}$ is straightforward.

---

4. For example, consider the model

$$y_i = a + bx_i + \varepsilon_i, \ i = 1, ..., N$$

where y_i is a scalar. Suppose (x_i, ε_i) are i.i.d. $N(0, \Sigma)$, where

$$\Sigma = \begin{pmatrix} \sigma_{xx} & \sigma_{x\varepsilon} \\ \sigma_{x\varepsilon} & \sigma_{\varepsilon\varepsilon} \end{pmatrix}$$

so that x_i is endogenous because it is correlated with ε_i. In this case the minimum mean squared error predictor of y_i given x_i is

$$E(y_i|x_i) = a + bx_i + \frac{\sigma_{x\varepsilon}}{\sigma_{xx}} x_t \ \text{ since } E(\varepsilon_i|x_i) = \frac{\sigma_{x\varepsilon}}{\sigma_{xx}} x_t.$$

Thus if the predictor of y_i based on x_i is $a + bx_i$, one would be ignoring the correlation of x_i and ε_i.

5. For a proof of these statements, and the list of assumptions, see Kelejian and Piras (2011). They also report a Monte Carlo study where the asymptotic equivalence of the two predictors is highlighted.

12.5 THE AUGMENTED EQUATION AND THE J-TEST

As indicated, the J-test is based on augmenting the null model in (12.2.1) with the predictions of y based on the alternative models. Let

$$\hat{y}_{1,G} = [\hat{y}_1^{(A)}, \dots, \hat{y}_G^{(A)}]. \tag{12.5.1}$$

Then the augmented equation is

$$\begin{aligned} y &= X\beta_1 + \rho_1 Wy + Y\beta_2 + \hat{y}_{1,G}\,\gamma + u \\ &= ZC + u, \;\; u = R\varepsilon \end{aligned} \tag{12.5.2}$$

where γ is a parameter vector whose value, under H_0, is $\gamma = 0$, and where $Z = (X, Wy, Y, \hat{y}_{1,G})$, and $C' = (\beta_1', \rho_1, \beta_2', \gamma')$.

The J-Test

To test the hypothesis that $\gamma = 0$ the augmented equation in (12.5.2) must be estimated. Unless unrealistic assumptions concerning the joint distribution of y and Y are made, the estimation will be instrumental variables. The instrument matrix can be taken as

$$\Psi = (\Phi, \Phi_1, \dots, \Phi_G)_{LI} \tag{12.5.3}$$

where Φ, Φ_1, ..., and Φ_G are defined in (12.2.3) and (12.3.2).[6]

Since the error terms in the null model are specified nonparametrically, C in (12.5.2) is estimated by 2SLS. Let $P_\Psi = \Psi(\Psi'\Psi)^{-1}\Psi'$ and let $\hat{Z} = P_\Psi Z$. Then the 2SLS estimator of C is

$$\hat{C} = (\hat{Z}'\hat{Z})^{-1}\hat{Z}'y. \tag{12.5.4}$$

Given the null model, it is left as an exercise at the end of this chapter (hints are given) to show that, under reasonable conditions,

$$N^{1/2}(\hat{C} - C) \xrightarrow{D} N(0, \Gamma\Omega_{\Psi RR'\Psi}\Gamma') \tag{12.5.5}$$

where

$$\begin{aligned} \Gamma &= p\lim[(N^{-1}\hat{Z}'\hat{Z})^{-1}(N^{-1}Z'\Psi)(N^{-1}\Psi'\Psi)^{-1}], \\ N^{-1}\hat{Z}'\hat{Z} &= N^{-1}Z'\Psi(\Psi'\Psi)^{-1}\Psi'Z, \end{aligned}$$

6. Actually, the parameters of the alternative models can be estimated by any technique as long as the estimated parameters converge in probability to finite constants and other technical assumptions described in Kelejian and Piras (2014) hold. However, the power of the test should be higher if the parameters are estimated by a technique which is consistent under the stated assumptions of each model.

and where

$$\Omega_{\Psi RR'\Psi} = p\lim N^{-1}\Psi' RR'\Psi.$$

As in Chapter 9, let $d_{ij,N}$ be a distance measure based on a sample of size N between the ith and jth units, and let d_N be a cutoff measure defining neighbors. Then, in practice inferences can be based on the finite sample approximation

$$\begin{aligned} \hat{C} &\simeq N(C, N^{-1}\hat{\Gamma}\hat{\Omega}_{\Psi RR'\Psi}\hat{\Gamma}'), \\ \hat{\Gamma} &= N(\hat{Z}'\hat{Z})^{-1}(Z'\Psi)(\Psi'\Psi)^{-1}, \\ \hat{\Omega}_{\Psi RR'\Psi} &= N^{-1}\Psi'\bar{K}\Psi, \end{aligned} \tag{12.5.6}$$

where the (i, j)th element of $\bar{K}$ is $\hat{u}_i\hat{u}_j k(\frac{d_{ij,N}}{d_N})$, where $k(\frac{d_{ij,N}}{d_N})$ is often taken as the Parzen kernel; see Section 9.4.

The J-test of H_0 against H_1 can be tested in terms of (12.5.6). That is, if γ is not significant at, say, the 5% level, then H_0 would be accepted at the 5% level.

Illustration 12.5.1: An application of the J-test

Using the DUI data, we want to test among two different model specifications that differ only in terms of the spatial weighting matrix. The model under the null is specified in terms of a spatial weighting matrix based on the queen contiguity criteria. The model under the alternative is specified in terms of a distance measure based on the six nearest neighbors.

As in one of the models in Illustration 6.7.1, the size of police force is treated as endogenous and instrumented through the election dummy variable. The estimation of the null model, which is the same as that in Illustration 6.7.1 is

$$\begin{aligned} \widehat{dui} = &-11.508(1.843) - 1.348(0.150)police - 0.000(0.003)nondui \\ &+ 0.092(0.006)vehicles + 0.397(0.095)dry + 0.196(0.055)wdui \end{aligned}$$

where standard errors are in the parentheses. Note that the estimated coefficients for the null model are exactly the same as those that we obtained in Illustration 6.7.1 when we also treated police as endogenous. However, the standard errors are different. These differences are due to the fact that we are assuming a nonparametric specification for the error term (see Chapter 9). Particularly, the HAC estimator is based on the distance measure relating to the six nearest neighbors. The kernel function is taken as the triangular kernel.

The specification under the alternative is the same except that its weighting matrix is different. The results obtained from the estimation of the alternative model are:

$$\widehat{dui} = -14.593(1.952) - 1.446(0.159)police - 0.000(0.003)nondui$$
$$+ 0.097(0.003)vehicles + 0.411(0.099)dry + 0.099(0.048)wdui.$$

Based on the results of the alternative model, the predictors can be calculated. In this example we only utilize the first predictor in (12.4.2), but the results with the other predictor are qualitatively similar. After calculating the predictor, the augmented equation can be determined, and estimated by 2SLS. In our example,the estimated coefficient corresponding to γ in (12.5.2) is $\hat{\gamma} = -1.465$ with an estimated standard error of 1.069. Therefore, since $|1.465/1.069| \simeq 1.37$, the alternative model is rejected, i.e., the weighting matrix is accepted as a binary contiguity using the queen criterion.

12.6 THE J-TEST: SAR ERROR TERMS

Consider again the model in (12.2.1) but now assume the researcher specifies the error terms as a spatial autoregressive (SAR) process

$$\begin{aligned} &H_0: \\ &y = X\beta_1 + \rho_1 W y + Y\beta_2 + u, \\ &u = \rho_2 W u + \varepsilon \end{aligned} \tag{12.6.1}$$

where the elements of ε are i.i.d. with mean and variance of 0 and σ_ε^2, respectively. Assume again that $(I_N - aW)$ is nonsingular for all $|a| < 1$, and the alternative models in (12.3.1).

In this case the J-test of H_0 against H_1 can be carried out as follows:

1. Estimate the null model by 2SLS using the IV set Φ with $r = 2$, in (12.2.3). Let $\hat{\beta}_1$, $\hat{\rho}_1$, and $\hat{\beta}_2$ be the estimators so obtained. Also, estimate all of the alternative models by an appropriate procedure according to their assumptions.

2. Obtain $\hat{u} = y - X\hat{\beta}_1 - \hat{\rho}_1 W y - Y\hat{\beta}_2$.

3. Use $\hat{u}$ to estimate ρ_2 as, say $\hat{\rho}_2$, using the GMM procedure described in Section 2.2.4 of Chapter 2.

4. Obtain the spatial Cochrane–Orcutt transform of the variables in the augmented model:

$$\begin{aligned} y(\hat{\rho}_2) &= y - \hat{\rho}_2 W y, \\ X(\hat{\rho}_2) &= X - \hat{\rho}_2 W X, \\ Wy(\hat{\rho}_2) &= Wy - \hat{\rho}_2 W^2 y, \end{aligned} \tag{12.6.2}$$

$$\begin{aligned} Y(\hat{\rho}_2) &= Y - \hat{\rho}_2 WY, \\ \hat{y}_{1,G}(\hat{\rho}_2) &= \hat{y}_{1,G} - \hat{\rho}_2 W \hat{y}_{1,G}, \\ Z(\hat{\rho}_2) &= [X(\hat{\rho}_2), Wy(\hat{\rho}_2), Y(\hat{\rho}_2), \hat{y}_{1,G}(\hat{\rho}_2)] \end{aligned}$$

where $\hat{y}_{1,G}$ is defined in (12.5.1).

5. Let $\hat{\varepsilon} = y(\hat{\rho}_2) - X(\hat{\rho}_2)\hat{\beta}_1 - \hat{\rho}_1 Wy(\hat{\rho}_2) - Y(\hat{\rho}_2)\hat{\beta}_2$ and estimate σ_ε^2 as

$$\hat{\sigma}_\varepsilon^2 = \hat{\varepsilon}'\hat{\varepsilon}/N. \tag{12.6.3}$$

6. Construct the augmented model as

$$\begin{aligned} y(\hat{\rho}_2) &\simeq X(\hat{\rho}_2)\beta_1 + \rho_1 Wy(\hat{\rho}_2) + Y(\hat{\rho}_2)\beta_2 + \hat{y}_{1,G}(\hat{\rho}_2)\,\gamma + \varepsilon \\ &= Z(\hat{\rho}_2)C + \varepsilon, \quad C' = (\beta_1', \rho_1, \beta_2', \gamma'). \end{aligned} \tag{12.6.4}$$

7. Let $P_\Psi = \Psi(\Psi\Psi)^{-1}\Psi$ where Ψ is defined in (12.5.3) and (12.3.2). Let $\hat{Z}(\hat{\rho}_2) = P_\Psi Z(\hat{\rho}_2)$. Now obtain the generalized spatial two stage least squares estimator of C in (12.6.4)

$$\hat{C} = (\hat{Z}(\hat{\rho}_2)'\hat{Z}(\hat{\rho}_2))^{-1}\hat{Z}(\hat{\rho}_2)'y(\hat{\rho}_2). \tag{12.6.5}$$

Under reasonable (and somewhat typical) assumptions Kelejian and Piras (2011) show that

$$N^{1/2}(\hat{C} - C) \xrightarrow{D} N(0, \sigma_\varepsilon^2 p \lim_{N\to\infty} [N^{-1}\hat{Z}(\hat{\rho}_2)'\hat{Z}(\hat{\rho}_2)]^{-1}). \tag{12.6.6}$$

Small sample inferences can be based on

$$\hat{C} \simeq N(C, \hat{\sigma}_\varepsilon^2[\hat{Z}(\hat{\rho}_2)'\hat{Z}(\hat{\rho}_2)]^{-1}) \tag{12.6.7}$$

where $\hat{\sigma}_\varepsilon^2$ is given in (12.6.3). Again, the null model would be accepted if γ is not statistically significant.

12.7 *J*-TEST AND NONLINEAR ALTERNATIVES

Consider again the null model in (12.2.1)

$$H_0: \tag{12.7.1}$$

$$\begin{aligned} y &= X\beta_1 + \rho_1 Wy + Y\beta_2 + u, \\ u &= R\varepsilon \end{aligned} \tag{12.7.2}$$

where, again, R is a nonstochastic matrix whose row and column sums are uniformly bounded in absolute value, and the elements of ε are i.i.d. with mean and variance of 0 and 1, respectively.

Also, before generalizing, assume there is only one alternative model which differs from the null in that it is loglinear with different regressors. The development of the test in this simple case will facilitate generalizations given below.

Let $\ln(y)' = (\ln(y_1), ..., \ln(y_N))$, and suppose the alternative to H_0 is

$$H_1 : \ln(y) = M_1\beta_{1,1} + \rho_{1,1}W_1 y + Y_1\beta_{2,1} + v_1 \tag{12.7.3}$$

where, for $J = 1$, M_1, $W_1 y$, and Y_1 are defined as in (12.3.1), v_1 the error vector, and the remaining notation should be evident. Note that the model in (12.7.3) is nonlinear in the endogenous variables. As suggested in Chapter 6, the instruments used to estimate this model should contain nonlinear forms of the available instruments.

The J-test requires a predictor of the dependent variable in the null model, y, based on the alternative model. Let M_{1i}, W_{1i}, and Y_{1i} be the ith rows of M_1, W_1, and Y_1, and let v_{1i} be the ith element of v_1. Then, the model in (12.7.3) implies

$$H_1 : y_i = \exp(M_{1i}\beta_{1,1} + \rho_{1,1}W_{1i}\ y + Y_{1i}\beta_{2,1})\exp(v_{1i}),\ i = 1, ..., N. \tag{12.7.4}$$

Let Φ_1 be an $N \times q_1$ matrix of observations on exogenous variables the researcher knows are in the system determining y, Y and Y_1. Let Φ_1^2 and M_1^2 be identical to Φ_1 and M_1 except that each element is squared. Let Ψ_1 be the matrix of instruments

$$\begin{aligned}\Psi_1 =&(M_1, M_1^2, \Phi_1, \Phi_1^2, W_1 M_1, W_1^2 M_1,\\ &W_1 M_1^2, W_1^2 M_1^2, W_1\Phi_1, W_1^2\Phi_1, W_1\Phi_1^2, W_1^2\Phi_1^2)_{LI}\end{aligned} \tag{12.7.5}$$

where the notation should be evident. Suppose (12.7.3) is estimated by 2SLS based on Ψ_1. Let the estimators of $\beta_{1,1}, \rho_{1,1}$ and $\beta_{2,1}$ be $\tilde{\beta}_{1,1}, \tilde{\rho}_{1,1}$ and $\tilde{\beta}_{2,1}$. Then one obvious predictor of y based on H_1 is[7]

$$\hat{y}_i^{(P)} = \exp(M_{1i}\tilde{\beta}_{1,1} + \tilde{\rho}_{1,1}W_{1i}\ y + Y_{1i}\tilde{\beta}_{2,1}),\ \ i = 1, ..., N. \tag{12.7.6}$$

Then, the J-test can be carried out in terms of the augmented model

$$\begin{aligned}y &= X\beta_1 + \rho_1 Wy + Y\beta_2 + \alpha\hat{y}^{(P)} + u\\ &= ZB + u\end{aligned} \tag{12.7.7}$$

where $Z = (X, Wy, Y, \hat{y}^{(P)})$ where $\hat{y}^{(P)}$ is a vector whose element are $\hat{y}_i^{(P)}$ and $B' = (\beta_1', \rho_1, \beta_2', \alpha)$.

7. Recall from Chapter 4 that a predictor such as that in (12.7.6) is naive in the sense that it does not account for the correlation of the endogenous variables with the error term. However, also recall that because the information set is large, it is a "reasonably" good predictor.

The augmented model in (12.7.7) can be estimated by 2SLS using the instruments

$$\Psi_{Aug} = (X, WX, W^2X, X^2, WX^2, W^2X^2, \Psi_1)_{LI}.$$

In particular, let $\hat{Z} = \Psi_{Aug}(\Psi'_{Aug}\Psi_{Aug})^{-1}\Psi'_{Aug}Z$. Then the 2SLS estimator of B in (12.7.7) is

$$\hat{B} = (\hat{Z}'\hat{Z})^{-1}\hat{Z}'y. \tag{12.7.8}$$

Under reasonable conditions, inferences can be based on the finite sample approximation

$$\hat{B} \simeq N(B, N\,\hat{F}\,\hat{\Omega}\hat{F}') \tag{12.7.9}$$

where $\hat{F} = (\hat{Z}'\hat{Z})^{-1}Z'\Psi_{Aug}(\Psi'_{Aug}\Psi_{Aug})^{-1}$ and $\hat{\Omega}$ is the HAC estimator of Ω where

$$\Omega = \lim_{N\to\infty} N^{-1}\Psi'_{Aug}RR'\Psi_{Aug}.$$

The test of H_0 against H_1 then relates to the significance of α.

A Generalization

Consider now the generalization of the J-test procedure to the case in which there are G alternative models, where some or all of the them are nonlinear. Specifically:

1. Estimate each of the alternative models by an appropriate procedure.

2. Based on the estimated parameters obtain a prediction based on each of the alternative models of the dependent vector in the null model. In many cases these predictors would be naive predictors.

3. Put these predicted values of the dependent variable based on the alternative models into the null model to obtain the augmented model.

4. Estimated the augmented model by 2SLS using all of the instruments relating to the null model as well as all of the instruments relating to the alternative models.

5. Test for the statistical significance of the predicted values. If they are not jointly significant, accept the null model. If they are significant, reject the null and conclude that the true model is one of the alternative models!

SUGGESTED PROBLEMS

1. Consider the model

$$y_i = a + x_i\beta + \varepsilon_i, \quad i = 1, ..., N \tag{12A.1}$$

where, using evident notation, x_i is an $1 \times k$ vector, and (x_i, ε_i) are i.i.d. $N(\mu, \Sigma)$ where $\mu' = (\mu_x, 0)$ and, using evident notation,

$$\Sigma = \begin{bmatrix} \underset{k\times k}{V_x} & \underset{k\times 1}{cov'(x_i, \varepsilon_i)} \\ \underset{1\times k}{cov(x_i, \varepsilon_i)} & \underset{1\times 1}{\sigma_\varepsilon^2} \end{bmatrix} \tag{12A.2}$$

Assume x_i is observed but ε_i is not.
Determine the minimum mean squared error predictor of y_i based on x_i, namely $E(y_i|x_i)$.

2. Suggest how you would estimate the parameters that enter the predictor obtained in problem 1. In doing this, assume that observations on an exogenous vector, z_i, are available, where z_i is in the system determining x_i. Also assume that z_i is an $1 \times r$ vector where $r \geq k$.

3. What is the feasible form of the minimum mean square error predictor obtained in problem 1.

4. Is the feasible predictor necessarily still the minimum mean square error predictor? (**Hint**) Consider the predictor obtained in problem 1 and compare it to the one obtained in problem 3.

5. Consider the model

$$y = X\beta + \lambda W y + u, \tag{12A.3}$$
$$u = R\varepsilon$$

where the elements of ε are i.i.d. $(0, \sigma_\varepsilon^2)$, R is unknown and the remaining specifications of the model are the usual ones. Suppose you think the weighting matrix W in (12A.3) should be row normalized, but you are not sure. Suggest a test of the hypothesis H_0 : W is row normalized, against H_1 : W is not row normalized.

Chapter 13

Endogenous Weighting Matrices: Specifications and Estimation

13.1 INTRODUCTORY COMMENTS

As was noted a number of times in previous chapters, the weighting matrix used to specify the intensity of the relationship between spatial units is typically assumed to be exogenous. The assumption of exogeneity of this matrix strongly influences the estimation and interpretation of the model under study. For example, all of the estimation procedures described in this book **thus far** have assumed and exogenous weighting matrix. This is even true for the emanating and vulnerability spillover indices which were described in Chapter 3. Specifically, if the weighting matrix were endogenous, the expressions given for the emanating and vulnerability indices would not correspond to the conditional means. This should become evident from the results below.

Unfortunately, in many cases this exogeneity assumption is not reasonable. As Anselin and Bera (1998) point out, if the elements of the weighting matrix involve socioeconomic variables, endogeneity issues could arise. As one example, extending the model of Baltagi and Levin (1986), Kelejian and Piras (2014) considered a spatial model explaining the demand for cigarettes within a state which accounts for cross state border shopping. Among other things, their weighting matrix involved prices of cigarettes both within and between states. In a demand framework, such a matrix is clearly endogenous, and that endogeneity was recognized by Kelejian and Piras (2014). As another example, in a study of a country's GDP fluctuations, Mukerji (2009) based her weighting matrix on trade shares between countries, which she recognized to be endogenous. Other illustrations of spatial models involving weighting matrices based on socioeconomic variables that may be endogenous are in the literature. For example, Cohen and Morrison (2004) base their weighting matrix on the share of the value of goods shipped between states. Conley and Ligon (2002) base their weighting matrix on transportation cost. As was done in Mukerji (2009), Kelejian et al. (2006) base their weighting matrix on trade shares, etc. In the context of the studies involved, in all of these cases issues relating to the endogeneity of the weighting matrix would arise.

Spatial Econometrics. http://dx.doi.org/10.1016/B978-0-12-813387-3.00013-5

In this chapter our discussion will mostly be based on the approach laid down by Kelejian and Piras (2014). For a different approach, see Qu and Lee (2015) who explicitly model the source of the endogeneity in order to obtain two sets of equations: one for the spatial autoregressive model, and the other one for the elements of the spatial weighting matrix.

13.2 THE MODEL

Consider the model

$$\begin{aligned} y &= X\beta_1 + \rho_1 Wy + Y\beta_2 + u \\ &= ZC + u, \\ u &= R\varepsilon \end{aligned} \tag{13.2.1}$$

where y is the $N \times 1$ vector of observations on the dependent variable, X is an $N \times k$ matrix of observations on exogenous variables, Y is an $N \times h$ matrix of observations on additional endogenous variables, $Z = (X, Wy, Y)$, $C' = (\beta_1', \rho_1, \beta_2')$, where W is the matrix of observations on an $N \times N$ weighting matrix whose elements are endogenous, the matrix R is an $N \times N$ unknown constant matrix, and the rest of the notation should be evident.

Assume that the elements of ε are i.i.d. with mean and variance of 0 and 1, respectively. In addition, assume that the row and column sums of R are uniformly bounded in absolute value and so the variance–covariance matrix of u is $\Omega_u = RR'$. Note that the model in (13.2.1) is reasonably general in that it allows for an endogenous weighting matrix, contains additional endogenous regressors, and has error terms which are specified nonparametrically.

Although the elements of W are endogenous, assume that its **row** sums are uniformly bounded in absolute value by 1. This would certainly be the case if the elements of W are trade shares. In other cases, typically the elements of a weighting matrix will be bounded in absolute value because of the formulation of the variables involved, and the row sums will be uniformly bounded in absolute value because the matrix will often be sparse. Recall from Section 2.3 that if the row sums of W are uniformly bounded in absolute value by 1, $(I_N - \alpha W)$ is nonsingular for all $|\alpha| < 1$ and so the model in (13.2.1) can be solved for y in terms of X, Y, and u. Recalling the discussion in Section 2.1.3, in other cases if the row sums are uniformly bounded in absolute value by another known constant, say α, then the row sum condition can easily be satisfied by dividing the weighting matrix by α.

13.3 ISSUES CONCERNING ERROR TERM SPECIFICATION

As indicated, the error term in (13.2.1) is specified nonparametrically. There are a number of reasons for this. First, recall the discussion in Chapter 9 that strongly suggested that the error term is the unknown part of a model and so there is no basis for it to be structurally specified. Second, if it is structurally specified, and that specification is not correct, the resulting estimators will typically contain biases, be inconsistent, etc. Third, as we will now show, if the weighting matrix is endogenous, typical specifications will lead to complications.

For example, suppose one assumes the error terms to be generated as

$$u = \rho_2 W u + \varepsilon \tag{13.3.1}$$

where $E(\varepsilon) = 0$ and $E(\varepsilon\varepsilon') = \sigma_\varepsilon^2 I_N$. Since the elements of W are endogenous, they will not be independent of the error terms and, in general, will be correlated with the error terms. To see the issues involved note that the model in (13.3.1) implies

$$u = (I_N - \rho_2 W)^{-1}\varepsilon. \tag{13.3.2}$$

Because W and ε are not independent, $E(u) \neq E(I_N - \rho W)^{-1}E(\varepsilon) = 0$. Instead,

$$\begin{aligned} E(u) &= E[(I_N - \rho_2 W)^{-1}\varepsilon] \\ &= \Psi \neq 0 \end{aligned} \tag{13.3.3}$$

where Ψ is an $N \times 1$ vector whose elements will generally be unknown functions of the set of exogenous variables, say S, that are in the system determining y, W, and Y. Thus, the mean of the error term will generally **not** be zero, and would generally not be a constant vector. Furthermore, unless very strong assumptions are made, the functions of the exogenous variables in Ψ will generally **not** be known, and so one would not be able to account for the nonzero mean of the error term. Even if the element functions in Ψ were known, observations on some of the exogenous variables involved would undoubtedly not be available. All of this means that a regression model such as that in (13.2.1), with an endogenous weighting matrix and an error term such as that in (13.3.1) would have more than enough difficulties to "inhibit" estimation. It should also be clear that the above comments apply to other typical specifications of the error term involving an endogenous weighting matrix, e.g., the SMA, SEC, etc.

13.4 FURTHER SPECIFICATIONS

In principle, if the nonzero elements of W and the variables in Y are endogenous, it is reasonable to assume that their observed values are determined in a system containing, among other things, exogenous variables. Some of these exogenous variables might relate to the elements of W, and some to the elements of Y. As an illustration, suppose the elements of W are trade shares. Then, trade shares might depend upon relative prices and income levels, which, in turn, may be endogenous. At the same time, trade shares might depend upon population levels in various countries, tariffs, and measures of social unrest which may be viewed as being exogenous.

Some of the exogenous variables in the system relating to the nonzero elements of W may appear in the matrix X in (13.2.1), and some may not. In addition, the researcher may have observations on some of these "outside the model" exogenous variables, but not on others.

Let the (i, j)th element of W be w_{ij}, $i, j = 1, ..., N$. Typically, many elements of the weighting matrix are defined to be zero, e.g., its diagonal elements, among others. Denote the nonzero elements of W as w_{ij}^*. In particular, $w_{ij}^* = w_{ij}$ if $w_{ij} > 0$. Then, consider the mean of w_{ij}^*, which we assume exists,[1]

$$E(w_{ij}^*) = f(p_{ij}, g_{ij}) \tag{13.4.1}$$

where p_{ij} is a $1 \times q$ row vector of exogenous variables for which observations are available, and g_{ij} is a row vector of all the other exogenous variables for which observations are not available. As an illustration of a variable that might appear in p_{ij}, suppose w_{ij}^* is the nonzero trade share between country i and country j. Then, using evident notation, one element of p_{ij} could be $pop_i/(pop_i + pop_j)$, where pop_i is the population in country i, etc.

The result in (13.4.1) implies

$$\begin{aligned} w_{ij}^* &= f(p_{ij}, g_{ij}) + \psi_{ij}, \\ E(\psi_{ij}) &= 0. \end{aligned} \tag{13.4.2}$$

The assumption in this section is that the mean of w_{ij}^*, namely $f(p_{ij}, g_{ij})$, can be approximated by a polynomial in the observable variables, p_{ij}, and the polynomial approximation is correlated with the mean function $f(p_{ij}, g_{ij})$ in (13.4.2).[2] For example, in practice, a researcher may consider the polynomial approximation

$$w_{ij}^* \simeq p_{ij}^a \gamma + v_{ij} \tag{13.4.3}$$

where p_{ij}^a is a $1 \times a$ vector of observable polynomial forms (squares, etc.) of the q variables in p_{ij}, γ is an $a \times 1$ parameter vector, and v_{ij} is an error term.

1. Note that the mean of w_{ij}^* may also entail time lagged values of some of endogenous variables. We do not focus on them because we do not suggest the use of time lagged dependent variables as instruments. The reason for this is that the evident extension of our nonparametric specification of the error term to a dynamic panel will prevent the use of lagged endogenous variables as instruments. These issues are discussed in Chapter 15.

2. For a full list of the formal assumptions, see Kelejian and Piras (2014).

Then, the assumption in this section is that the linear approximation, $p_{ij}^{a}\gamma$, is correlated with the mean function $f(p_{ij}, g_{ij})$ in (13.4.2).

For future reference, let $p_{ij}^{a} = (p_{ij,1}, ..., p_{ij,a})$ where $p_{ij,s}$, $s = 1, ..., a$ are the polynomial forms of the exogenous variables defining the row vector p_{ij}^{a}. Also let P_s, $s = 1, ..., a$ be identical to W except that if the (i, j)th element of W is not zero, it is replaced by $p_{ij,s}$. That is, if $w_{ij} \neq 0$, the (i, j)th element of P_s is $p_{ij,s}$, $s = 1, ..., a$. If the (i, j)th element of W is zero, the (i, j)th element of P_s is also zero. Note that P_s is an $N \times N$ matrix. Finally, let F be the $N \times c$, $c \geq h$ matrix of exogenous variables in the system relating to the variables in Y.

13.5 THE INSTRUMENT MATRIX

Because of the endogeneity of W and Y, and given the nonparametric specification of the error term, the model in (13.2.1) will be estimated by instrumental variables, e.g., ML and Bayesian methods are ruled out. At this point, we discuss some preliminaries, and give a summary of the variables involved in the estimation procedure.

First, let the $a \times 1$ vector γ in (13.4.3) be estimated by least squares, as say $\hat{\gamma}$, and denote the a elements of $\hat{\gamma}$ as $\hat{\gamma}_1, ..., \hat{\gamma}_a$. Note that $\hat{\gamma}_1, ..., \hat{\gamma}_a$ are scalars. Let $\hat{W}$ be identical to W except that all of the nonzero elements of W are replaced, **correspondingly**, by $p_{ij}^{a}\hat{\gamma} = p_{ij,1}\hat{\gamma}_1 + ... + p_{ij,a}\hat{\gamma}_a$, e.g., if $w_{ij} \neq 0$ then $\hat{w}_{ij} = p_{ij}^{a}\hat{\gamma}$; if $w_{ij} = 0$ then $\hat{w}_{ij} = 0$. The zeroes in $\hat{W}$ are the same as those in W. Since $\hat{\gamma}_1, ..., \hat{\gamma}_a$ are scalars, in this case $\hat{W}$ can be expressed as

$$\hat{W} = P_1\hat{\gamma}_1 + ... + P_a\hat{\gamma}_a. \tag{13.5.1}$$

Finally, the instrument matrix which will be used to estimate (13.2.1) is

$$\hat{H} = (X, F, \hat{W}X, \hat{W}F). \tag{13.5.2}$$

Since X is $N \times k$, the matrix $\hat{W}X$ can be expressed as

$$\begin{aligned} \hat{W}X &= (P_1X\hat{\gamma}_1 + ... + P_aX\hat{\gamma}_a) \\ &= S_{PX}\ \hat{A}_1 \end{aligned} \tag{13.5.3}$$

where

$$S_{PX} = (P_1X, ..., P_aX) \tag{13.5.4}$$

and

$$\hat{A}_1' = \begin{bmatrix} I_k\hat{\gamma}_1 & I_k\hat{\gamma}_2 & . & . & I_k\hat{\gamma}_a \end{bmatrix}. \tag{13.5.5}$$

Similarly, since F is an exogenous $N \times c$ matrix, $\hat{W}F$ can be expressed in a similar way as

$$\begin{aligned}\hat{W}F &= (P_1 F\hat{\gamma}_1 + ... + P_q F\hat{\gamma}_a) \\ &= S_{PF}\hat{A}_2\end{aligned} \tag{13.5.6}$$

where

$$S_{PF} = (P_1 F, ..., P_a F) \tag{13.5.7}$$

and

$$\hat{A}_2' = \begin{bmatrix} I_c\hat{\gamma}_1 & I_c\hat{\gamma}_2 & . & . & I_c\hat{\gamma}_a \end{bmatrix}. \tag{13.5.8}$$

Finally, in light of (13.5.3)–(13.5.8), the instrument matrix $\hat{H}$ in (13.5.2) can be expressed as

$$\begin{aligned}\hat{H} &= (X, F, S_{PX}, S_{PF})\hat{A} \\ &= H\hat{A}, \\ H &= (X, F, S_{PX}, S_{PF}),\end{aligned} \tag{13.5.9}$$

and where

$$\hat{A} = \begin{bmatrix} I_k & 0_{k\times c} & 0_{k\times k} & 0_{k\times c} \\ 0_{c\times k} & I_c & 0_{c\times k} & 0_{c\times c} \\ 0_{ak\times k} & 0_{ak\times c} & \hat{A}_1 & 0_{ak\times c} \\ 0_{ac\times k} & 0_{ac\times c} & 0_{ac\times k} & \hat{A}_2 \end{bmatrix}. \tag{13.5.10}$$

In passing note that, since $P_1, ..., P_a$ are exogenous, H is both exogenous and observable.

A Summary

A lot of notation was introduced, and so for the sake of clarity we provide a summary of all the variables introduced:

1. X is an exogenous and observable $N \times k$ matrix.

2. p_{ij} is an exogenous and observable $1 \times q$ row vector.

3. $w_{ij}^* = p_{ij}^a \gamma$ where p_{ij}^a is a $1 \times a$ row vector of polynomial forms of the elements of p_{ij}, and γ is an $a \times 1$ row vector of parameters.

4. The a scalar variables defining p_{ij}^a are $p_{ij}^a = (p_{ij,1}, ..., p_{ij,a})$.

5. The $N \times N$ matrix P_s is identical to W except that all of the nonzero elements of W are replaced, correspondingly, by $p_{ij,s}$, $s = 1, ..., a$.

6. The estimated mean of the endogenous weighting matrix is $\hat{W}$ where $\hat{W} = P_1\hat{\gamma}_1 + ... + P_a\hat{\gamma}_a$, where $\hat{\gamma}$ is estimated by OLS from (13.4.3), and $\hat{\gamma}' = (\hat{\gamma}_1, ..., \hat{\gamma}_a)$.
7. The exogenous and observable matrix F is $N \times c$ and relates to the exogenous variables in the system determining Y which is $N \times h$ and $c \geq h$.
8. The instrument matrix is $\hat{H} = (X, F, \hat{W}X, \hat{W}F)$ and is expressible as $\hat{H} = H\hat{A}$, where H is an exogenous matrix.

13.6 ESTIMATION AND INFERENCE

As indicated, since both W and Y are endogenous in (13.2.1), it is reasonable to assume that the joint distribution of the elements of W, Y, and y is not known. Therefore, the model (13.2.1) cannot be estimated by maximum likelihood, and so we again turn to IV estimation.

The steps of estimation are as follows:

1. Estimate γ in (13.4.3) by least squares to obtain $\hat{\gamma}$.
2. Given $\hat{\gamma}$ construct $\hat{w}_{ij}^* = p_{ij}^a\hat{\gamma}$.
3. Construct $\hat{W}$ which is identical to W except all nonzero elements in W are, correspondingly, replaced by $\hat{w}_{ij}^*$.
4. Construct the matrix of instruments H as

$$\hat{H} = (X, F, \hat{W}X, \hat{W}F). \tag{13.6.1}$$

5. Let $\hat{Z} = \hat{H}(\hat{H}'\hat{H})^{-1}\hat{H}'Z$. Then, the two stage least squares estimator of C in (13.2.1) is

$$\hat{C} = (\hat{Z}'\hat{Z})^{-1}\hat{Z}'y. \tag{13.6.2}$$

Inferences can be based on

$$\begin{aligned} &\hat{C} \simeq N(C, N^{-1}\,\hat{\Gamma}\hat{Q}_{HRRH}\hat{\Gamma}'), \\ &\hat{\Gamma} = N(\hat{Z}'\hat{Z})^{-1}Z'\hat{H}\,(\hat{H}'\hat{H})^{-1}\hat{A}' \end{aligned} \tag{13.6.3}$$

where $\hat{Q}_{HRRH}$ is the HAC estimator of $Q = \lim_{N\to\infty} N^{-1}H'RR'H$; see Chapter 9.

The distribution in (13.6.3) is the small sample approximation based on the corresponding large sample distribution. Let $p\lim_{N\to\infty}\hat{A} = A$ where the elements of A are based on the probability limit of $\hat{\gamma}$. Then, the large sample distribution is

$$N^{1/2}(\hat{C} - C) \xrightarrow{D} N(0, \Gamma_1 Q_{HRRH}\Gamma_1') \tag{13.6.4}$$

where

$$\Gamma_1 = p \lim_{N \to \infty} \hat{\Gamma} \tag{13.6.5}$$

and

$$Q_{HRRH} = p \lim_{N \to \infty} N^{-1} H' R R' H.$$

Illustration 13.6.1: Application to a cigarette demand model

In this illustration we consider a modified version of the dynamic panel data model estimated in Kelejian and Piras (2014) which was, in turn, a variation of the one considered in Baltagi and Levin (1986). A distinctive characteristic of both of those models was that consumer cigarette demand in each state was assumed to depend upon the cigarette price in neighboring states. In Kelejian and Piras (2014) this dependence was specified in terms of an endogenous spatial weighting matrix. We consider the same model in Kelejian and Piras (2014) except that we only use the last panel of their data (i.e., 1991).

The model is formulated as

$$\begin{aligned} \ln C_{i,1991} &= \beta_1 \ln C_{i,1990} + \beta_2 \ln p_{i,1991} + \beta_3 \ln I_{i,1991} \\ &\quad + \rho_1 \left[\sum_{j=1}^{46} \left(\frac{p_{j,1991}}{p_{i,1991}} d_{ij} \ln C_{j,1991} \right) \right] + u_{i,1991} \end{aligned}$$

where $i, j = 1, \ldots, 46$ denote states,[3] and the disturbance term $u_{i,1991}$ has the nonparametric specification considered above. Additionally, C_i is cigarette sales to persons of smoking age measured in packs per capita in state i and, therefore, is a measure of real per capita cigarette sales. p_i is the average retail price per pack of cigarettes in state i, and, finally, I_i is per capita disposable income in state i.

The spatial lag for cross-border cigarette shopping is specified in terms of a dummy variable, d_{ij}, and a price ratio. The dummy variable equals one if the two states have a common border and $p_j < p_i$, and zero otherwise. In other words, the model assumes that only neighboring states that have lower prices have an effect on the demand in state i. Since the price of cigarettes is endogenous in a demand model, the weighting matrix is also endogenous.

To instrument the endogenous spatial weighting matrix we used an intercept, the ratio of cigarette tax rates of the two states, the ratio of populations, the ratio of compensation per employees, and the distance between the two states measured in hundreds of miles.

3. The omitted states are Alaska, Colorado, Hawaii, North Carolina, and Oregon.

TABLE 13.6.1 Estimation results of the cigarette demand equation

	Coefficient	Std. Error	t-stat	$P > \|t\|$
$\ln(I_{i,1991})$	−0.0944	0.0530	−1.7813	0.0749
$W \ln(C_{i,1991})$	−0.0008	0.0029	−0.2973	0.7662
$\ln(C_{i,1990})$	0.8639	0.0601	14.3661	0.0000
$\ln(p_{i,1991})$	−0.2338	0.1255	−1.8626	0.0625

Additionally, in order to estimate the empirical model, we take income as the only exogenous variable in the model, and regard all of the other variables as endogenous. The instruments used in the two stage least squares procedure are the cigarette tax rate, population, compensation per employee, as well as the one period time lag of these three variables. We also take the instrument matrix as in (13.5.2).

Table 13.6.1 reports the estimation results of the cigarette demand equation. Standard errors are produced using a spatial HAC estimator with an Epanechnikov kernel. The only significant coefficient at the two tail 5% level is the coefficient of the time lag of the consumption variable. This coefficient is positive and significant, thus pointing to a certain persistence in smoking behavior. The coefficient of the price variable has the expected sign (since the demand, in general, is supposed to decrease when the price increases) but is not significant at the two tail 5% level. One might expect that an increase in income would increase the demand. On the other hand, higher levels of income might reflect higher levels of education, and if so, could induce lower levels of cigarette demand due to an awareness of health issues. In any event, the coefficient on the income variable is not significant at the two tail 5% level. Finally, the bootlegging effect found in Kelejian and Piras (2014) is not present when the model is estimated only for a single cross-section.

SUGGESTED PROBLEMS

1. Investigate whether or not the error term specification $u = R\varepsilon$, where $\varepsilon \sim N(0, \sigma^2 I_N)$ is consistent with the SAR model $u = \rho W u + \varepsilon$, if W is exogenous.

2. Consider the model

$$y = X\beta + \lambda W y + u,$$
$$u = R\varepsilon$$

where the elements of ε are i.i.d. (0, 1) and R is an unknown nonstochastic matrix. Suppose the sample size is $N = 81$, which is 9×9 squares. The units in the first row are numbered from 1 through 9, etc. Suppose the (i, j)th element of W is

$$w_{ij} = \exp(y_i + y_j)/(z_{i,1} + z_{j,2}) \text{ if } |i - j| \leq 2,$$
$$w_{ij} = 0 \text{ otherwise,}$$

where $z_{i,1}$ and $z_{j,2}$ are observed exogenous vectors.

(a) Write out the first row of the weighting matrix W.

(b) Describe how you would estimate this model.

(c) Suppose $z_{i,1}$ and $z_{i,2}$ are endogenous, and q_i is a vector of variables in the system determining $z_{i,1}$ and $z_{i,2}$. Describe how you would estimate this model.

3. Using (13.2.1) and (13.5.2),

(a) Show that $\hat{C}$ can be expressed as

$$N^{1/2}(\hat{C} - C) = (N^{-1}\hat{Z}'\hat{Z})^{-1} N^{-1} Z'\hat{H}(N^{-1}\hat{H}'\hat{H})^{-1} N^{-1/2}\hat{H}'R\varepsilon.$$

(b) Explain whether or not $\hat{H} = (X, F, \hat{W}X, \hat{W}F)$ as in (13.5.2) is an exogenous matrix.

Chapter 14

Systems of Spatial Equations

14.1 INTRODUCTORY COMMENTS

Although many spatial models relate to a single equation, in many cases some of the variables involved in those models are determined in a system of equations along with the dependent variable of the model.[1] Such single equation models are clearly in a limited information framework. There are, however, many examples of spatial simultaneous equations models with applications spreading over many fields of economics. However, in some of these studies all of the available information is not used. For example, Jeanty et al. (2010) considered a two-equation spatial simultaneous model of population migration and housing price dynamics. However, they did not estimate their model by a systems method. Instead, their equations were estimated by the general spatial 2SLS procedure that was described in Chapter 2. Another example of a systems model is the one given in Mukerji (2009). She considered a three-equation system explaining three endogenous variables: volatility of GDP growth rates across countries, the growth rate of a country's GDP per capita, and an index which describes a country's capital account openness. For each of these three endogenous variables, she specified a structural equation. These equations had additional endogenous variables. Her model was estimated by a "natural" systems generalization of the general spatial 2SLS procedure described in Chapter 2. Her estimation procedure, which is described below, was defined by Kelejian and Prucha (2004) as general spatial 3SLS, henceforth GS3SLS.[2] This is a systems instrumental variable procedure in that, as will become clear below, it takes into account potential cross-equation correlations of the error terms. At the time, Mukerji's estimation procedure was state-of-the-art.

One important point should be noted here. Since Mukerji's (2009) model had additional endogenous variables her model could not have been estimated

1. See, e.g., Kelejian and Prucha (2004), Fingleton and Le Gallo (2008), Mukerji (2009), Royuela (2011), Hoogstra (2012), Hoogstra et al. (2011), Lastauskas and Tatsi (2013), Jeanty et al. (2010), and Kelejian and Piras (2014), among others. These studies focus on more than one structural equation, or one structural equation which involves more than one endogenous variable. In such models the unspecified equations have implications for estimation which will become clear.

2. Because Mukerji's weighting matrix was assumed to be endogenous, her procedure should, perhaps, be viewed as an evident variation of GS3SLS. The GS3SLS is discussed in Section 14.8 below.

Spatial Econometrics. http://dx.doi.org/10.1016/B978-0-12-813387-3.00014-7

by maximum likelihood. As indicated earlier in this book, in general, if a model has more endogenous variables than equations it cannot be consistently estimated by maximum likelihood. The reason for this is that the joint distribution of the endogenous variables will involve unknown equations. Concerning this, we note that many single equation spatial models have been estimated by maximum likelihood under the assumption that all of the regressors are exogenous. Unfortunately, in many of these cases the exogeneity assumption can easily be called into question!

14.2 AN ILLUSTRATIVE TWO-EQUATIONS MODEL

Before presenting the description and procedures involved in a general G-equations model, we discuss a two-equations model. The extension of results to the general model is then presented.

We consider two specifications of the error term. In the first model the error term is specified nonparametrically. In the second, the error term is specified in terms of a spatial autoregressive model. Estimation details are given for both specifications.

14.3 THE MODEL WITH NONPARAMETRIC ERROR TERMS

Consider the two equations model

$$
\begin{aligned}
y_1 &= X_1\beta_1 + \rho_{1,11} W_{11} y_1 + \rho_{1,12} W_{12} y_2 + \rho_{1_{1,13},} y_2 + Y_1\delta_1 + u_1, \qquad (14.3.1)\\
y_2 &= X_2\beta_2 + \rho_{1,21} W_{21} y_1 + \rho_{1,22} W_{22} y_2 + \rho_{1,23} y_1 + Y_2\delta_2 + u_2
\end{aligned}
$$

where for $j = 1, 2$, y_j is an $N \times 1$ vector of observations on the dependent variable in the jth equation, X_j is an $N \times k_j$ matrix of observations on k_j exogenous variables that appear in the jth equation, W_{ji} is the $N \times N$ weighting matrix in the jth equation that relates y_j to y_i, Y_j is an $N \times q_j$ matrix of observations on q_j endogenous variables that are in the jth equation, δ_j are corresponding parameter vectors, u_j is the corresponding $N \times 1$ error term, and β_j, δ_j and $\rho_{1,ji}$ (for $i = 1, 2, 3$; $j = 1, 2$) are corresponding parameters.

Assume that the researcher does not know the equations determining Y_1 and Y_2. Because of this, and because the error terms will be specified nonparametrically, maximum likelihood cannot be considered. Therefore we will describe IV estimation for the two equation system in (14.3.1). Of course, the results given below can easily be restricted to the case in which additional endogenous variables are not present.

For future reference, note that since Y_1 and Y_2 are matrices of endogenous variables they feedback through a general system to y_1 and y_2, which are also clearly interrelated. Let Φ be the $N \times h$, $h \geq \max(q_1, q_2)$ matrix of observations on exogenous variables in that general system which do not appear in (14.3.1). Typically, researchers do not have data on all of the exogenous variables in that general system.

The two equation system in (14.3.1) can be stacked in two useful ways. The first way illustrates a property of the solution of the two equations for y_1 and y_2 in terms of $X_1, X_2, Y_1, Y_2, u_1, u_2$, and the weighting matrices. The second way is useful for estimation.

Let

$$\begin{aligned} y' &= (y_1', y_2'), \\ X &= diag_{i=1}^{2}(X_i), \\ \beta' &= (\beta_1', \beta_2'), \\ Y &= diag_{i=1}^{2}(Y_i), \\ \delta' &= (\delta_1', \delta_2'), \\ u' &= (u_1', u_2'), \end{aligned} \tag{14.3.2}$$

and, in order to describe the system in (14.3.1), let

$$W = \begin{bmatrix} \rho_{1,11} W_{11} & \rho_{1,12} W_{12} + \rho_{1,13} I_N \\ \rho_{1,21} W_{21} + \rho_{1,23} I_N & \rho_{1,22} W_{22} \end{bmatrix}. \tag{14.3.3}$$

Given this notation, the first stacked form of (14.3.1) which is useful for describing a property of the solution is

$$y = X\beta + Wy + Y\delta + u. \tag{14.3.4}$$

For example, assuming $(I_{2N} - W)$ is nonsingular,

$$y = (I_{2N} - W)^{-1}[X\beta + Y\delta + u]. \tag{14.3.5}$$

The result in (14.3.5), together with the definition of W in (14.3.3), implies that both y_1 and y_2 depend upon X_1, X_2, Y_1, and Y_2, as well as interactions of these terms with all four of the weighting matrices. Recall that Φ is the matrix of observed exogenous variables in the system determining Y_1 and Y_2. Then, the implication of (14.3.5) is that if the two-equation system is to be estimated by instrumental variables, the instruments should include the matrices X_1, X_2, and Φ, as well as products of these matrices with all four of the weighting matrices and, perhaps, their squares. Then, the instrument matrix, say H_*, for both equations could be taken as

$$H_* = [X_1, X_2, \Phi, W_{11}X_1, W_{12}X_1, W_{21}X_1, W_{22}X_1, \tag{14.3.6}$$

$$W_{11}X_2, W_{12}X_2, W_{21}X_2, W_{22}X_2,$$
$$W_{11}\Phi, W_{12}\Phi, W_{21}\Phi, W_{22}\Phi]_{LI}$$

where, for ease of notation, the squares of the weighting matrices are not indicated, and again, LI denotes the linearly independent columns of the corresponding matrix. Assume quite reasonably that the number of linearly independent columns in H_* is at least as large as the number of parameters in each of the two equation. Finally, let H be the stacked instrument matrix,

$$H = diag_{i=1}^{2}(H_*). \tag{14.3.7}$$

Now consider the second way of rewriting the model by stacking the two equations. In particular, let

$$\begin{aligned} y_j &= Z_j\gamma_j + u_j, \\ Z_j &= (X_j, W_{jj}y_j, W_{ji}y_i, y_i, Y_j), \\ \gamma_j &= (\beta_j', \rho_{1,j1}, \rho_{1,j2}, \rho_{1,j3}, \delta_j')', \\ j, i &= 1, 2;\ j \neq i, \end{aligned} \tag{14.3.8}$$

and correspondingly let

$$\begin{aligned} Z &= diag_{i=1}^{2}(Z_i), \\ \gamma &= (\gamma_1', \gamma_2')'. \end{aligned} \tag{14.3.9}$$

Given this notation, the second stacked version of the model which is useful for estimation is

$$y = Z\gamma + u. \tag{14.3.10}$$

The Error Term

For the model in (14.3.10), assume the error term, u, as defined in (14.3.2), is

$$u = R\varepsilon \tag{14.3.11}$$

where R is an unknown $2N \times 2N$ matrix, and ε is a $2N \times 1$ vector of innovations.

14.4 ASSUMPTIONS OF THE MODEL

Assumption 14.1. (a) The elements of ε are i.i.d. with mean and variance of 0 and 1, respectively, and finite fourth moment.[3] **(b)** The row and column sums of

3. This specification does not allow for triangular arrays. It is given here because it is intuitive. For a formal statement which allows for triangular arrays, see Section A.15 in the appendix on large sample theory.

the $2N \times 2N$ unknown exogenous matrix R are uniformly bounded in absolute value. **(c)** R is nonsingular.

Assumption 14.2. For N large enough X_1 and X_2, and therefore X, have full column rank.

Assumption 14.3. **(a)** $|\rho_{1,ij}| < 1.0$, $i = 1, 2$; $j = 1, 2, 3$. **(b)** The main diagonal elements of W are all zero. **(c)** The matrix $(I_{2N} - W)$ is nonsingular for all $|\rho_{1,ij}| < 1.0$. In addition, for all values of $\rho_{1,ij}$ stated in part (a), the row and column sums of W and $(I_{2N} - W)^{-1}$ are uniformly bounded in absolute value.

Assumption 14.4. The elements of the matrix of instruments H in (14.3.7) are uniformly bounded in absolute value. In addition, H has full column rank for N large enough.

Assumption 14.5.

$$
\begin{aligned}
&(A) \quad \lim_{N\to\infty} N^{-1} H'H = Q_{HH}, \qquad (14.4.1)\\
&(B) \quad \lim_{N\to\infty} N^{-1} H'RR'H = Q_{HRRH},\\
&(C) \quad p\lim_{N\to\infty} N^{-1} H'Z = Q_{HZ}
\end{aligned}
$$

where Q_{HH}, Q_{HRRH}, and Q_{HZ} have full column rank.

14.5 INTERPRETATION OF THE ASSUMPTIONS

The above five assumptions are reasonable. Parts (a) and (b) of Assumption 14.1 allow the error terms to be both spatially correlated and heteroskedastic in an unknown fashion. Parts (a)–(c) of Assumption 14.1, along with (14.3.11), imply that $E(uu') = RR'$ and RR' is nonsingular, and so no error term is a linear combination of the other error terms. Assumption 14.2 just rules out perfect multicollinearity. This is an underlying assumption in virtually every model. Among other things, Assumption 14.3 ensures that the two-equation system is complete in the sense that the two specified equations can be solved for the two dependent variables being explained. The force of Assumption 14.4 is that the instruments are uniformly bounded, and H does not contain redundancies. Assumption 14.5 is standard in most large sample analyses. Among other things, it rules out "peculiar" sequences of variables. An example of a variable that would violate Assumption 14.5 would be x_i whose values are:

$$1, 2, 2, 3, 3, 3, 1, 1, 1, 1, 2, 2, 2, 2, 2, 3, 3, 3, 3, 3, 3, \ldots. \qquad (14.5.1)$$

14.6 ESTIMATION AND INFERENCE

The form of the model to be estimated is (14.3.10) and (14.3.11). Let $\hat{Z} = H(H'H)^{-1}H'Z$ where H is defined in (14.3.7). Then, since the error term is nonparametrically specified as in (14.3.11), variations on a GLS procedure cannot be considered. Thus, the estimator of γ in (14.3.10) is just the 2SLS estimator, namely

$$\hat{\gamma} = (\hat{Z}'\hat{Z})^{-1}\hat{Z}'y. \tag{14.6.1}$$

Since $\hat{Z}'Z = \hat{Z}'\hat{Z}$, we leave it as an exercise to show that, given (14.3.10) and (14.3.11),

$$\begin{aligned} N^{1/2}(\hat{\gamma} - \gamma) &= N^{1/2}(\hat{Z}'\hat{Z})^{-1}\hat{Z}'R\varepsilon \qquad (14.6.2)\\ &= [(N^{-1}\hat{Z}'\hat{Z})^{-1}]\,[N^{-1}Z'H]\,[(N^{-1}H'H)^{-1}]N^{-1/2}H'R\varepsilon. \end{aligned}$$

It is also left as an exercise to show that, given Assumptions 14.1–14.5,

$$\begin{aligned} N^{1/2}(\hat{\gamma} - \gamma) &\xrightarrow{D} N(0, FQ_{HRRH}F'), \qquad (14.6.3)\\ F &= (Q'_{HZ}Q^{-1}_{HH}Q_{HZ})^{-1}Q'_{HZ}Q^{-1}_{HH}. \end{aligned}$$

Inference would be based on the finite sample approximation

$$\hat{\gamma} \simeq N(\gamma, N^{-1}\hat{F}\hat{Q}_{HRRH}\hat{F}) \tag{14.6.4}$$

where

$$\hat{F} = (\hat{Z}'\hat{Z})^{-1}\, Z'H\, (N^{-1}H'H)^{-1}$$

and $\hat{Q}_{HRRH}$ is the HAC estimator of Q_{HRRH}.

Note that since $\gamma' = (\gamma_1', \gamma_2')$ the result in (14.6.4) can be used not only to test hypotheses about γ_1 or γ_2, but also hypotheses relating to possible cross-equation restrictions. For example, suppose γ_1 is 3×1 and γ_2 is 5×1. Suppose the researcher wants to test the hypothesis, say H_0, that the second element of γ_1 is the same as the sum of the third and fourth elements of γ_2. This hypothesis can be expressed as

$$H_0 : S_1\gamma_1 - S_2\gamma_2 = 0 \tag{14.6.5}$$

where $S_1 = (0, 1, 0)$ and $S_2 = (0, 0, 1, 1, 0)$. The same hypothesis can also be expressed as

$$H_0 : [S_1, -S_2]\begin{bmatrix} \gamma_1 \\ \gamma_2 \end{bmatrix} = 0. \tag{14.6.6}$$

Let $S = [S_1, -S_2]$ and $\hat{\gamma}' = (\hat{\gamma}_1', \hat{\gamma}_2')$. Then, inferences would be based on

$$S\hat{\gamma} \simeq N(0, VC_{S\hat{\gamma}}), \quad (14.6.7)$$
$$VC_{S\hat{\gamma}} = S\,[N^{-1}\hat{F}\hat{Q}_{HRRH}\hat{F}]\,S'.$$

Thus, H_0 would be rejected at the 5% level if

$$S\hat{\gamma}\,[VC_{S\hat{\gamma}}]^{-1}\,S' > \chi_1^2(0.95). \quad (14.6.8)$$

Illustration 14.6.1: Volatility and financial development

In this example we use the data set from Mukerji (2009) to examine whether the impact of capital account convertibility on the volatility of economic growth depends on financial development. Mukerji (2009) estimated a system of three simultaneous equations. The dependent variables in these three equations are growth volatility, economic growth, and financial development.

The model specified in the original contribution was based on a panel of countries and four time periods, with each time period corresponding to a decade (1960–1969, 1970–1979, 1980–1989, and 1990–1999). The panel was unbalanced and therefore the estimation used in the original paper simply pooled the data. Dummies for the decades were included to account for this.

The system in matrix notation is described by the three following equations:

$$V = \alpha_0 + \alpha_1 K + \alpha_2 F + \alpha_3[(F, K)] + \alpha_4 G + \alpha_5 WV + X_1\alpha_6 + \varepsilon_1,$$
$$G = \beta_0 + \beta_1 K + \beta_2 F + \beta_3 V + \beta_4 WG + \beta_5 WV + X_2\beta_6 + \varepsilon_2,$$
$$F = \gamma_0 + \gamma_1 F_{-1} + \gamma_2 K + \gamma_3 G + X_3\gamma_4 + \varepsilon_3$$

where V is a vector of observations on the growth volatilities of countries; G is a vector of observations on the mean annual growth rates of real gross domestic product per capita; F is a vector of observations of average financial development of countries; F_{-1} is the time lag of F; K is a vector of indices of capital account openness of those countries; W is a spatial weighting matrix[4]; X_1, X_2, and X_3 are matrices of exogenous variables specific to each of the equations, and ε_1, ε_2 and ε_3 are vectors of spatially correlated error terms (see Mukerji (2009) for more details). In the original contribution, the instruments used were a dummy variable for diversified exporters, the ratio of initial investment to gross domestic product, initial secondary school enrollment, the average long term growth of trade partners, the average dispersion of growth

4. The weights of the spatial weighting matrix W consisted of average trade shares of the top 20 trading partners of each country in the sample. In this context W was then treated as endogenous and a variant of a gravity model was used to instrument the trade shares in the weighting matrix (for additional details, see Mukerji, 2009).

rates among sectors, the time lag of financial development, X_1, X_2, X_3, and the spatial lags of all of the exogenous variables.

Because the endogenous variables were assumed to be simultaneously determined, the disturbances in the three equations were assumed to be correlated. Mukerji (2009) used a GS3SLS procedure to consistently estimate the parameters of the model. Mukerji's results are reported in the first three columns of Table 14.6.1.[5] As a point of comparison, the last three columns are obtained by using the simultaneous estimation procedure with nonparametric error terms presented in Section 14.6. Clearly, we expect to see differences both in the estimated coefficients and in their standard errors. The reason for this is that the original system was estimated by GS3SLS, while the estimation procedure described in Section 14.6 is based on 2SLS. A glance at Table 14.6.1 reveals that very few of the variables in the volatility and growth equations present substantial differences between the two methods. For the financial development equation, things are a little bit more different, but the overall statistical significance is unchanged.

14.7 THE MODEL WITH SAR ERROR TERMS

In this section we assume that the error terms for the model in (14.3.1) and (14.3.8) are determined as

$$u_j = \rho_{2,j} M_j u_j + v_j, \qquad (14.7.1)$$
$$|\rho_{2,j}| < 1, \ j = 1, 2$$

where M_j is an observed $N \times N$ exogenous weighting matrix, and v_j is an $N \times 1$ vector of innovations. Again let $u' = (u_1', u_2')$, and let $v = (v_1', v_2')'$ be a random $2N \times 1$ vector. Then, the two equation error term system in (14.7.1) can be expressed as

$$\begin{bmatrix} u_1 \\ u_2 \end{bmatrix} = \begin{bmatrix} \rho_{2,1} M_1 & 0 \\ 0 & \rho_{2,2} M_2 \end{bmatrix} \begin{bmatrix} u_1 \\ u_2 \end{bmatrix} + \begin{bmatrix} v_1 \\ v_2 \end{bmatrix}, \qquad (14.7.2)$$

or

$$u = \begin{bmatrix} \rho_{2,1} I_N & 0 \\ 0 & \rho_{2,2} I_N \end{bmatrix} \begin{bmatrix} M_1 & 0 \\ 0 & M_2 \end{bmatrix} u + v.$$

5. A comparison between the results in Table 14.6.1 and those of Mukerji's original contribution reveals some minor differences. Those differences are due to the fact that the equation for financial development was estimated from a slightly different number of observations. This was due to missing values in some of the variables used to estimate the equations for volatility and growth. To keep things simple, we reestimated the model over the same number of observations for the three equations. The results reported in Table 14.6.1 reflect those changes.

TABLE 14.6.1 Results of a simultaneous equation model for volatility, growth, and financial development

	Growth	Volatility	FD	Growth	Volatility	FD
Constant	−3.219	8.285	−64.507	−3.711	8.058	−59.239
	(3.045)	(3.229)	(22.773)	(2.900)	(3.819)	(21.459)
Initial GDP pc/1000	0.000	0.000	0.001	0.000	0.000	0.001
	(0.000)	(0.000)	(0.000)	(0.000)	(0.000)	(0.000)
Initial inflation	0.000	−0.001	0.001	0.000	−0.001	0.000
	(0.001)	(0.001)	(0.004)	(0.000)	(0.001)	(0.002)
Initial trade share of GDP	0.000	−0.004	0.054	0.001	−0.004	0.069
	(0.006)	(0.007)	(0.047)	(0.007)	(0.006)	(0.059)
Democracy	−1.183	−1.363	−3.236	−1.158	−1.382	−4.775
	(0.598)	(0.619)	(4.446)	(0.537)	(0.682)	(3.631)
Black market premium	−0.272	0.177	−0.211	−0.287	0.166	−0.510
	(0.129)	(0.160)	(1.095)	(0.586)	(0.503)	(0.916)
Revolutions	−0.549	0.843	−0.007	−0.558	0.790	−0.252
	(0.496)	(0.555)	(3.916)	(0.586)	(0.503)	(3.732)
Gini	−0.024	0.035	0.385	−0.024	0.036	0.331
	(0.018)	(0.021)	(0.138)	(0.020)	(0.020)	(0.149)
Rate of change of trade	0.203	0.049	−0.486	0.203	0.047	−0.305
	(0.052)	(0.066)	(0.473)	(0.064)	(0.151)	(0.463)
SD rate of change of trade	−0.001	0.045	−0.142	−0.003	0.044	−0.135
	(0.017)	(0.019)	(0.132)	(0.020)	(0.049)	(0.135)
Log population	0.306	−0.413	2.209	0.340	−0.403	2.435
	(0.147)	(0.169)	(1.182)	(0.133)	(0.194)	(1.109)
SD inflation	−0.001	0.003	0.002	−0.001	0.003	0.002
	(0.001)	(0.001)	(0.010)	(0.001)	(0.001)	(0.005)
Initial investment	0.076			0.074		
	(0.026)			(0.026)		
Initial secondary education	0.012			0.010		
	(0.008)			(0.009)		
Diversified exporter		−0.475			−0.412	
		(0.304)			(0.271)	
Lagged financial development			0.904			0.931
			(0.065)			(0.077)
Dispersion of sectoral growth rate			2.503			1.529
			(1.114)			(1.076)
Volatility	−0.056			−0.048		
	(0.141)			(0.157)		
Growth		0.008	3.998		0.028	3.071
		(0.161)	(1.018)		(0.164)	(1.230)
FD	0.005	0.035		0.003	0.030	
	(0.009)	(0.013)		(0.008)	(0.016)	
Capital account openness	−0.187	2.445	6.611	−0.184	2.237	6.094
	(0.374)	(1.238)	(3.090)	(0.351)	(1.102)	(3.354)
Capital account openness × FD		−0.050			−0.046	
		(0.023)			(0.023)	
WG	0.769			0.753		
	(0.297)			(0.281)		
WV	−0.206	−0.278		−0.149	−0.242	
	(0.243)	(0.234)		(0.198)	(0.226)	

The random vector v accounts for cross-equation correlation. Specifically, let

$$v = (\Sigma_* \otimes I_N)\Psi \tag{14.7.3}$$
$$\Sigma_* \Sigma_*' = \Sigma,$$
$$\Sigma = \begin{bmatrix} \sigma_{11} & \sigma_{12} \\ \sigma_{12} & \sigma_{22} \end{bmatrix},$$

and where Ψ is a $2N \times 1$ random vector.

For this error specification assume the following:

Assumption 14.6. The elements of Ψ are i.i.d. with mean and variance of 0 and 1, respectively, and finite fourth moment.[6]

Assumption 14.7. **(a)** $|\rho_{2,j}| < 1$, $j = 1, 2$. **(b)** $|\sigma_{ii}| < c$, where c is a finite constant, $i = 1, 2$.

Assumption 14.8. **(a)** The diagonal elements of M_j are all zero, $j = 1, 2$. **(b)** The row and column sums of M_j and $(I_N - aM_j)^{-1}$ are uniformly bounded in absolute value for all $|a| < 1$, $j = 1, 2$.

Note that Assumption 14.6 and (14.7.3) imply

$$E(vv') = \Sigma_v \tag{14.7.4}$$
$$= (\Sigma \otimes I_N)$$

or, in more standard notation,

$$E(v_i v_j') = \sigma_{ij} I_2, \ i, j = 1, 2.$$

14.8 ESTIMATION AND INFERENCE: GS3SLS

An Illustration

The model in (14.3.8) and (14.3.10) with error terms defined by (14.7.1)–(14.7.3) has additional endogenous regressors and so it does not lend itself to maximum likelihood estimation. Again, an IV procedure will be used.

To illustrate the nature of the estimation procedure assume for the moment that the parameters in the error term process are known. Let

$$y_j(\rho_{2,j}) = (I_N - \rho_{2,j} M_j) y_j, \ j = 1, 2, \tag{14.8.1}$$
$$Z_j(\rho_{2,j}) = (I_N - \rho_{2,j} M_j) Z_j, \ j = 1, 2,$$

6. This specification does not allow for triangular arrays. It is given because it is intuitive. For a formal statement which allows for triangular arrays, see Section A.15 in the appendix on large sample theory.

$$y(\rho_2) = (y_1(\rho_{2,1})', y_2(\rho_{2,2})')',$$
$$Z(\rho_2) = diag_{j=1}^{2}[Z_j(\rho_{2,j})].$$

Then the model in (14.3.10), with error terms in (14.7.1)–(14.7.3) can be written as

$$y(\rho_2) = Z(\rho_2)\gamma + v, \qquad (14.8.2)$$
$$E(vv') = (\Sigma \otimes I_N).$$

The estimator of γ in (14.8.2) should account for the cross-equation correlation of the error terms. Let A be a 2×2 matrix that diagonalizes Σ, i.e., $A'\Sigma A = I_2$, so that $\Sigma^{-1} = AA'$. Let $P = (A \otimes I_N)$. Then

$$P'(\Sigma \otimes I_N)P = (A'\Sigma A \otimes I_N) \qquad (14.8.3)$$
$$= I_{2N}.$$

For future reference, note that an implication of (14.8.3) is

$$PP' = (A \otimes I_N)(A' \otimes I_N) \qquad (14.8.4)$$
$$= (\Sigma^{-1} \otimes I_N).$$

Multiplying the first line of (14.8.2) across by P' yields

$$P'y(\rho_2) = P'Z(\rho_2)\gamma + \xi, \qquad (14.8.5)$$
$$\xi = P'v$$

where $E(\xi) = 0$ and $E(\xi\xi') = I_{2N}$.

The ideal set of instruments for the system in (14.8.5) is

$$E[P'Z(\rho_2)] = P'E[Z(\rho_2)]. \qquad (14.8.6)$$

In general, unless the entire system is linear, and all of the model equations determining the additional endogenous regressors, namely Y_1 and Y_2, are known, an exact expression for $E[Z(\rho_2)]$ will not be available. However, $E[Z(\rho_2)]$ can be approximated in terms of the available data on the instruments. Specifically, the instrument matrix for both equations can be taken to be $H_{\&}$ where

$$H_{\&} = (H_*, M_1 H_*, M_2 H_*) \qquad (14.8.7)$$

with M_1 and M_2 being defined in (14.7.2) and H_* defined in (14.3.6). Let $H_{\#}$ be the block diagonal matrix of instruments

$$H_{\#} = diag_{j=1}^{2}(H_{\&}). \qquad (14.8.8)$$

Given $H_{\#}$, the evident approximation to $P'E[Z(\rho_2)]$ in (14.8.6) is

$$P'E\widehat{[Z(\rho_2)]} \simeq P'H_{\#}(H_{\#}'H_{\#})^{-1}H_{\#}'Z(\rho_2) \\ = P'\hat{Z}(\rho_2) \tag{14.8.9}$$

where $\hat{Z}(\rho_2) = H_{\#}(H_{\#}'H_{\#})^{-1}H_{\#}'Z(\rho_2)$. Given (14.8.9) and (14.8.4), the evident estimator of γ in (14.8.5) can be expressed as

$$\hat{\gamma} = [\hat{Z}(\rho_2)'PP'\hat{Z}(\rho_2)]^{-1}\hat{Z}(\rho_2)'PP'y(\rho_2) \\ = [\hat{Z}(\rho_2)'[\Sigma^{-1} \otimes I_N]\,\hat{Z}(\rho_2)]^{-1}\hat{Z}(\rho_2)'[\Sigma^{-1} \otimes I_N]\,y(\rho_2). \tag{14.8.10}$$

General Feasible Estimation: Extension to a G-Equation System

The estimator in (14.8.10) is not feasible because the parameters are not known. It also relates to only a two-equation system. However, given its development, the feasible counterpart which relates to a G-equation system should be evident.

To simplify notation in generalizing to G equations, suppose the regressor matrix in the jth equation is

$$Z_j = (X_j, W_{j*}y_{j*}, y_{j\bullet}, Y_j), \;\; j = 1, ..., G \tag{14.8.11}$$

where $W_{j*}y_{j*}$ is "shorthand" for the list of spatially lagged dependent variables that appear in the jth equation; and $y_{j\bullet}$ is "shorthand" for the list of dependent variables that appear in the jth equation (where y_j, of course, is excluded). For example, if the only spatially lagged dependent variables in the jth equation are y_j, y_1, and y_5, then $W_{j*}y_{j*} = (W_{jj}y_j, W_{j1}y_1, W_{j5}y_5)$.

Given this notation, and generalizing the above notation in an obvious way, the G-equation system is

$$y_j = Z_j\gamma_j + u_j, \;\; j = 1, ..., G, \\ u_j = \rho_{2,j}M_ju_j + v_j, \\ E(v_j) = 0, \;\; E(v_jv_j') = \sigma_{jj}I_N, \\ E(v_jv_i') = \sigma_{ji}I_G. \tag{14.8.12}$$

Now let Φ be the matrix of observations on the known exogenous variables that are in this general G-equation system, but not in (14.8.12), which generate the additional endogenous variables $Y_1, ..., Y_G$; see (14.8.11). Similarly, let the instrument matrix H_* as defined in (14.3.6) be extended to include all of the known and observed exogenous variables, as well as the products of these with all of the weighting matrices. In order to account for an SAR transformation described below related to the error terms, we extend this generalized G-equation systems version of H_* to H_{**}:

$$H_{**} = (H_*, M_1 H_*, M_2 H_*, ..., M_G H_*)_{LI}. \tag{14.8.13}$$

Finally, let the instrument matrix be

$$H_{IV} = diag_{j=1}^{G}(H_{**}). \tag{14.8.14}$$

Given this notation, for the G-equation system in (14.8.12), the calculation of the feasible generalized counterpart to $\hat{\gamma}$ in (14.8.10) is as follows:

Step 1. Estimate the jth equation by 2SLS to get $\hat{\gamma}_j$ using H_{IV} as defined in (14.8.14).

Step 2. Obtain the estimated residuals $\hat{u}_j = y_j - Z_j\hat{\gamma}_j$.

Step 3. Use $\hat{u}_j$ and the GMM procedure described in Chapter 2 to obtain $\hat{\rho}_{2,j}$.

Step 4. Use $\hat{\rho}_{2,j}$ and $\hat{u}_j$ to estimate Σ as follows:

$$\begin{aligned} \hat{v}_j &= \hat{u}_j - \hat{\rho}_{2,j} M_j \hat{u}_j, \\ \hat{\sigma}_{ij} &= N^{-1}\hat{v}_j'\hat{v}_i, \ i, j = 1, ..., G, \\ \hat{\Sigma} &= \{\hat{\sigma}_{ij}\}; \ \ i, j = 1, ..., G. \end{aligned} \tag{14.8.15}$$

Step 5. Calculate

$$\begin{aligned} y_j(\hat{\rho}_{2,j}) &= (I_N - \hat{\rho}_{2,j} W_{jj}) y_j, \\ Z_j(\hat{\rho}_{2,j}) &= (I_N - \hat{\rho}_{2,j} W_{jj}) Z_j, \\ y(\hat{\rho}_2) &= (y_1(\hat{\rho}_{2,1})', ..., y_G(\hat{\rho}_{2,G})')', \\ Z(\hat{\rho}_2) &= diag_{j=1}^{G}[Z_j(\hat{\rho}_{2,j})]. \end{aligned} \tag{14.8.16}$$

Step 6. Obtain the GS3SLS estimator of $\gamma' = (\gamma_j', ..., \gamma_G')'$ as

$$\hat{\gamma} = [\hat{Z}(\hat{\rho}_2)'[\hat{\Sigma}^{-1} \otimes I_N]\, \hat{Z}(\hat{\rho}_2)]^{-1} \hat{Z}(\hat{\rho}_2)'[\hat{\Sigma}^{-1} \otimes I_N]\, y(\hat{\rho}_2) \tag{14.8.17}$$

where $\hat{Z}(\hat{\rho}_2) = H_*(H_* H_*)^{-1} H_*' Z(\hat{\rho}_2)$.

Inferences can be based on the small sample approximation

$$\begin{aligned} \hat{\gamma} &\doteq N(\gamma, VC_{\hat{\gamma}}), \\ VC_{\hat{\gamma}} &= [\hat{Z}(\hat{\rho}_2)'[\hat{\Sigma}^{-1} \otimes I_N]\, \hat{Z}(\hat{\rho}_2)]^{-1}. \end{aligned} \tag{14.8.18}$$

SUGGESTED PROBLEMS

1. If $W_{12} = 0 = W_{21}$ and $\delta_1 = 0$ in (14.3.1), what IVs would you use to estimate the first equation in (14.3.1)?
2. If $W_{12} = 0 = W_{21}$ but $\delta_1 \neq 0$, how would your IVs change for the estimation of the first equation in (14.3.1)?
3. Suppose $\Sigma = I_2$ in (14.7.3). What would your estimator of γ in (14.8.2) be?
4. Given the result in (14.6.2), demonstrate the result in (14.6.3).

Chapter 15

Panel Data Models

15.1 INTRODUCTORY COMMENTS[1]

All of the previous chapters have been in a single panel framework. However, in recent years panel data sets have become available, and many, if not most, recent studies are based on them. Panel data come in various ways. The most typical form is a time series on the units being studied, e.g., instead of the dependent $N \times 1$ vector y, in a time series panel model the dependent vector would be $y_t, t = 1, ..., T$ where y_t is an $N \times 1$ vector of observations on the units being explained at time t. In most of these cases the number of units, N, is typically large relative to the number of time periods, T. Many, but not all, time series panels are balanced in that at each point in time, the number of units observed is the same.

Another type of panel relates to cross-sectional groups of units where each group contains, in many cases, a different number of units. One example would be a model explaining the grades of individual high school students in terms of various neighborhood and family characteristics, as well as the characteristics of the schools they attend. In this case the data set might relate to $G > 1$ schools and the number of students in the jth school might be N_j, $j = 1, ..., G$. Another example would be the case in which farming productivity of individual farmers is modeled in terms of various farming inputs (fertilizer, etc.) and spillover effects that reflect how a farmer may learn techniques from other farmers in the same village, but perhaps not from farmers in other villages. Again, the number of farmers may vary over the villages.

15.2 SOME IMPORTANT PRELIMINARIES

Let

$$Q_0 = (I_T - \frac{J_T}{T}) \otimes I_N, \tag{15.2.1}$$

1. There is a vast literature dealing with, or related to spatial panel data models. Some important references are Anselin et al. (2008), Arellano (2003), Baltagi (2005), Baltagi et al. (2003), Blundell and Bond (1998), Elhorst (2010, 2014), Kapoor et al. (2007), Lee and Yu (2010a,b, 2012a), Mutl and Pfaffermayr (2011), Pesaran and Tosetti (2011), and Piras (2013, 2014). See also Chapter 13 in the new edition of Baltagi's book and Chapter 30 in Pesaran (2015).

Spatial Econometrics. http://dx.doi.org/10.1016/B978-0-12-813387-3.00015-9

$$J_T = e_T e_T'$$

where $\otimes$ denotes the Kronecker product, e_T is the $T \times 1$ vector of ones, and let

$$Q_1 = \frac{J_T}{T} \otimes I_N. \tag{15.2.2}$$

Let F_t be any $N \times 1$ vector, and let $F = (F_1', ..., F_T')'$. Let $\bar{F} = T^{-1}(F_1 + ... + F_T)$, i.e., if t relates to time, then $\bar{F}$ is the time average of the T vectors, $F_1, ..., F_T$. Then, the matrix Q_0 is such that

$$Q_0 F = [(F_1 - \bar{F})', (F_2 - \bar{F})', ..., (F_1 - \bar{F})']'. \tag{15.2.3}$$

That is, premultiplying a vector such as F by the matrix Q_0 produces a vector of time deviations.

Now consider the multiplication of F be the matrix Q_1. In this case

$$Q_1 F = (e_T \otimes \bar{F}), \tag{15.2.4}$$

which is a vector identical to F except that each F_t is replaced by its time average.

Let G be any $N \times s$ matrix whose elements do not vary over time. Then, it is left to the reader to show that

$$\begin{aligned} Q_0 Q_0 &= Q_0, \\ Q_1 Q_1 &= Q_1, \\ Q_0 + Q_1 &= I_{NT}, \\ Q_0 Q_1 &= 0, \\ Q_0(e_T \otimes G) &= 0. \end{aligned} \tag{15.2.5}$$

15.3 THE RANDOM EFFECTS MODEL

There are a number of random effects panel data models which differ in at least two important respects. The first is their degree of generality which relates to the number and types of regressors in the model. The second relates to the degree of generality of the error term.

In the first case, the simplest model is the one in which all of the regressors are exogenous. In addition to exogenous variables, the more complex models in this case may also contain spatial lags in the dependent variable, as well as additional endogenous variables. Some of these variables may also be time lagged, making the model a dynamic panel data model. The simplest model in the second case would contain error terms which are i.i.d. $(0, \sigma^2)$. A more general model in this case might contain nonparametrically specified error terms which allow for heteroskedasticity as well as spatial correlation.

In this section we start with the simplest random effects model which only has exogenous regressors, and a structurally specified error term. Generalizations will be straightforward.

Consider the panel data model

$$\begin{aligned} y_t &= X_t\beta + u_t, \\ u_t &= \rho_2 W u_t + \varepsilon_t, \ |\rho_2| < 1, \\ \varepsilon_t &= \mu + v_t, \ t = 1, ..., T \end{aligned} \tag{15.3.1}$$

where y_t is the $N \times 1$ vector of observations on the dependent variable at time t, X_t is an $N \times k$ matrix of observations on k exogenous regressors at time t, W is an $N \times N$ weighting matrix, u_t is the corresponding $N \times 1$ error term, ε_t is the innovation vector which is the sum of an $N \times 1$ random vector, μ, which is not time dependent, and an $N \times 1$ random vector which is time dependent. The vector μ is often thought of as describing the random differences in the intercepts between units.

Let

$$\begin{aligned} y &= (y_1', ..., y_T')', \\ X &= (X_1', ..., X_T')', \\ u &= (u_1', ..., u_T')', \\ \varepsilon &= (\varepsilon_1', ..., \varepsilon_T')', \\ v &= (v_1', ..., v_T')'. \end{aligned} \tag{15.3.2}$$

Then the time stacked form of the model in (15.3.1) is

$$\begin{aligned} y &= X\beta + u, \\ u &= (I_T \otimes \rho_2 W)u + \varepsilon, \\ \varepsilon &= (e_T \otimes I_N)\mu + v. \end{aligned} \tag{15.3.3}$$

In the random effects model it is typically assumed that the elements of μ are i.i.d. with mean and variance of 0 and σ_μ^2, respectively, the elements of v are i.i.d. with mean and variance of 0 and σ_v^2, respectively, and the vectors μ and v are independent. Also, in order for the error vector u to have a solution in terms of the innovation vector ε, assume that $(I_N - aW)$ is nonsingular for all $|a| < 1$. An extensive formal set of assumptions is given in Kapoor et al. (2007).

Given these assumptions,

$$u = [I_{NT} - (I_T \otimes \rho_2 W)]^{-1}\varepsilon \tag{15.3.4}$$

$$= [I_T \otimes (I_N - \rho_2 W)^{-1}]\varepsilon,$$

since $I_{NT} = I_T \otimes I_N$. It follows from (15.3.4) that $E(u) = 0$ and $E(uu') = \Omega_u$ where

$$\Omega_u = [I_T \otimes (I_N - \rho_2 W)^{-1}]\Omega_\varepsilon [I_T \otimes (I_N - \rho_2 W)^{-1}]' \tag{15.3.5}$$

with Ω_ε being the VC matrix of ε. Since μ and v are independent, it then follows from the third line in (15.3.3) and (15.2.5) that

$$\begin{aligned} \Omega_\varepsilon &= \sigma_\mu^2 (e_T \otimes I_N)(e_T \otimes I_N)' + \sigma_v^2 I_{NT} \\ &= \sigma_\mu^2 (J_T \otimes I_N) + \sigma_v^2 I_{NT} \\ &= T\sigma_\mu^2 Q_1 + \sigma_v^2 I_{NT}. \end{aligned} \tag{15.3.6}$$

Since $Q_0 + Q_1 = I_{NT}$, we leave it to the reader to show that

$$\begin{aligned} \Omega_\varepsilon &= \sigma_v^2 Q_0 + \sigma_1^2 Q_1, \\ \sigma_1^2 &= \sigma_v^2 + T\sigma_\mu^2. \end{aligned} \tag{15.3.7}$$

Recalling (15.2.5), it is also left to the reader to show that

$$\begin{aligned} \Omega_\varepsilon^{-1} &= \sigma_v^{-2} Q_0 + \sigma_1^{-2} Q_1, \\ \Omega_\varepsilon^{-1/2} &= \sigma_v^{-1} Q_0 + \sigma_1^{-1} Q_1, \\ \sigma_v \Omega_\varepsilon^{-1/2} &= I_{NT} - \theta Q_1, \ \theta = 1 - \sigma_v/\sigma_1 \end{aligned} \tag{15.3.8}$$

where $\Omega_\varepsilon^{-1/2}\Omega_\varepsilon\Omega_\varepsilon^{-1/2} = I_{NT}$. The third line in (15.3.8) follows immediately by multiplying the second line across by σ_v, and then setting $Q_0 = I_{NT} - Q_1$.

Suppose ρ_2, σ_v^2, σ_μ^2, were known. Given this, $\Omega_\varepsilon^{-1/2}$ would also be known via (15.3.7). In this case one would estimate (15.3.3) by first transforming the model to eliminate the spatial correlation induced by the second line in (15.3.3), and then transforming the resulting model by premultiplying it across by $\Omega_\varepsilon^{-1/2}$. Specifically, let

$$\begin{aligned} y(\rho_2) &= y - (I_T \otimes \rho_2 W)y, \\ X(\rho_2) &= X - (I_T \otimes \rho_2 W)X, \\ u(\rho_2) &= u - (I_T \otimes \rho_2 W)u \end{aligned} \tag{15.3.9}$$

where, by (15.3.3), $u(\rho_2) = \varepsilon$. Applying this transformation to the first line in (15.3.3) would yield the model

$$y(\rho_2) = X(\rho_2)\beta + \varepsilon. \tag{15.3.10}$$

Given the VC matrix Ω_ε of ε in (15.3.7) and the results in (15.3.8), one would then premultiply (15.3.10) across by $\Omega_\varepsilon^{-1/2}$ to obtain

$$\begin{aligned}\Omega_\varepsilon^{-1/2}y(\rho_2) &= \Omega_\varepsilon^{-1/2}X(\rho_2)\beta + \Omega_\varepsilon^{-1/2}\varepsilon \\ &= \Omega_\varepsilon^{-1/2}X(\rho_2)\beta + \psi\end{aligned} \tag{15.3.11}$$

where $\psi = \Omega_\varepsilon^{-1/2}\varepsilon$. It follows from (15.3.7) and (15.3.8) that

$$\begin{aligned}E(\psi) &= 0, \\ E(\psi\psi') &= \Omega_\varepsilon^{-1/2}E(\varepsilon\varepsilon')\Omega_e^{-1/2} \\ &= \Omega_\varepsilon^{-1/2}\Omega_\varepsilon\Omega_\varepsilon^{-1/2} \\ &= I_{NT}.\end{aligned} \tag{15.3.12}$$

Thus, if $\rho_2, \sigma_v^2, \sigma_\mu^2$ were known, the estimation of β in the model in (15.3.3) may now be evident. Specifically, let

$$\begin{aligned}y^* &= \Omega_\varepsilon^{-1/2}y(\rho_2), \\ X^* &= \Omega_\varepsilon^{-1/2}X(\rho_2),\end{aligned} \tag{15.3.13}$$

so that the model in (15.3.11) can be expressed as

$$y^* = X^*\beta + \psi. \tag{15.3.14}$$

Given that ρ_2, σ_v^2, and σ_μ^2 are known, the estimator of β would just be the OLS estimator based on (15.3.14) which can be expressed as a GLS estimator based on (15.3.10), namely

$$\begin{aligned}\hat{\beta}_{GLS} &= (X^{*\prime}X^*)^{-1}X^{*\prime}y^* \\ &= [X(\rho_2)'\Omega_\varepsilon^{-1}X(\rho_2)]^{-1}X(\rho_2)'\Omega_\varepsilon^{-1}y(\rho_2).\end{aligned} \tag{15.3.15}$$

Under standard conditions given in Kapoor et al. (2007), $\hat{\beta}_{GLS}$ is consistent and asymptotically normal with the anticipated distribution. In particular,

$$\begin{aligned}(NT)^{-1/2}(\hat{\beta}_{GLS} - \beta) &\xrightarrow{D} N(0, VC), \\ VC &= \lim_{N\to\infty} (NT)[X(\rho_2)'\Omega_\varepsilon^{-1}X(\rho_2)]^{-1} \\ &= \lim_{N\to\infty} (NT)(X^{*\prime}X^*)^{-1}.\end{aligned} \tag{15.3.16}$$

Finite sample inferences would be based on the approximation

$$\begin{aligned}\hat{\beta}_{GLS} &\simeq N(\beta, [X(\rho_2)'\Omega_\varepsilon^{-1}X(\rho_2)]^{-1}) \\ &= N(\beta, [X^{*\prime}X^*]^{-1}).\end{aligned} \tag{15.3.17}$$

Sometimes for computational ease, researchers premultiply (15.3.10) across by $\sigma_v \Omega_\varepsilon^{-1/2} = I_{NT} - \theta Q_1$, and then estimate the resulting model by OLS. Let

$$y_{\rho_2,\theta} = (I_{NT} - \theta Q_1) y(\rho_2), \qquad (15.3.18)$$
$$X_{\rho_2,\theta} = (I_{NT} - \theta Q_1) X(\rho_2).$$

In this case the estimator is

$$\hat{\beta}_{GLS,1} = (X'_{\rho_2,\theta} X_{\rho_2,\theta})^{-1} X'_{\rho_2,\theta} y_{\rho_2,\theta}. \qquad (15.3.19)$$

We leave it as an exercise to show that $\hat{\beta}_{GLS,1} = \hat{\beta}_{GLS}$, so that inferences based on $\hat{\beta}_{GLS,1}$ are the same as those based on $\hat{\beta}_{GLS}$.

The estimators $\hat{\beta}_{GLS}$ and $\hat{\beta}_{GLS,1}$ are not feasible because ρ_2, σ_v^2, and σ_μ^2 are not known. Let $\hat{\rho}_2$, $\hat{\sigma}_v^2$, and $\hat{\sigma}_\mu^2$ be any consistent estimators of $\rho_2, \sigma_v^2, \sigma_\mu^2$, and let

$$\hat{\sigma}_1^2 = \hat{\sigma}_v^2 + T\hat{\sigma}_\mu^2, \qquad (15.3.20)$$
$$\hat{\Omega}_\varepsilon = \hat{\sigma}_v^2 Q_0 + \hat{\sigma}_1^2 Q_1.$$

Then the feasible GLS estimator of β is $\hat{\beta}_{FGLS}$ where

$$\hat{\beta}_{FGLS} = [X(\hat{\rho}_2)' \hat{\Omega}_\varepsilon^{-1} X(\hat{\rho}_2)]^{-1} X(\hat{\rho}_2)' \hat{\Omega}_\varepsilon^{-1} y(\hat{\rho}_2) \qquad (15.3.21)$$

with

$$X(\hat{\rho}_2) = X - (I_T \otimes \hat{\rho}_2 W) X,$$
$$y(\hat{\rho}_2) = y - (I_T \otimes \hat{\rho}_2 W) y.$$

Then, under reasonable conditions, Kapoor et al. (2007) show that $\hat{\beta}_{FGLS}$ is consistent and asymptotically normal with the same distribution as that of $\hat{\beta}_{GLS}$. In particular,

$$(NT)^{-1/2} (\hat{\beta}_{FGLS} - \beta) \xrightarrow{D} N(0, VC), \qquad (15.3.22)$$
$$VC = \lim_{N \to \infty} (NT)[X(\rho_2)' \Omega_\varepsilon^{-1} X(\rho_2)]^{-1}.$$

Small sample inferences can be based on the approximation

$$\hat{\beta}_{FGLS} \simeq N(\beta, [X(\hat{\rho}_2)' \hat{\Omega}_\varepsilon^{-1} X(\hat{\rho}_2)]^{-1}). \qquad (15.3.23)$$

The Estimation of ρ_2, σ_v^2, and σ_μ^2

Clearly, the empirical implementation of the above results requires consistent estimators of ρ_2, σ_v^2, and σ_μ^2. Kapoor et al. (2007) suggest consistent estimators based on moment conditions. These moment conditions are a generalization of those given in Section 2.2.4 in reference to the GMM procedure for the estimation of ρ_2.

In reference to u and ε in (15.3.3), let

$$\begin{aligned} \bar{u} &= (I_T \otimes W)u, \\ \bar{\bar{u}} &= (I_T \otimes W)\bar{u}, \\ \varepsilon &= u - \rho_2 \bar{u}, \\ \bar{\varepsilon} &= \bar{u} - \rho_2 \bar{\bar{u}}. \end{aligned} \tag{15.3.24}$$

Also, based on (15.3.3), let $\hat{\beta} = (X'X)^{-1}X'y$ and $\hat{u} = y - X\hat{\beta}$, and correspondingly let

$$\begin{aligned} \widehat{\bar{u}} &= (I_T \otimes \rho_2 W)\hat{u}, \quad \widehat{\bar{\bar{u}}} = (I_T \otimes \rho_2 W)\widehat{\bar{u}}, \\ \hat{\varepsilon} &= \hat{u} - \rho_2 \widehat{\bar{u}}, \quad \widehat{\bar{\varepsilon}} = \widehat{\bar{u}} - \rho_2 \widehat{\bar{\bar{u}}}. \end{aligned} \tag{15.3.25}$$

Then results given in Kapoor et al. (2007) imply, for $T \geq 2$,

$$\begin{bmatrix} \frac{1}{N(T-1)}\varepsilon' Q_0 \varepsilon \\ \frac{1}{N(T-1)}\bar{\varepsilon}' Q_0 \bar{\varepsilon} \\ \frac{1}{N(T-1)}\bar{\varepsilon}' Q_0 \varepsilon \\ \frac{1}{N}\varepsilon' Q_1 \varepsilon \\ \frac{1}{N}\bar{\varepsilon}' Q_1 \bar{\varepsilon} \\ \frac{1}{N}\bar{\varepsilon}' Q_1 \varepsilon \end{bmatrix} = \begin{bmatrix} \sigma_\nu^2 \\ \sigma_\nu^2 \frac{1}{N} Tr(W'W) \\ 0 \\ \sigma_1^2 \\ \sigma_1^2 \frac{1}{N} Tr(W'W) \\ 0 \end{bmatrix} + \begin{bmatrix} \delta_1 \\ \delta_2 \\ \delta_3 \\ \delta_4 \\ \delta_5 \\ \delta_6 \end{bmatrix}, \tag{15.3.26}$$

$$E(\delta_i) = 0, \ i = 1, ..., 6.$$

Setting $\varepsilon = u - \rho_2 \bar{u}$ and $\bar{\varepsilon} = \bar{u} - \rho_2 \bar{\bar{u}}$, and replacing u, $\bar{u}$, and $\bar{\bar{u}}$, with their respective expressions in (15.3.25), namely $\hat{u}, \widehat{\bar{u}}$, and $\widehat{\bar{\bar{u}}}$, the feasible form of the expressions in (15.3.26) is

$$\begin{bmatrix} \frac{1}{N(T-1)}(\hat{u} - \rho_2 \widehat{\bar{u}})' Q_0 (\hat{u} - \rho_2 \widehat{\bar{u}}) \\ \frac{1}{N(T-1)}(\widehat{\bar{u}} - \rho_2 \widehat{\bar{\bar{u}}})' Q_0 (\widehat{\bar{u}} - \rho_2 \widehat{\bar{\bar{u}}}) \\ \frac{1}{N(T-1)}(\widehat{\bar{u}} - \rho_2 \widehat{\bar{\bar{u}}})' Q_0 (\hat{u} - \rho_2 \widehat{\bar{u}}) \\ \frac{1}{N}(\hat{u} - \rho_2 \widehat{\bar{u}})' Q_1 (\hat{u} - \rho_2 \widehat{\bar{u}}) \\ \frac{1}{N}(\widehat{\bar{u}} - \rho_2 \widehat{\bar{\bar{u}}})' Q_1 (\widehat{\bar{u}} - \rho_2 \widehat{\bar{\bar{u}}})') \\ \frac{1}{N}(\widehat{\bar{u}} - \rho_2 \widehat{\bar{\bar{u}}})' Q_1 (\hat{u} - \rho_2 \widehat{\bar{u}}) \end{bmatrix} = \begin{bmatrix} \sigma_\nu^2 \\ \sigma_\nu^2 \frac{1}{N} Tr(W'W) \\ 0 \\ \sigma_1^2 \\ \sigma_1^2 \frac{1}{N} Tr(W'W) \\ 0 \end{bmatrix} + \begin{bmatrix} \hat{\delta}_1 \\ \hat{\delta}_2 \\ \hat{\delta}_3 \\ \hat{\delta}_4 \\ \hat{\delta}_5 \\ \hat{\delta}_6 \end{bmatrix} \tag{15.3.27}$$

where $\hat{\delta}_J$, $J = 1, ..., 6$ are residuals.

If the quadratic forms in (15.3.27) are multiplied out, e.g., $(\hat{u}-\rho_2\widehat{\bar{u}})'Q_0(\hat{u}-\rho_2\widehat{\bar{u}}) = \hat{u}'Q_0\hat{u} + \rho_2^2\widehat{\bar{u}}'Q_0\widehat{\bar{u}} - 2\rho_2\hat{u}'Q_0\widehat{\bar{u}}$, the six equations in (15.3.27) can be expressed in a form that is more conducive to estimation. Specifically, let

$$\gamma = \begin{bmatrix} \rho_2 \\ \rho_2^2 \\ \sigma_v^2 \\ \sigma_1^2 \end{bmatrix}, \quad \hat{\delta} = \begin{bmatrix} \hat{\delta}_1 \\ \hat{\delta}_2 \\ \hat{\delta}_3 \\ \hat{\delta}_4 \\ \hat{\delta}_5 \\ \hat{\delta}_6 \end{bmatrix}, \quad S = \begin{bmatrix} \frac{1}{N(T-1)}\hat{u}'Q_0\hat{u} \\ \frac{1}{N(T-1)}\widehat{\bar{u}}'Q_0\widehat{\bar{u}} \\ \frac{1}{N(T-1)}\hat{u}'Q_0\widehat{\bar{u}} \\ \frac{1}{N}\hat{u}'Q_1\hat{u} \\ \frac{1}{N}\widehat{\bar{u}}'Q_1\widehat{\bar{u}} \\ \frac{1}{N}\hat{u}'Q_1\widehat{\bar{u}} \end{bmatrix}, \tag{15.3.28}$$

$$M = \begin{bmatrix} \frac{2}{N(T-1)}\hat{u}'Q_0\widehat{\bar{u}} & \frac{-1}{N(T-1)}\widehat{\bar{u}}'Q_0\widehat{\bar{u}} & 1 & 0 \\ \frac{2}{N(T-1)}\widehat{\bar{\bar{u}}}'Q_0\widehat{\bar{u}} & \frac{-1}{N(T-1)}\widehat{\bar{\bar{u}}}'Q_0\widehat{\bar{\bar{u}}} & \frac{1}{N}Tr(W'W) & 0 \\ \frac{1}{N(T-1)}[\hat{u}'Q_0\widehat{\bar{\bar{u}}} + \widehat{\bar{u}}'Q_0\widehat{\bar{u}}] & \frac{-1}{N(T-1)}\widehat{\bar{u}}'Q_0\widehat{\bar{\bar{u}}} & 0 & 0 \\ \frac{2}{N}\hat{u}'Q_1\widehat{\bar{u}} & \frac{-1}{N}\widehat{\bar{u}}'Q_1\widehat{\bar{u}} & 0 & 1 \\ \frac{2}{N}\widehat{\bar{\bar{u}}}'Q_1\widehat{\bar{u}} & \frac{-1}{N}\widehat{\bar{\bar{u}}}'Q_1\widehat{\bar{\bar{u}}} & 0 & \frac{1}{N}Tr(W'W) \\ \frac{1}{N}[\hat{u}'Q_1\widehat{\bar{\bar{u}}} + \widehat{\bar{u}}'Q_1\widehat{\bar{u}}] & \frac{-1}{N}\widehat{\bar{u}}'Q_1\widehat{\bar{\bar{u}}} & 0 & 0 \end{bmatrix}.$$

Then, the six equations in (15.3.27) can be expressed as

$$S = M\gamma + \hat{\delta}. \tag{15.3.29}$$

Kapoor et al. (2007) show that consistent estimators of σ_v^2 and ρ_2 can be obtained by nonlinear least squares based only on the first three equations in (15.3.29), namely by finding

$$\text{argmin}_{\sigma_v^2,\rho_2}[\hat{\delta}_1^2 + \hat{\delta}_2^2 + \hat{\delta}_3^2]. \tag{15.3.30}$$

Let $\hat{\rho}_2$ and $\hat{\sigma}_v^2$ be the resulting estimators of ρ_2 and σ_v^2. Then a consistent estimator of σ_1^2 can be obtained from the fourth equation in (15.3.29):

$$\hat{\sigma}_1^2 = \frac{1}{N}(\hat{u} - \hat{\rho}_2\widehat{\bar{u}})'Q_1(\hat{u} - \hat{\rho}_2\widehat{\bar{u}}). \tag{15.3.31}$$

Kapoor et al. (2007) also suggested a more efficient GLS-type estimators of ρ_2, σ_v^2, and σ_1^2 which are based on all six equations in (15.3.29). Assuming normality of the innovation vector ε in (15.3.3), $\varepsilon \sim N(0, \Omega_\varepsilon)$ where Ω_ε is given in (15.3.7), they obtained the VC matrix of $\delta' = (\delta_1, ..., \delta_6)$ in (15.3.26), namely

$$V_\delta = \begin{bmatrix} \frac{1}{T-1}\sigma_v^4 & 0 \\ 0 & \sigma_1^4 \end{bmatrix} \otimes D, \tag{15.3.32}$$

$$D = \begin{bmatrix} 2 & 2Tr(\frac{W'W}{N}) & 0 \\ 2Tr(\frac{W'W}{N}) & 2Tr(\frac{W'WW'W}{N}) & Tr(\frac{W'W(W'+W)}{N}) \\ 0 & Tr(\frac{W'W(W'+W)}{N}) & Tr(\frac{WW+W'W)}{N}) \end{bmatrix}.$$

Let $\hat{V}_\delta$ be identical to V_δ except that σ_v^4 and σ_1^4 are now replaced by their corresponding consistent estimators obtained from (15.3.29) and (15.3.31). Then the nonlinear GLS-type estimators are determined by finding

$$\text{argmin}_{\rho_2,\sigma_v^2,\sigma_1^2}[\hat{\delta}'\hat{V}_\delta^{-1}\hat{\delta}] = \text{argmin}_{\rho_2,\sigma_v^2,\sigma_1^2}(S - M\gamma)'\hat{V}_\delta^{-1}(S - M\gamma). \quad (15.3.33)$$

Given consistent estimators of ρ_2, σ_v^2, and σ_1^2, inferences concerning β would be based on (15.3.23).

Illustration 15.3.1: The effect of public capital on gross state product

In the present illustration we use the well-known Munnell (1990) data set on public capital productivity in 48 US states observed over 17 years (from 1970 to 1986). Munnell (1990) specifies a Cobb–Douglas production function that relates the gross state product (gsp) to the input of public capital including highways and streets (pcap), private capital stock based on the estimates released by the Bureau of Economic Analysis (pc), labor (employment in nonagricultural sectors) input (emp), and state unemployment rates (unemp) added to capture business cycle effects. Baltagi and Pinnoi (1995) find that the OLS and the between panel estimators show that the sign of the public capital variable is positive and significant; whereas the within effect estimator as well as the GLS estimator find that public capital is not significant.[2] In other words, after con-

2. To describe the within and between estimators, consider the model in (A). Using evident notation let

$$(A) \quad y_{it} = \alpha + x_{it}\beta + \mu_i + \varepsilon_{it},$$
$$i = 1, ..., N, \ t = 1, ..., T,$$

where x_{it} is a $1 \times k$ row vector, etc. Let

$$\bar{y}_i = T^{-1}\sum_{t=1}^{T} y_{it}, \ \bar{x}_{i.} = T^{-1}\sum_{t=1}^{T} x_{it},$$
$$\check{y}_{it} = (y_{it} - \bar{y}_i), \ \check{x}_{i.} = (x_{it} - \bar{x}_{i.}).$$

Then the model in (A) implies

$$(B) \quad \check{y}_{it} = \check{x}_{it}\beta + \check{\varepsilon}_{it}, \ i = 1, ..., N, \ t = 1, ..., T,$$

since α and μ_i cancel, and where $\check{\varepsilon}_{it}$ is the transformed error term.
The within estimator of β is the OLS estimator based on (B). The between estimator of β is the OLS estimator of β in the regression of $\bar{y}_i$ on the constant and $\bar{x}_{i.}, i = 1, ..., N$.

trolling for state specific effects, public capital is no longer significant and plays no role in production. The same data set was also used in Millo and Piras (2012) to illustrate their R library dealing with spatial panel data models. The spatial weighting matrix used by Millo and Piras (2012) in their illustration is a simple row-standardized binary contiguity matrix. This weighting matrix is also the one we use in this illustration.

The estimates obtained using (15.3.1) and following the procedure described in the previous section are reported below:

$$\begin{aligned}\widehat{\ln(gsp)} &= 2.227(0.135) + 0.054(0.022)\ln(pcap) + 0.257(0.021)\ln(pc)\\ &\quad + 0.728(0.025)\ \ln(emp) - 0.004(0.001)\ unemp.\end{aligned}$$

The estimated value for ρ_2 is 0.548, and $\sigma_v^2 = 0.001$, $\sigma_1^2 = 0.088$, and $\theta = 0.887$. All the coefficients in the regression equation are significant and have the expected sign. This means that when the error term accounts for spatial correlation as specified in (15.3.1), the variable reflecting public sector capital has a positive and significant effect. The value of the spatial coefficient ρ_2 is positive (and its magnitude is quite large!). However, the procedure discussed above does not determine the statistical significance of the estimator of ρ_2.

15.4 A GENERALIZATION OF THE RANDOM EFFECTS MODEL

The model considered in Section 15.3 does not have a spatial lag in the dependent variable, nor does it have additional endogenous variables. In this section we expand that model to include these complications. Fortunately, the extensions are straightforward.

Consider the model

$$\begin{aligned} y &= X\beta_1 + \rho_1(I_T \otimes W)y + Y\beta_2 + u \qquad (15.4.1)\\ &= Z\gamma + u,\\ Z &= (X, (I_T \otimes W)y, Y),\ \gamma' = (\beta_1', \rho_1, \beta_2'),\\ u &= (I_T \otimes \rho_2 W)u + \varepsilon,\\ \varepsilon &= (e_T \otimes I_N)\mu + v \end{aligned}$$

where y, X, u, ε, and v are defined in a manner corresponding to (15.3.2), and $Y' = (Y_1', ..., Y_T')$ where $Y_t, t = 1, ..., T$ is an $N \times h$ matrix of additional endogenous variables. Let the specifications of W, u, ε, and v be exactly what they were in reference to (15.3.3). Also, let Φ be an $NT \times r$ matrix of observable exogenous variables the researcher knows to be in the system determining Y,

Typically, the within estimator is considered in a fixed effects framework (Section 15.5 below); the between estimator is typically in a random effects framework.

$r \geq h$. The variables defining Φ need not be the only exogenous variables in that system.

Because the spatial lag of y and Y are endogenous, least squares estimation of the model will not produce consistent estimators. Since we do not assume that the equations determining Y are known, maximum likelihood and Bayesian methods are not considered. Thus, we again turn to an IV procedure. Particularly, we use the equations in (15.3.27) to estimate ρ_2, σ_v^2, and σ_1^2.

Estimation of ρ_2, σ_v^2 and σ_1^2: An Outline

Following Baltagi and Liu (2011) and Piras (2013), we first multiply the model across by Q_0 and estimate $Q_0 u$ using the instrument matrix H_* where

$$H_* = Q_0[(X, (I_T \otimes W)X, (I_T \otimes W^2)X, \Phi, (I_T \otimes W)\Phi, (I_T \otimes W^2)\Phi]_{LI}. \tag{15.4.2}$$

We then multiply the model across by Q_1 and estimate $Q_1 u$ using the instrument matrix H_+ where

$$H_+ = Q_1[(X, (I_T \otimes W)X, (I_T \otimes W^2)X, \Phi, (I_T \otimes W)\Phi, (I_T \otimes W^2)\Phi]_{LI}. \tag{15.4.3}$$

The estimates of $Q_0 u$ and $Q_1 u$ can then be used via (15.3.27)–(15.3.29) to estimate ρ_2, σ_v^2, and σ_1^2. Given these estimates, the model is then transformed to account for the spatial lag in u, and the VC matrix of ε. That transformed model is then estimated using the instrument matrix $H_\#$ where

$$H_\# = (H_*, H_+).$$

Model Estimation: Details

Premultiplying the regression model in (15.4.1) across by Q_0 yields

$$\begin{aligned} Q_0 y &= Q_0 X\beta_1 + \rho_1(I_T \otimes W)Q_0 y + Q_0 Y\beta_2 + Q_0 u \\ &= Q_0 Z\gamma + Q_0 u. \end{aligned} \tag{15.4.4}$$

Under reasonable conditions, (15.4.4) can be consistently estimated by 2SLS using the instrument matrix H_* defined in (15.4.2). Specifically, let $P_{H_*} = H_*(H_*' H_*)^{-1} H_*'$ and $\hat{Z}_* = P_{H_*} Q_0 Z$. Then, the 2SLS estimator of γ based on (15.4.4) is

$$\hat{\gamma}_* = (\hat{Z}_*' \hat{Z}_*)^{-1} \hat{Z}_*' Q_0 y \tag{15.4.5}$$

and the estimate of $Q_0 u$ is

$$\widehat{Q_0 u} = Q_0 y - Q_0 Z\hat{\gamma}_*. \tag{15.4.6}$$

Note that although Q_0u can be estimated by this procedure, u cannot be estimated if X contains variables which only vary cross-sectionally. Therefore Q_1u cannot be estimated with the results based on the regression in (15.4.4). For example, suppose $X = (X_1, X_2)$ and correspondingly let $\beta_1' = (\beta_{1,1}', \beta_{1,2}')$. Suppose X_1 is $NT \times k_1$ whose elements vary over both cross-sections and time, and let $X_2 = (e_T \otimes M)$ where M is an $N \times k_2$ matrix whose elements do not vary over time. Recalling (15.2.5), $Q_0X = (Q_0X_1, 0)$ and so $Q_0X\beta_1 = Q_0(X_1, X_2)\beta_1 = Q_0X_1\beta_{1,1}$. The parameter vector $\beta_{1,2}$ would not appear in (15.4.4), and so u could not be estimated from the estimation results corresponding to (15.4.4).

In order to estimate Q_1u the model in (15.4.1) is multiplied across by Q_1 to obtain

$$\begin{aligned} Q_1y &= Q_1X\beta_1 + \rho_1(I_T \otimes W)Q_1y + Q_1Y\beta_2 + Q_1u \\ &= Q_1Z\gamma + Q_1u. \end{aligned} \tag{15.4.7}$$

Let $P_{H_+} = H_+(H_+'H_+)^{-1}H_+'$ and $\tilde{Z}_+ = P_{H_+}Q_1Z$. Then

$$\tilde{\gamma}_+ = (\tilde{Z}_+'\tilde{Z}_+)^{-1}\tilde{Z}_+'Q_1y \tag{15.4.8}$$

and Q_1u is then estimated as

$$\widetilde{Q_1u} = Q_1y - Q_1Z\tilde{\gamma}_+. \tag{15.4.9}$$

Given $\widehat{Q_0u}$ in (15.4.6) and $\widetilde{Q_1u}$ in (15.4.9), the equations in (15.3.27)–(15.3.29) can be used to estimate ρ_2, σ_v^2, and σ_1^2 as, say, $\breve{\rho}_2, \breve{\sigma}_v^2$, and $\breve{\sigma}_1^2$, respectively.

Finally, consider the estimation of (15.4.1). Let

$$\begin{aligned} y(\breve{\rho}_2) &= y - (I_T \otimes \breve{\rho}_2W)y, \\ Z(\breve{\rho}_2) &= Z - (I_T \otimes \breve{\rho}_2W)Z, \end{aligned}$$

and

$$\begin{aligned} y_{\breve{\rho}_2,\breve{\theta}} &= (I_{NT} - \breve{\theta}Q_1)y(\breve{\rho}_2), \\ Z_{\breve{\rho}_2,\breve{\theta}} &= (I_{NT} - \breve{\theta}Q_1)Z(\breve{\rho}_2) \end{aligned} \tag{15.4.10}$$

where $\breve{\theta} = 1 - \breve{\sigma}_v/\breve{\sigma}_1$. Note that in these transformations one is first transforming to account for spatial correlation, and then transforming again to account for the covariance matrix of ε.

Let $P_\# = H_\#(H_\#'H_\#)^{-1}H_\#'$ and

$$\breve{Z}_{\breve{\rho}_2,\breve{\theta}} = P_\#Z_{\breve{\rho}_2,\breve{\theta}}.$$

Then, the proposed estimator of γ is

$$\check{\gamma} = (\check{Z}'_{\check{\rho}_2,\check{\theta}} \check{Z}_{\check{\rho}_2,\check{\theta}})^{-1} \check{Z}'_{\check{\rho}_2,\check{\theta}} y_{\check{\rho}_2,\check{\theta}}. \tag{15.4.11}$$

Small sample inferences would be based on the finite sample approximation

$$\check{\gamma} \simeq N[\gamma, (\check{Z}'_{\check{\rho}_2,\check{\theta}} \check{Z}_{\check{\rho}_2,\check{\theta}})^{-1}]. \tag{15.4.12}$$

Illustration 15.4.1: A model of crime in North Carolina

The example considered in this illustration is based on a well known panel data set initially used by Cornwell and Trumbull (1994). The authors specify an economic model for crime relating the crime rate (lcrmrte) to a number of proxy variables meant to control for the return to legal opportunities. In addition, they also include a set of deterrent variables such as probability of arrest, probability of conviction conditional on arrest, and probability of imprisonment conditional on conviction. The panel reports information on counties in North Carolina and covers a fairly large time period ranging from 1981 to 1987.

The dependent variable in the model is crime per capita (lcrmrte). Some of the main explanatory variables are deterrents to crime. Specifically, the probability of arrest (lprbarr) is proxied by the ratio of arrest to offenses; the ratio of convictions to arrest is a proxy for the probability of conviction (lprbconv), and, finally, the proportion of total convictions resulting in prison sentences is a proxy for the probability of imprisonment (lprbpris). The model also includes a measure of sanction severity (lavgsen) measured by the average prison sentence as well as the number of police per capita (lpolpc). All the other variables are either observable county characteristics, or controls for the relative return to legal activities.

The relative return to legal activities is captured by the average weekly wage in the county in various sectors, such as construction (lwcon); transportation, utilities, and communications (lwtuc); wholesale and retail trade (lwtrd); finance, insurance, and real estate (lwfir); services (lwser); manufacturing (lwmfg); and federal (lwfed), state (lwsta), and local government (lwloc). A dummy variable (urban) controls for differences in participation in the legal sector that may occur between urban and rural environment. A similar role is played by a density variable (ldensity) which measures the ratio between county population and county land area.

The model also includes the proportion of the male population between the ages of 15–24 (lpctymle), and the proportion of the minority population (lpctmin). Finally, time dummies are included as well as two other dummy variables (central and western regional) are added in order to consider regional or cultural factors that may affect the crime rate. All variables, except for the dummy variables, are on logarithmic scale.

Cornwell and Trumbull (1994) were concerned about the endogeneity of police per capita (lpolpc) and the probability of arrest. For this reason they suggested an instrumental variable procedure based on two additional instruments: the logarithm of the offense mix (lomix) and the logarithm of per capita tax ratio (lpctaxr). Offense mix was defined as the ratio of crimes involving face-to-face contacts (such as, for example, robbery) to crimes that do not involve face-to-face contacts. The assumption implicitly made by using this instrument is that the chance to capture a criminal when the criminal can be identified is higher. The inclusion of the second instrument is based on the argument that counties with residents who had greater preferences for law enforcement were also willing to pay higher taxes to found larger police force.

Results based on (15.4.11) are reported below[3]:

$$
\begin{aligned}
\widehat{lcrmrte} = & -0.624(1.145) + 0.372(0.048) lpolpc - 0.333(0.060) lprbarr \\
& - 0.276(0.032)\, lprbconv - 0.161(0.034)\, lprbpris \\
& - 0.013(0.025)\, lavgsen + 0.452(0.049)\, ldensity \\
& - 0.008(0.037)\, lwcon + 0.040(0.017)\, lwtuc \\
& - 0.009(0.039)\, lwtrd - 0.006(0.027)\, lwfir \\
& + 0.005(0.019)\, lwser - 0.194(0.075)\, lwmfg \\
& - 0.081(0.141)\, lwfed - 0.027(0.098)\, lwsta \\
& + 0.137(0.111)\, lwloc - 0.068(0.117)\, lpctymle \\
& + 0.187(0.036)\, lpctmin - 0.220(0.091)\, west \\
& + 0.137(0.111)\, central - 0.068(0.117)\, urban.
\end{aligned}
$$

The estimated value of ρ_1 is 0.269 and it is strongly statistically significant (with standard error 0.070). The estimated value for ρ_2 is negative (−0.254) and the estimates of the two variance components σ_v^2 and σ_1^2 are 0.018 and 0.264, respectively. A closer look at the results show that the probability of arrest, the probability of conviction, the probability of imprisonment, and the measure of sanction severity all have the expected negative sign. However, only three of them are statistically significant (i.e., the probability of arrest, the probability of conviction, and the probability of imprisonment). The variable measuring the police per capita is positive and statistically significant. This is to say that in counties where the number of police per capita is higher, the crime rate is generally lower. Both regional dummies and the density variable are strongly significant. On the other hand, only a few of the variables that are meant to capture the return to legal opportunities are significant (i.e., the average weekly

3. The coefficients of the time dummies are not reported.

wage in manufacturing sector). One thing is worth noticing here. As it was for cross-sectional models, the presence of ρ_1 complicates the interpretation of the other coefficients. In a model without spatial lags, and without additional endogenous variables, the coefficients would be interpreted as elasticities. On the other hand, in the absence of additional endogenous variables, for models such as that in (15.4.1), the interpretation of the coefficients is a bit different.[4] Some of the software that implements the estimation of spillover effects in models involving spatial lags, but no additional endogenous variables, is available in R or Matlab, among other packages.

15.5 THE FIXED EFFECTS MODEL

Essentially, the fixed effects model differs from the random effects model in that it conditionalizes on intercept differences between units. That is, instead of assuming stochastic conditions for the elements of a vector such as μ, as in (15.3.1), the fixed effects model simply assumes the elements of μ are fixed constants, i.e., each unit has its own fixed intercept. Without further assumptions, the fixed effect vector μ is a parameter vector of the model.

Essentially, the random effects model is a special case of the fixed effects model. In the fixed effects model it does not matter how the intercepts were generated as long as they are uniformly bounded in absolute value. That is, these fixed effects were generated and we just conditionalize on their generated values. The random effects model is based on specific assumptions about how the intercepts were generated, such as those in (15.3.1). These assumptions can be tested using a modified version of the Hausman specification test; see, e.g., Mutl and Pfaffermayr (2011).

Consider the fixed effects model

$$
\begin{aligned}
y_t &= X_t\beta_1 + \rho_1 W y_t + Y_t\beta_2 + \mu + u_t, \\
u_t &= \rho_2 W u_t + v_t, \ t = 1, \ldots, T
\end{aligned}
\tag{15.5.1}
$$

where, at time t, y_t is an $N \times 1$ vector of observations on the dependent variable, X_t is an $N \times k$ matrix of observations on k exogenous variables whose values vary over both cross-sectional units and time, Y_t is an $N \times h$ matrix of additional endogenous variables, β_1 is a $k \times 1$ parameter vector, β_2 is a $h \times 1$ parameter vector, W is an $N \times N$ exogenous weighting matrix, ρ_1 and ρ_2 are

4. Spillover effects in models which have additional endogenous variables are more complex. The reason for this is that the system involving these variables also involves the dependent variable of the model being considered, as well as exogenous variables. Therefore spillover effects relate not to the single equation being considered, but to the complete system. At present, there are no results in the spatial literature relating to this.

scalar parameters, μ is an $N \times 1$ vector of fixed effects, u_t is the disturbance term, and v_t is an $N \times 1$ vector of stochastic innovations. Also, let Φ be an $NT \times r$ matrix of **observable** exogenous variables the researcher knows to be in the system determining $Y = (Y_1', ..., Y_T')'$, $r \geq h$. The variables defining Φ need not be the only exogenous variables in that system.

At this point, assume $|\rho_1| < 1$, $|\rho_2| < 1$, and $(I_N - aW)$ is nonsingular for all $|a| < 1$. Let $v = (v_1', ..., v_T')'$. Then, the assumption on the innovation vector is that the elements of v, say v_{it}, are i.i.d. over both $i = 1, ..., N$ and $t = 1, ..., T$ with mean and variance of 0 and σ_v^2, respectively, and finite fourth moment. Again, this assumption does not account for triangular arrays, and is given only to simplify the presentation. For a formal counterpart which does account for triangular arrays, see the central limit theorem in Section A.15 of Appendix A, as well as in Kapoor et al. (2007). Finally, at this point the development below is based on the assumption that N is "large" relative to T, i.e., the large sample results are based on $N \to \infty$ and T being finite.

A Note on Identification

Before continuing we note that in a fixed effects model, the coefficients of regressors whose values do not vary over time are not identified. This is the case whether those variables are exogenous or endogenous. For example, suppose (15.5.1) were extended to

$$y_t = S\beta_0 + X_t\beta_1 + \rho_1 W y_t + Y_t\beta_2 + \mu + u_t, \; t = 1, ..., T \tag{15.5.2}$$

where S is an $N \times k_s$ regressor matrix whose values do not vary over time. Since $S\beta_0$ is a time invariant $N \times 1$ vector the model in (15.5.2) reduces to

$$y_t = X_t\beta + \rho_1 W y_t + Y_t\beta_2 + \mu_1 + u_t, \; t = 1, ..., T \tag{15.5.3}$$

where $\mu_1 = \mu + S\beta_0$. In a sense, μ_1 could be viewed as a "new" fixed effects vector! Clearly, at best μ_1, but not μ or β_0, can be estimated, although not consistently.

Issues Relating to the Fixed Effects Vector

The time pooled version of the model in (15.5.1) is

$$\begin{aligned} y &= X\beta_1 + \rho_1(I_T \otimes W)y + Y\beta_2 + (e_T \otimes I_N)\mu + u, \\ u &= \rho_2(I_T \otimes W)u + v \end{aligned} \tag{15.5.4}$$

where e_T is an $T \times 1$ vector of unit elements and

$$y = (y_1', ..., y_T')',$$

$$X = (X_1', ..., X_T')',$$
$$Y = (Y_1', ..., Y_T')',$$
$$u = (u_1', ..., u_T')',$$
$$v = (v_1', ..., v_T')'.$$

Since μ is an $N \times 1$ parameter vector, the number of regression parameters in (15.5.4) is $(k + h + 1 + N) \to \infty$ as $N \to \infty$. The elements of μ cannot be consistently estimated since T is assumed to be finite. To see this note that even if, in (15.5.4), $\beta_1 = 0, \rho_1 = \rho_2 = 0$, and $\beta_2 = 0$, the vector μ cannot be consistently estimated. For example, in this case the model in (15.5.4) reduces to

$$y = (e_T \otimes I_N)\mu + v. \tag{15.5.5}$$

The model in (15.5.5) is a linear regression model with an exogenous regressor matrix, $(e_T \otimes I_N)$, and an error vector whose elements are i.i.d. $(0, \sigma_v^2)$. If, in addition, v is normally distributed, the maximum likelihood estimator of μ would be an efficient estimator, and would just be the OLS estimator, say $\hat{\mu}$, namely

$$\begin{aligned} \hat{\mu} &= [(e_T' \otimes I_N)(e_T \otimes I_N)]^{-1}(e_T' \otimes I_N)y \\ &= \frac{1}{T}\sum_{t=1}^{T} y_t = \bar{y}. \end{aligned} \tag{15.5.6}$$

The properties of $\hat{\mu}$ are easily determined by substituting (15.5.5) into the first line of (15.5.6):

$$\begin{aligned} \hat{\mu} &= [(e_T' \otimes I_N)(e_T \otimes I_N)]^{-1}(e_T' \otimes I_N)] \, [(e_T \otimes I_N)\mu + v] \\ &= \mu + [(e_T' \otimes I_N)(e_T \otimes I_N)]^{-1}(e_T' \otimes I_N)]v. \end{aligned} \tag{15.5.7}$$

Clearly,

$$\begin{aligned} E(\hat{\mu}) &= \mu, \\ VC_{\hat{\mu}} &= \sigma_v^2[(e_T' \otimes I_N)(e_T \otimes I_N)]^{-1} \\ &= \frac{\sigma_v^2}{T} I_N. \end{aligned} \tag{15.5.8}$$

It should be evident that issues relating to the consistency of $\hat{\mu}$ involve T. For example, if N is assumed to be given, and $T \to \infty$, then by (15.5.8) $VC_{\hat{\mu}} \to 0$, and since $\hat{\mu}$ is unbiased, Chebyshev's inequality in Section A.3 of Appendix A implies that $\hat{\mu}$ is consistent, $\hat{\mu} \xrightarrow{P} \mu$. Now let $\hat{\mu}_i$, $i = 1, ..., N$ be the ith element of $\hat{\mu}$ and consider the case in which $N \to \infty$ and $T \to \infty$. In this case (15.5.8) implies $E(\hat{\mu}_i) = \mu_i$ and $var(\hat{\mu}_i) \to 0$, and so again Chebyshev's inequality implies $\hat{\mu}_i \xrightarrow{P} \mu_i, i = 1, ..., N$.[5]

In most spatial models the sample configuration considered is $N \to \infty$ with T being fixed. This is one of the basic assumptions we have used in this chapter. Because in this case a consistent estimator of the fixed effects vector μ does not exist, the model is typically transformed to eliminate μ. This permits a simpler focus on the parameters in (15.5.4) which can be consistently estimated, as we show below.

Eliminating Fixed Effects and Obtaining Instruments

Premultiplying (15.5.4) across by Q_0 and noting that (15.2.5) implies $Q_0(e_T \otimes I_N) = 0$ yields

$$\begin{aligned} Q_0 y &= Q_0 X\beta_1 + \rho_1 Q_0 (I_T \otimes W) y + Q_0 Y \beta_2 + Q_0 u \\ &= Q_0 X\beta_1 + \rho_1 (I_T \otimes W) Q_0 y + Q_0 Y \beta_2 + Q_0 u \\ &= Q_0 Z\gamma + Q_0 u \end{aligned} \tag{15.5.9}$$

and

$$Q_0 u = \rho_2 (I_T \otimes W) Q_0 u + Q_0 v \tag{15.5.10}$$

where $Q_0 Z = [Q_0 X, (I_T \otimes W) Q_0 y, Q_0 Y]$ and $\gamma = (\beta_1', \rho_1, \beta_2')'$. Assuming that $[I_{NT} - a(I_T \otimes W)]$ is nonsingular for all $|a| < 1$, the second line in (15.5.9) implies

$$Q_0 y = [I_{NT} - \rho_1 (I_T \otimes W)]^{-1} [Q_0 X\beta_1 + Q_0 Y\beta_2 + Q_0 u], \tag{15.5.11}$$

and so the expected value of $Q_0 y$ is

$$E[Q_0 y] = [I_{NT} - \rho_1 (I_T \otimes W)]^{-1} [Q_0 X\beta_1 + Q_0 E(Y)\beta_2]. \tag{15.5.12}$$

The suggested matrix of instruments for estimating γ in (15.5.9) based on (15.5.12) is

$$H_* = Q_0 [X, (I_T \otimes W) X, (I_T \otimes W^2) X, \Phi, (I_T \otimes W)\Phi, (I_T \otimes W^2)\Phi]_{LI} \tag{15.5.13}$$

5. In this case $N \to \infty$ and we are **not** saying that $\hat{\mu} \xrightarrow{P} \mu$ as $N \to \infty$ because this "limit" makes no sense. The reason for this is that μ is an $N \times 1$ vector and so, in the limit, μ cannot even be defined – there is no upper limit to ∞.

where, again, Φ is the $NT \times r$ matrix of **observable** exogenous variables that are in the system determining Y, and where higher powers than 2 could be used.[6]

Estimation

The estimation procedure takes place in three steps. In the first step a consistent but inefficient estimator, say $\hat{\gamma}$, of γ in (15.5.9) is determined. Then, $\hat{\gamma}$ is used to estimate the error vector in (15.5.9), namely Q_0u. In the second step the estimator of Q_0u is used to estimate the parameters ρ_2 and σ_v^2. In the third step the model in (15.5.9) is transformed to account for the spatial correlation, and then a more efficient estimator of γ is obtained. An expression is then given which enables finite sample inferences.

Step 1

Let $P_{H_*} = H_*(H_*'H_*)^{-1}H_*'$ and $\hat{Z}_* = P_{H_*}Q_0Z$. Then, the 2SLS estimator of γ in (15.5.9), based on the instruments in (15.5.13) is

$$\hat{\gamma} = (\hat{Z}_*'\hat{Z}_*)^{-1}\hat{Z}_*'Q_0y. \tag{15.5.14}$$

Under standard conditions, $\hat{\gamma}$ can easily be shown to be consistent, $\hat{\gamma} \xrightarrow{P} \gamma$. Given $\hat{\gamma}$, the evident estimator of Q_0u in (15.5.9) is

$$\widehat{Q_0u} = Q_0y - Q_0Z\hat{\gamma}. \tag{15.5.15}$$

For future reference note that

$$\begin{aligned} Q_0\widehat{Q_0u} &= Q_0Q_0y - Q_0Q_0Z\hat{\gamma} \\ &= Q_0y - Q_0Z\hat{\gamma} \\ &= \widehat{Q_0u}. \end{aligned} \tag{15.5.16}$$

Step 2

Given $\widehat{Q_0u}$, the parameters ρ_2 and σ_v^2 can be consistently estimated using the first three equations in Kapoor et al. (2007). For example, noting from (15.2.5) that $Q_0' = Q_0$ and $Q_0^2 = Q_0$, the empirical form of the first three equations in their paper can be expressed in terms of $\widehat{Q_0u}$ in (15.5.15) as

$$\begin{aligned} \frac{1}{N(T-1)}(Q_0\hat{u} - \rho_2 Q_0\hat{\bar{u}})'(Q_0\hat{u} - \rho_2 Q_0\hat{\bar{u}}) &= \sigma_v^2 + \hat{\delta}_1, \\ \frac{1}{N(T-1)}(Q_0\hat{\bar{u}} - \rho_2 Q_0\hat{\bar{\bar{u}}})'(Q_0\hat{\bar{u}} - \rho_2 Q_0\hat{\bar{\bar{u}}}) &= \sigma_v^2 \frac{1}{N} Tr(W'W) + \hat{\delta}_2, \end{aligned} \tag{15.5.17}$$

6. Again, because the model has additional endogenous variables, maximum likelihood or Bayesian methods cannot be implemented unless the entire system generating the endogenous variables is known!

$$\frac{1}{N(T-1)}(Q_0\widehat{\bar{u}} - \rho_2 Q_0\widehat{\bar{\bar{u}}})'(Q_0\hat{u} - \rho_2 Q_0\widehat{\bar{u}}) = 0 + \hat{\delta}_3$$

where $\hat{\delta}_i, i = 1, 2, 3$ are error terms.[7] The estimators of ρ_2 and σ_v^2, say $\breve{\rho}_2$ and $\breve{\sigma}_v^2$, are then obtained by nonlinear least squares, namely by finding

$$\arg\min_{\rho_2, \sigma_v^2} (\hat{\delta}_1^2 + \hat{\delta}_2^2 + \hat{\delta}_3^2). \tag{15.5.18}$$

Let

$$\begin{aligned}
\widehat{\bar{u}}_0 &= (I_T \otimes W)\hat{u}_0, \\
\widehat{\bar{\bar{u}}}_0 &= (I_T \otimes W)\widehat{\bar{u}}_0, \\
\hat{u}_0 &= \widehat{Q_0 u}.
\end{aligned}$$

Note that in light of (15.5.16) the three equations in (15.5.17) can also be expressed as

$$\begin{aligned}
&\frac{1}{N(T-1)}(\hat{u}_0 - \rho_2\widehat{\bar{u}}_0)'(\hat{u}_0 - \rho_2\widehat{\bar{u}}_0) = \sigma_v^2 + \hat{\delta}_1, \\
&\frac{1}{N(T-1)}(\widehat{\bar{u}}_0 - \rho_2\widehat{\bar{\bar{u}}}_0)'(\widehat{\bar{u}}_0 - \rho_2\widehat{\bar{\bar{u}}}_0) = \sigma_v^2 \frac{1}{N} Tr(W'W) + \hat{\delta}_2, \\
&\frac{1}{N(T-1)}(\widehat{\bar{u}}_0 - \rho_2\widehat{\bar{\bar{u}}}_0)'(\hat{u}_0 - \rho_2\widehat{\bar{u}}_0) = 0 + \hat{\delta}_3,
\end{aligned} \tag{15.5.19}$$

since $Q_0(I_T \otimes \rho_2 W) = (I_T \otimes \rho_2 W)Q_0$.

Step 3

Finally, one needs to transform the variables in (15.5.9) in order to account for spatial correlation. Specifically, let

$$y_{\breve{\rho}_2} = Q_0 y - (I_T \otimes \breve{\rho}_2 W)Q_0 y, \tag{15.5.20}$$

7. For example, since Q_0 is symmetric and idempotent, any quadratic form such as $M'Q_0M$ can be expressed as

$$\begin{aligned}
M'Q_0M &= M'Q_0'Q_0M \\
&= (Q_0M)'(Q_0M).
\end{aligned}$$

Using this, the first equation in Kapoor et al. (2007) can be written as

$$\begin{aligned}
\frac{1}{N(T-1)}\varepsilon'Q_0\varepsilon &= \frac{1}{N(T-1)}(Q_0\varepsilon)'(Q_0\varepsilon) \\
&= \sigma_v^2 + \delta_1
\end{aligned}$$

where $\varepsilon = u - \rho(I_T \otimes W)u$ is the innovation vector, and $E(\delta_1) = 0$. Thus, to estimate $\varepsilon'Q_0\varepsilon$ one only has to estimate $Q_0\varepsilon$.

$$Z_{\breve{\rho}_2} = Q_0 Z - (I_T \otimes \breve{\rho}_2 W) Q_0 Z.$$

Applying this transformation to (15.5.9) yields the approximation model

$$y_{\breve{\rho}_2} \dot{\simeq} Z_{\breve{\rho}_2}\gamma + Q_0 v \tag{15.5.21}$$

where the approximation **would be perfect if** $\breve{\rho}_2 = \rho_2$.

Let

$$\check{Z}_{\breve{\rho}_2} = P_{H_*} Z_{\breve{\rho}_2} \tag{15.5.22}$$

where $P_{H_*} = H_*(H_*' H_*)^{-1} H_*'$ and H_* is defined in (15.5.13). Then, the suggested estimator of γ in (15.5.21) is

$$\check{\gamma} = (\check{Z}_{\breve{\rho}_2}' \check{Z}_{\breve{\rho}_2})^{-1} \check{Z}_{\breve{\rho}_2}' y_{\breve{\rho}_2}. \tag{15.5.23}$$

Straightforward calculations will demonstrate the consistency of $\check{\gamma}$, as well as its asymptotic normality. Small sample inferences can be based on the finite sample approximation

$$\check{\gamma} \simeq N[\gamma, \hat{\sigma}_v^2 (\check{Z}_{\breve{\rho}_2}' \check{Z}_{\breve{\rho}_2})^{-1}] \tag{15.5.24}$$

where $\hat{\sigma}_v^2$ is a consistent estimator of σ_v^2. One such estimator is $\breve{\sigma}_v^2$ which is determined by the GMM approach described by (15.5.18). Another one is based on (15.5.21). Let

$$\widehat{Q_0 v} = y_{\breve{\rho}_2} - Z_{\breve{\rho}_2}\check{\gamma}. \tag{15.5.25}$$

Then, under reasonable conditions, another consistent estimator of σ_v^2 is $\hat{\sigma}_v^2$ where

$$\hat{\sigma}_v^2 = \frac{1}{N(T-1)} (\widehat{Q_0 v})'(\widehat{Q_0 v}). \tag{15.5.26}$$

Illustration 15.5.1: A fixed effects version of the model of crime

We consider again the model of crime in North Carolina and the three-step procedure described above for the fixed effects model. Furthermore, for that model we consider the two additional instruments (offense mix and per capita tax ratio) to control for the endogeneity of police per capita and the probability of arrest.

Results from the estimation are reported below:

$$\begin{aligned} \widehat{lcrmrte} = &\, 0.427(0.106) lpolpc - 0.250(0.113) lprbarr \\ & - 0.246(0.065)\, lprbconv - 0.142(0.048)\, lprbpris \\ & - 0.007(0.027)\, lavgsen + 0.417(0.289)\, ldensity \end{aligned}$$

$$
\begin{aligned}
&-0.042(0.039)\, lwcon + 0.038(0.018)\, lwtuc \\
&-0.017(0.040)\, lwtrd - 0.009(0.028)\, lwfir \\
&+0.017(0.020)\, lwser - 0.307(0.124)\, lwmfg \\
&-0.332(0.185)\, lwfed + 0.056(0.117)\, lwsta \\
&+0.173(0.120)\, lwloc + 0.316(0.387)\, lpctymle.
\end{aligned}
$$

The value of $\rho_1 = 0.370$ is strongly statistically significant (with standard error 0.181). The estimated value of ρ_2 is negative (-0.254), and the estimated value of the variance component σ_v^2 is 0.018. These two values are extremely similar to those obtained in Illustration 15.4.1 in the previous section. As for the deterrent variables (i.e., the probability of arrest, the probability of conviction, the probability of imprisonment and the measure of sanction severity) all have the expected negative sign and are (in absolute value) lower than those obtained in the random effect model of Illustration 15.4.1. The variable measuring the level of police per capita is also statistically significant and has the expected positive sign.

Clearly, the dummy variables west, central, and urban, as well as all the other variables that do not vary over time, are wiped out when we apply the fixed effect transformation, and, therefore, their coefficients are not identified.

A Dynamic Version of the Fixed Effects Model

Another specification of the fixed effects panel data model is a variation of a dynamic random effects model given by Baltagi et al. (2014b).[8] The model we discuss here is a dynamic version of the model in (15.5.1) but it does not have additional endogenous variables.

Using evident notation the model is

$$
\begin{aligned}
y_t &= X_t\beta + \rho_1 W y_t + \theta y_{t-1} + \mu + u_t, \\
u_t &= \rho_2 W u_t + v_t, \; t = 1, \ldots, T
\end{aligned}
\tag{15.5.27}
$$

where y_t is an $N \times 1$ vector, μ is an $N \times 1$ fixed effects vector, etc. The elements of the $NT \times 1$ vector $v' = (v_1', \ldots, v_T')'$ are assumed to be i.i.d. $(0, \sigma_v^2)$.

Following Baltagi et al. (2014b), the fixed effects vector μ can be eliminated by time differencing (15.5.27) to obtain

$$
\begin{aligned}
\Delta y_t &= \Delta X_t\beta + \rho_1 W \Delta y_t + \theta \Delta y_{t-1} + \Delta u_t, \\
\Delta u_t &= \rho_2 W \Delta u_t + \Delta v_t, \; t = 1, \ldots, T
\end{aligned}
\tag{15.5.28}
$$

8. See also Arellano and Bond (1991).

where $\Delta y_t = y_t - y_{t-1}$, etc.[9] The error vector Δu_t in (15.5.28) can be expressed as

$$\Delta u_t = [I_N - \rho_2 W]^{-1} \Delta v_t. \tag{15.5.29}$$

Since $E(\Delta v_t y'_{t-s}) = 0$ for all $s \leq t-2$ implies $E(\Delta u_t y'_{t-s}) = 0$ for all $s \leq t-2$, in their framework Baltagi et al. (2014b) suggest the use of time lagged dependent as well as exogenous variables as instruments to estimate their model. Many steps in their procedure would carry over to the estimation of (15.5.28). The overall procedure is interesting, but a little bit tedious. It also depends crucially on the assumption that the elements of v_t are i.i.d. $(0, \sigma_v^2)$ over both $i = 1, ..., N$ and $t = 1, ..., T$. We do not describe the details of the procedure because in Section 15.6 we present a general panel data fixed effects model which contains both (15.5.1) and (15.5.27) as special cases.

15.6 A GENERALIZATION OF THE FIXED EFFECTS MODEL

The fixed effects model in (15.5.1) is generalized in this section. This generalization involves a nonparametric specification of the error term, as well as the contemporaneous presence of additional endogenous regressors, and a dynamic term in the model. Ironically, formal large sample results are available and easily obtained for this generalized model! The reason for this is that the nonparametric specification of the error term precludes the use of lagged dependent variables as instruments. Again, the large sample theory described in this section relates to the case in which $N \to \infty$ and T is fixed.

The nonparametric specification of the error term is especially important and, as we strongly suggested in Chapter 9. It is indicative of a "new wave" of spatial research. For the convenience of readers who may not have read Chapter 9, we outline the arguments given in that chapter. Further details are given in Chapter 9.

As we mentioned in Chapter 9, in time series econometrics, researchers used to specify heteroskedasticity in terms of a known function of exogenous regressors and a parameter vector, say θ,

$$\sigma_i^2 = f(x_i, \theta),\ i = 1, ..., N, \tag{15.6.1}$$

in order to reduce the number of parameters.[10] At the time, the general understanding was that without an assumption such as (15.6.1) the variance–

9. Baltagi et al. (2014b) eliminate their random effects vector because its elements are correlated with the time lagged dependent variable. So, although their model is quite different than ours in that they have random effects while our model here has fixed effects, the approach taken for estimation is quite similar.

10. Note that in a panel context, the expression in (15.6.1) can be further complicated if, for example, time lagged variables are considered.

covariance matrix of the estimators could not be consistently estimated. The assumed reason for this was that it would involve N unknown variances, which would be viewed as unknown parameters, where N is the size of the sample. Given an assumption such as (15.6.1), those kinds of model were estimated by ML, or by an iterative method in which one would first estimate the model ignoring the heteroskedasticity, then use the estimated squares of the residuals to estimate θ, and then account for the heteroskedasticity by dividing the model across by $[f(x_i, \hat{\theta})]^{1/2}$. This was the approach followed years ago before the influential paper of White (1980). White (1980) pointed out that estimation procedures based on structural specifications of the variances, such as (15.6.1), introduce biases. Among other things, his suggestion was to estimate the model ignoring the heteroskedasticity and then estimate the resulting VC matrix of the estimators by a robust procedure (HAC). His procedure essentially assumed a nonparametric specification of the error term variances. Nowadays it is rare to find a study in which models involving heteroskedasticity are estimated by assuming a structure such as (15.6.1).

In both applied and theoretical spatial modeling it is extremely common for researchers to assume a particular structure for their error terms. Two common structures assumed are the spatial autoregressive (SAR) and the spatial moving average (SMA) models, etc. We recommend again that spatial researchers take a lesson from the heteroskedasticity literature and **stop** modeling their error terms structurally – the error terms are the unknown parts of the model!

In this section we specify the error terms nonparametrically in such a way that it allows for very general patterns of heteroskedasticity, as well as spatial and time correlation. The resulting VC matrix of the estimators is estimated by an HAC procedure.

Consider the model

$$y_t = X_t\beta_1 + P_t\beta_2 + \rho_1 W y_t + \alpha y_{t-1} + Y_t\beta_3 + \mu + u_t, \qquad (15.6.2)$$
$$t = 1, ..., T$$

where, at time t, y_t is the $N \times 1$ vector of observations on the dependent variable, X_t is an $N \times k_x$ matrix of observations on exogenous variables, P_t is an $N \times T$ matrix of observations on T time dummy variables, W is an observed $N \times N$ exogenous weighting matrix, Y_t is an $N \times k_Y$ matrix of observations on endogenous regressors, μ is an $N \times 1$ vector of fixed effects, and u_t is the corresponding $N \times 1$ disturbance vector. The parameter vectors are β_1, β_2, and β_3 which are respectively $k_x \times 1, k_P \times 1$, and $k_Y \times 1$. The parameters ρ_1, and α are scalars. For ease of presentation, assume the available data are from $t = 0, ..., T$ so that y_t, y_{t-1}, X_t, Y_t, and P_t are observed for all $t = 1, ..., T$.

Stacking the variables of the model over time, let

$$
\begin{aligned}
y &= (y_1', ..., y_T')', \\
X &= (X_1', ..., X_T')', \\
P &= (P_1', ..., P_T')', \\
y_- &= (y_0', ..., y_{T-1}')', \\
u &= (u_1', ..., u_T')'.
\end{aligned}
$$

Given these definitions, the stacked form of the model is

$$
\begin{aligned}
y &= X\beta_1 + P\beta_2 + \rho_1(I_T \otimes W)y + \alpha y_- + Y\beta_3 + (e_T \otimes \mu) + u \\
&= Z\gamma + (e_T \otimes \mu) + u
\end{aligned} \tag{15.6.3}
$$

where e_T is a $T \times 1$ vector of unit elements, and

$$
\begin{aligned}
Z &= (X, P, (I_T \otimes W)y, y_-, Y), \\
\gamma &= (\beta_1', \beta_2', \rho_1, \alpha, \beta_3').
\end{aligned}
$$

Since consistent estimators of the elements of the fixed effects vector μ are not possible, the fixed effects vector will be eliminated from the model. As we saw in Section 15.5, there are at least two "typical" ways of doing this. One is to take time differences; the other is to premultiply the model across by Q_0. In this section we eliminate the fixed effects by premultiplying the model across by Q_0. Specifically,

$$
\begin{aligned}
Q_0 y &= Q_0 Z\gamma + Q_0 u, \\
y^* &= Z^*\gamma + u^*,
\end{aligned} \tag{15.6.4}
$$

since $Q_0(e_T \otimes \mu) = 0$, and where $y^* = Q_0 y$, $Z^* = Q_0 Z$, and $u^* = Q_0 u$.

Instead of assuming a structural form of spatial correlation and heteroskedasticity for the error term, we assume

$$
u_t = \sum_{j=1}^{t} R_{tj}\varepsilon_j, \quad t = 1, ..., T \tag{15.6.5}
$$

where the R_{tj} is an $N \times N$ unknown exogenous matrix, $j = 1, ..., T$, and ε_j, $j = 1, ..., T$ are $N \times 1$ random innovation vectors. The expression in (15.6.5) implies that the error vector in time period t, namely u_t, can be expressed as a weighted sum of random innovation $N \times 1$ vectors, ε_j, relating to periods $j = 1, ..., t$. In matrix terms (15.6.5) can be expressed as

$$
u = R\varepsilon, \tag{15.6.6}
$$

$$\begin{bmatrix} u_1 \\ \vdots \\ u_T \end{bmatrix} = \begin{bmatrix} R_{11} & 0 & . & . & . & 0 \\ R_{21} & R_{22} & 0 & . & . & 0 \\ . & . & . & 0 & . & . \\ . & . & . & . & 0 & . \\ . & . & . & . & . & 0 \\ R_{T1} & R_{T2} & . & . & . & R_{TT} \end{bmatrix} \begin{bmatrix} \varepsilon_1 \\ \vdots \\ \varepsilon_T \end{bmatrix}$$

where R is the $NT \times NT$ matrix whose (i, j)th block is the $N \times N$ matrix R_{ij}, $i, j = 1, ..., T$.

Let Φ be an $NT \times h, h \geq k_Y$ matrix of observations on exogenous variables that are not in (15.6.3), but are in the system determining Y. As described in earlier models, the variables in Φ may only be a subset of the variables in that system.

The parameters in the model in (15.6.3) cannot be estimated by maximum likelihood or by Bayesian techniques unless all the equations determining Y are known. Therefore, as for earlier models the estimation procedure will be instrumental variables.

Let $H_* = [Q_0X, Q_0P, Q_0\Phi]$. Then the IV matrix is H, where

$$\begin{aligned} H &= \{H_*, (I_T \otimes W)Q_0H_*, ..., (I_T \otimes W^r)Q_0H_*\}_{LI} \qquad (15.6.7) \\ &= \{H_*, (I_T \otimes W)Q_0X, (I_T \otimes W)Q_0P, (I_T \otimes W)Q_0\Phi, ..., (I_T \otimes W^r)Q_0\Phi\} \end{aligned}$$

where typically $r = 2$ and $Q_0Q_0 = Q_0$. For future reference, note that $H'Q_0u = H'u = H'R\varepsilon$, since $Q_0^2 = Q_0$, and so $Q_0H = H$.

The assumptions underlying the large sample theory for the parameter estimators of this model are given below. These assumptions are intuitive, and are sufficient for the large sample results presented below.

Assumption 15.1. The elements of ε are i.i.d. with mean and variance of 0 and 1, respectively, and have finite fourth moment.[11]

Assumption 15.2. The unknown exogenous matrix R in (15.6.4) is nonsingular.

Assumption 15.3. The elements of H in (15.6.7) are uniformly bounded in absolute value.

Assumption 15.4. $(I_N - aW)$ is nonsingular for all $|a| < 1$.

Assumption 15.5. The large sample theory relates to $N \to \infty$, while T remains fixed and finite. Assume the following limits

$$(A) \quad \lim_{N\to\infty} (NT)^{-1}H'H = \Omega_{HH},$$

11. Again, this does not account for triangular arrays; see Section A.15 in the appendix on large sample theory, or Kapoor et al. (2007) for specifications that do account for triangular arrays.

$$(B)\quad \lim_{N\to\infty} (NT)^{-1}H'RR'H = \Omega_{HRRH},$$

$$(C)\quad p\lim_{N\to\infty} (NT)^{-1}H'Z^* = p\lim_{N\to\infty} (NT)^{-1}H'Z = \Omega_{HZ},$$

$$(D)\quad p\lim_{N\to\infty} (NT)^{-1}Z^{*\prime}Z^* = p\lim_{N\to\infty} (NT)^{-1}Z'Q_0Z = \Omega_{ZQ_0Z}$$

where Ω_{HH}, Ω_{HRRH}, and Ω_{ZQ_0Z} are nonsingular finite matrices, and Ω_{HZ} has full column rank.

Implications of the Assumptions

Assumption 15.1 implies that the VC matrix of the disturbance term u specified in (15.6.6) is

$$E(uu') = RR'. \tag{15.6.8}$$

The implication of (15.6.8) is that the disturbance term may be both spatially and time correlated, as well as heteroskedastic. Furthermore since R is unknown, very general patterns of spatial and time correlation, as well as heteroskedasticity, are consistent with (15.6.8). Another implication of (15.6.8) is that time lagged dependent variables **cannot** be included in the set of instruments because general patterns of time correlation are consistent with (15.6.8) and hence all time lagged endogenous variables must be viewed as endogenous.

Effectively, (C) of Assumption 15.5 is an identification condition. The remaining assumptions are somewhat standard and imply, among other things, that the model in (15.6.4) is complete in that it can be solved for y in terms of the remaining variables of the model (Assumption 15.4). They also rule out peculiar sequences of the exogenous variables (Assumption 15.5). For example, let $x_{i,t}$ be the first regressor in X_t. Then (A) of Assumption 15.5 rules out sequences such as

$$x_{1,t} = 1, x_{2,t} = 5; x_{3,t} = 7; x_{4,t} = 1, x_{5,t} = 5, x_{6,t} = 7, x_{8,t} = 1, \ldots.$$

Estimation and Large Sample Properties

The model in (15.6.4) can be estimated by 2SLS, and the asymptotic VC matrix can be estimated by an HAC procedure. Let $\hat{Z}^* = P_H Z^*$ where $P_H = H(H'H)^{-1}H'$. Then, the 2SLS estimator of γ in (15.6.4) is

$$\hat{\gamma} = (\hat{Z}^{*\prime}\hat{Z}^*)^{-1}\hat{Z}^{*\prime}y^*. \tag{15.6.9}$$

Given (15.6.4) it follows that

$$\begin{aligned}&(NT)^{1/2}(\hat{\gamma} - \gamma)\\ &= (NT)(\hat{Z}^{*\prime}\hat{Z}^*)^{-1}(NT)^{-1/2}\hat{Z}^{*\prime}u^*\end{aligned} \tag{15.6.10}$$

$$= (NT)[Z^{*\prime}H(H'H)^{-1}H'Z^*]^{-1}Z^{*\prime}H(H'H)^{-1}(NT)^{-1/2}H'u$$
$$= [(NT)^{-1}Z'H(H'H)^{-1}H'Z]^{-1}Z'H(H'H)^{-1}(NT)^{-1/2}H'R\varepsilon$$

again, since $Q_0^2 = Q_0$. Note that there are no parameters of the error term that have to be estimated in order to obtain $\hat{\gamma}$.

The large sample distribution of $\hat{\gamma}$ is

$$\begin{aligned}
&(NT)^{1/2}(\hat{\gamma} - \gamma) \xrightarrow{D} N(0, VC_{\hat{\gamma}}), \\
&VC_{\hat{\gamma}} = S\Omega_{HRRH}S', \\
&S = [\Omega'_{HZ}\Omega_{HH}^{-1}\Omega_{HZ}]^{-1}\Omega'_{HZ}\Omega_{HH}^{-1}, \\
&\Omega_{HRRH} = \lim_{N\to\infty}(NT)^{-1}H'RR'H.
\end{aligned} \tag{15.6.11}$$

The proof for the result in (15.6.11) is straightforward.

In finite sample inferences can be based on

$$\hat{\gamma} \simeq N[\gamma, (NT)^{-1}\widehat{VC}_{\hat{\gamma}}] \tag{15.6.12}$$

where

$$\begin{aligned}
&\widehat{VC}_{\hat{\gamma}} = \hat{S}\,\hat{\Omega}_{HRRH}\hat{S}', \\
&\hat{S} = [(NT)^{-1}Z'H(H'H)^{-1}H'Z]^{-1}Z'H(H'H)^{-1},
\end{aligned}$$

and where $\hat{\Omega}_{HRRH}$ is the HAC estimator of Ω_{HRRH}. In constructing this HAC estimator, RR' should be viewed as the VC matrix of the error term u; see Chapter 9.

Illustration 15.6.1: A dynamic model of cigarette consumption

In this illustration we use a dynamic demand model for cigarettes. The data set is based on a panel over the period 1964–1992 for 46 US states and was originally used for the first time (over a limited period) in Baltagi and Levin (1986). The authors estimated a dynamic demand for cigarettes to address various policy issues. One of their main findings is that cigarette sales are negatively affected by the average price of cigarettes with a price elasticity of −0.2. They also found that the income effect is not relevant. A nice feature of their model is that cigarette sales in each state is related to the lowest cigarette price in neighboring states. This price variable, which in a sense is similar to a spatially lagged dependent variable, was meant to capture cross-state shopping by cigarette consumers as well as a "bootlegging" effect. This bootlegging effect was found to be positive and statistically significant in their model. Baltagi and Levin (1992) improved the results of their previous analysis by considering an extended time frame. They also considered different ways of modeling the bootlegging effect. In fact, they studies the sensitivity of their results by replacing their minimum price variable with a maximum neighboring price variable.

In this example we formulate a slightly modified version of the model considered by Baltagi and Levin (1992) in which we replace their minimum price with an average price variable based on the six nearest neighbors states; we also consider the spatial lag of cigarette consumption.

More specifically, the model that we estimate in this example is

$$\begin{aligned}\ln C_{it} &= \beta_1 \ln C_{it-1} + \beta_2 \ln p_{it} + \beta_3 \ln I_{it} \\ &+ \beta_4 \sum_{j=1}^{46} w_{ij} \ln p_{jt} + \lambda \sum_{j=1}^{46} w_{ij} \ln C_{jt} + \mu_i + \delta_t + u_{it}\end{aligned}$$

where $i = 1, \ldots, 46$ denotes states, $t = 1, \ldots, 29$ denotes time periods. C_{it} is cigarette sales per capita in constant dollars to persons of smoking age in state i at time t; p_{it} is the real price of cigarettes; I_{it} is real per capita disposable income; w_{ij} is an element of the spatial weighting matrix; μ_i is the fixed effect for state i, and δ_t is the fixed time effect for period t. The error term u_{it} is assumed to have the nonparametric specification described in (15.6.6).

In order to estimate the model, we use the 2SLS procedure described in Section 15.6. The matrix of instruments is specified as

$$H = Q_0[X, X_-, (I_T \otimes W)X, (I_T \otimes W^2)X, (I_T \otimes W)X_-, (I_T \otimes W^2)X_-, \Delta]$$

where X is the $NT \times 2$ matrix of observations on the price variable $\ln p_{it}$, and the income variable $\ln I_{it}$, X_- is the time lag of the variables in X, and Δ is a matrix of the time dummy variables.

Results from the estimation using the matrix H are reported below (except for the time dummies):

$$\begin{aligned}\widehat{\ln C} &= 0.643(0.037) \ln C_- - 0.437(0.045) \ln p + 0.166(0.032) \ln I \\ &+ 0.177(0.097) W \ln p + 0.217(0.056) W \ln C.\end{aligned}$$

A glance at the results shows that the coefficients of the (time) lagged consumption variable, and of price and income have the expected signs and are also statistically significant. In fact, one would expect that consumption habits are persistent, the price effect on demand is negative, and the income effect is positive. However, it should be stressed once more that these coefficients cannot be interpreted as elasticities because of the presence of the spatially lagged dependent variable whose coefficient is positive and significant.[12] The average price

12. Obtaining the elasticity for this dynamic panel data model would be even more complicated than usual. For an example of a dynamic panel, see Parent and LeSage (2010).

of the six nearest neighbors state is not statistically significant at the usual 5% level.

A final point relates to statistical inference. Standard errors are produced using the spatial HAC estimator with a Parzen kernel. In doing this we specify a variable bandwidth based on the distance to the six nearest neighbors.

15.7 TESTS OF PANEL MODELS: THE J-TEST

In this section we focus on testing the null panel data fixed effects model against a set of alternatives using the J-test, which was described in Chapter 12 in a single panel framework. The results in this section should demonstrate the ease of extending the results in Chapter 12 to a panel framework.

The Null Model

The assumed null model is the same as the general model specified in Section 15.6. The time stacked form of that model in (15.6.3) and its error term specification in (15.6.6) are repeated here for the convenience of the reader:

$$\begin{aligned} y &= X\beta_1 + P\beta_2 + \rho_1(I_T \otimes W)y + \alpha y_- + Y\beta_3 + (e_T \otimes \mu) + u \qquad (15.7.1)\\ &= Z\gamma + (e_T \otimes \mu) + u, \\ Z &= (X, P, (I_T \otimes W)y, y_-, Y), \quad \gamma = (\beta_1', \beta_2', \rho_1, \alpha, \beta_3'), \\ u &= R\varepsilon \end{aligned}$$

where y is the $NT \times 1$ vector of observations on the dependent variable, X is the $NT \times k_x$ matrix of observations on exogenous variables which vary over both time and cross-sections, P is an $NT \times T$ matrix of observations on T time dummy variables, W is an observed $N \times N$ exogenous weighting matrix, Y is an $NT \times k_Y$ matrix of observations on endogenous regressors, μ is an $N \times 1$ vector of fixed effects, and u is an $NT \times 1$ disturbance vector. The parameter vectors are β_1, β_2, and β_3 which are respectively $k_x \times 1$, $k_P \times 1$, and $k_Y \times 1$. The parameters ρ_1 and α are scalar. For ease of presentation, assume the available data are from $t = 0, ..., T$ so that y_t, y_{t-1}, X_t, Y_t, and P_t are observed for all $t = 1, ..., T$. The assumptions for the error term and for R are the same as in Section 15.6 and so

$$E(uu') = RR'. \qquad (15.7.2)$$

As in Section 15.6, the elements of the fixed effects vector μ cannot be consistently estimated, and so μ is eliminated from the model. There are at least two "typical" ways of doing this. One is to take time differences as was done in Section 15.5, and the other is to premultiply the model across by Q_0, as was done in Section 15.6. In this section we use the Q_0 method, which turns out to be convenient.

Premultiplying the fixed effects model in (15.7.1) by Q_0 yields

$$
\begin{aligned}
Q_0 y &= Q_0 Z\gamma + Q_0 u, \\
y^* &= Z^* \gamma + u^*,
\end{aligned} \tag{15.7.3}
$$

since $Q_0(e_T \otimes \mu) = 0$, and where $y^* = Q_0 y$, $Z^* = Q_0 Z$, and $u^* = Q_0 u$. The model in (15.7.3) can be viewed as the final form of the null model.

The Alternative Models

Suppose there are G alternative models, where $G \geq 1$ is finite. Also, suppose the researcher specifies these alternatives in the general form as (15.7.1)

$$
\begin{aligned}
y &= X_J \beta_{J,1} + P\beta_{J,2} + \rho_{J,1}(I_T \otimes W_J)y + \alpha_J y_- + Y_J \beta_{J,3} \\
&\quad + (e_T \otimes \mu_J) + u_J \\
&= Z_J \gamma_J + (e_T \otimes \mu_J) + u_J, \; Z_J = (X_J, P, (I_T \otimes W_J)y, y_-, Y_J), \\
u_J &= R_J \varepsilon_J, \quad J = 1, ..., G
\end{aligned} \tag{15.7.4}
$$

where, using evident notation, X_J and Y_J are respectively the $NT \times k_{J,x}$ and $NT \times k_{J,Y}$ matrices of observations on the exogenous and endogenous variables in the Jth alternative model, W_J is the corresponding weighting matrix, etc. The unit specific vector, μ_J, can be either a random or a fixed effects vector. Note that some alternative models may only differ from the null in terms of their weighting matrix, others may only differ in their set of regressors, while others may differ in both!

As in Chapter 12, the J-test is based on augmenting the null model with predictions of the dependent variable based on the alternative models, and then testing for the significance of those augmenting variables. The dependent vector in the final form of the null model is $y^* = Q_0 y$. Therefore, the J-test in this panel data framework is based on testing for the significance of predictions of $Q_0 y$ based on the alternative models.

Premultiplying (15.7.4) by Q_0 yields

$$
\begin{aligned}
y^* &= Z_J^* \gamma_J + u_J^*, \\
Z_J^* &= Q_0 Z_J, \\
u_J^* &= Q_0 u_J.
\end{aligned} \tag{15.7.5}
$$

The Augmented Model

Let $\hat{\gamma}_J$ be the researcher's estimator of γ_J based on his/her assumptions of the Jth alternative model, $J = 1, ..., G$. As described in Chapter 12, there are at least two ways of predicting the dependent vector based on the Jth model. One is just the estimated right-hand side of that model based on $\hat{\gamma}_J$. The other is based on the reduced form. Under reasonable conditions, Kelejian and Piras (2016b) show that, in a panel data framework, if there is only one alternative, $G = 1$, the asymptotic power of the test is the same for these two types of predictors. They also give Monte Carlo results which suggest that in finite samples the power is roughly the same for these two types of predictors even if $G > 1$. Because the predictor based on the estimated right-hand side is computationally simpler in that it does not involve inverting a matrix, we suggest its use.

Let $\hat{y}_J^* = Z_J^* \hat{\gamma}_J = Q_0 Z_J \hat{\gamma}_J$ be the predicted value of the dependent vector based on the Jth model, $J = 1, ..., G$. Let

$$\begin{aligned} \hat{Y}_{1,G}^* &= (\hat{y}_1^*, ..., \hat{y}_G^*), \\ \delta' &= (\delta_1', ..., \delta_G') \end{aligned} \tag{15.7.6}$$

where δ is a parameter vector. Then the augmented model is

$$\begin{aligned} y^* &= Z^* \gamma + \hat{Y}_{1,G}^* \delta + u^* \\ &= M^* \ F + u^* \end{aligned} \tag{15.7.7}$$

where $M^* = (Z^*, \hat{Y}_{1,G}^*)$ and $F = (\gamma', \delta')'$. Recalling (15.7.1) and (15.7.3), $u^* = Q_0 u = Q_0 R \varepsilon$.

Let H be an instrument matrix (whose elements are specified below), $P_H = H(H'H)^{-1}H'$, and $\hat{M}^* = P_H M^*$. Then, the 2SLS estimator of F based on (15.7.7) is $\hat{F}$ where

$$\hat{F} = (\hat{M}^{*\prime} \hat{M}^*)^{-1} \hat{M}^{*\prime} y^*. \tag{15.7.8}$$

The Instruments

In a manner similar to Chapter 6, let Φ_J be the $NT \times h_J$ matrix of observations on the exogenous variables the researcher knows to be in the system determining Y_J, and assume that $h_J \geq k_{J,Y}$. Also, let $X_{J,-}$ and $\Phi_{J,-}$ be identical to X_J and Φ_J except that each element now is lagged by one time period. Let $\Gamma_J = (X_J, \Phi_J, X_{J,-}, \Phi_{J,-})$ and let

$$\Psi_J = (\Gamma_J, (I_T \otimes W_J)\Gamma_J, ..., (I_T \otimes W_J^r)\Gamma_J)_{LI}, \ J = 1, ..., G, \tag{15.7.9}$$

where r would typically be taken as $r = 2$.

Similarly, let Φ be the $NT \times h$ matrix of observations on the exogenous variables the researcher knows to be in the system determining Y in the null model, $h \geq k_Y$. Also, let X_- and Φ_- be identical to X and Φ except that now each element is lagged by one time period. Let $\Gamma = (X, \Phi, X_-, \Phi_-)$ and

$$\Psi = (\Gamma, P, (I_T \otimes W)\Gamma, ..., (I_T \otimes W^r)\Gamma), \tag{15.7.10}$$

where typically $r = 2$. Then, the instrument matrix for estimating the augmented model is

$$H = Q_0(\Psi, \Psi_1, ..., \Psi_G)_{LI}. \tag{15.7.11}$$

Assumptions

The assumptions relating to the augmented model are quite similar to those in Section 15.6. Specifically, with respect to the augmented model in (15.7.7) assume Assumptions 15.1, 15.2, 15.3, and 15.4. Assumption 15.5 is replaced by[13]

Assumption 15.6. The large sample theory relates to $N \to \infty$, while T remains fixed and finite, and

$$\begin{aligned}
&(A) \quad \lim_{N\to\infty} (NT)^{-1} H'H = \Omega_{HH}, \\
&(B) \quad \lim_{N\to\infty} (NT)^{-1} H'RR'H = \Omega_{HRRH}, \\
&(C) \quad p\lim_{N\to\infty} (NT)^{-1} H'M^* = \Omega_{HM^*}, \\
&(D) \quad p\lim_{N\to\infty} (NT)^{-1} M^{*\prime}M^* = \Omega_{M^*M^*}
\end{aligned}$$

where $\Omega_{HH}, \Omega_{HRRH}$, and $\Omega_{M^*M^*}$ are nonsingular finite matrices, and Ω_{HM^*} has full column rank.

Given Assumptions 15.1–15.4 and 15.6, it is straightforward to show that

$$\begin{aligned}
&(NT)^{1/2}(\hat{F} - F) \xrightarrow{D} N(0, VC_{\hat{F}}), \\
&VC_{\hat{F}} = S\,\Omega_{HRRH}\,S', \\
&S = p\lim_{N\to\infty} (NT(\hat{M}^{*\prime}\hat{M}^*)^{-1}\Omega'_{HM^*}\Omega_{HH}^{-1}), \\
&p\lim_{N\to\infty} NT(\hat{M}^{*\prime}\hat{M}^*)^{-1} = (\Omega'_{HM^*}\Omega_{HH}^{-1}\Omega_{HM^*})^{-1}.
\end{aligned} \tag{15.7.12}$$

Small sample inferences can be based on the large sample approximation[14]

$$\hat{F} \simeq N(F, \hat{S}\,\hat{\Omega}_{HRRH}\,\hat{S}'), \tag{15.7.13}$$

13. The assumptions below are "high" level assumptions which should be more than adequate to convince the reader of the large sample result given below. More technical readers should see the list of assumptions given in Kelejian and Piras (2016a and 2016b).
14. See Fingleton and Palombi (2015) for an alternative approach based on bootstrap methods.

$$\hat{S} = (\hat{M}^{*\prime}\hat{M}^{*})^{-1}M^{*\prime}H,$$

and where $\hat{\Omega}_{HRRH}$ is the HAC estimator of Ω_{HRRH}.

Illustration 15.7.1: A J-test application of the dynamic model of cigarette consumption

Kelejian and Piras (2016b) developed a J-test for dynamic panel models with fixed effects and nonparametric error terms. In their paper there is an empirical application based on the same dynamic model of cigarette consumption that was used in Illustration 15.6.1.

The model under the null was specified as

$$\ln C_{it} = \alpha_1 \ln C_{it-1} + \alpha_2 \ln p_{it} + \alpha_3 \ln I_{it} + \alpha_4 \ln \bar{p}_{it} + \mu_i + \delta_t + u_{it}$$

where the variable description can be found in Illustration 15.6.1, and $\bar{p}$ is the minimum price used by Baltagi and Levin (1992).

The model under H_1 was identical to the one in Illustration 15.6.1. Following the J-test procedure described in this section Kelejian and Piras (2016b) found that at the 5% level, the J-test rejected the null model since the chi-squared variable $= 19.063 > \chi_1^2 = 3.841$. They concluded that the cross-state purchases are better captured by the model under the alternative that includes the spatial lag of the dependent variable!

SUGGESTED PROBLEMS

1. Demonstrate the results given in (15.2.5), namely

$$\begin{aligned} Q_0 Q_0 &= Q_0, \\ Q_1 Q_1 &= Q_1, \\ Q_0 + Q_1 &= I_{NT}, \\ Q_0 Q_1 &= 0, \\ Q_0(e_T \otimes G) &= 0. \end{aligned} \tag{15.2.5}$$

2. Demonstrate the results given in (15.3.6) and (15.3.7), namely

$$\begin{aligned} \Omega_\varepsilon &= \sigma_\mu^2 (e_T \otimes I_N)(e_T \otimes I_N)' + \sigma_v^2 I_{NT} \\ &= \sigma_\mu^2 (J_T \otimes I_N) + \sigma_v^2 I_{NT} \\ &= T\sigma_\mu^2 Q_1 + \sigma_v^2 I_{NT} \\ &= \sigma_v^2 Q_0 + \sigma_1^2 Q_1, \\ \sigma_1^2 &= \sigma_v^2 + T\sigma_\mu^2. \end{aligned} \tag{15.3.6}$$

3. Let a and b be nonzero constants. Demonstrate that the inverse of

$$aQ_0 + bQ_1$$

is

$$a^{-1}Q_0 + b^{-1}Q_1.$$

4. In reference to model (15.4.1),

(a) What would be required in order for the model in (15.4.1) to be estimated by maximum likelihood?

(b) Suppose $r < h$ in (15.4.1). Can the model still be estimated? Explain why, or why not.

Appendix A

Introduction to Large Sample Theory*

The need for large sample theory is evident. When models contain endogenous regressors, such as spatially lagged dependent variables, or variables which are endogenously related to the dependent variable in the model being considered, the finite sample distribution of parameter estimators is typically not known. One recourse is to obtain the large sample distribution and to use it to approximate the finite sample distribution. This is the approach which is taken in this book.

The material below on large sample theory is meant to be user friendly and intuitive. It is sufficient to understand the discussions relating to large sample theory in this text. It should also enable the reader to read a good part of the literature, as well as determine the large sample distribution of certain estimators he/she may wish to consider.

As in most things, large sample theory comes in various degrees of complexity. The material below would have to be supplemented in order to fully understand the large sample proofs given in some of the articles whose results are reviewed in this book.

A.1 AN INTUITIVE INTRODUCTION

Let $X_1, ..., X_N$ be a random sample from a population which has a mean of μ and a variance of σ^2. Let

$$\bar{X}_N = N^{-1} \sum_{i=1}^{N} X_i. \tag{A.1.1}$$

Then we can think of a sequence of variables

$$\bar{X}_1, \bar{X}_2, \bar{X}_3, \ldots. \tag{A.1.2}$$

$*$ Large sample theory is well documented in the literature. A number of the basic concepts presented in this appendix are also covered in Judge et al. (1985, Chapter 5). Other useful discussion are given in Dhrymes (1970), Greene (2003, Chapter 5), and Hogg and Craig (1995, Chapter 5). More advanced presentations are given in Pötscher and Prucha (1997), White (1984), and Bierens (1994).

Spatial Econometrics. http://dx.doi.org/10.1016/B978-0-12-813387-3.00025-1

Note the following:

$$E\bar{X}_N = \mu, \qquad (A.1.3)$$
$$var(\bar{X}_N) = \sigma^2/N.$$

Thus, the mean of $\bar{X}_N$ remains at μ, and its variance tends to zero in the limit. On an intuitive level, it would follow that the probability that $\bar{X}_N$ will deviate from its mean, namely μ, by any amount must decrease to zero as $N \to \infty$.

Now consider the sequence of variables

$$Z_N = N^{1/2}(\bar{X}_N - \mu), \ N = 1, 2, \dots. \qquad (A.1.4)$$

For this variable we have

$$E(Z_N) = 0, \qquad (A.1.5)$$
$$var(Z_N) = \sigma^2$$

so that, as $N \to \infty$, the mean of Z_N remains at zero, but its variance does not collapse to zero! It should be evident that, in this case, the values of Z_N need not condense around its mean, namely zero, as $N \to \infty$. Using material developed later we can show, in this case, that the cumulative distribution function (CDF) of Z_N converges to that of the normal distribution whose mean and variance are 0 and σ^2, respectively. As a preview of material to come, in this case we might express this convergence as

$$Z_N \xrightarrow{D} N(0, \sigma^2). \qquad (A.1.6)$$

The expression in (A.1.6) is, typically, read as Z_N converges in distribution to $N(0, \sigma^2)$. Note that this convergence is with respect to CDF functions. At a later point we will consider some technical points relating to this form of convergence.

Notice that the result in (A.1.6) relates to the limiting CDF and **not** to a limiting density. One reason for this is that more than one density corresponds to the same CDF. As an example, let the random variable X have the density $f(x), x > 0$. Let

$$g(x) = f(x), \ \text{for all } x > 0 \qquad (A.1.7)$$
$$\text{except at} \quad x = 5,$$
$$g(5) = f(5) + 3.$$

Then, $g(x)$ is a density and has the same CDF as $f(x)$ since $\Pr(X = 5) = 0$. Clearly, there are infinitely many such "peculiar" densities that have the same

CDF as $f(x)$. As an illustration, let A be any set of real positive numbers such that $\Pr(X \in A) = 0$ and define $h(x) = f(x)$, for all $x > 0$ except that for each element in A, $h(x)$ is defined as an arbitrary positive number. Then, again, $h(x)$ implies the same CDF as $f(x)$.

A.2 APPLICATION OF THE LARGE SAMPLE RESULT IN (A.1.6)

In many cases the exact density of $\bar{X}_N$, or Z_N in (A.1.4), is very difficult to obtain in the finite sample case, i.e., when N is finite. In such cases the result in (A.1.6) is often used to obtain an approximation. For example, one would typically assume, for the finite value of N in the sample, that Z_N is approximately normal,

$$Z_N \dot{\simeq} N(0, \sigma^2), \tag{A.2.1}$$

and, since $\bar{X}_N = \mu + \frac{Z_N}{N^{1/2}}$, that

$$\bar{X}_N \dot{\simeq} N(\mu, \frac{\sigma^2}{N}). \tag{A.2.2}$$

In such cases, an estimate of σ^2 would be obtained, say $\hat{\sigma}^2$, and then the small sample approximation to the density of $\bar{X}_N$ would be taken as

$$\bar{X}_N \dot{\simeq} N(\mu, \frac{\hat{\sigma}^2}{N}). \tag{A.2.3}$$

The result in (A.2.3) can be used to make approximate inferences concerning μ. For example, an approximate 95% confidence interval for μ based on (A.2.3) would be

$$\bar{X}_N \pm 1.96 \frac{\hat{\sigma}}{N^{1/2}}. \tag{A.2.4}$$

A final point on notation should be made. In the framework described above, $\bar{X}_N$ can be viewed as an estimator for μ, and so we could replace $\bar{X}_N$ with $\hat{\mu}_N$. Using this change of notation, Z_N as defined in (A.1.4) can be expressed as

$$Z_N = N^{1/2}(\hat{\mu}_N - \mu). \tag{A.2.5}$$

Recalling (A.1.4), the result in (A.1.6) would typically be expressed as

$$N^{1/2}(\hat{\mu}_N - \mu) \xrightarrow{D} N(0, \sigma^2). \tag{A.2.6}$$

A.3 MORE FORMALISM: CONVERGENCE IN PROBABILITY

Let S be a random variable whose mean and variance are μ_S and σ_S^2, respectively. Then Chebyshev's theorem, which is often given in the form of an inequality, implies[1]

$$\Pr(|S - \mu_S| > \delta) \leq \frac{\sigma_S^2}{\delta^2} \tag{A.3.1}$$

for all $\delta > 0$. Note, that (A.3.1) applies to all variables which have a finite mean and variance.

Consider again $\bar{X}_N$ as defined in (A.1.1), and recall that $E(\bar{X}_N) = \mu$ and $var(\bar{X}_N) = \sigma^2/N$. Applying Chebyshev's inequality to $\bar{X}_N$ yields

$$\Pr(|\bar{X}_N - \mu| > \delta) \leq \frac{\sigma^2}{N\delta^2} \tag{A.3.2}$$

so that for all $\delta > 0$

$$\lim_{N \to \infty} \Pr(|\bar{X}_N - \mu| > \delta) = 0. \tag{A.3.3}$$

Somewhat intuitively, the result in (A.3.3) implies that the probability that $\bar{X}_N$ will deviate from μ by any amount, tends to zero as the sample size increases beyond limit. This is often described verbally as $\bar{X}_N$ converges to μ in probability, or the probability limit of $\bar{X}_N$ is μ. The result in (A.3.3) is often written as

$$p \lim_{N \to \infty} \bar{X}_N = \mu \tag{A.3.4}$$

or, when it's understood that $N \to \infty$, simply as

$$p \lim \bar{X}_N = \mu, \tag{A.3.5}$$

or sometimes as

$$\bar{X}_N \xrightarrow{P} \mu. \tag{A.3.6}$$

In general, we will say that an estimator of a parameter c, say $\hat{c}_N$, where N is the sample size, is consistent if $\hat{c}_N \xrightarrow{P} c$. For example, given the results above, $\bar{X}_N$ is a consistent estimator for μ. To simplify notation, we will often (but not always) omit reference to the sample size when describing an estimator, e.g., $\hat{c}$ instead of $\hat{c}_N$.

Sufficient Conditions for Consistency

As we have seen from the above, Chebyshev's inequality implies that a sufficient conditions for an estimator based on a sample of size N, say $\hat{b}_N$, to be consistent

1. Hogg and Craig (1995, pp. 68–69) give a nice discussion of Chebyshev's theorem which extends the brief discussion given here.

for b are:

$$E(\hat{b}_N) = b, \qquad \text{(A.3.7)}$$
$$\lim_{N\to\infty} var(\hat{b}_N) = 0.$$

Simplifying notation by dropping the subscript N, slightly weaker conditions for consistency are

$$\lim_{N\to\infty} E(\hat{b}) = b, \qquad \text{(A.3.8)}$$
$$\lim_{N\to\infty} var(\hat{b}) = 0.$$

To see this, suppose $E(\hat{b}) = C_N$ where N is the sample size, and $C_N \to b$ as $N \to \infty$. Also, suppose the condition in (A.3.8) relating to the variance of $\hat{b}$ holds. Then, a more general version of Chebyshev's inequality implies that

$$\begin{aligned}\Pr(|\hat{b} - b| > \delta) &\leq \frac{E(\hat{b} - b)^2}{\delta^2} \qquad \text{(A.3.9)}\\ &= \frac{1}{\delta^2} E[(\hat{b} - C_N) + (C_N - b)]^2\\ &= E(\hat{b} - C_N)^2 + [C_N - b]^2\\ &= var(\hat{b}) + [C_N - b]^2 \to 0,\end{aligned}$$

since in (A.3.9) the cross-product term when multiplying out the square on the second line is zero: $E(\hat{b} - C_N)(C_N - b) = (C_N - b)E(\hat{b} - C_N) = 0$ and $[C_N - b]^2 \to 0$. Clearly, the conditions in (A.3.8) imply $\hat{b} \xrightarrow{P} b$.

We also note that the conditions in (A.3.7), or in (A.3.8), are sufficient but **not** necessary for convergence in probability. We now give an example which illustrates this.

Suppose the X_N is a discrete random variable and its density is

$$\Pr(X_N = c) = 1 - 1/N^{\alpha};$$
$$\Pr(X_N = N) = 1/N^{\alpha},$$

where $\alpha > 0$ and $N \geq 1$. Then, as $N \to \infty$,

$$\begin{aligned}\Pr(|X_N - c| > \delta) &= \Pr(X_N = N) \qquad \text{(A.3.10)}\\ &= \frac{1}{N^{\alpha}}\\ &\to 0,\end{aligned}$$

and so

$$X_N \xrightarrow{P} c. \tag{A.3.11}$$

On the other hand,

$$\begin{aligned} E(X_N) &= c[1 - \frac{1}{N^\alpha}] + N^{1-\alpha} \\ &\to c, \text{ if } \alpha > 1; \\ &\to c + 1, \text{ if } \alpha = 1; \\ &\to \infty, \text{ if } 0 < \alpha < 1. \end{aligned} \tag{A.3.12}$$

Clearly, if $\alpha \leq 1$, X_N does not satisfy conditions such as (A.3.7) or (A.3.8), but is, nevertheless, consistent for c.

Convergence to a Random Variable

The above discussion concerning convergence in probability relates to convergence to a constant. One generalization of this is convergence in probability to a random variable. Specifically, we will say that the sequence Z_N converges in probability to a random variable Z if

$$\lim_{N\to\infty} \Pr[|Z_N - Z| > \delta] = 0 \tag{A.3.13}$$

for all $\delta > 0$. Clearly, the result in (A.3.13) implies that in the limiting case $N \to \infty$, probability statements about Z_N must be the same as corresponding probability statements for Z because the probability that they differ tends to zero. We will formalize this below. At this point note that (A.3.13) implies, among other things, that if $\Pr(|Z| < 5.0) = 0.2$, then $\lim_{N\to\infty} \Pr(|Z_N| < 5.0) = 0.2$.

A.4 KHINCHINE'S THEOREM

As still another illustration that the Chebyshev conditions in (A.3.7) are not necessary for convergence in probability we state, without proof, a theorem due to Khinchine; see Theil (1971, pp. 360–361). Specifically, let $Z_1, ..., Z_N$ be a sequence of i.i.d. variables (i.e., a random sample) having mean μ. The variance **need not** be finite. Let

$$\bar{Z}_N = N^{-1} \sum_{i=1}^{N} Z_i. \tag{A.4.1}$$

Then

$$\bar{Z}_N \xrightarrow{P} \mu. \tag{A.4.2}$$

A.5 AN IMPORTANT PROPERTY OF CONVERGENCE IN PROBABILITY

Suppose $X_N \xrightarrow{P} c$, and $q(\cdot)$ is continuous at c. Then a theorem due to Slutsky[2] states that

$$q(X_N) \xrightarrow{P} q(c), \tag{A.5.1}$$

and so

$$p\lim q(X_N) = q(p\lim X_N). \tag{A.5.2}$$

As an example, if $X_N \xrightarrow{P} 2$, then $\exp(X_N) \xrightarrow{P} \exp(2)$. Using evident notation, the result in (A.5.2) holds. Indeed, since $q(\cdot)$ is continuous at c,

$$|q(X_N) - q(c)| < \delta_1 \tag{A.5.3}$$

if

$$|X_N - c| < \delta_2, \tag{A.5.4}$$

and the consistency of X_N implies that

$$\Pr(|X_N - c| < \delta_2) \to 1. \tag{A.5.5}$$

Asymptotic Unbiasedness

We say that an estimator, say $\hat{b}$ for b, is asymptotically unbiased if

$$\lim_{N\to\infty} E(\hat{b}) = b. \tag{A.5.6}$$

As we have seen, the conditions in (A.3.7) are sufficient for consistency, but not necessary. Therefore, it could be the case that $\hat{b}$ is consistent for b, yet asymptotically biased. This is important to note because it is sometimes assumed that consistency implies asymptotic unbiasedness.

A.6 A MATRIX ILLUSTRATION OF CONSISTENCY

Consider the model

$$y = XB + \varepsilon \tag{A.6.1}$$

where

1. $X_{N\times k}$ has rank k for N large enough;
2. X is nonstochastic;
3. $E(\varepsilon) = 0$;

2. See Greenberg and Webster (1983, p. 8).

4. $E(\varepsilon\varepsilon') = \sigma^2 I_N$;
5. $(X'X)^{-1} \to 0$.

Note, using evident notation, if $k = 1$ then

$$X'X = \Sigma_{i=1}^{N} x_i^2. \tag{A.6.2}$$

In most cases our data will be such that

$$\Sigma_{i=1}^{N} x_i^2 \to \infty \text{ as } N \to \infty, \tag{A.6.3}$$

and so Condition 5 above is reasonable.

Let

$$\hat{B} = (X'X)^{-1} X'y. \tag{A.6.4}$$

Then, given our assumptions, it follows that

$$\begin{aligned} E(\hat{B}) &= B, \\ VC_{\hat{B}} &= \sigma^2 (X'X)^{-1} \to 0, \end{aligned} \tag{A.6.5}$$

so $\hat{B}$ is unbiased, and its VC matrix tends to a zero matrix. Let $\hat{B} = (\hat{b}_1, ..., \hat{b}_k)'$. The implication of (A.6.5) is that $E(\hat{b}_i) = b_i$, and since the diagonal elements of $VC_{\hat{B}}$ are the variances which all tend to zero, Chebyshev's inequality implies

$$\hat{b}_i \xrightarrow{P} b_i, i = 1, ..., k. \tag{A.6.6}$$

We usually write (A.6.6) as

$$\hat{B} \xrightarrow{P} B. \tag{A.6.7}$$

A.7 GENERALIZATIONS OF SLUTSKY-TYPE RESULTS

Suppose $\underset{q\times 1}{X_N} \xrightarrow{P} \underset{q\times 1}{A}$. Consider a function of X_N, say $Q(X_N)$, which is continuous at A. Then

$$Q(X_N) \xrightarrow{P} Q(A), \tag{A.7.1}$$

or

$$p \lim_{N\to\infty} Q(X_N) = Q(p \lim_{N\to\infty} X_N). \tag{A.7.2}$$

Example 1. If

$$\hat{a} \xrightarrow{P} a, \tag{A.7.3}$$

$$\hat{b} \xrightarrow{P} b$$

then

$$\exp(\hat{a}\,\hat{b}) \xrightarrow{P} \exp(a\,b). \tag{A.7.4}$$

In a small sample framework, if $E(\hat{a}) = a$ and $E(\hat{b}) = b$, it will generally be the case that $E(\hat{a}\hat{b}) \neq (ab)$. However, (A.7.1) implies that, in general, if $\hat{a}$ is consistent for a, and $\hat{b}$ is consistent for b, then $\hat{a}\hat{b}$ is consistent for ab, and $\hat{a}^2\hat{b}^2$ is consistent for a^2b^2, etc. Thus, in many cases consistency is simpler to work with than expectations.

Example 2. If

$$\underset{m\times m}{F_N} \xrightarrow{P} F \tag{A.7.5}$$

then, assuming the inverses exist,

$$F_N^{-1} \xrightarrow{P} F^{-1}. \tag{A.7.6}$$

Basically, each element of F_N^{-1} is a continuous function of the elements of F_N, and these converge to the corresponding elements of F.

Example 3. If

$$\underset{m\times q}{F_N} \xrightarrow{P} F, \tag{A.7.7}$$

$$\underset{q\times r}{H_N} \xrightarrow{P} H$$

then

$$F_N H_N \xrightarrow{P} FH. \tag{A.7.8}$$

In the example above m, q, and r are constants, i.e., they do not depend on N. If they did, problems could arise, and so Slutsky-type results should not be assumed. For example, suppose $F_N = (1, 1, ..., 1)_{1\times N}$ and $H_N' = (1/N + 1/N^2, 1/N + 1/N^2, ..., 1/N + 1/N^2)_{1\times N}$. Then we **cannot** apply Slutsky-type results and say, since

$$H_N' \to (0, 0, ...), \tag{A.7.9}$$

that $F_N H_N \to 0$ because, in this case, $F_N H_N$ involves an infinite sum and so

$$F_N H_N = \sum_{i=1}^{N} (\frac{1}{N} + \frac{1}{N^2}) = 1 + \frac{1}{N} \to 1. \tag{A.7.10}$$

A.8 A NOTE ON THE LEAST SQUARES MODEL

The least squares model is sometimes specified as

$$y = X\beta + \varepsilon \tag{A.8.1}$$

where

1. $\text{rank}(X) = k$;
2. $X_{N \times k}$ is nonstochastic;
3. $E(\varepsilon) = 0$;
4. $E(\varepsilon\varepsilon') = \sigma^2 I_N$;
5. $N^{-1}X'X \to Q_{xx}$ where Q_{xx} is finite and nonsingular.

Note that assumption 5 implies

$$\begin{aligned}(X'X)^{-1} &= N^{-1}(N^{-1}X'X)^{-1} \\ &\to 0\, Q_{xx}^{-1} = 0.\end{aligned} \tag{A.8.2}$$

Thus, assumption 5 yields $(X'X)^{-1} \to 0$, and all our results relating to an earlier model go through here, e.g., $\hat{\beta} = (X'X)^{-1}X'y \xrightarrow{P} \beta$ since we would again have $E(\hat{\beta}) = \beta$ and $VC_{\hat{\beta}} = \sigma^2(X'X)^{-1} \to 0$.

A.9 CONVERGENCE IN DISTRIBUTION

Again, let Z_N, $N = 1, 2, \dots$ be a sequence of $q \times 1$ random vectors with corresponding CDFs:

$$\begin{aligned}&Z_1, Z_2, \dots, Z_N, \dots, \\ &F_1(z), F_2(z), \dots, F_N(z), \dots\end{aligned} \tag{A.9.1}$$

where $z = (z_1, \dots, z_q)'$. We will say that Z_N converges in distribution to the random $q \times 1$ vector Z whose CDF is $F(\cdot)$, if, for all $\delta > 0$, there is an N^* such that at all points of continuity

$$|F_N(z) - F(z)| < \delta \quad \text{for all } N > N^*. \tag{A.9.2}$$

If (A.9.2) holds, we indicate that Z_N converges in distribution to Z as

$$Z_N \xrightarrow{D} Z. \tag{A.9.3}$$

In this case $F(z)$ is called the asymptotic, or limiting, distribution of Z_N. The usefulness of this, as we will see below, is that in many cases the exact small sample distribution of Z_N, namely $F_N(z)$, is very difficult to determine, but

$F(z)$ is often easily obtainable. In these cases we typically use $F(z)$ to construct an approximation to $F_N(z)$ and then use that approximation to make "approximate" probability statements about Z_N when N is finite.[3]

A.10 RESULTS ON CONVERGENCE IN DISTRIBUTION

1. If $Z_N \xrightarrow{P} Z$ then $\Pr(|Z_N - Z|) > \delta) \to 0$ and so

$$Z_N \xrightarrow{D} Z, \tag{A.10.1}$$

that is, convergence in probability implies convergence in distribution. In a less formal way, this was already discussed in reference to (A.3.13). The reverse, however, is not generally true. That is, in general convergence in distribution does not imply convergence in probability. On an intuitive level, just because two variables have the same distribution, limiting or otherwise, does not imply that probability statements relating to differences between these variables are, or tend to, zero. For example, let Z_1 and Z_2 be independent normally distributed random variables each having mean and variance 0 and $1/2$, respectively. Then, $Z_1 - Z_2 = N(0, 1)$. Thus, $\Pr(|Z_1 - Z_2| > 0) = 0.5$, i.e., even though Z_1 and Z_2 have the same distribution, $\Pr(|Z_1 - Z_2| > 0) \neq 0$, nor does it tend to zero.

There is, however, an exception. In particular, if a sequence Z_N converges in distribution to a constant, then Z_N also converges in probability to that constant. An example may be helpful. Suppose $Z_N \sim N(c, \frac{1}{N})$. Then clearly $Z_N \xrightarrow{D} N(c, 0)$, which we would write as $Z_N \xrightarrow{D} c$, which in turn implies $\lim_{N\to\infty} \Pr(|Z_N - c| > \delta) = 0$, which is convergence in probability. Pulling results together:

$$\text{If } Z_N \xrightarrow{D} const \tag{A.10.2}$$

then

$$Z_N \xrightarrow{P} const.$$

2. Let C_N be a $q \times r$ sequence of matrices such that $C_N \xrightarrow{P} C$, where C is a constant $q \times r$ matrix. Let Z_N be an $r \times 1$ sequence of random vectors such that $Z_N \xrightarrow{D} Z$. Then

$$C_N Z_N \xrightarrow{D} CZ. \tag{A.10.3}$$

The result in (A.10.3) is one illustration of the continuous mapping theorem.

3. An illustration relating to the issue "at all points of continuity" is given in Amemiya (1985, pp. 85–86).

An example may clarify the intuitive nature of (A.10.3). Suppose $q = r = 1$ so that C_N is a scalar. Then, if $C_N \xrightarrow{P} 3$ and $Z_N \xrightarrow{D} N(\mu, \sigma^2)$, we obtain $C_N Z_N \xrightarrow{D} N(3\mu, 9\sigma^2)$. In the multivariate case, suppose $Z_N \xrightarrow{D} N(\mu, V)$ and $C_N \xrightarrow{P} C$. Then $C_N Z_N \xrightarrow{D} N(C\mu, CVC')$. Again, on a formal level, these convergence results relate to the CDFs of the indicated variables.

3. A random variable having an F distribution with r and $N-k$ degrees of freedom, $F_{r,N-k}$, can be expressed in the form

$$\begin{aligned} F_{r,N-k} &= \frac{\chi_r^2/r}{\chi_{N-k}^2/(N-k)} \\ &= [\frac{1}{\chi_{N-k}^2/(N-k)}]\chi_r^2/r \end{aligned} \tag{A.10.4}$$

where the χ_r^2 and χ_{N-k}^2 are independent chi-squared variables with r and $N-k$ degrees of freedom, respectively. Since

$$\begin{aligned} E(\chi_{N-k}^2) &= N-k, \\ var(\chi_{N-k}^2) &= 2(N-k), \end{aligned} \tag{A.10.5}$$

we have

$$\begin{aligned} E[\chi_{N-k}^2/(N-k)] &= 1, \\ var[\chi_{N-k}^2/(N-k)] &= 2/(N-k) \to 0 \\ &\text{as } N \to \infty, \end{aligned} \tag{A.10.6}$$

and so, by Chebyshev's inequality,

$$p \lim_{N\to\infty} \chi_{N-k}^2/(N-k) = 1. \tag{A.10.7}$$

Then, from (A.10.3) we have

$$F_{r,N-k} \xrightarrow{D} \chi_r^2/r, \tag{A.10.8}$$

which, of course, also implies $rF_{r,N-k} \xrightarrow{D} \chi_r^2$.

A.11 CONVERGENCE IN DISTRIBUTION: SLUTSKY-TYPE RESULTS

(A) If $\underset{q\times 1}{X_N} \xrightarrow{D} X$, where X is a $q \times 1$ random vector, and $g(\cdot)$ is a continuous q-dimensional function, then

$$g(X_N) \xrightarrow{D} g(X). \tag{A.11.1}$$

As an example, if $q = 1$ and

$$X_N \xrightarrow{D} N(0,1), \tag{A.11.2}$$

then[4]

$$X_N^2 \xrightarrow{D} \chi_1^2. \tag{A.11.3}$$

(B) As another example, if $q = 2$ and

$$\begin{bmatrix} X_N \\ Y_N \end{bmatrix} \xrightarrow{D} N(0, I_2) \tag{A.11.4}$$

then

$$X_N^2 + Y_N^2 \xrightarrow{D} \chi_2^2. \tag{A.11.5}$$

(C) If

$$\underset{q\times 1}{X_N} \xrightarrow{D} N(\mu, V), \tag{A.11.6}$$

where V is nonsingular, and

$$\hat{V}_N \xrightarrow{P} V, \tag{A.11.7}$$

$$\hat{\mu}_N \xrightarrow{P} \mu,$$

where $\hat{V}_N$ and $\hat{\mu}_N$ are estimators of V and μ, then

$$(X_N - \hat{\mu}_N)'\hat{V}_N^{-1}(X_N - \hat{\mu}_N) \xrightarrow{D} \chi_q^2. \tag{A.11.8}$$

Many Wald tests are based on the result in (A.11.8).

A.12 CONSTRUCTING FINITE SAMPLE APPROXIMATIONS

Consider the model

$$y = X\beta + \varepsilon \tag{A.12.1}$$

where the elements of ε are i.i.d. $(0, \sigma^2)$, the elements of X are uniformly bounded in absolute value, and $N^{-1}(X'X) \to Q_{xx}$ where Q_{xx} is nonsingular.

4. For future reference, note that the sum of squares of r jointly independent normal variables, all having zero mean and unit variance, has a χ_r^2 distribution:

$$\chi_r^2 \overset{D}{=} \sum_{i=1}^{r} X_i^2; \; X_i \text{ are i.i.d. } N(0,1).$$

Then the central limit theorem given in Section A.15 dealing with large sample theory implies that

$$N^{-1/2}X'\varepsilon \xrightarrow{D} N(0, \sigma^2 Q_{xx}). \tag{A.12.2}$$

Now consider the OLS estimator of β, namely $\hat{\beta} = (X'X)^{-1}X'y$. The model in (A.12.1) implies

$$N^{1/2}(\hat{\beta} - \beta) = [N(X'X)^{-1}][N^{-1/2}X'\varepsilon]. \tag{A.12.3}$$

Clearly, $N^{-1}(X'X) \to Q_{xx}$ implies $(N^{-1}X'X)^{-1} \to Q_{xx}^{-1}$. Let $\Psi \sim N(0, \sigma^2 Q_{xx})$. Then, given the result in (A.12.2) and (A.10.3), it follows that

$$\begin{aligned} N^{1/2}(\hat{\beta} - \beta) &\xrightarrow{D} \sigma^2 Q_{xx}^{-1}\Psi \\ &= N(0, Q_{xx}^{-1}). \end{aligned} \tag{A.12.4}$$

The distribution in (A.12.4) is the asymptotic, or large sample, distribution of $\hat{\beta}$.

Since the distribution of ε has not been specified, the finite sample distribution of $\hat{\beta}$ cannot be determined from the above assumptions. Therefore, tests of hypotheses, etc., cannot be carried out. In these cases, researchers often use the asymptotic distribution of $\hat{\beta}$ to approximate its finite sample distribution. Tests of significance, etc., are then based on this approximation. We now illustrate the way in which this is typically done.

Let $Z_N = N^{1/2}(\hat{\beta} - \beta)$ so that

$$\hat{\beta} = \frac{1}{\sqrt{N}} Z_N + \beta. \tag{A.12.5}$$

Then, the approximation made is that Z_N is approximately normal for the sample value of N,

$$Z_N \dot{\sim} N(0, \sigma^2 Q_{xx}^{-1}), \tag{A.12.6}$$

and so, from (A.12.5) and (A.12.6),

$$\hat{\beta} \dot{\sim} N(\beta, \sigma^2 N^{-1} Q_{xx}^{-1}). \tag{A.12.7}$$

The matrix Q_{xx} is then estimated as

$$\hat{Q}_{xx} = N^{-1}X'X. \tag{A.12.8}$$

Based on standard results, σ^2 is estimated as

$$\hat{\sigma}^2 = \frac{(y - X\hat{\beta})'(y - X\hat{\beta})}{N - k}. \tag{A.12.9}$$

Putting the results in (A.12.6)–(A.12.9) together, the approximation to the finite sample distribution of $\hat{\beta}$ is

$$\hat{\beta} \dot{\sim} N[\beta, \hat{\sigma}^2(X'X)^{-1}]. \tag{A.12.10}$$

As an illustration, let the ith elements of $\hat{\beta}$ and β be $\hat{\beta}_i$ and β_i, respectively. Let the ith diagonal element of $\hat{\sigma}^2(X'X)^{-1}$ be $\hat{\sigma}^2_{\hat{\beta}_i}$. Then, based on the approximation in (A.12.10), an approximate 95% confidence interval for β_i will be $\hat{\beta}_i \pm 1.96\hat{\sigma}_{\hat{\beta}_i}$.

A.13 A RESULT RELATING TO NONLINEAR FUNCTIONS OF ESTIMATORS

Suppose $\hat{C}$ is a $k \times 1$ estimator, based on a sample of size N, of the $k \times 1$ vector of parameters, C. Suppose

$$N^{1/2}(\hat{C} - C) \xrightarrow{D} N(0, V) \tag{A.13.1}$$

where V is nonsingular. Let

$$q(\hat{C}) = \begin{bmatrix} q_1(\hat{C}) \\ \vdots \\ q_r(\hat{C}) \end{bmatrix} \tag{A.13.2}$$

be an $r \times 1$ vector of functions, $r \leq k$. Assume that these functions are continuous in a neighborhood of the true value of C and have continuous first derivatives in that neighborhood. Then

$$N^{1/2}[q(\hat{C}) - q(C)] \xrightarrow{D} N(0, \underset{r\times k}{(\frac{\partial q}{\partial C'})} \underset{k\times k}{V} \underset{k\times r}{(\frac{\partial q}{\partial C'})'}) \tag{A.13.3}$$

where

$$\frac{\partial q}{\partial C'} = \begin{bmatrix} \frac{\partial q_1}{\partial C'} \\ \vdots \\ \frac{\partial q_r}{\partial C'} \end{bmatrix}_{r\times k}$$

and where

$$\frac{\partial q_i}{\partial C'} = [\frac{\partial q_i}{\partial C_1}, ..., \frac{\partial q_i}{\partial C_k}]_{1\times k};\ i = 1, ..., r.$$

Based on (A.13.3), small sample inferences would be based on the approximation

$$q(\hat{C}) \dot{\sim} N[q(C), N^{-1}\widehat{VC}], \tag{A.13.4}$$
$$\widehat{VC} = [(\underset{r\times k}{\frac{\partial q}{\partial C'}}) \underset{k\times k}{V} (\underset{k\times r}{\frac{\partial q}{\partial C'}})']_{\hat{C}}.$$

Since the functions are nonlinear, the VC matrix in (A.13.3) will typically involve the elements of C. The notation in (A.13.4) indicates that the elements of C involved in the $r \times r$ matrix $\widehat{VC}$ are to be replaced by the corresponding elements of $\hat{C}$.

The (very) useful result in (A.13.4) can be easily proven by expanding each of the r functions in $q(\hat{C})$ via the mean value theorem about the true vector, C, and expressing the result in vector form:

$$N^{1/2}[q(\hat{C}) - q(C)] = \frac{\partial q(C)}{\partial C'}|_{\tilde{C}} \, N^{1/2}[\hat{C} - C] \tag{A.13.5}$$

where $\tilde{C}$ is, element by element, between $\hat{C}$ and C. Since $\hat{C} \xrightarrow{P} C$, it follows that $\tilde{C} \xrightarrow{P} C$. Since the functions are continuous in a neighborhood of C, and have continuous first derivatives, it follows from (A.7.1) that

$$\frac{\partial q(C)}{\partial C'}|_{\tilde{C}} \xrightarrow{P} \frac{\partial q(C)}{\partial C'}. \tag{A.13.6}$$

The result in (A.13.3) follows from (A.13.1), (A.13.5), (A.13.6), and (A.10.2).

An Illustration

Suppose $\hat{b}$ is an estimator of the scalar parameter b which is in the interval $0 < b < 1$. Suppose the sample size is N and

$$N^{1/2}(\hat{b} - b) \xrightarrow{D} N(0, \sigma_{\hat{b}}^2), \tag{A.13.7}$$
$$\hat{\sigma}_{\hat{b}}^2 \xrightarrow{P} \sigma_{\hat{b}}^2.$$

Suppose we are interested in the multiplier in a typical Keynesian macro model, namely $m = (1 - b)^{-1}$, and take our estimator of m as

$$\hat{m} = (1 - \hat{b})^{-1}. \tag{A.13.8}$$

Then

$$\frac{\partial m}{\partial b} = (1 - b)^{-2} = m^2 \tag{A.13.9}$$

and so, via (A.13.3), the large sample distribution of $\hat{m}$ would be

$$N^{1/2}(\hat{m} - m) \xrightarrow{D} N(0, \sigma_{\hat{b}}^2 \frac{\partial m}{\partial b} \frac{\partial m}{\partial b}) \quad (A.13.10)$$
$$= N(0, \sigma_{\hat{b}}^2 m^4).$$

Therefore, based on (A.13.4), inferences concerning m would be based on the approximation

$$\hat{m} \dot{\sim} N(m, \frac{\hat{\sigma}_{\hat{b}}^2 \hat{m}^4}{N}). \quad (A.13.11)$$

As an illustration, an approximate 95% confidence interval for m would be $\hat{m} \pm 1.96 \frac{\hat{\sigma}_{\hat{b}} \hat{m}^2}{N^{1/2}}$.

A.14 ORDERS IN PROBABILITY

A sequence of random variables, say $Z_i, i = 1, ..., N$, is said to be at most of order N^k in probability, written as

$$Z_N = 0_P(N^k) \quad (A.14.1)$$

if, for every $\varepsilon > 0$, there exits an N^* such that

$$\Pr(N^{-k}|Z_N| > N^*) \leq \varepsilon \text{ for all } N. \quad (A.14.2)$$

We also say that Z_N is of smaller order in probability than N^k, written as

$$Z_N = o_P(N^k), \quad (A.14.3)$$

if

$$p \lim_{N \to \infty} N^{-k} Z_N = 0. \quad (A.14.4)$$

If $Z_N = 0_P(N^k)$, on an intuitive level one can think of $N^{-k} Z_N$ as being bounded in probability. It should be clear from (A.14.2) that if $Z_N = 0_P(N^k)$, then for all $\delta > 0$

$$p \lim_{N \to \infty} N^{-k-\delta} Z_N = 0. \quad (A.14.5)$$

Therefore, if $Z_N = 0_P(N^k)$ then $Z_N = o_P(N^{k+\delta})$ for all $\delta > 0$. For instance, if $Z_N = 0_P(N^2)$, then $Z_N = o_P(N^3)$, $Z_N = o_P(N^4)$, etc.

To illustrate these concepts, let $u_{N,1}$ be i.i.d. $N(\mu_1, \sigma_1^2)$, and $u_{N,2}$ be i.i.d. $N(\mu_2, \sigma_2^2)$ where μ_1, μ_2, σ_1^2, and σ_2^2 are finite. Then

$$\text{if } Z_{N,1} = u_{N,1}, \text{ then } Z_{N,1} \text{ is } 0_P(N^0); \text{ and } o_P(N^\delta), \delta > 0; \quad (A.14.6)$$

$$\text{if } Z_{N,2} = N^2 u_{N,1} - 3N u_{N,2}, \text{ then } Z_{N,2} \text{ is } 0_P(N^2);\ o_P(N^3);$$
$$\text{if } Z_{N,3} = N^{-1/2} u_{N,1} + N^{-1/5} u_{N,2}, \text{ then } Z_{N,3} \text{ is } 0_P(N^{-1/5});\ o_P(1).$$

To see why $Z_{N,3} = 0_P(N^{-1/5})$, note that

$$N^{1/5} Z_{N,3} = N^{-0.3} u_{N,1} + u_{N,2} \quad (A.14.7)$$
$$\xrightarrow{P} u_{N,2}.$$

As will become clear from the algebra below, on an intuitive level, $0_P(N^k)$ is "like $\leq aN^k$", while $o_P(N^k)$ is "like $< bN^k$" where a and b are constants.

Some Algebra

Let

$$X_N = 0_P(N^k),\ Z_N = 0_P(N^J) \quad (A.14.8)$$

where $k > J > 0$. Let L_N be any sequence such that $L_N \to 0$. Then, for all s

$$\begin{aligned} &(a)\ L_N(N^{-k} X_N) \to 0, \\ &(b)\ X_N + Z_N = 0_P(N^k), \\ &(c)\ X_N Z_N = 0_P(N^{k+J}), \\ &(d)\ (X_N)^s = 0_P(N^{ks}). \end{aligned} \quad (A.14.9)$$

Similarly, if $X_N = o_P(N^k)$, $Z_N = o_P(N^J)$ and $k > J$, then

$$\begin{aligned} &(a)\ X_N + Z_N = o_P(N^k), \\ &(b)\ X_N Z_N = o_P(N^{k+J}), \\ &(c)\ (X_N)^s = o_P(N^{ks}). \end{aligned} \quad (A.14.10)$$

Finally, if $X_N = 0_P(N^k)$ and $Z_N = o_P(N^J)$ then

$$X_N Z_N = o_P(N^{k+J}), \quad (A.14.11)$$

and also

$$X_N Z_N = 0_P(N^{k+J}).$$

An Application: Quality of Small Sample Approximations

Suppose

$$(\varepsilon_N, u_N, v_N) \text{ are i.i.d. } N(0, I_3). \quad (A.14.12)$$

Consider

$$Z_N = a_0 \frac{\varepsilon_N}{\sqrt{N}} + a_1 \frac{u_N}{N} + a_2 \frac{v_N}{N^{3/2}} \tag{A.14.13}$$

where a_0, a_1, and a_2 are finite constants. Then the exact finite sample distribution of Z_N is

$$Z_N \sim N(0, \frac{a_0^2}{N} + \frac{a_1^2}{N^2} + \frac{a_2^2}{N^3}). \tag{A.14.14}$$

Clearly, in finite samples, the variance of Z_N will depend quite strongly on the magnitudes of the three parameters, a_0, a_1, and a_2. On the other hand, consider the large sample distribution of Z_N. This would be determined as follows. First, note that

$$\begin{aligned} \sqrt{N} Z_N &= \sqrt{N}[a_0 \frac{\varepsilon_N}{\sqrt{N}} + a_1 \frac{u_N}{N} + a_2 \frac{v_N}{N^{3/2}}] \\ &= a_0 \varepsilon_N + a_1 \frac{u_N}{\sqrt{N}} + a_2 \frac{v_N}{N} \end{aligned} \tag{A.14.15}$$

and, since

$$\begin{aligned} \frac{u_N}{N^{1/2}} &= \frac{1}{N^{1/2}} 0_P(1) \to 0, \\ \frac{v_N}{N} &= \frac{1}{N} 0_P(1) \to 0, \end{aligned} \tag{A.14.16}$$

it follows that $p \lim_{N \to \infty} [\sqrt{N} Z_N - a_0 \varepsilon_N] \xrightarrow{P} 0$ and so

$$\sqrt{N} Z_N \xrightarrow{P} a_0 \varepsilon_N. \tag{A.14.17}$$

Since, by (A.14.12), $\varepsilon_N \sim N(0, 1)$, and convergence in probability implies convergence in distribution, it follows from (A.14.17) that

$$\sqrt{N} Z_N \xrightarrow{D} N(0, a_0^2). \tag{A.14.18}$$

Therefore, the small sample approximation based on the large sample distribution in (A.14.18) would be

$$Z_N \dot{\sim} N(0, \frac{a_0^2}{N}). \tag{A.14.19}$$

Clearly, unless N is quite large, (A.14.19) would be a poor approximation to the exact distribution in (A.14.14) if a_0^2 were small relative to a_1^2 or a_2^2. Of course, that approximation would improve as N increases!

A.15 TRIANGULAR ARRAYS: A CENTRAL LIMIT THEOREM

Let N be the size of the sample. Then, as described in Section 2.1.1, a triangular array is a sequence, say $Z_{1,N}, ..., Z_{N,N}$, in which each of the N variables depends not only upon its order in the sequence, but also upon the sample size. In Section 2.1.1 examples were given, and it was suggested that most, if not all, of the data underlying spatial models are in the form of triangular arrays. For the convenience of the reader, we state the central limit theorem which was given in Kelejian and Prucha (1998) and accounts for triangular arrays.

> *"Let $\{v_{i,n}, 1 \leq i \leq n, n \geq 1\}$ be a triangular array of identically distributed random variables. Assume that the random variables $\{v_{i,n}, 1 \leq i \leq n\}$ are (jointly) independently distributed for each n with $E(v_{i,n}) = 0$ and $E(v_{i,n}^2) = \sigma^2 < \infty$. Let $\{a_{ij,n}, 1 \leq i \leq n, n \geq 1\}$, $j = 1, \ldots, k$, be triangular arrays of real numbers that are bounded in absolute value. Further, let*
>
> $$v_n = \begin{bmatrix} v_{1,n} \\ \vdots \\ v_{n,n} \end{bmatrix}, \qquad A_n = \begin{bmatrix} a_{11,n} & \cdots & a_{1k,n} \\ \vdots & & \vdots \\ a_{n1,n} & \cdots & a_{nk,n} \end{bmatrix}.$$
>
> *Assume that $\lim_{n\to\infty} n^{-1} A_n' A_n = Q_{AA}$ is a finite and nonsingular matrix. Then $n^{-1/2} A_n' v_n \xrightarrow{D} N(0, \sigma^2 Q_{AA})$."*

Because researchers sometimes think in terms of notation, we give an illustration of the CLT in terms of familiar notation, and assumptions. Suppose the elements of the $N \times k$ regressor matrix X_N all form triangular arrays, are uniformly bounded in absolute value, and $N^{-1} X_N' X_N \to Q_{xx}$ where the $k \times k$ matrix Q_{xx} is finite and nonsingular. These assumptions are typically made. Suppose the elements of a disturbance vector, $\varepsilon_N = (\varepsilon_{1,N}, ..., \varepsilon_{N,N})'$ all form triangular arrays, and for each N, are i.i.d. with mean and variance 0 and σ^2, respectively, where σ^2 is finite. Note that the elements of ε_N need not be independent of those of ε_{N+s} if $s \neq 0$. Then

$$N^{-1} X_N' \varepsilon_N \to N(0, \sigma^2 Q_{xx}). \tag{A.15.1}$$

Appendix B

Spatial Models in R

B.1 INTRODUCTION

Only a few years ago estimating spatial models was challenging for at least a couple of reasons. On the one hand, the issues related to the estimation of the spatial model (particularly the presence of the Jacobian term in ML) were an enormous obstacle in estimation involving large datasets. In addition, there was a serious lack of available software.

With the advent of **SpaceStat** (Anselin, 1992), the estimation of spatial models became easier. However, at that time, the computational power was not comparable to that of modern computers.

In the last decades, the situation has evolved rapidly under both perspectives, and nowadays there are various statistical software to conduct spatial econometric analysis. Many functionalities to deal with cross-sectional estimation have recently been introduced in `Stata`'s user-written **sppack** commands (Drukker et al., 2013b,c,d). The `Matlab Spatial Econometrics toolbox` developed by LeSage contains basic as well as more advanced functions related to the Bayesian approach. Finally, `PySAL` (based on `Python`) contains lots of estimation functions that can also be accessed from `GeoDaSpace` (Anselin and Rey, 2014).

In this appendix we give a brief review of the statistical computer program R, which is a freely available language and environment for statistical computing, distributed under the General Public License (GPL).[1] Additionally, it is available for Microsoft Windows, for a variety of Linux platforms, and for Mac OS X.

The purpose of this appendix is to get the reader started with R in order to be able to reproduce most of the examples in the book. The reader is assumed to have a working installation of the software and all the three packages that will be used in this appendix, **spdep**, **sphet**, and **splm**. Those are the three main libraries to perform spatial analysis on lattice data with R.

This appendix is organized as follows. In the next section we start with an overview of R as a computing environment. This first part is meant to be a quick introduction to R. The second part focuses on how to read data and spatial

1. It is obtainable from the CRAN network at https://cran.r-project.org/.

Spatial Econometrics. http://dx.doi.org/10.1016/B978-0-12-813387-3.00026-3

weighting matrix into R. Finally, we will show how to perform the estimation of cross-sectional as well as spatial panel data models using code from three libraries.

B.2 INTRODUCTORY TOOLS

Vectors

The function concatenate (`c()`) is the basic function to generate vectors. Vectors are the basic objects in R. The function concatenate works with all types of vectors (numeric, string, and logical vectors). The arguments of the function can be vectors themselves:

```
R> z <- c(3, 2.1, 4.55, 3, 9)
R> e <- c(1, 2, 3, 4, 5)
R> p <- c(z, e)
R> names1 <- c("price", "sqrft", "bed", "bath")
R> names2 <- c("price", "sqrft", "bed", "bath")
R> names <- c(names1 , names2)
R> names

[1] "price" "sqrft" "bed"   "bath"  "price" "sqrft" "bed"   "bath"
```

The function `sort()` orders the elements of a numeric vector, as shown in the following example:

```
R> z <- c(3, 2.1, 4.55, 3, 9)
R> zdec <- sort(z, decreasing = TRUE)
R> zdec

[1] 9.00 4.55 3.00 3.00 2.10
```

The argument `decreasing` sets the order of the vector: If it is `TRUE`, the vector is ordered from the highest to the lowest (decreasing order).

Subsetting the elements of a vector (or any other object) is an important characteristic of any programming language. The way to index vectors in R is pretty straightforward, and requires the operator `[]`. For example, we can create a new vector taking the third element of the original vector as follows:

```
R> p <- z[3]
R> p

[1] 4.55
```

There are also ways of taking more than one element of a vector. Some of them are illustrated in the examples below:

```
R> u <- z[1:3]
R> u

[1] 3.00 2.10 4.55

R> u1 <- z[c(1,5)]
R> u1

[1] 3 9

R> u2 <- z[-c(1,2)]
R> u2

[1] 4.55 3.00 9.00
```

Two very useful functions to create vectors are `seq()` and `rep()`. `seq()` takes two mandatory and three optional arguments. The only required arguments are `from` and `to`: the starting and ending values of the sequence. One can also specify the argument `by` to adjust the increment of the sequence.

```
R> q <- seq(from = 1, to = 10,  by = 2)
R> q

[1] 1 3 5 7 9
```

The function `rep()` replicates the value of its first argument. The argument can be any R object. A few possible uses are illustrated in the following examples:

```
R> tmp <- rep(7, times = 4)
R> tmp

[1] 7 7 7 7

R> rep(q, times = 2)

[1] 1 3 5 7 9 1 3 5 7 9

R> rep(q, each = 2)

[1] 1 1 3 3 5 5 7 7 9 9
```

The first line creates a vector that repeats the number 7 four times. When the first argument is a vector, as in the second and third example, one can decide to replicate the entire vector or the elements of the vector.

The examples so far have only shown a few ways of generating vectors in R. There are, however, more sophisticated ways such as random number generators. A wide range of functions to generate random variables from different distributions are available in R. Our examples below only take advantage of the functions to generate vectors from the normal distribution. Thus, we encourage the reader to look at the various statistical distributions available in R. The syntax to generate random numbers is very intuitive. The simplest way to create a random vector from a normal distribution is by typing the following instruction

```
R>  n_100 <- rnorm(100)
```

which will draw a random sample of 100 observations from a standardized normal distribution. Clearly, R can generate values from a normal distribution with any mean and standard deviation:

```
R> n_100 <- rnorm(100, mean = 2, sd = 5)
R> summary(n_100)

Min.      1st Qu.     Median      Mean     3rd Qu.      Max.
-10.70000  -0.06118   2.50000   2.82900   5.55200  14.40000

R> dim(n_100)

NULL
```

The function dim( ) is used to assign or, as in this case, to check the dimension of an object. Interestingly, vectors are objects of NULL dimension. In the next section we will learn about objects with specific dimensions such as array and matrix.

Arrays and Matrices

Arrays are important R objects that can be defined with more than two dimensions. They can be seen as multidimensional matrices. In the following example we generate a vector of 30 observations from a normal distribution and then organize it into an array( ) of dimensions $5 \times 2 \times 3$:

```
R> p <- rnorm(30)
R> p <- array(p, c(5, 2, 3))
R> p

, , 1
[,1]        [,2]
[1,] -1.18950799  0.9190818
[2,] -0.51682079  1.6926400
[3,] -0.54807580  0.7713957
[4,] -0.03545199  0.8159488
[5,]  0.22168010 -1.2231760
, , 2
[,1]        [,2]
[1,] -1.06853048 -1.0053414
[2,]  0.02420646 -1.6946084
[3,]  0.17123001  0.8229905
[4,] -0.41222236 -1.9589639
[5,]  1.17490806 -1.2850768
, , 3
[,1]        [,2]
[1,] -0.242196915 -1.5395892
```

```
[2,]  1.628539315  0.5759114
[3,] -1.872581443 -0.2161676
[4,] -0.005236255  0.9349243
[5,] -0.346328524  0.2256075
```

Matrices in R are special cases of arrays with only two dimensions. An obvious way to generate a matrix is starting from a vector and splitting up its elements in rows and columns. This can be achieved with the function `matrix()`.

```
R> d <- seq(1,16)
R> mat1 <- matrix(d, nrow = 4, ncol = 4)
R> mat1

[,1] [,2] [,3] [,4]
[1,]    1    5    9   13
[2,]    2    6   10   14
[3,]    3    7   11   15
[4,]    4    8   12   16

R> mat2 <- matrix(d, nrow = 4, ncol = 4, byrow = TRUE)
R> mat2

[,1] [,2] [,3] [,4]
[1,]    1    2    3    4
[2,]    5    6    7    8
[3,]    9   10   11   12
[4,]   13   14   15   16

R> dim(mat2)

[1] 4 4
```

There are two other functions that create matrices from vectors, `rbind()` and `cbind()`. In the following example, we generate three random vectors of three elements each. The function `rbind()` combines the vectors to form the rows of the resulting matrix.

```
R> a <- rnorm(3)
R> b <- rnorm(3)
R> c <- rnorm(3)
R> M <- rbind(a,b,c)
R> M

[,1]        [,2]        [,3]
a -1.0913244 2.0476226  1.7654977
b -1.7182593 0.4384462 -1.5483322
c -0.8413423 0.5034061 -0.8779302
```

It is also possible to combine the vectors into columns by using the corresponding function `cbind()`. Using the matrix generated in the previous example, the commands to obtain the number of rows and columns of the matrix are:

```
R> ncol(M)

[1] 3

R> nrow(M)

[1] 3
```

We can also transpose the matrix using the function `t()`, and calculate the row and column sums by using the functions `rowSums()` and `colSums()`.

```
R> t(M)

a                 b          c
[1,] -1.091324 -1.7182593 -0.8413423
[2,]  2.047623  0.4384462  0.5034061
[3,]  1.765498 -1.5483322 -0.8779302

R> rowSums(M)

a             b         c
2.721796 -2.828145 -1.215866

R> colSums(M)

[1] -3.6509261  2.9894749 -0.6607647
```

Subsetting a matrix is very intuitive and not very different from what we saw for vectors. Let us say that we want to single out the element that belongs to the second row and the third column of the matrix. Then we write

```
R> mat1[2, 3]

[1] 10
```

To select an entire row (or column) we can write

```
R> sr <- M[2,]
R> sr

[1] -1.7182593  0.4384462 -1.5483322

R> tc <- M[,3]
R> tc

a              b           c
1.7654977 -1.5483322 -0.8779302
```

Another convenient function is the function `diag()`. If the only argument of the function is a scalar, say n, the result will be an identity matrix of dimension $N \times N$, as in the following example where n is set to five:

```
R> diag(5)

[,1] [,2] [,3] [,4] [,5]
[1,]    1    0    0    0    0
[2,]    0    1    0    0    0
[3,]    0    0    1    0    0
[4,]    0    0    0    1    0
[5,]    0    0    0    0    1
```

When the argument of `diag()` is a vector, the function will generate a matrix whose diagonal elements are the elements of the vector:

```
R> xvec <- seq(1, 5)
R> diag(xvec)

[,1] [,2] [,3] [,4] [,5]
[1,]    1    0    0    0    0
[2,]    0    2    0    0    0
[3,]    0    0    3    0    0
[4,]    0    0    0    4    0
[5,]    0    0    0    0    5
```

Finally, if the argument is a matrix, the diagonal is extracted and assigned to a new object:

```
R> B <- matrix(seq(1,16), 4, 4)
R> B

[,1] [,2] [,3] [,4]
[1,]    1    5    9   13
[2,]    2    6   10   14
[3,]    3    7   11   15
[4,]    4    8   12   16

R> db <- diag(B)
R> db

[1]  1  6 11 16
```

R offers a full range of basic matrix operations. Suppose that A and B are two matrices of the same dimension. Then, the operators sum and difference will return element-by-element sum and difference of the two matrices.

```
R> A <- matrix(1:9, 3, 3)
R> A

[,1] [,2] [,3]
[1,]    1    4    7
[2,]    2    5    8
[3,]    3    6    9
```

```
R> B <- matrix(1:9, 3, 3)
R> B

[,1] [,2] [,3]
[1,]    1    4    7
[2,]    2    5    8
[3,]    3    6    9

R> A+B

[,1] [,2] [,3]
[1,]    2    8   14
[2,]    4   10   16
[3,]    6   12   18

R> A-B

[,1] [,2] [,3]
[1,]    0    0    0
[2,]    0    0    0
[3,]    0    0    0
```

A matrix can also be multiplied (or divided) by a scalar:

```
R> v <- 2
R> A*v

[,1] [,2] [,3]
[1,]    2    8   14
[2,]    4   10   16
[3,]    6   12   18

R> A/v

[,1] [,2] [,3]
[1,]  0.5  2.0  3.5
[2,]  1.0  2.5  4.0
[3,]  1.5  3.0  4.5
```

Matrix algebra requires special notation. The use of the operator for matrix multiplication (%*%) is illustrated in the following example:

```
R> Mat <- matrix(1:9, 3, 3)
R> vec_1 <- matrix(1:3, 1, 3)
R> vec_1 %*% Mat

[,1] [,2] [,3]
[1,]   14   32   50
```

Let us now show how to estimate a linear model by OLS in R. In order to be able to do this, we first need to generate the data. In the following example, we generate y from the standard normal distribution. The matrix of explanatory variables X consists of a constant term as well as four additional columns generated from a uniform distribution over $(-5, 5)$.

```
R> X <- cbind(1, matrix(runif(100,-5, 5), 25,4))
R> y <- rnorm(25)
```

There are various ways to implement OLS in R using matrix algebra.[2] We are going to illustrate three different alternatives. The first and most complex way uses the following lines of code:

```
R> Xt <- t(X)
R> XpX <- Xt%*%X
R> XpXi <- solve(XpX)
R> Xpy <- Xt%*%y
R> b <- XpXi%*%Xpy
```

The first line takes the transpose of X, and the second line multiplies X' by X. When only an argument is specified, the function `solve()` takes the inverse of that argument. After multiplying X' and y, we have all the elements to calculate b.

Fortunately, there is a function in R that calculates the cross-product between two matrices. The second solution takes advantage of this function:

```
R>  XpX2 <- crossprod(X)
R> Xpy2 <- crossprod(X,y)
R> XpXi2 <- solve(XpX2)
R> b2 <- XpXi2%*%Xpy2
```

Finally, the third solution takes advantage of the fact that if `solve()` is specified with two arguments, then the function solves the equation $a\% * \%X = b$ where a and b are the two arguments:

```
R> b3 <- solve(crossprod(X), crossprod(X,y))
R> all.equal(b, b2, b3)

[1] TRUE
```

All three methods give the same result.

Among the possible operations between matrices, there exists a function that performs the Kronecker product:

2. Later on in this appendix we show the usage of the function `lm()` as the general function for estimating linear models.

```
R> x <- array(1:3, c(1,3))
R> A <- matrix(1:9, 3, 3)
R> kronecker(x, A)

[,1] [,2] [,3] [,4] [,5] [,6] [,7] [,8] [,9]
[1,]    1    4    7    2    8   14    3   12   21
[2,]    2    5    8    4   10   16    6   15   24
[3,]    3    6    9    6   12   18    9   18   27
```

Finally, the eigenvalues and eigenvectors of a matrix are calculated by the function `eigen()`:

```
R> A <- matrix((1:16), 4, 4)
R> eigen(A)

$values
[1]  3.620937e+01 -2.209373e+00  1.599839e-15  7.166935e-16
$vectors
[,1]           [,2]        [,3]       [,4]
[1,] 0.4140028  0.82289268 -0.5477226  0.1125155
[2,] 0.4688206  0.42193991  0.7302967  0.2495210
[3,] 0.5236384  0.02098714  0.1825742 -0.8365883
[4,] 0.5784562 -0.37996563 -0.3651484  0.4745519
```

B.3 READING DATA AND CREATING WEIGHTS

There are various alternatives to reading data into R. We will see two different ways, loading existing data and reading external files.[3]

R has a myriad of built-in data. Typing `data()` in the console will produce a list of available data sets. An extensive number of them are associated with specific libraries.[4] For example, one of the datasets available from **spdep** is the Boston dataset (Harrison and Rubinfeld, 1978). Using a hedonic housing price specification, the authors wanted to estimate the demand for air quality improvements. The dataset contains information on housing attributes, including accessibility, structure and neighborhoods characteristics, and air pollution concentrations. In the original study data are aggregated at census tracts level for the Boston Standard Metropolitan Area in 1970.[5]

---

3. There is a very convenient library named **foreign** that allows the interface with a variety of different softwares including, STATA, SAS, Octave, SPSS, among others.

4. To access the dataset from all the installed libraries one should type `data(package = .packages(all.available = TRUE))`.

5. However, the original dataset was modified over the years (see, for example, Gilley and Pace, 1996) to fix some errors. The one available from **spdep** includes all the modifications made to the original dataset.

The simplest way to load a dataset is via

```
R> library(spdep)
R> data(boston)
R> ls()

[1] "boston.c"    "boston.soi" "boston.utm"
```

If we do a list of the current objects in the work space, we see that three files have been loaded. The `boston.c` file is the dataset itself, `boston.utm` is a matrix of point coordinates (projected to UTM zone 19), and, finally, `boston.soi` is a sphere of influence neighbors list.

A summary of the data can be produced in the following way:

```
R> summary(boston.c[,2:4])

TOWNNO          TRACT            LON
Min.   : 0.00   Min.   :   1   Min.   :-71.29
1st Qu.:26.25   1st Qu.:1303   1st Qu.:-71.09
Median :42.00   Median :3394   Median :-71.05
Mean   :47.53   Mean   :2700   Mean   :-71.06
3rd Qu.:78.00   3rd Qu.:3740   3rd Qu.:-71.02
Max.   :91.00   Max.   :5082   Max.   :-70.81
```

We can also write the data frame to the disk using the function `write.csv()`, where the first argument is the R object containing the data set, and the second argument is the name of the file that R creates

```
R> write.csv(boston.c, "bostondata.csv")
```

One of the more general functions to read external files is `read.table()`. This function reads a file in table format and creates a specific R object called `data.frame`. In the previous example we stored `boston.c` into a file that we named "bostondata.csv". In the example below we are creating a new object (`data1`) using the function `read.table()` to read the "bostondata.csv".

```
R> data1 <- read.table("bostondata.csv", header = TRUE, sep = ",")
R> class(data1)

[1] "data.frame"
```

The first argument is the name of the file. The argument `header` (whose default value is false) is a logic vector to determine whether the first line of the file contains the names of the variables. The separator can be set by the argument `sep`.[6]

6. There are many other arguments to the function `read.table()`, reason for which we strongly encourage the readers to consult the help page of the function.

In Chapter 1 we saw that spatial weighting matrices are an essential component in spatial models. We also reviewed some typical specifications of weighting matrices for Monte Carlo studies. We now focus on how to generate some of those matrices in R. The creation of the weighting matrix in R can be approached stepwise: The first step is to decide the criteria to determine who the neighbors are, while the second step is to decide the actual weight to assign to each neighbor. At first sight this process can appear cumbersome but has an important advantage. When the number of spatial units is high, storing an $N \times N$ matrix can be unfeasible due to the volume of information that one is trying to store. Most of the spatial weighting matrices are sparse in that each observations only has a limited number of neighbors. This is the reason why in R spatial weighting matrices are classified in objects named `listw`. Basically, `listw` objects are made up of two lists where each element (of the list) corresponds to a row of the spatial weighting matrices. The first list stores the id's of the neighbors (this corresponds to the information of the column of the spatial weighting matrix), while the second list includes the actual weights assigned to those elements.

A neighbors list for regular grids using the rook contiguity criterion can be generated by the function `cell2nb()`

```
R> Wnbr <- cell2nb(nrow = 3, ncol = 3, type = "rook")
R>  summary(Wnbr)
```

```
Neighbour list object:
Number of regions: 9
Number of nonzero links: 24
Percentage nonzero weights: 29.62963
Average number of links: 2.666667
Link number distribution:
2 3 4
4 4 1
4 least connected regions:
1:1 3:1 1:3 3:3 with 2 links
1 most connected region:
2:2 with 4 links
```

The first two arguments set the dimension of the regular grid, while the third argument set the nature of contiguity. Queen neighbors can be obtained by changing the option `type` to queen. There is a `summary()` method available for objects of class nb. The summary reports some information on the number of regions, percentage of nonzero elements, and a distribution of the number of links, among other things.

Another criteria to generate weights from a regular grid that we saw in Chapter 1 was called "h-ahead and h-behind". Such neighbors can be obtained with the function `circular` available from **sphet**:

```
R> library(sphet)
R> Wncircular <- circular(nrow = 5, ncol = 5, ab =  2)
```

If R was only able to generate a spatial weighting matrix from regular grid that would be considered a huge limitation for real-world applications. Fortunately, there are quite a few options to read shape files and generate spatial weighting matrices. However, we only review one of these options (that is part of the library `maptools`) since other details on this issue would be beyond the scope of our book.

The function `readShapeSpatial()` reads a shape file and generates an object of class `SpatialPolygonsDataFrame`.[7]

```
R> library(maptools)
R> e80 <- readShapeSpatial("elect80")
R> class(e80)

[1] "SpatialPolygonsDataFrame"
attr(,"package")
[1] "sp"
```

Once the shape file has been read, it is possible to generate the list of neighbors by mean of the function `poly2nb()`:

```
R> e80_queen <- poly2nb(e80, queen = TRUE)
```

Finally, the function that generates k-nearest neighbors spatial weights matrices reads a set of coordinates, calculates the distance between each pair of observations, and generates a list of the k-nearest neighbors for each observation (in the example below k is set to 5). In the following example we use the coordinates in `boston.utm`.

```
R> Bos.knn <- knearneigh(boston.utm, k = 5)
R> Bos.nb <- knn2nb(Bos.knn)
```

Once the list of neighbors has been established, the next step is to assign a weight to each relationship. The `nb2listw()` function takes a neighbors object and converts it into a weights object. In **spdep**, various styles of weights are allowed (controlled by the argument `style`). In particular, if the argument `style` is set to `W`, the weights for each observation are standardized to sum to unity.[8]

Our example uses the object `Bos.nb` that we generated previously

```
R> Bos.listw <- nb2listw(Bos.nb, style = "W")
R> class(Bos.listw)

[1] "listw" "nb"
```

7. The `SpatialPolygonsDataFrame` is the same dataset obtainable from **spdep** by loading the data `elect80`.

8. Other options ranges from a binary scheme to a general list of weights defined by the user.

B.4 ESTIMATING SPATIAL MODELS

Cross-Sectional Models

In this subsection we demonstrate how to estimate a linear regression model in R, and then move to the estimation of cross-sectional spatial models. We will start with the general model and then proceed to all the "restricted" versions of it. We review both ML and IV estimation. The examples are illustrated with the support of the Boston data. Harrison and Rubinfeld (1978) investigated various methodological issues related to the use of housing data to estimate the demand for clean air. As we already mentioned, the data consist of 506 units of observation. The complete list of variables includes median values of owner-occupied homes (CMEDV); per-capita crime rate (CRIM); nitric oxides concentration (NOX); average number of rooms (RM); proportion of residential land zoned for lots over 25,000 sq. ft (ZN); proportion of nonretail business acres per town (INDUS); Charles River dummy variable (CHAS); proportion of units built prior to 1940 (AGE); weighted distances to five Boston employment centers (DIS); index of accessibility to highways (RAD); property-tax rate (TAX); pupil–teacher ratios (PTRATIO); proportion of African Americans (B); and percentage of the lower status of the population (LSTAT).

Since the only purpose of this appendix is the illustration of various commands in R, we only consider a limited number of explanatory variables such as per-capita crime rate; (the square of) nitric oxides concentration; average number of rooms; proportions of units built prior to 1940; and proportion of African Americans.

Typically, the ingredients to fit a model in R are a model-fitting function, a brief description of the model, and a `data.frame` object containing the variables. For a linear regression, we make use of the function `lm()`. The description of the model is a `formula` object that we define once and for all as:

```
R> fm = log(CMEDV) ~ CRIM + NOX2 + RM + AGE + B
```

Most fitting functions, including `lm()`, take a few additional arguments. However, most of the additional arguments are only optional and provide either a more detailed description of the model or some control parameters for the fitting algorithm.

The model fitted with the function `lm()` is then reported with the function `summary()`:

```
R> B_ols <- lm(formula = fm, data = boston.c)
R> summary(B_ols)

Call:
lm(formula = fm, data = boston.c)
```

```
Residuals:
Min       1Q   Median      3Q      Max
-0.91457 -0.11368 -0.01545  0.10990  1.33712
Coefficients:
Estimate Std. Error t value Pr(>|t|)
(Intercept)  1.2345646  0.1311112   9.416  < 2e-16 ***
CRIM        -0.0130720  0.0014858  -8.798  < 2e-16 ***
NOX2        -0.2622690  0.1170193  -2.241 0.025448 *
RM           0.2861582  0.0166834  17.152  < 2e-16 ***
AGE         -0.0019237  0.0005478  -3.512 0.000485 ***
B            0.0007429  0.0001365   5.441 8.33e-08 ***
---
Signif. codes:  0 '***' 0.001 '**' 0.01 '*' 0.05 '.' 0.1 ' ' 1
Residual standard error: 0.2497 on 500 degrees of freedom
Multiple R-squared:  0.6297,    Adjusted R-squared:  0.626
F-statistic: 170.1 on 5 and 500 DF,  p-value: < 2.2e-16
```

As we observed in Chapter 2, the general model can be estimated both by ML and IV. The function that implements the ML is named `sacsarlm()`. In the following example we specify the only three mandatory arguments: the formula, the data frame, and the spatial weighting matrix (`listw`):

```
R> B_f_ml <- sacsarlm(formula = fm, data = boston.c,
listw = Bos.listw)
R> summary(B_f_ml)

Call:sacsarlm(formula = fm, data = boston.c, listw = Bos.listw)
Residuals:
Min         1Q     Median       3Q       Max
-0.948279 -0.060184 -0.003493  0.055914  0.793689
Type: sac
Coefficients: (asymptotic standard errors)
Estimate  Std. Error z value  Pr(>|z|)
(Intercept)  1.53252419  0.28447321  5.3872 7.155e-08
CRIM        -0.00396912  0.00106416 -3.7298 0.0001916
NOX2        -0.47514507  0.14755481 -3.2201 0.0012813
RM           0.22243814  0.01221855 18.2049 < 2.2e-16
AGE         -0.00346966  0.00049038 -7.0755 1.489e-12
B            0.00080873  0.00011941  6.7725 1.265e-11
Rho: 0.073484
Asymptotic standard error: 0.077794
z-value: 0.9446, p-value: 0.34486
Lambda: 0.82513
Asymptotic standard error: 0.03316
z-value: 24.883, p-value: < 2.22e-16
LR test value: 444.4, p-value: < 2.22e-16
Log likelihood: 209.3649 for sac model
ML residual variance (sigma squared): 0.021466, (sigma: 0.14651)
Number of observations: 506
```

```
Number of parameters estimated: 9
AIC: -400.73, (AIC for lm: 39.674)
```

There are more arguments that the reader can access throughout the help file of `sacsarlm()`. Many of these arguments improve upon the numerical optimization for more complicated likelihoods.[9] In this section, we just want to emphasize two of them, `listw2` and `method`. For the unrestricted model, it is possible to specify two different spatial weighting matrices: one that multiplies the dependent variable (`listw`), and one for the autocorrelated error term (`listw2`). The argument `method` is related to the computation of the Jacobian term. The default is to use the eigenvalues but other options are available (either exact or approximated). An explanation of those methods was given in Chapter 2 where we also referenced LeSage and Pace (2009).

The summary of the results is pretty self-explanatory and since the aim of this appendix is to illustrate the software application, we avoid any comments of the results. At this point, we should only notice that the results above refer to λ and ρ, where λ is the coefficient that multiplies the spatial lag of the dependent variable, and ρ is the coefficient of the spatially autocorrelated error term.

The IV estimation of the complete model is performed by the function `gstsls()`.[10] Also in this case there is an option to specify two different spatial weighting matrices. It is also possible to pick among different optimization algorithms.[11] For ease of presentation, in the following example we only specify the three mandatory arguments:

```
R> B_f_iv <- gstsls(formula = fm, data = boston.c,
listw = Bos.listw)
R> summary(B_f_iv)

Call:gstsls(formula = fm, data = boston.c, listw = Bos.listw)
Residuals:
Min            1Q        Median         3Q         Max
-0.8755972 -0.0651889 -0.0094776  0.0600763  0.8498660
Type: GM SARAR estimator
Coefficients: (GM standard errors)
Estimate  Std. Error z value  Pr(>|z|)
Rho_Wy         0.35838430  0.06756789  5.3041 1.133e-07
(Intercept)  0.50804320  0.22530979  2.2549   0.02414
CRIM          -0.00497143  0.00116178 -4.2792 1.876e-05
```

9. A recommendation for unexperienced users would be to leave those argument to their default values. In most cases, indeed, the default values perform pretty well.
10. `gstsls()` uses the moment conditions of Kelejian and Prucha (1999) that were described in Chapter 2. However, there is a more general function (`spreg()`) available from **sphet**. This function implements different moment conditions (i.e., those derived in Drukker et al., 2013a; and Kelejian and Prucha, 2010a). A description of `spreg()` can be found in Bivand and Piras, 2015.
11. All those additional features of the function are explained in the help file.

```
NOX2         -0.16053078  0.12439377 -1.2905    0.19688
RM            0.22780347  0.01290285 17.6553 < 2.2e-16
AGE          -0.00253036  0.00047697 -5.3051 1.126e-07
B             0.00071970  0.00011922  6.0368 1.572e-09
Lambda: 0.56303
Residual variance (sigma squared): 0.024946, (sigma: 0.15794)
GM argmin sigma squared: 0.025356
Number of observations: 506
Number of parameters estimated: 9
```

The next example illustrates how to estimate a special case of the model (i.e., when $\rho_1 = 0$) using the function `errorsarlm()`:

```
R> B_e_ml <- errorsarlm(formula = fm, data = boston.c,
listw = Bos.listw)
R> summary(B_e_ml)

Call:errorsarlm(formula = fm, data = boston.c, listw = Bos.listw)
Residuals:
Min          1Q       Median          3Q         Max
-0.9425659 -0.0609690 -0.0032992  0.0556162  0.7903949
Type: error
Coefficients: (asymptotic standard errors)
Estimate  Std. Error z value  Pr(>|z|)
(Intercept)  1.78149784  0.11577977 15.3870 < 2.2e-16
CRIM        -0.00396183  0.00105887 -3.7415 0.0001829
NOX2        -0.51437566  0.14407947 -3.5701 0.0003569
RM           0.22111383  0.01208871 18.2909 < 2.2e-16
AGE         -0.00353550  0.00048899 -7.2303 4.821e-13
B            0.00081427  0.00011915  6.8340 8.260e-12
Lambda: 0.84662, LR test value: 443.62, p-value: < 2.22e-16
Asymptotic standard error: 0.022083
z-value: 38.338, p-value: < 2.22e-16
Wald statistic: 1469.8, p-value: < 2.22e-16
Log likelihood: 208.9741 for error model
ML residual variance (sigma squared): 0.021191, (sigma: 0.14557)
Number of observations: 506
Number of parameters estimated: 8
AIC: -401.95, (AIC for lm: 39.674)
```

IV estimation of the same model is described in the following example:

```
R> B_e_iv <- GMerrorsar(formula = fm, data = boston.c,
listw = Bos.listw)
R> summary(B_e_iv)

Call:GMerrorsar(formula = fm, data = boston.c, listw = Bos.listw)
Residuals:
Min         1Q     Median        3Q        Max
-0.997154 -0.141609 -0.033334  0.104619  1.304224
```

```
Type: GM SAR estimator
Coefficients: (GM standard errors)
Estimate  Std. Error z value  Pr(>|z|)
(Intercept)  1.70091612  0.12136448 14.0149 < 2.2e-16
CRIM        -0.00494544  0.00119179 -4.1496 3.330e-05
NOX2        -0.46634888  0.14639303 -3.1856  0.001445
RM           0.22843119  0.01360314 16.7925 < 2.2e-16
AGE         -0.00329912  0.00053404 -6.1777 6.504e-10
B            0.00082924  0.00013160  6.3013 2.952e-10
Lambda: 0.73949 (standard error): 0.070179 (z-value): 10.537
Residual variance (sigma squared): 0.02737, (sigma: 0.16544)
GM argmin sigma squared: 0.027514
Number of observations: 506
Number of parameters estimated: 8
```

Finally, a model where $\rho_2 = 0$ can be estimated by ML using the function `lagsarlm()`:

```
R> B_l_ml <- lagsarlm(formula = fm, data = boston.c,
listw = Bos.listw)
R> summary(B_l_ml)
```

```
Call:lagsarlm(formula = fm, data = boston.c, listw = Bos.listw)
Residuals:
Min         1Q     Median        3Q        Max
-0.590881 -0.084008 -0.014851  0.072212  0.965309
Type: lag
Coefficients: (asymptotic standard errors)
Estimate  Std. Error z value  Pr(>|z|)
(Intercept) -2.8341e-01  1.0138e-01 -2.7955  0.005182
CRIM        -5.1305e-03  1.0146e-03 -5.0567 4.265e-07
NOX2         4.5634e-02  7.9414e-02  0.5746  0.565537
RM           1.8609e-01  1.2321e-02 15.1035 < 2.2e-16
AGE         -9.2723e-04  3.7536e-04 -2.4703  0.013501
B            4.2564e-04  9.3837e-05  4.5360 5.734e-06
Rho: 0.68437, LR test value: 346.31, p-value: < 2.22e-16
Asymptotic standard error: 0.02654
z-value: 25.786, p-value: < 2.22e-16
Wald statistic: 664.92, p-value: < 2.22e-16
Log likelihood: 160.3184 for lag model
ML residual variance (sigma squared): 0.028039, (sigma: 0.16745)
Number of observations: 506
Number of parameters estimated: 8
AIC: -304.64, (AIC for lm: 39.674)
LM test for residual autocorrelation
test value: 55.959, p-value: 7.3941e-14
```

The same model can be estimated by an IV procedure using the function `stsls()`

```
R> B_1_iv <- stsls(formula = fm, data = boston.c,
listw = Bos.listw)
R> summary(B_1_iv)
```

```
Call:stsls(formula = fm, data = boston.c, listw = Bos.listw)
Residuals:
Min         1Q     Median        3Q        Max
-0.660165 -0.081843 -0.016141  0.081650  1.110205
Coefficients:
Estimate  Std. Error t value  Pr(>|t|)
Rho            0.41766735  0.05927230  7.0466 1.834e-12
(Intercept)  0.30815487  0.16447993  1.8735  0.060998
CRIM          -0.00822533  0.00131439 -6.2579 3.901e-10
NOX2          -0.07435740  0.09215968 -0.8068  0.419763
RM             0.22508634  0.01527407 14.7365 < 2.2e-16
AGE           -0.00131554  0.00042186 -3.1184  0.001818
B              0.00054926  0.00010654  5.1556 2.528e-07
Residual variance (sigma squared): 0.035427, (sigma: 0.18822)
```

Panel Models

In this final subsection we illustrate the use of the function `spgm()` to estimate spatial panel data models. `spgm()` is a wrapper function available from **splm** that deals with the estimation of the general model as well as all the reduced forms (i.e., when either ρ_1, ρ_2, or β_2 in equation (15.4.1) are zero). Furthermore, `spgm()` is able to accommodate both fixed and random effects.

Clearly, the Boston data cannot be used to illustrate panel models since that data set is only available for a single time period. For this reason we use a well known panel data set initially employed by Cornwell and Trumbull (1994) to estimate a crime model in North Carolina. The data consists of observations on 90 counties in North Carolina observed for a time period that ranges from 1981 to 1987.

After loading the libraries **plm** and **splm**, the data can be accessed with the command `data(Crime)`:

```
R> library(plm)
R> library(splm)
R> data(Crime)
R> names(Crime)
```

```
[1] "county"  "year"    "crmrte"   "prbarr"   "prbconv" "prbpris"
[7] "avgsen"  "polpc"   "density" "taxpc"    "region"  "smsa"
[13] "pctmin"  "wcon"    "wtuc"     "wtrd"     "wfir"    "wser"
[19] "wmfg"    "wfed"    "wsta"     "wloc"     "mix"     "pctymle"
```

The dependent variable in the model is crime per-capita (`crmrte`). Some of the main explanatory variables are deterrents to crime. Specifically, the probability of arrest (`prbarr`) is proxied by the ratio of arrest to offenses; the ratio of convictions to arrest is a proxy for the probability of conviction (prbconv), and, finally, the proportion of total convictions resulting in prison sentences is a proxy for the probability of imprisonment (prbpris). The model includes a measure of sanction severity (avgsen) measured by the average prison sentence as well as the number of police per capita (polpc).

The relative return to legal activities is captured by the average weekly wage in the county in various sectors, such as construction (wcon); transportation, utilities, and communications (wtuc); wholesale and retail trade (wtrd); finance, insurance, and real estate (wfir); services (wser); manufacturing (wmfg); and federal (wfed), state (wsta), and local government (wloc). The model also includes the proportion of the male population between the ages of 15–24 (pctymle), and the proportion of the minority population (pctmin). The density variable (density) measures the ratio between county population and county land area. All the variables mentioned so far are in logarithm.

There are two additional variables in the data set, namely region and smsa. Those two variables are used to create three different dummy variables: urban, west, and central. This is illustrated by the following lines of code:

```
R> Crime$west <- ifelse(Crime$region == "west", 1, 0)
R> Crime$central <- ifelse(Crime$region == "central", 1, 0)
R> Crime$urban <- ifelse(Crime$smsa == "yes", 1, 0)
```

Time dummies are also created (the excluded year to avoid the dummy variables trap is 1981) and added to the dataset. Finally, the dataset is sorted first by year and then by county.

```
R> for (i in 82 : 87){
+  assign(paste("d", i, sep=""), ifelse(Crime$year == i, 1, 0))
+  }
R> dum <- cbind(d82, d83, d84, d85, d86, d87)
R> Crime$dum <- dum
R> crime <- Crime[order(Crime$year, Crime$county),]
```

Next we generate the formula in the usual way and take the logarithm of all the variables (except for the dummies):

```
R> fm <- log(crmrte) ~  log(prbconv)+ log(prbpris) +
+  log(avgsen)+ log(density) + log(wcon) +
+  log(wtuc)+ log(wtrd) + log(wfir) + log(wser) +
+  log(wmfg) + log(wfed) + log(wsta) + log(wloc) +
+  log(pctymle) + log(pctmin) + west + central +
+  urban + dum
```

At this point an attentive reader may have noted that two of the variables listed above are not explicitly considered in the formula object. This is due to the potential endogeneity problem of police per capita (polpc) and the probability of arrest (prbarr).

The additional instruments are the logarithm of the offense mix (mix) and the logarithm of per capita tax ratio (taxpc).

Both the endogenous variables and the additional instruments have to be specified as two additional arguments of the function spgm(), namely endog and instruments. The next two lines of code illustrate how to do this.

```
R> endog = ~ log(polpc) + log(prbarr)
R> instruments = ~ log(taxpc) + log(mix)
```

Note the sign ~ before the variables in each expression typical in all formula objects.

In order to create the spatial weighting matrix in terms of the five nearest neighbors, we first read the (polygon) shape file named north_carol, then, using the function coordinates(), we create the object coord that stores the longitude and latitude of the centroids of each county. The function knearneigh() determine a list of the k-nearest neighbors observations for each county that is then transformed in an object of class nb by the function knn2nb(). Finally, the function nb2listw() creates the weighting matrix in terms of a listw object.

```
R> shapel <- readShapePoly("north_carol")
R> coord <- coordinates(shapel)
R> knn <- knearneigh(coord, k = 5)
R> nbnc <- knn2nb(knn)
R> nc_listw <- nb2listw(nbnc)
```

As we anticipated the function spgm() deals with the estimation of panel models. There are various arguments of the function but we will comment only on a few of them pointing the reader to the help file of the function. As it is typical in R, the first argument is a formula object that is a description of the model to be estimated. The data set may be specified with the argument data. The index argument should be left to the default value (i.e., NULL) provided that the first two columns in the data are the individual and time indexes. The two arguments listw and listw2 are the two spatial weighting matrices (respectively the one that multiplies the dependent variable and the error term). If listw2 is not specified, listw will be used both for the dependent variable and the error term. The argument model distinguish between within and random effects estimators. lag and spatial.error are set to TRUE to estimate the complete model. The arguments endog and instruments allow for the presence of additional endogenous variables and instruments (which can also be spatially lagged). Finally, to reproduce the fixed effects estimation of Section 15.5 the `method` should be set to `"w2sls"`, while to reproduce the random effects estimation of Section 15.4 the `method` should be set to `"ec2sls"`.

The next command describes the estimation of the complete model by fixed effects. The `model` is set to `within` and the `moments` are those described in equation (15.3.33).

```
R> fes <- spgm(fm, data = crime, listw = nc_listw,
+  model = "within", lag = T, spatial.error = T,
+  method= "w2sls", endog = endog,
+  instruments = instruments, lag.instruments = T,
+  moments = "fullweights")
R> summary(fes)
```

```
Spatial panel fixed effects GM model
Call:
spgm(formula = fm, data = crime, listw = nc_listw, model = "within",
lag = T, spatial.error = T, moments = "fullweights", endog = endog,
instruments = instruments, lag.instruments = T, method = "w2sls")
Residuals:
Min. 1st Qu.  Median    Mean 3rd Qu.    Max.
1.01    2.99    3.18    3.17    3.41    4.32
Estimated spatial coefficient, variance components and theta:
Estimate
rho        -0.254286
sigma^2_v  0.018094
Spatial autoregressive coefficient:
Estimate Std. Error t-value Pr(>|t|)
lambda  0.37041    0.18087  2.0479  0.04057 *
Coefficients:
Estimate Std. Error t-value  Pr(>|t|)
log(polpc)     0.4272067  0.1063037  4.0187 5.851e-05 ***
log(prbarr)   -0.2502110  0.1126204 -2.2217 0.0263022 *
log(prbconv) -0.2461538  0.0654893 -3.7587 0.0001708 ***
log(prbpris) -0.1418214  0.0482029 -2.9422 0.0032591 **
log(avgsen)  -0.0072827  0.0268078 -0.2717 0.7858819
log(density)  0.4175251  0.2895354  1.4421 0.1492876
log(wcon)    -0.0417410  0.0391591 -1.0659 0.2864526
log(wtuc)     0.0377545  0.0176901  2.1342 0.0328245 *
log(wtrd)    -0.0168634  0.0404437 -0.4170 0.6767070
log(wfir)    -0.0090857  0.0279407 -0.3252 0.7450472
log(wser)     0.0166432  0.0196920  0.8452 0.3980131
log(wmfg)    -0.3074218  0.1242875 -2.4735 0.0133806 *
log(wfed)    -0.3323302  0.1851797 -1.7946 0.0727116 .
log(wsta)     0.0557962  0.1168988  0.4773 0.6331457
log(wloc)     0.1727744  0.1197381  1.4429 0.1490383
log(pctymle)  0.3160977  0.3873447  0.8161 0.4144641
dumd82        0.0165919  0.0238288  0.6963 0.4862421
dumd83       -0.0246687  0.0365653 -0.6746 0.4999006
dumd84       -0.0229325  0.0498720 -0.4598 0.6456408
dumd85       -0.0052982  0.0646087 -0.0820 0.9346430
```

```
dumd86         0.0221351  0.0780757  0.2835 0.7767877
dumd87         0.0531318  0.0948486  0.5602 0.5753604
---
Signif. codes:  0 '***' 0.001 '**' 0.01 '*' 0.05 '.' 0.1 ' ' 1
```

The following model is again a fixed effects but the error term is not spatially autocorrelated:

```
R> fes <- spgm(fm, data = crime, listw = nc_listw,
+  model = "within", lag = T, spatial.error = F,
+  method= "w2sls", endog = endog,
+  instruments = instruments, lag.instruments = T,
+  moments = "fullweights")
R> summary(fes)

Call:
spgm(formula = fm, data = crime, listw = nc_listw, model = "within",
lag = T, spatial.error = F, moments = "fullweights", endog = endog,
instruments = instruments, lag.instruments = T, method = "w2sls")
Residuals:
Min          1Q      Median          3Q         Max
-0.5740092 -0.0673813 -0.0028763  0.0713752  0.4883877
Coefficients:
Estimate Std. Error t value  Pr(>|t|)
log(polpc)     0.4676677  0.1145836  4.0815 4.475e-05
log(prbarr)   -0.2951640  0.1238724 -2.3828 0.0171812
lambda         0.2729852  0.2044295  1.3354 0.1817613
log(prbconv)  -0.2734338  0.0704183 -3.8830 0.0001032
log(prbpris)  -0.1545504  0.0521132 -2.9657 0.0030203
log(avgsen)   -0.0036232  0.0277266 -0.1307 0.8960314
log(density)   0.4186425  0.3152569  1.3279 0.1841977
log(wcon)     -0.0464178  0.0408117 -1.1374 0.2553854
log(wtuc)      0.0445631  0.0196304  2.2701 0.0232010
log(wtrd)     -0.0129971  0.0416968 -0.3117 0.7552656
log(wfir)     -0.0057517  0.0289980 -0.1983 0.8427735
log(wser)      0.0164790  0.0204688  0.8051 0.4207763
log(wmfg)     -0.3366902  0.1292669 -2.6046 0.0091978
log(wfed)     -0.3706083  0.1894600 -1.9561 0.0504498
log(wsta)      0.0569072  0.1211453  0.4697 0.6385384
log(wloc)      0.2177977  0.1246634  1.7471 0.0806224
log(pctymle)   0.2992991  0.4045068  0.7399 0.4593539
dumd82         0.0177870  0.0277685  0.6405 0.5218182
dumd83        -0.0334837  0.0416174 -0.8046 0.4210733
dumd84        -0.0330545  0.0559562 -0.5907 0.5547076
dumd85        -0.0165296  0.0703409 -0.2350 0.8142141
dumd86         0.0123064  0.0828864  0.1485 0.8819693
dumd87         0.0449656  0.0995485  0.4517 0.6514882
Residual variance (sigma squared): 0.016561, (sigma: 0.12869)
```

Below is an example of fixed effects model with a spatially autocorrelated error term but no spatial lag:

```
R> fele <- spgm(fm, data = crime, listw = nc_listw,
+  model = "within", lag = F, spatial.error = TRUE,
+  method= "w2sls", endog = endog,
+  instruments = instruments, lag.instruments = T )
R> summary(fele)

Spatial panel fixed effects GM model
Call:
spgm(formula = fm, data = crime, listw = nc_listw, model = "within",
lag = F, spatial.error = TRUE, endog = endog,
instruments = instruments, lag.instruments = T, method = "w2sls")
Residuals:
Min. 1st Qu.  Median    Mean 3rd Qu.    Max.
0.508   2.490   2.700   2.670   2.930   3.620
Estimated spatial coefficient, variance components and theta:
[1] 0.0057477
Coefficients:
Estimate Std. Error t-value Pr(>|t|)
log(polpc)     0.5503574  0.2282601  2.4111  0.01590 *
log(prbarr)   -0.4622388  0.2444075 -1.8913  0.05859 .
log(prbconv)  -0.3555144  0.1421759 -2.5005  0.01240 *
log(prbpris)  -0.2116991  0.0873939 -2.4224  0.01542 *
log(avgsen)    0.0041167  0.0283458  0.1452  0.88453
log(density)   0.2704138  0.3940456  0.6862  0.49256
log(wcon)     -0.0332931  0.0403693 -0.8247  0.40953
log(wtuc)      0.0424188  0.0202220  2.0977  0.03594 *
log(wtrd)     -0.0188346  0.0408068 -0.4616  0.64440
log(wfir)     -0.0065543  0.0289747 -0.2262  0.82104
log(wser)      0.0150574  0.0214249  0.7028  0.48218
log(wmfg)     -0.2937053  0.1550841 -1.8938  0.05825 .
log(wfed)     -0.3905922  0.2202554 -1.7734  0.07617 .
log(wsta)      0.0150813  0.1335455  0.1129  0.91009
log(wloc)      0.2274617  0.1411529  1.6115  0.10708
log(pctymle)   0.4509414  0.4512184  0.9994  0.31761
dumd82         0.0301003  0.0308368  0.9761  0.32901
dumd83        -0.0447094  0.0378981 -1.1797  0.23811
dumd84        -0.0475428  0.0503691 -0.9439  0.34523
dumd85        -0.0226687  0.0672736 -0.3370  0.73614
dumd86         0.0155414  0.0840171  0.1850  0.85325
dumd87         0.0645800  0.1074801  0.6009  0.54794
---
Signif. codes:  0 '***' 0.001 '**' 0.01 '*' 0.05 '.' 0.1 ' ' 1
```

Finally, the following is an example of a random effects model for the full model:

```
R> rel <- spgm(fm, data = crime, listw = nc_listw,
+   model = "random", lag = T, spatial.error = T,
+   method= "ec2sls", endog = endog,
+   instruments = instruments, lag.instruments = T )
R> summary(rel)
```

```
Call:
spgm(formula = fm, data = crime, listw = nc_listw, model = "random",
lag = T, spatial.error = T, endog = endog, instruments = instruments,
lag.instruments = T, method = "ec2sls")
Residuals:
Min.  1st Qu.   Median     Mean  3rd Qu.     Max.
-1.36000 -0.13500  0.00324  0.00023  0.15200  1.11000
Coefficients:
Estimate Std. Error t-value  Pr(>|t|)
log(polpc)     0.3724972  0.0484813  7.6833 1.550e-14 ***
log(prbarr)   -0.3335397  0.0607076 -5.4942 3.925e-08 ***
lambda         0.2699027  0.0700254  3.8544 0.0001160 ***
(Intercept)   -0.6240857  1.1452489 -0.5449 0.5857985
log(prbconv)  -0.2764480  0.0320922 -8.6142 < 2.2e-16 ***
log(prbpris)  -0.1607962  0.0340476 -4.7227 2.327e-06 ***
log(avgsen)   -0.0135835  0.0252715 -0.5375 0.5909201
log(density)   0.4527401  0.0487741  9.2824 < 2.2e-16 ***
log(wcon)     -0.0084332  0.0372932 -0.2261 0.8210980
log(wtuc)      0.0399603  0.0173188  2.3073 0.0210359 *
log(wtrd)     -0.0091618  0.0392464 -0.2334 0.8154170
log(wfir)     -0.0063858  0.0273422 -0.2335 0.8153351
log(wser)      0.0054519  0.0188215  0.2897 0.7720734
log(wmfg)     -0.1936043  0.0747789 -2.5890 0.0096249 **
log(wfed)     -0.0814508  0.1414625 -0.5758 0.5647661
log(wsta)     -0.0266134  0.0980204 -0.2715 0.7859996
log(wloc)      0.1365891  0.1113866  1.2263 0.2201005
log(pctymle)  -0.0682851  0.1168727 -0.5843 0.5590396
log(pctmin)    0.1865774  0.0364748  5.1152 3.133e-07 ***
west          -0.2205528  0.0907647 -2.4299 0.0151013 *
central       -0.2094642  0.0561089 -3.7332 0.0001891 ***
urban         -0.1950307  0.1019866 -1.9123 0.0558356 .
dumd82         0.0049908  0.0207350  0.2407 0.8097934
dumd83        -0.0660894  0.0263175 -2.5112 0.0120312 *
dumd84        -0.0803101  0.0331209 -2.4248 0.0153189 *
dumd85        -0.0787971  0.0449746 -1.7520 0.0797676 .
dumd86        -0.0639599  0.0548972 -1.1651 0.2439846
dumd87        -0.0425662  0.0653856 -0.6510 0.5150446
---
Signif. codes:  0 '***' 0.001 '**' 0.01 '*' 0.05 '.' 0.1 ' ' 1
```

Answer Manual

A Review of Four Frequently Used Results

These four results are used at various points in this answer manual. For the convenience of the reader, we review them here.

(i) Let a be a scalar. Then

$$Tr(a) = a. \tag{R.1}$$

(ii) Let the product of the matrices A and B be a square matrix. Then

$$Tr(AB) = Tr(BA). \tag{R.2}$$

The condition that AB is a square matrix does not imply that A and B must also be square. For example, let A be $r \times h$ and let B be $h \times r$. Then AB is a square $r \times r$ matrix, and BA is a square $h \times h$ matrix.

(iii) Let A be an $N \times N$ matrix, and let some, or all, of its elements be random. Let the ith diagonal element of A be a_{ii}, $i = 1, ..., N$. Then

$$E(Tr(A)) = Tr(E(A)). \tag{R.3}$$

To see this note that $Tr(A) = a_{11} + a_{22} + ... + a_{NN}$. Therefore $E(Tr(A)) = E(a_{11}) + ... + E(a_{NN}) = Tr(E(A))$.

(iv) Let δ be an $N \times 1$ random vector whose mean and VC matrix are 0 and Σ, respectively. Let C be a constant $N \times N$ matrix. Then

$$E(\delta' C \delta) = Tr(\Sigma C). \tag{R.4}$$

To see this first note that $\delta' C \delta$ is a scalar, and so by (R.1), $\delta' C \delta = Tr(\delta' C \delta)$. Therefore, using (R.2) and (R.3), $E(\delta' C \delta) = E(Tr(\delta' C \delta)) = E(Tr(\delta \delta' C)) = Tr(E(\delta \delta' C)) = Tr(\Sigma C)$.

Answers to the Problem Sets

Chapter 1

1. If w_{ij} is generally defined as $w_{ij} = \alpha g_{ij}$ then the (i, j)th element of the row normalized weighting matrix is

$$\frac{\alpha g_{ij}}{\sum_{j=1}^{N} \alpha g_{ij}} = \frac{\alpha g_{ij}}{\alpha \sum_{j=1}^{N} g_{ij}} = \frac{g_{ij}}{\sum_{j=1}^{N} g_{ij}}.$$

2. If, in general, $w_{ij} = F(ag_{ij})$ where F is the normal CDF and a is an unknown parameter, then the weighting matrix W will not be observable and the model in (1.2.1) will not be a model, which is linear in the parameter because of a.

3. It is reasonable to assume that the GDPs of neighboring countries are related because of trade, etc. Thus, one such model might be

$$GDP_i = a_0 + a_1 CAP_i + a_2 ED_i + a_3 W_{i.} GDP + X_i + u_i$$

where CAP_i is a measure of country $i's$ capital stock, ED_i is a measure of its human capital, $W_{i.}$ is the ith row of a weighting matrix whose jth element could be a distance measure between the ith and jth countries, GDP is an $N \times 1$ vector of the N GDPs of the studied countries, X_i is a row vector of other relevant variables, and u_i is the error term.

4. The answer is 3, which relates to a corner unit.

5. If the matrix is row normalized, the third row is

$$\begin{bmatrix} 1/4, & 1/4, & 0, & 1/4, & 1/4, & 0, & 0, & 0, & 0, & 0 \end{bmatrix}.$$

Chapter 2

1. Since $u = (I_N + \rho W)\varepsilon$, it follows that $VC_u = E(uu') = \sigma^2 (I_N + \rho W)(I_N + \rho W)'$. Let $\bar{u} = Wu$, and note, since W is a weighting matrix, that $Tr(W) = 0$. Then GMM equations could be based on the moments:

$$\begin{aligned} 1.\ E[u'u] &= E[\varepsilon'(I_N + \rho W)'(I_N + \rho W)\varepsilon] \\ &= Tr\left[E(\varepsilon\varepsilon')(I_N + \rho W)'(I_N + \rho W)\right] \\ &= \sigma^2 Tr[(I_N + \rho W)'(I_N + \rho W)] \\ &= \sigma^2 N + \sigma^2 \rho^2 Tr[W'W]. \end{aligned} \tag{2A.1}$$

2. $$E[\bar{u}'u] = E[u'W'u] = Tr(E[uu']W')$$
$$= \sigma^2 Tr[(I_N + \rho W)(I_N + \rho W)'W']$$
$$= \sigma^2 Tr[W' + \rho(W'W' + WW') + \rho^2 WW'W']$$
$$= \sigma^2 \rho Tr[W'W' + WW'] + \sigma^2\rho^2 Tr[WW'W'].$$

3. $$E[\bar{u}'\bar{u}] = E[u'W'Wu] = Tr[E(uu')W'W]$$
$$= \sigma^2 Tr[(I_N + \rho W)(I_N + \rho W)'W'W]$$
$$= \sigma^2 Tr[W'W] + \sigma^2 \rho Tr[W'W'W + WW'W]$$
$$+ \sigma^2\rho^2 Tr[WW'W'W].$$

Let $\hat{u}$ be the estimated value of u and let $\widehat{\bar{u}} = W\hat{u}$. Then, the parameter vector $\gamma' = (\sigma^2, \sigma^2\rho, \sigma^2\rho^2)$ could be estimated by either OLS or by nonlinear least squares from the equations in (2A.2):

$$N^{-1}\hat{u}'\hat{u} = \sigma^2 + \sigma^2\rho^2 A_1 + \delta_1, \tag{2A.2}$$
$$N^{-1}\widehat{\bar{u}}' u = (\sigma^2\rho)A_2 + (\sigma^2\rho^2)A_3 + \delta_2,$$
$$N^{-1}\widehat{\bar{u}}'\widehat{\bar{u}} = \sigma^2 A_1 + \sigma^2\rho A_4 + +\sigma^2\rho^2 A_5 + \delta_3$$

where δ_1, δ_2, and δ_3 are error terms and

$$A_1 = N^{-1}Tr[W'W],\ A_2 = N^{-1}Tr[W'W' + WW'], \tag{2A.3}$$
$$A_3 = N^{-1}Tr[WW'W'],\ A_4 = N^{-1}Tr[W'W'W + WW'W],$$
$$A_5 = N^{-1}Tr[WW'W'W].$$

2. First note that $u = (I_N - \rho W)^{-1}(I_N + \lambda W)\varepsilon$ and $\bar{u} = Wu = W(I_N - \rho W)^{-1}(I_N + \lambda W)\varepsilon$. To simplify notation let $D = (I_N - \rho W)^{-1}(I_N + \lambda W)$. Then similarly to problem 1, the moment conditions for the GMM estimation are:

$$E(u'u) = E(\varepsilon' D' D\varepsilon) = \sigma^2 Tr(D'D), \tag{2A.4}$$
$$E(u'\bar{u}) = E(\varepsilon' DWD\varepsilon) = \sigma^2 Tr(DWD),$$
$$E(\bar{u}'\bar{u}) = E(\varepsilon' D'W'WD\varepsilon) = \sigma^2 Tr(D'W'WD).$$

The remainder of the procedure, while tedious, follows along the lines of problem 1.

3. **(a)** To estimate the model in (P.3), define the instrument matrix

$$H = (X, W_1X, W_2X, MX, ..., M_1^r X) \tag{2A.5}$$

where typically $r = 2$. Use the 2SLS procedure to estimate the error term u as $\hat{u}$. Obtain $\widehat{\bar{u}} = M\hat{u}$, and use the GMM approach to estimate ρ as $\hat{\rho}$. Let $Z = (X, W_1 y, W_2 y)$ and $\gamma' = (\beta', \lambda_1, \lambda_2)$. Then transform the model in (P.3) as

$$(y - \hat{\rho} M) \simeq (Z - \hat{\rho} M Z)\gamma + \varepsilon. \tag{2A.6}$$

Let $Z^* = (Z - \hat{\rho} M Z)$ and $\hat{Z}^* = H(H'H)^{-1}H'Z^*$. Then estimate γ as

$$\hat{\gamma} = (\hat{Z}^{*\prime}\hat{Z}^*)^{-1}\hat{Z}^{*\prime}(y - \hat{\rho} M). \tag{2A.7}$$

(b) If we know that $\rho = 0$, then the estimator of γ would be

$$\tilde{\gamma} = (\hat{Z}'\hat{Z})^{-1}\hat{Z}'y \tag{2A.8}$$

where $\hat{Z} = H_1(H_1'H_1)^{-1}H_1'Z$ and

$$H_1 = (X, W_1 X, W_2 X, ..., W_1^r X, W_2^r X) \tag{2A.9}$$

with, typically, $r = 2$. The large sample distribution would be

$$N^{1/2}(\tilde{\gamma} - \gamma) \xrightarrow{D} N[0, \sigma^2 N(\hat{Z}'\hat{Z})^{-1}]. \tag{2A.10}$$

4. Let $Q_1 = (I_N - \lambda_1 W_1 - \lambda_2 W_2)^{-1}$ and $Q_2 = (I_N - \rho M)^{-1}$. Then the solution of the model for y is $y = Q_1 X\beta + Q_1 Q_2 \varepsilon$. Therefore, assuming normality of ε,

$$\begin{aligned} y &= N(Q_1 X\beta, \sigma^2 Q_1 Q_2 Q_2' Q_1') \\ &= N(Q_1 X\beta, \sigma^2 V), \quad V = Q_1 Q_2 Q_2' Q_1', \end{aligned} \tag{2A.11}$$

and so the likelihood is

$$L = \frac{1}{(\sigma^2)^{N/2}|V|^{1/2}} \exp[\frac{1}{\sigma^2}(y - Q_1 X\beta)'[V]^{-1}(y - Q_1 X\beta)]. \tag{2A.12}$$

The log-likelihood is

$$\begin{aligned} \ln(L) = &\frac{1}{\sigma^2}(y - Q_1 X\beta)'[V]^{-1}(y - Q_1 X\beta) \\ &- \frac{N}{2}\ln(\sigma^2) - \ln(|V|^{1/2}). \end{aligned} \tag{2A.13}$$

Note that $\ln(|V|) = \ln(|Q_1 Q_2 Q_2' Q_1'|) = \ln\left[|Q_1 Q_2||Q_2' Q_1'|\right] = \ln(|Q_1 Q_2|^2)$, and so $\ln(|V|^{1/2}) = \ln(|Q_1 Q_2|)$. Also the VC matrix of u is $V_u =$

$\sigma^2(Q_2Q_2')$. The log-likelihood is therefore

$$\ln(L) = \frac{1}{\sigma^2}(y - Q_1X\beta)'[V]^{-1}(y - Q_1X\beta) \\ - \frac{N}{2}\ln(\sigma^2) \ - \ln(|Q_1Q_2|). \tag{2A.14}$$

The first order conditions for β and the MLE of β are respectively

$$\frac{\partial \ln(L)}{\partial \beta}|_{\hat{\beta}} = 2X'\hat{Q}_1'\hat{V}^{-1}\hat{Q}_1X\hat{\beta} - 2X'\hat{Q}_1'\hat{V}^{-1}y = 0, \\ \hat{\beta} = [X'\hat{Q}_1'\hat{V}^{-1}\hat{Q}_1X]^{-1}X'\hat{Q}_1'\hat{V}^{-1}y \tag{2A.15}$$

where $\hat{Q}_1 = (I_N - \hat{\lambda}_1W_1 - \hat{\lambda}_2W_2)^{-1}$, $\hat{V} = (\hat{Q}_1\hat{Q}_2\hat{Q}_2'\hat{Q}_1')$, and $\hat{Q}_2 = (I_N - \hat{\rho}M)^{-1}$ where $\hat{\lambda}_1, \hat{\lambda}_2, \hat{\rho}$ are the MLEs of λ_1, λ_2, and ρ.

5. $|\lambda_1| + |\lambda_2| < 1$.

6. The IV matrix could be taken as $H = (X, WX, W^2X)$. Then write the model as

$$y = Z\gamma + u, \\ u = (I_N + \rho W)\varepsilon \tag{2A.16}$$

where $Z = (X, Wy)$ and $\gamma' = (\beta', \lambda)$. Let $\hat{Z} = H(H'H)^{-1}H'Z$ and recall that $\hat{Z}'Z = \hat{Z}'\hat{Z}$. Then estimate γ as

$$\hat{\gamma} = (\hat{Z}'\hat{Z})^{-1}\hat{Z}'y \\ = (\hat{Z}'\hat{Z})^{-1}\hat{Z}'[Z\gamma + u] \\ = \gamma + (N^{-1}\hat{Z}'\hat{Z})^{-1}N^{-1}\hat{Z}'(I_N + \rho W)\varepsilon. \tag{2A.17}$$

To show consistency note that, under typical assumptions,

$$p\lim\hat{\gamma} = \gamma + p\lim\{(N^{-1}\hat{Z}'\hat{Z})^{-1}[N^{-1}\hat{Z}'\varepsilon + \rho N^{-1}\hat{Z}'W\varepsilon]\}. \tag{2A.18}$$

Consider the terms on the right-hand side of (2A.18). Under typical assumptions,

$$N^{-1}\hat{Z}'\hat{Z} = (N^{-1}Z'H)\,(N^{-1}H'H)^{-1}(N^{-1}H'Z) \\ = Q_{HZ}'Q_{HH}^{-1}Q_{HZ}. \tag{2A.19}$$

Also

$$p\lim(N^{-1}\hat{Z}'\varepsilon) = p\lim[N^{-1}Z'H(N^{-1}H'H)^{-1}N^{-1}H'\varepsilon] \tag{2A.20}$$

$$= Q'_{HZ} Q_{HH}^{-1} [p \lim N^{-1} H' \varepsilon]$$
$$= 0.$$

Similar manipulations will show that $p \lim \rho N^{-1} \hat{Z}' W \varepsilon = 0$. It follows from (2A.18) that $\hat{\gamma}$ is consistent.

Chapter 3

1. Let $G = (I_N - \rho_1 W_1 - \rho_2 W_2)^{-1}$, and consider the $N \times k$ matrix $X = [X_1, ..., X_k]$, where X_i is the ith column of X. Let the jth element of X_i be $x_{j,i}$; this corresponds to the value of the ith regressor in country j.
The solution for y is

$$\begin{aligned} y &= G[X\beta + u] \\ &= G\{[X_1, ..., X_k]\beta + u\}, \\ \beta' &= (\beta_1, ..., \beta_k). \end{aligned} \tag{3A.1}$$

If the value of the first regressor in country j were to change, the emanating effects on the other countries would be

$$\frac{\partial y_s}{\partial x_{j,1}} = G_{s,j}\beta_1, \quad s = 1, ..., N; s \neq j. \tag{3A.2}$$

The vulnerability effect of country 1 to a change in the value of the first regressor in all countries other than country 1 is

$$\sum_{q=2}^{N} \frac{\partial y_1}{\partial x_{q,1}} = G_{1,q}\beta_1, \quad s = 1, ..., N. \tag{3A.3}$$

2. To solve the model for y_1, substitute the model for y_2 into the first equation to get

$$\begin{aligned} y_1 &= X_1\beta_1 + \lambda_1 W_1 y_1 + \alpha_1[X_2\beta_2 + y_1\alpha_2 + u_2] + u_1 \\ &= G^*[X_1\beta_1 + \alpha_1 X_2\beta_2 + \alpha_1 u_2 + u_1] \end{aligned} \tag{3A.4}$$

where $G^* = (I_N - \lambda_1 W_1 - \alpha_1\alpha_2 I_N)^{-1}$. The emanating and vulnerability effects with respect to the first unit of y_1 can be obtained from (3A.2) and (3A.3) by replacing G with G^*.

3. The emanating effects are $\partial y_s / \partial x_1 = W_{s1}\beta_2$. The vulnerability effects are $\sum_{q=2}^{N} \partial y_1 / \partial x_q = \sum_{q=2}^{N} W_{1q}\beta_2$.

4. Again, to solve the model, let $G = (I_N - \rho_1 W_1 - \rho_2 W_2)^{-1}$. Let α be the percentage change in the exogenous variables. Then, the change in y_s, $s > 1$, with respect to the uniform percentage change, α, is

$$\Delta y_s = \alpha[G_{s,1}|\beta_1|x_{1,1} + ... + G_{s1}|\beta_k|x_{1,k}]. \tag{3A.5}$$

Chapter 4

1. **(a)** Since $y = (I_N - \rho_1 W)^{-1}[X\beta + u]$ and $u = (I_N - \rho_2 W)^{-1}\varepsilon$, the VC matrix of y is

$$V_y = \sigma_\varepsilon^2 (I_N - \rho_1 W)^{-1}(I_N - W\rho_2)^{-1}(I_N - \rho_2 W')^{-1}(I_N - \rho_1 W')^{-1} \tag{4A.1}$$

and

$$var(w_{N.}y) = w_{N.}V_y w'_{N.}. \tag{4A.2}$$

(b) $E(w_{N.}y) = w_{N.}E(y) = w_{N.}(I_N - \rho_1 W)^{-1}X\beta$.

(c) y_{-N} is given in (4.2.13) and u_N is given in (4.2.9). Since $E(u_N) = 0$, and u_N is a scalar $u_N = u'_N$. Therefore

$$\begin{aligned} cov(u_N, y_{-N}) &= E(y_{-N}u_N) \\ &= E[I_{-N,N}(I - \rho_1 W)^{-1}(I - \rho_2 W)^{-1}\varepsilon\varepsilon'(I_N - \rho_2 W)^{-1'}_{N.}] \\ &= \sigma^2 I_{-N,N}(I - \rho_1 W)^{-1}(I - \rho_2 W)^{-1}(I_N - \rho_2 W)^{-1'}_{N.}. \end{aligned} \tag{4A.3}$$

2. Let $M = (I_N - \lambda_1 W_1 - \lambda_2 W_2)^{-1}$. Then note that

$$\begin{aligned} y &= MX\beta + M\varepsilon, \\ y_N &= M_{N.}X\beta + M_{N.}\varepsilon, \\ W_1 y &= W_1 MX\beta + W_1 M\varepsilon, \\ W_2 y &= W_2 MX\beta + W_2 M\varepsilon. \end{aligned} \tag{4A.4}$$

Then from (4.2.1)

$$\begin{aligned} E(y_N|X, W_1 y, W_2 y) &= M_{N.}X\beta + M_{N.}E(\varepsilon|X, W_1 y, W_2 y) \\ &= M_{N.}X\beta + M_{N.}C_{\varepsilon,(W_1 y, W_2 y)}V^{-1}_{(W_1 y, W_2 y)} * \\ &\quad [(W_1 y, W_2 y) - (W_1 MX\beta, W_2 MX\beta)] \end{aligned} \tag{4A.5}$$

and where the covariance matrix, $C_{\varepsilon,(W_1y,W_2y)}$, and the VC matrix, $V^{-1}_{(W_1y,W_2y)}$, respectively are

$$C_{\varepsilon,(W_1y,W_2y)} = E(\varepsilon\varepsilon' M' W_1'), E(\varepsilon\varepsilon' M' W_2') \tag{4A.6}$$
$$= (\sigma^2 M' W_1', \sigma^2 M' W_2')$$

and

$$V_{(W_1y,W_2y)} = \sigma^2 \begin{pmatrix} W_1 M M' W_1' & W_1 M M' W_2' \\ W_2 M M' W_1' & W_2 M M' W_2' \end{pmatrix}.$$

Note that since y_N is a scalar and $M_{N.}$ is a row vector, $C_{\varepsilon,(W_1y,W_2y)}$ must be expressed as an $N \times 2N$ matrix in order for the term on the right-hand side of (4A.5) be conformable for multiplication with $V^{-1}_{(W_1y,W_2y)}$ which is a $2N \times 2N$ matrix. Clearly, the right-hand side of (4A.5) will be a scalar because $M_{N.}$ is a row vector, and β and the term in brackets are column vectors.

3. Since X is nonstochastic, it can be ignored when applying (4.1.3). In particular, expressing the problem in the notation of (4.1.3) yields

$$E[E(y_N|X, Wy)] = \underset{Wy}{E}[\underset{y_N|Wy}{E}(y_N)] \tag{4A.7}$$
$$= E(y_N) = (I_N - \lambda W)^{-1}_{N.} X\beta.$$

Chapter 5

1. (a) The main problem is that the model is nonlinear in the parameters because of α, and formal results relating to such nonlinear spatial models are scarce. One might try the maximum likelihood procedure. In this case

$$y = (I_N - \lambda W)^{-1} X\beta + (I_N - \lambda W)^{-1}(I_N - \rho W)^{-1}\varepsilon \tag{5A.1}$$

and so, assuming $\varepsilon \sim N(0, \sigma^2 I_N)$,

$$y = N((I_N - \lambda W)^{-1} X\beta, \sigma_\varepsilon^2 \Omega_{\lambda,\rho,\alpha}) \tag{5A.2}$$

where $\Omega_{\lambda,\rho,\alpha} = (I_N - \lambda W)^{-1}(I_N - \rho W)^{-1}(I_N - \rho W')^{-1}(I_N - \lambda W')^{-1}$. Since the maximization of the likelihood corresponding to (5A.1) involves λ, ρ, α, β, and σ^2, it involves quite a bit of tediousness, especially for nonsparse weighting matrices.

(b) No. The model would not be a nonlinear spatial model and it can be estimated using standard procedures.

(c) Additional estimation issues would not arise since d is known.

2. Yes. If N_J did not vary over $J = 1, ..., G$ the model would not be useful. It would be extremely unlikely that the number of students in all the schools were the same.

Chapter 6

1. The second equation can also be written as

$$y_{i2} = b_1 + b_2 x_i + b_3 x_i^2 + b_4 x_i^3 + \varepsilon_{i2}, i =, ..., N, \tag{6A.1}$$

or

$$y_2 = X\beta + \varepsilon,$$

where $b_3 = b_4 = 0$, $X = (e_N, X, X^2, X^3)$ is the $N \times 4$ matrix of observations on the regressors in (6A.1) where X^J is the $N \times 1$ vector of observations on x_i raised to the Jth power, $J = 1, 2, 3$, etc. The first stage of 2SLS estimation of (6A.1) would be to do OLS and obtain the predicted values of y_2 by regressing it on all of the predetermined variables X, that is,

$$\hat{y}_2 = X\,\hat{\beta}, \qquad \hat{\beta} = (X'X)^{-1}X'y_2 \tag{6A.2}$$

where, using evident notation, $\hat{\beta}' = (\hat{b}_1, ..., \hat{b}_4)$.
Substituting (6A.1) into (6A.2) yields

$$\hat{\beta} = \beta + (X'X)^{-1}X'\varepsilon \tag{6A.3}$$

and so

$$E(\hat{\beta}) = \beta, \qquad E(\hat{\beta} - \beta)(\hat{\beta} - \beta)' = \sigma^2 (X'X)^{-1}. \tag{6A.4}$$

Under typical assumptions, $(X'X)^{-1} \to 0$. It follows from Chebyshev's inequality that $\hat{\beta} \xrightarrow{P} \beta = (b_1, b_2, 0, 0)'$. On an intuitive level, this means that in large samples $\hat{y}_2 = (e_N, X)(b_1, b_2)'$ and therefore the rank of the second stage regressor matrix (6.2.4) used to estimate (6.2.1) would only be 2, and thus be singular.

2. Let X be the $N \times 1$ vector whose ith value is x_i. Then, the ith row of the instrument matrix would be $[1, x_i, \exp(x_i), x_i \exp(x_i)]$.

3. **(a)** The minimum mean squared error (MMSE) of prediction is the conditional mean. If ε_{i2} is i.i.d. $N(0, \sigma_2^2)$, recall that $E[\exp(\varepsilon_{i2})] =$

$\exp(\sigma_2^2/2) > 0$ since $\exp(c) > 1$ for all $c > 0$, since $\exp(0) = 1$. Then, since the parameters are known, the MMSE predictor of y_{i1} is

$$\begin{aligned} E(y_{i1}) &= a_1 + a_2 \exp(b_1 + b_2 x_i) E[\exp(\varepsilon_{i2})] + a_3 x_i \\ &= a_1 + a_2 \exp(b_1 + b_2 x_i) \exp(\sigma_2^2/2) + a_3 x_i. \end{aligned} \tag{6A.5}$$

Therefore the predictor obtained by setting the error terms equal to zero is biased. The bias is

$$Bias_i = a_2 \exp(b_1 + b_2 x_i)[\exp(\sigma_2^2/2) - 1]. \tag{6A.6}$$

(b) In light of (6A.6), the bias will clearly be related to x_i – it is not a fixed constant.

Chapter 7

1. (a) Write the model in matrix form as $y = Xc + \varepsilon$, where the ith row of X is $(1, x_i^2)$, etc. Since y and X are part of the data, the posterior of c is

$$P(c|data) \propto \exp[\frac{1}{6}(y - Xc)'(y - Xc)]. \tag{7A.1}$$

Let $\hat{c} = (X'X)^{-1}X'y$. Using (7.5.1),

$$P(c|data) \propto \exp[\frac{1}{6}(\hat{c} - c)'X'X(\hat{c} - c)] \tag{7A.2}$$

and so $c \sim N[\hat{c}, 3(X'X)^{-1}]$. That is, the mean of c is just the least squares estimator of c. The VC matrix of c is exactly what it would be in the non-Bayesian framework, namely $3(X'X)^{-1}$.

(b) Again, let $\hat{c} = (X'X)^{-1}X'y$, and recall that $X'(y - X\hat{c}) = 0$. Also, let $\hat{\varepsilon} = (y - X\hat{c})$. Then the joint posterior for σ and c is

$$\begin{aligned} &P(c, \sigma|data) \\ &\propto \frac{1}{\sigma^{N+1}} \exp[-\frac{1}{2\sigma^2}(y - Xc)'(y - Xc)] \\ &\propto \frac{1}{\sigma^{N+1}} \exp[-\frac{1}{2\sigma^2}[(y - X\hat{c} + X\hat{c} - Xc)'(y - X\hat{c} + X\hat{c} - Xc)]] \\ &\propto \frac{1}{\sigma^{N+1}} \exp[-\frac{1}{2\sigma^2}[\hat{\varepsilon}'\hat{\varepsilon} + (\hat{c} - c)'X'X(\hat{c} - c)]] \\ &\propto \left[\frac{1}{\sigma^{N-2}} \exp[\frac{1}{2\sigma^2}(\hat{\varepsilon}'\hat{\varepsilon})]\right]\left[\frac{1}{\sigma^2} \exp[\frac{1}{2\sigma^2}(c - \hat{c})'X'X(c - \hat{c})]\right] \\ &\propto g_1(\sigma|data)g_2(\sigma, c|data) \end{aligned} \tag{7A.3}$$

where $g_1(\sigma|data) = (1/\sigma^{N-2})\exp[\frac{1}{2\sigma^2}\hat{\varepsilon}'\hat{\varepsilon}]$ and $g_2(\sigma, c|data) = (1/\sigma^2)\exp[\frac{1}{2\sigma^2}(\hat{c}-c)'X'X(\hat{c}-c)]$. Clearly, the conditional of c given σ is normal with mean and VC matrix $\hat{c}$ and $\sigma^2(X'X)^{-1}$, respectively, and so

$$\int_{-\infty}^{\infty} g_2(\sigma, c|data)dc \propto const. \tag{7A.4}$$

Therefore the marginal of σ is proportional to $g_1(\sigma|data)$, which implies that its marginal is an inverted gamma; see, e.g., (7.5.30) and (7.5.31).

2. (a) Express the model with obvious notation as $y = Z_\lambda c + \varepsilon$, where $Z_\lambda = (e_N, F_\lambda)$, e_N is an $N \times 1$ vector of one, F_λ is an $N \times 1$ vector whose ith element is $\exp(\lambda x_i^2)$, and $c = (a, b)$. Let $\hat{c}_\lambda = (Z_\lambda' Z_\lambda)^{-1} Z_\lambda' y$ and $\hat{\varepsilon}_\lambda = y - Z_\lambda \hat{c}_\lambda$. Given that λ and σ are known constants, the posterior $P(c|data)$ is, using (7A.3) and evident notation, given by

$$\begin{aligned} &P(c|data) \\ &\propto \frac{1}{\sigma^{N+1}}\exp[-\frac{1}{2\sigma^2}(\hat{\varepsilon}_\lambda'\hat{\varepsilon}_\lambda + (\hat{c}_\lambda - c)'Z_\lambda'Z_\lambda(\hat{c}_\lambda - c))] \\ &\propto \exp[-\frac{1}{2\sigma^2}(\hat{c}_\lambda - c)'Z_\lambda'Z_\lambda(\hat{c}_\lambda - c)]. \end{aligned} \tag{7A.5}$$

Thus, in this case $P(c|data)$ is normal with mean and VC matrix $\hat{c}_\lambda$ and $\sigma^2(Z_\lambda' Z_\lambda)^{-1}$, respectively.

(b) Let $\gamma = (c, \lambda)$ and recall that $c = (a, b)$. In this case the joint posterior for γ and σ is

$$\begin{aligned} P(\gamma, \sigma|data) &\propto \frac{1}{\sigma^{N+1}}\exp[-\frac{1}{2\sigma^2}(y - Z_\lambda c)'(y - Z_\lambda c)] \\ &\propto \frac{1}{(\sigma^2)^{\frac{N+1}{2}}}\exp[-\frac{1}{2\sigma^2}(y - Z_\lambda c)'(y - Z_\lambda c)]. \end{aligned} \tag{7A.6}$$

Manipulations identical to (7A.3) imply

$$\begin{aligned} &P(\gamma, \sigma|data) \\ &\propto \frac{1}{(\sigma^2)^{\frac{N+1}{2}}}\exp[-\frac{1}{2\sigma^2}(\hat{\varepsilon}_\lambda'\hat{\varepsilon}_\lambda + (\hat{c}_\lambda - c)'Z_\lambda'Z_\lambda(\hat{c}_\lambda - c))] \\ &\propto \frac{1}{(\sigma^2)^{\frac{N+1}{2}}}\exp[-\frac{A_{c,\lambda}}{2\sigma^2}] \end{aligned} \tag{7A.7}$$

where $A_{c,\lambda} = \hat{\varepsilon}'_\lambda \hat{\varepsilon}_\lambda + (\hat{c}_\lambda - c)' Z'_\lambda Z_\lambda (\hat{c}_\lambda - c)$. Thus, using (7.5.23)–(7.5.26), we get

$$P(\gamma|data) \propto \int_0^\infty \frac{1}{(\sigma^2)^{\frac{N+1}{2}}} \exp[-\frac{A_{c,\lambda}}{2\sigma^2}] d\sigma \tag{7A.8}$$
$$\propto A_{c,\lambda}^{-N/2}$$
$$\propto [\hat{\varepsilon}'_\lambda \hat{\varepsilon}_\lambda + (\hat{c}_\lambda - c)' Z'_\lambda Z_\lambda (\hat{c}_\lambda - c)]^{-N/2}.$$

Since λ is also unknown and random, the expression for $P(\gamma, \sigma|data)$ given in (7A.8) is not a multivariate t; see (7.5.28). Its normalizing constant can be obtained by numerical procedures.

3. **(a)** If σ^2 were not specified, the VC matrix of u would be $\rho^2\sigma^2(I_N + W)(I_N + W')$. In this case one would define $\phi^2 = \rho^2\sigma^2$, and estimate ϕ^2. The parameters ρ and σ^2 would not be separately identified. So the "restriction" that $\sigma^2 = 1$ simply avoids introducing a parameter which cannot be estimated.

(b) Let $V = (I_N + W)(I_N + W')$, $\hat{\beta} = (X'V^{-1}X)^{-1}X'V^{-1}y$, and $\hat{\varepsilon} = y - X\hat{\beta}$. Note that $V' = V$. Also note that

$$X'V^{-1}\hat{\varepsilon} = X'V^{-1}[y - X(X'V^{-1}X)^{-1}X'V^{-1}y] \tag{7A.9}$$
$$= X'V^{-1}y - X'V^{-1}y$$
$$= 0.$$

Then, the posterior of β and ρ is

$$P(\beta, \rho|data) \tag{7A.10}$$
$$\propto \frac{1}{\rho^N} \exp[-\frac{1}{2\rho^2}(y - X\beta)'V^{-1}(y - X\beta)]$$
$$\propto \frac{1}{\rho^N} \exp[-\frac{1}{2\rho^2}(y - X\hat{\beta} + X\hat{\beta} - X\beta)'V^{-1}(y - X\hat{\beta} + X\hat{\beta} - X\beta)]$$
$$\propto \frac{1}{\rho^N} \exp[-\frac{1}{2\rho^2}(\hat{\varepsilon}'\hat{\varepsilon} + (\beta - \hat{\beta})X'V^{-1}X(\beta - \hat{\beta}))].$$

Note that the part relating to β is in the form of a multivariate normal with mean $\hat{\beta}$ and VC matrix $\rho^2(X'V^{-1}X)^{-1}$.

(c) The posterior of ρ is

$$P(\rho|data) \tag{7A.11}$$
$$\propto \frac{1}{\rho^N} \exp[-\frac{1}{2\rho^2}(\hat{\varepsilon}'\hat{\varepsilon})] \int_\beta \exp[-\frac{1}{2\rho^2}((\beta - \hat{\beta})X'V^{-1}X(\beta - \hat{\beta}))] d\beta$$

$$\propto \frac{1}{\rho^{N+k}} \exp[-\frac{1}{2\rho^2}(\hat{\varepsilon}'\hat{\varepsilon})]$$

if β is a $k \times 1$.

4. Clearly, $X'Q'QX + 8FX = X'Q'QX - 2F^*X$, where $F^* = -4F$. Then using (7.5.1) the completed quadratic is

$$(X - (Q'Q)^{-1}F^{*\prime})'Q'Q(X - (Q'Q)^{-1}F^{*\prime}) - F^*(Q'Q)^{-1}F^{*\prime}. \quad (7A.12)$$

5. Since $g(x)$ is concave in the interval $(0, 25)$, one could estimate the value of G based on a sampling procedure in terms of

$$G = \int_0^{25} \frac{g(x)}{f(x)} f(x)dx, \quad (7A.13)$$

$$f(x) = \frac{1}{c}[\ln(50) + x^{1/2}],$$

$$c = 25\ln(50) + \frac{2}{3}(25)^{3/2}$$

$$\doteq 180.84.$$

Let $r(x) = g(x)/f(x)$. If $x_1, ..., x_N$ is a random sample from $f(x)$ then

$$\hat{G} = N^{-1}\sum_{i=1}^{N} r(x_i), \quad i = 1, ..., N. \quad (7A.14)$$

Chapter 8

1. $E(XZ) = \frac{1}{2}E(Z|X = 1) + \frac{1}{2}E(Z|X = 2)$.
2. **(a)** Let

$$v = 1 \text{ if } \hat{a}_1 + \hat{a}_2 \leq 0.9, \quad (8A.1)$$
$$v = 0 \text{ if } \hat{a}_1 + \hat{a}_2 > 0.9.$$

Also, let $p_1 = \Pr(v = 1)$ and $p_0 = \Pr(v = 0)$, and note that $E(v) = p_1$. The pretest estimator of $A = a_1 + a_2$ is

$$\hat{A} = v(\hat{a}_1 + \hat{a}_2) + (1 - v)0.9 \quad (8A.2)$$
$$= 0.9 - 0.9v + v(\hat{a}_1 + \hat{a}_2)$$

and so

$$E(\hat{A}) = 0.9 - 0.9E(v) + E[v(\hat{a}_1 + \hat{a}_2)] \quad (8A.3)$$
$$= 0.9 - 0.9p_1 + E[(\hat{a}_1 + \hat{a}_2)|(\hat{a}_1 + \hat{a}_2) \leq 0.9]p_1.$$

(b) Using evident notation, let S be the test statistic, and let H_0 be accepted if $S \leq S^{0.95}$, and H_1 be accepted if $S > S^{0.95}$. Let

$$\lambda = 1 \text{ if } S \leq S^{0.95}, \qquad (8A.4)$$
$$\lambda = 0 \text{ if } S > S^{0.95}.$$

Then

$$p\lim(\hat{A}|H_1) = p\lim(\lambda)p\lim(\hat{a}_1 + \hat{a}_2) + [1 - p\lim(\lambda)]0.9 \qquad (8A.5)$$
$$= 0.9$$

since $p\lim(\lambda) = 0$.

3. (a) Again using evident notation, let S be the test statistic, and assume that H_0 is accepted if $S \leq S^{0.95}$ and H_1 is accepted if $S > S^{0.95}$. Let

$$\phi = 1 \text{ if } H_0 \text{ is rejected}, \qquad (8A.6)$$
$$\phi = 0 \text{ if } H_0 \text{ is accepted},$$

and assume that the pretest estimator of λ_2 is

$$\tilde{\lambda}_2 = \phi\hat{\lambda}_{2,1} + (1 - \phi)\hat{\lambda}_{2,2}. \qquad (8A.7)$$

Note, under typical assumptions, and assuming that $\lambda_2 \neq 0$, $p\lim[\phi|H_1] = 1$, and so $p\lim[\hat{\lambda}_{2,1}|H_1] = \lambda_2$. Thus,

$$p\lim[\tilde{\lambda}_2|H_1] \qquad (8A.8)$$
$$= p\lim[\phi|H_1]p\lim[\hat{\lambda}_{2,1}|H_1] + (1 - p\lim[\phi|H_1])p\lim[\hat{\lambda}_{2,2}|H_1]$$
$$= \lambda_2.$$

(b) Again define ϕ as in (8A.6). Recall that under H_0 ϕ converges to a (0, 1) binary variable; see, e.g., Section 8.5. Let Φ denote that limiting binary variable. Again let the pretest estimator of λ_2 be as defined in (8A.7). Note that under typical conditions $p\lim[\hat{\lambda}_{2,1}|H_0] = p\lim[\hat{\lambda}_{2,2}|H_0] = \lambda_2$. It follows that

$$p\lim[\tilde{\lambda}_2|H_0] \qquad (8A.9)$$
$$= p\lim[\phi|H_0]p\lim[\hat{\lambda}_{2,1}|H_0] + (1 - p\lim[\phi|H_0])p\lim[\hat{\lambda}_{2,2}|H_0]$$
$$= \Phi\lambda_2 + (1 - \Phi)\lambda_2 = \lambda_2.$$

Thus, $\tilde{\lambda}_2$ is consistent.

4. Let $\tilde{W}$ be the estimated value of W, and let $W = \tilde{W} + \Delta_W$. In this case the researcher's considered model would be

$$y = X\beta + \lambda \tilde{W} y + \delta \tag{8A.10}$$

where $\delta = \varepsilon + \lambda \Delta_W\, y$, but the researcher would "not recognize", or account for, the term $\lambda \Delta_W\, y$ as part of the error term. Some problems relating to the term Δ_W are:

(a) Δ_W is endogenous because it is based on the elements of y which is obviously endogenous.

(b) The endogeneity problem of Δ_W is compounded because it is multiplied by y.

(c) There may also be a severe pretest problem because the estimated matrix $\tilde{W}$ may be arrived at by pretesting procedures.

5. Let

$$\begin{aligned} &\lambda = 1 \text{ if } H_0 \text{ is rejected,} \\ &\lambda = 0 \text{ if } H_0 \text{ is accepted.} \end{aligned} \tag{8A.11}$$

Then the pretest estimator of b based on the later data is

$$\tilde{b} = \lambda \hat{b}_1 + (1 - \lambda)\hat{b}_2 \tag{8A.12}$$

where $\hat{b}_1$ is obtained from M_1 and $\hat{b}_2$ is obtained from M_2. In this case λ is based entirely on the first part of the sample and so is independent of $\hat{b}_1$ and $\hat{b}_2$. Therefore

$$\begin{aligned} E(\tilde{b}|H_0) &= E(\lambda|H_0)E(\hat{b}_1|H_0) + (1 - E(\lambda|H_0))E(\hat{b}_2|H_0) \\ &= E(\lambda|H_0)[E(\hat{b}_1|H_0) - E(\hat{b}_2|H_0)] + E(\hat{b}_2|H_0) \\ &= E(\lambda|H_0)[b - b] + b = b. \end{aligned} \tag{8A.13}$$

Chapter 9

1. **(a)** Suppose X is an $N \times 1$ vector. Also let $|x_i| \le c_x$ and $|\sigma_i^2| \le c_\sigma$ where c_x and c_σ are finite constants. Then

$$N^{-1}X'DX = N^{-1}\sum_{i=1}^{N} x_i^2\sigma_i^2 \le c_x^2 c_\sigma^2 < \infty. \tag{9A.1}$$

(b) If X is an $N \times 1$ vector whose elements are

$$1, 2, 3, 1, 1, 2, 2, 3, 3, 1, 1, 1, 2, 2, 2, 3, 3, 3, 1, 1, 1, 1, \ldots, \tag{9A.2}$$

the product $N^{-1}X'DX$ will not converge because it will keep being dominated by the later sequences.

(c)

$$N^{-1}\sum_{i=1}^{N} x_i^2\hat{u}_i^2 = N^{-1}\sum_{i=1}^{N}[x_i^2u_i^2 + x_i^4\Delta_N^2 - 2x_i^3u_i\Delta_N] \qquad (9A.3)$$

$$= N^{-1}X'DX + N^{-1}\sum_{i=1}^{N} x_i^4\Delta_N^2 - 2N^{-1}\sum_{i=1}^{N} x_i^3u_i\Delta_N.$$

Consider $N^{-1}\sum_{i=1}^{N} x_i^4\Delta_N^2$. Since x_i is uniformly bounded in absolute value, say by c_x, $N^{-1}\sum_{i=1}^{N} x_i^4\Delta_N^2 \le c_x^2\Delta_N^2 \xrightarrow{P} 0$.

Now consider the second term, say $-2N^{-1}\sum_{i=1}^{N} x_i^3u_i\Delta_N = -2\Delta_N N^{-1}\sum_{i=1}^{N} x_i^3u_i$. Let $\Phi = N^{-1}\sum_{i=1}^{N} x_i^3u_i$ and note that

$$E(\Phi) = N^{-1}\sum_{i=1}^{N} x_i^3E(u_i) = 0 \qquad (9A.4)$$

and since u_i is not autocorrelated,

$$Var(\Phi) = N^{-2}\sum_{i=1}^{N} x_i^6\sigma_i^2 \le N^{-1}c_x^6c_\sigma^2 \to 0 \qquad (9A.5)$$

and so, by Tchebyshev's inequality, $\Phi \xrightarrow{P} 0$. In addition, since $\Delta_N \xrightarrow{P} 0$, it clearly follows from (9A.3) that $N^{-1}X'\hat{D}X - N^{-1}X'DX \xrightarrow{P} 0$.

2. If $\sum_{i=1}^{s}|\rho_i \max(i)| < 1$ then (9.2.1) can be written as $u = Au + \varepsilon$ where $A = \sum_{i=1}^{s}\rho_i W_i$, and where the row sums of A are uniformly bounded in absolute value less than 1. Therefore the roots of A are all less than 1; see, e.g., the discussion of Geršgorin's Theorem in Section 2.1.2. Therefore $u = (I_N - A)^{-1}\varepsilon$, where $(I_N - A)^{-1} = I_N + A + A^2 + \ldots$.

3. The change in G would be to add σ_{13} in the first row; σ_{24} in the second row; σ_{13} and σ_{35} in the third row, etc. In brief, just add the terms σ_{ij} where $|i - j| = 2$.

4. If a country, say country 2, is a central trading country which all other countries trade with, regardless of their geographical distance to country 2, then the second column sum in the weighting matrix may not be uniformly bounded in absolute value.

5. For the Epanechnikov kernel $K(x) = 1 - x^2$ if $0 \leq x \leq 1$ and $K(x) = 0$ if $x > 1$, we clearly have

$$\begin{aligned} K(0) &= 1, \\ K(x) &= 0 \text{ if } x > 1, \\ |K(x) - 1| &= |1 - x^2 - 1| \\ &= |x^2| \leq cx^2 \end{aligned} \tag{9A.6}$$

where $c = 1$.

Chapter 10

1. From (10.5.1) and (10.5.2),

$$y_3 = (I_N - \rho_1 W)_{3.}^{-1} X\beta + (I_N - \rho_1 W)_{3.}^{-1} P_3 \varepsilon \tag{10A.1}$$

where $N = N_1 + N_2 + N_3$, $P_3 = (P_{31}, P_{32}, P_{33})$, and $(I_N - \rho_1 W)_{3.}^{-1}$ are the last N_3 rows of $(I_N - \rho_1 W)^{-1}$. Thus

$$\begin{aligned} &(N_1 + N_2)^{-1/2} H_{2.2}' W_{23} y_3 \\ &= (N_1 + N_2)^{-1/2} H_{2.2}' W_{23}[(I_N - \rho_1 W)_{3.}^{-1} X\beta + \\ &(I_N - \rho_1 W)_{3.}^{-1} P_3 \varepsilon]. \end{aligned} \tag{10A.2}$$

For future reference, let q be the number of columns in $H_{2.2}$. Consider now the first term on the right-hand side of (10A.2), namely the $q \times k$ matrix $H_{2.2}' W_{23}(I_N - \rho_1 W)_{3.}^{-1} X$. Assuming, as usual, that the row and column sums of $(I_N - \rho_1 W)^{-1}$ and W are uniformly bounded in absolute value, the elements of the $q \times N_3$ matrix $H_{2.2}' W_{23}$ are all uniformly bounded by a finite constant. Similarly, the elements of the $N_3 \times k$ matrix $(I_N - \rho_1 W)_{3.}^{-1} X$ are uniformly bounded by a finite constant. It follows from **Point 4** following (2.1.4.4) in Chapter 2 that the elements of the matrix $H_{2.2}' W_{23}(I_N - \rho_1 W)_{3.}^{-1} X$ are at most of order N_3. Since $N_3/(N_1 + N_2)^{1/2} \to 0$, it follows that

$$(N_1 + N_2)^{-1/2} H_{2.2}' W_{23}(I_N - \rho_1 W)_{3.}^{-1} X\beta \to 0. \tag{10A.3}$$

Now consider the second term on the right-hand side of (10A.2), say

$$\delta = (N_1 + N_2)^{-1/2} H_{2.2}' W_{23}[(I_N - \rho_1 W)_{3.}^{-1} P_3 \varepsilon]. \tag{10A.4}$$

Clearly, $E(\delta) = 0$. Recalling that $\sigma^2 = 1$, the VC matrix of δ is

$$VC_\delta = (N_1 + N_2)^{-1}[H'_{2.2}W_{23}]FF'[H'_{2.2}W_{23}]' \tag{10A.5}$$
$$F = [(I_N - \rho_1 W)^{-1}_{3.} P_3].$$

Clearly, the elements of the $q \times N_3$ matrix $H'_{2.2}W_{23}$ are uniformly bounded in absolute value. The row and column sums of the matrix FF' are uniformly bounded in absolute value since those of $(I_N - \rho_1 W)^{-1}_{3.}$ and of P_3 are also bounded. It follows from Point 4 following (2.1.4.4) that the elements of the $q \times q$ VC matrix VC_δ are at most of order N_3. Therefore $VC_\delta \to 0$ if $N_3/(N_1 + N_2)^{1/2} \to 0$. It follows from Tchebyshev's inequality and (10A.2)–(10A.5) that

$$p\lim(N_1 + N_2)^{-1/2} H'_{2.2}W_{23}y_3 \to 0. \tag{10A.6}$$

2.

$$\begin{aligned} &E(\hat{c}_r|\varphi) \\ &= E(\hat{c}_{OLS}|\varphi) - [M'_{(1)}M_{(1)}]^{-1}R' \left\{R[M'_{(1)}M_{(1)}]^{-1}R'\right\}^{-1} * \\ &[RE(\hat{c}_{OLS}|\varphi) - \mu] \\ &= c - [M'_{(1)}M_{(1)}]^{-1}R' \left\{R[M'_{(1)}M_{(1)}]^{-1}R'\right\}^{-1} [Rc - \mu] \\ &= c \end{aligned} \tag{10A.7}$$

since $Rc - \mu = 0$.

3. Using (10.2.8) express $\hat{c}_r$ as

$$\hat{c}_r = [I - [M'_{(1)}M_{(1)}]^{-1}R' \left\{R[M'_{(1)}M_{(1)}]^{-1}R'\right\}^{-1} R]\hat{c}_{OLS} + Q \tag{10A.8}$$

where Q is a constant vector which does not involve $\hat{c}_{OLS}$. Let $G = I - H$ where $H = [M'_{(1)}M_{(1)}]^{-1}R' \left\{R[M'_{(1)}M_{(1)}]^{-1}R'\right\}^{-1} R$. Then $\hat{c}_r = G\hat{c}_{OLS}$ and so

$$\begin{aligned} VC_{\hat{c}_r} &= GVC_{OLS}G' \\ &= [I - H]VC_{OLS}[I - H]' \\ &= VC_{OLS} - VC_{OLS}H' - HVC_{OLS} + HVC_{OLS}H'. \end{aligned} \tag{10A.9}$$

The expression for $VC_{\hat{c}_r}$ in (10.2.9) follows by recalling that $VC_{OLS} = \sigma^2_\varepsilon[M'_{(1)}M_{(1)}]^{-1}$, and (tediously) multiplying out the terms in (10A.9).

4. Because normality would imply that $g(z_i\lambda)$ is linear and so consistency would then require that $N_1 \to \infty$. If the conditional mean were nonlinear, as one might expect for many joint distributions, consistency could be achieved if $N_1 \to \infty$, or if $N_2 \to \infty$. That is, one could have consistency even if N_1 remained bounded.
5. Let $\gamma = (a, \lambda)'$. Then, $\frac{\partial F}{\partial \gamma}$ is an $N \times 2$ matrix whose ith row is (first differentiating with respect to a and then λ)

$$[\exp(\lambda x_i), ax_i \exp(\lambda x_i)], \quad i = 1, ..., N. \tag{10A.10}$$

6. In the conditional mean formula given in (4.2.2) Z_1 and Z_2 are column vectors. If Z_1 and Z_2 were row vectors, respectively, $1 \times q_1$ and $1 \times q_2$, the conditional mean formula would be

$$\underset{1\times q_1}{E(Z_1|Z_2)} = \underset{1\times q_1}{\mu_1} + \underset{1\times q_2}{(Z_2 - \mu_2)} \underset{q_2\times q_2}{V_{22}^{-1}} \underset{q_2\times q_1}{V_{21}} \tag{10A.11}$$

where μ_1 and μ_2 are the unconditional means of Z_1 and Z_2, V_{22} is the VC matrix of Z_2, and the s, r element of V_{21} is $cov(Z_{2,s}, Z_{1,r})$, $s = 1, ..., q_2$ and $r = 1, ..., q_1$.

Applying (10A.11) to the expression in (10.2.2), where x_i is a scalar and z_i is a $1 \times p$ row vector, and x_i and z_i have zero means

$$\underset{1\times 1}{E(x_i|z_i)} = \underset{1\times p}{z_i} \underset{p\times p}{V_{zz}^{-1}} \underset{p\times 1}{V_{z,x}} \tag{10A.12}$$

where the notation should be evident.

Chapter 11

1. Since $h(\varepsilon_1, ..., \varepsilon_N)$ is scale free, $h(\frac{\varepsilon_1}{a}, ..., \frac{\varepsilon_N}{a}) = h(\varepsilon_1, ..., \varepsilon_N)$, where a is any constant. The joint moment generating function of $h(\varepsilon_1, ..., \varepsilon_N)$ and $Q = \sum_{i=1}^{N} {\varepsilon_i}^2$ for the case in which ε is i.i.d. $N(0, \sigma^2)$ is

$$\begin{aligned}\phi(t_1, t_2) &= E[e^{t_1 h(\varepsilon_1,...,\varepsilon_N)} e^{t_2 \Sigma_{i=1}^N \varepsilon_i^2}] \\ &= \int \frac{e^{t_1 h(\varepsilon_1,...,\varepsilon_N)}}{(2\pi)^{N/2}} e^{t_2 \Sigma_{i=1}^N {\varepsilon_i}^2} e^{-\frac{1}{2\sigma^2} \Sigma_{i=1}^N \varepsilon_i^2} d\varepsilon\end{aligned} \tag{11A.1}$$

where $d\varepsilon = d\varepsilon_1 ... d\varepsilon_N$. It follows from (11A.1) that

$$\begin{aligned}\phi(t_1, t_2) &= \int \frac{e^{t_1 h(\varepsilon_1,...,\varepsilon_N)}}{(2\pi)^{N/2}} e^{t_2 \Sigma_{i=1}^N {\varepsilon_i}^2 - \frac{1}{2\sigma^2} \Sigma_{i=1}^N \varepsilon_i^2} d\varepsilon \\ &= \int e^{t_1 h(\varepsilon_1,...,\varepsilon_N)} \frac{1}{(2\pi)^{N/2}} e^{[-\frac{1}{2}(\frac{1}{\sigma^2} - 2t_2) \Sigma_{i=1}^N \varepsilon_i^2]} d\varepsilon.\end{aligned} \tag{11A.2}$$

Let $z_i = (\frac{1}{\sigma^2} - 2t_2)^{1/2}\varepsilon_i$ and note that $d\varepsilon_i/dz_i = (\frac{1}{\sigma^2} - 2t_2)^{-1/2}, i = 1, ..., N$ and so, using evident notation, $d\varepsilon/dz = (\frac{1}{\sigma^2} - 2t_2)^{-N/2}$. Substituting z_i for ε_i into (11A.2), and recalling that $h(\varepsilon_1, ..., \varepsilon_N)$ is scale free, yields

$$\begin{aligned}\phi(t_1, t_2) &= \frac{1}{(\frac{1}{\sigma^2} - 2t_2)^{N/2}} \int e^{t_1 h(z_1,...,z_N)} e^{-\frac{1}{2}\Sigma_{i=1}^N z_i^2} dz \qquad (11A.3)\\ &= \frac{1}{(\frac{1}{\sigma^2} - 2t_2)^{N/2}} E[e^{t_1 h(z_1,...,z_N)}]\\ &= g_1(t_1)g_2(t_2).\end{aligned}$$

2. Recall that for any two matrices, say A and B, whose product is a square matrix, $Tr(AB) = Tr(BA)$. From (11.3.10)

$$\begin{aligned}E(I) &= c_1 Tr[P_x W] \qquad (11A.4)\\ &= c_1 Tr[X(X'X)^{-1}X'W]\\ &= c_1 Tr[X'WX(X'X)^{-1}]\\ &\propto c_1\end{aligned}$$

since, under typical assumptions, the elements of the $k \times k$ matrix $X'WX$ are of order N, and those of the $k \times k$ matrix $(X'X)^{-1}$ are of order N^{-1}, e.g., it is typically assumed that $N^{-1}(X'X) \to \Omega_{xx}$ which is a finite matrix. Now consider c_1 and note that

$$\begin{aligned}c_1 &= \frac{-N}{(N-k)\,[Tr(W'W + WW)]^{1/2}} \qquad (11A.5)\\ &= \frac{-N}{(N-k)} \frac{1}{[Tr(W'W + WW)]^{1/2}} \to 0\end{aligned}$$

since $\frac{-N}{(N-k)} \to -1$ and $[Tr(W'W + WW)]^{1/2} \to \infty$. It follows that $E(I) \to 0$. The reader can challenge his/her understanding by giving a similar "demonstration" that $var(I) \to 1$.

3. No as the function is not continuous, and its derivatives with respect to the elements of β are not continuous.

4. **(a)** Let L be the log-likelihood, and $£$ be the Lagrangian. Then $£$ is

$$£ = L(\beta) + \lambda'(R\beta - r) \qquad (11A.6)$$

where λ is a $h \times 1$ vectors of multipliers. The first order conditions are:

$$\frac{\partial £}{\partial \beta}|_{\hat{\beta}_r,\hat{\lambda}} = \frac{\partial L}{\partial \beta}|_{\hat{\beta}_r,\hat{\lambda}} + \frac{\partial \lambda' R\beta}{\partial \beta}|_{\hat{\beta}_r,\hat{\lambda}} \qquad (11A.7)$$

$$= -\frac{1}{2}[-2X'y + 2X'X\hat{\beta}_r] + R'\hat{\lambda}$$
$$= 0$$

where $\hat{\beta}_r$ is the restricted least squares estimator of β, and

$$\frac{\partial \pounds}{\partial \lambda}|_{\hat{\beta}_r, \hat{\lambda}} = R\hat{\beta}_r - r \qquad (11A.8)$$
$$= 0.$$

Multiplying the second line of (11A.7) across by $R(X'X)^{-1}$, and noting that (11A.8) implies $R\hat{\beta}_r = r$, we get

$$-\frac{1}{2}[-2R(X'X)^{-1}X'y + 2R\hat{\beta}_r] + R'\hat{\lambda} \qquad (11A.9)$$
$$= [R\hat{\beta}_{OLS} - r] + R(X'X)^{-1}R'\hat{\lambda} = 0.$$

The solution for $\hat{\lambda}$ from (11A.9) is

$$\hat{\lambda} = (R(X'X)^{-1}R')^{-1}[R\hat{\beta}_{OLS} - r]. \qquad (11A.10)$$

Substituting (11A.10) into the second line of (11A.7) yields

$$[X'y - X'X\hat{\beta}_r] + R'(R(X'X)^{-1}R')^{-1}[R\hat{\beta}_{OLS} - r] = 0 \qquad (11A.11)$$

and solving for $\hat{\beta}_r$ gives

$$\hat{\beta}_r = (X'X)^{-1}X'y \qquad (11A.12)$$
$$+ (X'X)^{-1}R'(R(X'X)^{-1}R')^{-1}[R\hat{\beta}_{OLS} - r]$$
$$= \hat{\beta}_{OLS} + (X'X)^{-1}R'(R(X'X)^{-1}R')^{-1}[R\hat{\beta}_{OLS} - r].$$

(b) The information matrix is

$$-E[\frac{\partial^2 \pounds}{\partial \beta \partial \beta'}] = -E\left[\frac{\partial(\frac{\partial \pounds}{\partial \beta})}{\partial \beta'}\right] = -E\left[\left(\frac{\partial(\frac{\partial \pounds}{\partial \beta})}{\partial \beta}\right)'\right] \qquad (11A.13)$$

which, in light of the second line in (11A.7), is just

$$-E[\frac{\partial^2 \pounds}{\partial \beta \partial \beta'}] = \frac{\partial[X'y - X'X\beta]}{\partial \beta} \qquad (11A.14)$$
$$= X'X.$$

We also need $\frac{\partial L}{\partial \beta}|_{\hat{\beta}_r}$ to determine the Lagrangian multiplier test. In light of the second line of (11A.7) and (11A.12), it should be evident that

$$\begin{aligned}
&\frac{\partial L}{\partial \beta}|_{\hat{\beta}_r} \quad (11A.15)\\
&= X'y - X'X\hat{\beta}_r\\
&= X'y - X'X[\hat{\beta}_{OLS} + (X'X)^{-1}R'(R(X'X)^{-1}R')^{-1}[R\hat{\beta}_{OLS} - r]]\\
&= R'(R(X'X)^{-1}R')^{-1}[R\hat{\beta}_{OLS} - r].
\end{aligned}$$

Thus, given (11A.14) and (11A.15), using the Lagrangian multiplier test statistics in (11.7.8), say TS; at the 5% level the hypothesis $H_0 : R\beta = r$ would be rejected if $TS > \chi^2(0.95)$.

Chapter 12

1. Using the conditional mean results in (4.2.2) of Chapter 4, the MMSE is

$$\begin{aligned}
E(y_i|x_i) &= a + x_i\beta + E(\varepsilon_i|x_i) \quad (12A.1)\\
&= a + x_i\beta + \underset{1\times k}{cov(\varepsilon_i, x_i)}\underset{k\times k}{V_{x_i}^{-1}}\underset{k\times 1}{(x_i' - \mu_x')}.
\end{aligned}$$

2. The parameters a and β can be estimated, say as $\hat{a}$ and $\hat{\beta}$, by 2SLS using the instruments $(1, x_i, z_i)$. The parameters relating to x_i can be estimated as

$$\begin{aligned}
\hat{\mu}_x' &= N^{-1}\sum_{i=1}^{N} x_i', \quad (12A.2)\\
\hat{V}_{x_i} &= N^{-1}\sum_{i=1}^{N} x_i'x_i.
\end{aligned}$$

The covariance row vector $cov(\varepsilon_i, x_i)$ can be estimated as

$$\begin{aligned}
\widehat{cov}(\varepsilon_i, x_i) &= N^{-1}\sum_{i=1}^{N} \hat{\varepsilon}_i x_i, \quad (12A.3)\\
\hat{\varepsilon}_i &= y_i - \hat{a} - x_i\hat{\beta}, \quad i = 1, ..., N.
\end{aligned}$$

3. The feasible form of the MMSE predictor of y_i is

$$y_i^P = \hat{a} + x_i\hat{\beta} + \widehat{cov}(\varepsilon_i, x_i)\hat{V}_{x_i}^{-1}(x_i' - \hat{\mu}_x'). \quad (12A.4)$$

4. The MMSE predictor of y_i conditional on x_i is $E(y_i|x_i)$, which is given in (12A.1). That predictor is based on the true values of the parameters involved. The feasible predictor given in (12A.4) is based on the estimated values of those parameters. In general, $E(y_i|x_i, \hat{a}, \hat{\beta}, \widehat{cov}(\varepsilon_i, x_i), \hat{V}_{x_i}^{-1}) \neq E(y_i|x_i)$, and so (12A.4) will not necessarily be the MMSE predictor of y_i.

5. Let the row normalized weighting matrix be W_1, and the matrix which is not row normalized be W_2. Note that W_1 and W_2 are identical, except that W_1 is row normalized. Since there are no other issues than the weighting matrix, the model based on W_1 is identical to the model based on W_2, except for the weighting matrix.
The model based on W_2 is

$$y = X\beta + \lambda W_2 y + u. \qquad (12A.5)$$

Given the specification $u = R\varepsilon$, the model in (12A.5) could be estimated by 2SLS to obtain $\hat{\beta}_2$ and $\hat{\lambda}_2$. In doing this, use the instrument set $H_2 = (X, W_2 X, W_2^2 X)$. Then, obtain the predicted value of y,

$$\hat{y}^P = X\hat{\beta}_2 + \hat{\lambda}_2 W_2 y. \qquad (12A.6)$$

A J-test of H_0 against H_1 would be in terms of the augmented model

$$y = X\beta + \lambda W_2 y + \alpha \hat{y}^P + u. \qquad (12A.7)$$

This model can be estimated by 2SLS in terms of the instruments $H = (H_1, W_1 X, W_1^2 X)$. Let $\hat{\alpha}/\hat{\sigma}_\alpha$ be the t-ratio relating to α, where $\hat{\sigma}_\alpha$ is the square root of the last diagonal element of the HAC estimator of the VC matrix of $\hat{\gamma} = (\hat{\beta}, \hat{\lambda}, \hat{\alpha})$. Then, at the 5% level if $|\hat{\alpha}/\hat{\sigma}_\alpha| > 1.96$ one would reject H_0.

Chapter 13

1. The SAR model can be written as $u = (I_N - \rho W)^{-1}\varepsilon$. It is typically assumed that the row and column sums of $(I_N - \rho W)^{-1}$ are uniformly bounded in absolute value, and that the elements of ε are i.i.d. $(0, \sigma_\varepsilon^2)$. Thus, the SAR model is a special case of the model specifying $u = R\varepsilon$ where R is an $N \times N$ matrix whose row and column sums are uniformly bounded in absolute value, and the elements of ε, say ε_i, are i.i.d. (0, 1). Note that if ε_i has a variance of σ_ε^2, then $u = R\varepsilon$ implies $u = (\sigma_\varepsilon R)(\frac{1}{\sigma_\varepsilon}\varepsilon) = R^*\varepsilon^*$ where the row and column sums of R^* are uniformly bounded in absolute value and the elements of ε^* are i.i.d. (0, 1).

2. **(a)** The first row of W is $[0, w_{1,2}, w_{1,3}, 0, 0, ..., 0]$ where

$$w_{ij} = \exp[(y_i + y_j)/(z_{i,1} + z_{j,2})] \text{ if } |i - j| \leq 2, \qquad (13A.1)$$
$$w_{ij} = 0, \text{ otherwise.}$$

(b) Clearly, W is endogenous because it is based on the dependent vector, and so it cannot be directly used in a typical fashion in the instrument matrix.
To estimate the model, the instruments can be based on X, X^2, z_1, z_1^2, z_2, z_2^2 and, perhaps higher powers, where z_1 and z_2 are the vectors of observations on $z_{i,1}$ and $z_{i,2}$ and X^2, z_1^2, z_2^2 are exactly the same as X, z_1 and z_2 except that each element is squared.
The instruments described below will involve a "predicted" value of W, say $\hat{W}$. Two forms of $\hat{W}$ can be considered. One imposes the zeroes in W and is described in the text by (13.4.2)–(13.5.10). This formulation is tedious but **"probably"** more efficient than the more direct, and simpler formulation described here which does not impose the zeroes but is more "user friendly."[1]
Let H_1 be

$$H_1 = [X, X^2, z_1, z_1^2, z_2, z_2^2]. \tag{13A.2}$$

Then, an alternative to the predicted value of W described in Section 13.5 is $\hat{W} = H_1(H_1'H_1)^{-1}H_1'W$. The instrument matrix which can be used to estimate the model is

$$H = (H_1, \hat{W}H_1). \tag{13A.3}$$

Rewrite the model as

$$\begin{aligned} y &= ZC + u, \\ Z &= (X, Wy), \quad C = (\beta', \lambda)', \end{aligned} \tag{13A.4}$$

and let $\hat{Z} = H(H'H)^{-1}H'Z$ The estimator of C is

$$\hat{C} = (\hat{Z}'\hat{Z})^{-1}\hat{Z}'y. \tag{13A.5}$$

(c) If z_1 and z_2 are endogenous, and if a matrix of observations on q_i is available, say q, then the estimation of the model can be done in exactly the same way as described above in point (b) except that in place of z_1, z_1^2, z_2, z_2^2, H_1 would involve the matrix q.

3. (a) First note that $P_{\hat{H}} = \hat{H}(\hat{H}'\hat{H})^{-1}\hat{H}'$ is symmetric and idempotent, i.e., $P_{\hat{H}}P_{\hat{H}} = P_{\hat{H}}$, and so $\hat{Z}'Z = Z'P_{\hat{H}}Z = Z'P_{\hat{H}}P_{\hat{H}}Z = \hat{Z}'\hat{Z}$. Then from

1. To date, there are no small sample Monte Carlo results relating to the efficiencies obtained by the use of the two forms of $\hat{W}$ described in this problem. One strongly suspects that the more zeroes W has, the more efficient the estimators based on $\hat{W}$ described in (13.4.2)–(13.5.10) will be.

(13.2.1) and (13.6.2),

$$\begin{aligned}\hat{C} &= (\hat{Z}'\hat{Z})^{-1}\hat{Z}'[ZC + u] \\ &= C + (\hat{Z}'\hat{Z})^{-1}\hat{Z}'R\varepsilon.\end{aligned} \tag{13A.6}$$

Therefore

$$N^{1/2}(\hat{C} - C) = N(\hat{Z}'\hat{Z})^{-1}[N^{-1}Z'\hat{H}][N(\hat{H}'\hat{H})^{-1}][N^{-1/2}\hat{H}'R\varepsilon]. \tag{13A.7}$$

(b) In light of (13A.3), $\hat{H}$ depends upon W, i.e., $\hat{W} = H_1(H_1'H_1)^{-1}H_1'W$, which depends upon the dependent variable. Thus, $\hat{H}$ is endogenous.

Chapter 14

1. Note that even with the restrictions, the equations are interrelated because of appearance of y_1 in the second equation, and y_2 in the first. However, under the restrictions, there are no additional endogenous variables. To estimate the first equation, use the instrument matrix

$$H = (X_1, W_{11}X_1, W_{11}^2X_1, X_2, W_{22}X_2, W_{22}^2X_2) \tag{14A.1}$$

where we have not indicated cross-products which could also be used, namely $W_{11}W_{22}X_1$, etc.

2. If $\delta_1 \neq 0$ then there are additional endogenous variables in the first equation. In this case one could estimate the first equation by expanding the instrument H as $H_1 = (H, \Phi, W_{11}\Phi, W_{11}^2\Phi, W_{22}\Phi, W_{22}^2\Phi)$.

3. Estimate $\rho_{2,1}$ and $\rho_{2,2}$ in the usual way, that is, estimate each equation by 2SLS, obtain the residuals, and use the GMM procedure to obtain $\hat{\rho}_{2,1}$ and $\hat{\rho}_{2,2}$. The instrument matrix could be taken to be H in (14.3.7). Then in (14.8.10) replace $\hat{Z}(\rho_2)$ by $\hat{Z}(\hat{\rho}_2)$ and $y(\rho_2)$ by $y(\hat{\rho}_2)$ which would be defined by (14.8.1). Replace Σ by I_2 in (14.8.10). Then the resulting estimator of γ is

$$\hat{\gamma} = (\hat{Z}(\hat{\rho}_2)'\hat{Z}(\hat{\rho}_2))^{-1}\hat{Z}(\hat{\rho}_2)'y(\hat{\rho}_2). \tag{14A.2}$$

4. Recall that $\hat{Z} = H(H'H)^{-1}H'Z$ and $H(H'H)^{-1}H'$ is symmetric idempotent. Given the result in (14.6.2),

$$\begin{aligned}&N^{1/2}(\hat{\gamma} - \gamma) \\ &= ([N^{-1}Z'H][N\ (H'H)^{-1}][N^{-1}H'Z])^{-1}[N^{-1}Z'H]* \\ &(N^{-1}H'H)^{-1}[N^{-1/2}H'u].\end{aligned} \tag{14A.3}$$

Assumptions 14.1–14.5 imply

$$([N^{-1}Z'H][N(H'H)^{-1}][N^{-1}H'Z])^{-1} \tag{14A.4}$$
$$\xrightarrow{P} (Q'_{HZ}Q^{-1}_{HH}Q_{HZ})^{-1},$$
$$N^{-1}Z'H \xrightarrow{P} Q'_{HZ},$$
$$N^{-1}H'H \xrightarrow{P} Q_{HH}.$$

Recall from (14.3.11) that $u = R\varepsilon$. By the central limit theorem in (A.15.1) of the appendix on large sample theory,

$$N^{-1/2}H'R\varepsilon \xrightarrow{D} N(0, Q_{HRRH}). \tag{14A.5}$$

The result in (14.6.3) then follows from (14A.4), (14A.5), and the result (A.10.3) in the appendix on large sample theory.

Chapter 15

1.

$$Q_0Q_0 = [(I_T - \frac{J_T}{T}) \otimes I_N][(I_T - \frac{J_T}{T}) \otimes I_N] \tag{15A.1}$$
$$= (I_T - \frac{J_T}{T})(I_T - \frac{J_T}{T}) \otimes I_N I_N.$$

Since $e'_T e_T = T$, $J_T J_T = e_T(e'_T e_T)e'_T = T(e_T e'_T) = TJ_T$, it follows that $(I_T - \frac{J_T}{T})(I_T - \frac{J_T}{T}) = (I_T - \frac{J_T}{T})$ and so $Q_0Q_0 = Q_0$.
Now consider Q_1Q_1 and recall that $J_T J_T = TJ_T$. Then

$$Q_1Q_1 = [\frac{J_T}{T} \otimes I_N][\frac{J_T}{T} \otimes I_N] \tag{15A.2}$$
$$= \frac{J_T}{T}\frac{J_T}{T} \otimes I_N$$
$$= \frac{J_T}{T} \otimes I_N = Q_1.$$

Now consider $Q_0 + Q_1 = [(I_T - \frac{J_T}{T}) \otimes I_N] + [\frac{J_T}{T} \otimes I_N] = I_T \otimes I_N = I_{NT}$, and $Q_0Q_1 = [(I_T - \frac{J_T}{T}) \otimes I_N][\frac{J_T}{T} \otimes I_N] = (\frac{J_T}{T} - \frac{J_T J_T}{T^2}) \otimes I_N = (\frac{J_T}{T} - \frac{J_T}{T}) \otimes I_N = 0$.
Finally, compute $Q_0(e_T \otimes G) = [(I_T - \frac{J_T}{T}) \otimes I_N](e_T \otimes G) = [(e_T - \frac{J_T e_T}{T}) \otimes G] = (e_T - e_T) \otimes G = 0$.

2.

$$\begin{aligned}\Omega_\varepsilon &= \sigma_\mu^2(e_T \otimes I_N)(e_T \otimes I_N)' + \sigma_v^2 I_{NT} \\ &= \sigma_\mu^2(e_T e_T' \otimes I_N) + \sigma_v^2 I_{NT} \\ &= \sigma_\mu^2(J_T \otimes I_N) + \sigma_v^2 I_{NT} \\ &= \sigma_\mu^2 T(\frac{J_T}{T} \otimes I_N) + \sigma_v^2 I_{NT} \\ &= T\sigma_\mu^2 Q_1 + \sigma_v^2 I_{NT} \\ &= \sigma_v^2 Q_0 + \sigma_1^2 Q_1\end{aligned} \tag{15A.3}$$

where $\sigma_1^2 = \sigma_v^2 + T\sigma_\mu^2$.
To see the equivalence of the last two lines in (15A.3), note that

$$\sigma_v^2 Q_0 + \sigma_1^2 Q_1 = [\sigma_v^2(I_T - \frac{J_T}{T}) \otimes I_N] + (\sigma_v^2 + T\sigma_\mu^2)(\frac{J_T}{T} \otimes I_N). \tag{15A.4}$$

Bringing together the terms involving σ_v^2, we have

$$\begin{aligned}&[\sigma_v^2(I_T - \frac{J_T}{T}) \otimes I_N] + \sigma_v^2(\frac{J_T}{T} \otimes I_N) \\ &= \sigma_v^2(I_T \otimes I_N) = \sigma_v^2 I_{NT}.\end{aligned} \tag{15A.5}$$

The remaining term in (15A.4) is

$$T\sigma_\mu^2(\frac{J_T}{T} \otimes I_N) = T\sigma_\mu^2 Q_1. \tag{15A.6}$$

The equivalence of the last two lines in (15A.3) follows from (15A.5) and (15A.6).

3. Using the results in (15A.1), $(aQ_0 + bQ_1)(a^{-1}Q_0 + b^{-1}Q_1) = Q_0Q_0 + ab^{-1}Q_0Q_1 + ba^{-1}Q_1Q_0 + Q_1Q_1 = Q_0 + Q_1 = I_{NT}$.

4. **(a)** The equations determining the variables in Y must be known.

(b) Yes, the model in (15.4.1) can still be estimated because the number of linearly independent columns (instruments) obtained from the general system determining Y, namely $[(I_T \otimes W)\Phi, (I_T \otimes W^2)\Phi]$, can still be greater than h, the number of variables in Y. In a sense each variable in the system generating the elements of Y is "probably" correlated with many of the other variables in that general system. However, if $r < h$, the instruments used in this manner will probably be weak.

References

[1] Abreu, M., de Groot, H. and Florax, R. 2005. Space and Growth: A Survey of Empirical Evidence and Methods. *Région et Développement*, 21: 12-43.

[2] Afifi, A. and Elashoff, R. 1966. Missing Observations in Multivariate Statistics I. Review of the Literature. *Journal of the American Statistical Association*, 61: 595-604.

[3] Afifi, A. and Elashoff, R. 1967. Missing Observations in Multivariate Statistics II. Point Estimation in Linear Regression. *Journal of the American Statistical Association*, 62: 10-29.

[4] Ajilore, O. and Smith, J. 2011. Ethnic Fragmentation and Police Spending. *Applied Economic Letters*, 18(4): 329-332.

[5] Amaral, P. and Anselin, L. 2014. Finite Sample Properties of Moran's I Test for Spatial Autocorrelation in Tobit Models. *Papers in Regional Sciences*, 93(4): 773-781.

[6] Amaral, P., Arribas-Bel, D. and Anselin, L. 2013. Testing for Spatial Error Dependence in Probit Models. *Letters in Spatial and Resource Sciences*, 6(2): 91-101.

[7] Amemiya, T. 1985. *Advanced Econometrics*. Cambridge: Harvard University Press.

[8] Andrews, D. 1991. Heteroscedasticity and Autocorrelation Consistent Covariance Matrix Estimation. *Econometrica*, 59: 817-858.

[9] Angeriz, A., McCombie, J. and Roberts, M. 2009. Increasing Returns and the Growth of Industries in the EU Regions: Paradoxes and Conundrums. *Spatial Economic Analysis*, 4: 127-148.

[10] Anselin, L. 2011. Estimation of Spatial Error Autocorrelation With and Without Heteroskedasticity. *Manuscript*.

[11] Anselin, L. 2009. Spatial Regression. In *The Sage Handbook of Spatial Analysis*, Forthering-ham, A.S. and Rogerson, P.A. (eds.), pp. 255-275. *Manuscript*.

[12] Anselin, L. 2002. Under the Hood Issues in the Specification and Interpretation of Spatial Regression Models. *Agricultural Economics*, 27: 247-267.

[13] Anselin, L. 2001. Rao's Score Test in Spatial Econometrics. *Journal of Statistical Planning and Inference*, 97: 113-139.

[14] Anselin, L. 1992. SpaceStat Tutorial. A Workbook for Using SpaceStat in the Analysis of Spatial Data. *Manuscript*.

[15] Anselin, L. 1988. *Spatial Econometrics: Methods and Models*. Boston: Kluwer Academic Publishers.

[16] Anselin, L. 1986. Non-Nested Tests on the Weight Structure in Spatial Autoregressive Models: Some Monte Carlo Results. *Journal of Regional Science*, 26: 267-284.

[17] Anselin, L. and Bera, A. 1998. Spatial Dependence in Linear Regression Models With an Introduction to Spatial Econometrics. In *The Handbook of Applied Economic Statistics*, Ullah, A. and Giles, D. (eds.). New York: Marcel Dekker, pp. 237-289.

[18] Anselin, L. and Florax, R. (eds.) 1995a. *New Directions in Spatial Econometrics*. London: Springer.

[19] Anselin, L. and Florax, R. 1995b. Small Sample Properties of Tests for Spatial Dependence in Regression Models. In *New Directions in Spatial Econometrics*, Anselin, L. and Florax, R. (eds.). New York, NY: Springer.

[20] Anselin, L., Florax, R. and Rey, S. (eds.) 2004. *Advances in Spatial Econometrics*. New York: Springer.

[21] Anselin, L., Le Gallo, J. and Jayet, H. 2008. Spatial Panel Econometrics. In *The Econometrics of Panel Data, Fundamentals and Recent Developments in Theory and Practice*, Matyas, L. and Sevestre, P. (eds.), 3rd ed. Dordrecht: Kluwer, pp. 901-969.

[22] Anselin, L. and Lozano-Gracia, N. 2008. Errors in Variables and Spatial Effects in Hedonic House Price Models of Ambient Air Quality. *Empirical Economics*, 34(1): 5-34.

[23] Anselin, L. and Moreno, R. 2003. Properties of Tests for Spatial Error Components. *Regional Science and Urban Economics*, 33(5): 595-618.

[24] Anselin, L. and Rey, R. 2014. *Modern Spatial Econometrics in Practice: A Guide to GeoDa, GeoDaSpace and PySAL*. Chicago: GeoDa Press.

[25] Anselin, L. and Rey, S. 1991. Properties of Tests for Spatial Dependence in Linear Regression Models. *Geographical Analysis*, 23: 110-131.

[26] Arbia, G. 2014. *A Primer for Spatial Econometrics: With Applications in R*. New York: Palgrave Macmillan.

[27] Arbia, G. 2006. *Spatial Econometrics: Statistical Foundations and Applications to Regional Convergence*. Berlin: Springer.

[28] Arbia, G., Le Gallo, J. and Piras, G. 2008. Does Evidence on Regional Economic Convergence Depend on the Estimation Strategy? Outcomes From Analysis of a Set of NUTS2 EU Regions. *Spatial Economic Analysis*, 3: 209-224.

[29] Arellano, M. 2003. *Panel Data Econometrics*. Oxford: Oxford University Press.

[30] Arellano, M. and Bond, S. 1991. Some Tests of Specification for Panel Data: Monte Carlo Evidence and an Application to Employment Equations. *Review of Economic Studies*, 58: 277-297.

[31] Autant-Bernard, C. and LeSage, J. 2011. Quantifying Knowledge Spillovers Using Spatial Econometric Models. *Journal of Regional Science*, 51: 471-496.

[32] Badinger, H. and Egger, P. 2011. Estimation of Higher-Order Spatial Autoregressive Cross-Section Models With Heteroscedastic Disturbances. *Papers in Regional Science*, 90: 213-235.

[33] Baltagi, B. 2005. *Econometric Analysis of Panel Data*, 3rd ed. Hoboken: John Wiley & Sons, Ltd.

[34] Baltagi, B., Bresson, G. and Pirotte, A. 2012. Forecasting With Spatial Panel Data. *Computational Statistics and Data Analysis*, 56: 3381-3397.

[35] Baltagi, B., Egger, P. and Pfaffermayr, M. 2008. A Monte Carlo Study for Pure and Pretest Estimators of a Panel Data Model With Spatially Autocorrelated Disturbances. *Annales d'Économie et de Statistique*, 87/88: 11-38.

[36] Baltagi, B., Fingleton, B. and Pirotte, A. 2014a. Spatial Lag Models With Nested Random Effects: An Instrumental Variable Procedure With an Application to English House Prices. *Journal of Urban Economics*, 80: 76-86.

[37] Baltagi, B., Fingleton, B. and Pirotte, A. 2014b. Estimating and Forecasting With a Dynamic Spatial Panel Data Model. *Oxford Bulletin of Economics and Statistics*, 76: 112-138.

[38] Baltagi, B. and Levin, D. 1986. Estimating Dynamic Demand for Cigarettes Using Panel Data: The Effects of Bootlegging, Taxation and Advertising Reconsidered. *The Review of Economics and Statistics*, 68: 148-155.

[39] Baltagi, B. and Levin, D. 1992. Cigarette Taxation: Raising Revenues and Reducing Consumption. *Structural Change and Economic Dynamics*, 3: 321-335.

[40] Baltagi, B. and Li, D. 2006. Prediction in the Panel Data Model With Spatial Correlation: The Case of Liquor. *Spatial Economic Analysis*, 1: 175-185.

[41] Baltagi, B. and Li, D. 2004. Testing for Linear and Log-Linear Models Against Box–Cox Alternatives With Spatial Lag Dependence. *Advances in Econometrics*, 18: 35-74.
[42] Baltagi, B. and Pinnoi, N. 1995. Public Capital Stock and State Productivity Growth: Further Evidence From an Error Components Model. *Empirical Economics*, 20(2): 351-359.
[43] Baltagi, B. and Liu, L. 2011. Instrumental Variable Estimation of a Spatial Autoregressive Panel Model With Random Effects. *Economics Letters*, 111: 135-137.
[44] Baltagi, B., Song, S. and Koh, W. 2003. Testing Panel Data Regression Models With Spatial Error Correlation. *Journal of Econometrics*, 117: 123-150.
[45] Banerjee, S., Carlin, B.P. and Gelfand, A.E. 2003. *Hierarchical Modeling and Analysis for Spatial Data*. Chapman and Hall/CRC.
[46] Barry, R.P. and Pace, R.K. 1999. Monte Carlo Estimates of the Log Determinant of Large Sparse Matrices. *Linear Algebra and its Applications*, 289: 41-54.
[47] Bartels, C. and Hordijk, L. 1977. On the Power of the Moran Contiguity Coefficient in Testing for Spatial Correlation Among Regression Disturbances. *Regional Science and Urban Economics*, 7: 83-101.
[48] Bavaud, F. 1998. Models for Spatial Weights: A Systematic Look. *Geographic Analysis*, 30: 153-171.
[49] Beron, K. and Vijverberg, W. 2004. Probit in a Spatial Context: A Monte Carlo Analysis. In *Advances in Spatial Econometrics. Methodology, Tools and Applications*, Anselin, L., Florax, R. and Rey, S. (eds.). Berlin: Springer, pp. 169-195.
[50] Besag, J., York, J. and Mollie, A. 1991. Bayesian Image Restoration, With Two Applications in Spatial Statistics. *Annals of the Institute of Statistical Mathematics*, 43: 1-20.
[51] Bierens, H. 1994. *Topics in Advanced Econometrics: Estimation, Testing, and Specification of Cross-Section and Time Series Models*. Cambridge University Press.
[52] Bivand, R. 2002. Spatial Econometrics Functions in R: Classes and Methods. *Journal of Geographical Systems*, 4(4): 405-421.
[53] Bivand, R. and Piras, G. 2015. Comparing Implementations of Estimation Methods for Spatial Econometrics. *Journal of Statistical Software*, 63(18): 1-36.
[54] Blundell, R. and Bond, S. 1998. Initial Conditions and Moment Restrictions in Dynamic Panel Data Models. *Journal of Econometrics*, 87: 115-143.
[55] Bolduc, D., Laferriere, R. and Santarossa, G. 1995. Spatial Autoregressive Error Components in Travel Flow Models: An Application to Aggregate Mode Choice. In *New Directions in Spatial Econometrics*, Anselin, L. and Florax, R. (eds.). Berlin: Springer.
[56] Borcard, D. and Legendre, P. 2002. All Scale Spatial Analysis of Ecological Data by Means of Principal Coordinates of Neighboring Matrices. *Ecological Modelling*, 153: 51-68.
[57] Brockwell, P. and Davis, R. 1991. *Time Series: Theory and Methods*, second ed. Berlin: Springer-Verlag.
[58] Brueckner, J.K. 2003. Strategic Interactions Among Governments: An Overview of Empirical Studies. *International Regional Science Review*, 26: 175-188.
[59] Burridge, P. 2012. Improving the J Test in the SARAR Model by Likelihood-Based Estimation. *Spatial Economic Analysis*, 7: 75-107.
[60] Burridge, P. 1980. On the Cliff–Ord Test for Spatial Correlation. *Journal of the Royal Statistical Society, B*, 42: 107-108.
[61] Cameron, S. and Trivedi, P. 2005. *Microeconometrics*. Cambridge: Cambridge University Press.
[62] Case, A., Hines Jr., J.R. and Rosen, H. 1993. Budget Spillovers and Fiscal Policy Interdependence: Evidence From the States. *Journal of Public Economics*, 52: 285-307.
[63] Case, A. 1991. Spatial Patterns in Household Demand. *Econometrica*, 59: 953-966.
[64] Casella, G. and George, E.I. 1992. Explaining the Gibbs Sampler. *American Statistician*, 46: 167-174.

[65] Cliff, A. and Ord, J. 1981. *Spatial Process: Models and Applications*. London: Pion.

[66] Cliff, A. and Ord, J. 1973. *Spatial Autocorrelation*. London: Pion.

[67] Cliff, A. and Ord, J. 1972. Testing for Spatial Autocorrelation Among Regression Residuals. *Geographic Analysis*, 4: 267-284.

[68] Cochrane, D. and Orcutt, G. 1949. Applications of Least Squares Regressions to Relationships Containing Autocorrelated Error Terms. *Journal of the American Statistical Association*, 44: 32-61.

[69] Cohen, J. and Morrison, P.C. 2004. Public Infrastructure Investment, Interstate Spatial Spillovers, and Manufacturing Costs. *The Review of Economics and Statistics*, 86: 551-560.

[70] Conley, T. and Dupor, B. 2003. A Spatial Analysis of Sectoral Complementarity. *Journal of Political Economy*, 111: 311-352.

[71] Conley, T. and Ligon, E. 2002. Economic Distance, Spillovers and Cross Country Comparison. *Journal of Economic Growth*, 7: 157-187.

[72] Cornwell, C. and Trumbull, W.N. 1994. Estimating the Economic Model of Crime With Panel Data. *The Review of Economics and Statistics*, 76(2): 360-366.

[73] Corrado, L. and Fingleton, B. 2012. Where Is the Economics in Spatial Econometrics? *Journal of Regional Science*, 52: 210-239.

[74] Cressie, N.A.C. 1993. *Statistics for Spatial Data*. New York: Wiley.

[75] Dall'Erba, S., Percoco, M. and Piras, G. 2008. The European Regional Growth Process Revisited. *Spatial Economic Analysis*, 3(1): 7-25.

[76] Das, D., Kelejian, H. and Prucha, I. 2003. Finite Sample Properties of Estimators of Spatial Autoregressive Models With Autoregressive Disturbances. *Papers in Regional Science*, 82: 1-26.

[77] Dastoor, N. 1983. Some Aspects of Testing Non-Nested Hypothesis. *Journal of Econometrics*, 21: 213-228.

[78] Davidson, R. and MacKinnon, J. 1981. Several Tests for Model Specification in the Presence of Alternative Hypotheses. *Econometrica*, 49: 781-794.

[79] de Jong, R.M. and Davidson, J. 2000. Consistency of Kernel Estimators of Heteroscedastic and Autocorrelated Covariance Matrices. *Econometrica*, 68: 407-423.

[80] Dhrymes, P. 1978. *Econometrics: Statistical Foundation and Applications*. New York: Harper and Row.

[81] Dhrymes, P. 1970. *Introductory Econometrics*. New York: Springer-Verlag.

[82] Di Tella, R. and Schargrodsky, E. 2004. Do Police Reduce Crime? Estimates Using the Allocation of Police Forces After a Terrorist Attack. *American Economic Review*, 94(1): 115-133.

[83] Douc, R., Guillin, A., Marin, J. and Robert, C. 2007. Convergence of Adaptive Mixtures of Importance Sampling Schemes. *The Annals of Statistics*, 35: 420-448.

[84] Driscoll, J. and Kraay, A. 1998. Consistent Covariance Matrix Estimation With Spatially Dependent Panel Data. *The Review of Economics and Statistics*, 80: 549-560.

[85] Drukker, D.M., Egger, P. and Prucha, I.R. 2013a. On Two-Step Estimation of a Spatial Autoregressive Model With Autoregressive Disturbances and Endogenous Regressors. *Econometric Reviews*, 32(5–6): 686-733.

[86] Drukker, D.M., Peng, H., Prucha, I.R. and Raciborski, R. 2013b. Creating and Managing Spatial-Weighting Matrices With the spmat Command. *Stata Journal*, 13(2): 242-286.

[87] Drukker, D.M., Prucha, I.R. and Raciborski, R. 2013c. A Command for Estimating Spatial-Autoregressive Models With Spatial-Autoregressive Disturbances and Additional Endogenous Variables. *Stata Journal*, 13(2): 287-301.

[88] Drukker, D.M., Prucha, I.R. and Raciborski, R. 2013d. Maximum Likelihood and Generalized Spatial Two-Stage Least-Squares Estimators for a Spatial-Autoregressive Model With Spatial-Autoregressive Disturbances. *Stata Journal*, 13(2): 221-241.

[89] Dubin, R. 2004. Spatial Lags and Spatial Errors Revisited: Some Monte Carlo Evidence. In *Advances in Econometrics: Spatial and Spatiotemporal Econometrics*, LeSage, J. and Pace, K. (eds.). Emerald.

[90] Dubin, R. 1992. Spatial Autocorrelation and Neighborhood Quality. *Regional Science and Urban Economics*, 22(3): 433-452.

[91] Dubin, R. 1995. Estimating Spatial Models With Spatial Dependence. In *New Directions in Spatial Econometrics*, Anselin, L. and Florax, R. (eds.). New York: Springer, pp. 229-238.

[92] Easterly, W. and Levine, R. 1998. Troubles With the Neighbours: Africa's Problem, Africa's Opportunity. *Journal of African Economics*, 7: 120-142.

[93] Elhorst, P. 2014. *Spatial Econometrics: From Cross Sectional Data to Spatial Panels*. New York: Springer.

[94] Elhorst, P. 2010. Dynamic Panels With Endogenous Interactions Effects When T Is Small. *Regional Science and Urban Economics*, 40: 272-282.

[95] Elhorst, P. 2009. Spatial Panel Data Models. In *Handbook of Applied Spatial Analysis*, Fischer, M. and Getis, A. (eds.). Berlin, Heidelberg: Springer, pp. 377-407.

[96] Elhorst, P. 2005. Unconditional Maximum Likelihood Estimation of Linear and Log-Linear Dynamic Models for Spatial Panels. *Geographical Analysis*, 37: 85-106.

[97] Elhorst, P., Lacombe, D. and Piras, G. 2012. On Model Specification and Parameter Space Definitions in Higher Order Spatial Econometric Models. *Regional Science and Urban Economics*, 42(1): 211-220.

[98] Fingleton, B. 2008a. A Generalized Method of Moments Estimator for a Spatial Panel Model With an Endogenous Spatial Lag and Spatial Moving Average Error Terms. *Spatial Economic Analysis*, 3: 27-44.

[99] Fingleton, B. 2008b. Housing Supply, Housing Demand, and Affordability. *Urban Studies*, 45(8): 1545-1563.

[100] Fingleton, B. and Le Gallo, J. 2008. Estimating Spatial Models With Endogenous Variables, a Spatial Lag and Spatially Dependent Disturbances: Finite Sample Properties. *Papers in Regional Science*, 87: 319-339.

[101] Fingleton, B. and Palombi, S. 2015. Bootstrap J Test for Panel Models With Spatially Dependent Error Components, a Spatial Lag and Additional Endogenous Variables. *Spatial Economic Analysis*, 11(1): 7-26.

[102] Fisher, F. 1966. *The Identification Problem in Econometrics*. Huntington, N.Y.: R.E. Krieger Publishing Company.

[103] Fischer, M., Bartkowska, M., Riedl, A., Sardadvar, S. and Kunnert, A. 2009. The Impact of Human Capital on Regional Labor Productivity in Europe. *Letters in Spatial and Resource Sciences*, 2: 97-108.

[104] Florax, R. and de Graaff, T. 2004. The Performance of Diagnostic Tests for Spatial Dependence in Linear Regression Models. In *Advances in Spatial Econometrics*, Anselin, L. and Florax, R. (eds.). New York: Springer, pp. 29-66.

[105] Florax, R., Folmer, H. and Rey, S. 2003. Specification Searches in Spatial Econometrics: The Relevance of Hendry's Methodology. *Regional Science and Urban Economics*, 33(5): 557-579.

[106] Fujita, M., Krugman, P. and Venables, A. 1999. *The Spatial Economy: Cities, Regions and International Trade*. Cambridge: MIT Press.

[107] Gallant, R. and White, H. 1988. *A Unified Theory of Estimation and Inference for Nonlinear Dynamic Models*. New York: Basil Blackwell.

[108] Gelfand, A.E. and Smith, A.F.M. 1990. Sampling-Based Approaches to Calculating Marginal Densities. *Journal of the American Statistical Association*, 85: 398-409.

[109] Geweke, J. 1992. Evaluating the Accuracy of Sampling Based Approaches to the Calculation of Posterior Moments. In *Bayesian Statistics 4*, Bernardo, J.M., Berger, J.O., Dawid, A.P. and Smith, A.F.M. (eds.). Oxford University Press, pp. 169-193.

[110] Geweke, J. 2005. *Contemporary Bayesian Econometrics and Statistics*. New York: John Wiley & Sons Inc.

[111] Gilley, O.W. and Pace, R.K. 1996. On the Harrison and Rubinfeld Data. *Journal of Environmental Economics and Management*, 31: 403-405.

[112] Godfrey, L. 1983. Testing Non-Nested Models After Estimation by Instrumental Variables or Least Squares. *Econometrica*, 51: 355-366.

[113] Goldberger, A.S. 1962. Best Linear Unbiased Prediction in the Generalized Linear Regression Model. *Journal of the American Statistical Association*, 57: 369-375.

[114] Golubov, B.I. 1981. On Abel–Poisson Type and Riesz Means. *Annals of Mathematics*, 7: 161-194.

[115] Greenberg, E. and Webster, C. 1983. *Advanced Econometrics: A Bridge to the Literature*. New York: Wiley.

[116] Greene, W. 2003. *Econometric Analysis*, 5th ed. New York: Prentice Hall.

[117] Griffith, D. 1985. An Evaluation of Techniques for Boundary Effects in Spatial Statistical Analysis: Contemporary Methods. *Geographical Analysis*, 17: 81-88.

[118] Griffith, D. 1983. The Boundary Value Problem in Spatial Statistical Analysis. *Journal of Regional Science*, 23: 377-387.

[119] Griffith, D. and Amrhein, C. 1983. An Evaluation of Techniques for Boundary Effects in Spatial Statistical Analysis: Traditional Methods. *Geographic Analysis*, 15: 352-360.

[120] Haining, R. 1990. *Spatial Data Analysis in the Social and Environmental Sciences*. Cambridge: Cambridge University Press.

[121] Halleck Vega, S. and Elhorst, J.P. 2015. The SLX Model. *Journal of Regional Science*, 55: 339-363.

[122] Harrison Jr., D. and Rubinfeld, D.L. 1978. Hedonic Housing Prices and the Demand for Clean Air. *Journal of Environmental Economics and Management*, 5: 81-102.

[123] Heckman, J. 1979. Sample Selection Bias as a Specification Error. *Econometrica*, 47(1): 153-161.

[124] Hepple, L. 2004. Bayesian Model Choice in Spatial Econometrics. In *Advances in Econometrics, Vol. 18: Spatial and Spatiotemporal Econometrics*, LeSage, J. and Pace, R.K. (eds.). Boston: Elsevier.

[125] Hogg, R. and Craig, A. 1995. *Introduction to Mathematical Statistics*, 5th ed. Englewood Cliffs: Prentice Hall.

[126] Hondroyiannis, G., Kelejian, H. and Tavlas, G. 2009. Spatial Aspects of Contagion Among Emerging Economies. *Spatial Economic Analysis*, 4: 191-211.

[127] Hoogstra, G. 2012. Gender, Space, and the Location Changes of Jobs and People: A Spatial Simultaneous Equations Analysis. *Geographic Analysis*, 44: 47-64.

[128] Hoogstra, G., vanDijk, J. and Florax, R. 2011. Determinants of Variation in Population-Employment Interaction Finding: A Quasi-Experimental Meta-Analysis. *Geographic Analysis*, 43: 14-37.

[129] Horn, R. and Johnson, C. 1985. *Matrix Analysis*. New York: Cambridge University Press.

[130] Jeanty, P., Partridge, M. and Irwin, E. 2010. Estimation of a Spatial Simultaneous Equation Model of Population Migration and Housing Price Dynamics. *Regional Science and Urban Economics*, 40: 343-352.

[131] Jeffreys, H. 1961. *Theory of Probability*, 3rd ed. Oxford: Clarendon.

[132] Judge, G. and Bock, M. 1978. *The Statistical Implications of Pre-Test and Stein-Rule Estimators in Econometrics*. Amsterdam: North Holland.

[133] Judge, G., Griffiths, W., Hill, R., Lutkepohl, H. and Lee, T.C. 1985. *The Theory and Practice of Econometrics*, second ed. New York: Wiley.

[134] Judge, G. and Yancey, T. 1986. *Improved Methods of Inference Econometrics*. Amsterdam: North Holland.

[135] Kapoor, M., Kelejian, H. and Prucha, I. 2007. Panel Data Models With Spatially Correlated Error Components. *Journal of Econometrics*, 140: 97-130.

[136] Kelejian, H. 2016. Critical Issues in Spatial Models: Error Term Specifications, Additional Endogenous Variables, Pre-Testing, and Bayesian Analysis. *Letters in Spatial and Resource Sciences*, 9(1): 113-136.

[137] Kelejian, H. 2008. A Spatial J-Test for Model Specification Against a Single or a Set of Non-Nested Alternatives. *Letters in Spatial and Resource Sciences*, 1: 3-11.

[138] Kelejian, H. 1971. Two Stage Least Squares and Econometric Models Linear in the Parameters but Non Linear in the Endogenous Variables. *Journal of the American Statistical Association*, 66: 373-374.

[139] Kelejian, H. 1969. Missing Observations in Multivariate Regression: Efficiency of a First-Order Method. *Journal of the American Statistical Association*, 64: 1609-1616.

[140] Kelejian, H., Murrell, P. and Shepotylo, O. 2013. Spatial Spillovers in the Development of Institutions. *Journal of Development Economics*, 102: 297-315.

[141] Kelejian, H. and Mukerji, P. 2011. Important Indices in Spatial Models. *Papers in Regional Science*, 90: 693-702.

[142] Kelejian, H. and Piras, G. 2016a. An Extension of the J-Test to a Spatial Panel Data Framework. *Journal of Applied Econometrics*, 31(2): 387-402.

[143] Kelejian, H. and Piras, G. 2016b. A J Test for Dynamic Panel Model With Fixed Effects, and Nonparametric Spatial and Time Dependence. *Empirical Economics*, 51(4): 1581-1605.

[144] Kelejian, H. and Piras, G. 2014. Estimation of Spatial Models With Endogenous Weighting Matrices, and an Application to a Demand Model for Cigarettes. *Regional Science and Urban Economics*, 46: 140-149.

[145] Kelejian, H. and Piras, G. 2011. An Extension of Kelejian's J-Test for Non-Nested Spatial Models. *Regional Science and Urban Economics*, 41: 281-292.

[146] Kelejian, H. and Prucha, I. 2010a. Specification and Estimation of Spatial Autoregressive Models With Autoregressive and Heteroskedastic Disturbances. *Journal of Econometrics*, 157: 53-67.

[147] Kelejian, H. and Prucha, I. 2010b. Spatial Models With Spatially Lagged Dependent Variables and Incomplete Data. *Journal of Geographical Systems*, 12: 241-257.

[148] Kelejian, H. and Prucha, I. 2007a. HAC Estimation in a Spatial Framework. *Journal of Econometrics*, 140: 131-154.

[149] Kelejian, H. and Prucha, I. 2007b. The Relative Efficiencies of Various Predictors in Spatial Models Containing Spatial Lags. *Regional Science and Urban Economics*, 37: 283-432.

[150] Kelejian, H. and Prucha, I. 2004. Estimation of Simultaneous Systems of Spatially Interrelated Cross Sectional Equations. *Journal of Econometrics*, 118: 27-50.

[151] Kelejian, H. and Prucha, I. 2001. On the Asymptotic Distribution of the Moran I Test Statistic With Applications. *Journal of Econometrics*, 104: 219-257.

[152] Kelejian, H. and Prucha, I. 1999. A Generalized Moments Estimator for the Autoregressive Parameter in a Spatial Model. *International Economic Review*, 40: 509-533.

[153] Kelejian, H. and Prucha, I. 1998. A Generalized Spatial Two Stage Least Squares Procedure for Estimating a Spatial Autoregressive Model With Autoregressive Errors. *Journal of Real Estate Finance and Economics*, 17: 99-121.

[154] Kelejian, H., Prucha, I. and Yuzefovich, Y. 2006. Estimation Problems in Models With Spatial Weighting Matrices Which Have Blocks of Equal Elements. *Journal of Regional Science*, 46: 507-517.

[155] Kelejian, H., Prucha, I. and Yuzefovich, Y. 2004. Instrumental Variable Estimation of a Spatial Autoregressive Model With Autoregressive Disturbances: Large and Small Sample Results. In *Advances in Econometrics, Vol. 18: Spatial Spatiotemporal Econometrics*, Pace, K. and LeSage, J. (eds.). New York: Elsevier.

[156] Kelejian, H. and Yuzefovich, Y. 2004. Properties of Tests for Spatial Error Components: A Further Analysis. In *Spatial Econometrics and Spatial Statistics*, Getis, A., Mur, J. and Zoller, H.G. (eds.). Basingstoke, Hampshire, England: Palgrave, Macmillan, pp. 135-149 (Chapter 7).

[157] Kelejian, H. and Robinson, D. 2004. The Influence of Spatially Correlated Heteroskedasticity on Tests for Spatial Correlation. In *New Advances in Spatial Econometrics*, Anselin, L., Florax, R. and Rey, S. (eds.). Berlin: Springer, pp. 79-98.

[158] Kelejian, H. and Robinson, D. 1995. Spatial Correlation: A Suggested Alternative to the Autoregressive Model. In *New Direction in Spatial Econometrics*, Anselin, L. and Florax, R.J.G.M. (eds.). New York, NY: Springer.

[159] Kelejian, H. and Robinson, D. 1993. Spatial Autocorrelation: A New Computationally Simple Test With an Application to Per Capita County Police Expenditures. *Regional Science and Urban Economics*, 22: 317-331.

[160] Kelejian, H., Tavlas, G. and Hondroyiannis, G. 2006. A Spatial Modeling Approach to Contagion Among Emerging Economies. *Open Economies Review*, 17: 423-441.

[161] Kim, C.W., Phipps, T.T. and Anselin, L. 2003. Measuring the Benefits of Air Quality Improvement: A Spatial Hedonic Approach. *Journal of Environmental Economics and Management*, 45(1): 24-39.

[162] Kim, M.S. and Sun, Y. 2011. Spatial Heteroskedasticity and Autocorrelation Consistent Estimation of Covariance Matrix. *Journal of Econometrics*, 160: 349-371.

[163] King, M. 1981. A Small Sample Property of the Cliff–Ord Test for Spatial Correlation. *Journal of the Royal Statistical Association B*, 43: 263-264.

[164] Kmenta, J. 1986. *Elements of Econometrics*. New York: Macmillan.

[165] Koop, G. 2003. *Bayesian Econometrics*. John Wiley & Sons Ltd.

[166] Koopman, S.J., Shephard, N. and Creal, D.D. 2009. Testing the Assumptions Behind Importance Sampling. *Journal of Econometrics*, 149: 2-11.

[167] Koopmans, T. 1942. Serial Correlation and Quadratic Forms in Normal Variables. *Annals of Mathematical Statistics*, 13: 14-33.

[168] Kovandzic, T. and Sloan, J.J. 2002. Police Levels and Crime Rates Revisited: A County-Level Analysis from Florida (1980–1998). *Journal of Criminal Justice*, 30: 65-76.

[169] Lambert, D., Florax, R. and Cho, S. 2008. *Bandwidth Selection for Spatial HAC and Other Robust Covariance Estimators*. Working Paper 8-10. Purdue University, College of Agriculture, Department of Agricultural Economics.

[170] Lancaster, T. 2004. *An Introduction to Modern Bayesian Econometrics*. Malden: Blackwell.

[171] Lastauskas, P. and Tatsi, E. 2013. *Spatial Nexus in Crime and Unemployment in Times of Crisis*. Cambridge Working Papers in Economics No. 1359.

[172] Lee, L.F. 2007. GMM and 2SLS Estimation of Mixed Regressive, Spatial Autoregressive Models. *Journal of Econometrics*, 137: 489-514.

[173] Lee, L.F. 2004. Asymptotic Distributions of Quasi-Maximum Likelihood Estimators for Spatial Econometric Models. *Econometrica*, 72: 1899-1926.

[174] Lee, L.F. 2003. Best Spatial Two-Stage Least Squares Estimators for a Spatial Autoregressive Model With Autoregressive Disturbances. *Econometric Reviews*, 22: 307-335.

[175] Lee, L.F. and Liu, X. 2010. Efficient GMM Estimation of Higher Order Spatial Autoregressive Models With Autoregressive Disturbances. *Econometric Theory*, 26: 187-230.

[176] Lee, L.F., Liu, X. and Lin, X. 2010. Specification and Estimation of Social Interaction Models With Network Structures. *Econometrics Journal*, 13: 145-176.

[177] Lee, L.F. and Yu, J. 2012a. Spatial Panels: Random Components Versus Fixed Effects. *International Economic Review*, 53(4): 1369-1412.

[178] Lee, L.F. and Yu, J. 2012b. QML Estimation of Spatial Dynamic Panel Data Models With Time Varying Spatial Weights Matrices. *Spatial Economic Analysis*, 7: 31-74.

[179] Lee, L.F. and Yu, J. 2010a. A Spatial Dynamic Panel Data Model With Both Time And Individual Fixed Effects. *Econometric Theory*, 26(2): 564-597.
[180] Lee, L.F. and Yu, J. 2010b. Estimation of Spatial Autoregressive Panel Data Models With Fixed Effects. *Journal of Econometrics*, 154(2): 165-185.
[181] Lenze, D.L. 2000. Forecast Accuracy and Efficiency: An Evaluation of Ex Ante Substate Long-Term Forecasts. *International Regional Science Review*, 23: 201-226.
[182] LeSage, J. 1999. *The Theory and Practice of Spatial Econometrics, Spatial Econometrics Library*. On line: http://www.spatial-econometrics.com/.
[183] LeSage, J. and Fischer, M. 2008. Spatial Growth Regressions: Model Specification, Estimation and Interpretation. *Spatial Economic Analysis*, 3: 275-304.
[184] LeSage, J. and Pace, R.K. 2009. *Introduction to Spatial Econometrics*. New York: CRC Press.
[185] LeSage, J. and Pace, R.K. (eds.) 2004. *Spatial and Spatiotemporal Econometrics*. New York: Elsevier.
[186] Levitt, S. 1997. Using Electoral Cycles in Police Hiring to Estimate the Effect of Police on Crime. *American Economic Review*, 87(3): 270-290.
[187] Lindley, D.V. 1965. *Introduction to Probability and Statistics From a Bayesian Viewpoint, Part 2. Inference*. Cambridge: Cambridge University Press.
[188] Lindley, D.V. 1961. The Use of Prior Probability Distributions in Statistical Inference and Decisions. In *Proceedings of the Fourth Berkeley Symposium on Mathematical Statistics and Probability, Vol. I*, Neyman, J. (ed.), pp. 453-468.
[189] Little, R. 1992. Regression With Missing X's: A Review. *Journal of the American Statistical Association*, 87: 1227-1237.
[190] MacKinnon, J., White, H. and Davidson, R. 1983. Test for Model Specification in the Presence of Alternative Hypotheses: Some Further Results. *Journal of Econometrics*, 21: 53-70.
[191] Maddala, G.S. 1983. *Limited Dependent and Qualitative Variables in Econometrics*. Cambridge: Cambridge University Press.
[192] Marvell, T. and Moody, C.E. 1996. Specification Problems, Police Levels, and Crime Rates. *Criminology*, 34(4): 609-646.
[193] Millo, G. and Piras, G. 2012. splm: Spatial Panel Data Models in R. *Journal of Statistical Software*, 47(1): 1-38.
[194] Mood, A., Graybill, F. and Boes, D. 1974. *Introduction to the Theory of Statistics*. Boston: McGraw–Hill.
[195] Moran, P. 1948. The Interpretation of Statistical Maps. *Journal of the Royal Statistical Society, B*, 10: 243-251.
[196] Moran, P. 1950. Notes on Continuous Stochastic Phenomena. *Biometrika*, 37: 17-23.
[197] Mukerji, P. 2009. Ready for Capital Account Convertibility? *Journal of International Money and Finance*, 28: 1006-1021.
[198] Munnell, A.H. 1990. Why Has Productivity Growth Declined? Productivity and Public Investment. *New England Economic Review*, 3-22.
[199] Mutl, J. and Pfaffermayr, M. 2011. The Hausman Test in a Cliff and Ord Panel Model. *Econometrics Journal*, 14: 48-76.
[200] Mur, J. and Angulo, A. 2006. The Spatial Durbin Model and the Common Factor Tests. *Spatial Economic Analysis*, 1: 207-226.
[201] Newey, W. and West, K. 1987. A Simple, Positive Semi-Definite Heteroskedastic and Autocorrelated Consistent Covariance Matrix. *Econometrica*, 55: 703-708.
[202] Ord, J. 1975. Estimation Methods for Models of Spatial Interaction. *Journal of the American Statistical Association*, 70: 120-126.
[203] Pace, R.K. and LeSage, J. 2008. A Spatial Hausman Test. *Economics Letters*, 101: 282-284.
[204] Pace, R.K. and LeSage, J. 2004. Chebyshev Approximation of Log-Determinants of Spatial Weight Matrices. *Computational Statistics & Data Analysis*, 45: 179-196.

[205] Parent, O. and LeSage, J. 2010. A Spatial Dynamic Panel Model With Random Effects Applied to Commuting Times. *Transportation Research Part B: Methodological*, 44(5): 633-645.

[206] Persson, T. and Tabellini, G. 2009. Democratic Capital: The Nexus of Political and Economic Change. *American Economic Journal: Macroeconomics*, 1(2): 88-126.

[207] Pesaran, H.M. 2015. *Time Series and Panel Data Econometrics*. Oxford University Press.

[208] Pesaran, H.M. 1982. Comparison of Local Power of Alternative Tests of Non-Nested Regression Models. *Econometrica*, 50: 1287-1305.

[209] Pesaran, H.M. 1974. On the General Problem of Model Selection. *Review of Economic Studies*, 41: 153-171.

[210] Pesaran, H.M. and Deaton, A. 1978. Testing Non-Nested Non-Linear Regression Models. *Econometrica*, 46: 677-694.

[211] Pesaran, H.M. and Tosetti, E. 2011. Large Panels With Common Factors and Spatial Correlations. *Journal of Econometrics*, 161: 182-202.

[212] Pesaran, H.M. and Weeks, M. 2001. Non-Nested Hypothesis Testing: An Overview. In *A Companion to Theoretical Econometrics*, Baltagi, B. (ed.). Malden: Blackwell Publishers.

[213] Pinkse, J. 2004. Moran-Flavored Tests With Nuisance Parameters. In *Advances in Spatial Econometrics: Methodology, Tools and Applications*, Anselin, L., Florax, R. and Rey, S. (eds.). New York: Springer, pp. 67-77.

[214] Pinkse, J., Slade, M.E. and Brett, C. 2002. Spatial Price Competition: A Semiparametric Approach. *Econometrica*, 70: 1111-1153.

[215] Piras, G. 2013. Efficient GMM Estimation of a Cliff and Ord Panel Data Model With Random Effects. *Spatial Economic Analysis*, 8(3): 370-388.

[216] Piras, G. 2014. Impact Estimates for Static Panel Data Models in R. *Letters in Spatial and Resource Sciences*, 7: 213-223.

[217] Piras, G., Postiglione, P. and Aroca, P. 2012. Specialization, R&D and Productivity Growth: Evidence From EU Regions. *Annals of Regional Sciences*, 49: 35-51.

[218] Piras, G. and Prucha, I. 2014. Finite Sample Properties of Pre-Test Estimators of Spatial Models. *Regional Science and Urban Economics*, 46: 103-116.

[219] Pötscher, B. and Prucha, I. 2000. Basic Elements of Asymptotic Theory. In *A Companion to Theoretical Econometrics*, Baltagi, B. (ed.). Basil Blackwell.

[220] Pötscher, B. and Prucha, I. 1997. *Dynamic Nonlinear Econometrics Models*. New York: Springer.

[221] Powers, E.L. and Wilson, J.K. 2004. Access Denied: The Relationship Between Alcohol Prohibition and Driving Under the Influence. *Sociological Inquiry*, 74(3): 318-337.

[222] Qu, X. and Lee, L.F. 2015. Estimating a Spatial Autoregressive Model With an Endogenous Spatial Weight Matrix. *Journal of Econometrics*, 184(2): 209-232.

[223] Raiffa, H. and Schlaifer, R. 1961. *Applied Statistical Decision Theory*. Boston: Division of Research, Graduate School of Business Administration, Harvard University.

[224] Resnik, P. and Hardisty, E. 2010. *Gibbs Sampling for the Uninitiated*. On line: www.umiacs.umd.edu/~resnik/pubs/LAMP-TR-153.pdf.

[225] Royuela, V. 2011. Modelling Quality of Life and Population Growth. The Case of the Barcelona Metropolitan Area. *Spatial Economic Analysis*, 6: 83-109.

[226] Schmidt, P. 1976. *Econometrics*. New York: Marcel Dekker.

[227] Seldadyo, H., Elhorst, J.P. and De Haan, J. 2010. Geography and Governance: Does Space Matter? *Papers in Regional Science*, 89: 625-640.

[228] Shroder, M. 1995. Games the States Don't Play: Welfare Benefits and the Theory of Fiscal Federalism. *The Review of Economics and Statistics*, 77: 183-191.

[229] Smith, T.E. 2014. *Notebook on Spatial Data Analysis*. http://www.seas.upenn.edu/~ese502/#notebook.

[230] Song, H. 2011. *Posterior Simulation: Chapter 11 of Bayesian Data Analysis by Andrew Gelman*. Department of Mathematics and Statistics, Queen's University. On line: http://www.mast.queensu.ca/~wburr/seminar/files/July13.pdf.

[231] Stakhovych, S. and Bijmolt, T. 2009. Specification of Spatial Models: A Simulation Study on Weights Matrices. *Papers in Regional Science*, 88: 389-408.

[232] Theil, H. 1971. *Principles of Econometrics*. New York: Wiley.

[233] Vigil, R. 1998. *Interactions Among Municipalities in the Provision of Police Services: A Spatial Econometric Approach*. Ph.D. Thesis. University of Maryland.

[234] Wallace, T. 1977. Pre-Test Estimation in Regression: A Survey. *American Journal of Agricultural Economics*, 59: 431-443.

[235] Walsh, B. 2004. *Markov Chain Monte Carlo and Gibbs Sampling*. Lecture Notes for EEB 581, Version April 2004. On line: http://www.stat.columbia.edu/~liam/teaching/neurostat-spr11/papers/mcmc/mcmc-gibbs-intro.pdf.

[236] Wang, W. and Lee, L. 2013. Estimation of Spatial Panel Data Models With Randomly Missing Data in the Dependent Variable. *Regional Science and Urban Economics*, 43: 521-538.

[237] White, H. 1984. *Asymptotic Theory for Econometricians*. Orland: Academic Press.

[238] White, H. 1980. A Heteroskedastic-Consistent Covariance Estimator and a Direct Test for Heteroskedasticity. *Econometrica*, 48: 817-848.

[239] Wooldridge, J.M. 2013. *Introductory Econometrics: A Modern Approach*, Fifth edition South-Western, Cengage Learning.

[240] Yu, J., De Jong, R. and Lee, L.F. 2008. Quasi-Maximum Likelihood Estimators for Spatial Dynamic Panel Data With Fixed Effects When Both n and T Are Large. *Journal of Econometrics*, 146: 118-134.

[241] Zellner, A. 1971. *An Introduction to Bayesian Inference in Econometrics*. London: John Wiley and Sons.

Index

D

E

F

G

H

I

J

K

L

M

N

T

U

V

W

Printed in the United States
By Bookmasters